Zezhong Peng

July 17 · 1987

MD · U·S·A·

SWITCHING AND FINITE
AUTOMATA THEORY

有著作權 ＊ 翻印必究

原著者：ZVI KOHAVI
發行者：林　　在　　高
發行所：中 央 圖 書 出 版 社
　　　　台北市重慶南路一段一四一號
總經銷：中 央 圖 書 供 應 社
　　　　台北市重慶南路一段一四一號
　　電　話：3315726 · 3719893
　　劃撥帳戶：0000914-6
行政院新聞局出版事業登記證，局版台業字第〇九二〇號
印刷所：國 順 文 具 印 刷 行
　　　　板橋市中正路216巷2弄13號
中 華 民 國 七 十 二 年 八 月 一 版
定　價 NT$

SWITCHING AND FINITE AUTOMATA THEORY

Second Edition

ZVI KOHAVI

Departments of Electrical Engineering
and Computer Science
TECHNION–Israel Institute of Technology

McGraw-Hill Book Company
New York
CENTRAL BOOK COMPANY
Taipei, Taiwan

SWITCHING AND FINITE
AUTOMATA THEORY

1234567890 DODO 78321098

This book was set in Modern 8A by Bi-Comp, Incorporated.
The editors were Julienne V. Brown and Madelaine Eichberg;
the production supervisor was Charles Hess.
New drawings were done by Fine Line Illustrators, Inc.
R. R. Donnelley & Sons Company was printer and binder.

Library of Congress Cataloging in Publication Data

Kohavi, Zvi.
    Switching and finite automata theory.

    (McGraw-Hill computer science series)
    Includes bibliographical references and index.
    1. Sequential machine theory. 2. Switching theory.
I. Title.
QA267.5.S4K64 1978   629.8'9   77-13703
ISBN 0-07-035310-7

Contents

★ Sections marked with a star may be omitted without loss of continuity.

Preface

The subject of switching and finite automata theory needs no introduction. It has become a part of every computer science and electrical engineering curriculum, and rightly so. It provides techniques useful in a wide variety of applications and helps develop *a way of thinking* that leads to understanding of the structure, behavior, and limitations and capabilities of logical machines. In this book I have tried to cover the whole subject, starting with introductory material and leading to the more advanced topics, assuming a minimal technical background on the part of the reader. I did not attempt to provide detailed techniques for the design of specific circuits, but rather to formulate methods and to develop algorithms that can be applied to a broad class of problems. For once such general principles are understood, the relevance of specific procedures and their applicability to given problems are a matter of engineering decisions.

I have endeavored to provide a logical and rigorous presentation with a minimum of formalism. Accordingly, theorems are proved and algorithms are carefully developed, but only after an intuitive understanding of the procedures involved has been achieved by means of illustrative examples. Throughout I have assumed that the reader of this book is a computer scientist, a logical designer, or a communication or control engineer. Applications and examples are drawn accordingly from these fields. Most of the material is not new, although many subjects appear for the first time in an introductory text. A listing of the main sources upon which I have drawn, as well as some historical notes, is provided at the end of each chapter. These references are just the basic ones, and should not be considered a comprehensive bibliography.

The book is divided into three parts. The first part, which consists of Chapters 1 and 2, provides some introductory background. The second part is devoted to combinational logic, and the third part is concerned with finite automata. The book is organized so that many of its chapters cover specific topics and they are not prerequisite for subsequent chapters.

In this category are Chapters 6, 7, 8, 11, 12, 13, 14, 15, 16, and their selection in a course outline depends on the preferences of the instructor. Sections marked with a star ($\bigstar$) may be omitted without loss of continuity.

The book is self-contained as a text. At present much of this material is customarily taught in graduate courses, but from my experience at the Polytechnic Institute of New York, the Massachusetts Institute of Technology, and the Technion most of it can be taught at the junior or senior level in computer science or electrical engineering departments. The book is intended as a text for a two-semester sequence. The first semester can be devoted to "classical" switching theory [Chapters 1, 3 (Sections 3-1 to 3-4), and 4 through 11], and the second semester devoted primarily to finite automata theory [Chapters 2, and 12 through 16]. Other organizations of the material into one-semester or two-semester courses are possible, keeping in mind the following prerequisites: Chapters 3 (excluding Section 3-5), 4, and 5 are prerequisite for the entire book. Chapters 9 and 10 (excluding Section 10-4) are prerequisite for Chapters 12 through 16.

In revising the book some chapters have undergone a major revision, while others required only minor changes. Chapters 5 and 9 have been updated to reflect the general use of integrated circuits in logical design. Chapters 8 and 13 have been revised and expanded to reflect the importance of testing circuits and of designing more reliable circuits. In an era where computers are used to execute algorithms and perform experiments, it is of utmost importance to establish that the computations will indeed terminate and to provide bounds for their length. The development of bounds on the length of various experiments has therefore been further emphasized by providing new proofs in appendixes and problems in Chapters 10, 13, and 14. The problem sets, which were originally quite extensive, have been further expanded. They range from simple numerical examples to natural extensions of the ideas presented in the text.

The first edition of this book has been used in many universities and departments and I received numerous helpful comments. I am grateful for all of them. My gratitude is due to M. Yoeli of the Technion and E. J. Smith of the Polytechnic Institute of New York, who stimulated my first interest in the subject of switching and automata theory. I also wish to thank I. Kohavi, I. Koren, S. Patil, R. Riesenfeld, and C. L. Seitz for their helpful comments and many valuable suggestions. I am indebted to the electrical engineering department at M.I.T. which provided a stimulating atmosphere for writing the first edition, and to the Technion and the computer science department at the University of Utah for making the revised edition possible.

Special gratitude is due to C. L. Liu of the University of Illinois for his thorough review of the entire manuscript and his invaluably discerning technical criticism, which significantly improved this book. I also thank Karen Evans for her excellent typing of the manuscript and for drawing the figures. Last but not least, I wish to thank my wife, Sima, for her help and understanding.

Zvi Kohavi

SWITCHING AND FINITE AUTOMATA THEORY

Part one
Preliminaries

1
Number Systems and Codes

This chapter deals with the representation of numerical data, with emphasis on those representations which use only two symbols, 0 and 1. Described are special methods of representing numerical data, affording protection against various transmission errors and component failures.

1-1 NUMBER SYSTEMS

Convenient as the decimal number system generally is, its usefulness in machine computation is limited because of the nature of practical electronic devices. In most present digital machines the numbers are represented, and the arithmetic operations performed, in a different number system, called the binary number system. This section is concerned with the representation of numbers in various systems and with methods of conversion from one system to another.

Number representation

An ordinary decimal number actually represents a polynomial in powers of 10. For example, the number 123.45 represents the polynomial

$$123.45 = 1 \cdot 10^2 + 2 \cdot 10^1 + 3 \cdot 10^0 + 4 \cdot 10^{-1} + 5 \cdot 10^{-2}$$

This method of representing decimal numbers is known as the *decimal number system*, and the number 10 is referred to as the *base* (or *radix*) of the system. In a system whose base is b, a positive number N represents the polynomial

$$N = a_{q-1}b^{q-1} + \cdots + a_0b^0 + \cdots + a_{-p}b^{-p}$$

$$= \sum_{i=-p}^{q-1} a_i b^i$$

where the base b is an integer greater than 1, and the a's are integers in the range $0 \leq a_i \leq b - 1$. The sequence of digits $a_{q-1}a_{q-2} \cdots a_0$ constitutes the *integral part* of N, while the sequence $a_{-1}a_{-2} \cdots a_{-p}$ constitutes the *fractional part* of N. Thus p and q designate the number of digits in the fractional and integral parts, respectively. The integral and fractional parts are usually separated by a *radix point*. The digit a_{-p} is referred to as the *least significant digit*, while a_{q-1} is called the *most significant digit*.

When the base b equals 2, the number representation is referred to as the *binary number system*. For example, the binary number 1101.01 represents the polynomial

$$1101.01 = 1 \cdot 2^3 + 1 \cdot 2^2 + 0 \cdot 2^1 + 1 \cdot 2^0 + 0 \cdot 2^{-1} + 1 \cdot 2^{-2}$$

that is,

$$1101.01 = \sum_{i=-2}^{3} a_i 2^i$$

where $a_{-2} = a_0 = a_2 = a_3 = 1$ and $a_{-1} = a_1 = 0$.

A number N in base b is usually denoted $(N)_b$. Whenever the base is not specified, base 10 is implicit. Table 1-1 shows the representations of integers 0 through 15 in several number systems.

The *complement* of a digit a, denoted a', in base b is defined as

$$a' = (b - 1) - a$$

That is, the complement a' is the difference between the largest digit in base b and the digit a. In the binary number system, since $b = 2$, $0' = 1$ and $1' = 0$. In the decimal number system the largest digit is 9. Thus, for example, the complement† of 3 is $9 - 3 = 6$.

Conversion of bases

Suppose that some number N, which we wish to express in base b_2, is presently expressed in base b_1. In converting a number from base b_1 to

---

† In the decimal system the complement is also referred to as the 9's *complement*. In the binary system it is also known as the 1's *complement*.

Table 1-1   Representations of integers

	Base			
2	4	8	10	12
0000	0	0	0	0
0001	1	1	1	1
0010	2	2	2	2
0011	3	3	3	3
0100	10	4	4	4
0101	11	5	5	5
0110	12	6	6	6
0111	13	7	7	7
1000	20	10	8	8
1001	21	11	9	9
1010	22	12	10	α
1011	23	13	11	β
1100	30	14	12	10
1101	31	15	13	11
1110	32	16	14	12
1111	33	17	15	13

base b_2, it is convenient to distinguish two cases. In the first case, $b_1 < b_2$, and consequently base-b_2 arithmetic can be used in the conversion process. The conversion technique involves expressing the number $(N)_{b_1}$ as a polynomial in powers of b_1 and evaluating the polynomial using base-b_2 arithmetic.

Example We wish to express the numbers $(432.2)_8$ and $(1101.01)_2$ in base 10.

$$(432.2)_8 = 4 \cdot 8^2 + 3 \cdot 8^1 + 2 \cdot 8^0 + 2 \cdot 8^{-1} = (282.25)_{10}$$
$$(1101.01)_2 = 1 \cdot 2^3 + 1 \cdot 2^2 + 0 \cdot 2^1 + 1 \cdot 2^0 + 0 \cdot 2^{-1} + 1 \cdot 2^{-2}$$
$$= (13.25)_{10}$$

In both cases the arithmetic operations are done in base 10. ∎

When $b_1 > b_2$ it is more convenient to use base-b_1 arithmetic. The conversion procedure will be proved by considering separately the integral and fractional parts of N. Let $(N)_{b_1}$ be an integer whose value in *base b_2* is given by

$$(N)_{b_1} = a_{q-1}b_2{}^{q-1} + a_{q-2}b_2{}^{q-2} + \cdots + a_1b_2{}^1 + a_0b_2{}^0$$

To find the values of the a_i's, let us divide (base b_1) the above polynomial by b_2.

$$\frac{(N)_{b_1}}{b_2} = \underbrace{a_{q-1}b_2{}^{q-2} + a_{q-2}b_2{}^{q-3} + \cdots + a_1}_{Q_0} + \frac{a_0}{b_2}$$

Thus the least significant digit of $(N)_{b_2}$, i.e., a_0, is equal to the first remainder. The next significant digit, a_1, is obtained by dividing the quotient Q_0 by b_2, i.e.,

$$\left(\frac{Q_0}{b_2}\right)_{b_1} = \underbrace{a_{q-1}b_2{}^{q-3} + a_{q-2}b_2{}^{q-4} + \cdots}_{Q_1} + \frac{a_1}{b_2}$$

The remaining a's are evaluated by repeated divisions of the quotients until Q_{q-1} is equal to zero. If N is finite, the process must terminate.

Example The above conversion procedure is now applied to convert $(548)_{10}$ to base 8.   The r_i's in the table below denote the remainders. The first entries in the table are 68 and 4, corresponding, respectively, to the quotient Q_0 and the first remainder from the division of $(548/8)_{10}$.   The remaining entries are found by successive divisions.

Q_i	r_i
68	$4 = a_0$
8	$4 = a_1$
1	$0 = a_2$
	$1 = a_3$

Thus $(548)_{10} = (1044)_8$.

In a similar manner we obtain the conversion of $(345)_{10}$ to $(1333)_6$, as illustrated in the table below.

Q_i	r_i
57	$3 = a_0$
9	$3 = a_1$
1	$3 = a_2$
	$1 = a_3$

Indeed, $(1333)_6$ can be reconverted to base 10, i.e.,

$$(1333)_6 = 1 \cdot 6^3 + 3 \cdot 6^2 + 3 \cdot 6^1 + 3 \cdot 6^0 = 345 \quad \blacksquare$$

If $(N)_{b_1}$ is a fraction, a dual procedure is employed. $(N)_{b_1}$ can be expressed in base b_2 as

$$(N)_{b_1} = a_{-1}b_2^{-1} + a_{-2}b_2^{-2} + \cdots + a_{-p}b_2^{-p}$$

The most significant digit, a_{-1}, can be obtained by multiplying the polynomial by b_2, i.e.,

$$b_2 \cdot (N)_{b_1} = a_{-1} + a_{-2}b_2^{-1} + \cdots + a_{-p}b_2^{-p+1}$$

If the above product is less than 1, then a_{-1} equals 0; if the product is greater than or equal to 1, then a_{-1} is equal to the integral part of the product. The next most significant digit, a_{-2}, is found by multiplying the fractional part of the above product by b_2 and determining its integral part, and so on. This process does not necessarily terminate, since it may not be possible to represent the fraction in base b_2 with a finite number of digits.

Example To convert $(0.3125)_{10}$ to base 8, multiply

$$0.3125 \cdot 8 = 2.5000 \qquad \text{hence} \qquad a_{-1} = 2$$
$$0.5000 \cdot 8 = 4.0000 \qquad \text{hence} \qquad a_{-2} = 4$$

Thus $(0.3125)_{10} = (0.24)_8$.
Similarly, the computation below proves that $(0.375)_{10} = (0.011)_2$.

$$0.375 \cdot 2 = 0.750 \qquad \text{hence} \qquad a_{-1} = 0$$
$$0.750 \cdot 2 = 1.500 \qquad \text{hence} \qquad a_{-2} = 1$$
$$0.500 \cdot 2 = 1.000 \qquad \text{hence} \qquad a_{-3} = 1 \quad \blacksquare$$

Example To convert $(432.354)_{10}$ to binary, we first convert the integral part and next the fractional part.

Q_i	r_i
216	$0 = a_0$
108	$0 = a_1$
54	$0 = a_2$
27	$0 = a_3$
13	$1 = a_4$
6	$1 = a_5$
3	$0 = a_6$
1	$1 = a_7$
	$1 = a_8$

Hence $(432)_{10} = (110110000)_2.$

$$0.354 \cdot 2 = 0.708 \qquad \text{hence} \qquad a_{-1} = 0$$
$$0.708 \cdot 2 = 1.416 \qquad \text{hence} \qquad a_{-2} = 1$$
$$0.416 \cdot 2 = 0.832 \qquad \text{hence} \qquad a_{-3} = 0$$
$$0.832 \cdot 2 = 1.664 \qquad \text{hence} \qquad a_{-4} = 1$$
$$0.664 \cdot 2 = 1.328 \qquad \text{hence} \qquad a_{-5} = 1$$
$$0.328 \cdot 2 = 0.656 \qquad \text{hence} \qquad a_{-6} = 0$$
$$a_{-7} = 0$$

etc.

Hence $(0.354)_{10} = (0.0101101 \ldots)_2$. The conversion is usually carried up to the desired accuracy. In our example reconversion to base 10 shows that

$$(110110000.0101101)_2 = (432.3515)_{10} \quad \blacksquare$$

A considerably simpler conversion procedure may be employed in converting octal numbers (i.e., numbers in base 8) to binary, and vice versa. Since $8 = 2^3$, each octal digit can be expressed by three binary digits. For example, $(6)_8$ can be expressed as $(110)_2$, etc. The procedure of converting a binary number into an octal number is to partition the binary number into groups of three digits, starting from the binary point, and to determine the octal digit corresponding to each group.

Example

$$(123.4)_8 = (001 \quad 010 \quad 011.100)_2$$
$$(1010110.0101)_2 = (001 \quad 010 \quad 110.010 \quad 100) = (126.24)_8 \quad \blacksquare$$

A similar procedure may be employed in conversions from binary to hexadecimal (base 16), except that four binary digits are needed to represent a single hexadecimal digit. In fact, whenever a number is converted from base b_1 to base b_2, where $b_2 = b_1{}^k$, then k digits of that number are grouped and may be represented by a single digit from base b_2.

Binary arithmetic

The binary number system is widely used in digital systems. Although a detailed study of digital arithmetic is beyond the scope of this book, we shall present the elementary techniques of binary arithmetic. The basic arithmetic operations are summarized in Table 1-2, where the sum and carry, difference and borrow, and product are computed for every combination of the binary digits (abbreviated *bits*) 0 and 1. For a more comprehensive discussion of computer arithmetic the reader may consult Ref. 1.

Table 1-2 Elementary binary operations

Bits		Sum	Carry	Difference	Borrow	Product
a	b	$a + b$		$a - b$		$a \cdot b$
0	0	0	0	0	0	0
0	1	1	0	1	1	0
1	0	1	0	1	0	0
1	1	0	1	0	0	1

Binary addition is performed in a manner similar to that of decimal addition. Corresponding bits are added, and if a carry 1 is produced, it is added to the binary digits at the left.

Example

$$
\begin{array}{ll}
1111 & = \text{carries of } 1 \\
1111.01 & = (15.25)_{10} \\
+ \\
\underline{0111.10} & = (\ 7.50)_{10} \\
10110.11 & = (22.75)_{10} \quad \blacksquare
\end{array}
$$

In subtraction, if a borrow of 1 occurs and the next left digit of the minuend is 1, it is changed to 0, and the subtraction is continued in the usual manner. If, however, the next left digit of the minuend is 0, it is changed to 1, as is each successive minuend digit to the left which is equal to 0. The first minuend digit to the left which is equal to 1 is changed to 0, and the subtraction is continued.

Example

$$
\begin{array}{ll}
1 & = \text{borrows of } 1 \\
10010.11 & = (18.75)_{10} \\
- \\
\underline{01100.10} & = (12.50)_{10} \\
00110.01 & = (\ 6.25)_{10} \quad \blacksquare
\end{array}
$$

Just as in decimal numbers, multiplication of binary numbers is performed by successive addition, while division is done by successive subtraction.

Example   Multiply the binary numbers below.

$$11001.1 = (25.5)_{10}$$
$$\times$$
$$110.1 = (\ 6.5)_{10}$$

$$
\begin{array}{r}
11001\ 1 \\
000000 \\
110011 \\
110011 \\
\hline
10100101.11 = (165.75)_{10} \quad \blacksquare
\end{array}
$$

Example   Divide the binary number 1000100110 by 11001.

$$
\begin{array}{r}
10110 = \text{quotient} \\
11001\sqrt{1000100110} \\
11001 \\
\hline
00100101 \\
11001 \\
\hline
0011001 \\
11001 \\
\hline
00000 = \text{remainder} \quad \blacksquare
\end{array}
$$

1-2 BINARY CODES

Although the binary number system has many practical advantages and is widely used in digital computers, in many cases it is convenient to work with the decimal number system, especially when the communication between man and machine is extensive, since most numerical data generated by man are in terms of decimal numbers. To simplify the communication problem between man and machine, a number of codes have been devised so that the decimal digits are represented by sequences of binary digits.

Weighted codes

In order to represent the 10 decimal digits 0, 1, . . . , 9 it is necessary to use at least four binary digits. Since there are 16 combinations of four binary digits, of which only 10 combinations are used, it is possible to form a very large number of distinct codes. Of particular importance is the class of *weighted codes*, whose main characteristic is that each binary digit is assigned a "weight," and for each group of four bits, the sum of the weights of those binary digits whose value is 1 is equal to the decimal digit which they represent. In other words, if w_1, w_2, w_3, and w_4 are the weights of the binary digits and x_1, x_2, x_3, x_4 are the corresponding digit values, then the decimal digit $N = w_4x_4 + w_3x_3 + w_2x_2 + w_1x_1$ is represented by the binary sequence $x_4x_3x_2x_1$. A sequence of binary digits which represents a decimal digit is called a *code word*. Thus the above sequence $x_4x_3x_2x_1$ is the code word for N. A number of weighted, four-digit binary codes are shown in Table 1-3.

Table 1-3   Examples of weighted binary codes

Decimal digit	8	4	2	1	2	4	2	1	6	4	2	−3
					$w_4w_3w_2w_1$							
0	0	0	0	0	0	0	0	0	0	0	0	0
1	0	0	0	1	0	0	0	1	0	1	0	1
2	0	0	1	0	0	0	1	0	0	0	1	0
3	0	0	1	1	0	0	1	1	1	0	0	1
4	0	1	0	0	0	1	0	0	0	1	0	0
5	0	1	0	1	1	0	1	1	1	0	1	1
6	0	1	1	0	1	1	0	0	0	1	1	0
7	0	1	1	1	1	1	0	1	1	1	0	1
8	1	0	0	0	1	1	1	0	1	0	1	0
9	1	0	0	1	1	1	1	1	1	1	1	1

The binary digits in the first code in Table 1-3 are assigned the weights 8, 4, 2, 1. As a result of this weight assignment, the code word that corresponds to each decimal digit is the binary equivalence of that digit; e.g., 5 is represented by 0101, and so on. This code is known as the BCD (*Binary-Coded-Decimal*) code. For each of the codes in Table 1-3 the decimal digit that corresponds to a given code word is equal to the sum of the weights in those binary positions which are 1's. Thus, in the second code, where the weights are 2, 4, 2, 1, decimal 5 is represented by 1011, corresponding to the sum $2 \cdot 1 + 4 \cdot 0 + 2 \cdot 1 + 1 \cdot 1 = 5$. The weights assigned to the binary digits may also be negative, as is shown by the code $(6,4,2,-3)$. In this code, decimal 5 is represented by 1011, since $6 \cdot 1 + 4 \cdot 0 + 2 \cdot 1 - 3 \cdot 1 = 5$.

It is apparent that the representations of some decimal numbers in the $(2,4,2,1)$ and $(6,4,2,-3)$ codes are not unique. For example, in the $(2,4,2,1)$ code, decimal 7 may be represented by 1101 as well as by 0111. Adopting the representations shown in Table 1-3 causes the codes to become self-complementing. A code is said to be *self-complementing* if the code word of the 9's complement of N, i.e., $9 - N$, can be obtained from the code word of N by interchanging all the 1's and 0's. For example, in the $(6,4,2,-3)$ code, decimal 3 is represented by 1001, while decimal

6 is represented by 0110. In the (2,4,2,1) code, decimal 2 is represented by 0010, while decimal 7 is represented by 1101. Note that the BCD code is not self-complementing. It can be shown that a necessary condition for a weighted code to be self-complementing is that the sum of the weights must equal 9. There exist only four positively weighted self-complementing codes, namely, (2,4,2,1), (3,3,2,1), (4,3,1,1), (5,2,1,1). In addition, there exist 13 self-complementing codes with positive and negative weights.

Nonweighted codes

There are many nonweighted binary codes, two of which are shown in Table 1-4. The *Excess*-3 code is formed by adding 0011 to each BCD code word. Thus, for example, the representation of decimal 7 in Excess-3 is given by 0111 + 0011 = 1010. The Excess-3 code is a self-complementing code, and it possesses a number of properties that made it practical in earlier decimal computers.

Table 1-4   Nonweighted binary codes

Decimal digit	Excess-3				Cyclic			
0	0	0	1	1	0	0	0	0
1	0	1	0	0	0	0	0	1
2	0	1	0	1	0	0	1	1
3	0	1	1	0	0	0	1	0
4	0	1	1	1	0	1	1	0
5	1	0	0	0	1	1	1	0
6	1	0	0	1	1	0	1	0
7	1	0	1	0	1	0	0	0
8	1	0	1	1	1	1	0	0
9	1	1	0	0	0	1	0	0

In many practical applications, e.g., analog-to-digital conversion, it is desirable to use codes in which all successive code words differ in only one digit. Codes that have such a property are referred to as *cyclic codes*. The second code in Table 1-4 is an example of such a code. (Note that in this, as in all cyclic codes, the code word representing the decimal digits 0 and 9 differ in only one digit.) A particularly important cyclic code is the *Gray code*. A four-bit Gray code is shown in Table 1-5. The feature that makes this cyclic code useful is the simplicity of the procedure for converting from the binary number system into the Gray code.

Table 1-5   The complete four-bit Gray code

Decimal number	Gray g_3	g_2	g_1	g_0	Binary b_3	b_2	b_1	b_0
0	0	0	0	0	0	0	0	0
1	0	0	0	1	0	0	0	1
2	0	0	1	1	0	0	1	0
3	0	0	1	0	0	0	1	1
4	0	1	1	0	0	1	0	0
5	0	1	1	1	0	1	0	1
6	0	1	0	1	0	1	1	0
7	0	1	0	0	0	1	1	1
8	1	1	0	0	1	0	0	0
9	1	1	0	1	1	0	0	1
10	1	1	1	1	1	0	1	0
11	1	1	1	0	1	0	1	1
12	1	0	1	0	1	1	0	0
13	1	0	1	1	1	1	0	1
14	1	0	0	1	1	1	1	0
15	1	0	0	0	1	1	1	1

Let $g_n \cdots g_2 g_1 g_0$ denote a code word in the $(n + 1)$st-bit Gray code, and let $b_n \cdots b_2 b_1 b_0$ designate the corresponding binary number, where the subscripts 0 and n denote the least significant and most significant digits, respectively. Then, the ith digit g_i can be obtained from the corresponding binary number as follows:

$$g_i = b_i \oplus b_{i+1} \qquad 0 \le i \le n - 1$$
$$g_n = b_n$$

where the symbol $\oplus$ denotes the *modulo-2 sum*, which is defined as follows:

$$0 \oplus 0 = 0 \qquad 1 \oplus 1 = 0 \qquad 0 \oplus 1 = 1 \qquad 1 \oplus 0 = 1$$

For example, the Gray code word which corresponds to the binary number 101101 is found to be 111011 in the following manner:

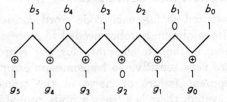

To convert from Gray code to binary, start with the leftmost digit and proceed to the least significant digit, making $b_i = g_i$ if the number of 1's preceding g_i is even, and making $b_i = g_i'$ if the number of 1's preceding g_i is odd. (Note that zero 1's is an even number of 1's.) For example, the (Gray) code word 1001011 represents the binary number 1110010. The proofs that the preceding conversion procedures indeed work are left to the reader as an exercise.

The n-bit Gray code is a member of a class called *reflected codes*. The term "reflected" is used to designate codes which have the property that the n-bit code can be generated by reflecting the $(n - 1)$st-bit code, as illustrated in Fig. 1-1. The two-bit Gray code is shown in Fig. 1-1a. The three-bit Gray code can be obtained by reflecting the two-bit code about an axis at the end of the code, and assigning a most significant bit of 0 above the axis and of 1 below the axis. The four-bit Gray code is obtained in the same manner from the three-bit code, as shown in Fig. 1-1c.

00	0 00	0. 000
01	0 01	0 001
11	0 11	0 011
10	0 10	0 010
	1 10	0 110
	1 11	0 111
	1 01	0 101
	1 00	0 100
		1 100
		1 101
		1 111
		1. 110
		1 010
		1 011
		1 001
		1 000
(a)	(b)	(c)

Fig. 1-1 Reflection of Gray codes.

1-3 ERROR DETECTION AND CORRECTION

In the codes presented so far, each code word consists of four binary digits, which is the minimum number needed to represent the 10 decimal digits. Such codes, although adequate for the representation of the decimal digits, are very sensitive to transmission errors that may occur because of equipment failure or noise in the transmission channel. In any practical system there is always a finite probability of the occurrence of a single error. The probability that two or more errors will occur simultaneously, although nonzero, is substantially smaller. We therefore restrict our discussion mainly to the detection and correction of single errors.

Error-detecting codes

In a four-bit binary code, the occurrence of a single error in one of the binary digits may result in another, incorrect but valid, code word. For example, in the BCD code, if an error occurs in the least significant digit of 0110, the code word 0111 results, and since it is a valid code word, it is incorrectly interpreted by the receiver. If a code possesses the property that the occurrence of any single error transforms a valid code word into an invalid code word, it is said to be a *(single)-error-detecting code*. Two error-detecting codes are shown in Table 1-6.

The error detection in either of the codes of Table 1-6 is accomplished by a *parity check*. The basic idea in the parity check is to add an extra digit to each code word of a given code, so as to make the number of 1's in each code word either odd or even. In the codes of Table 1-6 we have used *even parity*. The even-parity BCD code is obtained directly from the BCD code of Table 1-3. The added bit, denoted p, is called *parity bit*. The *2-out-of-5 code* consists of all 10 possible combinations of two 1's in a five-bit code word. With the exception of the code word for decimal 0, the 2-out-of-5 code of Table 1-6 is a weighted code and can be derived from the (1,2,4,7) code.

Table 1-6   Error-detecting codes

Decimal digit	Even-parity BCD 8 4 2 1 p					2-out-of-5 0 1 2 4 7				
0	0	0	0	0	0	0	0	0	1	1
1	0	0	0	1	1	1	1	0	0	0
2	0	0	1	0	1	1	0	1	0	0
3	0	0	1	1	0	0	1	1	0	0
4	0	1	0	0	1	1	0	0	1	0
5	0	1	0	1	0	0	1	0	1	0
6	0	1	1	0	0	0	0	1	1	0
7	0	1	1	1	1	1	0	0	0	1
8	1	0	0	0	1	0	1	0	0	1
9	1	0	0	1	0	0	0	1	0	1

In each of the codes in Table 1-6 the number of 1's in a code word is even. Now, if a single error occurs, it transforms the valid code word into an invalid one, thus making the detection of the error straightforward.

Although the parity check is intended only for the detection of single errors, it in fact detects any odd number of errors and some even number of errors. For example, if the code word 10100 is received in an even-parity BCD message, it is clear that the message is erroneous, although the parity check is satisfied. We cannot determine, however, the original transmitted word.

In general, to obtain an n-bit error-detecting code, no more than half of the possible 2^n combinations of digits can be used. The code words are chosen in such a manner that, in order to change one valid code word into another valid code word, at least two digits must be complemented. In the case of four-bit codes, this constraint means that only 8 valid code words can be formed of the 16 possible combinations. Thus, to obtain an error-detecting code for the 10 decimal digits, at least 5 binary digits are needed. It is useful to define the *distance* between two code words as the number of digits that must change in one word so that the other word results. For example, the distance between 1010 and 0100 is three, since the two code words differ in three bit positions. The *minimum distance* of a code is the smallest number of bits in which any two code words differ. Thus the minimum distance of the BCD or the Excess-3 codes is one, while that of the codes in Table 1-6 is two. Clearly, *a code is an error-detecting code if and only if its minimum distance is two or more.*

Error-correcting codes

For a code to be error-correcting, its minimum distance must be further increased. For example, consider the three-bit code which consists of only two valid code words, 000 and 111. If a single error occurs in the first code word, it can be changed to 001, 010, or 100. The second code word can be changed due to a single error to 110, 101, or 011. Note that in each case the invalid code words are different. Clearly, this code is error-detecting, since its minimum distance is three. Moreover, if we assume that only a single error can occur, then this error can be located and corrected, since every error results in an invalid code word that can be associated with only one of the valid code words. Thus the two code words 000 and 111 constitute an error-correcting code whose minimum distance is three. In general, a code is said to be an *error-correcting code* if the correct code word can always be deduced from the erroneous word. In this section we shall discuss a single type of error-correcting codes, known as the *Hamming codes*.

If the minimum distance of a code is three, then any single error changes a valid code word into an invalid one, which is a distance one away from the original code word and a distance two from any other valid code word. Therefore, in a code with minimum distance of three, any single error is correctable *or* any double error detectable. Similarly, a code whose minimum distance is four may be used for either single-error correction *and* double-error detection *or* triple-error detection. The key to error correction is that it must be possible to *detect* and *locate* erroneous digits. If the location of an error has been determined, then by complementing the erroneous digit the message is corrected.

The basic principles in constructing a Hamming error-correcting code are as follows. To each group of m *information*, or *message, digits*, k *parity checking digits*, denoted $p_1, p_2, \ldots, p_k$, are added to form an $(m + k)$-digit code. The location of each of the $m + k$ digits within a code word is assigned a decimal value, starting by assigning a 1 to the most significant digit and $m + k$ to the least significant digit. k parity checks are performed on selected digits of each code word. The result of each parity check is recorded as 1 or 0, depending, respectively, on whether an error has or has not been detected. These parity checks make possible the development of a binary number, $c_1 c_2 \cdots c_k$, whose value when an error occurs is equal to the decimal value assigned to the location of the erroneous digit, and is equal to zero if no error occurs. This number is called the *position* (or *location*) *number*.

The number k of digits in the position number must be large enough to describe the location of any of the $m + k$ possible single errors, and must in addition take on the value zero to describe the "no error" condition. Consequently, k must satisfy the inequality $2^k \geq m + k + 1$. Thus, for example, if the original message is in BCD, where $m = 4$, then $k = 3$ and at least three parity checking digits must be added to the BCD code. The resultant error-correcting code thus consists of seven digits. In this case, if the position number is equal to 101, it means that an error has occurred in position 5. If, however, the position number is equal to 000, the message is correct.

In order to be able to specify the checking digits by means of only message digits and independently of each other, they are placed in positions $1, 2, 4, \ldots, 2^{k-1}$. Thus, if $m = 4$ and $k = 3$, the checking digits are placed in positions 1, 2, and 4, while the remaining positions contain the original (BCD) message bits. For example, in the code word **1100**110 the checking digits (in boldface) are $p_1 = 1$, $p_2 = 1$, $p_3 = 0$, while the message digits are 0, 1, 1, 0, which correspond to decimal 6.

We shall now show how the Hamming code is constructed, by constructing the code for $m = 4$ and $k = 3$. As discussed above, the parity checking digits must be so specified that, when an error occurs, the position number will take on the value assigned to the location of the erroneous digit. Table 1-7 lists the seven error positions and the corresponding values of the position number. It is evident that if an error occurs in position 1, or 3, or 5, or 7, the least significant digit, i.e., c_3, of the position number must be equal to 1. If the code is constructed so that in every code word the digits in positions 1, 3, 5, and 7 have even parity, then the occurrence of a single error in any one of these positions will cause an odd parity. In such a case the least significant digit of the position number is recorded as 1. If no error occurs among these digits, the parity check will show an even parity, and the least significant digit of the position number is recorded as 0.

Table 1-7   Position numbers

Error position	Position number		
	c_1	c_2	c_3
0 (no error)	0	0	0
1	0	0	1
2	0	1	0
3	0	1	1
4	1	0	0
5	1	0	1
6	1	1	0
7	1	1	1

From Table 1-7 we observe that an error in position 2, or 3, or 6, or 7 should result in the recording of a 1 in the center of the position number. Hence the code must be designed so that the digits in positions 2, 3, 6, and 7 have even parity. Again, if the parity check of these digits shows an odd parity, the corresponding position number digit, i.e., c_2, is set to 1; otherwise it is set to 0. Finally, if an error occurs in position 4, or 5, or 6, or 7, the most significant digit of the position number, i.e., c_1, should be a 1. Therefore, if digits 4, 5, 6, and 7 are designed to have even parity, an error in any one of these digits will be recorded as a 1 in the most significant digit of the position number. To summarize:

p_1 is selected so as to establish even parity in positions 1, 3, 5, 7.
p_2 is selected so as to establish even parity in positions 2, 3, 6, 7.
p_3 is selected so as to establish even parity in positions 4, 5, 6, 7.

The code can now be constructed by adding the appropriate checking digits to the message digits. Consider, for example, the message 0100 (i.e., decimal 4).

Position:	1	2	3	4	5	6	7
	p_1	p_2	m_1	p_3	m_2	m_3	m_4

	1	2	3	4	5	6	7
Original BCD message:			0		1	0	0
Parity check in positions 1,3,5,7 requires $p_1 = 1$:	1		0		1	0	0
Parity check in positions 2,3,6,7 requires $p_2 = 0$:	1	0	0		1	0	0
Parity check in positions 4,5,6,7 requires $p_3 = 1$:	1	0	0	1	1	0	0
Coded message:	1	0	0	1	1	0	0

p_1 is set equal to 1 so as to establish even parity in positions 1, 3, 5, and 7. Similarly, it is evident that p_2 must be a 0 and p_3 a 1, so that even parity is established in positions 2, 3, 6, and 7 and 4, 5, 6, and 7. The Hamming code for the decimal digits coded in BCD is shown in Table 1-8.

Table 1-8   Hamming code for BCD

Decimal digit	Position	1	2	3	4	5	6	7
		p_1	p_2	m_1	p_3	m_2	m_3	m_4
0		0	0	0	0	0	0	0
1		1	1	0	1	0	0	1
2		0	1	0	1	0	1	0
3		1	0	0	0	0	1	1
4		1	0	0	1	1	0	0
5		0	1	0	0	1	0	1
6		1	1	0	0	1	1	0
7		0	0	0	1	1	1	1
8		1	1	1	0	0	0	0
9		0	0	1	1	0	0	1

The error location and correction is performed in the following manner. Suppose, for example, that the sequence 1101001 is transmitted but, due to an error in the fifth position, the sequence 1101101 is received. The location of the error can be determined by performing three parity checks as follows:

Position:	1	2	3	4	5	6	7	
Message received:	1	1	0	1	1	0	1	
4-5-6-7 parity check:				1	1	0	1	$c_1 = 1$ since parity is odd
2-3-6-7 parity check:		1	0			0	1	$c_2 = 0$ since parity is even
1-3-5-7 parity check:	1		0		1		1	$c_3 = 1$ since parity is odd

Thus the position number formed of $c_1c_2c_3$ is 101, which means that the location of the error is in position 5. To correct the error, the digit in position 5 is complemented, and the correct message 1101001 is obtained.

It is easy to prove that the Hamming code constructed as shown above is a code whose distance is three. Consider, for example, the case where the two original four-bit code words differ in only one position, e.g., 1001 and 0001. Since each message digit appears in at least two parity checks, the parity checks that involve the digit in which the two code words differ will result in different parities, and hence different checking digits will be added to the two words, making the distance between them equal to three. For example, consider the two code words below.

Position:	1	2	3	4	5	6	7
	p_1	p_2	m_1	p_3	m_2	m_3	m_4
First word:			1		0	0	1
Second word:			0		0	0	1
First word with parity bits:	0	0	1		0	0	1
Second word with parity bits:	1	1	0		0	0	1

The two words differ in only m_1 (i.e., position 3). Parity checks 1-3-5-7 and 2-3-6-7 for these two words will give different results. Therefore the parity-checking digits p_1 and p_2 must be different for these words. Clearly, the foregoing argument is valid in the case where the original code words differ in two of the four positions. Thus the Hamming code has a distance of three.

If the distance is increased to four, by adding a parity bit to the code in Table 1-8, so that all eight digits will have even parity, the code may be used for single-error correction and double-error detection in the following manner. Suppose that two errors occur; then the overall parity check is satisfied but the position number (determined as before from the first seven digits) will indicate an error. Clearly, such a situation indicates the existence of a double error. The error positions, however, cannot be located. If only a single error occurs, the overall parity check will detect it. Now, if the position number is 0, then the error is in the last parity bit; otherwise it is in the position given by the position number. If all four parity checks indicate even parities, then the message is correct.

NOTES AND REFERENCES

The material on number systems is available in almost all elementary texts on algebra, switching theory, and digital computers. An extensive discussion of computer arithmetic is available in Flores [1]. Binary codes have been studied in the early 1950's by numerous authors. A listing of many four-bit weighted codes is given in Richards [3]. The material on error-correcting codes is due to Hamming [2].

1. Flores, I.: "The Logic of Computer Arithmetic," Prentice-Hall, Inc., Englewood Cliffs, N.J., 1963.
2. Hamming, R. W.: Error Detecting and Error Correcting Codes, *Bell System Tech. J.*, vol. 29, pp. 147–160, April, 1950.
3. Richards, R. K.: "Arithmetic Operations in Digital Computers," D. Van Nostrand Company, Inc., Princeton, N.J., 1955.

PROBLEMS

1-1. Convert the following numbers:
- (a) $(1431)_8$ to base 10
- (b) 11001010.0101 to base 10
- (c) 11001101.0101 to base 8 and to base 4
- (d) $(1984)_{10}$ to base 8
- (e) $(1776)_{10}$ to base 6
- (f) $(53.1575)_{10}$ to base 2
- (g) $(3.1415\cdots)_{10}$ to base 8 and to base 2

1-2. (a) Given that $(16)_{10} = (100)_b$, determine the value of b. (b) Given that $(292)_{10} = (1204)_b$, determine the value of b.

1-3. Given the binary numbers $a = 1010.1$, $b = 101.01$, $c = 1001.1$, perform the following binary operations:
- (a) $a + c$
- (b) $a - b$
- (c) $a \cdot c$
- (d) a/b

1-4. Each of the following arithmetic operations is correct in at least one number system. Determine the possible bases of the numbers in each operation.
- (a) $1234 + 5432 = 6666$
- (b) $41/3 = 13$
- (c) $33/3 = 11$
- (d) $23 + 44 + 14 + 32 = 223$
- (e) $302/20 = 12.1$
- (f) $\sqrt{41} = 5$

1-5. In the following series, the same integer is expressed in different number systems. Determine the missing member of the series.

10,000, 121, 100, ?, 24, 22, 20, . . .

1-6. (a) Encode each of the 10 decimal digits 0, 1, . . . , 9 by means of the following weighted binary codes:

$$
\begin{array}{rrrr}
6 & 3 & 1 & -1 \\
7 & 3 & 2 & -1 \\
7 & 3 & 1 & -2 \\
5 & 4 & -2 & -1 \\
8 & 7 & -4 & -2
\end{array}
$$

(b) Determine which of the above codes is self-complementing.

1-7. (a) Prove that in every positively weighted code one of the weights must be 1, a second weight must be either 1 or 2, and the sum of the weights must be equal to or greater than 9.

(b) Show by listing all such codes that there are only 17 positively weighted codes, of which only 4 are self-complementing.

1-8. (a) Prove that in a self-complementing code the sum of the weights must be 9.

(b) Show the weights of three different four-bit self-complementing codes whose only negative weight is -4.

1-9. The following were suggested as the first code words in a cyclic code. In each case either complete the code or show that it cannot be completed. Each code sequence must contain the set of all possible code words, and the last code word must be a unit distance from the first.

(a) 000, 001, 011, 111
(b) 000, 010, 011, 111, 101
(c) 000, 010, 110, 111
(d) 0000, 0100, 0101, 1101, 1111, 1011, 1010

1-10. Given a Gray code word $g_n \cdot \cdot \cdot g_2 g_1 g_0$, prove that the ith digit of the corresponding binary number $b_n \cdot \cdot \cdot b_2 b_1 b_0$ is given by

$$
b_i = g_n \oplus g_{n-1} \oplus g_{n-2} \oplus \cdot \cdot \cdot \oplus g_i
$$
$$
b_n = g_n
$$

Hint: Prove first that if $x \oplus y = z$, then $x \oplus z = y$ and $y \oplus z = x$, where x, y, and z are binary variables.

1-11. The message below has been coded in the Hamming code of Table 1-8 and transmitted through a noisy channel. Decode the message assuming that at most a single error has occurred in each code word.

$$
1\ 0\ 0\ 1\ 0\ 0\ 1\ 0\ 1\ 1\ 1\ 0\ 0\ 1\ 1\ 1\ 1\ 0\ 1\ 1\ 0\ 0\ 0\ 1\ 1\ 0\ 1\ 1
$$

1-12. Construct a seven-bit error-correcting code to represent the decimal digits by augmenting the Excess-3 code and by using *odd*-1 parity check.

1-13. Consider the following four codes:

Code A	Code B	Code C	Code D
0001	000	01011	000000
0010	001	01100	001111
0100	011	10010	110011
1000	010	10101	
	110		
	111		
	101		
	100		

(a) Which of the following properties is satisfied by each of the above codes?

(i) Detects single errors

(ii) Detects double errors

(iii) Detects triple errors

(iv) Corrects single errors

(v) Corrects double errors

(vi) Corrects single and detects double errors

(b) How many words can be added to code A without changing its error-detection and correction capabilities? Give a possible set of such words. Is this set unique?

2
Sets, Relations, and Lattices

The objective of this chapter is twofold: to develop in an informal manner the properties of partially ordered sets and lattices, and to furnish the algebraic concepts necessary for the understanding of later chapters. The chapter develops in an intuitive manner the notions of sets, relations, and partial ordering, which together form the basis for the presentation of some results from lattice theory and, in Chap. 3, Boolean algebras. The chapter is by no means a complete treatment of the subjects, but rather a survey of some of the results to the extent that they bear upon material developed in later chapters.

2-1 SETS

A set S is intuitively defined as a collection of distinct objects. IBM computers, the readers of this book, and the prime numbers are examples of sets. The objects that form a set are called the *elements*, or *members*, of that set, and the set is said to *contain* them. The membership of an element a in a set A is denoted by $a \in A$ to mean "a is an element of

A." A set which has no element is called *empty set*, or *null set*, and is denoted ϕ. The elements contained in a set are either listed explicitly or described by their properties. This is accomplished by placing the elements or the describing property in braces.

Example   The set of all even numbers between 1 and 10 is written as

$\{2,4,6,8,10\}$

The infinite set of all positive, even numbers can be described by

$\{2,4,6, \ldots\}$

The set

{all readers of this book who live in Antarctica}

is in all likelihood empty.   ■

Two sets A and B are *equal*, or *identical*, if they contain precisely the same elements. The equality of two sets is denoted by $A = B$. A set A is said to be a *subset* of B if every element of A is also an element of B. If B contains at least one element which is not contained in A, then A is said to be a *proper subset* of B. We use the notation $A \subseteq B$ to indicate that A is a subset of B, and $A \subset B$ to indicate that A is a proper subset of B. Thus the collection of female students in a university is a proper subset of the set of all students. The collection of students understanding the lecture in a class, on the other hand, is not necessarily a proper subset of all the students sitting in that class, since it may happen that they all understand the lecture. The sets that we shall consider in each particular discussion are subsets of a corresponding set U, which we shall call the *universe*.

Example   In the rolling of a die the universe of the possible outcomes is the set consisting of all six faces of the die, $f_1, f_2, \ldots, f_6$, *i.e.*,

$U = \{f_1, f_2, f_3, f_4, f_5, f_6\}$

Clearly, U has $2^6 = 64$ subsets, namely,

$\phi, \{f_1\}, \ldots, \{f_6\}, \{f_1, f_2\}, \ldots, \{f_5, f_6\}, \{f_1, f_2, f_3\}, \ldots, U$ ■

New sets can be generated by operating on existing sets. The *union*, or *sum*, of two sets A and B, designated $A + B$ or $A \cup B$, is the set containing all elements which are members of either *A or B or* both. The *intersection*, or *product*, of two sets A and B, designated AB or $A \cap B$, is the set containing precisely those elements which are members of both *A and B*. The *absolute complement* (or simply *complement*) A' of a set

A is the set containing the elements of the universe that are not contained in A.

Two sets A and B are *disjoint*, or *mutually exclusive*, if they have no common element, i.e., $AB = \phi$. For example, if we let A be the set of female students, and B be the set of male students, then the union $A + B$ yields the entire student body. The intersection $AB = \phi$ is the null set, for obvious reasons, and since $U = A + B$, then $A' = B$ and $B' = A$.

A common way of describing graphically various sets is by *Venn diagram*, shown in Fig. 2-1, where the universe is represented by a square, and the elements of the sets are represented by the interiors of the corresponding circles. The intersection and union of A and B are shown by the shaded areas of Fig. 2-1a and b, respectively.

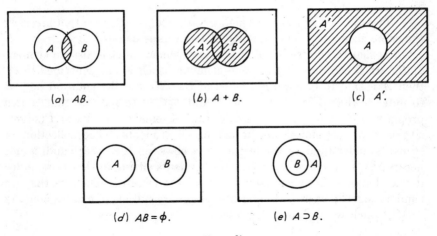

(a) AB.   (b) $A + B$.   (c) A'.

(d) $AB = \phi$.   (e) $A \supset B$.

Fig. 2-1 Venn diagrams.

2-2 RELATIONS

The concepts of equivalence relations and partitions, which are presented in this section, are very useful in the study of finite-state machines, and are essential for the understanding of their structural properties.

An *ordered pair* (a,b) is a pair of elements with a specific order associated with them. A father and his son, a teacher and a student, are examples of ordered pairs. The first element a is the first *coordinate* of the pair, while the second element b is its second coordinate. A convenient way of describing a set of ordered pairs is by means of a directed graph.

Example The graph of Fig. 2-2 describes the set of ordered pairs
$\{(a,a),(a,b),(b,a),(b,c),(c,a)\}$. ∎

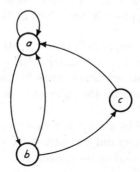

Fig. 2-2 Graphical representation of a set of ordered pairs.

In a similar manner we define the notion of an *ordered triple* (a,b,c), where a is the first coordinate, b is second, and c is third. Extending the definition to n elements yields the notion of an *ordered n-tuple* $(a_1,a_2, \ldots ,a_n)$. The ith element a_i of an ordered n-tuple is referred to as its *ith coordinate.*

It is often necessary to consider sets whose members are ordered pairs. Such a set of ordered pairs is called a *binary relation.* If R is a binary relation and the pair (a,b) is an element of R, we write $a \, R \, b$ to indicate that a *is related to* b by R. We often specify the relation R by the property that relates the members of each of its ordered pairs. For example, the binary relation "is less than" is denoted by $a < b$, "is equal to" is denoted by $a = b$, and so on.

If A and B are two sets, then the *cartesian product* of A and B, denoted $A \times B$, is the set containing all ordered pairs (a,b), such that $a \in A$ and $b \in B$. It is evident that any subset of $A \times B$ is a binary relation, and it is referred to as a *relation from A to B.*

Example Let $A = \{p,q\}$ and $B = \{r,s,t\}$; then

$$A \times B = \{(p,r),(p,s),(p,t),(q,r),(q,s),(q,t)\} \quad ∎$$

A relation from a set A to A is called a *relation in A*, and it is a subset of the cartesian product $A \times A$, that is, $R \subseteq A \times A$. The cartesian product $A \times A$ is usually denoted A^2, $A \times A \times A$ is denoted A^3, etc. A relation R in a set A is *reflexive* if it contains (a,a) for every $a \in A$; it is *symmetric* if the existence of the ordered pair (a,b) in R

implies the existence of (b,a). A relation is *antisymmetric* if for every ordered pair (a,b) it contains, where $a \neq b$, it does not contain the pair (b,a). In other words, if both (a,b) and (b,a) are contained in an antisymmetric relation, then $a = b$. A relation R is *transitive* if the existence of (b,a) and (a,c) in R implies the existence of (b,c).

Example The relation $\{(a,a),(b,b),(a,b)\}$ in the set $\{a,b\}$ is reflexive, and transitive, but not symmetric. The relation $\{(a,b),(b,a)\}$ is symmetric, but not transitive since it does not contain the pair (a,a) which is implied by the pairs (a,b) and (b,a). ■

A binary relation R in a set S is called an *equivalence relation* (*in S*) if it is reflexive, symmetric, and transitive. Two elements related by an equivalence relation are said to be *equivalent*.

Example The relation = is an equivalence relation, since it satisfies the following for all a, b, and c in R:

Reflexive: $a = a$

Symmetric: If $a = b$, then $b = a$

Transitive: If $a = b$ and $b = c$, then $a = c$ ■

The equivalence relation actually partitions the elements of a set into *disjoint* subsets, so that all members of a subset are equivalent and members of different subsets are not equivalent. These disjoint subsets are called *equivalence classes*, and they play an important role in the study of finite-state machines.

Example The relation of parallelism between lines in the plane is an equivalence relation. In particular, the equivalence relation for the lines of Fig. 2-3 is

$$R = \{(a,a),(b,b),(c,c),(d,d),(e,e),(f,f),(a,b),(b,a),(a,c),(c,a),$$
$$(b,c),(c,b),(d,e),(e,d)\}$$

The equivalence classes are $\{a,b,c\}$, $\{d,e\}$, and $\{f\}$, and are denoted by $\{\overline{a,b,c};\overline{d,e};\overline{f}\}$. ■

A relation which is reflexive and symmetric, but not transitive, is called a *compatibility relation*. Two elements related by a compatibility relation are said to be *compatible*. A consequence of the nontransitivity of the compatibility relation is that it classifies the elements of a set into *nondisjoint* subsets, so that all members of a subset are compatible. These subsets are called *compatibility classes*.

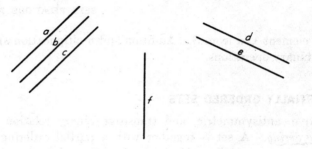

Fig. 2-3 Lines in a plane.

Definition 2-1. A *partition* π on a set S is a collection of disjoint subsets whose set union is S. The disjoint subsets are called the *blocks* of π.

$\#(\pi)$ is the number of blocks in π, and $\rho(\pi)$ denotes the number of elements in the largest block. If every block of π contains precisely the same number of elements, the partition is said to be *uniform*.

Since an equivalence relation partitions the elements of a set into disjoint subsets, it defines, or *induces*, a partition on that set. For example, the equivalence relation corresponding to Fig. 2-3 induces the partition $\pi = \{\overline{a,b,c}; \overline{d,e}; \overline{f}\}$. It is quite obvious that the converse is also true and every partition on S defines an equivalence relation in that set.

A binary relation F in a set S of ordered pairs is called a *function* if and only if the existence of two pairs (a,b) and (a,c) in F, such that their first coordinates are identical, implies $b = c$. In other words, a function is a set of ordered pairs in which no two pairs have the same first coordinate. A *function from set A to set B* is one which associates with each element a in A exactly one element b in B so that $(a,b) \in F$.

Example If $A = \{a_1, a_2, a_3\}$ and $B = \{b_1, b_2\}$, then $\{(a_1, b_1), (a_2, b_2), (a_3, b_1)\}$ is a function from A to B, while $\{(a_1, b_1), (a_2, b_2), (a_3, b_1), (a_3, b_2)\}$ is not, since it assigns two elements of B to a_3. ∎

A function from set A to itself is called a *unary operation* in A, and it serves to assign to every element in A a unique element from A. Similarly, a *binary operation* is a function from A^2 to A, and it assigns to every ordered pair of A^2 a unique element from A. In general, an *n-ary operation* in A is a function from A^n to A.

Example Consider the set S of positive, real numbers. The function *square root* is a unary operation which assigns to each a in S

an element $\sqrt{a}$ from S.   Addition and multiplication are examples of binary operations.

2-3 PARTIALLY ORDERED SETS

A reflexive, antisymmetric, and transitive binary relation is called a _partial ordering_.   A set S together with a partial ordering relation is referred to as a _partially ordered set_.   A very useful example of partial ordering is the "is less than or equal to" relation.   If (a,b) is an element of a partially ordered set, we usually say that a is less than or equal to b, even if no numerical values are associated with a or b.

Example   The partial ordering $\leq$ satisfies the following for all a, b, and c in S:

Reflexive: $a \leq a$

Antisymmetric: $a \leq b$ and $b \leq a$.implies $a = b$

Transitive: if $a \leq b$ and $b \leq c$, then $a \leq c$ ∎

A partition π_1 on S is said to be "smaller than or equal to" π_2 on S, denoted $\pi_1 \leq \pi_2$, if and only if each pair of elements which are in a common block of π_1 are also in a common block of π_2.   Two partitions π_1 and π_2 are said to be _incomparable_ if $\pi_1 \nleq \pi_2$ and $\pi_2 \nleq \pi_1$.

Example   Consider the set S and three partitions on S.

$$S = \{a,b,c,d,e,f,g,h,i\}$$
$$\pi_1 = \{\overline{a,b}; \overline{c,d}; \overline{e,f}; \overline{g,h,i}\}$$
$$\pi_2 = \{\overline{a,f}; \overline{b,c}; \overline{d,e}; \overline{g,h}; \overline{i}\}$$
$$\pi_3 = \{\overline{a,b,e,f}; \overline{c,d}; \overline{g,h,i}\}$$

Clearly, $\pi_1 \leq \pi_3$, but π_1 and π_2 are incomparable, as are π_2 and π_3.   ∎

If for every pair of elements a, $b \in S$ either $a \leq b$ or $b \leq a$, then the set S is _totally ordered_ by the binary relation $\leq$.   For example, the set of all prime numbers is totally ordered by the $\leq$ relation.   On the other hand, the set of partitions $\{\pi_1,\pi_2,\pi_3\}$, defined in the preceding example, is partially ordered, since no ordering by the relation $\leq$ exists between π_1 and π_2.

A convenient way of displaying the ordering relation among the elements of an ordered set S is by means of a graph whose vertices represent the elements of the set.   Vertex a is drawn in a higher level than vertex b whenever $b < a$, that is, $b \leq a$ but $b \neq a$. Vertex a is in a higher level immediately adjacent to vertex b if $b < a$ and there is no element c in S such that $b < c < a$. In such cases a is said to *cover* b. The graph is called a *Hasse graph* or *Hasse diagram*.

It is always possible to reconstruct a partial ordering from the Hasse diagram. This is accomplished by observing that each upward path from vertex b to vertex a corresponds to $b < a$, which in turn may be denoted $b \leq a$.

Example The partial ordering displaying the divisibility relation among all positive integers dividing the number 45, so that the quotient is an integer, is shown in Fig. 2-4a. ■

Example Let $S = \{(0,0),(0,1),(1,0),(1,1)\}$ and define the ordering relation as follows:

$$(a_1,a_2) \leq (b_1,b_2) \qquad \text{if and only if} \qquad a_1 \leq b_1 \text{ and } a_2 \leq b_2$$

Clearly, S is not a totally ordered set, under the above-defined ordering, since $(0,1)$ and $(1,0)$ are not related. The graphical description of the partial ordering is given in Fig. 2-4b. ■

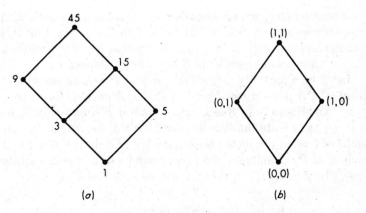

Fig. 2-4 Hasse diagrams for partially ordered sets.

Consider the partially ordered set S and the given relation $\leq$. If $a \leq b$ for every element b in S, then a is said to be a *least member* of the set S. Not every set has a least member (see, for example, Fig. 2-5), but whenever it does exist, it is unique. In order to prove the uniqueness of the least member, assume that for some S there exist two least members,

a_1 and a_2. Since $a_1 \leq b$ for every element b in S, then $a_1 \leq a_2$. Similarly, since $a_2 \leq b$, then $a_2 \leq a_1$. Consequently, $\leq$ being an antisymmetric relation, $a_1 = a_2$. Similarly, if $b \leq a$ for all b in S, then a is said to be a *greatest member* of S; and if such a member exists, it is unique. In the two graphs of Fig. 2-4, the least and greatest elements are shown in the lowest and highest levels, respectively.

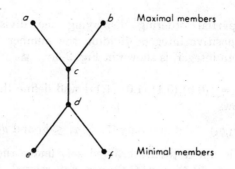

Fig. 2-5 A Hasse diagram without least or greatest elements.

Whenever the least member does not exist, it is convenient to define a *minimal member* a in S such that for no b in S is $b < a$; that is, there is no smaller element, but there may exist another unrelated minimal member in S. A *maximal member* in S is similarly defined.

Let S be a partially ordered set, and let P be a subset of S; then an element s in S is an *upper bound* of P if and only if, for every p in P, $p \leq s$. An element s in S is a *lower bound* of P if and only if, for every p in P, $s \leq p$. Note that s is not necessarily a member of P. An upper bound s of P is said to be the *least upper bound* (lub) if $s \leq s'$ for all upper bounds s' of P. Similarly, the lower bound s in S is called *greatest lower bound* (glb) if and only if, for all lower bounds s' of P, $s' \leq s$.

Example Consider the subset $P = \{3,5\}$ of the set

$$S = \{1,3,5,9,15,45\}$$

described in Fig. 2-4a. The upper bounds are 15 and 45; the lub is 15. The glb is 1. In the partially ordered set described in Fig. 2-5, the subset $P = \{a,b\}$ has no upper bound, but it has four lower bounds, c, d, e, and f, of which c is the glb. For the subset $P = \{b,f\}$, b is the lub, while f is the glb. ∎

2-4 LATTICES

Lattices play an important role in characterizing various computation models. In particular, it will be shown later that a Boolean algebra is nothing but a lattice with a few specific properties.

Definition 2-2. A partially ordered set in which every pair of elements has a unique glb and a unique lub is called a *lattice*.

Example The partially ordered sets described in Fig. 2-4 are lattices, while the one described in Fig. 2-5 is not. ∎

A consequence to Definition 2-2 is that each finite lattice has both a least and a greatest element, which are denoted 0 and 1, respectively. Thus, for each element a of the lattice,

$$a \leq 1 \quad \text{and} \quad 0 \leq a$$

Example The lattice of all subsets of the set $S = \{a,b,c\}$, under the ordering relation of set inclusion, is shown in Fig. 2-6, where $\{a,b,c\} = 1$ and $\phi = 0$. ∎

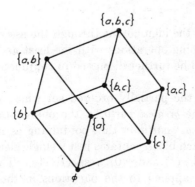

Fig. 2-6 Lattice of the subsets of $\{a,b,c\}$.

Because of the uniqueness of the lub and the glb, they may be viewed as binary operations, which assign to each ordered pair of elements their lub and glb. The first operation, called *sum*, or *join*, is denoted by + or ∨; the second operation, called *product*, or *meet*, is denoted by $\wedge$ or $\cdot$. Thus

$$a + b = \text{lub}(a,b)$$
$$a \cdot b = \text{glb}(a,b)$$

By definition, the lub and glb satisfy the idempotent and commutative laws, i.e.,

Idempotency: $a \cdot a = a + a = a$

Commutativity: $a \cdot b = b \cdot a$ and $a + b = b + a$

In addition, they satisfy the absorption law and are associative, i.e.,

Absorption: $a + a \cdot b = a$ and $a \cdot (a + b) = a$

Associativity: $a \cdot (b \cdot c) = (a \cdot b) \cdot c$ and $a + (b + c) = (a + b) + c$

In order to prove the validity of the absorption law, recall that $a \cdot b$ defines the glb of a and b, and thus $a \cdot b \leq a$. Hence $a + a \cdot b$, which defines the lub of a and $a \cdot b$, is clearly a. The dual property is verified in an analogous manner. The proof that the operations are associative is left to the reader as an exercise (see Prob. 2-3).

The following properties are valid for every finite lattice:

$$a + 0 = a \qquad a \cdot 0 = 0$$

and

$$a \cdot 1 = a \qquad a + 1 = 1$$

The duality of the idempotent through the associative laws, as well as that of the foregoing operations with the least and greatest elements, is apparent, and will be further discussed in conjunction with the subject of Boolean algebras.

Now consider the partially ordered set whose elements are partitions. Define as the *greatest partition* the one containing just a single block, and as the *least partition* that containing as many blocks as elements, i.e., where each block contains just a single element. These partitions are designated $\pi(I)$ and $\pi(0)$, respectively. The binary operations of lub and glb are applied to the partitions in the following manner. The sum (or join) $\pi_1 + \pi_2$ is obtained by including in every block those elements of π_1 and π_2 which are chain-connected;† the product (or meet) $\pi_1 \cdot \pi_2$ is obtained by intersecting the blocks of the individual partitions. As a consequence, under the above-defined operations, the set of all partitions constitutes a lattice. It can be shown that these sum and product

---

† Two subsets (or blocks) S_1 and S_n are said to be *chain-connected* if and only if there exists a sequence of subsets $S_1, S_2, \ldots, S_n$ such that

$$S_i \cdot S_{i+1} \neq \phi \qquad i = 1, 2, \ldots, n - 1$$

operations follow directly from the partition inclusion relation and indeed yield the lub and glb, respectively. But the proof is beyond the scope of this book.

Example Let $\pi_1 = \{\overline{a,b}; \overline{c,d,e}; \overline{f,h}; \overline{g,i}\}$ and $\pi_2 = \{\overline{a,b,c}; \overline{d,e}; \overline{f,g}; \overline{h,i}\}$; then

$$\pi_1 + \pi_2 = \{\overline{a,b,c,d,e}; \overline{f,g,h,i}\}$$

and

$$\pi_1 \cdot \pi_2 = \{\overline{a,b}; \overline{c}; \overline{d,e}; \overline{f}; \overline{g}; \overline{h}; \overline{i}\} \quad \blacksquare$$

The distributive law is not necessarily valid for arbitrary lattices, as shown by the lattice in Fig. 2-7. A lattice is said to be *distributive* if and only if

$$a \cdot (b + c) = a \cdot b + a \cdot c$$
$$a + (b \cdot c) = (a + b)(a + c)$$

Example Consider the following set of partitions:

$$\pi_0 = \{\overline{a}; \overline{b}; \overline{c}\} = \pi(0) \qquad \pi_1 = \{\overline{a,b}; \overline{c}\} \qquad \pi_2 = \{\overline{a}; \overline{b,c}\}$$
$$\pi_3 = \{\overline{a,c}; \overline{b}\} \qquad \pi_4 = \{\overline{a,b,c}\} = \pi(I)$$

The product $\pi_1 \cdot (\pi_2 + \pi_3) = \pi_1$, but $\pi_1 \cdot \pi_2 + \pi_1 \cdot \pi_3 = \pi_0$; consequently, the lattice, which is shown in Fig. 2-7, is not distributive. $\blacksquare$

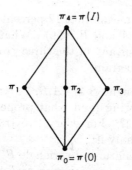

Fig. 2-7 A nondistributive lattice.

If for each element a in the lattice there exists an element a' such that

$$a \cdot a' = 0 \qquad \text{and} \qquad a + a' = 1$$

the lattice is said to be *complemented.* The element a' is said to be a *complement* of a, and vice versa. For example, the lattice of subsets of $\{a,b,c\}$ shown in Fig. 2-6 is distributive and complemented.

NOTES AND REFERENCES

The material covered in this chapter is available in many good books on modern algebra; among these are Birkhoff and MacLane [2] and Mostow, Sampson, and Meyer [3]. A classical reference, though an advanced one, is "Lattice Theory" by Birkhoff [1].

1. Birkhoff, G.: "Lattice Theory," American Mathematical Society Colloquium Publications, vol. 25, Providence, R.I., 1948.
2. Birkhoff, G., and S. MacLane: "A Survey of Modern Algebra," 3d ed., The Macmillan Company, New York, 1965.
3. Mostow, G. D., J. H. Sampson, and J. Meyer: "Fundamental Structures of Algebra," McGraw-Hill Book Company, New York, 1963.

PROBLEMS

2-1. In an examination there are three problems, A, B, and C. In the following tabulation are the percentages of students who received credit for solving one or more problems.

A: 40	A, B: 12	A, B, C: 4
B: 30	A, C: 8	
C: 30	B, C: 6	

(For example, A, B: 12 means that 12 percent of the students received credit for both problems A and B, etc.) What percent of the students received no credit at all for any of the three problems?

Hint: Use a Venn diagram.

2-2. Consider a set of triangles $S = \{A, B, \ldots\}$ in a plane. What kind of relations are the following (and what properties do they have, e.g., reflexive, symmetric, etc.)? For every two triangles A and B in S, A and B are related if and only if:

   (a) Triangle A is congruent to triangle B

   (b) Triangle A has area in common with triangle B

   (c) Triangle A is similar to triangle B

   (d) Triangle A is entirely inside of or the same as triangle B

   (e) Triangle A has a side equal to or smaller than the smallest side of triangle B

   (f) Triangle A has a side equal to or smaller than the smallest side of triangle B but has at least as much area as triangle B

$\sqrt{}$ **2-3.** Prove that the lub and glb operations are associative; that is, for all a, b, and c of any lattice

$$a + (b + c) = (a + b) + c \qquad \text{and} \qquad a \cdot (b \cdot c) = (a \cdot b) \cdot c$$

Hint: Use the uniqueness of the lub and the glb of (a,b,c).

$\sqrt{}$ **2-4.** Given the following three partitions on the set $\{a,b,c,d,e,f,g,h,i,j,k\}$:

$$\pi_1 = \{\overline{a,b,c}; \overline{d,e}; \overline{f}; \overline{g,h,i}; \overline{j,k}\}$$
$$\pi_2 = \{\overline{a,b}; \overline{c,g,h}; \overline{d,e,f}; \overline{i,j,k}\}$$
$$\pi_3 = \{\overline{a,b,c,f}; \overline{d,e}; \overline{g,h,i,j,k}\}$$

(a) Find $\pi_1 + \pi_2$ and $\pi_1 \cdot \pi_2$.

(b) Find $\pi_1 + \pi_3$ and $\pi_1 \cdot \pi_3$.

(c) Find a partition that is greater than π_1 and smaller than π_3.

(d) Can you find a partition that is greater than π_2 and smaller than π_3?

2-5. Prove that if a complemented lattice is not distributive, the complements of its elements are not necessarily unique. And conversely, if for some element in the lattice the complement is not unique, the lattice is not distributive.

$\sqrt{}$ **2-6.** For each of the lattices described by the diagrams in Fig. P2-6, determine whether it is a distributive and/or complemented lattice. If the lattice is complemented, identify the complementary elements. Which diagram corresponds to a total ordering?

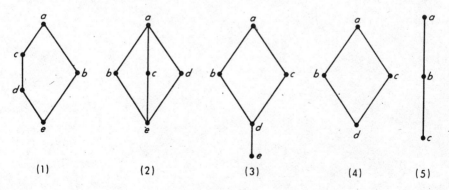

(1)   (2)   (3)   (4)   (5)

Fig. P2-6

Part Two
Combinational Logic

3
Switching Algebra and Its Applications

The second part of this book is devoted to *combinational logic* and deals with the various aspects of analysis and design of combinational switching circuits. The particular characteristic of a *combinational switching circuit* is that its outputs are functions of only the present circuit inputs. First, switching algebra is introduced as the basic mathematical tool essential in dealing with the problems encountered in the study of switching circuits. Switching expressions are defined and are found to be instrumental in describing the logical properties of switching circuits. Systematic simplification procedures of these expressions are next presented, leading to more economical circuits. Logical design is studied with special attention to conventional logic, contact circuits, and threshold logic. Finally, various problems of reliable design are examined, such as prevention of hazards and malfunctions, fault detection and correction, and improvements of circuit reliability.

In the present chapter, after developing a switching algebra from the simplest set of basic postulates, we show its applications in the study of switching circuits, as well as in the calculus of propositions. Finally, this switching algebra is shown to be a special case of Boolean algebra.

3-1 SWITCHING ALGEBRA

The basic concepts of switching algebra will be introduced by means of a set of postulates, from which we shall derive useful theorems and develop the necessary tools that will enable us to manipulate and simplify algebraic expressions.

Fundamental postulates

The basic postulate of switching algebra is the existence of a two-valued switching variable which can take any of the two distinct values 0 and 1. Precisely stated, if x is a switching variable, then

$$x \neq 0 \quad \text{if and only if} \quad x = 1$$
$$x \neq 1 \quad \text{if and only if} \quad x = 0$$

These values are often referred to as the *truth values* of x.

A *switching algebra* is an algebraic system consisting of the set $\{0,1\}$, two binary† operations called OR and AND and denoted by the symbols $+$ and $\cdot$, respectively, and one unary operation called NOT and denoted by a prime, $'$. The definitions of the OR and AND operations are as follows:

OR operation	AND operation
$0 + 0 = 0$	$0 \cdot 0 = 0$
$0 + 1 = 1$	$0 \cdot 1 = 0$
$1 + 0 = 1$	$1 \cdot 0 = 0$
$1 + 1 = 1$	$1 \cdot 1 = 1$

The OR combination of two switching variables $x + y$ is equal to 1 if the value of either x *or* y *or* both is 1. The AND combination of these variables $x \cdot y$ is equal to 1 if and only if the values of x *and* y are 1. The OR operation is very often called *logical sum* (or simply *sum*), or *union*, and may also be denoted by $\cup$ or $\vee$. The AND operation is referred to as *logical multiplication* (or *product*), or *intersection*, and is also denoted by $\cap$ or $\wedge$. We shall generally omit the dot $\cdot$ and write xy to mean $x \cdot y$.

† A *binary operation* on a set of elements is a rule which assigns a unique element from the set to each ordered pair of elements from the set. A *unary operation* is a rule which assigns to every element in the set another element from the set (see Sec. 2-2).

The NOT operation, which is also known as *complementation*, is defined as follows:

$$0' = 1$$

$$1' = 0$$

The preceding postulates and the definitions of the switching operations enable us to derive many useful theorems and to develop the entire algebraic structure so that it may be advantageously applied to switching circuits.

Basic properties

The first property which drastically differs from the algebra of real numbers, and accounts for the special characteristics of switching algebra, is the idempotence law:

Idempotency: $x + x = x$ (3-1)

$x \cdot x = x$ (3-1')

To prove this property we shall employ *perfect induction*. Perfect induction is a method of proof whereby a theorem is verified for every possible combination of values that the variables may assume. Since x is a two-valued variable, $x + x = x$ may assume the values $1 + 1 = 1$ and $0 + 0 = 0$. The equations being identities clearly verifies the validity of Eq. (3-1), and similarly for Eq. (3-1'), $1 \cdot 1 = 1$ and $0 \cdot 0 = 0$.

If x is a switching variable, then

$x + 1 = 1$ (3-2)

$x \cdot 0 = 0$ (3-2')

$x + 0 = x$ (3-3)

$x \cdot 1 = x$ (3-3')

The following two pairs of relations establish the commutativity and associativity of the switching operations. The convention adopted for parenthesizing is that of ordinary algebra, where $x + y \cdot z$ means $x + (y \cdot z)$ and not $(x + y) \cdot z$. Let x, y, and z be switching variables; then

Commutativity: $x + y = y + x$ (3-4)

$x \cdot y = y \cdot x$ (3-4')

Associativity: $(x + y) + z = x + (y + z)$ (3-5)

$(x \cdot y) \cdot z = x \cdot (y \cdot z)$ (3-5')

In addition, for every switching variable x,

Complementation: $x + x' = 1$ (3-6)

$x \cdot x' = 0$ (3-6')

The properties established by Eqs. (3-2) through (3-6') can be proved by the method of perfect induction. The actual proofs are left to the reader as exercises. It is the associative law which enables us to extend the definitions of the AND and OR operations to more than two variables; i.e., we write $T = x + y + z$ to mean that T equals 1 if any of x, y, or z, or any combination thereof, equals 1.

In switching algebra multiplication distributes over addition, and addition distributes over multiplication—a property known as the distributive law.

Distributivity: $x \cdot (y + z) = x \cdot y + x \cdot z$ (3-7)

$x + y \cdot z = (x + y) \cdot (x + z)$ (3-7')

To verify Eq. (3-7) for every possible combination of values of x, y, and z, it is convenient to tabulate these combinations in a table called *truth table,* or *table of combinations.* Since every variable may assume one of two values, 0 or 1, the truth table for the three variables contains $2^3 = 8$ combinations. These combinations are tabulated in the leftmost column of Table 3-1. The value of $x(y + z)$ is computed for every possible combination of x and $y + z$. The value of $xy + xz$ is computed independently by adding the entries in columns xy and xz. Since the two different methods of computation yield identical results, as shown in the two rightmost columns, Eq. (3-7) is verified.

Table 3-1 Proof by perfect induction of Eq. (3-7)

x y z	xy	xz	$y + z$	$x(y + z)$	$xy + xz$
0 0 0	0	0	0	0	0
0 0 1	0	0	1	0	0
0 1 0	0	0	1	0	0
0 1 1	0	0	1	0	0
1 0 0	0	0	0	0	0
1 0 1	0	1	1	1	1
1 .1 0	1	0	1	1	1
1 1. 1	1	1	1	1	1

We observe that all the preceding properties are grouped in pairs. Within each pair one statement can be obtained from the other by interchanging the OR and AND operations and replacing the constants 0 and 1 by 1 and 0, respectively. Any two statements or theorems which have this property are called *dual,* and this quality of duality which characterizes switching algebra is known as the *principle of duality.* It stems from the symmetry of the postulates and definitions of switching algebra with respect to the two operations and the two constants. The implication of the concept of duality is that it is necessary to prove only one of each pair of statements, and its dual is henceforth proved.

Switching expressions and their manipulation

By a *switching expression* we mean the combination of a finite number of switching variables (x, y, etc.) and constants (0,1) by means of the switching operations ($+$, $\cdot$, and $'$). More precisely, any switching constant or variable is a switching expression, and if T_1 and T_2 are switching expressions, then so are T'_1, T'_2, $T_1 + T_2$, and $T_1 T_2$. No other combinations of variables and constants are switching expressions.

The properties to be presented in Eqs. (3-8) through (3-10') provide the basic tools for the simplification of switching expressions. They establish the notion of redundancy, and like all the preceding properties, they appear in dual forms. Equation (3-8) and its dual (3-8') express the absorption law of switching algebra.

Absorption: $x + xy = x$ $\hspace{5cm}$ (3-8)

$$x(x + y) = x \hspace{5cm} (3\text{-}8')$$

The method of proof by perfect induction is an effective one, as long as the number of combinations for which the statement is to be verified is small. In other cases algebraic procedures are more appropriate, such, for example, as are demonstrated in the following proofs.

Proof: $x + xy = x1 + xy$ $\hspace{1.5cm}$ [by Eq. (3-3')]

$\hspace{2cm} = x(1 + y)$ $\hspace{1.5cm}$ [by Eq. (3-7)]

$\hspace{2cm} = x1$ $\hspace{2.6cm}$ [by Eqs. (3-2) and (3-4)]

$\hspace{2cm} = x$ $\hspace{2.9cm}$ [by Eq. (3-3')] ∎

Another property of switching expressions, important in their simplification, is the following:

$$x + x'y = x + y \hspace{5cm} (3\text{-}9)$$

$$x(x' + y) = xy \hspace{5cm} (3\text{-}9')$$

Proof: $x + x'y = (x + x')(x + y)$ $\hspace{1cm}$ [by Eq. (3-7')]

$\hspace{2cm} = 1(x + y)$ $\hspace{2cm}$ [by Eq. (3-6)]

$\hspace{2cm} = x + y$ $\hspace{2.5cm}$ [by Eqs. (3-3') and (3-4')] ∎

The consensus theorem is noteworthy in that it is used frequently in the simplification of switching expressions.

Consensus:
$$xy + x'z + yz = xy + x'z \tag{3-10}$$
$$(x + y)(x' + z)(y + z) = (x + y)(x' + z) \tag{3-10'}$$

Proof:
$$\begin{aligned}
xy + x'z + yz &= xy + x'z + yz1 \\
&= xy + x'z + yz(x + x') \\
&= xy + x'z + xyz + x'yz \\
&= xy(1 + z) + x'z(1 + y) \\
&= xy + x'z \quad \blacksquare
\end{aligned}$$

The preceding properties permit a variety of manipulations on switching expressions. In particular, they enable us (whenever possible) to convert an expression into an equivalent one with fewer literals, where by *literal* we mean an appearance of a variable or its complement. For example, while the left-hand side of Eq. (3-10) consists of six literal appearances, its right-hand side consists of only four appearances. If the value of a switching expression is independent of the value of some literal x_i, then x_i is said to be *redundant*. Equations (3-1) through (3-10') provide, among other things, the tools for manipulating expressions so as to eliminate redundant literals.

Example Simplify the expression $T(x,y,z) = x'y'z + yz + xz$ by eliminating redundant literals.

$$\begin{aligned}
x'y'z + yz + xz &= z(x'y' + y + x) \\
&= z(x' + y + x) \\
&= z(y + 1) \\
&= z1 \\
&= z
\end{aligned}$$

Hence $T(x,y,z)$ is actually independent of the values of x and y, and depends only on z. $\blacksquare$

It is important to observe that no inverse operations are defined in switching algebra, and consequently, no cancellations are allowed. For example, if $A + B = A + C$, the equality of B and C is not implied;

in fact, if $A = B = 1$ and $C = 0$, then $1 + 1 = 1 + 0$ but $B \neq C$. Similarly, B is not necessarily-equal to C if $AB = AC$.

De Morgan's theorems

The rules governing the complementation operations are summarized by the following three theorems:

Involution: $\qquad (x')' = x$ $\hfill$ (3-11)

Proof: Obvious by perfect induction. ■

$$(x + y)' = x' \cdot y' \hfill (3\text{-}12)$$
$$(x \cdot y)' = x' + y' \hfill (3\text{-}12')$$

Proof: By perfect induction. The proof follows from the truth table of Table 3-2, where $(x + y)'$ and $x'y'$ are computed independently, and are shown to be identical for all possible combinations of values of x and y. ■

Table 3-2   Truth table for proof of Eq. (3-12)

x y	x'	y'	$x + y$	$(x + y)'$	$x'y'$
0 0	1	1	0	1	1
0 1	1	0	1	0	0
1 1	0	0	1	0	0
1 0	0	1	1	0	0

Equations (3-12) and (3-12') are known as *De Morgan's theorems* for two variables. In general, De Morgan's theorems state that *the complement of any expression can be obtained by replacing each variable and element with its complement, and at the same time interchanging the OR and AND operations,* that is,

$$[f(x_1, x_2, \ldots, x_n, 0, 1, +, \cdot)]' = f(x_1', x_2', \ldots, x_n', 1, 0, \cdot, +) \hfill (3\text{-}13)$$

The proof of the general De Morgan's theorem follows immediately from Eq. (3-12) and mathematical induction on the number of operations.

Example   In order to simplify the expression

$$T(x,y,z) = (x + y)[x'(y' + z')]' + x'y' + x'z'$$

it is necessary to first apply De Morgan's theorem and multiply out the expressions in parentheses.

$$\begin{aligned}
T(x,y,z) &= (x + y)(x + yz) + x'y' + x'z' \\
&= (x + xyz + yx + yz) + x'y' + x'z' \\
&= x + yz + x'y' + x'z' \\
&= x + yz + y' + z' \\
&= x + z + y' + z' \\
&= x + y' + 1 \\
&= 1
\end{aligned}$$

Hence $T = 1$ independently of the values of the variables. ■

Example   Prove the following identity.

$$xy + x'y' + yz = xy + x'y' + x'z$$

From the application of Eq. (3-10) to $x'y' + yz$ it follows that the term $x'z$ may be added to the left-hand side of the equation; i.e., the equation becomes

$$xy + x'y' + yz + x'z = xy + x'y' + x'z$$

Another application of Eq. (3-10) to the first, third, and fourth terms in the augmented left-hand side of the equation shows that yz is redundant. The elimination of yz results in the left-hand side of the equation being identical with its right-hand side (i.e., both consist of identical terms), and thus the proof is complete. ■

3-2   SWITCHING FUNCTIONS

Definitions

Let $T(x_1, x_2, \ldots, x_n)$ be a switching expression. Since each of the variables $x_1, x_2, \ldots, x_n$ can independently assume any one of the two values 0 or 1, there are 2^n combinations of values to be considered in determining the values of T. In order to determine the value of an expression for a given combination, it is only necessary to substitute the values for the variables in the expression. For example, if $T(x,y,z) = x'z + xz' + x'y'$, then, for the combination $x = 0, y = 0, z = 1$, the value of the expression is 1 because $T(0,0,1) = 0'1 + 01' + 0'0' = 1$.

In a similar manner the value of T may be computed for every combination, as shown in the right-hand column of Table 3-3.

Table 3-3 Truth table for
$$T(x,y,z) = x'z + xz' + x'y'$$

x	y	z	T
0	0	0	1
0	0	1	1
0	1	0	0
0	1	1	1
1	0	0	1
1	0	1	0
1	1	0	1
1	1	1	0

If we now repeat the above procedure and construct the truth table for the expression $x'z + xz' + y'z'$, we find that it is identical with that of Table 3-3. Hence, for every possible combination of variables, the value of the expression $x'z + xz' + x'y'$ is identical with the value of $x'z + xz' + y'z'$. Thus different switching expressions may represent the same assignment of values specified by the right-hand column of a truth table. The values assumed by an expression for all the combinations of the variables $x_1, x_2, \ldots, x_n$ define a switching function. In other words, a *switching function* $f(x_1,x_2, \ldots ,x_n)$ is a correspondence which associates an element of the algebra with each of the 2^n combinations of the variables $x_1, x_2, \ldots, x_n$. This correspondence is best specified by means of a truth table. Note that each truth table defines only one switching function, although this function may be expressed in a number of ways.

The complement $f'(x_1,x_2, \ldots ,x_n)$ is a function whose value is 1 whenever the value of $f(x_1,x_2, \ldots ,x_n)$ is 0, and 0 whenever the value of f is 1. The sum of two functions $f(x_1,x_2, \ldots ,x_n)$ and $g(x_1,x_2, \ldots ,x_n)$ is 1 for every combination in which either f or g or both equal 1, while their product is equal to 1 if and only if both f and g equal 1. If a function $f(x_1,x_2, \ldots ,x_n)$ is specified by means of a truth table, its complement is obtained by complementing each entry in column f. New functions which are equal to the sum $f + g$ and product fg are obtained by adding or multiplying corresponding entries in columns f and g.

Example Two functions $f(x,y,z)$ and $g(x,y,z)$ are specified in columns f and g of Table 3-4. The complement f', the sum $f + g$, and product fg are specified in the corresponding columns. ■

Table 3-4   Illustration of addition, multiplication, and complementation of switching functions

x	y	z	f	g	f'	$f + g$	fg
0	0	0	1	0	0	1	0
0	0	1	0	1	1	1	0
0	1	0	1	0	0	1	0
0	1	1	1	1	0	1	1
1	0	0	0	1	1	1	0
1	0	1	0	0	1	0	0
1	1	0	1	1	0	1	1
1	1	1	1	0	0	1	0

Simplification of expressions

The truth table assigns to each combination of variable values a specific switching element. Consequently, all the properties of switching elements [Eqs. (3-1) through (3-13)] are valid when elements are replaced by expressions. For example, $xy + xyz = xy$ by virtue of the property established in Eq. (3-8).

Example   Simplify the expression

$$T(A,B,C,D) = A'C' + ABD + BC'D + AB'D' + ABCD'$$

First apply the consensus theorem [Eq. (3-10)] to the first three terms of T, letting x, y, and z replace A', C', and BD, respectively. As a result the third term, $BC'D$, is redundant. Next apply the distributive law [Eq. (3-7)] to the fourth and fifth terms. This gives the expression $AD'(B' + BC)$. Letting x and y replace B' and C, respectively, and applying Eq. (3-9) yields $AD'(B' + C)$. No other literal is redundant; thus the simplest expression for T is

$$T = A'C' + A[BD + D'(B' + C)] \quad \blacksquare$$

Example   Simplify the expression

$$T(A,B,C,D) = A'B + ABD + AB'CD' + BC$$

First apply Eq. (3-9) to the first two terms and to the last two terms. This yields

$$T = A'B + BD + ACD' + BC$$

The next step in the simplification is not as obvious; in order to simplify T it is first necessary to expand it. Since $BC = (A + A')BC$, we have

$$T = A'B + BD + ACD' + ABC + A'BC$$

The application of Eq. (3-8) to the first and last terms results in the elimination of the last term. Now apply Eq. (3-10) to the second, third, and fourth terms, letting x, y, and z replace D, B, and AC, respectively. This step eliminates ABC and yields

$$T = A'B + BD + ACD' \quad \blacksquare$$

Canonical forms

Truth tables have been shown to be the means for describing switching functions. An expression representing a switching function is derived from the table by finding the sum of all the terms that correspond to those combinations (i.e., rows) for which the function assumes the value 1. Each term is a product of the variables on which the function depends. Variable x_i appears in uncomplemented form in the product if it has the value 1 in the corresponding combination, and it appears in complemented form if it has the value 0. For example, the product term which corresponds to row 3 of Table 3-5, where the values of x, y, and z are 0, 1, and 1, is $x'yz$. The sum of all product terms for the function defined by Table 3-5 is

$$f(x,y,z) = x'y'z' + x'yz' + x'yz + xyz' + xyz$$

A product term which contains each of the n variables as factors in either complemented or uncomplemented form is called a *minterm*. Its characteristic property is that it assumes the value 1 for exactly one combination of the variables. If we assign to each of the n variables a fixed, arbitrary value of 0 or 1, then of the 2^n minterms, one and only one will have the value 1, while all the remaining $2^n - 1$ minterms will have the value 0, because they differ by at least one literal whose value is 0 from the term whose value is 1. The sum of all minterms derived from those rows for which the value of the function is 1 takes on the value 1 or 0 according to the value assumed by f. Therefore this sum is in fact an algebraic representation of f. An expression of this type is called a *canonical sum of products*, or a *disjunctive normal* expression.

Switching functions are usually expressed in a compact form, obtained by listing the decimal codes associated with the minterms for which $f = 1$. The decimal codes are derived from the truth tables by regarding each row as a binary number; e.g., the minterm $x'yz'$ is associated with row 010, which, when interpreted as a binary number, is equal to 2.   The function defined by Table 3-5 can thus be expressed as

$$f(x,y,z) = \Sigma(0,2,3,6,7)$$

where $\Sigma(\ \ )$ means that $f(x,y,z)$ is the sum of all the minterms whose decimal code is given within the parentheses.

Table 3-5   Truth table for the function
$$f(x,y,z) = x'y'z' + x'yz' + x'yz + xyz' + xyz$$

Decimal code	x	y	z	f
0	0	0	0	1
1	0	0	1	0
2	0	1	0	1
3	0	1	1	1
4	1	0	0	0
5	1	0	1	0
6	1	1	0	1
7	1	1	1	1

A switching function can also be expressed as a product of sums. This is accomplished by considering those combinations for which the function is to have the value 0.   For example, the sum term $x + y + z'$ has the value 1 for all combinations of x, y, and z, except $x = 0$, $y = 0$, and $z = 1$, where it has the value 0.   Any similar term assumes the value 0 for only one combination.   Consequently, a product of such sum terms will assume the value 0 for precisely those combinations for which the individual terms are 0.   For all other combinations the product-of-sum terms will have value 1.   A sum term which contains each of the n variables in either a complemented or an uncomplemented form is called a *maxterm*.   An expression formed of the product of all maxterms for which the function takes on the value 0 is called a *canonical product of sums*, or a *conjunctive normal* expression.

In each maxterm, variable x_i appears in uncomplemented form if it has the value 0 in the corresponding row in the truth table, and it appears in complemented form if it has the value 1.   For example, the maxterm which corresponds to the row whose decimal code is 1 of Table 3-5 is $x + y + z'$.   The canonical product-of-sums expression for the function defined by Table 3-5 is given by

$$f(x,y,z) = (x + y + z')(x' + y + z)(x' + y + z')$$

This function can also be expressed in a compact form by listing the combinations for which f is to have the value 0, i.e.,

$$f(x,y,z) = \Pi(1,4,5)$$

where $\Pi(\quad)$ means that $f(x,y,z)$ is the product of all maxterms whose decimal code is given within the parentheses.

One way of obtaining the canonical forms of any switching function is by means of *Shannon's expansion theorem*, which states that any switching function $f(x_1,x_2, \ldots ,x_n)$ can be expressed as

$$f(x_1,x_2, \ldots ,x_n) = x_1 \cdot f(1,x_2, \ldots ,x_n) + x_1' \cdot f(0,x_2, \ldots ,x_n)$$

$$\text{(3-14)}$$

$$f(x_1,x_2, \ldots ,x_n) = [x_1 + f(0,x_2, \ldots ,x_n)] \cdot [x_1' + f(1,x_2, \ldots ,x_n)]$$

$$\text{(3-14')}$$

Proof: By perfect induction. Let x_1 be equal to 1; then x_1' equals 0 and Eq. (3-14) becomes an identity, i.e.,

$$f(1,x_2, \ldots ,x_n) = 1 \cdot f(1,x_2, \ldots ,x_n)$$

Similarly, substituting $x_1 = 0$ and $x_1' = 1$ also reduces Eq. (3-14) to an identity, and thus the theorem is proved. ■

If we now apply the expansion theorem with respect to variable x_2 to each of the two terms in Eq. (3-14), we obtain

$$\begin{aligned} f(x_1,x_2, \ldots ,x_n) &= x_1x_2f(1,1,x_3, \ldots ,x_n) + x_1x_2'f(1,0,x_3, \ldots ,x_n) \\ &+ x_1'x_2f(0,1,x_3, \ldots ,x_n) + x_1'x_2'f(0,0,x_3, \ldots ,x_n) \end{aligned}$$

The expansion of the function about the remaining variables yields the disjunctive normal form. In a similar manner, repeated applications of the dual expansion theorem [Eq. (3-14')] to $f(x_1,x_2, \ldots ,x_n)$ about its variables $x_1, x_2, \ldots , x_n$ yield the conjunctive normal form.

A simpler and faster procedure for obtaining the canonical sum-of-products form of a switching function is summarized as follows:

1. Examine each term; if it is a minterm, retain it, and continue to the next term.
2. In each product which is not a minterm, check the variables that do not occur; for each x_i that does not occur, multiply the product by $(x_i + x_i')$.
3. Multiply out all products and eliminate redundant terms.

Example Let us determine the canonical sum-of-products form for $T(x,y,z) = x'y + z' + xyz$.

$$\begin{aligned} T &= x'y + z' + xyz \\ &= x'y(z + z') + (x + x')(y + y')z' + xyz \\ &= x'yz + x'yz' + xyz' + xy'z' + x'yz' + x'y'z' + xyz \\ &= x'yz + x'yz' + xyz' + xy'z' + x'y'z' + xyz \quad ■ \end{aligned}$$

The canonical product-of-sums form is obtained in a dual manner by expressing the function as a product of factors, and adding to each factor in which the variable x_i is missing, the product $x_i x_i'$. The expansion into canonical form is obtained by repeated applications of Eq. (3-7').

Example Let us determine the canonical product-of-sums form of $T(x,y,z) = x'(y' + z)$.

$$T = x'(y' + z)$$
$$= (x' + yy' + zz')(y' + z + xx')$$
$$= [(x' + y + z)(x' + y + z')(x' + y' + z)(x' + y' + z')]$$
$$[(x + y' + z)(x' + y' + z)]$$
$$= (x' + y + z)(x' + y + z')(x' + y' + z)(x' + y' + z')$$
$$(x + y' + z) \quad \blacksquare$$

In some instances it is desirable to transform a function from one form to the other. This transformation can be accomplished by writing the truth table and using the previously described techniques. An alternative method, which is based on the involution theorem $(x')' = x$, is illustrated by the following example.

Example Find the canonical product-of-sums form for the function

$$T(x,y,z) = x'y'z' + x'y'z + x'yz + xyz + xy'z + xy'z'$$
$$T = (T')' = [(x'y'z' + x'y'z + x'yz + xyz + xy'z + xy'z')']'$$

The complement T' consists of those minterms which are not contained in the expression for T, i.e.,

$$T = [x'yz' + xyz']'$$
$$= (x + y' + z)(x' + y' + z) \quad \blacksquare$$

Functional properties

From the foregoing discussion we may conclude that *the canonical sum-of-products form of a switching function is unique (up to commutation).* In order to prove this assertion, suppose that there exist two different canonical sum-of-products forms expressing f. Since we are assuming the forms to be different, they must differ by at least one minterm; that is, there must be at least one set of values for the variables $x_1, x_2, \ldots, x_n$ for which one form results in $f(x_1, x_2, \ldots, x_n) = 0$, while the other form yields $f(x_1, x_2, \ldots, x_n) = 1$, a result which contradicts the assumption that both forms express the same function. (Note that according to the commutativity law there actually exist more than one such canonical form, but we shall regard them all as identical.)

Two switching functions, $f_1(x_1,x_2, \ldots ,x_n)$ and $f_2(x_1,x_2, \ldots ,x_n)$, are said to be *logically equivalent* (or simply *equivalent*) if and only if both functions have the same value for each and every combination of the variables $x_1, x_2, \ldots , x_n$. Thus

 Two switching functions are equivalent if and only if their canonical sum-of-products forms are identical.

Consequently, in order to prove an identity of two functions, it is sufficient to expand both functions to their canonical forms and to compare the outcomes.

In a similar manner it can be shown that every switching function may be expressed *uniquely* in a canonical product-of-sums form, and that two switching functions are equivalent if and only if their canonical product-of-sums forms are identical. From here on we shall confine our discussion to the sum-of-products form, since the applicability of subsequent results to the dual form is understood.

Let the binary constant a_i be the value of the function $f(x_1,x_2, \ldots , x_n)$ for the combination of variables whose decimal code is i. Then every switching function can be expressed in the form

$$f(x_1,x_2, \ldots ,x_n) = a_0 x_1' x_2' \cdots x_n' + a_1 x_1' x_2' \cdots x_n$$
$$+ \cdots + a_r x_1 x_2 \cdots x_n$$

A factor a_i is set to 1 (or 0) if the corresponding minterm is (or is not) contained in the canonical form of the function. There are $r = 2^n$ coefficients, each of which can have two values, 0 and 1; hence there are 2^{2^n} possible assignments of values to the coefficients, and thus *there exist 2^{2^n} switching functions of n variables.*

Example Tabulate the functions of two variables.

The canonical sum-of-products form of a function of two variables is given by

$$f(x,y) = a_0 x' y' + a_1 x' y + a_2 x y' + a_3 x y$$

There are $2^{2^2} = 16$ functions corresponding to the 16 possible assignments of 0's and 1's to $a_0, a_1, a_2,$ and a_3. The functions are given in Table 3-6. There are six nonsimilar functions, $f = 0, f = 1,$ and $f = x$, which are known as the trivial functions, while $f = xy$, $f = x + y$, and $f = xy + x'y'$ are known as the nontrivial ones. Any other function may be obtained from these six by complementation or by interchange of variables. For example, $x'y + xy'$ can be obtained from $xy + x'y'$ by interchanging x and x'. ■

Table 3-6   List of functions of two variables

a_3 a_2 a_1 a_0	$f(x,y)$	Name of function	Symbol
0 0 0 0	0	Inconsistency	
0 0 0 1	$x'y'$	NOR(dagger)	$x \downarrow y$
0 0 1 0	$x'y$		
0 0 1 1	x'	NOT	x'
0 1 0 0	xy'		
0 1 0 1	y'		
0 1 1 0	$x'y + xy'$	EXCLUSIVE OR (modulo-2 addition)	$x \oplus y$
0 1 1 1	$x' + y'$	NAND(Sheffer stroke)	$x \mid y$
1 0 0 0	xy	AND	$x \cdot y$
1 0 0 1	$xy + x'y'$	Equivalence	$x \equiv y$
1 0 1 0	y		
1 0 1 1	$x' + y$	Implication	$x \rightarrow y$
1 1 0 0	x		
1 1 0 1	$x + y'$	Implication	$y \rightarrow x$
1 1 1 0	$x + y$	OR	$x + y$
1 1 1 1	1	Tautology	

The EXCLUSIVE-OR operation

The *EXCLUSIVE OR*, denoted $\oplus$, is a binary operation on the set of switching elements. It assigns the value 1 to two arguments if and only if they have complementary values; that is, $A \oplus B = 1$ if either A or B is 1, but not when both A and B are 1. It is evident that the EXCLUSIVE-OR operation assigns to each pair of elements its modulo-2 sum; consequently, it is often called the *modulo-2 addition* operation. The following properties of the EXCLUSIVE OR are direct consequences of its definition:

Commutativity: $A \oplus B = B \oplus A$

Associativity: $(A \oplus B) \oplus C = A \oplus (B \oplus C) = A \oplus B \oplus C$

Distributivity: $(AB) \oplus (AC) = A(B \oplus C)$

If $A \oplus B = C$, then $\begin{cases} A \oplus C = B \\ B \oplus C = A \\ A \oplus B \oplus C = 0 \end{cases}$

In general, the modulo-2 addition of an even number of elements whose value is 1 is 0, and the modulo-2 addition of an odd number of elements whose value is 1 is 1. The usefulness of the modulo-2-addition operation will become evident in subsequent chapters, and especially in the analysis and design of linear sequential machines.

Functionally complete operations

It has been demonstrated that every switching function can be expressed in a canonical sum-of-products form, where each expression consists of a finite number of switching variables, constants, and operations $+$, $\cdot$, $'$.

Definition 3-1 A set of operations is said to be *functionally complete* (or *universal*) if and only if every switching function can be expressed entirely by means of operations from this set.

The set $\{+, \cdot, '\}$ is clearly functionally complete; moreover, by means of De Morgan's theorem it can be shown that the set $\{+, '\}$ is also functionally complete. Since $x \cdot y = (x' + y')'$, the operations $+$ and $'$ can replace the $\cdot$ in any switching function, and therefore the set $\{+, '\}$ is functionally complete. In a similar way it can be shown that the set $\{\cdot, '\}$ is also functionally complete. Many functionally complete sets of operations exist, among the more important of which are the NAND and NOR operations.

Example Prove that the NOR operation is functionally complete.

A common method for proving completeness of an operation is to show that it is capable of generating each of the operations of a set that is already known to be functionally complete, for example, the $\{+, '\}$ or the $\{\cdot, '\}$.

Since $x \downarrow y = x'y'$ (see Table 3-6), then

$$x \downarrow x = x'x' = x'$$
$$(x \downarrow y) \downarrow (x \downarrow y) = (x'y')' = x + y \quad \blacksquare$$

In order to implement switching functions, it is sufficient to find a set of devices capable of implementing a functionally complete set of operations. In general, because of manufacturing and maintenance advantages, it is desirable to obtain uniformity and reduce the cost of the implementation by selecting a minimal set of such devices. The devices implementing the NAND and NOR operations have numerous advantages, can be manufactured quite inexpensively, and since each of them is functionally complete, they serve as the major component presently used in logical design.

3-3 ISOMORPHIC SYSTEMS

In this section we shall discuss the relationship between switching algebra, the calculus of propositions, and the algebra of series-parallel switching circuits.

Two algebraic systems, each consisting of a set of elements and one or more operations which satisfy a given set of postulates, are said to be *isomorphic* if the following are satisfied. First, for every operation in one system there exists a corresponding operation in the second system, although it may be denoted in a different way. To each element x_i in one system there corresponds a unique element y_i in the second system, and vice versa. Consequently, if both systems have finite sets of elements, then they have the same number of elements. Finally, if in every postulate of the first system, each x_i is replaced by the corresponding y_i, and every operation is replaced by the corresponding operation from the second system, then the resulting postulate must be a valid one for the second system. In other words, two algebraic systems are isomorphic if and only if they are identical except for the labels and symbols used to represent the operations and elements.

The algebra of series-parallel circuits and the calculus of propositions will be shown to be isomorphic to switching algebra; therefore all the properties of the latter system are valid for the former ones.

Series-parallel switching circuits

A switching circuit consists of "gates" through which information flows. This information may take the form of electric signals, water, pressure, or some other quantity. A *gate* is a two-state device capable of switching from one state which permits the flow of information to the other state which blocks it, and vice versa. Physically, this gate may be an electromechanical switch which is either open or closed, a magnetic core either energized or not, a pneumatic device which may be in either compressed or released state, and so on.

We shall associate with each gate a two-valued variable (x, y, etc.), which is in a primed form if the gate normally permits the flow of information, and is in an unprimed form if the gate normally blocks that flow. If two gates operate so that they are always in the same state, they are associated with the same variable and denoted by the same letter. If they operate so that one is always permitting the flow of information when the other is blocking it, and vice versa, the first is denoted by a primed letter, say x', while the second is denoted by the same unprimed letter, i.e., x. In general, primed letters are reserved for those gates which normally, i.e., before the circuit is activated, allow the flow of information, while unprimed letters are assigned to gates which normally block that flow. If a gate permits the flow of information, the literal associated with it takes on the value 1, and if it blocks that flow, the literal takes on the value 0.

The parallel connection of two gates is denoted by $x + y$, and their series connection is denoted by xy, as shown in Fig. 3-1. The circuits of Fig. 3-1, as well as the circuit which consists of a single gate, are said to be *elementary series-parallel* circuits. Any switching circuit which is constructed of either a series or a parallel connection of two or more elementary series-parallel circuits is called *series-parallel*. In other words, a circuit is series-parallel if it can be decomposed into either two subcircuits in series or two subcircuits in parallel; these subcircuits, which are also series-parallel, may be again decomposed as before, and so on until each subcircuit consists of only an elementary series-parallel circuit.

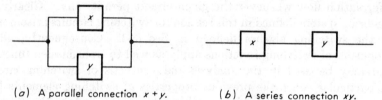

(a) A parallel connection $x + y$.   (b) A series connection xy.

Fig. 3-1 Basic connections of switching circuits.

Associated with each circuit we define a *transmission function*, which assumes the value 1 when there is a path from one terminal to the other terminal through which information flows, and assumes the value 0 if there is no such path. The transmission function is said to *represent* the circuit, and the circuit is said to be a *realization* of the function. A transmission function is usually denoted by the letter T.

In order to determine the value of the transmission function representing the parallel circuit in Fig. 3-1a, we observe that a path exists between the two circuit terminals if either gate x or gate y or both allow the flow of information, that is, T is 1 if either x or y is 1 or both x and y are 1. The circuit blocks the flow of information if both x and y block such a flow, i.e., x and y are 0. These properties of the transmission function are tabulated in Table 3-7. In a similar manner we observe that the transmission function which represents the series circuit of Fig. 3-1b is 1 if and only if both gates x and y permit the flow of information, i.e., x is 1 and y is 1.

**Table 3-7 Definition of
transmission functions**

x y	$x + y$	xy
0 0	0	0
0 1	1	0
1 0	1	0
1 1	1	1

From Table 3-7 and from the preceding discussion it is evident that a complete analogy exists between the OR and AND operations defined in Sec. 3-1 and, respectively, the operations $x + y$ and xy which define the transmission functions of parallel and series switching circuits. Moreover, since the transmission function of a gate must be either 0 or 1, then $x = 1$ if and only if $x' = 0$, and $x = 0$ if and only if $x' = 1$. Thus the *complement* of a given circuit is one which blocks all paths of information flow whenever the given circuit permits any. Clearly, the algebraic system defined in this section for switching circuits is isomorphic to the switching algebra defined in Sec. 3-1. Consequently, all the properties of switching functions apply as well to transmission functions, and may be used in the analysis and synthesis of switching circuits. In particular, since the previous properties of switching elements [Eqs. (3-1) through (3-14')] hold true when expressions replace the elements, we may conclude that the transmission function of a circuit consisting of a series connection of two subcircuits whose transmission functions are T_1 and T_2 is $T_1 T_2$. Similarly, the transmission function of a circuit composed of two parallel subcircuits T_1 and T_2 is $T_1 + T_2$.

Example The transmission function of the circuit in Fig. 3-2a is given by

$$T = xy' + (x' + y)z$$

Simple algebraic manipulation yields the reduced form

$$T = xy' + z$$

which represents the simpler circuit shown in Fig. 3-2b. ∎

An important application of the theory of switching circuits is to relay circuits in which contacts act as gates and information is transmitted by means of electric current. The properties of relay circuits, their analysis and design, are studied in Chap. 5.

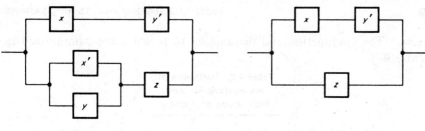

(a) Original circuit.   (b) Simplified circuit.

Fig. 3-2 Simplification of a switching circuit.

Propositional calculus

A *proposition* is a declarative statement which may be either true or false, but never both.   For example, the temperature is 100 degrees, the turtle runs faster than the hare, the sum of 2 and 3 equals 4, etc.   With every proposition we associate a variable, denoted p, q, etc., which assumes the value 1 if the proposition is true, and assumes the value 0 if it is false.   Thus the proposition 0 is always false, while the proposition 1 is always true.

New propositions may be derived from existing ones.   Consider, for example, the propositions "the sun is shining" and "the sun is not shining."   It seems evident that if the first proposition is true, then the second one is false, and vice versa.   A proposition is said to be a *negation* of another proposition if when one is false the other is true. Thus the negation p' of a proposition p is defined to be 1 if p is 0, and to be 0 if p is 1.

Two propositions p and q may be combined to form new propositions.   For example, if p designates the proposition "the temperature is above 60 degrees" and q designates "the humidity is over 50 percent," then we may form the proposition "the temperature is above 60 degrees *and* the humidity is over 50 percent" by combining p and q with a connective *and*.   In general, the *conjunction of p and q*, denoted pq, is the proposition "p and q."   The proposition pq is true whenever both p and q are true, and it is false whenever either one or both p and q are false.

Propositions may also be combined by means of a connective *or*. For example, the preceding propositions, when thus combined, yield the proposition "either the temperature is above 60 degrees or the humidity is over 50 percent."   In general, the *disjunction of p and q*, denoted $p + q$, is the proposition "either p or q or both," where the words "or both" are omitted and the "or" is defined to be the *inclusive or*. From its definition it follows that the proposition $p + q$ is true whenever either p or q or both are true, and is false whenever both p and q are false.   The conjunction and disjunction of p and q are summarized in Table 3-8.

Table 3-8   Definition of the conjunction and disjunction of p and q

p q	pq	$p + q$
0 0	0	0
0 1	0	1
1 0	0	1
1 1	1	1

The analogy between the calculus of propositions and switching algebra is now apparent; in fact they are isomorphic algebraic systems. Consequently, we may speak of variables and functions in precisely the same way as before.

Example   An air-conditioning system of a storage warehouse is to be turned on if one or more of the following three conditions occurs:

1. The weight of the stored material is less than 100 tons, the relative humidity is at least 60 percent, and the temperature is above 60 degrees;
2. The weight of the stored material is 100 tons or more and the temperature is above 60 degrees;
3. The weight of the stored material is less than 100 tons and the barometer stands at 30 or over.

Let A denote the proposition that the air conditioning is turned on.   It is our objective to specify A in terms of the following four propositions:

W designates weight of 100 tons or more.
H designates relative humidity of at least 60 percent.
T designates temperature above 60 degrees.
P designates barometric pressure of 30 or more.

From condition 1 we find that A is 1 if $W'HT$ is 1; from condition 2 we conclude that the air conditioning is turned on if WT is 1; and condition 3 is represented by $W'P$.   Consequently, an expression for A is

$$A = W'HT + WT + W'P$$

This expression may be simplified by applying Eq. (3-9) to yield

$$A = HT + WT + W'P$$
$$= T(H + W) + W'P$$

Hence the air-conditioning system is turned on if the temperature is above 60 degrees and either the weight is at least 100 tons or the humidity is at least 60 percent, or if the weight is less than 100 tons and the barometer stands at 30 or over. ■

3-4 ELECTRONIC-GATE NETWORKS

So far we have studied methods of deriving switching functions, manipulating them, and eliminating all redundancies from them. We consider now the problem of realizing switching functions by means of electronic devices. We shall introduce briefly the building blocks of these devices, deferring reference to their actual physical properties to Chap. 5.

Electronic gates generally receive voltages as inputs and produce output voltages. The precise values of these voltages are not significant toward determination of the logical operation of the gates; in fact, these values vary from circuit to circuit and from device to device. The significant point is that these voltages are restricted to two ranges of values, "high" and "low." Thus two-valued variables may be used to represent these voltages. By convention we shall associate the switching constants 1 and 0 with the higher and lower voltages, respectively.

Electronic gates are constructed of two-state switching devices, each capable of either permitting a flow of current or blocking it. In order to implement any switching function, these gates must be capable of implementing a functionally complete set of operations.

One set of basic gates, capable of implementing the three operations AND, OR, and NOT, is shown in Fig. 3-3. The *AND gate* has two or more inputs, and one output which assumes the value 1 if and only if all the inputs are 1. Thus, if the input values are a, b, and c, the output value is given by $T_1 = abc$. Similarly, the *OR gate* produces an output 1 if one or more of its inputs is 1, and thus its output may be characterized by $T_2 = a + b + c$. The *NOT gate* has one input, and one output whose value is the complement of the input value; i.e., its output is 1 if its input is 0, and 0 if its input is 1.

Gate networks are constructed of interconnections of gates, where the output of one gate is used to drive the inputs of others. As an example, consider the network of Fig. 3-4, which implements the function $A = T(H + W) + W'P$ describing the preceding air-conditioning control system. The inputs to this network may come from various

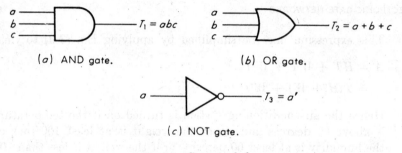

(a) AND gate. (b) OR gate.

(c) NOT gate.

Fig. 3-3 Gate symbols.

thermometers, humidity-measurement devices, a barometer, and a scale, while its output turns on (or off) the air conditioner.

The preceding discussion has served to introduce the basic electronic-gate logic. A more comprehensive study of the analysis and synthesis of switching circuits is deferred to Chap. 5.

★3-5 BOOLEAN ALGEBRAS

In Chap. 2 we established the properties of partially ordered sets and lattices; we shall now define a Boolean algebra, and subsequently show its relationship to the switching algebra defined in Sec. 3-1.

Definition 3-2 A *Boolean algebra B* is a distributive and complemented lattice.

Since a Boolean algebra is defined as a special lattice, all the lattice properties derived in Chap. 2 are applicable in any Boolean algebra. Accordingly, we can now summarize the properties of Boolean algebras as follows:

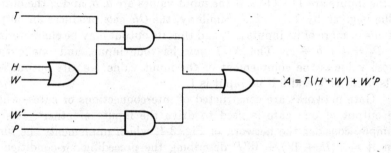

Fig. 3-4 Gate network.

▶ A Boolean algebra B is a set of elements a, b, c, . . . , together with two binary operations, $+$ and $\cdot$, which satisfy the idempotent, commutative, absorption, and associative laws, and are mutually distributive. B contains two bounds, 0 and 1, which are the least and greatest elements, respectively. B has a unary operation of complementation, which assigns to every element in B its complement.

We shall now prove that *the complement a' of any element a in B is unique;* that is, there exists only one element a' such that $a + a' = 1$ and $a \cdot a' = 0$. Suppose that there exists some element a which possesses two complements, b_1 and b_2, satisfying the above properties, i.e.,

$$a + b_1 = 1 \qquad a + b_2 = 1$$
$$a \cdot b_1 = 0 \qquad a \cdot b_2 = 0$$

Then

$$b_1 = b_1 \cdot 1 = b_1 \cdot (a + b_2) = b_1 \cdot a + b_1 \cdot b_2 = 0 + b_1 \cdot b_2 = b_1 \cdot b_2$$

Similar argument shows that $b_2 = b_1 \cdot b_2$. Consequently, $b_1 = b_2$, which proves the uniqueness of the complement, and provides the justification for defining the unary complement operation. An immediate corollary is that the complement of a' is a, i.e., $(a')' = a$.

To find the complements of the elements 0 and 1, note that by definition $0 + 0' = 1$, but by virtue of the definition of the lub it follows that $0' = 1$. Thus

$$0' = 1 \qquad \text{and} \qquad 1' = 0$$

Example Prove De Morgan's theorem for two variables.

$$(a + b)' = a' \cdot b'$$
$$(a \cdot b)' = a' + b'$$

We have to show that $(a + b)(a' \cdot b') = 0$ and $(a + b) + a' \cdot b' = 1$ (As before, we shall subsequently omit the $\cdot$ symbol.)

$$(a + b)(a'b') = aa'b' + ba'b' = 0 + a'bb' = 0 + 0 = 0$$

Applying the distributive law to $(a + b) + a'b'$ yields

$$(a + b) + a'b' = (a + b + a')(a + b + b') = (b + 1)(a + 1) = 1$$

The dual property is verified in an analogous manner. ■

We shall now show that the switching algebra defined in Sec. 3-1 is a two-valued Boolean algebra. Define a Boolean algebra which consists of just two elements, 0 and 1, with the usual binary operations $+$ and $\cdot$, and the complementation operation $'$. If the algebra is to satisfy all lattice properties and Definition 3-2, it must follow the operations shown in Table 3-9. For example, to show that the operation $\cdot$ is commutative, it is necessary to show that it is commutative for each one of the four ways of selecting values for the two elements, that is, for every combination of values $ab = ba$. It is evident that Table 3-9 defines a Boolean algebra which is isomorphic to the switching algebra defined in Sec. 3-1.

**Table 3-9   Definition of a Boolean algebra
which is isomorphic to the switching algebra**

$+$	0	1		$\cdot$	0	1	
0	0	1		0	0	0	$0' = 1$
1	1	1		1	0	1	$1' = 0$

Example The algebraic system defined in Table 3-10 is a Boolean algebra. The elements 0 and 1 satisfy the definitions of the least and greatest bounds, namely, that for every element x in B, $x + 0 = x$ and $x + 1 = 1$. The elements a and b are complements of each other since they satisfy the requirement that $a + b = 1$ and $a \cdot b = 0$. Finally, it is easy to verify that this system defines a distributive lattice by showing that, for every combination of elements, the operations are idempotent, commutative, and associative, and that they distribute over each other. ∎

Table 3-10   A Boolean algebra

$+$	0	1	a	b		$\cdot$	0	1	a	b	
0	0	1	a	b		0	0	0	0	0	$0' = 1$
1	1	1	1	1		1	0	1	a	b	$1' = 0$
a	a	1	a	1		a	0	a	a	0	$a' = b$
b	b	1	1	b		b	0	b	0	b	$b' = a$

NOTES AND REFERENCES

The first significant contribution in the area of switching theory was made by Shannon [3] in 1938. He developed the algebra of switching circuits and showed its relation to the calculus of propositions and Boolean algebra [1]. Further developments of switching theory were made by numerous

authors in the 1940's and 1950's, in particular in a second paper by
Shannon [4], in a book by Keister, Ritchie, and Washburn [2], and in a
report by the staff of Harvard University Computation Laboratory [5].

1. Boole, G.: "An Investigation of the Laws of Thought," Dover Publications, Inc.,
   New York, 1854.
2. Keister, W., S. A. Ritchie, and S. Washburn: "The Design of Switching Circuits,"
   D. Van Nostrand Company, New York, 1951.
3. Shannon, C. E.: A Symbolic Analysis of Relay and Switching Circuits, *Trans.
   AIEE*, vol. 57, pp. 713–723, 1938.
4. Shannon, C. E.: The Synthesis of Two-terminal Switching Circuits, *Bell System
   Tech. J.*, vol. 28, pp. 59–98, 1949.
5. Staff of the Computation Laboratory: "Synthesis of Electronic Computing and
   Control Circuits," Annals 27, Harvard University Press, Cambridge, Mass.,
   1951.

PROBLEMS

3-1. Prove the properties in Eqs. (3-2) through (3-6).

3-2. Using mathematical induction, prove De Morgan's theorem for n variables,

$$[f(x_1, x_2, \ldots, x_n, 0, 1, +, \cdot)]' = f(x_1', x_2', \ldots, x_n', 1, 0, \cdot, +)$$

3-3. Simplify the following algebraic expressions:
   (a) $x' + y' + xyz'$
   (b) $(x' + xyz') + (x' + xyz')(x + x'y'z)$
   (c) $xy + wxyz' + x'y$
   (d) $a + a'b + a'b'c + a'b'c'd + \cdots$
   (e) $xy + y'z' + wxz'$
   (f) $w'x' + x'y' + w'z' + yz$

3-4. Find, by inspection, the complement of each of the following expressions and *then* simplify it.
   (a) $x'(y' + z')(x + y + z')$
   (b) $(x + y'z')(y + x'z')(z + x'y')$
   (c) $w' + (x' + y + y'z')(x + y'z)$

3-5. Demonstrate, without using perfect induction, whether or not each of the following equations is valid.
   (a) $(x + y)(x' + y)(x + y')(x' + y') = 0$
   (b) $xy + x'y' + x'yz = xyz' + x'y' + yz$
   (c) $xyz + wy'z' + wxz = xyz + wy'z' + wxy'$
   (d) $xy + x'y' + xy'z = xz + x'y' + x'yz$

3-6. Given $AB' + A'B = C$, show that $AC' + A'C = B$.

3-7. Find the values of the two-valued variables A, B, C, and D by solving the set of simultaneous equations

$$A' + AB = 0$$
$$AB = AC$$
$$AB + AC' + CD = C'D$$

3-8. Prove that if $w'x + yz' = 0$, then

$$wx + y'(w' + z') = wx + xz + x'z' + w'y'z$$

3-9. Define the connective $*$ for the two-valued variables A, B, and C as follows:

$$A * B = AB + A'B'$$

Let $C = A * B$. Determine which of the following is valid:
   (a) $A = B * C$
   (b) $B = A * C$
   (c) $A * B * C = 1$

3-10. Determine the canonical sum-of-products representation of the functions:
   (a) $f(x,y,z) = z + (x' + y)(x + y')$
   (b) $f(x,y,z) = x + (x'y' + x'z)'$

3-11. Show the truth table for each of the following functions and find its simplest (i.e., with minimum number of literals) product-of-sums form.
   (a) $f(x,y,z) = xy + xz$
   (b) $f(x,y,z) = x' + yz'$

3-12. By adding redundant factors or terms to the expression $uvw + uwxy + uvxz + xyz$, it may be simplified as follows:

$$uvw + uwxy + uvxz + xyz = uw(v + xy) + xz(uv + y)$$
$$= uw(uv + xy) + xz(uv + xy)$$
$$= (uw + xz)(uv + xy)$$

Factor each of the following expressions into a product of two factors so that it is expressed with the least number of literals.
   (a) $wxyz + w'x'y'z' + w'xy'z + wx'yz'$
   (b) $vwx + vwyz + wxy + vxyz$

3-13. The dual f_d of a function $f(x_1,x_2, \ldots ,x_n)$ is obtained by interchanging the operations of logical addition and multiplication and by interchanging the constants 0 and 1 within any expression for that function.

(a) Show that $f_d = f'(x'_1, x'_2, \ldots, x'_n)$.

(b) Find a three-variable function that is its own dual. Such a function is called *self-dual*.

(c) Prove that for any function f and any two-valued variable A, which may or may not be a variable in f, the function

$$g = Af + A'f_d$$

is self-dual.

3-14. (a) Show that $f(A,B,C) = A'BC + AB' + B'C'$ is a universal operation.

(b) Assuming that a constant value 1 is available, show that $f(A,B) = A'B$ (together with the constant) is a universal operation.

3-15. For each of the following prove or show a counter example.

(a) If $A \oplus B = 0$, then $A = B$

(b) If $A \oplus C = B \oplus C$, then $A = B$

(c) $A \oplus B = A' \oplus B'$

(d) $(A \oplus B)' = A' \oplus B = A \oplus B'$

(e) $A \oplus (B + C) = (A \oplus B) + (A \oplus C)$

(f) If $A \oplus B \oplus C = D$, then $A \oplus B = C \oplus D$ and $A = B \oplus C \oplus D$

3-16. Any function of two variables can be represented, with proper choice of truth values for the a's, as

$$f(x,y) = a_0 x'y' + a_1 x'y + a_2 xy' + a_3 xy$$

(a) Prove that each of the representations below can also be used to specify any function of two variables. Show how to obtain the b's and c's from the a's.

$$f(x,y) = b_0 \oplus b_1 y \oplus b_2 x \oplus b_3 xy$$
$$f(x,y) = c_0 x'y' \oplus c_1 x'y \oplus c_2 xy' \oplus c_3 xy$$

Hint: Compare coefficients by choosing proper values for x and y.

(b) Prove that if a function $f(x_1, x_2, \ldots, x_n)$ is represented in a canonical sum-of-products form, then all OR operations may be replaced by EXCLUSIVE-OR operations.

3-17. Prove that any function $f(x_1, x_2, \ldots, x_n)$ can be expressed in a complement-free form as follows:

$$f(x_1, x_2, \ldots, x_n) = d_0 \oplus d_1 x_1 \oplus d_2 x_2 \oplus \cdots \oplus d_n x_n$$
$$\oplus d_{n+1} x_1 x_2 \oplus d_{n+2} x_1 x_3 \oplus \cdots \oplus d_{n(n+1)/2} x_{n-1} x_n$$
$$\oplus d_{[n(n+1)/2]+1} x_1 x_2 x_3 \oplus \cdots \oplus d_{2^n-1} x_1 x_2 \cdots x_n$$

where $d_0, d_1, \ldots, d_{2^n-1}$ are two-valued variables.

3-18. Prove that the expansion of any switching function of n variables $f(y_1, y_2, \ldots, y_s, z_1, z_2, \ldots, z_{n-s})$ with respect to the variables $z_1, z_2, \ldots, z_{n-s}$ is given by

$$f(y_1, y_2, \ldots, y_s, z_1, z_2, \ldots, z_{n-s})$$
$$= \sum_{i=1}^{2^{n-s}-1} f_i(y_1, y_2, \ldots, y_s) g_i(z_1, z_2, \ldots, z_{n-s})$$

where

$$f_0(y_1, y_2, \ldots, y_s) = f(y_1, y_2, \ldots, y_s, 0, 0, \ldots, 0)$$
$$f_1(y_1, y_2, \ldots, y_s) = f(y_1, y_2, \ldots, y_s, 0, 0, \ldots, 1)$$
$$\cdots \cdots \cdots \cdots \cdots \cdots \cdots \cdots \cdots \cdots \cdots$$
$$f_{2^{n-s}-1}(y_1, y_2, \ldots, y_s) = f(y_1, y_2, \ldots, y_s, 1, 1, \ldots, 1)$$

and where $g_i(z_1, z_2, \ldots, z_{n-s})$ is the product term whose decimal representation is i, e.g., $g_0 = z_1' z_2' \cdots z_{n-s}'$. Note that the distinction between the y's and the z's is only for convenience and has no other significance.

Hint: Use Shannon's expansion theorem [Eq. (3-14)] and finite induction on s.

3-19. The *majority function* $M(x,y,z)$ is equal to 1 when two or three of its arguments equal 1, that is,

$$M(x,y,z) = xy + xz + yz = (x + y)(x + z)(y + z)$$

(a) Show that $M[a,b,M(c,d,e)] = M[M(a,b,c),d,M(a,b,e)]$.

(b) Show that $M(x,y,z)$, together with the complementation operation and the constant 0, forms a functionally complete set of operations.

(c) Find the simplest switching expression $f(A,B,C,D)$ corresponding to the network of Fig. P3-19.

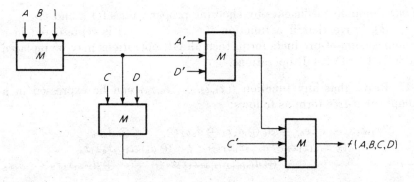

Fig. P3-19

3-20. A safe has five locks, v, w, x, y, and z, all of which must be unlocked for the safe to open. The keys to the locks are distributed among five executives in the following manner:

Mr. A has keys for locks v and x
Mr. B has keys for locks v and y
Mr. C has keys for locks w and y
Mr. D has keys for locks x and z
Mr. E has keys for locks v and z

(a) Determine the minimal number of executives required to open the safe.

(b) Find all the combinations of executives that can open the safe. Write an expression $f(A,B,C,D,E)$ which specifies when the safe can be opened as a function of what executives are present.

(c) Who is the "essential executive" without whom the safe cannot be opened?

3-21. You are presented with a set of requirements under which an insurance policy will be issued. The applicant must be:

1. A married female 25 years old or over, or
2. A female under 25, or
3. A married male under 25 who has not been involved in a car accident, or
4. A married male who has been involved in a car accident, or
5. A married male 25 years or over who has not been involved in a car accident.

The variables w, x, y, and z assume the truth value 1 in the following cases:

$w = 1$ if applicant has been involved in a car accident
$x = 1$ if applicant is married
$y = 1$ if applicant is a male
$z = 1$ if applicant is under 25

(a) You are asked to find an algebraic expression which assumes the value 1 whenever the policy should be issued.

(b) Simplify algebraically the above expression and suggest a simpler set of requirements.

3-22. Five soldiers, A, B, C, D, and E, volunteer to perform an important military task if their following conditions are satisfied:

1. Either A or B or both must go.
2. Either C or E, but not both, must go.
3. Either both A and C go or neither goes.
4. If D goes, then E must also go.
5. If B goes, then A and D must also go.

Define the variables A, B, C, D, E so that an unprimed variable will mean that the corresponding soldier has been selected to go. Determine the expression which specifies the combinations of the volunteers who can get the assignment.

3-23. (a) Show a series-parallel network which realizes the transmission function $T = A(B + C'D') + A'B'$.

(b) Show an AND, OR, NOT gate network which realizes the function $T = A'B + AB'C + B'C'$, assuming that only unprimed inputs are available.

3-24. Prove that a Boolean algebra of three elements $B = \{0,1,a\}$ cannot exist.

3-25. Prove that for every Boolean algebra:
(a) $a + a'b = a + b$
(b) If $a + b = a + c$ and $a' + b = a' + c$, then $b = c$
(c) If $a + b = a + c$ and $ab = ac$, then $b = c$

3-26. Prove that the partial ordering of all positive integers dividing the number 30 is a Boolean algebra of eight elements $B = \{1,2,3,5,6,10,15,30\}$.
(a) Draw the corresponding Hasse diagram.
(b) Define the binary operations by their operations on the integers.
(c) For each element a in B, specify its complement a'.

3-27. An alternative definition of Boolean algebra is by means of the *Huntington postulates*, which are given as follows:

Definition A Boolean algebra is a set B of elements $a, b, c, \ldots$ with the following properties:

1. B has two binary operations $+$ and $\cdot$ which satisfy the idempotent laws $a + a = a$ and $a \cdot a = a$, the commutative laws $a + b = b + a$ and $a \cdot b = b \cdot a$, the associative laws $a \cdot (b \cdot c) = (a \cdot b) \cdot c$ and $a + (b + c) = (a + b) + c$, and the absorption laws $a \cdot (a + b) = a$ and $a + (a \cdot b) = a$.

2. The operations are mutually distributive:

$$a \cdot (b + c) = (a \cdot b) + (a \cdot c) \text{ and } a + (b \cdot c) = (a + b) \cdot (a + c)$$

3. There exist in B two universal bounds 0 and 1 which satisfy

$$0 + a = a \qquad 0 \cdot a = 0 \qquad 1 + a = 1 \qquad 1 \cdot a = a$$

4. B has a unary operation of complementation, which assigns to every element a in B an element a' in B, such that

$$a \cdot a' = 0 \qquad a + a' = 1$$

Derive the following properties of Boolean algebra directly from the Huntington postulates:

(a) For each a in B, there exists a *unique* a' in B.
(b) For every a in B, $(a')' = a$.
(c) For every Boolean algebra, $0' = 1$ and $1' = 0$.
(d) In any Boolean algebra

$$(a + b)' = a' \cdot b' \qquad \text{and} \qquad (a \cdot b)' = a' + b'$$

4
Minimization
of
Switching Functions

A switching function can usually be represented by a number of expressions. Our aim in this chapter will be to develop procedures for obtaining a minimal expression for any such function, after establishing some criteria for minimality. In the preceding chapter we dealt with simplification of switching expressions by means of algebraic manipulations. The deficiency of this method is that it does not constitute an algorithm and is ineffective for expressions of even a small number (e.g., four or five) of variables. The methods to be introduced in this chapter partly overcome these limitations. The presented map method is very effective for hand simplification of expressions of up to five or six variables, while the tabulation procedure is suitable for machine computation and yields minimal expressions.

4-1 INTRODUCTION

Our aim in simplifying a switching function $f(x_1, x_2, \ldots, x_n)$ is to *find an expression* $g(x_1, x_2, \ldots, x_n)$ *which is equivalent to f and which mini-*

mizes some cost criteria. There are various criteria to determine minimal cost; the most common are:

1. Minimum number of appearances of literals. (Recall that a *literal* is a variable in complemented or uncomplemented form.)
2. Minimum number of literals in a sum-of-products (or product-of-sums) expression.
3. Minimum number of terms in a sum-of-products expression, provided there is no other such expression with the same number of terms and with fewer literals.

In subsequent discussions we shall adopt the third criterion and restrict our attention to the sum-of-products form. Of course, dual results can be obtained by employing the product-of-sums form instead. Note that the expression $xy + xz + x'y'$ is a minimal one according to our criterion, although it may be written as $x(y + z) + x'y'$, which requires fewer literals.

Consider the minimization of the function $f(x,y,z)$ below. The combination of the first and second product terms yields $x'z'(y + y') = x'z'$. Similarly, the combinations of the second and third, fourth and fifth, fifth and sixth terms yield a reduced expression for f.

$$f(x,y,z) = \underbrace{x'yz'} + \underbrace{x'y'z' + xyz'} + \underbrace{x'yz} + \underbrace{xyz + xy'z}$$

$$f(x,y,z) = \qquad x'z' + y'z' \qquad + \qquad yz + xz$$

This expression is said to be in an irredundant form, since any attempt to reduce it, either by deleting any of the four terms or by removing a literal, will yield an expression which is not equivalent to f. In general, a sum-of-products expression, from which no term or literal can be deleted without altering its logical value, is called an *irredundant, or irreducible, expression.*

The above reduction procedure is not unique, and a different combination of terms may yield different reduced expressions. In fact, if we combine the first and second terms of f, the third and sixth, the fourth and fifth, we obtain the expression

$$f(x,y,z) = x'z' + xy' + yz$$

In a similar manner, by combining the first and fourth terms, the second and third, the fifth and sixth, we obtain a third irredundant expression,

$$f(x,y,z) = x'y + y'z' + xz$$

While all three expressions are irredundant, only the latter two are minimal. Consequently, *an irredundant expression is not necessarily minimal, nor is the minimal expression always unique.* It is therefore desirable to develop procedures for generating the set of all minimal expressions, so that the appropriate one may be selected according to other criteria (e.g., distribution of gate loads, etc.).

4-2 THE MAP METHOD

The algebraic procedure of combining various terms and applying to them the rule $Aa + Aa' = A$ becomes very tedious as the number of terms and variables increases. The map method presented in this section and the tabulation procedure in Sec. 4-4 provide systematic methods for combining terms and determining minimal expressions.

Representation of functions

A *Karnaugh map* is, actually, a modified form of a truth table in which the arrangement of the combinations is particularly convenient. The maps for functions of three and four variables are shown in Fig. 4-1. The column headings are labeled with the four combinations of the two corresponding variables. The row headings correspond to the binary values of z in the three-variable map, and to the values of yz in the four-variable map. Each n-variable map consists of 2^n cells (squares), representing all possible combinations of these variables. The decimal codes which correspond to these combinations are shown in Fig. 4-1a and c. We shall subsequently refer to particular cells by their decimal codes.

The function value associated with a particular combination is entered in the corresponding cell. For example, the map of the function $f(x,y,z) = \Sigma(2,6,7)$ is shown in Fig. 4-1b, where the value 1 is entered in cells 2, 6, and 7. A blank cell means that for the corresponding combination the value of the function is 0. The minterm which corresponds to a particular cell is determined as in the truth table. Variable x_i appears in uncomplemented form in the product if it has the value 1 in the corresponding cell, and it appears in complemented form if it has value 0. For example, cell 6 in the three-variable map corresponds to xyz', and in the four-variable map it corresponds to $w'xyz'$. Figure 4-1d shows the map for the function $f(w,x,y,z) = \Sigma(4,5,8,12,13,14,15)$.

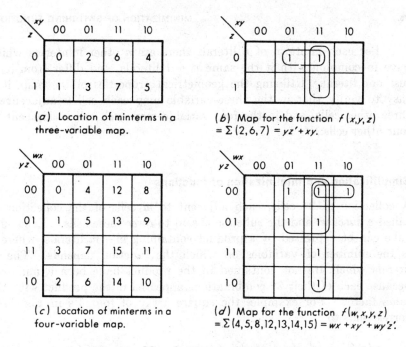

(a) Location of minterms in a
three-variable map.

(b) Map for the function $f(x,y,z)$
$= \Sigma(2,6,7) = yz' + xy$.

(c) Location of minterms in a
four-variable map.

(d) Map for the function $f(w,x,y,z)$
$= \Sigma(4,5,8,12,13,14,15) = wx + xy' + wy'z'$.

Fig. 4-1   Maps for three and four variables.

The cyclic code used in listing the combinations as column and row headings is of particular importance. As a result of this coding, cells which have a common side correspond to combinations that differ by the value of just a single variable. In general, two cells which differ in just one variable value are said to be *adjacent*, and play a major role in the simplification process, because they may be combined by means of the rule $Aa + Aa' = A$, where A denotes a product of literals, and a denotes a single literal. For the purpose of determining adjacencies, it is useful to regard the three-variable map as the surface of a cylinder formed by joining the left and right sides of the map. Similarly, the four-variable map is regarded as an open face of a torus; that is, the left and right sides of the map are joined, as are its top and bottom. This results, for example, in cell 8 being adjacent to cells 0 and 10, in addition to its obvious adjacency to cells 9 and 12.

The product term, corresponding to two adjacent cells for which the function is to have the value 1, is obtained by writing down the product of all those variables whose values are the same in the two cells, deleting that variable which is complemented in one cell and uncomplemented in the other. For example, the term which corresponds to cells 2 and 6 of Fig. 4-1b is yz', since $x'yz' + xyz' = yz'$.

For each minterm of n literals there are n other minterms which have in common with it the same $n - 1$ literals, and differ from it in just one literal. Utilizing the geometrical properties of the map, it is easy to verify that in the three-variable map each cell is adjacent to three other cells, and in the four-variable map each cell is adjacent to four other cells.

Simplification and minimization of functions

A collection of 2^m cells, each adjacent to m cells of the collection, is called a *subcube*, and the subcube is said to *cover* these cells. Each subcube can be expressed by a product containing $n - m$ literals, where n is the number of variables on which the function depends. The m literals which are not contained in the product have been eliminated, because each of their 2^m combinations appeared in the product with the same factor. For example, the square array of four 1's in Fig. 4-1d corresponds to

$$w'xy'z' + w'xy'z + wxy'z' + wxy'z$$
$$= xy'(w'z' + w'z + wz' + wz) = xy'$$

Similarly, the product expressing the rectangular array of four 1's is wx, since the values of both w and x are the same in the four cells, while the value of yz is different in every cell.

Now consider the function f defined by the map of Fig. 4-1b. We could express f as the sum of three minterms. However, observing that the map consists of two pairs of adjacent cells, we can express f as the sum of two product terms:

$$f = yz' + xy$$

The use of cell 6 in forming both subcubes is justified by the idempotent law. In this example the corresponding algebraic manipulations leading to the same result are

$$f = x'yz' + xyz' + xyz$$
$$= x'yz' + xyz' + xyz' + xyz$$
$$= yz'(x' + x) + xy(z' + z)$$
$$= yz' + xy$$

In general, by the idempotent law, any cell may be included in as many subcubes as desired. For example, the function f defined by the map of Fig. 4-1d can be expressed as the sum of three products, corresponding to the three subcubes marked on the map, i.e.,

$$f = wx + xy' + wy'z'$$

From the preceding discussion we observe that a function f can be expressed as a sum of those product terms which correspond to the subcubes necessary to cover all its 1 cells. The number of product terms in the expression for f is equal to the number of subcubes, while the number of literals in each term is determined by the size of the corresponding subcube. In order to obtain a minimal expression, we must cover all the 1 cells with the smallest number of subcubes, such that each subcube is as large as possible. Hence a subcube contained in a larger subcube must never be selected. If there is more than one way of covering the map (i.e., its 1 cells) with the minimal number of subcubes, we must select the covering which consists of larger subcubes. Such selection guarantees that the corresponding expression is indeed minimal and that no other expression containing the same number of terms but fewer literals exists. A subcube contained in any combination of other subcubes already selected in the covering of the map is redundant by virtue of the consensus theorem [Eq. (3-10)].

The foregoing discussion suggests the following rules for obtaining simple expressions for f:

1. Start by covering with subcubes those 1's that cannot be combined with any other 1 cells, and continue to those which have only a single adjacent 1 cell, and thus can form subcubes of only two cells.
2. Next combine those 1's which yield subcubes of four, but are not part of any subcube of eight cells, and so on.
3. A minimal expression is one that corresponds to a collection of subcubes which are as large and as few in number as possible, so that every 1 cell in the map of the function is covered by at least one subcube.

Example   Two irredundant expressions for

$$f(w,x,y,z) = \Sigma(0,4,5,7,8,9,13,15)$$

are derived from the maps of Fig. 4-2. The expression derived from Fig. 4-2a is $f = x'y'z' + w'xy' + wy'z + xz$. Since none of the subcubes is contained either within a combination of other subcubes or within a larger subcube, this expression is irredundant.

However, since it does not contain the smallest number of terms, it is not a minimal expression. The expression derived from the map of Fig. 4-2b, $f = w'y'z' + wx'y' + xz$, is the unique minimal expression for f. There exist two more irredundant expressions for f, but neither of them is minimal. ∎

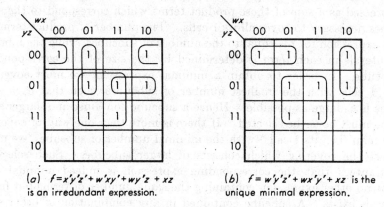

(a) $f = x'y'z' + w'xy' + wy'z + xz$
is an irredundant expression.

(b) $f = w'y'z' + wx'y' + xz$ is the
unique minimal expression.

Fig. 4-2   Two irredundant expressions for $f(w,x,y,z) = \Sigma(0,4,5,7,8,9,13,15)$.

Example   The function $f(w,x,y,z) = \Sigma(1,5,6,7,11,12,13,15)$ has only one irredundant form, as opposed to the preceding example. This unique minimal expression is derived from Fig. 4-3 and is found to be $f = wxy' + wyz + w'xy + w'y'z$. Note that the dotted subcube xz of four 1's becomes redundant if rule 1 is followed, since all its cells are covered by the other subcubes. ∎

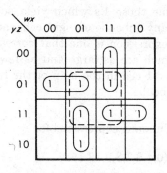

Fig. 4-3   Map for $f = wxy' + wyz + w'xy + w'y'z$.

So far we have specified a switching function by combining the 1 cells; clearly, it may equally well be specified by the 0 cells. In the latter case the expression yields the complement f' whose 1's are the 0's of f, and vice versa.

Determination of minimal product of sums

The minimization of functions expressed as product of sums is the dual procedure of that just developed for the sum-of-products form. An immediate question arises as to whether the number of literals required in the minimal expressions of both forms is the same. Supposing we have determined a minimal sum-of-products expression for f, does it imply that the minimal product-of-sums expression will require at least as many literals? The answer to this question is negative, as is shown subsequently.

Consider the function $f(w,x,y,z) = \Sigma(5,6,9,10)$. From the subcubes shown in Fig. 4-4a it is evident that no two 1 cells are adjacent. Thus f cannot be reduced, and its minimal sum-of-products form consists of 16 literals in four minterms.

$$f(w,x,y,z) = w'xy'z + w'xyz' + wx'y'z + wx'yz'$$

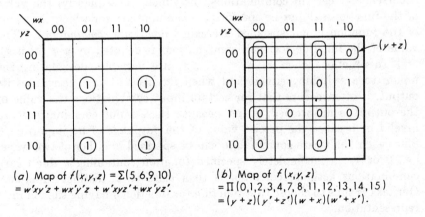

(a) Map of $f(x,y,z) = \Sigma(5,6,9,10)$
$= w'xy'z + wx'y'z + w'xyz' + wx'yz'$.

(b) Map of $f(x,y,z)$
$= \Pi(0,1,2,3,4,7,8,11,12,13,14,15)$
$= (y+z)(y'+z')(w+x)(w'+x')$.

Fig. 4-4 Minimal sum-of-products and product-of-sums forms.

The minimal product-of-sums expression for a function f is defined in an analogous manner to the definition of a minimal sum of products. It consists of a product of a minimum number of sum factors, provided there is no other such product with the same number of factors and with fewer literals. The product-of-sums expression is obtained from the map in the same way as from the truth table. A variable corresponding to a 1 is complemented, and a variable corresponding to a 0 is uncomplemented. Subcubes are formed of 0 cells instead of 1 cells and are selected in exactly the same manner as in the sum-of-products case. The minimal product-of-sums expression for f is derived from the map of Fig. 4-4b, i.e.,

$$f(w,x,y,z) = (y + z)(y' + z')(w + x)(w' + x')$$

This expression consists of only 8 literals versus 16 in the sum-of-products form. Hence, if a minimal expression is sought, regardless of its form, both forms must be determined, and the one with a smaller number of literals selected.

Don't-care combinations

So far the functions considered have been completely specified for every combination of the variables. There exist situations, however, where, while a function is to assume the value 1 for some combinations and the value 0 for others, it may assume either value for a number of combinations. Such situations may occur when the variables are not mutually independent; that is, dependency among the variables may preclude the occurrence of certain combinations, for which, consequently, the value of the function will not be specified. Combinations for which the value of the function is not specified are called *don't-care combinations*. The value of the function for such combinations is denoted by a ϕ (or a d).

In practice, when $x_1, x_2, \ldots, x_n$ are variables designating the inputs to a switching circuit and when $f(x_1,x_2, \ldots ,x_n)$ designates its output, it often occurs that for certain input combinations the value of the output is unspecified, either because these input combinations are invalid or because the precise value of the output is of no importance. Since each don't-care combination can be specified in either of two ways, i.e., 0 or 1, an incompletely specified function containing k don't-care combinations actually corresponds to a class of 2^k distinct functions. Our task is thus to choose that function (or functions) having the minimal representation.

When employing the map of an incompletely specified function, we assign the value 1 to selected don't-care combinations and the value 0 to others, in such a way as to increase the size of the selected subcubes whenever possible. No subcube containing only don't-care cells may be formed, because it is not required that the function equal 1 for these combinations.

Example   Design a code converter which converts BCD messages into Excess-3 code. The converter has four input lines carrying signals labeled w, x, y, and z, and four output lines carrying signals f_1, f_2, f_3, and f_4. The inputs and outputs correspond, respectively, to the BCD and Excess-3 coded messages. If the system operates properly, the input combinations will correspond to the decimal values 0 through 9, while the remaining six combinations 10 through 15 will never occur, and thus may be regarded as don't-care combinations. The code converter will be designed by considering each output function separately. The truth table specifying the codes is shown in Fig. 4-5a, and the resulting output functions are shown in Fig. 4-5b.

(a) Truth table for BCD and Excess-3 codes

Decimal number	BCD—inputs w x y z	Excess-3—outputs f_4 f_3 f_2 f_1
0	0 0 0 0	0 0 1 1
1	0 0 0 1	0 1 0 0
2	0 0 1 0	0 1 0 1
3	0 0 1 1	0 1 1 0
4	0 1 0 0	0 1 1 1
5	0 1 0 1	1 0 0 0
6	0 1 1 0	1 0 0 1
7	0 1 1 1	1 0 1 0
8	1 0 0 0	1 0 1 1
9	1 0 0 1	1 1 0 0

(b) Output functions:

$$f_1 = \Sigma(0,2,4,6,8) + \Sigma_\phi(10,11,12,13,14,15)$$

$$f_2 = \Sigma(0,3,4,7,8) + \Sigma_\phi(10,11,12,13,14,15)$$

$$f_3 = \Sigma(1,2,3,4,9) + \Sigma_\phi(10,11,12,13,14,15)$$

$$f_4 = \Sigma(5,6,7,8,9) + \Sigma_\phi(10,11,12,13,14,15)$$

Fig. 4-5 Specifications of a code converter.

The simplification of the output functions is accomplished by use of the corresponding maps, as shown in Fig. 4-6. The don't-care combinations are considered and specified in each function regardless of the specification in the other functions. Generally, the specification is done in such a way as to increase the size of the subcubes in the map, without making it necessary to select more subcubes than would be necessary if fewer don't-cares were

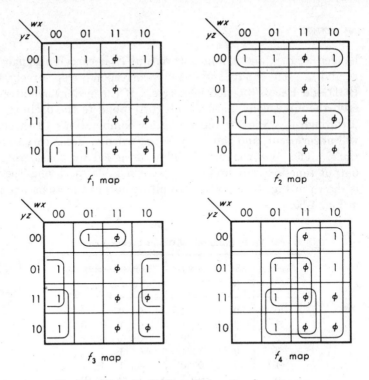

Fig. 4-6 Maps for BCD-to-Excess-3 code converter.

made 1's. The minimal functions derived from the maps are

$$f_1 = z'$$
$$f_2 = y'z' + yz$$
$$f_3 = x'y + x'z + xy'z'$$
$$f_4 = w + xy + xz$$

A gate network† realizing the code translator is shown in Fig. 4-7. Note that if, due to a malfunction in the message, an invalid input combination occurs, the output of the code converter will also be erroneous. ∎

A switching circuit in which a set of n input variables determines the values of two or more outputs is called a *multiple-output* (or *multi-*

---

† Any gate network which realizes a sum-of-products (or a product-of-sums) expression is called a *two-level* realization, since it consists of a level of AND (OR) gates driving a second level of OR (AND) gate. Thus the longest path through which any input signal must pass until it reaches the output consists of two gates. A measure of the complexity of a network is either the overall number of gates or the total number of gate inputs. For example, the network of Fig. 4-7 consists of 10 gates and 23 gate inputs.

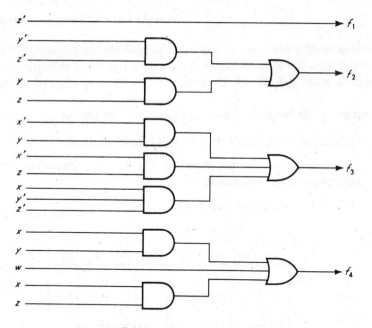

Fig. 4-7 BCD-to-Excess-3 code converter.

terminal) circuit. The above code converter is thus a four-output circuit.

The five-variable map

The minimization procedure described so far with respect to functions of three or four variables can be extended to the case of five or six variables. For functions of seven or more variables the map is very large and its value as an effective tool in the minimization procedure decreases, since it becomes very difficult to keep track of the adjacencies.

A five-variable map contains $2^5 = 32$ cells, as shown in Fig. 4-8. Each cell, in addition to its being adjacent to four other cells, can be

vwx\yz	000	001	011	010	110	111	101	100
00	0	4	12	8	24	28	20	16
01	1	5	13	9	25	29	21	17
11	3	7	15	11	27	31	23	19
10	2	6	14	10	26	30	22	18

Fig. 4-8 Five-variable map with locations of minterms.

combined with a fifth cell on the other side of the center symmetry line. Thus cell 9 in the map of Fig. 4-8 is adjacent to (and therefore may be combined with) cell 25, cell 15 is adjacent to 31, 4 to 20, and so on.

Example   With the aid of the map, minimize the function

$$f(v,w,x,y,z) = \Sigma(1,2,6,7,9,13,14,15,17,22,23,25,29,30,31)$$

From the subcubes shown in Fig. 4-9, we obtain the minimal sum-of-products expression

$$f(v,w,x,y,z) = x'y'z + wxz + xy + v'w'yz' \quad \blacksquare$$

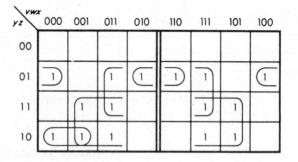

Fig. 4-9   Map for $f(v,w,x,y,z) = x'y'z + wxz + xy + v'w'yz'$.

The extension of the map to six variables is accomplished in a similar manner.   The map is a square consisting of 64 cells, where each cell is adjacent to six other cells.   The actual construction of the map, the determination of the appropriate row and column headings, and the locations of the minterms are left to the reader as an exercise.

4-3   MINIMAL FUNCTIONS AND THEIR PROPERTIES

In Sec. 4-1 we observed that there exists a distinction between irredundant and minimal expressions, and that neither of them is necessarily unique.   We shall now investigate the properties of these expressions and determine the characteristics of the product terms contained in a minimal sum-of-products expression.

Prime implicants

A switching function $f(x_1,x_2, \ldots ,x_n)$ is said to *cover* another function $g(x_1,x_2, \ldots ,x_n)$, denoted $f \supseteq g$, if f assumes the value 1 whenever g does.

Thus, if f covers g, then it has a 1 in every row of the truth table in which g has a 1. If f covers g and at the same time g covers f, then f and g are equivalent.

Let $f(x_1,x_2, \ldots ,x_n)$ be a switching function and $h(x_1,x_2, \ldots ,x_n)$ be a product of literals. If f covers h, then h is said to *imply* f, or h is said to be an *implicant* of f. The implication is often denoted $h \rightarrow f$.

Example If $f = wx + yz$ and $h = wxy'$, then f covers h and h implies f. ■

Definition 4-1 A *prime implicant* p of a function f is a product term which is covered by f, such that the deletion of any literal from p results in a new product which is not covered by f. Alternatively stated, p is a prime implicant if and only if p implies f, but does not imply any product with fewer literals which in turn also implies f. The set of all prime implicants of f will be denoted by P.

Example $x'y$ is a prime implicant of $f = x'y + xz + y'z'$, since it is covered by f and neither x' nor y alone implies f. ■

Theorem 4-1 *Every irredundant sum-of-products equivalent to f is a union of prime implicants of f.*

Proof: Let f^* be an irredundant sum-of-products expression equivalent to f, and suppose that f^* contains a product term φ which is not a prime implicant. Since φ is not a prime implicant, it is possible to replace it with another product which consists of fewer literals. Hence f contains redundant literals, which contradicts the initial assumption. ■

The next task is to generate the set of all prime implicants of f, and from this set to select those prime implicants whose union yields a minimal expression for f. Suppose that f is given in a canonical sum-of-products form; then by applying the *combining theorem* $Aa + Aa' = A$ to a pair of minterms, we obtain a product which implies f. Repeated applications of this theorem to all pairs of terms which differ in the value of just one variable yield a set of products, each of which implies f. A product which cannot be combined with any other product to yield a still smaller product, i.e., with fewer literals, is a prime implicant of f. Thus our first step in the determination of the minimal expression is a systematical combination of terms. The second step, that of selecting the minimal set of prime implicants, is in general more complicated, as will be demonstrated in the next section.

On the map an irreducible product corresponds to a subcube which is not contained in any larger subcube. Consequently, the set P of all prime implicants can be obtained by writing down the products corresponding to all the subcubes which are not contained in any larger subcubes.

Example Consider the map of $f(w,x,y,z) = \Sigma(0,4,5,7,8,9,13,15)$ given in Fig. 4-2. The set of all prime implicants of f is

$$P = \{xz, w'y'z', wx'y', x'y'z', w'xy', wy'z\}$$

Note that xyz is not a prime implicant since it implies xz. ■

Deriving minimal expressions

An inspection of the maps in Fig. 4-2 reveals that the prime implicant xz *must* be contained in any irredundant expression equivalent to f, since it is the only product which covers combinations 7 and 15. On the other hand, any other 1 cell is covered by two prime implicants, and consequently, none of them is essential for the specification of an irredundant expression.

A prime implicant p of a function f is said to be an *essential prime implicant* if it covers at least one minterm of f which is not covered by any other prime implicant. Since every minterm of f must be covered by an expression for f, all essential prime implicants must be contained in any irredundant expression for this function.

Example The prime implicants of the function

$$f(w,x,y,z) = \Sigma(4,5,8,12,13,14,15)$$

are all essential, as demonstrated by the map of Fig. 4-1d. ■

Example The map for the function $f(x,y,z) = \Sigma(0,2,3,4,5,7)$ is shown in Fig. 4-10; it is known as a *cyclic* prime implicant map, since no

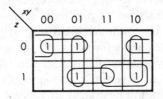

Fig. 4-10 A map for the function $f(x,y,z) = \Sigma(0,2,3,4,5,7)$.

prime implicant is essential, all prime implicants have the same size, and every cell is covered by exactly two prime implicants. The reader can verify by means of this map the results obtained in an algebraic manner in Sec. 4-1. ∎

Since every minterm covered by a nonessential prime implicant is covered by at least two prime implicants, then any nonessential prime implicant is covered by the sum of some prime implicants. For example, the prime implicant $w'xy'$ of the function whose map is shown in Fig. 4-2 is covered by the prime implicants xz and $w'y'z'$. An essential prime implicant, on the other hand, is not covered by any such sum.

When simplifying expressions by means of a map, we start by selecting the essential prime implicants, if any. This is accomplished by first forming the maximal subcubes of those 1's that can be combined to form only one subcube. Any other subcube, whose 1's are contained in any one or more of these subcubes, corresponds to a redundant term and need not be further considered. We thus arrive at the conclusion that

▶ The set of all essential prime implicants must be contained in any irredundant sum-of-products expression, while any prime implicant covered by the sum of the essential prime implicants must not be contained in an irredundant expression.

For example, the prime implicant xz of the function f of Fig. 4-3 is covered by the sum of four essential prime implicants and therefore must not be contained in any irredundant expression for f. We can thus summarize the procedure for obtaining a minimal sum-of-products expression for a function f:

1. Determine all essential prime implicants and include them in the minimal expression.
2. Remove from the list of prime implicants all those which are covered by the essential prime implicants.
3. If the set derived in step 1 covers all the minterms of f, then it is the unique minimal expression. Otherwise, select additional prime implicants so that the function f is covered completely and the total number and size of the prime implicants added are minimal.

The execution of step 3 is not always straightforward. While in most cases of a small number of variables it can be done by inspecting the map, in more complicated cases and when the number of variables is large, a more systematic method is needed. The prime implicant chart

presented in the next section is one of the possible aiding tools in the
search for a minimal expression.

4-4 THE TABULATION PROCEDURE FOR THE DETERMINATION OF PRIME IMPLICANTS

The map method described in the preceding sections is very useful for
functions of up to six variables.   In order to manipulate functions of a
larger number of variables, a more systematic procedure, preferably one
which can be carried out by a computing machine, is necessary.   The
tabulation procedure, known also as the Quine-McCluskey method of
reduction, satisfies the above requirements.   It is suitable for hand computation, and has also been programmed on various machines.

The binary representation

The fundamental idea on which this procedure is based is that repeated
applications of the combining theorem $Aa + Aa' = A$ on all adjacent
pairs of terms yield the set of all prime implicants, from which a minimal
sum may be selected.   The technique will be introduced by minimizing
the function

$$f_1(w,x,y,z) = \Sigma(0,1,8,9) = w'x'y'z' + w'x'y'z + wx'y'z' + wx'y'z$$

The first two and last two terms of f_1 can be combined to yield

$$f_1(w,x,y,z) = w'x'y'(z' + z) + wx'y'(z' + z)$$
$$= w'x'y' + wx'y'$$

This expression in turn can be combined, and we obtain

$$f_1(w,x,y,z) = x'y'(w' + w)$$
$$= x'y'$$

In the first step we obtained, for each of the two pairs of adjacent
terms, consisting of four literals per term, one term which consists of
three literals.   In the second step these two terms were combined again
and reduced to a single two-literal product.   A similar result can be
obtained by initially combining the first and third and the second and
fourth terms in the original function.   On the other hand, no combination
of the first and fourth or the second and third terms is possible, because
they are not adjacent.   Therefore our first task is to determine in a simple
and systematic way which terms can (or cannot) be combined, and to
carry out all possible such combinations.

Two k-variable terms can be combined into a single $(k - 1)$-variable
term if and only if they have in common $k - 1$ identical literals and differ

in just a single literal.   The combined term consists of the product of the $k - 1$ identical literals, while the variable, which is uncomplemented in one term and complemented in the other, is deleted.   Thus the terms $w'x'y'z'$ and $w'x'y'z$ can be combined to $w'x'y'$, while $w'x'y'z$ and $wx'y'z'$ cannot be combined, since they differ by two variables (i.e., w and z). If we consider the binary representation of the minterms, we observe that the necessary and sufficient condition for two minterms to be combinable is that their binary representations differ in just one position. For example, the representations for $w'x'y'z$ and $wx'y'z$ are 0001 and 1001, respectively.   The combined term is denoted -001, where the dash indicates that the variable w has been absorbed and the combined term is $x'y'z$.   The terms $w'x'y'z$ and $wx'y'z'$, on the other hand, cannot be combined, since their binary representations 0001 and 1000 differ in two positions, i.e., in the first and fourth digits.

For the binary representations of two minterms to be different in just one position, it is necessary that the number of their 1's differ by exactly one.   Consequently, to facilitate the combination process, the minterms are arranged in groups according to the number of 1's in their binary representation.   With the following steps the procedure becomes systematic:

1. Arrange all minterms in groups, such that all terms in the same group have the same number of 1's in their binary representation. Start with the least number of 1's and continue with groups of increasing numbers of 1's.   The number of 1's in a term is called the *index* of that term.
2. Compare every term of the lowest-index group with each term in the successive group; whenever possible, combine the two terms being compared by means of the combining theorem $Aa + Aa' = A$.   Repeat this by comparing each term in a group of index i with every term in the group of index $i + 1$, until all possible applications of the combining theorem have been exhausted.

   Two terms from adjacent groups are combinable if their binary representations differ by just a single digit in the same position; the combined term consists of the original fixed representation, with the different digit replaced by a dash (—).   A check mark ($\checkmark$) is placed next to every term which has been combined with at least one term.   (Note that each term may be combined with several terms, but only a single check is required.)
3. The terms generated in step 2 are now compared in the same fashion: a new term is generated by combining two terms which differ by only a single 1 *and* whose dashes are in the same position.

The process continues until no further combinations are possible. The remaining unchecked terms constitute the set of prime implicants of the function.

The entire procedure is, actually, a mechanized process for combining and reducing all adjacent pairs of terms. The unchecked terms are the prime implicants of f, since each implies f and is not covered by any other term with fewer literals. We shall illustrate the procedure by applying it to the function

$$f_2(w,x,y,z) = \Sigma(0,1,2,5,7,8,9,10,13,15)$$

The left-hand column of Fig. 4-11 consists of all minterms, arranged in groups of increasing indices. The reduced terms, after the first application of step 2, are given in the center column. For example, the combination of the terms 0000 and 0001 is recorded by writing 000– in its first row, where the dash indicates that variable z is redundant. The terms 0000 and 0001 in the left-hand column are now checked off. The same rule is applied repeatedly until all combinable terms are recorded in the center column.

Step (i)

	w	x	y	z	
0	0	0	0	0	✓
1	0	0	0	1	✓
2	0	0	1	0	✓
8	1	0	0	0	✓
5	0	1	0	1	✓
9	1	0	0	1	✓
10	1	0	1	0	✓
7	0	1	1	1	✓
13	1	1	0	1	✓
15	1	1	1	1	✓

Step (ii)

	w	x	y	z	
0,1	0	0	0	–	✓
0,2	0	0	–	0	✓
0,8	–	0	0	0	✓
1,5	0	–	0	1	✓
1,9	–	0	0	1	✓
2,10	–	0	1	0	✓
8,9	1	0	0	–	✓
8,10	1	0	–	0	✓
5,7	0	1	–	1	✓
5,13	–	1	0	1	✓
9,13	1	–	0	1	✓
7,15	–	1	1	1	✓
13,15	1	1	–	1	✓

Step (iii)

	w	x	y	z	
0,1,8,9	–	0	0	–	A
0,2,8,10	–	0	–	0	B
1,5,9,13	–	–	0	1	C
5,7,13,15	–	1	–	1	D

Fig. 4-11 Determination of the set of prime implicants for the function $f_2(w,x,y,z) = \Sigma(0,1,2,5,7,8,9,10,13,15)$.

The entire procedure is now repeated for the groups just formed in the center column. Again, only adjacent groups need be compared, and a new term is generated whenever two terms which differ in only one position and have their dashes in the same position are found. This procedure guarantees that the two combined terms actually consist of the same variables; that is, the same variable was deleted from both terms in the previous step. The new terms are recorded in the right-hand column, while the appropriate terms are checked off. For example, the term 000– can be combined with 100– to form –00–, which is recorded in the first row of the rightmost column.

While recording the terms in the rightmost column, we observe that each term is generated in two ways. For example, the term –00– is generated in the preceding manner, as well as by combining –000 and –001. Clearly, it is sufficient to record it once, but checks must be placed next to all four terms 000–, 100–, –000, and –001. The cause of this phenomenon is that every four-cell subcube can be formed by combining two adjacent two-cell subcubes, in two ways, as illustrated for the preceding example in Fig. 4-12.

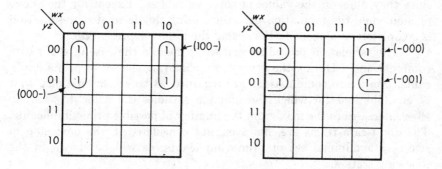

Fig. 4-12   Illustration of the two ways of generating a term.

The terms recorded in the right-hand column and labeled A, B, C, and D cannot be combined with any other term, and therefore form the set of prime implicants of f_2. From this set we must now select a minimal subset whose union is equivalent to f_2. This is accomplished by means of the prime implicant chart presented in the next section.

The decimal representation

The tabulation procedure can be further simplified by adopting the decimal code for the minterms, rather than their binary representation. Two minterms can be combined only if they differ by a power of 2, that is, only if the difference between their decimal codes is 2^i. The combined term consists of the same literals as the minterms, with the exception of the variable whose weight is 2^i, which is deleted. For example, if we consider the function $f_1(w,x,y,z) = \Sigma(0,1,8,9)$, the minterms 1 and 9 differ by $2^3 = 8$, and consequently, the variable w whose weight is 8 is deleted. This process, which is recorded by placing the weight of the redundant variable in parentheses, e.g., 1,9 (8), is nothing but a numerical way of describing the algebraic manipulation $w'x'y'z + wx'y'z = x'y'z$. Similarly, the combination of minterms 0 and 8 is written as 0,8 (8).

The condition that the decimal codes of two combinable terms must differ by a power of 2 is necessary but not sufficient. Two terms whose codes differ by a power of 2 but which have the same index cannot be combined, since they differ by more than one variable. Similarly, if a term with a smaller index has a higher decimal value than another term whose index is higher, then the two terms cannot be combined, although they may differ by a power of 2. For example, the terms 9 and 7 in Fig. 4-11, whose indices are 2 and 3, respectively, cannot be combined, since they differ in the values of three variables. Except for the above phenomenon, the tabulation procedure using the decimal representation is completely analogous to that using the binary representation.

The tabulation procedure can easily handle the case of don't-care combinations. During the process of generating the set of prime implicants, don't-care combinations are regarded as true combinations, that is, combinations for which the function assumes the value 1. This in effect increases to the maximum the number of possible prime implicants. The don't-care terms are, however, not considered in the next step of selecting a minimal set of prime implicants, as will be shown in the following section.

The tabulation procedure for generating the set of prime implicants for the function

$$f_3(v,w,x,y,z)$$
$$= \Sigma(13,15,17,18,19,20,21,23,25,27,29,31) + \Sigma_\phi(1,2,12,24)$$

is shown in Fig. 4-13. This set consists of eight prime implicants, denoted A through H, i.e.,

$$P = \{vz, wxz, vwx'y', vw'xy, vw'x'y, v'wxy, w'x'yz, w'x'y'z'\}$$

The selection of the prime implicants to be used in the minimal sum is accomplished with the aid of the prime implicant chart, presented in the next section.

1 ✓	1,17	(16)	H
2 ✓	2,18	(16)	G
12 ✓	12,13	(1)	F
17 ✓	17,19	(2)	✓
18 ✓	17,21	(4)	✓
20 ✓	17,25	(8)	✓
24 ✓	18,19	(1)	E
13 ✓	20,21	(1)	D
19 ✓	24,25	(1)	C
21 ✓	13,15	(2)	✓
25 ✓	13,29	(16)	✓
15 ✓	19,23	(4)	✓
23 ✓	19,27	(8)	✓
27 ✓	21,23	(2)	✓
29 ✓	21,29	(8)	✓
31 ✓	25,27	(2)	✓
(a)	25,29	(4)	✓
	15,31	(16)	✓
	23,31	(8)	✓
	27,31	(4)	✓
	29,31	(2)	✓
	(b)		

17, 19, 21, 23	(2, 4)	✓
17, 19, 25, 27	(2, 8)	✓
17, 21, 25, 29	(4, 8)	✓
13, 15, 29, 31	(2,16)	B
19, 23, 27, 31	(4, 8)	✓
21, 23, 29, 31	(2, 8)	✓
25, 27, 29, 31	(2, 4)	✓

(c)

17, 19, 21, 23, 25, 27, 29, 31   (2, 4, 8)   A

(d)

Fig. 4-13 Tabulation procedure using decimal notation.

4-5 THE PRIME IMPLICANT CHART

The *prime implicant chart* displays pictorially the covering relationships between the prime implicants and the minterms of the function. It consists of an array of u columns and v rows, where u and v designate the number of minterms for which the function takes on the value 1 and the number of prime implicants, respectively. The entries of the ith row in the chart consist of ✕'s placed at its intersections with the columns, corresponding to minterms covered by the ith prime implicant. For example, the prime implicant chart of $f_2(w,x,y,z) = \Sigma(0,1,2,5,7,8,9,10,13,15)$ is shown in Fig. 4-14. It consists of 10 columns corresponding to the minterms of f_2, and four rows which correspond to the prime implicants A, B, C, and D generated in Fig. 4-11. Row C contains four ✕'s in the intersections with columns 1, 5, 9, and 13, because these minterms are covered by prime implicant C. A row is said to *cover* the columns in which it has ✕'s.

The problem now is to *select a minimal subset of prime implicants such that each column contains at least one* ✕ *in the rows corresponding to the selected subset and the total number of literals in the prime implicants*

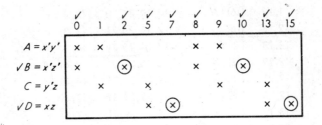

Fig. 4-14 Prime implicant chart for $f_2(w,x,y,z)$ of Fig. 4-11.

selected is as small as possible. These requirements guarantee that the union of the selected prime implicants is indeed equivalent to the original function f, and that no other expression containing fewer literals and equivalent to f can be found.

Essential rows

If any column contains just a single $\times$, the prime implicant corresponding to the row in which this $\times$ appears is essential, and consequently must be included in any irredundant expression for f. The $\times$ is circled, and a check mark is placed next to the essential prime implicant. The row which corresponds to an essential prime implicant is referred to as an *essential row*. Once an essential prime implicant has been selected, all the minterms it covers are checked off. For example, the essential prime implicant B covers, in addition to columns 2 and 10, columns 0 and 8. Consequently, columns 0, 2, 8, and 10 are checked off. If, after all essential prime implicants and their corresponding columns have been checked, the entire function is covered, i.e., every column is checked off, then the union of all essential prime implicants yields the minimal expression. If this is not the case, additional prime implicants are necessary.

The two essential prime implicants B and D of f_2 cover all the minterms except 1 and 9. These minterms may be covered by either prime implicant A or C, and since both are expressed with the same number of literals, we obtain two minimal expressions for f_2, namely,

$$f_2(w,x,y,z) = x'z' + xz + x'y'$$

and

$$f_2(w,x,y,z) = x'z' + xz + y'z$$

Don't-care combinations

Don't-care minterms need not be listed as column headings in the prime implicant chart, since they do not have to be covered by the minimal expression. By not listing them, we actually leave the specification of the don't-care terms open; that is, if a minimal expression contains a prime implicant derived from a don't-care combination, this amounts to specifying that combination as 1; otherwise, the don't-care combination is in effect assigned the value 0. The prime implicant chart thus yields a minimal expression of a function which covers all the *specified* minterms.

The prime implicant chart for the function

$$f_3(v,w,x,y,z)$$
$$= \Sigma(13,15,17,18,19,20,21,23,25,27,29,31) + \Sigma_\phi(1,2,12,24)$$

whose prime implicants have been computed in Fig. 4-13 is shown in Fig. 4-15.

	✓ 13	✓ 15	✓ 17	18	✓ 19	✓ 20	✓ 21	✓ 23	✓ 25	✓ 27	✓ 29	✓ 31
✓ $A = vz$			×		×		×	⊗	×	⊗	×	×
✓ $B = wxz$	×	⊗									×	×
$C = vwx'y'$									×			
✓ $D = vw'xy'$						⊗	×					
$E = vw'x'y$				×	×							
$F = v'wxy'$	×											
$G = w'x'yz'$				×								
$H = w'x'y'z$			×									

Fig. 4-15   Prime implicant chart for $f_3(v,w,x,y,z)$ of Fig. 4-13.

The selection of the nonessential prime implicants is facilitated by initial listing of the prime implicants in a descending order according to the number of minterms they cover. Thus prime implicants which are located in a higher group in the chart are expressed with fewer literals than those located in a lower group. A horizontal line across the chart separates one group from the other.

The essential prime implicants in the chart of Fig. 4-15 are A, B, and D. They cover all the specified minterms with the exception of 18. This last minterm can be covered by either prime implicant E or G, and since both have the same number of literals, two minimal expressions can be found, namely,

$$f_3(v,w,x,y,z) = vz + wxz + vw'xy' + vw'x'y$$

and

$$f_3(v,w,x,y,z) = vz + wxz + vw'xy' + w'x'yz'$$

Determination of the set of all irredundant expressions

So far we have been able to determine the minimal sum-of-products expressions by inspecting the prime implicant chart. In more complex cases, however, the inspection process becomes prohibitive, and different techniques are in order. As an illustration, consider the minimization of the function

$$f_4(v,w,x,y,z) = \Sigma(0,1,3,4,7,13,15,19,20,22,23,29,31)$$

The corresponding prime implicant chart is shown in Fig. 4-16a, where the essential prime implicants and all minterms covered by them have been checked off. While every irredundant expression must contain prime implicants A and C, none of them may contain B, since it covers only terms already covered by A and C. The reduced chart, which results after the removal of rows A, B, and C and all columns covered by them, is shown in Fig. 4-16b. Every column of the reduced chart contains two $\times$'s, and our task is to select a minimal number of additional prime implicants so as to cover the entire function.

	0	1	3 ✓	4	7 ✓	13 ✓	15 ✓	19 ✓	20	22	23 ✓	29 ✓	31 ✓
✓ $A = wxz$						⊗	×					⊗	×
$B = xyz$					×		×				×		×
✓ $C = w'yz$			×		×			⊗			×		
$D = vw'xy$										×	×		
$E = vw'xz'$									×	×			
$F = w'xy'z'$				×					×				
$G = v'w'x'z$		×	×										
$H = v'w'y'z'$	×			×									
$I = v'w'x'y'$	×	×											

(a) Prime implicant chart.

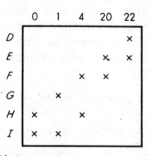

(b) Reduced prime implicant chart.

Fig. 4-16 Determination of all irredundant expressions for $f_4 = \Sigma(0,1,3,4,7,13,15,19,20,22,23,29,31)$.

Utilizing the techniques of propositional calculus, we associate a two-valued variable with each of the remaining prime implicants. The truth value of such a variable is 1 if the corresponding prime implicant is included in the irredundant expression, and is 0 if it is not. Define a *prime implicant function* p to be equal to 1 if each column is covered by at least one of the chosen prime implicants, and 0 if it is not. For example, column 0 can be covered by either row H or row I; consequently, one of them must be included in any irredundant expression. Similarly, either row G or row I must also be included, since only they have $\times$'s in column 1. Deriving the appropriate expressions from the remaining columns of Fig. 4-16b, we obtain the expression for p,

$$p = (H + I)(G + I)(F + H)(E + F)(D + E)$$

which can also be written as a sum of products,

$$p = EHI + EFI + DFI + EGH + DFGH$$

From the expression for p, we find that at least three rows are needed in order to cover the reduced chart, for example, rows E, H, and I, or rows E, F, and I, and so on. There are five irredundant expressions for f_4, corresponding to the five product terms for which p assumes the value 1. And since all the prime implicants which correspond to the rows of the reduced chart have the same number of literals, there are only four minimal expressions, corresponding to the first four terms in p. Each of these minimal expressions is obtained by forming the sum of the essential prime implicants A and C and a minimal number of prime implicants necessary to set p equal 1. Thus

$$f_4(v,w,x,y,z) = wxz + w'yz + vw'xz' + v'w'y'z' + v'w'x'y'$$
$$f_4(v,w,x,y,z) = wxz + w'yz + vw'xz' + w'xy'z' + v'w'x'y'$$
$$f_4(v,w,x,y,z) = wxz + w'yz + vw'xy + w'xy'z' + v'w'x'y'$$
$$f_4(v,w,x,y,z) = wxz + w'yz + vw'xz' + v'w'x'z + v'w'y'z'$$

The foregoing method for determining the irredundant sets of prime implicants can be applied directly to the prime implicant chart, instead of to the reduced chart. But the prime implicant function will be, in most cases, considerably simpler if, first, the essential rows and the columns covered by them are removed. Note that in deciding whether a product term in p corresponds to a minimal expression, two factors must be considered: the number of prime implicants and the number of literals in each such prime implicant.

Reduction of the chart

In general, prime implicant charts are not as simple as the preceding ones, and more elaborate techniques for manipulating them are required. Whenever our aim is limited to finding just one minimal expression rather than all minimal expressions, the selection of prime implicants may be considerably simplified. Consider the minimization of the function

$$f_5(v,w,x,y,z)$$
$$= \Sigma(1,3,4,5,6,7,10,11,12,13,14,15,18,19,20,21,22,23,25,26,27)$$

Its prime implicant chart is shown in Fig. 4-17a, where the essential prime implicants A, B, J, and K and all minterms covered by them have been checked off.

The reduced chart, which is obtained by removing the essential rows and the columns covered by them, is shown in Fig. 4-17b. Although none of the rows in the reduced chart is essential, some of them may be removed. For example, row H has an $\times$ in column 19, while row G has $\times$'s in columns 19 and 11. Since both prime implicants G and H belong to the same group in the chart, i.e., both are expressed with the same number of literals, the removal of row H cannot prevent us from finding at least one minimal expression. In other words, two expressions which are identical, except that one contains prime implicant G while the other contains H, will have the same number of literals; and since G covers the minterm covered by H, it can replace H in every expression for f_5 without affecting its logical value or its number of literals. Note that the converse is not true, since the removal of row G may leave column 11 without any $\times$ in a row whose corresponding prime implicant must be contained in the minimal expression.

A row U of a prime implicant chart is said to *dominate* another row V of that chart if U covers every column covered by V. Generalizing the preceding arguments, we conclude that, *if row U dominates row V and the prime implicant corresponding to row U does not have more literals than the prime implicant which corresponds to row V, then row V can be deleted from the chart.* Thus row I of Fig. 4-17b is deleted because it is dominated by row G, and similarly, rows D and F are removed because they are dominated by rows C and E, respectively. The final reduced chart is shown in Fig. 4-17c. It contains three rows, of which two (C and E) must be included in the minimal expression, since only they cover columns 18 and 10, respectively. Clearly, the inclusion of C and E is also sufficient, since they cover all the columns not covered by the essential prime implicants. The minimal expression for f_5 thus consists of the prime implicants A, B, J, K, C, and E, i.e.,

$$f_5(v,w,x,y,z) = w'x + v'x + v'w'z + vwx'z + vx'y + wx'y$$

Prime implicant chart (a):

	1	3	4	5	6	7	10	11	12	13	14	15	18	19	20	21	22	23	25	26	27
	✓	✓	✓	✓	✓	✓			✓	✓	✓	✓			✓	✓	✓	✓	✓		✓
✓ $A = w'x$			×	×	×	×									(×)	(×)	×	×			
✓ $B = v'x$			×	×	×	×			(×)	(×)	×	×									
$C = vx'y$													×	×						×	×
$D = vw'y$													×	×			×	×			
$E = wx'y$							×	×												×	×
$F = v'wy$							×	×			×	×									
$G = x'yz$		×						×						×							×
$H = w'yz$		×				×								×				×			
$I = v'yz$		×				×		×				×									
✓ $J = v'w'z$	(×)	×		×		×															
✓ $K = vwx'z$																			(×)		×

(a) Prime implicant chart.

Reduced prime implicant chart (b):

	10	11	18	19	26
C			×	×	×
D			×	×	
E	×	×			×
F	×	×			
G		×		×	
H				×	
I		×			

(b) Reduced prime implicant chart.

Final chart (c):

	10	11	18	19	26
	✓	✓	✓	✓	✓
✓ C			(×)	×	×
✓ E	(×)	×			×
G		×		×	

(c) Final chart.

Fig. 4-17 Minimization of
$$f_5 = \Sigma(1,3,4,5,6,7,10,11,12,13,14,15,18,19,20,21,22,23,25,26,27).$$

Prime implicant charts can also be reduced by removing certain columns. Consider, for example, columns 10 and 11 in Fig. 4-17b. In order to cover column 10, either row E or row F must be selected, whereby column 11 will also automatically be covered since it has ×'s in rows E and F. The converse is not true, since column 11 can also be covered by row G, but this will not cover column 10.

A column i in a prime implicant chart is said to *dominate* another column j of that chart if i has an × in every row in which j has an ×. Clearly, any minimal expression derived from a chart which contains both columns i and j can be derived from a chart which contains only the dominated column. Hence, *if column i dominates column j, then column i can be deleted from the chart without affecting the search for a minimal expression.* In fact, the removal of dominating columns does not prevent us from finding all minimal expressions.

101

Note that, when reducing columns, the *dominating* ones are removed, while of the rows, the *dominated* are deleted. The removal of dominated rows and dominating columns may alternate a number of times; that is, we may start by removing dominated rows and dominating columns. This in turn may create new dominated rows which can be removed, and so on.

The branching method

It may occur that a prime implicant chart has no essential prime implicants, dominated rows, or dominating columns. Whenever this happens, a different approach must be taken, called the *branching method*. Consider, for example, the function

$$f_6(w,x,y,z) = \Sigma(0,1,5,7,8,10,14,15)$$

whose map, which is cyclic, is given in Fig. 4-18a. Eight prime implicants of equal size are derived from the map and are shown in the chart of Fig. 4-18b, where each prime implicant covers two minterms, and each minterm is covered by two prime implicants. Such a chart is called a *cyclic* prime implicant chart.

In order to find a minimal expression for f_6, it is necessary to make an arbitrary selection of one row and then apply the above reduction procedure. Consider, for example, column 0 in the chart of Fig. 4-18b. It can be covered by either row A or row H; consequently, one of these rows must be included in any minimal expression. If row A is arbitrarily chosen, the chart of Fig. 4-18c results. In this chart row B is dominated by row C, and row H is dominated by row G. After removal of these dominated rows, we find that rows C and G must be selected, since only they cover columns 5 and 8 respectively. This selection in turn implies the inclusion of row E in the expression for f_6, i.e.,

$$f_6(w,x,y,z) = w'x'y' + w'xz + wxy + wx'z'$$

The entire process must now be repeated for row H as the initial selection. The removal of this row results in the chart of Fig. 4-18d. This chart is again reduced by removing the dominated rows A and G and including prime implicants B, D, and F in the expression for f_6.

$$f_6(w,x,y,z) = w'y'z + xyz + wyz' + x'y'z'$$

Since the two expressions for f_6 have the same number of literals, both are minimal.

In general, there is no guarantee that the initial arbitrary selection will result in a minimal expression. It is therefore necessary to repeat

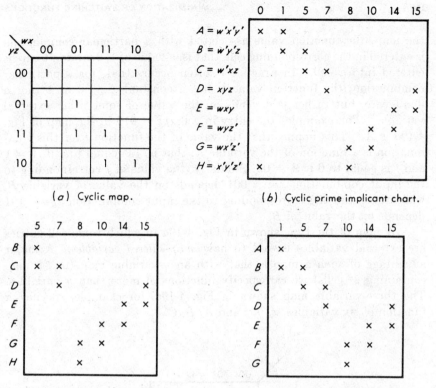

Fig. 4-18 Minimization of $f_6(w,x,y,z) = \Sigma(0,1,5,7,8,10,14,15)$ by the branching method.

the process for each row which could be substituted for the initially selected one.

Although the prime implicant chart of a function whose map is cyclic is always cyclic, it is possible to encounter cyclic charts in the process of reducing a prime implicant chart, which corresponds to a non-cyclic map. Moreover, a cyclic chart may result while applying the branching process and reducing another cyclic chart. Whenever such a situation occurs, another arbitrary row selection must be made, and all alternative expressions must be obtained, so that a minimal one may be selected.

4-6 MAP-ENTERED VARIABLES

The map can be made a considerably more powerful tool if we allow the entering of variables *into* the map cells. In the preceding utilization of the map, the function value associated with a particular combination is entered in the corresponding cell, that is, a value of 1, 0, or don't-care is entered into a cell. In practice it often occurs that, for a particular combination, the function value is not a constant (i.e., 0 or 1) nor a don't care, but rather it depends on the value of some other external variable. For example, the entry in cell $xyz = 010$ in the map of Fig. 4-19a is A. This implies that the value of the function f for this combination is a function of the variable A, that is, f is equal to 1 if $A = 1$ and f is equal to 0 if $A = 0$. Similarly, the value of f corresponding to the input combination $xyz = 001$ depends on the value of variable B, while the value of f corresponding to the input combination $xyz = 101$ depends on the value of B'.

A map of the type shown in Fig. 4-19a in which some cell entries are external variables is said to have *map-entered variables*. A major advantage of such a map is that with an n-variable map (i.e., a map containing 2^n cells) we can specify functions of more than n variables. The three-variable map shown in Fig. 4-19a, for example, specifies a function of six variables, x, y, z and A, B, C.

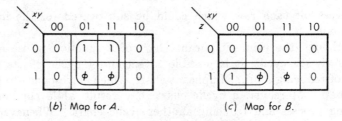

(a) Initial map.

(b) Map for A.   (c) Map for B.

Fig. 4-19 Deriving expressions from map-entered variables.

The product term that corresponds to a cell-entered variable is equal to the product of the variable entered into the cell and the combination that identifies the cell. For example, the product corresponding to cell 010 is $Ax'yz'$ and the product corresponding to cell 101 is $B'xy'z$.

The procedure for covering such a map and generating a simple expression for the corresponding function can be summarized as follows:

1. Treat all map-entered variables as 0's and find a minimal expression for the resulting map.
2. To cover the first map-entered variable, say A, treat all other map-entered variables as 0's and treat all 1's as don't-cares. Find a minimal cover for the resulting map.
3. Repeat step 2 for each and every map-entered variable. (Note that in this context a variable and its complement are treated as distinct variables, i.e., B and B' in Fig. 4-19a are distinct variables.)

Following this procedure we can find a minimal expression corresponding to the map in Fig. 4-19a. From step 1 it is evident that the 1 in the map is covered by the subcube yz. Step 2 for variable A is illustrated in Fig. 4-19b. Clearly, the corresponding term is Ay. Similarly, from Fig. 4-19c we obtain the term for B, namely, $Bx'z$. The terms for B' and C are found in a similar manner and the entire function is given by

$$f = yz + Ay + Bx'z + B'xz + Cxy'z'$$

NOTES AND REFERENCES

The problem of minimizing switching expressions has been studied extensively in the literature. The map method was introduced by Veitch [7] in 1952 and modified to its present form by Karnaugh [2]. The tabulation algorithm was developed by Quine [5, 6] and modified by McCluskey [3]. Tabular simplification of multiple-output circuits was treated by Bartee [1] and McCluskey and Schorr [4].

1. Bartee, T. C.: Computer Design of Multiple Output Logical Networks, *IRE Trans. Electron. Computers*, vol. EC-10, no. 1, pp. 21–30, March, 1961.
2. Karnaugh, M.: The Map Method for Synthesis of Combinational Logic Circuits, *Trans. AIEE*. pt. I, vol. 72, no. 9, pp. 593–599, 1953.
3. McCluskey, E. J., Jr.: Minimization of Boolean Functions, *Bell System Tech. J.*, vol. 35, no. 6, pp. 1417–1444, November, 1956.
4. McCluskey, E. J., and H. Schorr: Essential Multiple-Output Prime Implicants, in Mathematical Theory of Automata, *Proc. Polytech. Inst. Brooklyn Symp.*, vol. 12, pp. 437–457, April, 1962.
5. Quine, W. V.: The Problem of Simplifying Truth Functions, *Am. Math. Monthly*, vol. 59, no. 8, pp. 521–531, October, 1952.

6. Quine, W. V.: A Way to Simplify Truth Functions, *Am. Math. Monthly*, vol. 62, no. 9, pp. 627–631, November, 1955.
7. Veitch, E. W.: A Chart Method for Simplifying Truth Functions, *Proc. ACM*, Pittsburgh, May 2–3, 1952, pp. 127–133.

PROBLEMS

4-1. With the aid of a four-variable map derive minimal sum-of-products expressions for each of the following functions:

(a) $f_1(w,x,y,z) = \Sigma(0,1,2,3,4,6,8,9,10,11)$
(b) $f_2(w,x,y,z) = \Sigma(0,1,5,7,8,10,14,15)$
(c) $f_3(w,x,y,z) = \Sigma(0,2,4,5,6,8,10,12)$

4-2. (a) Find the minimal sum-of-products and minimal product-of-sums expressions for

$$f(w,x,y,z) = \Pi(1,4,5,6,11,12,13,14,15)$$

Is your answer unique?

(b) Determine the minimal sum-of-products expression for

$$f(w,x,y,z) = \Sigma(0,2,4,9,12,15) + \Sigma_\phi(1,5,7,10)$$

4-3. Given the function $T(w,x,y,z) = \Sigma(1,2,3,5,13) + \Sigma_\phi(6,7,8,9,11,15)$:

(a) Find a minimal sum-of-products expression.
(b) Find a minimal product-of-sums expression.
(c) Compare the expressions obtained in (a) and (b); if they do not represent identical functions, explain.

4-4. Find all minimal four-variable functions which assume the value 1 when the minterms 4, 10, 11, 13 are equal to 1, and assume the value 0 when the minterms 1, 3, 6, 7, 8, 9, 12, 14 are equal to 1.

4-5. Each of the following functions actually represents a set of four functions, corresponding to the various assignments of the don't-care terms.

$$f_1(w,x,y,z) = \Sigma(1,3,4,5,9,10,11) + \Sigma_\phi(6,8)$$

$$f_2(w,x,y,z) = \Sigma(0,2,4,7,8,15) + \Sigma_\phi(9,12)$$

(a) Find $f_3 = f_1 \cdot f_2$. How many functions does f_3 represent?
(b) Find $f_4 = f_1 + f_2$. How many functions does f_4 represent?
(c) Simplify the above functions, their product, and their sum.

4-6. Let $f = \Sigma(5,6,13)$ and $f_1 = \Sigma(0,1,2,3,5,6,8,9,10,11,13)$. Find f_2 such that $f = f_1 \cdot f_2'$. Is f_2 unique? If not, indicate all possibilities.

4-7. Given the network of Fig. P4-7, determine the functions f_2 and f_3 if $f_1 = xz' + x'z$ and the overall transmission function is to be

$$f(w,x,y,z) = \Sigma(0,4,9,10,11,12)$$

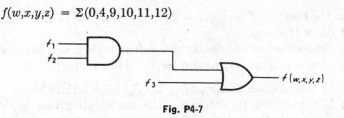

Fig. P4-7

4-8. A binary-coded-decimal (BCD) message appears in four input lines of a switching circuit. Design an AND, OR, NOT gate network which produces an output 1 whenever the input combination is 0, 2, 3, 5, or 8.

4-9. Find the simplest function $g(A,B,C,D)$ that will make the function $f = A'BC + (AC + B)D + g(A,B,C,D)$ self-dual.

Hint: Determine first the properties of maps of self-dual functions.

4-10. Use the map method to simplify each of the following functions:
(a) $f_1(v,w,x,y,z) = \Sigma(3,6,7,8,10,12,14,17,19,20,21,24,25,27,28)$
(b) $f_2(v,w,x,y,z) = \Sigma(0,1,2,4,5,9,11,13,15,16,18,22,23,26,29,30,31)$

4-11. The five-variable map can be constructed of two disjoint four-variable maps which correspond to the fifth variable and its complement, as shown in Fig. P4-11.

(a) Devise an algorithm which specifies the minimization procedure using such maps.

(b) Simplify the function

$$T(v,w,x,y,z) = \Sigma(1,2,6,7,9,13,14,15,17,22\ 23,25,29,30,31)$$

whose maps are given in Fig. P4-11.

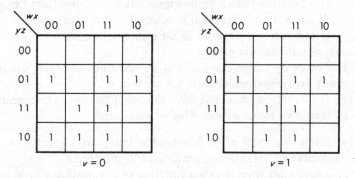

Fig. P4-11

4-12. Construct a six-variable map and show the representation of
$$T(u,v,w,x,y,z) = u'w'y' + uwy + w'xy'z$$

4-13. For the function $T(w,x,y,z) = \Sigma(0,1,2,3,4,6,7,8,9,11,15)$:
(a) Show the map.
(b) Find all prime implicants and indicate which are essential.
(c) Find a minimal expression for T. Is it unique?

4-14. Given the function $T(w,x,y,z) = \Sigma(1,3,4,5,7,8,9,11,14,15)$:
(a) Use the map to determine the set of all prime implicants. Indicate specifically the essential ones.
(b) Find three distinct minimal expressions for T.
(c) Find directly from the map the complement T'.
(d) Assume that only unprimed variables are available. Construct a circuit which realizes T and requires no more than 13 gate inputs and two NOT gates. (*Hint:* Use the result obtained in part *c*.)

4-15. Show maps for four-variable functions with the following specifications. If impossible, explain why.
(a) For each of the specifications below a function with eight minterms and:
(i) No essential prime implicants.
(ii) All its prime implicants are essential.
(b) Repeat (a) for functions with nine minterms.
(c) A function with an even number of prime implicants, of which exactly half are essential.
(d) A function with six prime implicants, of which four are essential and two are covered by the essential ones.

4-16. Prove or show a counter example to each of the following statements:
(a) If a function f has a unique minimal sum-of-products expression, then all its prime implicants are essential.
(b) If a function f has a unique minimal sum-of-products expression, then it also has a unique minimal product-of-sums expression.
(c) If the pairwise product of all prime implicants of f is 0, then it has a unique minimal expression.
(d) For every prime implicant p which is not essential, there is an irredundant expression which *does not* contain p.
(e) If a function f does not have any essential prime implicant, then it has at least two minimal sum-of-products forms.

4-17. (a) Show the map of an irreducible four-variable function whose sum-of-products representation consists of 2^3 minterms.
(b) Prove that there exists a function of n variables whose minimal sum-of-products form consists of 2^{n-1} minterms, and that no function,

when expressed in sum-of-products form, requires more than 2^{n-1} product terms.

(c) Derive a bound on the number of literals needed to express *any* n-variable function.

4-18. (a) Let $f(x_1, x_2, \ldots, x_n)$ be equal to 1 if and only if exactly k of the variables equal 1. How many prime implicants does this function have?

(b) Repeat (a) for the case where f assumes the value 1 if and only if k or more of the variables are equal to 1.

·(*Note:* The above functions are known as *symmetric*, and will be studied in Chap. 6.)

4-19. (a) Let $T(A,B,C,D) = A'BC + B'C'D$. Prove that *any* expression for T must contain at least one literal D or one literal D'.

(b) If in the minimal sum-of-products expression each variable appears either in a primed form or in an unprimed form, but not in both, the function is said to be *unate*. Prove that the minimal sum-of-products form of a unate function is unique.

(c) Is the converse true, i.e., if the minimal sum-of-products expression is unique, then the function is unate?

Hint: The function $f = w'z + x'y + x'z$ is unate. If you relabel the variables, the function may be transformed into another function whose variables are all in an unprimed form.

4-20. Use the tabulation procedure to generate the set of prime implicants and to obtain *all* minimal expressions for the following functions:
   (a) $f_1(w,x,y,z) = \Sigma(1,5,6,12,13,14) + \Sigma_\phi(2,4)$
   (b) $f_2(v,w,x,y,z) = \Sigma(0,1,3,8,9,13,14,15,16,17,19,24,25,27,31)$
   (c) $f_3(w,x,y,z) = \Sigma(0,1,4,5,6,7,9,11,15) + \Sigma_\phi(10,14)$
   (d) $f_4(v,w,x,y,z) = \Sigma(1,5,6,7,9,13,14,15,17,18,19,21,22,23,25,29,30)$
   (e) $f_5(w,x,y,z) = \Sigma(0,1,5,7,8,10,14,15)$

4-21. Apply the branching method to find a minimal expression for

$$f(v,w,x,y,z) = \Sigma(0,4,12,16,19,24,27,28,29,31)$$

4-22. (a) Prove that if x and y are switching variables, then:
   (i) $x + y = x \oplus y \oplus xy$
   (ii) $x' = x \oplus 1$

(b) Using the equations in (a), any switching expression can be converted to an equivalent expression containing only the operations EXCLUSIVE OR and AND. Demonstrate the conversion procedure by transforming the expression

$$f = xyz' + xy'z + x'z$$

(*c*) Derive a procedure to transform an expression containing the EXCLUSIVE-OR operation to an equivalent switching expression containing only AND, OR, and NOT operations. Apply your procedure to the expression

$$f = x \oplus y \oplus z$$

4-23. Consider the minimization of modulo-2 sum-of-products expressions by means of the map. Since, for every such expression, the following are valid,

$$x \oplus x \oplus \cdots \oplus x = \begin{cases} 0 & \text{for even number of } x\text{'s} \\ x & \text{for odd number of } x\text{'s} \end{cases}$$

$$xy \oplus xy' = x$$

then, when forming subcubes, every 1 cell *must* be included in an *odd* number of subcubes, while any 0 cell *may* be included in selected subcubes, as long as it is included in an *even* number of such subcubes. For example, the map for the function

$$f(x,y,z) = x'y'z' \oplus x'yz \oplus xy'z \oplus xyz'$$

is shown in Fig. P4-23. From the three subcubes shown, it is evident that the minimal expression is

$$f = x \oplus y \oplus z'$$

(*a*) Drive an algorithm for simplifying modulo-2 sum-of-products expressions by means of the map.†

(*b*) Apply your algorithm to simplify the following expressions:

$$f_1(w,x,y,z) = w'xy'z' \oplus w'xyz' \oplus wx'y'z \oplus wx'yz \oplus wxy'z' \oplus wxy'z$$

(Three terms containing seven literals constitute a minimum.)

$$f_2(w,x,y,z) = w'x'yz \oplus w'xy'z \oplus w'xyz' \oplus wx'y'z \oplus wx'yz' \oplus wxy'z'$$

(Five terms containing fourteen literals constitute a minimum.)

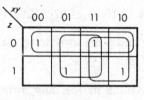

Fig. P4-23

---

† For reference see S. Even, I. Kohavi, and A. Paz, On Minimal Modulo 2 Sums of Products for Switching Functions, *IEEE Trans. Electron. Computers*, vol. EC-16, October, 1967.

4-24. The table shown in Fig. P4-24 is a prime implicant table for $f(a,b,c,d)$, in which some of the row and column headings are unknown. It is known, however, that the table has a row for each prime implicant of f and has a column for each minterm for which f has a value 1.

(a) Find with the aid of a map all the minterms and prime implicants that correspond, respectively, to the columns and rows with unknown headings.

(b) Is your solution to (a) unique?

(c) Write the minterms for which f must be equal to 0.

(d) Find a minimal expression for f.

	0	7	8	10	15	?	?
$A = b'd'$	×		×	×			
$B = ?$	×					×	
$C = bcd$		×			×		
$D = ?$					×		×
$E = ?$		×					
$F = ?$							×

Fig. P4-24

4-25. Given a combinational network with four inputs A, B, C, and D, three intermediate outputs Q, P, and R, and two outputs T_1 and T_2, as shown in Fig. P4-25.

(a) Assuming that G_1 and G_2 are both AND gates, show the map for the smallest function P_{min} (i.e., with minimum minterms) which makes it possible to produce T_1 and T_2.

(b) Show the maps for Q and R which correspond to the above P_{min}. Indicate explicitly the don't-care positions.

(c) Assuming that G_1 and G_2 are both OR gates, find the largest P_{max} and show the corresponding maps for Q and R.

(d) Can both T_1 and T_2 be produced if G_1 is an AND gate and G_2 an OR gate? Or when G_1 is an OR gate and G_2 an AND gate?

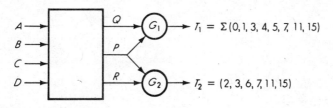

Fig. P4-25

4-26. Given the gate T whose logical properties are defined by the map in Fig. P4-26.

(a) Prove that, if the logical value 1 is given, then any switching function can be realized by means of T gates; that is, T gates plus the logical value 1 are functionally complete.

(b) Realize by means of two T gates the function

$$f(w,x,y,z) = \Sigma(0,1,2,4,7,8,9,10,12,15)$$

Hint: Realize the 0's of f.

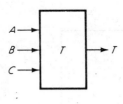
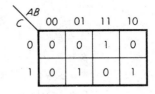

Fig. P4-26

5
Logical Design

The principal application of switching theory is in the design of digital circuits. The design of such circuits is commonly referred to as *logical* (or *logic*) *design*. Many different physical devices, such as magnetic cores, electromechanical relays, and pneumatic valves, exhibit behavior which permits them to be used as switching elements, but the majority of digital systems are constructed of electronic switching circuits. In this chapter we describe some components which are typical of the basic building blocks used in constructing digital systems. Switching algebra will be used to describe the logical behavior of networks composed of these building blocks as well as to manipulate and simplify switching expressions, thereby reducing the number of components used in the design. We shall be concerned with the *logical* functions that a circuit performs rather than with its electronic structure or behavior. Special attention is given to logic design with integrated circuits and to design of high-speed binary adders. These examples will introduce us to some of the practical aspects of logical design in which speed of operation, cost, and component limitations require ingenuity in arriving at a proper compromise.

5-1 DESIGN WITH BASIC LOGICAL GATES

Although modern digital systems are composed of a large number of components, they usually employ only a small number of different kinds of elementary circuits, called gates, whose task is to perform logical operations on the input signals. In Sec. 3-2 we showed that in order to implement any switching function, it is necessary to have a set of two-valued switching devices capable of implementing a functionally complete set of operations. The objective of this section is to present some of the more commonly used such devices.

Introductory definitions

Switching variables can be represented by voltage or current. We shall consider only the voltage representation, since that of the current is similar. It is customary to represent the switching constants 1 and 0 by higher and lower voltages, respectively. Such an assignment of voltages to the switching constants is referred to as *positive logic polarity*. The converse, that is, the representation of 1 and 0 by the lower and higher voltages, respectively, is referred to as *negative logic polarity*. Both of these representations are valid by virtue of the duality principle in switching algebra.

In practice, 0 and 1 do not correspond to specific, carefully controlled voltages, but to two voltage *ranges;* that is, there may be *nominal* "high" and "low," but these usually have tolerances in the order of hundreds of percent. "Low" might be −1.0 to +1.0 volt, and "high" +2.0 to +5.0 volts. Consequently, only the range of the signal is important, while its precise value is subject to changes due to temperature or variations in electronic parameters. This flexibility is important because it enables logic devices to employ simple circuits which operate correctly in spite of wide variations on circuit parameters and relatively large amount of noise on signal wires.

Circuits may be either *synchronous* or *asynchronous*. Synchronization is usually achieved by a timing device called *clock*, which produces a train of equally spaced pulses. The clock pulses are fed into the circuit in such a way that the various operations take place only with the arrival of the appropriate synchronization pulses. The clock for a particular circuit may have a number of outputs, on which pulses appear at certain intervals and with fixed relation between the pulses on the various outputs. This process ensures an orderly execution of the various operations and logical decisions to be made by the circuit. Asynchronous circuits, on the other hand, are usually faster because they are almost free-running and do not depend on the frequency of a clock, which in most cases is well below the speed of operation of a free-running gate. The orderly execution of operations in asychronous circuits is controlled by a number of *completion* and *initiation* signals, so that the completion signal of one operation initiates the execution of the next consecutive operation, and so on.

In practice, there is a maximum amount of current which can be drawn from a gate without affecting its operation. There is also a minimum amount of current necessary to drive each gate. Consequently, the number of gate inputs which can be driven by the output of a single gate is limited; the maximum of such number is called *fanout* and is usually specified by the manufacturer. The overloading of a gate will cause a serious deterioration in the signal value and may affect the circuit performance. A less critical, though still serious, restriction is the bound on the number of inputs which a single gate may have. This bound is referred to as the *fanin* of the gate and is also specified by the manufacturer.

The basic logical gates which implement the logical operations AND, OR, and NOT were introduced in Sec. 3-4. AND or OR gates are relatively simple to manufacture and they are often referred to as *diode logic*, since they can be constructed of diodes. The NOT gate, which is also called an INVERTER, is constructed of a transistor. Presently, these gates are manufactured as integrated circuits and the names "diode gates" or "transistor gates" have only historical values. In practice, time is required to propagate a signal through a gate, or to switch a gate output from one value to another. This delay, which is known as *propagation delay*, strongly affects the logical design. It may cause hazards and races which are discussed in subsequent chapters. In this introductory chapter we shall assume that the propagation delay is very small, and it will therefore generally be ignored.

In all conventional gates, the output of a gate is either connected to the input of another gate or it serves as an external circuit output. It is never connected to the output of another gate, since it may lead to a nondeterministic operation and to the destruction of the gate. There are special gates, known as *wired-OR* and *wired-AND*, in which special circuitry is provided so that their outputs can be directly connected. However, we shall not consider these gates, because in most cases they can be handled by using the same procedures valid for conventional gates.

Analysis of combinational circuits

To every combinational switching circuit there corresponds a Boolean function which describes the logical behavior of the circuit. The analysis of a circuit is concerned with determining the function which describes that circuit.

A combinational circuit is analyzed by tracing the output of each gate, starting from the circuit inputs and continuing toward each circuit output. This procedure is illustrated by the analysis of the circuit in Fig. 5-1, which is a minimal realization of a *full binary adder*. (A more

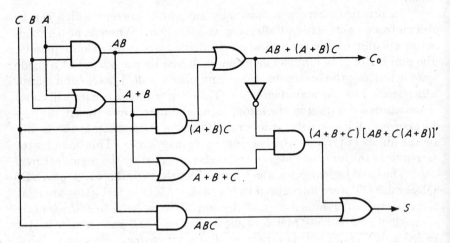

Fig. 5-1 Analysis of a full-adder gate circuit.

comprehensive discussion of the properties of this circuit is deferred to Sec. 5-4). The output designated C_0 is given by

$$C_0 = AB + (A + B)C$$
$$= AB + AC + BC$$

The second output designated S is found to be

$$S = (A + B + C)[AB + (A + B)C]' + ABC$$
$$= (A + B + C)(A' + B')(A' + C')(B' + C') + ABC$$
$$= AB'C' + A'BC' + A'B'C + ABC$$
$$= A \oplus B \oplus C$$

The circuit shown in Fig. 5-1 is referred to as a *multilevel realization*, because the incoming input signals must pass through several levels of gates until they reach the outputs. In this circuit the signals corresponding to A must pass as many as six levels of gates before reaching the output S. Multilevel circuits have several practical limitations. Since a finite delay is associated with each gate, propagation time of the input signals increases proportionally to the increase in the number of gate levels. The lengths of the various paths in a multilevel circuit are not always constant. Some paths are shorter than others, e.g., in Fig. 5-1, there is one path going from A to S of length two, while other paths from A to S range in length from four to six levels. Consequently, different propagation times are associated with the various paths, which may cause certain hazardous situations. Such situations are discussed in Chap. 8. A *two-level realization* overcomes these limitations, at the price of considerable increase in the number of gates required for the realization. Two-level realizations of some circuits are shown subsequently. In Chap. 8 we shall also show that the problem of testing a multilevel circuit for faults is considerably more complicated than the testing of two-level circuits.

Some simple design problems

In the preceding chapters we have introduced some of the most important tools that can be used in designing switching circuits. These tools include switching algebra, truth tables, and the minimization procedures. In this section we shall employ these tools to design and implement some simple circuits.

Example It is required to design a *parallel parity-bit generator*. This circuit must produce an output 1 if and only if an odd number of its inputs have value 1. As an illustration we shall design a parity-bit generator for three-bit code words; that is, the circuit has three

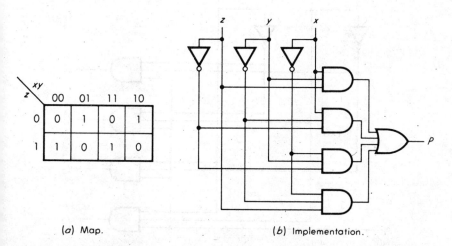

(a) Map.   (b) Implementation.

Fig. 5-2 Design of a parallel parity-bit generator.

inputs x, y, and z, and its output p must be equal to 1 whenever either only one of the inputs equals 1 or all three inputs are equal to 1. The map for this function is shown in Fig. 5-2a. Clearly,

$$p = x'y'z + x'yz' + xy'z' + xyz$$

A simple implementation of p is shown in Fig. 5-2b. ∎

Example An input line X to a *serial-to-parallel converter* receives a long sequence of binary digits which must be distributed into four different output lines, as specified by external control signals. Let C_1 and C_2 be the two control signals and let L_1, L_2, L_3, and L_4 denote the output lines. The truth table shown in Table 5-1 specifies

Table 5-1 Truth table and logical equations for
serial-to-parallel converter

Control		Output lines				Logical equations
C_1	C_2	L_1	L_2	L_3	L_4	
0	0	x	0	0	0	$L_1 = xC_1'C_2'$
0	1	0	x	0	0	$L_2 = xC_1'C_2$
1	0	0	0	x	0	$L_3 = xC_1C_2'$
1	1	0	0	0	x	$L_4 = xC_1C_2$

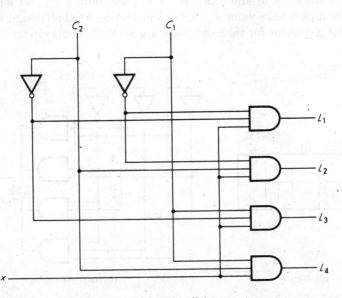

Fig. 5-3 A serial-to-parallel converter.

the logical values of the output lines for every combination of control signals. For example, if the control signals have values $C_1 = C_2 = 0$, then the input signals must be directed to L_1, and so on for other control signal values. The resulting logical equations are given in Table 5-1 and a two-level implementation is shown in Fig. 5-3. ■

5-2 LOGIC DESIGN WITH INTEGRATED CIRCUITS

So far we have developed the traditional techniques of logical design, where discrete gates have been used as the basic building blocks for implementing digital systems. Since the 1960's more modern devices, called *integrated circuits*, have been developed and they serve now as the main building blocks of all logical circuits. Integrated circuits are produced in *packages*, or *chips*, and are generally classified into three categories:

1. *Small Scale Integration*, or SSI, usually refers to packages containing single gates, e.g., AND, OR, NOT, NAND, NOR, XOR, or small packages containing two or four gates of the same type.
2. *Medium Scale Integration*, or MSI, are intermediate packages containing each up to about 100 gates and they usually realize some *standard* circuit which is very often used in logical design, e.g., code converters, adders, etc.
3. *Large Scale Integration*, or LSI, may contain many hundreds and thousands of gates in a single package. Some LSI circuits are standard, e.g., subsystems for computer control or for computer arithmetic unit, while other LSI circuits are manufactured to the specification of the logical designer. These latter circuits are usually very expensive to manufacture and they are economical only when large quantities of the same circuit are needed.

Integrated circuits have several important advantages over the older discrete components. First, they are relatively inexpensive; in fact, the integrated circuit cost becomes an increasingly small part of the total cost of a system. Second, they are more reliable and easily available. Presently, a logical designer will make every effort to incorporate as many standard MSI packages as possible in building a system, since their use will result in a lower cost, at the same time increasing the system's reliability and making it easier to maintain by simply replacing a defective package by a new one.

In this section we present several standard circuits which are all available as MSI packages and are very widely used in the computer technology. Although each of these circuits can be purchased separately and therefore may be viewed as a "black box," we shall show how to design each of these circuits. Their design will not only illustrate design techniques for other nonstandard circuits but also enhance our ability to use these circuits, to modify them, or to enlarge them by connecting several such packages.

Comparators

An *n-bit comparator* is a circuit which compares the magnitude of two numbers X and Y. It has three outputs f_1, f_2, and f_3 such that $f_1 = 1$ iff $X > Y$; $f_2 = 1$ iff $X = Y$; $f_3 = 1$ iff $X < Y$. As an example consider an elementary two-bit comparator, as shown in Fig. 5-4a. The circuit

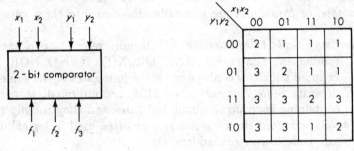

(a) Block diagram.

(b) Map for f_1, f_2, and f_3.

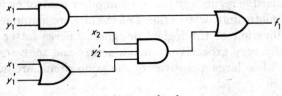

(c) Circuit for f_1.

Fig. 5-4 Designing a 2-bit comparator.

has four inputs x_1, x_2, y_1 and y_2, where x_1 and y_1 each denotes the most significant digit of X and Y respectively. The logical equations may be determined with the aid of the map of Fig. 5-4b, where the values 1, 2, and 3 are entered in the appropriate cells to denote, respectively, $f_1 = 1$, $f_2 = 1$, and $f_3 = 1$.

$$f_1 = x_1 x_2 y_2' + x_2 y_1' y_2' + x_1 y_1'$$
$$= (x_1 + y_1') x_2 y_2' + x_1 y_1'$$

$$f_2 = x_1'x_2'y_1'y_2' + x_1'x_2y_1'y_2 + x_1x_2'y_1y_2' + x_1x_2y_1y_2$$
$$= x_1'y_1'(x_2'y_2' + x_2y_2) + x_1y_1(x_2'y_2' + x_2y_2)$$
$$= (x_1'y_1' + x_1y_1)(x_2'y_2' + x_2y_2)$$
$$f_3 = x_2'y_1y_2 + x_1'x_2'y_2 + x_1'y_1$$
$$= x_2'y_2(y_1 + x_1') + x_1'y_1$$

The circuit for f_1 is shown in Fig. 5-4c. Similar circuits can be shown for f_2 and f_3.

The reader can verify that $X > Y$, that is, $f_1 = 1$, when the most significant bit of X is larger than that of Y, i.e., $x_1 > y_1$, or when the most significant bits are equal, but the least significant bit of X is larger than that of Y, namely, $x_1 = y_1$ and $x_2 > y_2$. In a similar way we can determine the conditions for $f_2 = 1$ and $f_3 = 1$. This line of reasoning can be further generalized to yield the logical equations for a four-bit comparator.

Four-bit comparators are available commercially as MSI packages, described as shown in Fig. 5-5a. A four-bit package has 11 inputs: four representing X, four representing Y, and three connected to the outputs f_1, f_2, and f_3 of the preceding stage. Three such packages can be connected in cascade, as shown in Fig. 5-5b, to obtain a 12-bit comparator. Initial conditions are inserted to the inputs of the comparator corre-

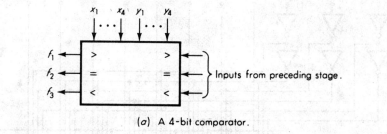

(a) A 4-bit comparator.

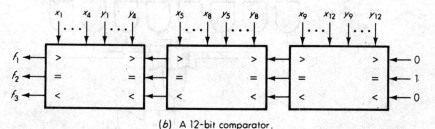

(b) A 12-bit comparator.

Fig. 5-5 Design of 12-bit comparator using three available MSI 4-bit comparators.

sponding to the least significant bits in such a way that the outputs of this comparator will depend only on the values of its own x's and y's.

Data selectors

A *multiplexer* is essentially an electronic switch that can connect one out of n inputs to the output. A most important application of the multiplexer is as a *data selector*. In general, a data selector has n *data input* lines $D_0, D_1, \ldots, D_{n-1}$, m *select digit* inputs $s_0, s_1, \ldots, s_{m-1}$, and

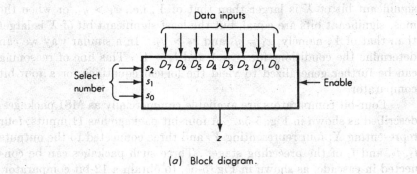

(a) Block diagram.

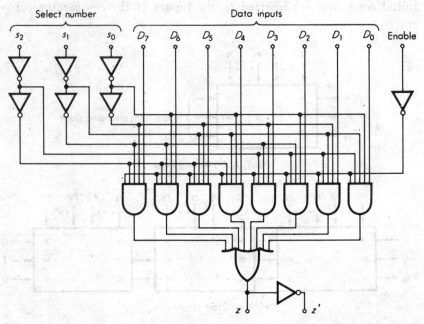

(b) Logic diagram.

Fig. 5-6 Data selector with eight data-input lines.

one output. The m-select digits form a binary *select number* ranging from 0 to $2^m - 1$, and when this number has the value k, then D_k is connected to the output. Thus this circuit selects one of n data input lines, according to the value of the select number, and in effect connects it to the output. Clearly, the number of select digits must equal $m = \log_2 n$, so that it can identify all the data inputs.

Data selectors have numerous applications. For example, they may be used to connect one out of n terminals to the computer input or to connect one out of n teletypes to the computer output, and so on. As we shall subsequently show, data selectors may also be used to implement all Boolean functions.

A block diagram for a data selector with eight data input lines is shown in Fig. 5-6a. The select number consists of the three digits $s_2 s_1 s_0$. Thus, for example, when $s_2 s_1 s_0 = 101$, then D_5 is to be connected to the output, and so on. The *Enable* (or *strobe*) input "enables" or turns the circuit on. A logic diagram for this data selector is shown in Fig. 5-6b. Such a unit is available as an MSI package, and it provides the complement of the output z' as well as the output z. The Enable input turns the circuit on when it assumes the value 0.

Implementing switching functions with data selectors

An important application of data selectors is the implementation of arbitrary switching functions. As an example we shall show how the functions of two variables can be implemented by means of the data selector of Fig. 5-7. Clearly, in this circuit if $s = 0$, then z assumes the value of D_0, and if $s = 1$, then z assumes the value of D_1. Thus, $z = sD_1 + s'D_0$. Now, suppose that we want to implement the EXCLUSIVE-OR opera-

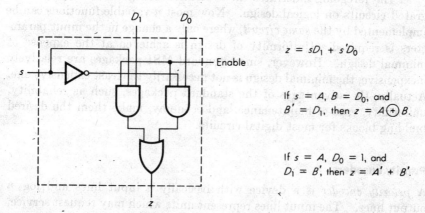

$$z = sD_1 + s'D_0$$

If $s = A$, $B = D_0$, and
$B' = D_1$, then $z = A \oplus B$.

If $s = A$, $D_0 = 1$, and
$D_1 = B'$, then $z = A' + B'$.

Fig. 5-7 Implementing two-variable functions with a data selector.

tion $A \oplus B$. This can be accomplished by connecting variable A to input s and variables B and B' to D_0 and D_1, respectively. In this case, $z = AB' + A'B = A \oplus B$. Similarly, if we want to implement the NAND operation $z = A' + B'$, we connect variable A to s and variable B' to D_1. D_0 is connected to a constant 1. Clearly, $z = AB' + A'1 = A' + B'$.

In a similar manner a judicial choice of the inputs will implement any of the 16 different two-variable functions. In general, to implement an n-variable function we require a data selector with $n - 1$ select inputs and 2^{n-1} data inputs. Hence, for example, to implement all three-variable functions, we require a data selector with two select inputs, s_1 and s_2, and $2^{3-1} = 4$ data inputs, D_0, D_1, D_2, and D_3. The output of such a data selector is equal to

$$z = s_1's_2'D_0 + s_1s_2'D_1 + s_1's_2D_2 + s_1s_2D_3$$

The reader can verify that, if we connect variables A and B to s_1 and s_2, respectively, and connect variables C and C' to D_0 and D_3, respectively, and assign D_1 the constant 1 and D_2 the constant 0, the circuit will realize the function $z = A'B'C + AB' + ABC' = AC' + B'C$.

In general, to implement an n-variable function, we assign $n - 1$ variables to the select inputs—one variable to each such input. The last variable and the constants 0 and 1 are assigned to the data inputs in such a way that together with the select-input variables they will yield the required function. Such an implementation is usually possible when at least one variable is available in both its complemented as well as uncomplemented forms; otherwise a larger data selector may be required. Implementations of functions of five or more variables are usually accomplished by means of a multilevel arrangement of several smaller standard data selectors.

The foregoing illustrates the revolution brought about by the integrated circuits on logical design. Now most n-variable functions can be implemented by the *same circuit*, where only a change in the input parameters is required. Uniformity of design is achieved at the expense of minimal design. However, since standard MSI packages are relatively inexpensive, the minimal design is not necessarily the least expensive one. Actually, the advantages of the standard packages, such as reliability, uniformity, ease of maintenance, and economy, make them the desired building blocks for most digital circuits.

Priority encoders

A *priority encoder* is a device with basically n input lines and $\log_2 n$ output lines. The input lines represent units which may request service, such as, for example, terminals in a time-sharing system. When two lines p_i and p_j, such that $i > j$, request service simultaneously, line p_i has the priority over line p_j. The encoder produces a binary output code indicating which of the input lines requesting service has the highest priority. An input line p_i indicates a request for service by assuming the value $p_i = 1$. A block diagram for an eight-input, three-output priority encoder is shown in Fig. 5-8a.

The truth table for this encoder is shown in Fig. 5-8b. In the first row only p_0 requests service and, consequently, the output code should be the binary number zero to indicate that p_0 has the priority. This is accomplished by setting $z_4 z_2 z_1 = 000$. The fourth row, for example, describes the situation where p_3 requests service, while p_0, p_1, and p_2 each may or may not request service simultaneously. This is indicated by the entry 1 in column p_3 and the don't-cares in columns p_0, p_1, and p_2. No request of a higher priority than p_3 is present at this time. Since in this situation p_3 has the highest priority, the output code must be the binary number three. Therefore, we set z_1 and z_2 to 1 while z_4 is set to 0. (Note that the binary number is given by $N = 4z_4 + 2z_2 + z_1$). In a similar manner the entire table is completed.

From the truth table we can derive the logic equations for z_1, z_2, and z_4. Starting with z_4, we find that

$$z_4 = p_4 p_5' p_6' p_7' + p_5 p_6' p_7' + p_6 p_7' + p_7$$

This equation can be simplified to

$$z_4 = p_4 + p_5 + p_6 + p_7$$

For z_2 and z_1 we find

$$z_2 = p_2 p_3' p_4' p_5' p_6' p_7' + p_3 p_4' p_5' p_6' p_7' + p_6 p_7' + p_7$$
$$= p_2 p_4' p_5' + p_3 p_4' p_5' + p_6 + p_7$$
$$z_1 = p_1 p_2' p_3' p_4' p_5' p_6' p_7' + p_3 p_4' p_5' p_6' p_7' + p_5 p_6' p_7' + p_7$$
$$= p_1 p_2' p_4' p_6' + p_3 p_4' p_6' + p_5 p_6' + p_7$$

An implementation of such an encoder is given in Fig. 5-8c. In this encoder, which is available as an MSI package, the inputs are given in a complemented form. The circuit has also an Enable signal and it contains an output z_0 which indicates whether any requests are present. Specifically, $z_0 = 0$ if there is no request and $z_0 = 1$ if there are one or more requests present. It is possible to combine several such encoders by means of external gating to handle more than eight inputs.

It is appropriate to note at this point that in the preceding implementation of switching functions by means of data selectors as well as in this priority encoder we may encounter "hazards" which can cause prob-

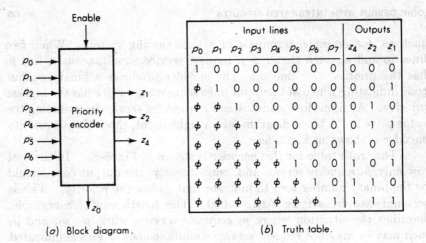

(a) Block diagram.

(b) Truth table.

Input lines								Outputs		
p_0	p_1	p_2	p_3	p_4	p_5	p_6	p_7	z_4	z_2	z_1
1	0	0	0	0	0	0	0	0	0	0
ϕ	1	0	0	0	0	0	0	0	0	1
ϕ	ϕ	1	0	0	0	0	0	0	1	0
ϕ	ϕ	ϕ	1	0	0	0	0	0	1	1
ϕ	ϕ	ϕ	ϕ	1	0	0	0	1	0	0
ϕ	ϕ	ϕ	ϕ	ϕ	1	0	0	1	0	1
ϕ	ϕ	ϕ	ϕ	ϕ	ϕ	1	0	1	1	0
ϕ	ϕ	ϕ	ϕ	ϕ	ϕ	ϕ	1	1	1	1

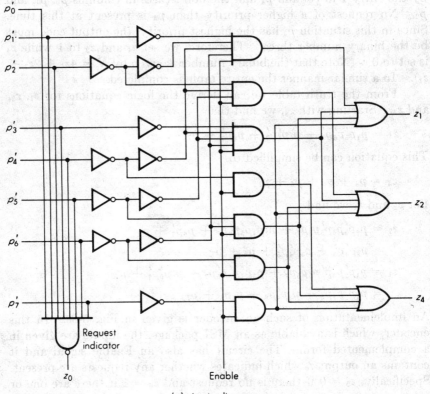

(c) Logic diagram.

Fig. 5-8 Design of a priority encoder.

lems during transient operations. These problems as well as methods to overcome them are discussed in Chap. 8.

Decoders

A *decoder* is a combinational circuit with n inputs and at most 2^n outputs. Its characteristic property is that *for every combination of input values only one output will be equal to 1 at the same time.* Decoders have a wide variety of applications in digital technology. They may be used to route input data to a specified output line, as, for example, is done in addressing core memory, where input data are to be stored in (or read from) a specified memory location. They serve for some code conversions. Or they may be used for data distribution, i.e., demultiplexing, as will be shown subsequently. Finally, decoders are also used as the basic building blocks in implementing arbitrary switching functions.

Figure 5-9a illustrates a basic 2-to-4 decoder. Clearly if w and x are the input variables, then each of the outputs corresponds to a different minterm of two variables. Two such 2-to-4 decoders plus a gate-switching matrix can be connected, as shown in Fig. 5-9b, to form a 4-to-16 decoder. Different switching matrices are available in various sizes and forms and are very widely used in the design of digital circuits.

Not all decoders have exactly 2^n outputs. Figure 5-10 describes a *decimal decoder* which converts information from BCD to decimal. It has four inputs w, x, y, and z, where w is the most significant and z the least significant digits; and 10 outputs, f_0 through f_9, corresponding to the decimal numbers. In designing this decoder we took advantage of the don't-care combinations, f_{10} through f_{16}, as can be verified by means of the map in Fig. 5-10b. Decimal decoders similar to the above are available as MSI packages. Another implementation of decimal decoders is by means of a partial-gate matrix, as shown in Fig. 5-11.

A decoder with exactly n inputs and 2^n outputs can also be used to implement any switching function. Each of the outputs of such a decoder realizes one distinct minterm. Thus, by connecting the appropriate outputs into an external OR gate, the required function will be realized. Figure 5-12 illustrates the implementation of the function $f(A,B,C,D) = \Sigma(1,5,9,15)$ by means of a complete decoder.

A decoder with one data input and n address inputs is called a *demultiplexer* and it directs the input data to any one of the 2^n outputs, as specified by the n-bit input address. A block diagram of a demultiplexer is shown in Fig. 5-13. A demultiplexer with four outputs is shown in Fig. 5-3.

Various types and sizes of decoders for a variety of applications are available as integrated MSI packages. When larger-size decoders are

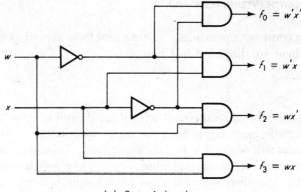

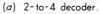

(a) 2-to-4 decoder.

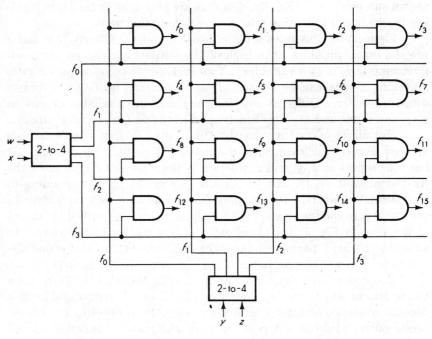

(b) Design of a 4-to-16 decoder.

Fig. 5-9 Illustration of n-to-2^n decoders.

needed, they can usually be formed by interconnecting several such smaller packages with (perhaps) some additional discrete logic. Larger decoders are also available as "Read-Only-Memories," or ROM, but their design will not be further discussed in this book.

128

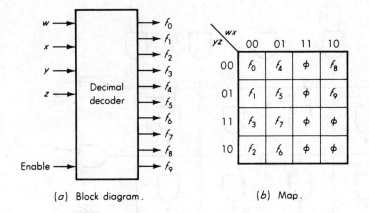

(a) Block diagram.

(b) Map.

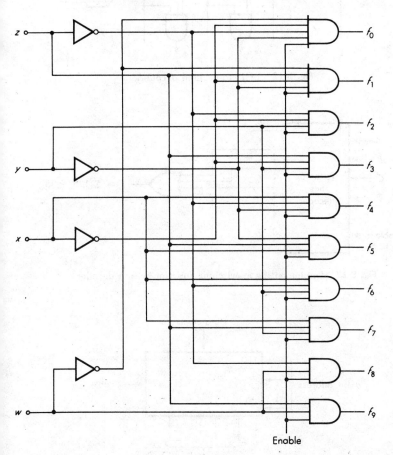

(c) Logic diagram.

Fig. 5-10 Design of a BCD-to-decimal decoder.

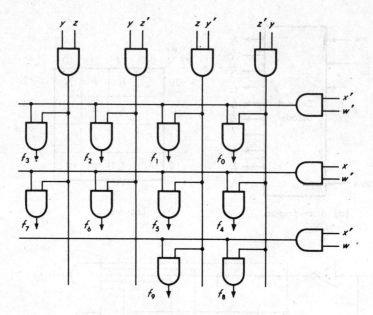

Fig. 5-11 BCD-to-decimal decoder.

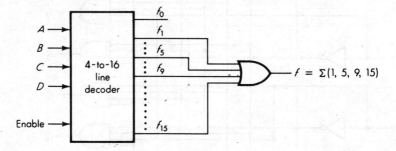

Fig. 5-12 Implementing a switching function with a decoder.

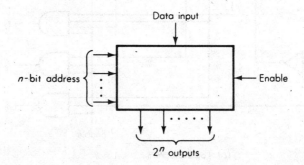

Fig. 5-13 A demultiplexer.

Seven-segment display

The conventional method for displaying decimal digits is by means of the *seven-segment display* shown in Fig. 5-14. The display consists of a BCD to seven-segment decoder and seven separate light segments (usually light-emitting diodes or crystals) each of which can be turned on and off independently of the others. The display receives its inputs in the form of BCD coded digits and is to transform these inputs so as to obtain the desired pattern of the corresponding decimal digit.

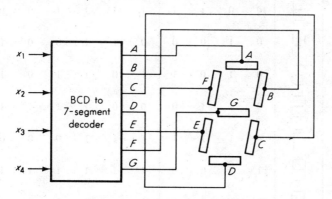

Fig. 5-14 Seven-segment display.

Table 5-2 can be viewed as the truth table for the output functions of the BCD-to-seven-segment decoder. The seven-segment code corresponding to each digit is determined directly from the pattern. For example, to display the decimal digit 2, segments A, B, G, E, D are turned on while segments C and F remain off. In a similar manner the entire seven-segment code is obtained. The segment excitation functions can now be determined directly from the table or by using maps. Note that there are six don't-care combinations identical to the ones shown in Fig. 5-10b. The expressions for the segment excitation functions are thus as follows:

$$A = x_1 + x_2'x_4' + x_2x_4 + x_3x_4$$
$$B = x_2' + x_3'x_4' + x_3x_4$$
$$C = x_2 + x_3' + x_4$$
$$D = x_2'x_4' + x_2'x_3 + x_3x_4' + x_2x_3'x_4$$
$$E = x_2'x_4' + x_3x_4'$$
$$F = x_1 + x_2x_3' + x_2x_4' + x_3'x_4'$$
$$G = x_1 + x_2'x_3 + x_2x_3' + x_3x_4'$$

Table 5-2   Seven-segment pattern and code

Decimal digit	Pattern	BCD code				Seven-segment code						
		x_1	x_2	x_3	x_4	A	B	C	D	E	F	G
1		0	0	0	1	0	1	1	0	0	0	0
2		0	0	1	0	1	1	0	1	1	0	1
3		0	0	1	1	1	1	1	1	0	0	1
4		0	1	0	0	0	1	1	0	0	1	1
5		0	1	0	1	1	0	1	1	0	1	1
6		0	1	1	0	0	0	1	1	1	1	1
7		0	1	1	1	1	1	1	0	0	0	0
8		1	0	0	0	1	1	1	1	1	1	1
9		1	0	0	1	1	1	1	0	0	1	1
0		0	0	0	0	1	1	1	1	1	1	0

The realization of the decoder is now straightforward. It can be either implemented as a conventional multiple-output circuit, or it may be implemented using a single 4-to-16 line decoder plus seven OR gates in a manner similar to that shown in Fig. 5-12. In practice, the seven-segment decoder is commercially available as a standard MSI package.

Sine generators

Trigonometric functions can either be generated sequentially or they may be produced by combinationa' circuits. Combinational sine generators are used whenever the sine funi ion must be evaluated fast and repeatedly.

A combinational sine generator receives as its input the angle and, in turn, produces the sine of that angle. The angle is given in radians converted to binary and the sine value is produced in binary. Naturally, the accuracy of the calculation is a function of the number of bits that describe the angles and the number of bits that provide the sine values.

In practical applications at least eight binary digits are required to describe the angles or the sine values. In our case, however, in order to simplify the computations, we shall consider a *four-bit sine generator*.

Let the sine function be $\sin(\pi x)$, where $0 \le x < 1$. The angle x will be described by the four binary digits x_1, x_2, x_3, x_4, where x_1 has a weight of $\frac{1}{2}$, x_2 of $\frac{1}{4}$, and so on. Thus, for example, to specify an angle of 45°, the input x must be equal to $\frac{1}{4}$, or $x = 0100$. To specify an angle of 30°, x must be equal to $\frac{1}{6}$. However, it is impossible to represent precisely this value with four bits, and the closest possible value is $\frac{3}{16}$ or $x = 0011$. The truth table of the sine generator is shown in Fig. 5-15a. The sine is given by the binary number $z = z_1 z_2 z_3 z_4$, such that $0 \le z < 1$ and z_1 has a weight of $\frac{1}{2}$, z_2 has a weight of $\frac{1}{4}$, and so on. The sine of 30° is equal to 0.5. Hence, the output values in row $x = 0011$ are specified to be $z = 1000$. Similarly, the sine of 45° is 0.707. Clearly, the closest output value would be $z = 1011$, which is equal to 0.6875. In a similar manner the entire truth table is constructed. Figure 5-15c illustrates the actual function specified by this table versus the sine function.

Angle x				$\sin(\pi x)$			
x_1	x_2	x_3	x_4	z_1	z_2	z_3	z_4
0	0	0	0	0	0	0	0
0	0	0	1	0	0	1	1
0	0	1	0	0	1	1	0
0	0	1	1	1	0	0	0
0	1	0	0	1	0	1	1
0	1	0	1	1	1	0	1
0	1	1	0	1	1	1	0
0	1	1	1	1	1	1	1
1	0	0	0	1	1	1	1
1	0	0	1	1	1	1	1
1	0	1	0	1	1	1	0
1	0	1	1	1	1	0	1
1	1	0	0	1	0	1	1
1	1	0	1	1	0	0	0
1	1	1	0	0	1	1	0
1	1	1	1	0	0	1	1

(a) Truth table.

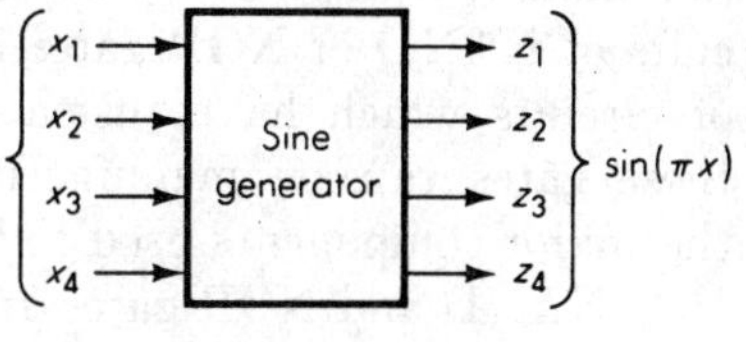

(b) Block diagram.

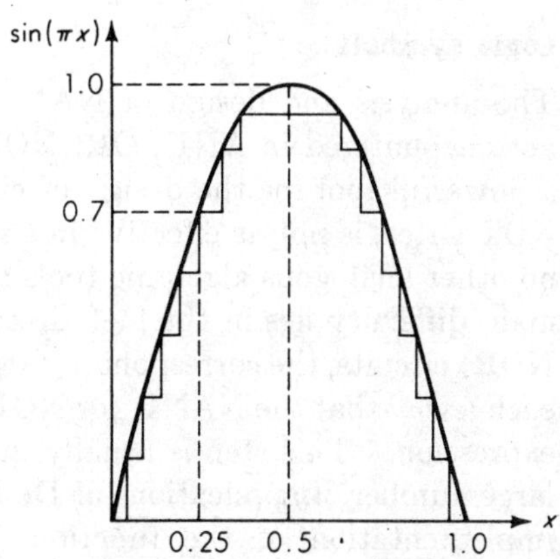

(c) Function generated versus sine wave.

Fig. 5-15 Designing a sine generator.

The logical equations specifying the outputs can be derived from a set of four maps that correspond to the truth tables and are as follows:

$$z_1 = x_1'x_2 + x_1x_2' + x_2x_3' + x_1'x_3x_4$$
$$z_2 = x_1x_2' + x_3x_4' + x_1'x_2x_4$$
$$z_3 = x_3x_4' + x_2x_3 + x_2x_4' + x_2'x_3'x_4 + x_1x_4'$$
$$z_4 = x_2'x_3'x_4 + x_2x_3'x_4' + x_1x_2'x_3' + x_1x_3x_4 + x_1'x_2x_4$$

The sine generator, which is a special-purpose code converter, can be implemented in a variety of ways, namely, as a conventional multiple-output circuit or by using a 4-to-16 line decoder plus the necessary OR gates. In practice, however, sine generators consisting of 10 or more input bits can be obtained as LSI packages.

5-3 NAND AND NOR CIRCUITS

In Sec. 3-2 we proved that the NAND and NOR operations are each functionally complete. It is highly desirable to construct digital circuits of NAND or NOR gates because of the simplicity and uniformity of circuits which have just a single primitive component. And since these gates can be manufactured quite inexpensively, they constitute the major components used today by logical designers.

NAND and NOR gates are also available as integrated circuit SSI packages. These packages vary in sizes and may contain from one to four gates per package.

Logic symbols

The analysis and design of NAND and NOR circuits poses difficulties not encountered in AND, OR, NOT logic. Switching algebra, which is a powerful tool for the design of circuits constructed of AND, OR, and NOT gates, is not as effective in the case of NAND and NOR logic, and no other analogous algebraic tools are available for the latter case. The main difficulty lies in the fact that in order to obtain simple NAND (or NOR) circuits, the corresponding algebraic expressions must be factored in such a way that the NAND (or NOR) operation will be the only one in the expression. This step is usually quite complicated because it involves a large number of applications of De Morgan's theorem. For example, the implementation of the function $T = A' + (B + C')(D' + EF')$ with AND, OR, NOT logic is straightforward, but its NAND-logic realization is not as evident. It can be, however, considerably simplified by expressing the function as $T = A|((B'|C)|(D|(E|F')))$. Evidently, the determination of this expression by algebraic means would be quite involved, but it may be avoided through the use of special symbols and simple circuit manipulations.

The interpretation and manipulation of logic diagrams, as well as the implementation of switching functions, becomes more evident if we use a system of symbols so that each logic gate can be represented by one of two symbols. This system, known as the MIL-STD-806B, is shown in Fig. 5-16. Each symbol is formed by combining the AND-gate or OR-gate symbol with an INVERSION symbol, which is indicated by a small circle.

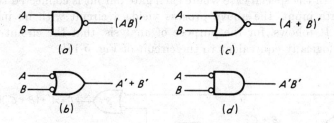

Fig. 5-16   NAND and NOR gate symbols.

The symbol in Fig. 5-16a represents a circuit that generates the complement of the AND combination of its inputs, i.e., $(AB)'$. The symbol of Fig. 5-16b, on the other hand, represents a circuit that generates the OR combination of its inverted inputs, i.e., $A' + B'$. Clearly, both symbols describe the NAND operation, but for reasons which will become more evident subsequently, we prefer to think in terms of AND, OR, and NOT. For example, when realizing the function $P + Q$, it is natural to think in terms of an OR operation, and consequently a gate of the type shown in Fig. 5-16b, whose inputs are P' and Q', is used to describe the real. .on of this function. Similar arguments explain the use of the ...bols shown in Fig. 5-16c and d for NOR gates.

The assignment of two symbols to represent the same gate circuit is confusing at first, but is very convenient, because it provides a deeper insight into the logical operations taking place within the circuit. It enables the designer to analyze a circuit constructed of NAND or NOR gates by employing the same techniques used for circuits consisting of AND, OR, and NOT gates. In other words, the main feature of this notation is that one circuit may be viewed as either an AND gate or an OR gate, depending on the required logical operation.

Analysis and synthesis of NAND-NOR network

The usefulness of having two symbols to represent a NAND gate will be demonstrated by the analysis of the circuit shown in Fig. 5-17a. Since every small circle represents an inversion, whenever a line connecting two gates has circles at both ends, *both* circles may be ignored, because their net logical effect is nil. Whenever a circuit has a line with a circle at one end and a switching variable (or expression) at the other end (e.g., input or output lines), it is logically equivalent to a circuit which has a connecting line from which the circle has been removed and the variable complemented. This process does not guarantee that all the inversion circles will be removed, but in most cases it ensures a considerably simpler circuit. In the special case where each gate output is connected to just a single gate input, the above process yields a circuit with no inversion circles. It follows, for the purpose of analysis, that the circuit of Fig. 5-17a is logically equivalent to the circuit of Fig. 5-17b.

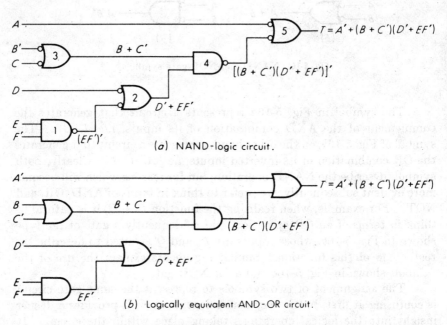

(a) NAND-logic circuit.

(b) Logically equivalent AND-OR circuit.

Fig. 5-17   Analysis of a NAND-logic circuit.

With some experience, circuits consisting of NAND or NOR logic can be analyzed directly, without actually converting the circuit to its equivalent AND-OR form. For example, gate 1 of Fig. 5-17a performs an AND operation and an inversion on its inputs E and F'. This is denoted by

$(EF')'$. Gate 2, on the other hand, performs the OR operation on the inverted inputs. Its output, therefore, is $D' + [(EF')']' = D' + EF'$. In a similar manner we find that the output of gate 3 is $B + C'$, while that of gate 4 is the complement of the AND combination of its inputs, as shown in the circuit of Fig. 5-17a. The analysis is completed by determining the OR combination of the complemented inputs to gate 5.

The logic diagram of Fig. 5-17a is characterized by the property that the polarities at all points match completely; that is, if a line connecting two gates has an inversion circle at one end, then it has also such a circle at the other end. As a result, the logically equivalent AND-OR circuit contains no inversion circles. In general, however, it may occur that a circled gate output will be connected to an uncircled gate input, or vice versa. In such cases, some of the inversion circles cannot be removed, and the logically equivalent circuit will consist of AND and OR, as well as NOT, gates, where each NOT gate replaces an inversion circle.

Consider the function $T = w(y + z) + xy'z'$ whose realization, which consists of four NAND gates, is shown in Fig. 5-18a. The choice of symbol to be used for each gate is dictated by the operation which that gate must perform. For example, gate 1 should produce the OR combination of $y + z$, and accordingly, the symbol of Fig. 5-16b is selected. Gate 2, on the other hand, is to produce the complement of the AND combination of w and $y + z$, and thus the symbol of Fig. 5-16a is chosen.

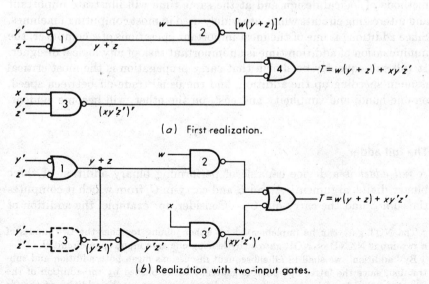

(a) First realization.

(b) Realization with two-input gates.

Fig. 5-18 Synthesis of a NAND circuit.

The symbols for the other gates are selected in a similar manner, and we find the output of gate 3 to be $(xy'z')'$, while that of gate 4 is the OR combination of its complemented inputs, that is, $T = w(y + z) + xy'z'$.

This circuit can also be realized with just two-input gates, as shown in Fig. 5-18b. (For the moment disregard the line connecting the outputs of gates 1 and 3.) In this circuit the output of gate 3 is the complement of the AND combination of its inputs, i.e., $(y'z')'$. The NOT† gate inverts this output, so that the input to gate 3' is $y'z'$. The outputs of gates 3' and 4 are established in a similar manner. At this point we observe that the inputs and functional operations of gates 1 and 3 are identical. We may therefore delete gate 3 after having connected its output to that of gate 1.

It must be emphasized that the assumed logic polarity and the symbols used to describe a circuit are important only insofar as the interpretation of the circuit is concerned; the circuit's actual operation is independent of the precise symbol used and the logic polarity assumed. In other words, the circuit "does not know" which symbols are used to describe it and whether we associate the constant 1 with the high voltage or vice versa.

5-4 DESIGN OF HIGH-SPEED ADDERS

The design of high-speed adders will serve as an example for studying methods of logical design and at the same time will illustrate important and interesting circuits which are widely used in most computing machines. Since addition‡ is one of the most important operations of a computer, the minimization of addition time is an important task of any logical designer. It will subsequently be shown that carry propagation is the most critical issue in speeding up the addition, and the usual trade-off between speed, on one hand, and simplicity and cost, on the other, will become evident.

The full adder

A *full adder* is a device capable of performing binary addition of three binary digits, arguments A and B and carry-in C, from which it computes the sum S and the carry-out C_0. Consider, for example, the addition of

---

† The NOT gate can be implemented by either joining together the two inputs of a two-input NAND or NOR gate or by leaving one gate input open-circuited.

‡ By "addition" we shall in all subsequent discussions mean both addition and subtraction, since the latter operation is generally accomplished by the addition of the inverted subtrahend in sign-and-magnitude machines, or by the addition of the 2's complement of the subtrahend in 2's-complement machines.

the following two binary numbers:

$$
\begin{array}{llll}
0 & 1 & 1 & \quad = \text{carry-in} \\
1 & 0 & 1 & 1 = \text{augend} \\
0 & 0 & 1 & 1 = \text{addend} \\
\hline
1 & 1 & 1 & 0 = \text{sum}
\end{array}
$$

The carries produced in the addition of the ith significant digits must be incorporated in the addition process of the $(i + 1)$st significant digits.

The truth table defining the input-output functional relationship for the full adder is shown in Fig. 5-19, as is its block-diagram representa-

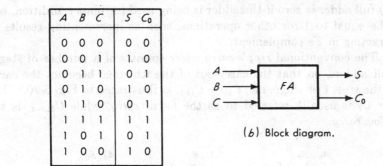

A	B	C	S	C_0
0	0	0	0	0
0	0	1	1	0
0	1	1	0	1
0	1	0	1	0
1	1	0	0	1
1	1	1	1	1
1	0	1	0	1
1	0	0	1	0

(*a*) Truth table for S and C_0.

(*b*) Block diagram.

Fig. 5-19 A full adder.

tion.   The logical equations for the sum and carry-out, derived from the truth table, are given by

$$
\begin{aligned}
S &= A'B'C + A'BC' + AB'C' + ABC \\
&= A \oplus B \oplus C \\
C_0 &= A'BC + ABC' + AB'C + ABC \\
&= AB + AC + BC
\end{aligned}
$$

A minimal realization of the full adder was shown in Fig. 5-2.   A NAND-logic realization is shown in Fig. P5-15.

The ripple-carry adder

In order to add two n-digit binary numbers, it is necessary to connect n stages of full adders so that each stage computes the corresponding sum and carry.   All high-speed adders are basically *parallel* devices, i.e., devices constructed of full adders which are connected in such a manner that all digits of the addend and augend are fed into them simultaneously. Hence the number of full adders required for a parallel implementation of an adder is equal to the word length n of the machine.

Let A_i and B_i be the ith digits of the two arguments being added, and let S_i be their sum; C_{0i} and C_i designate the carry-out of the ith full adder and the carry-in of that adder, respectively. The logical equations of the ith full adder are

$$S_i = A_i \oplus B_i \oplus C_i \qquad C_{0i} = A_iB_i + A_iC_i + B_iC_i$$

where $i = 0, 1, \ldots, n - 1$. The carry C_f into the zeroth (least significant) full adder is zero if the adder is being used for binary addition, but can be equal to 1 for other operations, such as incrementing results or subtracting in 2's complement.

The conventional *ripple-carry adder* consists of a number of stages of full adders, so that the carry-out of the ith stage becomes the carry into the $(i + 1)$st stage, i.e., $C_{0i} = C_{i+1}$, as illustrated in Fig. 5-20. The carry C_f is usually referred to as the *forced carry*, while $C_{0(n-1)}$ is the *overflow carry*.

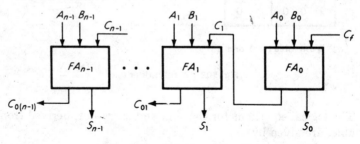

Fig. 5-20   A ripple-carry adder.

The time required to perform addition in the ripple-carry adder is the time required for the propagation (or ripple) of the carries in the stages. Although the carry will not propagate through all stages in every addition, the time allotted for the addition operation must be at least equal to the longest carry propagation time (plus addition time in the last full adder). The adder is assumed to produce the sum in a *fixed time* regardless of the actual carry or the numbers being added. If we assume that two time units are required for generating the carry in one (two-level) full-adder stage, then the fixed time that must be allotted to the n-stage ripple-carry adder is at least $2n$ units. This implies that the adder is part of a synchronous system and that the next summands must not be transferred into the adder until at least $2n$ time units have elapsed since the transfer of the current summands. In order to increase the speed of the adder, it is necessary to minimize the fixed time required for carry propagation.

The carry-lookahead adder

The *carry-lookahead adder* is a fixed-time adder, in which several stages are simultaneously examined and their carries are generated in parallel. The carry equation can be rewritten as follows.

Define D_i and T_i as the *generated* and *propagated* carry signals for the ith stage, where

$$D_i = A_i B_i$$
$$T_i = A_i \oplus B_i = A'_i B_i + A_i B'_i$$

Then

$$C_{0i} = D_i + T_i C_i \tag{5-1}$$

D_i equals 1 if a carry is generated in the ith stage, i.e., if $A_i = B_i = 1$. T_i equals 1 if either A_i or B_i, but not both, is equal to 1. If $T_i = 1$ and $C_i = 1$, then $C_{0i} = 1$; that is, the carry-out of the $(i - 1)$st stage will propagate uninterrupted through the ith stage into the $(i + 1)$st stage.

In order to generate the carries in a parallel manner, it is necessary to transform the recursive form of the carry function into a nonrecursive form. This can be achieved as follows:

$$C_{0i} = D_i + T_i C_i$$
$$C_i = C_{0(i-1)}$$
$$C_{0i} = D_i + T_i(D_{i-1} + T_{i-1}C_{i-1})$$
$$= D_i + T_i D_{i-1} + T_i T_{i-1}(D_{i-2} + T_{i-2}C_{i-2})$$
$$= D_i + T_i D_{i-1} + T_i T_{i-1} D_{i-2} + T_i T_{i-1} T_{i-2} C_{i-2}$$

If we continue this iteration, we are able to directly express the carry-out of the ith stage in terms of external inputs (i.e., excluding carries) of the preceding stages and the forced carry (note that $C_{i-i} = C_f$). Hence

$$C_{0i} = D_i + T_i D_{i-1} + T_i T_{i-1} D_{i-2}$$
$$+ \cdots + T_i T_{i-1} T_{i-2} \cdots T_0 C_f \tag{5-2}$$

Equation (5-2) actually defines the ith carry-out C_{0i} to be 1 if it has been generated in the ith stage (D_i) or originated in a preceding stage and propagated by all subsequent stages.

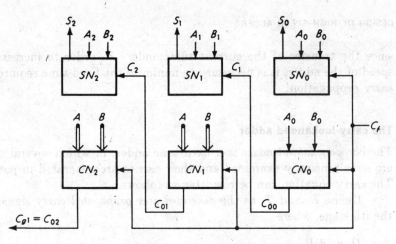

(a) Block diagram of initial three-stage group.

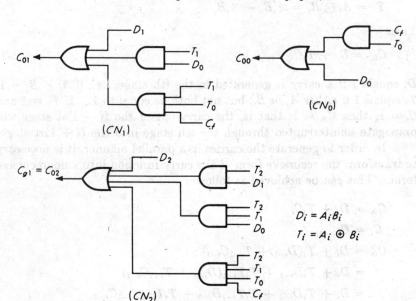

$$D_i = A_i B_i$$
$$T_i = A_i \oplus B_i$$

(b) The carry networks.

Fig. 5-21 Three-digit adder group with full carry lookahead.

The implementation of the above lookahead scheme for the entire adder is not practical, because it requires a very large number of gates and, in addition, for each stage of the adder it is necessary to have an OR gate with n inputs and n AND gates with 1 through n inputs. And since a modern computer may have 50-bit words, such a complete lookahead scheme cannot be economically accomplished. The limitation can be overcome, though at the expense of speed of computation, by dividing the n stages of the adder into groups, so that within each group a full carry lookahead as defined by Eq. (5-2) is achieved, while a ripple carry is maintained between the groups. For the purposes of illustration, let us consider groups consisting of three full-adder stages; i.e., group 1 consists of stages 0 through 2; group 2 consists of stages 3 through 5, etc. The carry-out of group k (and into group $k + 1$) will be denoted C_{gk}. The first three-stage group with full carry lookahead is shown in Fig. 5-21a, where the block diagram of each full adder is shown with its sum network (SN) and carry network (CN) separated. The details of the carry networks are given in Fig. 5-21b. The sum networks are the conventional ones, i.e., $S_i = T_i \oplus C_i$. The double-arrow inputs to carry network CN_i indicate that A_0 through A_i and B_0 through B_i are the inputs to that carry network.

It takes four time units to generate C_{g1}, because there are four levels of gates in CN_2. (Two units are required to produce T_i, and two units to compute C_{g1} in CN_2.) The generation of C_{g2} and any subsequent group carry requires only two time units, because the necessary generate (D_i) and propagate (T_i) signals are already available. Two additional time units are required in the final sum stage. Consequently, for an n-stage adder divided into three-stage groups with full lookahead within each group and ripple carry between groups, the longest propagation time is $4 + 2n/3$ units as compared with $2n$ units for the ripple-carry adder. A schematic diagram of a 30-digit adder with full lookahead within each three-digit group and ripple carry between groups is shown in Fig. 5-22. The lookahead adder requires about 50 percent additional hardware, a relatively small price for the threefold increase in speed.

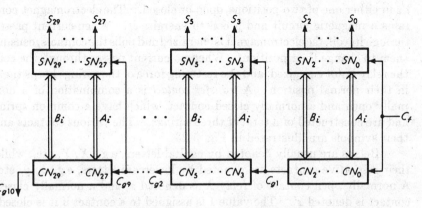

Fig. 5-22 Schematic diagram of a 30-digit adder with full lookahead within three-digit groups and ripple carry between groups.

The adder shown in Fig. 5-22 is called *one-level lookahead*. It is also possible to design adders with higher levels of lookahead. This is accomplished by designating a number of groups as a *section* and having a second level of lookahead to speed up the propagation of the carries between the groups within a section.

Presently, various MSI packages are available for the logical designer concerned with computer arithmetic operations. There are simple packages containing just a single full adder; and more complex ones containing a ripple-carry adder capable of adding two four-bit words. There are other MSI packages containing complete carry-lookahead circuitry. And finally, there are very complex LSI packages containing complete units capable of performing all the necessary arithmetic operations.

5-5 RELAY CONTACTS

Combinational networks constructed of relay contacts are typical examples of *bilateral* (or *branch-type*) *networks*, because they allow the flow of information in two directions. Circuits constructed of relay contacts are slower in operation than those constructed of electronic devices and are, therefore, not very useful in computer technology where speed of operation is of paramount importance. In numerous other applications, e.g., telephone exchanges and switchboards, control units for elevators, traffic lights, industrial control devices, and similar systems, relays are still useful building elements. The importance of bilateral networks is presently further enhanced because several solid-state devices act as bilateral elements.

A relay is an electromechanical device consisting of an electromagnet and a number of contacts. Each *contact* consists of two *springs* and may be in either one of two positions, open or closed. The electromagnet contains a magnetic circuit and a coil to energize it. When current passes through its coil, the electromagnet is energized and pulls the contacts, causing them to change their position. When no current passes through the coil, the relay is not energized, and the restoring force of the springs keeps them in their normal position. A *transfer contact* is a combination of a normally open and a normally closed contact, which have a common spring and are constructed of a total of three springs. The various contacts and their symbols are illustrated in Fig. 5-23.

Relays are usually denoted by capital letters, e.g., X, Y, etc., while their respective contacts are denoted by lowercase letters, e.g., x, y, etc. A normally open contact of relay X is denoted x, and a normally closed contact is denoted x'. The value 1 is assigned to a contact if it is closed, and the value 0 if it is open.

The analogy of relay contacts to the gates defined in Sec. 3-3 is

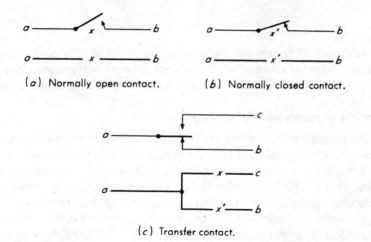

(a) Normally open contact.　　(b) Normally closed contact.

(c) Transfer contact.

Fig. 5-23 Relay contacts and their symbols.

evident. We may therefore utilize switching expressions to represent contact networks, and conversely, any switching expression can be realized by an appropriate connection of contacts. The transmission function of a circuit consisting of a parallel connection of two contacts x and y is $x + y$, whereas the one consisting of a serial connection of these contacts is xy. Thus the parallel and serial connections of contacts serve, respectively, as implementations of the OR and AND operations, as illustrated in Fig. 5-24.

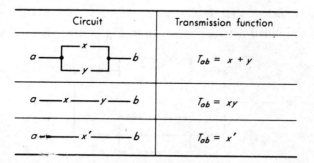

Circuit	Transmission function
$a \rule{0.5em}{0pt} \begin{smallmatrix} x \\ y \end{smallmatrix} \rule{0.5em}{0pt} b$	$T_{ab} = x + y$
$a \rule{1em}{0pt} x \rule{1em}{0pt} y \rule{1em}{0pt} b$	$T_{ab} = xy$
$a \rule{1em}{0pt} x' \rule{1em}{0pt} b$	$T_{ab} = x'$

Fig. 5-24 Implementation of the basic logical operations by means of contact networks.

5-6 ANALYSIS AND SYNTHESIS OF CONTACT NETWORKS

By analysis of a two-terminal contact network we mean the determination of its transmission function. For networks which have more than two terminals, the analysis involves determination of a transmission function for each pair of terminals. The synthesis problem of a contact network is the converse of its analysis; the desired network performance is specified by a switching expression, from which a corresponding circuit is derived.

Analysis of series-parallel networks

In the preceding section it was shown that the transmission function of a network, which consists of two contacts, x and y, in parallel, is $x + y$, and the transmission function of a network, consisting of the two contacts in series, is xy. Since the algebra of contact networks is isomorphic to switching algebra, the transmission function of two networks, T_1 and T_2, connected in series is $T_1 T_2$, and the transmission function of a parallel connection of these two networks is $T_1 + T_2$. Utilizing these properties, we can determine the transmission function of any series-parallel network by inspection.

Example Find the transmission function for the network of Fig. 5-25a. The network consists of a contact x' in series with another network, which contains two parallel subnetworks. The transmission function of the upper subnetwork can be written by inspection as $(y'z + z'y)w'$. The lower subnetwork contains three parallel branches, and therefore its transmission function is $w + y' + x'z'$. The overall transmission is given by

$$T_{ab}(w,x,y,z) = x'[(y'z + z'y)w' + w + y' + x'z']$$

This expression may be simplified to

$$T_{ab}(w,x,y,z) = x'(w + y' + z')$$

The simplified network is shown in Fig. 5-25b. ∎

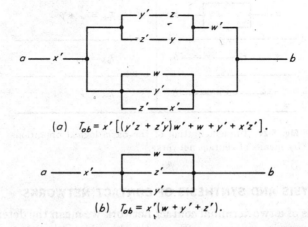

$$(a) \quad T_{ob} = x'\left[(y'z + z'y)w' + w + y' + x'z'\right].$$

$$(b) \quad T_{ob} = x'(w + y' + z').$$

Fig. 5-25 Analysis and simplification of a series-parallel contact network.

Using the procedure illustrated in the preceding example, we can associate a switching expression with every series-parallel contact network, and conversely, to every switching expression there corresponds a series-parallel contact network. This example also demonstrates that in order to simplify a contact network, it is advisable to first find its transmission function and then to simplify it whenever possible.

Analysis of non-series-parallel networks

A question now arises as to the relationship between switching expressions and non-series-parallel networks. The previously described analysis procedure is clearly not applicable to bridge-type networks (e.g., Fig. 5-26), and a different, more general, procedure must be developed. In the case of series-parallel networks, switching expressions provide information regarding the structure (or geometry) of the network as well as its transmission. Switching expressions can also be found which reflect the transmission properties, but not the structure, of non-series-parallel networks.

One way of determining the transmission function between two terminals of a given network is by tracing all paths from one terminal to the other. In the bridge network of Fig. 5-26, one path from terminal i to terminal j consists of a series connection of contacts w and x. The transmission through this path is 1 if both w and x are 1, i.e., closed. Hence this path can be expressed by the product wx. If we associate with each path from terminal i to terminal j a product of literals corresponding to the contacts encountered in the path, then the sum of all these products is the required transmission function T_{ij}. These paths are known as the *tie sets* of the network. Each tie set represents a minimal path between the two network terminals, so that whenever all the contacts in the path are closed, the transmission through the path is 1, regardless of the state of all other contacts in the network. Using this technique, the transmission function for the bridge network of Fig. 5-26a is found to be

$$T_{ij} = wx + wvz + yvx + yz$$

A dual technique is illustrated in Fig. 5-26b. Dotted lines are drawn through the network contacts, so as to separate in all possible ways terminal i from terminal j and to have the transmission T_{ij} equal to 0. For example, the transmission T_{ij} is 0 if both contacts w and y are open, regardless of the state of the other contacts in the network. Similarly, if w, v, and z are open, then T_{ij} is 0, and so on. If we express each such "cut" through the network by a sum of literals, e.g., $w + y$, then the product of all these sums is 0 whenever any of its factors is 0. For all other combinations the product will have the value 1. Consequently,

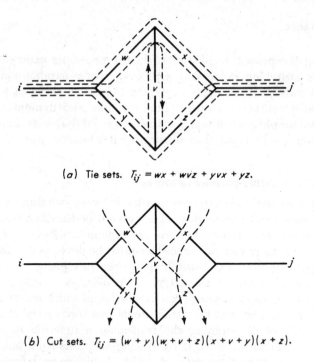

(a) Tie sets. $T_{ij} = wx + wvz + yvx + yz$.

(b) Cut sets. $T_{ij} = (w + y)(w + v + z)(x + v + y)(x + z)$.

Fig. 5-26   Analysis of a bridge network.

this product is a conjunctive expression for the transmission function of the network.   For the bridge network of Fig. 5-26b we thus have

$$T_{ij} = (w + y)(x + z)(w + v + z)(x + v + y)$$

The minimal sets of contacts which, when open, ensure that the network transmission is 0 are known as the *cut sets* of the network.   Thus no closed path can be found between terminals i and j of a given network whenever any of its cut sets equals 0.

In determining the tie sets, all paths containing a product of a variable and its complement, e.g., xx', are ignored.   Similarly disregarded are all sums containing a variable and its complement, e.g., $x + x'$, when determining the cut sets.

Synthesis of contact networks

The synthesis of a contact network that has given properties can be accomplished in several steps.   First, the requirements that the network is to satisfy are expressed algebraically in the form of switching expressions. For simple networks this can be done directly from the "verbal" description of the required properties; in other cases the truth table must be employed, and the switching expressions are derived from it. Next, these switching expressions are simplified as much as possible, and a corresponding series-parallel network is obtained. In general, although the expressions may be minimal, the corresponding series-parallel network may still be further simplified. Consequently, the final step in the synthesis procedure is the simplification of the contact network. Unfortunately, no effective techniques are available for carrying out this last step, and the ingenuity of the designer plays a major role in arriving at a minimal network.

A measure of cost in the design of a contact network is the number of springs of which the network is constructed. This number can be reduced by minimizing the number of literals in the corresponding algebraic expression and by using transfer contacts, which consist each of a normally closed and a normally open contact, connected to a common point and therefore requiring only three springs. A network is said to be *minimal* if it realizes the corresponding transmission function with as few springs as possible.

Consider the following problem. Four men, W, X, Y, and Z, own a company. Their shares in the company are

W: 40 percent X: 30 percent Y: 20 percent Z: 10 percent

A 60 percent majority of the shares is required to pass a resolution. Around their conference table are mounted four buttons, W, X, Y, and Z. Each man presses his button to vote in favor of, and releases it to oppose, the resolution under consideration. We want to design a circuit which signals whenever a resolution is passed, and we assume that each button is connected to as many contacts as necessary.

The transmission function corresponding to the desired circuit takes on the value 1 whenever a majority is obtained. It is evident that whenever W and X press their buttons, the resolution is passed, independently of the votes of Y and Z. Similarly, the pressing of W and Y or X and Y and Z is sufficient to activate the circuit and produce the signal. The transmission function is thus given by

$$T(w,x,y,z) = wx + wy + xyz = w(x + y) + xyz$$

A series-parallel realization of this expression, which requires 6 contacts or 12 springs, is shown in Fig. 5-27a.

When simplifying a contact network, extreme care must be taken to prevent the introduction of undesired paths through the network, which may change its transmission function. Such paths, called *sneak paths*, occur in contact networks because they are bilateral and allow

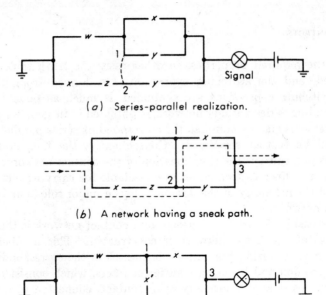

(a) Series-parallel realization.

(b) A network having a sneak path.

(c) A minimal bridge-type realization.

Fig. 5-27 Design of a signal-control circuit.

flow of current in two directions. This problem will now be illustrated by simplifying the network of Fig. 5-27a.

Referring to Fig. 5-27a we observe that it contains two parallel y contacts. Consequently, if nodes 1 and 2 are connected as suggested by the dotted line, one of the y contacts can be eliminated, and the network shown in Fig. 5-27b results. The tie sets of this network are found to be $wx + wy + xyz + xz$. Clearly, the path xz is not allowed, since it represents only 40 percent of the shares. This path, which is referred to as a sneak path, can be avoided if, instead of making a solid connection between nodes 1 and 2, a contact x' is connected between them, as shown in Fig. 5-27c. This contact acts in such a way as to make the connection between nodes 1 and 2 "one-way"; that is, the required path wy is unaffected because the transmission between nodes 1 and 3 is $x + x'y = x + y$, while the path through nodes 2, 1, and 3 is open, since it contains x and x' in series. In going from the network of Fig. 5-27a to that of Fig. 5-27c we actually traded a contact y for a contact x', which enables us to use a transfer contact for x and x' and thus save one spring. The network of Fig. 5-27c consists of 11 springs and is known to be a minimal realization of the corresponding transmission function.

Example Design a contact network, with four input relays, W, X, Y, and Z, which receives BCD numbers and produces a signal whenever the present number is 3 or a multiple of 3.

The map which specifies the transmission function of the desired network is shown in Fig. 5-28a. It contains three 1 cells in combinations 3, 6, and 9 and six don't-care combinations, corresponding to all invalid BCD code words. The minimal sum-of-products expression derived from the map is

$$T(w,x,y,z) = wz + xyz' + x'yz$$
$$= z(w + x'y) + xyz'$$

The corresponding series-parallel network is shown in Fig. 5-28b. In order to eliminate one of its y contacts, we check whether the connection shown by the dotted line can be made without introducing any undesired path. If we actually make the connection and eliminate one of the y contacts, we obtain the network of Fig. 5-28c where the only sneak path introduced is $z'xx'w$, which, since it is always open, has no effect on the transmission of the network.

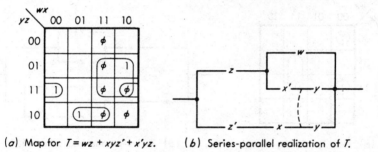

(a) Map for $T = wz + xyz' + x'yz$.   (b) Series-parallel realization of T.

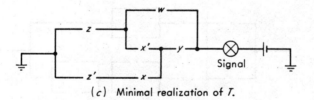

(c) Minimal realization of T.

Fig. 5-28 Realization of $T(w,x,y,z) = \Sigma(3,6,9) + \Sigma_\phi(10,11,12,13,14,15)$.

The network of Fig. 5-28c consists of 10 springs and is known to be a minimal realization of the function specified by the map of Fig. 5-28a. Note that in this case it is possible to obtain another (distinct) minimal realization from the product of sums, i.e.,

$$T(w,x,y,z) = (w + y)(x + z)(x' + z'). \quad \blacksquare$$

Example Design a minimal-contact network which realizes the function

$$T(w,x,y,z) = \Sigma(0,3,13,14,15)$$

With the aid of the map of Fig. 5-29a, the algebraic expression corresponding to T is found to be

$$T = wxy + wxz + w'x'y'z' + w'x'yz$$
$$= wx(y + z) + w'x'(y'z' + yz)$$

The corresponding series-parallel network, which requires 17 springs, is shown in Fig. 5-29b. If we interchange the locations of contacts x' and w', we may connect nodes 1 and 2 as shown in Fig. 5-29c. This connection has no logical effect on the transmission of the network, since $x'x = ww' = 0$; but it serves as a common point for w and w' as well as x and x', so that transfer contacts may be used. The lower branch of the network has been redrawn utilizing the identity $y'z' + yz = (y + z')(y' + z)$, and this enables us to combine the two parallel z contacts, as shown in Fig. 5-29d. ∎

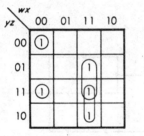

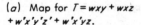

(a) Map for $T = wxy + wxz + w'x'y'z' + w'x'yz$.

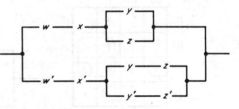

(b) Series-parallel realization of T.

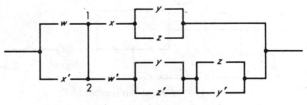

(c) An alternative series-parallel realization.

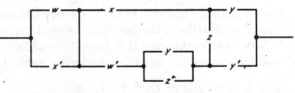

(d) A minimum-spring realization of T.

Fig. 5-29 Realization of $T(w,x,y,z) = \Sigma(0,3,13,14,15)$.

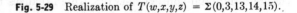

There exist several synthesis procedures for non-series-parallel contact networks.   Among the more important and interesting approaches are the applications of the theory of matrices and of graph theory to the synthesis problem.   These methods are available in various references among which are Refs. 4, 6, and 9.

NOTES AND REFERENCES

Information about the available integrated circuits and their applications can be found in the manufacturers' handbooks.   As examples see Refs. 11–13.   There are also numerous books on logical design; among which are Blakeslee [1], Brzozowski and Yoeli [2], Gschwind and McCluskey [5], Peatman [8], and many others.   A comprehensive review of high-speed adders is given in MacSorley [7].   The material on contact networks dates back to Shannon's original work [10].   An extensive treatment of such networks is available in Caldwell [3].

1. Blakeslee, T. R.: "Digital Design with Standard MSI and LSI," John Wiley & Sons, Inc., New York, 1975.
2. Brzozowski, J. A. and M. Yoeli: "Digital Networks," Prentice-Hall, Inc., Englewood Cliffs, N.J., 1976.
3. Caldwell, S. H.: "Switching Circuits and Logical Design," John Wiley & Sons, Inc., New York, 1958.
4. Gould, R.: Application of Graph Theory to the Synthesis of Contact Networks, Proceedings of an International Symposium on the Theory of Switching, pp. 244–292, Harvard University Press, Cambridge, Mass., 1959.
5. Gschwind, H. W. and E. J. McCluskey: "Design of Digital Computers," Springer-Verlag, New York, 1975.
6. Hohn, F. E., and L. R. Schissler: "Boolean Matrices and the Design of Combinational Relay Switching Circuits," Bell System Tech. J., vol. 34, no. 1, pp. 177–202, 1955.
7. MacSorley, O. L.: High-speed Arithmetic in Binary Computers, Proc. IRE, vol. 49, no. 1, pp. 67–91, January, 1961.
8. Peatman, J. B.: "The Design of Digital Systems," McGraw-Hill Book Company, New York, 1972.
9. Semon, W.: Matrix Methods in the Theory of Switching, Proceedings of an International Symposium on the Theory of Switching, pp. 13–50, Harvard University Press, Cambridge, Mass., 1959.
10. Shannon, C. E.: A Symbolic Analysis of Relay and Switching Circuits, Trans. AIEE, vol. 57, pp. 713–723, 1938.
11. Texas Instruments Staff: "The TTL Data Book," and "The Integrated Circuits Catalog," Texas Instruments Inc., Dallas, Texas, 1973.
12. Fairchild Semiconductor Staff: "The TTL Data Book" and "The TTL Applications Handbook," Fairchild Semiconductor, Mountain View, California, 1973.
13. Manuals by the staffs of RCA, Motorola, Intel, Signetics, National Semiconductors, and others.

PROBLEMS

5-1. Express T_1 and T_2 as functions of A, B, C, and D.

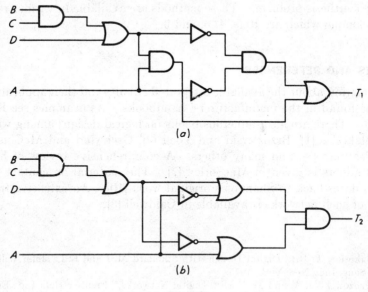

(a)

(b)

Fig. P5-1

5-2. (a) Design a two-level code converter from BCD to the *2-out-of 5 code* shown below.

(b) Design a two-level code converter from the *Ringtail code* shown below to BCD.

Decimal		2-out-of-5					Decimal		Ringtail				
0	$\rightarrow$	1	1	0	0	0	0	$\rightarrow$	0	0	0	0	0
1	$\rightarrow$	0	0	0	1	1	1	$\rightarrow$	0	0	0	0	1
2	$\rightarrow$	0	0	1	0	1	2	$\rightarrow$	0	0	0	1	1
3	$\rightarrow$	0	0	1	1	0	3	$\rightarrow$	0	0	1	1	1
4	$\rightarrow$	0	1	0	0	1	4	$\rightarrow$	0	1	1	1	1
5	$\rightarrow$	0	1	0	1	0	5	$\rightarrow$	1	1	1	1	1
6	$\rightarrow$	0	1	1	0	0	6	$\rightarrow$	1	1	1	1	0
7	$\rightarrow$	1	0	0	0	1	7	$\rightarrow$	1	1	1	0	0
8	$\rightarrow$	1	0	0	1	0	8	$\rightarrow$	1	1	0	0	0
9	$\rightarrow$	1	0	1	0	0	9	$\rightarrow$	1	0	0	0	0

5-3. Design a circuit with four inputs, x_1, x_2, x_3, x_4, and seven outputs, p_1, p_2, m_1, p_3, m_2, m_3, m_4, that receives BCD code words and generates the corresponding Hamming code words defined in Table 1-8.

5-4. You are supplied with just one NOT gate and an unlimited amount of diode gates, and are required to design a circuit which realizes the expression

$$T(w,x,y,z) = w'x + x'y + xz'$$

Only unprimed variables are available as inputs.

Hint: You may find the map of T helpful.

5-5. The tables shown below define two devices whose inputs and outputs may assume any one of the *three* values 0, 1, or 2.

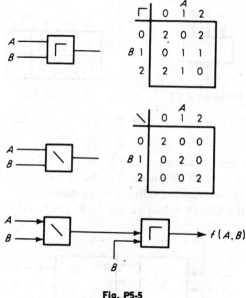

Fig. P5-5

Give the equivalent of a Karnaugh-map description of the function $f(A,B)$ realized by the network of Fig. P5-5.

5-6. A certain four-input gate, called a LEMON gate, realizes the switching function

$$LEMON(A,B,C,D) = BC(A + D)$$

Assuming that the input variables are available in both primed and unprimed form:

    (a) Show a realization of the function

$$f(w,x,y,z) = \Sigma(0,1,6,9,10,11,14,15)$$

with only three LEMON gates and one OR gate.

(b) Can all switching functions be realized with LEMON/OR logic?
    Hint: Draw the map for LEMON and utilize possible "patches"
on the map of f.

5-7. A three-input gate BOMB, whose characteristics are shown in Fig.
P5-7, has been mass-produced by an unfortunate company. Experimental evidence shows that the input combinations 101 and 010 cause the gate
to "explode." Your task is to determine whether the gate is completely
useless or can be externally modified so that it may be efficiently
used to implement any switching function without causing explosions.

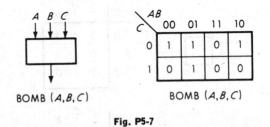

Fig. P5-7

5-8. Given the logic package A shown in Fig. P5-8, which operates as
follows: output $y_i = 1$ iff i inputs out of x_0, x_1, x_2 are equal to 1. Design
unit B so that the overall logic function of unit C will be to produce an
output $z_i = 1$ iff i inputs out of x_0, x_1, x_2, x_3 are equal to 1.

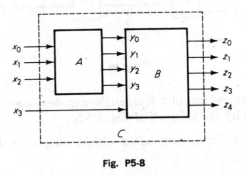

Fig. P5-8

5-9. Given the logic package A that compares the magnitudes of two
three-bit numbers, $X_3 = x_1x_2x_3$ and $Y_3 = y_1y_2y_3$, where x_3 and y_3 are the
least-significant bits. Package A has two outputs G_3 and S_3, such that,
$G_3 = 1$ iff $X_3 > Y_3$; $S_3 = 1$ iff $X_3 < Y_3$; and $G_3 = S_3 = 0$ iff $X_3 = Y_3$.
    (a) Design a logic unit B, so that together with package A it will
serve as a comparator for two four-bit numbers, $X_4 = x_1x_2x_3x_4$ and

$Y_4 = y_1 y_2 y_3 y_4$, as shown in Fig. P5-9. Find expressions for G_4 and S_4 in terms of the inputs to unit B and show a realization of these expressions by using only NAND gates.

(b) Show a realization of package A by means of only units of type B. Assume the constants 0 and 1 are available.

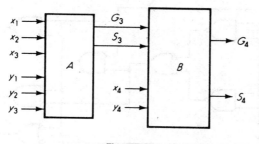

Fig. P5-9

5-10. Given the function $g(x_1,x_2,x_3,x_4) = \Sigma(4,6,7,15) + \Sigma_\phi(2,3,5,11)$. Realize g in the form shown in Fig. P5-10, i.e., find the correspondence between the x_i's and a, b, c, d, and determine the functions A, B, and C.

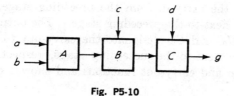

Fig. P5-10

5-11. A *half adder* is a device capable of performing addition of two bits. It has two binary inputs, A and B, and two outputs, S and C_0. (Note that there is no carry into the half adder.)

(a) Write truth tables which define the half adder and derive logical expressions for S and C_0.

(b) Assuming that only uncomplemented inputs are available, show an implementation of the half adder which requires only three two-input diode gates and one NOT gate.

(c) Under the above assumption, design the half adder using no more than five NAND or NOR gates, but not both.

5-12. Construct a full adder using only two half adders and one OR gate.

5-13. A *half subtractor* is a device capable of subtracting one binary digit from the other. Show a realization of the half subtractor using AND, OR, NOT logic.

5-14. Define a *full subtractor*, show its truth tables, and derive logical expressions for difference (D) and borrow (B) outputs.

5-15. Analyze the two-output circuit shown in Fig. P5-15. Indicate the logical expression associated with every gate output.

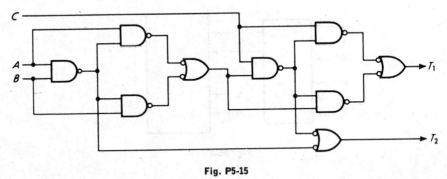

Fig. P5-15

5-16. Design a device capable of adding *three* binary digits simultaneously. The device has five inputs, as shown in Fig. P5-16. X, Y, and Z are the arguments, C_1 is the carry-in from the preceding stage, and C_2 is the carry-in from the next-to-the-preceding stage. The output S designates the sum, while C_{01} and C_{02} designate the carry-out to the succeeding stage and to the next-to-the-succeeding stage, respectively. Express explicitly the sum and carry-out functions and show a circuit diagram.

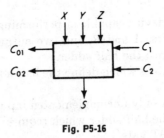

Fig. P5-16

5-17. The schematic diagram in Fig. P5-17 shows a multiplier capable of multiplying two two-digit binary numbers. a_0 and a_1, b_0 and b_1 designate the digits of the two arguments, while c_0, c_1, c_2, and c_3 designate the digits of the product. Design the combinational logic.

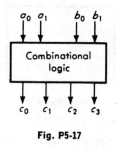

Fig. P5-17

5-18. The schematic diagram shown in Fig. P5-18 shows a *ternary full adder* that receives two ternary digits X and Y plus a carry-in C_i and produces the sum S in base 3 plus a carry-out C_0. The ternary digits are coded in binary; that is, each of the three ternary digits 0, 1, 2 is coded by two binary digits: 0 by 00, 1 by 01, and 2 by 10. Thus, for example, if X and Y are each equal to 2 in base 3 and C_i equals 1, the ternary full adder is required to perform the ternary addition of $(2)_3 + (2)_3 + (1)_3 = (12)_3$. Accordingly, the sum S must be 2 while the carry-out must be 1. Design the circuit assuming you have as many gates as necessary as well as binary half and full adders.

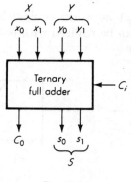

Fig. P5-18

5-19. A communication system is designed to transmit just two code words, $A = 0010$ and $B = 1101$. However, due to noise in the system, the received word can have as many as two errors. Design a combinational circuit that receives the words and can correct one error and detect the existence of two errors. Specifically, design the circuit in Fig. P5-19, so that output A will be equal to 1 if the received word is A; output B will be equal to 1 if the received word is B; and output C will be equal to 1 if the word received has two errors and thus cannot be corrected.

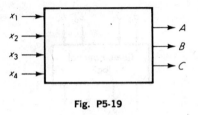

Fig. P5-19

5-20. (a) Find all cut and tie sets for the circuit shown in Fig. P5-20. What function T is realized by this circuit?

(b) Prove that *any* contact realization of T must contain at least one contact d. Generalize your arguments to determine the necessity of contacts for other literals.

(c) Find a minimum-contact, series-parallel realization for T.

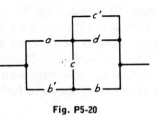

Fig. P5-20

5-21. Find minimal contact networks equivalent to the ones shown in Fig. P5-21. Network a can be realized with only 5 contacts, while network b requires 10 springs.

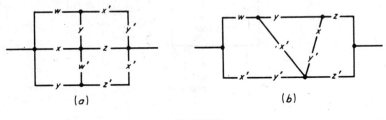

(a)   (b)

Fig. P5-21

5-22. For the network of Fig. P5-22, find an equivalent contact network with only 11 contacts. *Think!*

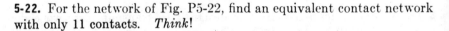
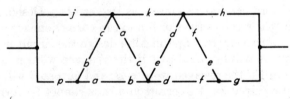

Fig. P5-22

5-23. Design a switching circuit which can turn a lamp *on* or *off* from three different locations independently. Denote the switches x, y, and z, as shown in Fig. P5-23. (Four transfer contacts are sufficient.)

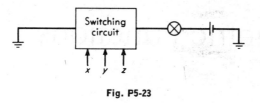

Fig. P5-23

5-24. For each of the following functions find a contact realization which requires as few springs as possible.

(a) $T(w,x,y,z) = \Sigma(0,4,6,8,9,12)$ (11 springs)
(b) $T(w,x,y,z) = \Sigma(3,7,8,9,13)$ (11 springs)
(c) $T(w,x,y,z) = \Sigma(5,6,7,9,10,11,13,14)$ (4 transfer contacts)
(d) $T(w,x,y,z) = \Sigma(5,6,9,10,11,12,13,14,15)$ (13 springs)
(e) $T(w,x,y,z) = \Sigma(5,6,7,9,10,11,12)$ (14 springs)

5-25. In a board of directors meeting four resolutions, A, B, C, and D, are up to a vote. The decision is complicated, however, by the fact that the resolutions are not mutually independent. In fact, the vote must be governed by the following rules:

1. Those who vote for resolution B must also vote for resolution C.
2. It is possible to vote for both resolutions A and C, only if a vote for either B or D is also cast.
3. Those who vote for either resolution C or D or vote against resolution A must vote for resolution B.

Each member of the board has four switches, A, B, C, and D, which he presses or releases, depending on whether he is in favor of or against the resolution under consideration. The switches of each member are the inputs to a contact circuit associated with that member. The circuit produces a red signal at the end of the vote if the member *did not* vote according to the rules. Design such a circuit with as few springs as possible.

6
Functional Decomposition and Symmetric Functions

In this chapter we discuss the *structural properties of switching functions*. One aspect of this problem, known as *functional decomposition*, is concerned with properties of functions which may be composed of several simpler functions. Utilizing these functional properties enables us to decompose large and complex circuits into a system of smaller subcircuits which may be readily available and economically maintained. Another structural property is the *symmetry* of certain switching functions with respect to some of their variables. The detection and identification of symmetries in switching functions and the design of symmetric circuits are also discussed in this chapter.

6-1 FUNCTIONAL DECOMPOSITION

By the term *functional decomposition* we refer to the process of expressing a switching function $f(x_1, x_2, \ldots, x_n)$ of n variables as a composition of a number of functions, each depending on less than n variables. The simplest type of decomposition can be obtained by applying Shannon's expansion theorem [Eq. (3-14)] to f, i.e.,

$$f(x_1,x_2, \ldots ,x_n) = x_1f(1,x_2, \ldots ,x_n) + x_1'f(0,x_2, \ldots ,x_n)$$

In this case $f(x_1,x_2, \ldots ,x_n)$ has been expressed as a composition of three functions, $\Phi(x_1) = x_1$, $g(x_2, \ldots ,x_n)$, and $h(x_2, \ldots ,x_n)$, i.e.,

$$f(x_1,x_2, \ldots ,x_n) = \Phi(x_1)g(x_2, \ldots ,x_n) + \Phi'(x_1)h(x_2, \ldots ,x_n)$$

This type of decomposition is referred to as trivial, since every switching function can be decomposed in such a way by means of Shannon's expansion theorem.

A switching function $f(x_1,x_2, \ldots ,x_n)$ is said to be (*simple*) *functionally decomposable* if and only if there exist functions F and Φ such that

$$f(x_1,x_2, \ldots ,x_n) = F[\Phi(y_1,y_2, \ldots ,y_s),z_1,z_2, \ldots ,z_r] \qquad (6\text{-}1)$$

where $1 < s \leq n - 1$, and the sets of variables $\{y_1, \ldots ,y_s\}$ and $\{z_1, \ldots ,z_r\}$ are subsets of $\{x_1,x_2, \ldots ,x_n\}$, so that their set union is equal to $\{x_1,x_2, \ldots ,x_n\}$; that is, the y's and z's are just convenient renamings of the x's.

If the sets $\{y_1, \ldots ,y_s\}$ and $\{z_1, \ldots ,z_r\}$ are disjoint, i.e., $r = n - s$, the decomposition is said to be *disjunctive*, to emphasize that no variables are common to both subsets. The functions $F[\Phi,z_1,z_2, \ldots ,z_r]$ and $\Phi(y_1,y_2, \ldots ,y_s)$ of $r + 1$ and s variables, respectively, are then said to represent a (*simple*) *disjunctive decomposition* of $f(x_1,x_2, \ldots ,x_n)$. In this book we shall be concerned only with simple, nontrivial disjunctive decompositions, whose pictorial representation is shown in Fig. 6-1.

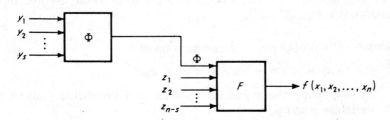

Fig. 6-1 Pictorial representation of a simple disjunctive decomposition for $f(x_1,x_2, \ldots ,x_n)$.

Example   The function $f(w,x,y,z) = \Sigma(0,2,3,7,9,10,11,14)$ can be decomposed as follows:

$$f(w,x,y,z) = w'x'z' + wx'z + w'yz + wyz'$$
$$= (w'z' + wz)x' + (w'z + wz')y$$

If we let

$$\Phi(w,z) = w'z' + wz$$

we obtain

$$f(w,x,y,z) = \Phi x' + \Phi'y$$
$$= F[\Phi(w,z),x,y] \quad \blacksquare$$

Decomposition by expansion

We shall now derive a procedure for decomposing switching functions, and show that the functional decomposition is an *intrinsic* property of switching functions; that is, it is independent of the particular form which the function may assume.   The procedure will be best understood by recognizing its analogy to repeated applications of Shannon's expansion theorem, whereby the expansion of the function $f(y_1,y_2, \ldots ,y_s,z_1,z_2, \ldots ,z_{n-s})$ about the variables $z_1,z_2, \ldots ,z_{n-s}$ is given by

$$f(y_1,y_2, \ldots ,y_s,z_1,z_2, \ldots ,z_{n-s})$$
$$= \sum_{i=0}^{2^{n-s}-1} f_i(y_1,y_2, \ldots ,y_s)g_i(z_1,z_2, \ldots ,z_{n-s}) \quad (6\text{-}2)$$

where

$$f_0(y_1,y_2, \ldots ,y_s) = f(y_1,y_2, \ldots ,y_s,0,0, \ldots ,0)$$
$$f_1(y_1,y_2, \ldots ,y_s) = f(y_1,y_2, \ldots ,y_s,0,0, \ldots ,1)$$
$$\cdots \cdots \cdots \cdots \cdots \cdots \cdots \cdots \cdots \cdots$$
$$f_{2^{n-s}-1}(y_1,y_2, \ldots ,y_s) = f(y_1,y_2, \ldots ,y_s,1,1, \ldots ,1)$$

and where $g_i(z_1,z_2, \ldots ,z_{n-s})$ is the product term whose decimal representation is i, e.g., $g_0 = z_1'z_2' \cdots z_{n-s}'$.

Example   Obtain the above decomposition of

$$f(w,x,y,z) = w'x'z' + wx'z + w'yz + wyz'$$

by employing the expansion theorem and expanding f about the variables x and y.

$$f(w,x,y,z) = \sum_{i=0}^{2^2-1} f_i(w,z)g_i(x,y)$$

where

$$f_0(w,z) = w'z' + wz$$
$$f_1(w,z) = w'z' + wz + w'z + wz' = 1$$
$$f_2(w,z) = 0$$
$$f_3(w,z) = w'z + wz'$$

and

$$g_0(x,y) = x'y' \qquad g_1(x,y) = x'y$$
$$g_2(x,y) = xy' \qquad g_3(x,y) = xy$$

Thus

$$f(w,x,y,z) = (w'z' + wz)x'y' + x'y + (w'z + wz')xy$$

Letting $w'z' + wz = \Phi$, we obtain

$$f(w,x,y,z) = \Phi x'y' + x'y + \Phi'xy$$

which may be reduced to

$$f(w,x,y,z) = \Phi x' + \Phi'y$$
$$= F[\Phi(w,z),x,y]$$

Hence the expansion of f about the variables x and y in effect results in a decomposition of f. ∎

The expansion of a function about its variables $z_1, z_2, \ldots, z_{n-s}$, and decomposing it if possible, can be accomplished in a more compact way by expressing it as a $2^{n-s} \times 2^s$ matrix. The column headings are the 2^s combinations of the variables $y_1, y_2, \ldots, y_s$ in *decimal order*, while the row headings are the 2^{n-s} combinations of the variables $z_1, z_2, \ldots, z_{n-s}$, also in decimal order. Each entry in the matrix corresponds to a unique configuration of $y_1, y_2, \ldots, y_s$ and $z_1, z_2, \ldots, z_{n-s}$, and hence to a unique minterm of an n-variable function. The entry of the matrix is 1 or 0 according to whether the corresponding minterm is, or is not, covered by the function. For example, the matrix which represents the function of the preceding example is shown in Fig. 6-2. It consists of four rows labeled 0,1,2,3, corresponding to $xy = 00,01,10,11$, respectively, and four columns similarly labeled and corresponding to combinations of wz. Note that only the arrangement of the variables, and the order in which the combinations are listed as row and column headings, distinguish this matrix from the Karnaugh map.

An inspection of the matrix of Fig. 6-2 reveals the values of $f_i(w,z)$ and the corresponding products $g_i(x,y)$. Row 0 corresponds to

xy \ wz	0	1	2	3
0	1	0	0	1
1	1	1	1	1
2	0	0	0	0
3	0	1	1	0

Fig. 6-2 A matrix representing the function $f = \Sigma(0,2,3,7,9,10,11,14)$.

$g_0(x,y) = x'y'$; the two 1 entries in row 0, columns 0 and 3, correspond to the function $f_0(w,z) = w'z' + wz$, and the complete term is thus given by $(w'z' + wz)x'y'$. It is important to observe that the values of wz in row 3 are the complements of those in row 0; therefore, if $\Phi(w,z)$ is chosen to be represented by $w'z' + wz$, then the term derived from row 3 is $\Phi'xy$. Similarly, from rows 1 and 2, we obtain the terms $x'y1$ and $xy'0$, respectively. These are precisely the terms we obtained earlier by employing the expansion theorem.

In decomposing the foregoing function, we aimed at a particular decomposition of the form $F[\Phi(w,z),x,y]$. In general, however, the initial information regarding the structure of the function to be decomposed is limited, and a more systematic procedure is required in order to detect possible decompositions.

Test for decomposability

Every disjunctive decomposition induces a two-block partition δ on the set of variables $\{x_1,x_2, \ldots ,x_n\}$, such that

$$\delta = \{\overline{y_1,y_2, \ldots ,y_s; z_1,z_2, \ldots ,z_{n-s}}\}$$

It is convenient to associate with such a partition an n-digit binary number, in which each y_i is represented by 0 and each z_i by 1. Clearly, with the set $\{x_1,x_2, \ldots ,x_n\}$, we can associate 2^n distinct partitions, corresponding to the binary numbers 0 through $2^n - 1$. A *partition matrix* for a function $f(x_1,x_2, \ldots ,x_n)$ and a partition δ is defined to consist of 2^s columns labeled 0 through $2^s - 1$, and 2^{n-s} rows labeled 0 through $2^{n-s} - 1$. The columns correspond to the 2^s combinations of the y's, and the rows correspond to the 2^{n-s} combinations of the z's. Each position in the matrix thus corresponds to a unique combination of the variables $x_1, x_2, \ldots , x_n$. The element in a given position is 0 or 1 according to the value of the function for the corresponding combination. The number of distinct rows in the partition matrix is called its *row multiplicity* and is designated by μ; the *column multiplicity* is defined analogously and is designated by ν.

166

Example The partition matrix for $f(w,x,y,z) = w'x'z' + wx'z + w'yz + wyz'$ and for $\delta = \{w,z; x,y\}$ is shown in Fig. 6-2. Its row multiplicity is $\mu = 4$, and its column multiplicity is $\nu = 2$. ∎

By combining all identical columns of the partition matrix, we obtain a *reduced matrix* which has 2^s rows and ν columns. Clearly, it has at most 2^ν distinct rows, since each row corresponds to a binary number whose value is in the range $0, \ldots, 2^\nu - 1$. And because identical rows in the reduced matrix correspond to identical rows in the partition matrix, we obtain the relation $\mu \leq 2^\nu$. Similarly, it can be shown that $\nu \leq 2^\mu$ by reversing the roles of the rows and columns. As a result, if $\nu = 1$ and $\mu \leq 2$, then every row must be trivial, i.e., contains either only 0's or only 1's. Conversely, if every row contains only 0's or only 1's, then all columns must be identical, i.e., $\nu = 1$ and $\mu \leq 2$.

If $\nu = 2$, then $\mu \leq 4$, and the reduced matrix may have rows 00,01,10, and 11. Obviously, if $\nu = 2$, at least one of the rows must be nontrivial and contain either 01 or 10; otherwise all columns would be identical, contrary to our assumption. Suppose that one row, designated Φ, in the reduced matrix contains the entries 01. The remaining three rows, 10,00, and 11, will then be designated Φ' **0**, and **1**, respectively. Corresponding rows in the partition matrix are similarly designated. The elements of row Φ' in the partition matrix are each the complement of the corresponding elements in row Φ. The elements in row **0** are all 0's, while those in row **1** are all 1's. Similarly, if $\mu \leq 4$ and at least one nontrivial row (i.e., 01 or 10) appears in the reduced matrix, then $\nu = 2$. Consequently, $\nu = 2$ *if and only if* $\mu \leq 4$ *and one nontrivial row Φ exists, and no rows other than* Φ', **0**, *and* **1** *appear in the partition matrix.* The foregoing conclusions lead to the fundamental theorem which establishes the connection between partition matrices and functional decomposition.

heorem 6-1 *A switching function $f(x_1,x_2, \ldots ,x_n)$ is decomposable, so that $f(x_1,x_2, \ldots ,x_n) = F[\Phi(y_1,y_2, \ldots ,y_s),z_1,z_2, \ldots ,z_{n-s}]$ if and only if its partition matrix corresponding to $\delta = \{y_1,y_2, \ldots ,y_s; z_1,z_2, \ldots ,z_{n-s}\}$ has column multiplicity $\nu \leq 2$.*

Proof: Suppose that $\nu = 2$; then at least one nontrivial row exists in the partition matrix. Designate one such row by Φ and its complement (if any) by Φ'. These rows yield the functions $\Phi(y_1,y_2, \ldots ,y_s)$ and its complement $\Phi'(y_1,y_2, \ldots ,y_s)$. The remaining rows are designated **0** or **1** according to whether their entries are all 0's or all 1's. The function $F(\Phi,z_1,z_2, \ldots ,z_{n-s})$ is constructed in the following way. Let φ_i be the minterm of F whose decimal representation is i; $\varphi_i = 1$ if it is included in

$F(\Phi,z_1,z_2, \ldots ,z_{n-s})$. The ith row of the partition matrix corresponds to the product $g_i(z_1, \ldots ,z_{n-s})$ of Eq. (6-2), and thus yields the values of the variables $z_1,z_2, \ldots ,z_{n-s}$ of φ_i and $\varphi_{i+2^{n-s}}$, which differ only in the value of Φ. (Recall that the weight of Φ in the decimal representation of F is 2^{n-s}.) The values of φ_i and $\varphi_{i+2^{n-s}}$ are determined by row i, according to Table 6-1.

Table 6-1   **Rules for determining the components of the decomposed function** F

Row i	φ_i	$\varphi_{i+2^{n-s}}$
0	0	0
1	1	1
Φ	0	1
Φ'	1	0

The case $\nu = 1$ is simple. Only the first two rows of Table 6-1 are used, and the designation of a row as Φ is made arbitrarily.

It is evident that the functions $F(\Phi,z_1,z_2, \ldots ,z_{n-s})$ and $\Phi(y_1,y_2, \ldots ,y_s)$ determined by this scheme constitute a simple disjunctive decomposition of $f(x_1,x_2, \ldots ,x_n)$. Consequently, $\nu \leq 2$ is a sufficient condition for functional decomposition. To show that it is also a necessary condition, suppose that f is decomposable, i.e.,

$$f(x_1,x_2, \ldots ,x_n) = F[\Phi(y_1,y_2, \ldots ,y_s),z_1,z_2, \ldots ,z_{n-s}] \qquad (6\text{-}3)$$

By the expansion theorem, f can be expressed as

$$f(x_1,x_2, \ldots ,x_n) = \sum_{i=0}^{2^{n-s}-1} f_i(y_1,y_2, \ldots ,y_s)g_i(z_1,z_2, \ldots ,z_{n-s})$$

Since this expansion is unique, the products f_i can be either $\Phi(y_1,y_2, \ldots ,y_s)$, Φ', 1, or 0. No other f_i may exist if f can be expressed in the form of Eq. (6-3). Therefore the partition matrix corresponding to $\delta = \{y_1,y_2, \ldots ,y_s; \overline{z_1,z_2, \ldots ,z_{n-s}}\}$ consists of at most four distinct rows, Φ, Φ', **1**, and **0**, and thus, by the foregoing arguments, $\nu \leq 2$ and the proof is complete. ∎

Theorem 6-1 establishes necessary and sufficient conditions for a switching function to be functionally decomposable. In addition, it provides the procedure for constructing the decomposed function.

Example   Consider again the function $f(w,x,y,z) = \Sigma(0,2,3,7,9,10,11,14)$, whose partition matrix is given in Fig. 6-2. Its column multiplicity

$\nu = 2$, and thus it is decomposable. Let the nontrivial row 0 be selected as Φ; then $\Phi(w,z) = w'z' + wz$, because row 0 has 1 entries in columns 0 and 3. Since row 3 is the complement of row 0, it represents Φ', while rows 1 and 2 correspond to **1** and **0**, respectively. From row 0 of the matrix and row Φ of Table 6-1, we conclude that $\varphi_0 = 0$ and $\varphi_4 = 1$. From row 1 of the matrix and row **1** of Table 6-1, we find $\varphi_1 = \varphi_5 = 1$, and similarly, from row 2, $\varphi_2 = \varphi_6 = 0$. Row 3, which is Φ', yields the values of $\varphi_3 = 1$ and $\varphi_7 = 0$. Thus

$$F(\Phi,x,y) = \varphi_1 + \varphi_3 + \varphi_4 + \varphi_5 = \Sigma(1,3,4,5)$$
$$= \Phi'x'y + \Phi'xy + \Phi x'y' + \Phi x'y$$
$$= \Phi'y + \Phi x'$$

Such a decomposition is clearly identical with that found by the expansion theorem.

If the nontrivial row 3 of the partition matrix is specified as Φ, then $\Phi(w,z) = w'z + wz'$, and the decomposed function is found to be

$$G(\Phi,x,y) = \Sigma(0,1,5,7)$$
$$= \Phi'x'y' + \Phi'x'y + \Phi x'y + \Phi xy$$
$$= \Phi'x' + \Phi y$$

By substituting the appropriate expressions for Φ, it is easy to verify that F and G are identical functions. ■

The foregoing example illustrates the following property of decomposable functions whose column multiplicity $\nu = 2$. *If $f(x_1,x_2, \ldots ,x_n)$ is decomposable into $F(\Phi,z_1,z_2, \ldots ,z_{n-s})$ and $\Phi(y_1,y_2, \ldots ,y_s)$, then it is also decomposable into $G(\Phi',z_1,z_2, \ldots ,z_{n-s})$ and $\Phi'(y_1,y_2, \ldots ,y_s)$, where $G_i = \varphi_{i+2}{}^{n-s}$ and $\varphi_i = G_{i+2}{}^{n-s}$.* ($G_i$ denotes the minterm of G whose decimal value is i.)

Another corollary which follows directly from the preceding theorem is that *if $f(x_1,x_2, \ldots ,x_n)$ is decomposable into $F(\Phi,z_1,z_2, \ldots ,z_{n-s})$ and $\Phi(y_1,y_2, \ldots ,y_s)$, then $f'(x_1,x_2, \ldots ,x_n)$ is decomposable into $F'(\Phi,z_1,z_2, \ldots ,z_{n-s})$ and $\Phi(y_1,y_2, \ldots ,y_s)$.* Thus, for a given partition, either f and its complement are both decomposable or neither is. The case of $\nu = 1$ is a special one in which f is independent of Φ.

Decomposition charts

The foregoing theorem establishes necessary and sufficient conditions for a switching function to be disjunctively decomposable—conditions expressed in terms of the partition matrices. The decomposability-detection procedure is, however, complicated by the large number of partition matrices that a switching function possesses. In fact, to each n-variable function there correspond 2^n such matrices. This number can be reduced by observing that the transpose of a partition matrix is also a partition matrix, and thus each matrix, when viewed sideways, corresponds to another matrix. Consequently, for each n-variable function, 2^{n-1} matrices must be tested. These tests are facilitated by the use of standard decomposition charts.

A *decomposition chart* for a function of n variables consists of 2^{n-1} subcharts, corresponding to the partition matrices. Each subchart has 2^n entries, which are the integers 0 to $2^n - 1$. The integer associated with each entry represents the decimal value of the corresponding minterm. A function is entered on the chart by circling on every subchart those entries corresponding to minterms for which the function assumes the value 1. Each subchart is then checked *normally and sideways* to determine whether it exhibits a decomposition. This is done by either testing if $\nu \leq 2$ or by checking whether rows Φ, Φ', **0**, and **1** are the only ones to appear. The four-variable decomposition chart corresponding to the function $f(w,x,y,z) = \Sigma(1,3,6,10,13,15)$ is shown in Fig. 6-3. (The labels of the rows and columns have been omitted, and are understood to follow the decimal ordering.)

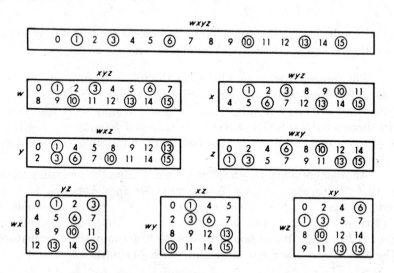

Fig. 6-3 Four-variable decomposition chart for $f(w,x,y,z) = \Sigma(1,3,6,10,13,15)$.

The topmost matrix corresponds to the trivial partition where $s = 0$, and it serves only for recording the function. The four 2×8 matrices when viewed sideways correspond to trivial decompositions for which $s = 1$. All other matrices are capable of exhibiting nontrivial decompositions, whether viewed normally or sideways.

An inspection of the chart reveals that the function is disjunctively decomposable, that is,

$$f(w,x,y,z) = F[\Phi(w,x),y,z]$$

because the lower-left matrix, when viewed sideways, has column multiplicity 2. This matrix contains three nontrivial rows, two of which are identical. Let us designate rows 1 and 3 as Φ; consequently, row 2 is Φ', while row 0 is **0**. From this matrix and Table 6-1 we obtain the values for the minterms φ_i, namely,

$$\varphi_0 = \varphi_4 = 0 \quad \varphi_1 = 0 \quad \varphi_5 = 1 \quad \varphi_2 = 1 \quad \varphi_6 = 0 \quad \varphi_3 = 0 \quad \varphi_7 = 1$$

Thus

$$\begin{aligned}
F(\Phi,y,z) &= \varphi_2 + \varphi_5 + \varphi_7 = \Sigma(2,5,7) \\
&= \Phi'yz' + \Phi y'z + \Phi yz \\
&= \Phi'yz' + \Phi z
\end{aligned}$$

where

$$\Phi(w,x) = w'x' + wx$$

The decomposition chart enables us to specify don't-care combinations so as to achieve, whenever possible, the desired functional decomposability. This is accomplished by specifying the don't-care entries in such a way that at least one of the matrices will satisfy the conditions set by Theorem 6-1.

Example Consider the five-variable decomposition chart shown in Fig. 6-4. The function

$$f(v,w,x,y,z) = \Sigma(3,4,5,7,9,15,17,21,22,28,29)$$
$$+ \Sigma_\phi(10,13,14,18,23,27,30,31)$$

is represented by the matrices corresponding to the trivial partition and to $\{v,w,y; \overline{x,z}\}$. The latter matrix is shown again in Fig. 6-5 with all its entries well defined; that is, don't-care entries specified as 1's are circled, while those specified as 0's are ignored.

The completely specified matrix contains only two distinct columns and thus reveals a possible decomposition of f into

$$f(v,w,x,y,z) = F[\Phi(v,w,y),x,z]$$

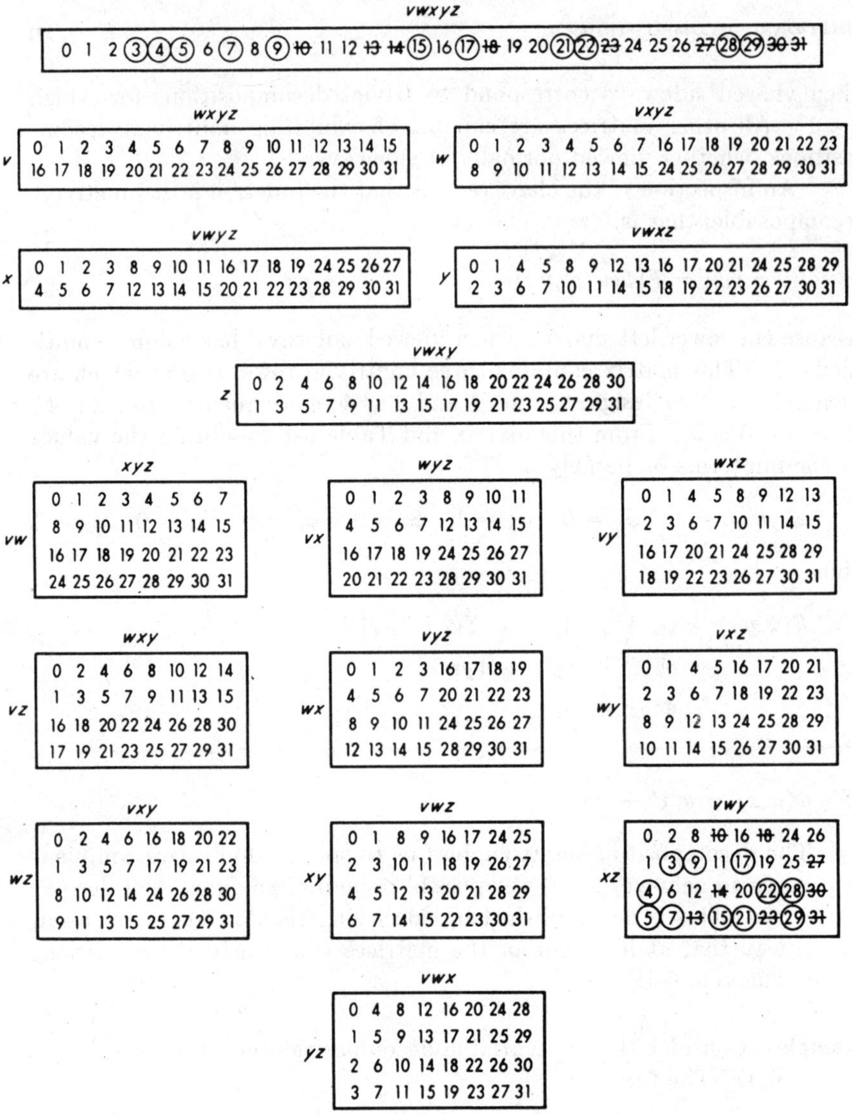

vwxyz

```
0 1 2 (3)(4)(5) 6 (7) 8 (9) ~~10~~ 11 12 ~~13~~ ~~14~~ (15) 16 (17) ~~18~~ 19 20 (21)(22) ~~23~~ 24 25 26 ~~27~~ (28)(29) ~~30~~ ~~31~~
```

v — wxyz

```
0  1  2  3  4  5  6  7  8  9  10 11 12 13 14 15
16 17 18 19 20 21 22 23 24 25 26 27 28 29 30 31
```

w — vxyz

```
0 1 2  3  4  5  6  7  16 17 18 19 20 21 22 23
8 9 10 11 12 13 14 15 24 25 26 27 28 29 30 31
```

x — vwyz

```
0 1 2 3 8  9  10 11 16 17 18 19 24 25 26 27
4 5 6 7 12 13 14 15 20 21 22 23 28 29 30 31
```

y — vwxz

```
0 1 4 5 8  9  12 13 16 17 20 21 24 25 28 29
2 3 6 7 10 11 14 15 18 19 22 23 26 27 30 31
```

z — vwxy

```
0 2 4 6 8 10 12 14 16 18 20 22 24 26 28 30
1 3 5 7 9 11 13 15 17 19 21 23 25 27 29 31
```

vw — xyz

```
0  1  2  3  4  5  6  7
8  9  10 11 12 13 14 15
16 17 18 19 20 21 22 23
24 25 26 27 28 29 30 31
```

vx — wyz

```
0  1  2  3  8  9  10 11
4  5  6  7  12 13 14 15
16 17 18 19 24 25 26 27
20 21 22 23 28 29 30 31
```

vy — wxz

```
0  1  4  5  8  9  12 13
2  3  6  7  10 11 14 15
16 17 20 21 24 25 28 29
18 19 22 23 26 27 30 31
```

vz — wxy

```
0  2  4  6  8  10 12 14
1  3  5  7  9  11 13 15
16 18 20 22 24 26 28 30
17 19 21 23 25 27 29 31
```

wx — vyz

```
0  1  2  3  16 17 18 19
4  5  6  7  20 21 22 23
8  9  10 11 24 25 26 27
12 13 14 15 28 29 30 31
```

wy — vxz

```
0  1  4  5  16 17 20 21
2  3  6  7  18 19 22 23
8  9  12 13 24 25 28 29
10 11 14 15 26 27 30 31
```

wz — vxy

```
0  2  4  6  16 18 20 22
1  3  5  7  17 19 21 23
8  10 12 14 24 26 28 30
9  11 13 15 25 27 29 31
```

xy — vwz

```
0 1 8  9  16 17 24 25
2 3 10 11 18 19 26 27
4 5 12 13 20 21 28 29
6 7 14 15 22 23 30 31
```

xz — vwy

```
0    2  8  ~~10~~ 16 ~~18~~ 24    26
1   (3)(9) 11 (17) 19 25  ~~27~~
(4)  6 12 ~~14~~ 20 (22)(28) ~~30~~
(5)(7) ~~13~~ (15)(21) ~~23~~(29) ~~31~~
```

yz — vwx

```
0 4 8  12 16 20 24 28
1 5 9  13 17 21 25 29
2 6 10 14 18 22 26 30
3 7 11 15 19 23 27 31
```

Fig. 6-4 A five-variable decomposition chart.

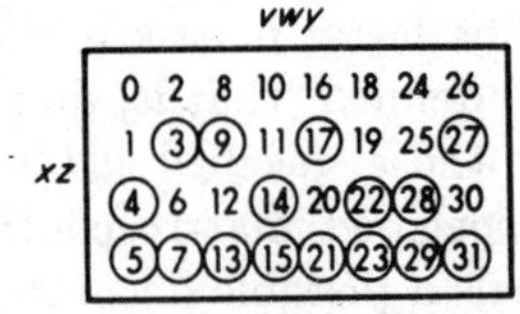

xz — vwy

```
0    2  8  10  16 18 24   26
1   (3)(9) 11 (17) 19 25  (27)
(4)  6 12 (14) 20 (22)(28) 30
(5)(7)(13)(15)(21)(23)(29)(31)
```

Fig. 6-5 Completely specified partition matrix.

Designating row 1 as Φ results in row 2 being Φ', while rows 0 and 3 correspond to **0** and **1**, respectively. Thus

$$\Phi(v,w,y) = v'w'y + v'wy' + vw'y' + vwy$$
$$= v \oplus w \oplus y$$

The minterms of $F(\Phi,x,z)$ are found with the aid of Table 6-1 and yield

$$F(\Phi,x,z) = \varphi_2 + \varphi_3 + \varphi_5 + \varphi_7 = \Sigma(2,3,5,7)$$
$$= \Phi'xz' + \Phi'xz + \Phi x'z + \Phi xz$$
$$= \Phi'x + \Phi z \quad \blacksquare$$

In this section we have developed the theory of simple disjunctive functional decompositions and presented a test for detecting such properties. The determination of more complex types of disjunctive decompositions, namely,

$$f(x_1,x_2, \ldots ,x_n)$$
$$= F[\Phi(y_1,y_2, \ldots ,y_s),\psi(w_1,w_2, \ldots ,w_r),z_1,z_2; \ldots ,z_{n-r-s}]$$

or

$$f(x_1,x_2, \ldots ,x_n)$$
$$= F[\Phi\{y_1,y_2, \ldots ,y_s,\psi(w_1,w_2, \ldots ,w_r)\},z_1,z_2, \ldots ,z_{n-r-s}]$$

is in general complicated, since it involves the testing and manipulating of a large number of submatrices. An extensive discussion of such disjunctive decompositions, as well as nondisjunctive ones, is available in a book by Curtis [4], mainly devoted to functional decomposition.

6-2 SYMMETRIC NETWORKS

General synthesis procedures for non-series-parallel or for multiple-output networks are not yet available. These problems are, however, solved for the particular case of networks specified by means of symmetric functions. Symmetric functions occur very often while synthesizing practical circuits: the functional description of a number of decoders, the sum and carry and the difference and borrow functions in binary addition and subtraction, all are examples of symmetric functions widely used in practical applications. The non-series-parallel realization of symmetric functions is straightforward and in most cases more economical than any series-parallel realization of the same function.

Properties of symmetric functions

In this section we shall develop the algebraic structure of symmetric functions and utilize it in the next section for the synthesis of symmetric networks.

Definition 6-1   A switching function of n variables $f(x_1, x_2, \ldots, x_n)$ is called *symmetric* (or *totally symmetric*) if and only if it is invariant under any permutation of its variables; it is called *partially symmetric* in the variables x_i, x_j, where $\{x_i, x_j\}$ is a subset of $\{x_1, x_2, \ldots, x_n\}$, if and only if the interchange of the variables x_i, x_j leaves the function unchanged.

Example $f(x,y,z) = x'y'z + xy'z' + x'yz'$ is symmetric.

$$f(x,y,z) = x'y'z + xy'z'$$

is partially symmetric in the variables x and z, since

$$x'y'z + xy'z' = z'y'x + zy'x'$$

but interchanging x and y yields $x'y'z + xy'z' \neq y'x'z + yx'z'$.   ∎

We shall be concerned only with totally symmetric functions.   For a discussion of partially symmetric functions the reader may consult Ref. 6.

Example   The function

$$f(x_1, x_2, x_3) = x_1'x_2'x_3' + x_1 x_2' x_3 + x_1' x_2 x_3$$

is not symmetric with respect to the variables x_1, x_2, and x_3, but it is symmetric with respect to the variables x_1, x_2, and x_3'.   In other words, f is not invariant, for example, under an interchange of the variables x_1 and x_3, i.e., $x_3'x_2'x_1' + x_3 x_2' x_1 + x_3' x_2 x_1 \neq f$, but it is invariant under the interchange of the variables x_1, x_3'; i.e., $x_3 x_2' x_1 + x_3' x_2' x_1' + x_3 x_2 x_1' = f$, as well as the variables x_1, x_2 and x_2, x_3'.   ∎

The variables in which a function is symmetric are called the *variables of symmetry*.   It is not always easy to determine the variables of symmetry, if any, for a given function.   This problem will be discussed later.

Theorem 6-2   *The necessary and sufficient condition for a function $f(x_1, x_2, \ldots, x_n)$ to be symmetric is that it may be specified by a set* *of numbers $\{a_1, a_2, \ldots, a_k\}$, where $0 \leq a_i \leq n$, such that it assumes the value 1 when and only when a_i of the variables are equal to 1. The numbers in the set $\{a_1, a_2, \ldots, a_k\}$ are called the a-numbers.*

Proof: Assume that $f(x_1, x_2, \ldots, x_n)$ is symmetric and is equal to 1 when some a_i variables are equal to 1. But since it is invariant under any permutation of the variables, it is equal to 1 when *any* a_i variables are equal to 1. And conversely, if f can be specified by a set of a-numbers, then any permutation of the variables will merely relabel the variables, but cannot change these a-numbers. Thus the function is invariant under any permutation of its variables, and it is therefore symmetric. ∎

A symmetric function is denoted $S_{a_1 a_2}, \ldots, a_k(x_1, x_2, \ldots, x_n)$, where S designates the property of symmetry, the subscripts $a_1, a_2, \ldots, a_k$ designate the a-numbers, and $(x_1, x_2, \ldots, x_n)$ designate the variables of symmetry.

Example The function $f(x,y,z) = x'y'z + x'yz' + xy'z'$ assumes the value 1 when and only when any one out of its three variables is equal to 1. This function is thus denoted $S_1(x,y,z)$. Similarly, the symmetric function $S_{1,3}(x,y,z)$ is $f(x,y,z) = xyz + x'y'z + xy'z' + x'yz'$. ∎

From Theorem 6-2 we can derive many properties of symmetric functions, most of which are given without proofs, since their validity follows directly from that theorem.

Let M and N designate two sets of a-numbers; then the sum and product of two symmetric functions, $S_M(x_1, x_2, \ldots, x_n)$ and $S_N(x_1, x_2, \ldots, x_n)$, which have the same variables of symmetry, are symmetric and equal to

$$S_M(x_1, x_2, \ldots, x_n) + S_N(x_1, x_2, \ldots, x_n) = S_{M \cup N}(x_1, x_2, \ldots, x_n)$$

$$S_M(x_1, x_2, \ldots, x_n) \cdot S_N(x_1, x_2, \ldots, x_n) = S_{M \cap N}(x_1, x_2, \ldots, x_n)$$

where $M \cup N$ and $M \cap N$ correspond, respectively, to the union and intersection of the sets of the a-numbers. These relations follow directly from the definitions of the sum (OR) and product (AND) in switching algebra, where for any particular combination of variables the sum of two functions is 1 if either function or both are equal to 1; and the product of two functions is equal to 1 if and only if both functions are 1 for the combination under consideration.

Example   Let $f_1(w,x,y,z) = S_{0,2,4}(w,x,y,z)$ and $f_2(w,x,y,z) = S_{3,4}(w,x,y,z)$; then

$$f_3(w,x,y,z) = f_1 + f_2 = S_{0,2,3,4}(w,x,y,z)$$
$$f_4(w,x,y,z) = f_1 \cdot f_2 = S_4(w,x,y,z) \quad \blacksquare$$

The complement $S'_M(x_1,x_2, \ldots ,x_n)$ of a symmetric function $S_M(x_1,x_2, \ldots ,x_n)$ is also a symmetric function whose a-numbers are those numbers included in the set $\{0,1, \ldots ,n\}$ and not included in M. Thus, for example, $S'_{0,2,4}(w,x,y,z) = S_{1,3}(w,x,y,z)$.

The application of Shannon's expansion theorem to a symmetric function renders

$$S_M(x_1,x_2, \ldots ,x_n) = x'_1 S_M(0,x_2, \ldots ,x_n) + x_1 S_M(1,x_2, \ldots ,x_n)$$

The function $S_M(1,x_2, \ldots ,x_n)$ is a symmetric one, in which the value of one variable has been set equal to 1. Consequently, the value of the function will become 1 if, for all a_i in M, any $a_i - 1$ of the remaining $n - 1$ variables will be equal to 1. The function $S_M(1,x_2, \ldots ,x_n)$ is thus symmetric with respect to $n - 1$ variables, where each a-number is replaced by a corresponding $(a - 1)$-number. A similar argument about $S_M(0,x_2, \ldots ,x_n)$ yields the *expansion theorem for symmetric functions*, as follows:

$$S_{a_1,a_2, \ldots ,a_k}(x_1,x_2, \ldots ,x_n)$$
$$= x'_1 S_{a_1,a_2, \ldots ,a_k}(x_2, \ldots ,x_n) + x_1 S_{a_1-1,a_2-1, \ldots ,a_k-1}(x_2, \ldots ,x_n)$$

where the a-number n (if it exists) is eliminated from the first term, since it is a function of only $n - 1$ variables; similarly, the a-number 0 (if it exists) is eliminated from the second term.

Synthesis of symmetric networks

The basic network for symmetric functions is shown in Fig. 6-6. The network is drawn completely for three variables, and its extension to n variables is indicated. It is a multiple-output network consisting of a single input (grounded) and $n + 1$ outputs, numbered 0 through n, corresponding to the $n + 1$ possible a-numbers. A network which realizes a symmetric function is called a *symmetric network*.

The contacts of a symmetric network are arranged in such a way that ground can propagate from the input terminal in just two directions, from bottom to top and from left to right. Contacts of operated relays shift the ground upward to the successive levels, while contacts of unoperated relays shift the ground to the right. These properties of sym-

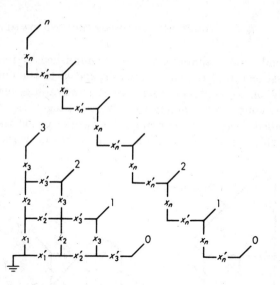

Fig. 6-6 Basic contact symmetric network.

metric networks make it possible to simplify the networks in various ways, without introducing sneak paths.

A symmetric network for three variables is shown in Fig. 6-7. Its outputs are numbered 0 through 3, corresponding to the four a-numbers, where output terminal a_i is grounded when and only when any a_i relays are operated. In order to realize the function $S_{1,3}(x_1,x_2,x_3)$, it is necessary to join the output terminals labeled 1 and 3, as shown by the dotted lines in Fig. 6-7. It is evident that all contacts leading only to unused terminals may be deleted. Hence contact x_3', which leads to output terminal 0, and the transfer contact leading to output terminal 2 are both deleted. The simplified network is shown in Fig. 6-8a.

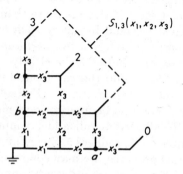

Fig. 6-7 Basic symmetric network for three variables illustrating connections for $S_{1,3}(x_1,x_2,x_3)$.

177

A second type of simplification is accomplished by recognizing that the transmissions from the two vertices a and a' to the output terminal depend only on x_3 contacts; therefore it is advantageous to eliminate one of the x_3 contacts by joining these vertices together. This method, which is called *folding* the symmetric network, yields the network of Fig. 6-8b, which in this example is the minimal network. The trans-

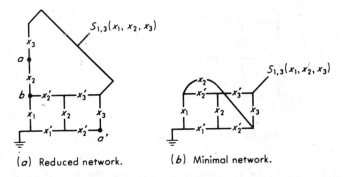

(*a*) Reduced network.   (*b*) Minimal network.

Fig. 6-8   Synthesis of a symmetric network.

mission from vertex b to the output terminal remains unchanged, since any path from vertex b through vertex a is now replaced by an identical path through vertex a'. From the tie sets of the network it can be verified that the transmission function is equal to 1 when either one or three of the relays are energized, i.e.,

$$T(x_1,x_2,x_3) = S_{1,3}(x_1,x_2,x_3) = x_1x_2x_3 + x_1x_2'x_3' + x_1'x_2x_3' + x_1'x_2'x_3$$

In general, two or more vertices can be connected together to make a folding of the symmetric network possible if all paths from each vertex to the output are identical. If there is more than one network output, the foregoing rule must be valid for every such output. Two vertices which have this property are referred to as *equivalent*.

The sum function of a full adder is clearly a symmetric function, namely, $S = S_{1,3}(x_1,x_2,x_3)$ while the carry-out function, which is also symmetric, is equal to $C_0 = S_{2,3}(x_1,x_2,x_3)$. Full adders, which are available as MSI packages, can also be used to implement many larger symmetric functions. Recall that a full adder counts the number of incoming 1's, out of three, and produces a binary number corresponding to this count. Using this property, we may combine several full adders to count the number of 1's out of any arbitrary number of inputs. As an example, let us design a circuit realizing the symmetric function

$$f(x_1, \ldots ,x_7) = S_{1,3,6}(x_1,x_2, \ldots ,x_7)$$

The arrangement of full adders shown in the left-hand part of Fig. 6-9 actually adds the values of the binary digits $x_1, x_2, \ldots, x_7$ and produces the sum in a binary form. Thus, for example, if five out of the seven variables have value 1, then $k_4 = 1$, $k_2 = 0$, and $k_1 = 1$, yielding the binary number 5, i.e., $k_4 k_2 k_1 = 101$. The right-hand part of Fig. 6-9 generates the required function f, according to the a numbers. It is a circuit which produces an output $f = 1$, when the input combinations k_4, k_2, k_1 have values identical with the a-numbers. Accordingly, in our example, f must be 1 when the input combinations are: $k_4 k_2 k_1 = 001$, 011, or 110. Thus, $f = k_4' k_1 + k_4 k_2 k_1'$. Note that, although the realization of f shown in Fig. 6-9 is not the minimal one, it is very inexpensive to implement since it mainly consists of readily available MSI circuits.

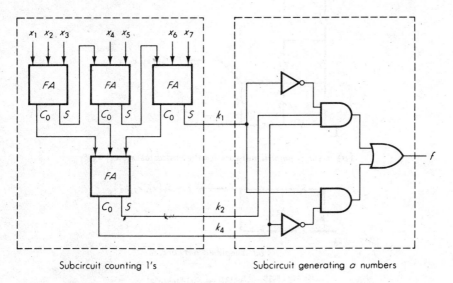

Subcircuit counting 1's   Subcircuit generating a numbers

Fig. 6-9   Realizing the symmetric circuit $f = s_{1,3,6}(x_1, \ldots, x_7)$.

Complemented variables of symmetry

So far we have considered the synthesis of symmetric functions for which the variables of symmetry were all unprimed, i.e., $x_1 x_2, \ldots, x_n$. As shown before, functions may be symmetric with respect to primed as well as unprimed variables. For example, the function

$$T(x_1, x_2, x_3) = x_1' x_2' x_3' + x_1 x_2' x_3 + x_1' x_2 x_3$$

is not symmetric with respect to the variables x_1, x_2, and x_3, but has been shown to be symmetric with respect to the variables x_1, x_2, and x_3' or with respect to the variables x_1', x_2', and x_3.

$$T(x_1,x_2,x_3) = S_1(x_1,x_2,x_3') = S_2(x_1',x_2',x_3)$$

The realization of functions some of whose variables of symmetry are complemented is analogous to the previously described technique. The only exception is in the basic symmetric network, where the contacts which correspond to complemented variables of symmetry are complemented; that is, a normally closed contact replaces a normally open one, and vice versa. The network realizing $S_1(x_1,x_2,x_3')$ is shown in Fig. 6-10.

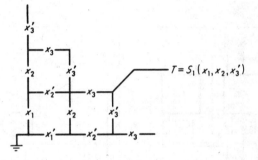

(a) Basic symmetric network for the variables x_1, x_2, x_3'.

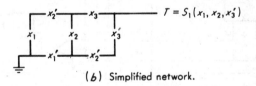

(b) Simplified network.

Fig. 6-10 Design of $S_1(x_1,x_2,x_3')$.

6-3 IDENTIFICATION OF SYMMETRIC FUNCTIONS

If the variables of symmetry of a switching function are not mixed, that is, they are all either primed or unprimed, the determination whether a given function is symmetric is relatively simple. It can be accomplished by expanding the function to a canonical form and counting whether or not the number of minterms corresponding to each a-number is $n!/(n-a)!a!$, which is the formula for the number of combinations of n elements taken a at a time. If, however, the variables of symmetry are mixed, the foregoing method will fail, and different techniques must be employed. One such technique is presented subsequently.

The switching function to be tested for symmetry is written as a table in which all the minterms contained in the function are listed by their binary representation. For example, the function

$$f(x,y,z) = \Sigma(1,2,4,7)$$

is written as shown:

x	y	z	$a^\#$
0	0	1	1
0	1	0	1
1	0	0	1
1	1	1	3
2	2	2	

The arithmetic sum of each column in the table is computed and written under the column. This sum is referred to as *column sum*. The number of 1's in each row is written in the corresponding position in column $a^\#$. This number is called *row sum*.

If an n-variable function is symmetric and one of its row sums is equal to some number a, then, by definition, there must exist $n!/(n-a)!a!$ rows which have the same row sum. This formula specifies the binomial coefficients, and thus the row sums in column $a^\#$ are the a-numbers of the function, whose variables of symmetry are written at the head of the columns. If all row sums occur the required number of times, then all column sums are identical. For the above function all column sums equal 2, and there are two row sums, 1 and 3, that must be checked for "sufficient occurrence," i.e.,

$$\frac{3!}{(3-1)!1!} = 3 \qquad \frac{3!}{(3-3)!3!} = 1$$

Both row sums occur the required number of times; therefore the function is symmetric and can be expressed as $S_{1,3}(x,y,z)$.

The function

$$f(w,x,y,z) = \Sigma(0,1,3,5,8,10,11,12,13,15)$$

written in table form is shown in Fig. 6-2a.

Since the column sums are not all the same, further tests must be made to determine if the function is symmetric, and if it is, to find its variables of symmetry. The column sums can be made the same by complementing the columns corresponding to variables x and y, as shown in Table 6-2b. The properties of the function are not altered by complementation of the entries of a column and the variable at its head. The new column

Table 6-2 Test for symmetry

w	x	y	z		w	x'	y'	z	$a^{\#}$		w'	x	y	z'	$a^{\#}$
0	0	0	0		0	1	1	0	2		1	0	0	1	2
0	0	0	1		0	1	1	1	3		1	0	0	0	1
0	0	1	1		0	1	0	1	2		1	0	1	0	2
0	1	0	1		0	0	1	1	2		1	1	0	0	2
1	0	0	0		1	1	1	0	3		0	0	0	1	1
1	0	1	0		1	1	0	0	2		0	0	1	1	2
1	0	1	1		1	1	0	1	3		0	0	1	0	1
1	1	0	0		1	0	1	0	2		0	1	0	1	2
1	1	0	1		1	0	1	1	3		0	1	0	0	1
1	1	1	1		1	0	0	1	2		0	1	1	0	2
6	4	4	6		6	6	6	6			4	4	4	4	
	(a)						(b)						(c)		

sums are now computed and are found to be identical. The row sums are determined next and entered in column $a^{\#}$. Each row sum is tested by the binomial coefficients formula for sufficient occurrence, i.e.,

$$\frac{4!}{(4-2)!2!} = 6 \qquad \frac{4!}{(4-3)!3!} = 4$$

Since all row sums occur the required number of times, the function defined by Table 6-2b is symmetric, its variables of symmetry are w, x', y', and z, and its a-numbers are 2 and 3; that is,

$$f(w,x,y,z) = S_{2,3}(w,x',y',z)$$

If columns w and z are complemented, instead of columns x and y, Table 6-1c results, and since all its row sums occur the required number of times, f can also be expressed as

$$f(w,x,y,z) = S_{1,2}(w',x,y,z')$$

A more involved identification process is encountered while testing for symmetry the function

$$f(w,x,y,z) = \Sigma(0,3,5,10,12,15)$$

The column sums of Table 6-3a are all identical, but row sum 2 does not occur six times as required. A difficulty arises because the column sums do not offer any clue as to which columns, if any, should be complemented. One way of overcoming this difficulty is by expanding the function about any one of its variables.

The expansion of a function can be accomplished in tabular form, as shown in Table 6-3b, where the function has been expanded about w.

Table 6-3   A test involving an expansion of the function

w	x	y	z	$a^{\#}$
0	0	0	0	0
0	0	1	1	2
0	1	0	1	2
1	0	1	0	2
1	1	0	0	2
1	1	1	1	4
3	3	3	3	

(a)

w	x	y	z
0	0	0	0
0	0	1	1
0	1	0	1
	1	1	2
1	0	1	0
1	1	0	0
1	1	1	1
	2	2	1

(b)

w	x'	y'	z	$a^{\#}$
0	1	1	0	2
0	1	0	1	2
0	0	1	1	2
1	1	0	0	2
1	0	1	0	2
1	0	0	1	2
3	3	3	3	

(c)

The terms containing w' and those containing w are grouped separately, and the column sums for variables x, y, and z in each group are computed. In both groups we observe that if either column z or columns x and y are complemented, then the function corresponding to each group is found to be symmetric. Consequently, f can be expressed as

$$f(w,x,y,z) = w'S_1(x,y,z') + wS_2(x,y,z')$$

which, by the expansion theorem for symmetric functions, can be expressed as

$$f(w,x,y,z) = S_2(w',x,y,z')$$

Another expression, $f(w,x,y,z) = S_2(w,x',y',z)$, can be obtained by complementing columns x and y of Table 6-3a, as shown in Table 6-3c.

When testing a function for symmetry, all column sums are computed first. If more than two different sums occur, the function is not symmetric, because no complementation of selected columns can be made so as to yield a table whose column sums are all the same. If two different column sums occur, say p and q, a necessary condition for the function to be symmetric is that the number of 0's in the columns whose column sum is q is equal to p. If these columns are now complemented, their column sums will be p. In other words, the sum of the two column sums, i.e., $p + q$, must be equal to the number of rows in the table. For example, in Table 6-2a, $4 + 6 = 10$.

If all column sums are identical, the row sums are determined and checked for sufficient occurrence. If they satisfy the binomial coefficients formula, the given function is symmetric; if they do not satisfy the formula, two cases may occur: (1) The column sum is not equal to one-half the number of rows in the table; consequently, no complementation of any number of columns will yield a table in which all column sums are identical, and thus the function is not symmetric. (2) The column sums are equal to one-half the number of rows in the table, in which case the expansion technique may be employed to determine whether or not the function is symmetric.

Following the above arguments, the procedure for identifying symmetric functions can be summarized as follows:

1. Obtain column sums.
    (a) If more than two different sums occur, the function is not symmetric.
    (b) If two different sums occur, compare the total of these two sums with the number of rows in the table: if they are not equal, the function is not symmetric; if they are equal, complement the columns corresponding to either one of the column sums (preferably the one of fewer occurrences) and continue to step 2.
    (c) If all column sums are identical, compare their sum with one-half the number of rows in the table. If they are not equal, continue to step 2; if they are equal, continue to step 3.
2. Obtain row sums and check each for sufficient occurrence; that is, if a is a row sum and n is the number of variables, then that row sum must occur $n!/(n - a)!a!$ times.
    (a) If any row sum does not occur the required number of times, the function is not symmetric.
    (b) If all row sums occur the required number of times, the function is symmetric, its a-numbers are given by the different row sums in column $a^{\#}$, and its variables of symmetry are given at the top of the table.
3. Obtain row sums and check each for sufficient occurrence.
    (a) If all row sums occur the required number of times, the function is symmetric.
    (b) If any row sum does not occur the required number of times, expand the function about any of its variables; that is, find functions g and h such that $f = x'g + xh$. Write g and h in tabular form and find their column sums. Determine all variable complementations required for the identifications of symmetries in g and h. Test f under the same variable complementations. If all row sums occur the required number of times, f is symmetric; if any row sum does not occur the required number of times, f is not symmetric.

NOTES AND REFERENCES

The main results in functional decomposition were presented by Ashenhurst [1], whose original terminology has been followed in Sec. 6-1. The decomposition chart is due to Singer [11]. Other aspects of functional decomposition were studied by Semon [10], and Roth and Karp [9]. Nondisjunctive and complex decompositions were treated extensively by Curtis [4]. Symmetric functions are discussed extensively by Caldwell [3]. The problem of identifying symmetric functions has been studied by Caldwell [2], Marcus [6], and McCluskey [7]. Additional properties of symmetric functions derived from group theory can be found in Harrison [5] and Povarov [8].

1. Ashenhurst, R. L.: The Decomposition of Switching Functions, Proceedings of an International Symposium on the Theory of Switching, April 2–5, 1957, *Ann. Computation Lab., Harvard Univ.*, vol. 29, pp. 74–116, 1959.
2. Caldwell, S. H.: Recognition and Identification of Symmetric Functions, *Trans. AIEE, Commun. Electron.*, pt. II, vol. 73, pp. 142–146, May, 1954.
3. Caldwell, S. H.: "Switching Circuits and Logical Design," John Wiley & Sons, Inc., New York, 1958.
4. Curtis, H. A.: "A New Approach to the Design of Switching Circuits," D. Van Nostrand Company, Inc., Princeton, N.J., 1962.
5. Harrison, M. A.: "Introduction to Switching and Automata Theory," McGraw-Hill Book Company, New York, 1965.
6. Marcus, M. P.: The Detection and Identification of Symmetric Switching Functions, *IRE Trans. Electron. Computers*, vol. EC-5, no. 4, pp. 237–239, December, 1956.
7. McCluskey, E. J., Jr.: Detection of Group Invariance or Total Symmetry of a Boolean Function, *Bell System Tech. J.*, vol. 35, pp. 1445–1453, November, 1956.
8. Povarov, G. N.: A Mathematical Theory for the Synthesis of Contact Networks with One Input and *k* Outputs, Proceedings of an International Symposium on the Theory of Switching, April 2–5, 1957, *Ann. Computation Lab., Harvard Univ.*, vol. 30, pp. 74–94, 1959.
9. Roth, J. P., and R. M. Karp: Minimization over Boolean Graphs, *IBM J. Res. Develop.*, vol. 6, no. 2, pp. 227–238, April, 1962.
10. Semon, W.: Characteristic Numbers and Their Use in the Decomposition of Switching Functions, *Proc. ACM*, Pittsburgh, 1952, pp. 273–280.
11. Singer, T.: Some Uses of Truth Tables, Proceedings of an International Symposium on the Theory of Switching, pt. I, pp. 125–133, Harvard University Press, Cambridge, Mass., 1959.

PROBLEMS

6-1. Construct the decomposition chart for the function

$$f(w,x,y,z) = \Sigma(1,3,5,7,8,11,13,15)$$

Indicate all possible decompositions, and determine specifically the functions F and Φ such that $f(w,x,y,z) = F[\Phi(x,y),w,z]$.

6-2. The function $f(v,w,x,y,z) = \Sigma(4,7,8,11,13,14,23,27,28,29,30)$ can be decomposed to the form $F[\Phi(v,y,z),w,x]$. Determine the functions F and Φ.

6-3. For each of the following functions, specify the don't-care combinations and determine the functions F and Φ so that it is disjunctively decomposable as follows:

$$(a) \quad f(v,w,x,y,z) = \Sigma(4,8,10,16,21,27,28) + \Sigma_\phi(1,5,23,25,30,31)$$
$$= F[\Phi(v,x,z),w,y]$$
$$(b) \quad f(v,w,x,y,z) = \Sigma(1,2,7,9,10,17,19,26,31) + \Sigma_\phi(0,15,20,23,25)$$
$$= F[\Phi(v,w,y),x,z]$$

6-4. (a) Let $f = S_M(x_1,x_2, \ldots ,x_n)$ be a symmetric function of n variables. Prove that its complement f' is also a symmetric function of n variables whose a-numbers are those numbers included in the set $\{0,1, \ldots ,n\}$ but not included in M.

(b) Determine the complements of the following functions:

(i) $f_1 = S_{1,3}(x_1,x_2,x_3,x_4)$

(ii) $f_2 = S_{0,1,2}(x_1,x_2,x_3)$

6-5. (a) Prove that there are 2^{n+1} symmetric functions of n variables. *Hint:* Determine the number of possible subsets of a-numbers.

(b) Find all symmetric functions of two variables and show for each function its a-numbers.

6-6. (a) Prove that

$$S_{a_1,a_2, \ldots ,a_k}(x_1,x_2, \ldots ,x_n) = S_{\alpha_1,\alpha_2, \ldots ,\alpha_k}(x_1',x_2', \ldots ,x_n')$$

where

$$\alpha_1 = n - a_1$$
$$\alpha_2 = n - a_2$$
$$\cdots \cdots \cdots$$
$$\alpha_k = n - a_k$$

(b) Demonstrate the above result in the case of

$$f(w,x,y,z) = S_{0,3,4}(w',x',y',z')$$

6-7. Prove that the basic symmetric circuit contains $(n + 1)n/2$ transfer contacts, where n is the number of variables.

Hint: Prove by verifying for some k variables and induction to $k + 1$.

6-8. Can the don't-care entries in the map of Fig. P6-8 be so chosen that $f(x,y,z)$ becomes a self-dual symmetric function with respect to x, y, z? With respect to x', y, z? Complete the map in each case when the answer is yes.

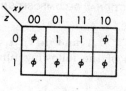

Fig. P6-8

6-9. It can be shown that a function $f(x_1, x_2, \ldots, x_n)$ is symmetric if and only if

$$f(x_1, x_2, \ldots, x_n) = f(x_2, x_1, x_3, \ldots, x_n)$$

and

$$f(x_1, x_2, \ldots, x_n) = f(x_2, x_3, \ldots, x_n, x_1)$$

Verify this assertion in the case of

$$f(w', x, y, z) = wx'y'z' + wxyz + w'x'yz + w'xy'z + w'xyz'$$

6-10. Utilizing the expansion theorem, express the following as symmetric functions:

    (a) $A'S_{0,1,4}(B,C,D,E) + AS'_{0,3,4}(B,C,D,E)$
    (b) $A'S_{0,1,4}(B,C,D,E) + AS_{0,3,4}(B,C,D,E)$
    (c) $A'S_{0,1,4}(B,C,D,E) + AS_{0,3,4}(B',C',D',E')$

Hint: The property established in Prob. 6-6 may prove helpful.

6-11. For each of the following functions find a contact-network realization with minimum number of contacts.

    (a) $S_{1,4}(w,x,y,z)$
    (b) $S_{0,1,3}(w,x,y,z)$
    (c) $S_{2,3,5}(v,w',x,y',z)$

6-12. Find a minimal contact network which realizes the symmetric function $S_{1,3}(x_1,x_2,x_3,x_4,x_5)$.

    Hint: Compare the circuit obtained from a direct realization with that obtained by utilizing the property established in Prob. 6-6.

6-13. Realize the symmetric function $S_{2,4}(x_1,x_2,x_3,x_4,x_5)$ using any combination of three gates from the set AND, OR, NOT, and EXCLUSIVE OR. Assume that both the variables and their complements are available as inputs.

6-14. Realize each of the functions below using full adders and gates.

    (a) $f_1(x_1, \ldots, x_5) = S_{3,4,5}(x_1, \ldots, x_5)$
    (b) $f_2(x_1, \ldots, x_7) = S_{2,4,6}(x_1, \ldots, x_7)$
    (c) $f_3(x_1, \ldots, x_9) = S_{1,3,5,7,9}(x_1, \ldots, x_9)$

6-15. (a) Let $f_1(x_1,x_2, \ldots ,x_n)$ and $f_2(x_1,x_2, \ldots ,x_n)$ be both symmetric functions. Which of the following functions is also necessarily symmetric?

$$f_1 + f_2; f_1 \cdot f_2; f_1 \oplus f_2$$

(b) Under what conditions will the above functions be symmetric if f_1 is symmetric, but f_2 is not?

6-16. Show that the following functions are symmetric. Find a two-output realization which uses only five transfer contacts.

$$T_1(x,y,z) = \Sigma(1,2,4,7) \qquad T_2(x,y,z) = \Sigma(0,3,5,6)$$

6-17. Design a minimal, three-output contact network to realize the functions shown below. Ten transfer contacts should be sufficient.

$$T_1(w,x,y,z) = \Sigma(0,1,2,4,8)$$
$$T_2(w,x,y,z) = \Sigma(3,5,6,9,10,12)$$
$$T_3(w,x,y,z) = \Sigma(7,11,13,14,15)$$

6-18. Determine which of the following functions is symmetric and identify its a-numbers and variables of symmetry.

(a) $f(x_1,x_2,x_3,x_4,x_5) = \Sigma(0,3,5,6,10,12,15,18,20,23,25,30)$
(b) $f(x_1,x_2,x_3) = \Sigma(0,2,3,4,5,7)$
(c) $f(x_1,x_2,x_3,x_4) = \Sigma(0,5,6,9,10,15)$

7
Threshold Logic

So far we have been concerned with logical design of switching circuits constructed of electronic gates or bilateral devices. There exists another type of switching device, called the threshold element. Presently, threshold elements are not as fast to operate or as easy to manufacture as conventional gates, and consequently they are of very limited usefulness. However, the study of threshold logic leads to many important theoretical results concerning switching function. Moreover, recently new types of threshold elements have been developed and consequently the study of threshold logic may prove beneficial from the practical point of view as well.

Circuits constructed of threshold elements usually consist of fewer components and simpler interconnections than the corresponding circuits implemented with conventional gates. But while the input-output relations of circuits constructed of conventional gates can be specified by switching algebra, different algebraic means must be developed for threshold circuits. In this chapter we shall study the properties of threshold elements and present necessary and sufficient conditions for a switching function to be realizable by just a single element. The general synthesis procedure, that of synthesizing switching circuits using only threshold elements, is very complicated and is briefly introduced in Sec. 7-2.

7-1 INTRODUCTORY CONCEPTS

The usefulness of threshold logic, or of any other new logic in digital systems design, is determined by the availability, cost, and capabilities of the basic building blocks, as well as by the existence of effective synthesis procedures. In this section we shall study the properties of the threshold element, determine its limitations and capabilities, and develop a synthesis procedure.

The threshold element

A *threshold element*, or *gate*, has n two-valued inputs, $x_1, x_2, \ldots, x_n$, and a single two-valued output, y. Its internal parameters are a *threshold* T and *weights* $w_1, w_2, \ldots, w_n$, where each weight w_i is associated with a particular input variable x_i. The values of the threshold T and the weights w_i ($i = 1, 2, \ldots, n$) may be any real, finite, positive or negative numbers. The input-output relation of a threshold element is defined as follows:

$$y = 1 \quad \text{if and only if} \quad \sum_{i=1}^{n} w_i x_i \geq T$$

$$y = 0 \quad \text{if and only if} \quad \sum_{i=1}^{n} w_i x_i < T \tag{7-1}$$

where the sum and product operations are the conventional arithmetic ones. The sum $\sum_{i=1}^{n} w_i x_i$ is called the *weighted sum* of the element. The symbol representing a threshold element is shown in Fig. 7-1.

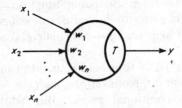

Fig. 7-1 Symbol for a threshold element.

Example The input-output relation of the threshold element shown in Fig. 7-2 is given in Table 7-1. The weighted sum is computed in the center column for every input combination. A 1 is entered in the output column in every row for which the weighted sum is

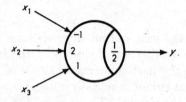

Fig. 7-2 A threshold element.

greater than or equal to $\frac{1}{2}$ (because $T = \frac{1}{2}$), and a 0 is entered in all remaining rows. From the input-output relation (Table 7-1) it is evident that this threshold element realizes the switching function

$$y = f(x_1,x_2,x_3) = \Sigma(1,2,3,6,7)$$
$$= x_1'x_3 + x_2 \quad \blacksquare$$

Table 7-1 Input-output relation of the gate shown in Fig. 7-2

Input variables			Weighted sum	Output
x_1	x_2	x_3	$-x_1 + 2x_2 + x_3$	y
0	0	0	0	0
0	0	1	1	1
0	1	0	2	1
0	1	1	3	1
1	0	0	−1	0
1	0	1	0	0
1	1	0	1	1
1	1	1	2	1

The threshold element, defined algebraically by the relation (7-1), can be constructed physically in various ways. Consider, for example, the resistor-transistor gate shown in Fig. 7-3. If the input resistances

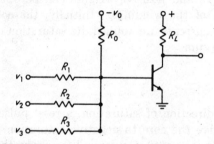

Fig. 7-3 Resistor-transistor threshold element.

are not equal, then the gate output depends on a weighted sum of the inputs, where these weights are functions of the input resistances, the input voltages, and the particular combination of inputs whose logical value is 1. The input circuit is actually a linear summer which computes the weighted sum of the inputs. The threshold of the gate is determined by resistor R_0 and the voltage source v_0. Since all resistances have positive values, this gate is capable of providing only positive weights.

Another realization of a threshold element, which provides both positive and negative weights, is by means of a magnetic core, as shown in Fig. 7-4, where there is a magnetic core with $n + 3$ windings. The value of each input variable x_i is determined by the presence or absence

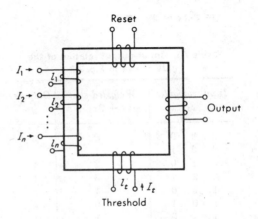

Fig. 7-4 Magnetic-core threshold element.

of current in the ith winding, and the corresponding weight w_i is a function of the number of turns l_i. The threshold T is determined by the constant current I_t, the number of turns l_t, and their direction, while the value of the output y is determined by the magnetization state of the core. Both negative and positive weights can be obtained, depending upon the direction of the windings. Initially, the core is in negative saturation. When currents are applied, its saturation direction depends on the value of the sum

$$\sum_{i=1}^{n} I_i l_i + I_t l_t$$

To determine the direction of saturation, a reset pulse is applied, sufficiently large to drive the core to negative saturation. If at that time the core is positively saturated, a pulse will appear on the output winding. If, on the other hand, the core is negatively saturated when a reset pulse appears, no pulse will appear on the output winding. The presence or absence of a pulse on the output winding corresponds, respectively, to output values 1 or 0. Other realizations of threshold elements by means of tunnel diodes, parametrons, etc., are also possible.

Capabilities and limitations of threshold logic

From the definition of threshold elements it is evident that they are more powerful than conventional diode and transistor gates. Their higher capability is manifested by the ability of *single* threshold elements to realize a larger class of functions than is realizable by any one conventional gate. In fact, a threshold element can be considered a generalization of the conventional gates, because any of the latter can be realized by a single threshold element. A two-input NAND gate, for example, can be realized by a single threshold element with weights -1, -1, and threshold $T = -1\frac{1}{2}$, as shown in Fig. 7-5. Similarly, a threshold gate whose weights are unity and whose threshold $T = \frac{1}{2}$ realizes the OR operation, and so on. Since NAND is a functionally complete operation, any switching function can be realized by threshold elements alone.

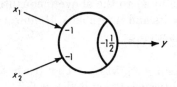

Fig. 7-5 A threshold gate realizing the NAND operation.

Because of the wide range of weights and threshold combinations, there is a large class of switching functions which can be realized by single threshold elements. As to whether every switching function is realizable by only one threshold element, the answer is *no*, as will be shown by the following example. Suppose that $f(x_1,x_2,x_3,x_4) = x_1x_2 + x_3x_4$ is realizable by a threshold element, with weights w_1, w_2, w_3, w_4, and threshold T. Then the output of this element must be 1 for input combinations $x_1x_2x_3'x_4'$ and $x_1'x_2'x_3x_4$, and 0 for input combinations $x_1'x_2x_3x_4'$ and $x_1x_2'x_3'x_4$. Thus

$$\left.\begin{array}{l} w_1 + w_2 \geq T \\ w_3 + w_4 \geq T \end{array}\right\} \Rightarrow w_1 + w_2 + w_3 + w_4 \geq 2T \tag{7-2}$$

$$\left.\begin{array}{l} w_2 + w_4 < T \\ w_1 + w_3 < T \end{array}\right\} \Rightarrow w_1 + w_2 + w_3 + w_4 < 2T \tag{7-3}$$

Clearly, the requirements in inequalities (7-2) and (7-3) are conflicting, and no threshold value can satisfy them. Consequently, $f = x_1x_2 + x_3x_4$ cannot be realized by a single threshold element.

In light of the fact that not every switching function is realizable by just a single threshold element, we now formulate the basic problem of threshold logic as follows:

▶ Given a switching function $f(x_1, x_2, \ldots, x_n)$, determine whether or not it is realizable by a single threshold element, and if it is, find appropriate weights and threshold.

A switching function that can be realized by a single threshold element is called a *threshold function*.

A straightforward approach to the identification problem of threshold functions is to derive from the truth table a set of 2^n linear, simultaneous inequalities and to solve them. From the input combinations for which $f = 1$, we derive all the weighted sums which must exceed or equal the threshold T, and from the input combinations for which $f = 0$, we derive all the weighted sums which must be less than T. If a solution (not necessarily unique) to the above inequalities exists, it provides the values for the weights and threshold. If, however, no solution exists, f is not a threshold function.

Example Let $f(x_1, x_2, x_3) = \Sigma(0,1,3)$. The truth table and the corresponding inequalities are given in Table 7-2.

Table 7-2 Truth table with linear inequalities for $f = \Sigma(0,1,3)$

Combination	x_1	x_2	x_3	f	Inequality
0	0	0	0	1	$0 \geq T$
1	0	0	1	1	$w_3 \geq T$
2	0	1	0	0	$w_2 < T$
3	0	1	1	1	$w_2 + w_3 \geq T$
4	1	0	0	0	$w_1 < T$
5	1	0	1	0	$w_1 + w_3 < T$
6	1	1	0	0	$w_1 + w_2 < T$
7	1	1	1	0	$w_1 + w_2 + w_3 < T$

From the inequality which corresponds to combination 0 we observe that T must be negative, and so must w_2 and w_1 (see combinations 2 and 4). From combinations 3 and 5 we conclude that

w_2 must be greater than w_1, and from combination 1 we conclude that w_3 is greater than or equal to T. Thus we are able at this point to establish the relation

$$w_3 \geq T > w_2 > w_1$$

where only w_3 may be positive. If we restrict the weights to integer values and want to use weights of smallest magnitude, we obtain

$$w_2 = -1 \qquad w_1 = -2 \qquad T = -\tfrac{1}{2}$$

It is easy to verify that if we choose $w_3 = 1$, all the inequalities are satisfied. f is therefore a threshold function. ■

For an n-variable switching function there are 2^n linear inequalities, some of which may usually be eliminated because they are implied by the others (e.g., if inequalities 2 and 4 in Table 7-2 are satisfied, then, since T is negative, inequality 6 is automatically implied, and similarly, inequality 7 is implied by 2 and 5). Although any set of linear inequalities can be either solved or shown by various methods to be inconsistent, it is desirable to further explore those properties of threshold functions that will make possible the development of more effective identification procedures. These properties will be investigated in the next section.

The realization of other, nonthreshold switching functions, whose corresponding AND-OR networks may be quite complex, can often be accomplished with just a few threshold elements. Thus the use of threshold elements may result, among other things, in a considerable reduction in the number of gates, inputs, and components, as well as in the size of the final circuit.

One of the limitations of threshold logic is its sensitivity to variations in circuit parameters. Resistance values may change by as much as 20 percent of their nominal value; input and supply voltages may also vary by an appreciable amount; and consequently, the weighted sum for a particular combination, especially with a large number of inputs, may deviate from its prescribed value so as to cause a circuit malfunction. Restrictions must therefore be imposed on the maximum allowable number of inputs and on the threshold value T. Care must be taken to increase the difference between the values of the weighted sums for which f must equal 1, and the values of the weighted sums for which f must equal 0.

Another major problem which limits the practical usefulness of threshold logic is the lack of effective synthesis procedures. The outward appearance of a switching function gives no indication as to how it may be expressed in a way that will enable the designer to specify the required number of elements, their weights and thresholds, and their interconnections. A great deal of research effort has been devoted to finding synthesis procedures for threshold logic, but a satisfactory one is yet to be found.

Elementary properties

In the discussions to follow, a threshold element will be specified by its input variables and a *weight-threshold vector*

$$V = \{w_1, w_2, \ldots, w_n; T\}$$

Thus the threshold element of Fig. 7-2 is completely specified by its input variables x_1, x_2, x_3 and $V = \{-1, 2, 1; \frac{1}{2}\}$.

Consider the function $f(x_1, x_2, \ldots, x_n)$, which is realized by a single threshold element $V_1 = \{w_1, w_2, \ldots, w_j, \ldots, w_n; T\}$ whose inputs are $x_1, x_2, \ldots, x_j, \ldots, x_n$. Now suppose that one of the inputs, say x_j, is complemented. We shall show that the same function f is realizable by a single threshold element $V_2 = \{w_1, w_2, \ldots, -w_j, \ldots, w_n; T - w_j\}$ whose inputs are $x_1, x_2, \ldots, x_j', \ldots, x_n$.

From the inequalities in (7-1) and from V_1, we find that whenever

$$w_j x_j + \sum_{i \neq j} w_i x_i \begin{cases} \geq T & \text{then } f = 1 \\ < T & \text{then } f = 0 \end{cases} \qquad (7\text{-}4)$$

When V_2 replaces V_1 and x_j' replaces x_j, we find that if

$$-w_j x_j' + \sum_{i \neq j} w_i x_i \begin{cases} \geq T - w_j & \text{then } g = 1 \\ < T - w_j & \text{then } g = 0 \end{cases} \qquad (7\text{-}5)$$

where g is the function realized by the element V_2. To prove that g and f are identical functions, let $x_j = 0$ so that $x_j' = 1$. Then Eqs. (7-4) and (7-5) become identical. Next, let $x_j = 1$ so that $x_j' = 0$. Again Eqs. (7-4) and (7-5) are identical. Consequently, both f and g assume for each input combination identical values, and thus are identical functions.

The above property leads to several important conclusions. If a function is realizable by a single threshold element, then by an appropriate selection of complemented and uncomplemented input variables, it is possible to obtain a realization by an element whose weights have any desired *sign* distribution. Therefore, *if a function is realizable by a single threshold element, then it is realizable by an element with only positive weights.* Clearly, this assertion is valid only if the input variables are available in both forms. Consequently, although threshold elements constructed of resistor-transistor logic can be manufactured only with positive weights, they may be used to implement any switching function.

We shall next show that if a function $f(x_1,x_2, \ldots ,x_n)$ is realizable by a single threshold element whose weight-threshold vector is $V_1 = \{w_1,w_2, \ldots ,w_n; T\}$, then its complement $f'(x_1,x_2 \ldots ,x_n)$ is realizable by a single threshold element whose weight-threshold vector is $V_2 = \{-w_1,-w_2, \ldots ,-w_n; -T\}$.

From the inequalities in (7-1) and from V_1 we obtain†

$$\sum_{i=1}^{n} w_i x_i > T \qquad \text{where } f = 1$$

$$\sum_{i=1}^{n} w_i x_i < T \qquad \text{where } f = 0$$

(7-6)

Multiplying both sides of (7-6) by -1 yields

$$\sum_{i=1}^{n} (-w_i)x_i < -T \qquad \text{whenever } f = 1 \text{ or } f' = 0$$

$$\sum_{i=1}^{n} (-w_i)x_i > -T \qquad \text{whenever } f = 0 \text{ or } f' = 1$$

(7-7)

Clearly, the inequalities in (7-7) demonstrate that f' is realizable by the element whose weight-threshold vector is V_2.

7-2 SYNTHESIS OF THRESHOLD NETWORKS

Our principal goal in this section is the development of methods for the identification and realization of threshold functions. Before proceeding with this general study, we shall present a number of properties of threshold functions which provide the theoretical background necessary for the development of simpler and more effective synthesis procedures. We shall primarily be concerned with the synthesis of threshold functions, but attention will also be given to the realization of nonthreshold functions by means of threshold elements.

Unate functions

A function $f(x_1,x_2, \ldots ,x_n)$ is said to be *positive in* a variable x_i if there exists a disjunctive or conjunctive expression for the function in which x_i appears only in uncomplemented form. Analogously, $f(x_1,x_2, \ldots ,x_n)$

---

† The following argument becomes simpler if we restrict the values of the weights and threshold so that for no input combination will the weighted sum be exactly equal to T.

is said to be *negative in* x_i if there exists a disjunctive or conjunctive expression for f in which x_i appears only in complemented form. If f is either positive or negative in x_i, then it is said to be *unate in* x_i.

Example   The function $f = x_1x_2' + x_2x_3'$ is positive in x_1 and negative in x_3, but is not unate in x_2. ∎

If a function $f(x_1,x_2, \ldots ,x_n)$ is unate in each one of its variables, then it is called *unate.* Thus a function is unate if it can be represented by a disjunctive or conjunctive expression in which no variable appears in both its complemented and uncomplemented forms.

Example   The function $f = x_1'x_2 + x_1x_2x_3'$ is unate because a disjunctive expression for f exists which satisfies the above definition, namely, $f = x_1'x_2 + x_2x_3'$. On the other hand, the function $f = x_1x_2' + x_1'x_2$ is clearly not unate in any of its variables. ∎

If $f(x_1,x_2, \ldots ,x_n)$ is positive in x_i, then it can be expressed as

$$f(x_1,x_2, \ldots ,x_n) = x_i g_1(x_1, \ldots ,x_{i-1},x_{i+1}, \ldots ,x_n) + h_1(x_1, \ldots ,x_{i-1},x_{i+1}, \ldots ,x_n) \quad (7\text{-}8)$$

Similarly, if $f(x_1,x_2, \ldots ,x_n)$ is negative in x_i, then it can be expressed as

$$f(x_1,x_2, \ldots ,x_n) = x_i' g_2(x_1, \ldots ,x_{i-1},x_{i+1}, \ldots ,x_n) + h_2(x_1, \ldots ,x_{i-1},x_{i+1}, \ldots ,x_n) \quad (7\text{-}9)$$

By definition, if a function f can be expressed by Eq. (7-8) [Eq. (7-9)], then it is positive (negative) in x_i. Hence *the existence of two such functions g_1 and h_1 (g_2 and h_2) is a necessary and sufficient condition for f to be positive (negative) in x_i.*

Geometrical representation

Unate functions have several interesting properties, which are best illustrated by a geometrical representation of these functions. An *n-cube* contains 2^n vertices, each of which represents an assignment of values to the n variables and thus corresponds to a minterm. A line is drawn between every pair of vertices which differ in just one variable, and no other lines are drawn. The vertices corresponding to true minterms, that is, for which the function assumes the value 1, are called *true vertices*, while those corresponding to false minterms are called *false vertices*. The analogy between the *n*-cube and the map methods for representing switching functions is evident.

Example The three-cube representation of the function $f = x'y' + xz$
is shown in Fig. 7-6. The heavier lines connecting the two pairs
of true vertices [(1,1,1) and (1,0,1), and (0,0,1) and (0,0,0)] represent
the subcubes xz and $x'y'$. ∎

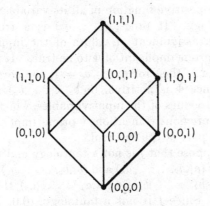

Fig. 7-6 A three-cube representation
of $f = x'y' + xz$.

It is convenient to define a partial-ordering relation between the vertices of the n-cube, so that

$$(a_1,a_2, \ldots ,a_n) \leq (b_1,b_2, \ldots ,b_n)$$

if and only if, for all i, $a_i \leq b_i$. As shown in Chap. 2, this partially ordered
set of vertices is a lattice and the vertices $(0,0, \ldots ,0)$ and $(1,1, \ldots ,1)$
are, respectively, the least vertex and the greatest vertex of the lattice.
As in any partial ordering, some pairs of vertices may be incomparable,
for example, $(0,0, \ldots ,0,1)$ and $(1,0, \ldots ,0,0)$.

Without loss of generality we shall subsequently restrict our attention to unate functions which are positive in all their variables, that is,
functions without any complemented variables. Such a restriction is
justified because every complemented variable in a unate function may
be relabeled, e.g., $x_i' \rightarrow y_i$, etc., and obviously, the resulting function is
unate if and only if the original one is. For example, the unate function
$x_1'x_2x_3' + x_2x_3'x_4$ may be converted to $x_1x_2x_3 + x_2x_3x_4$, using the relabeling
$x_1' \rightarrow x_1$ and $x_3' \rightarrow x_3$. By reconverting the latter function, it is possible
to determine the original one.

Theorem 7-1 *A switching function $f(x_1,x_2, \ldots ,x_n)$ is unate if and only
if it is not a tautology† and the above partial ordering exists, so that*

† A *tautology* is a function which is equal to 1 for all combinations of its variables.

for every pair of vertices $(a_1, a_2, \ldots, a_n)$ *and* $(b_1, b_2, \ldots, b_n)$, *if* $(a_1, a_2, \ldots, a_n)$ *is a true vertex and* $(b_1, b_2, \ldots, b_n) \geq (a_1, a_2, \ldots, a_n)$, *then* $(b_1, b_2, \ldots, b_n)$ *is also a true vertex of f.*

Proof: Suppose that f is unate. Let us find an expression Φ, representing f as a positive function in all its variables. Obviously, Φ is not a tautology. If $(a_1, a_2, \ldots, a_n)$ is a true vertex, then it represents an assignment of values of the input variables which causes some prime implicant of Φ to be true. If $(b_1, b_2, \ldots, b_n) \geq (a_1, a_2, \ldots, a_n)$, then for every $a_i = 1$, the corresponding $b_i = 1$. Therefore, since Φ is positive, $(b_1, b_2, \ldots, b_n)$ also represents an assignment of values of the input variables, which causes to be true at least the previously mentioned prime implicant. This proves the "only if" part of the theorem.

Now suppose that f is not a tautology and that for every pair of its vertices $(a_1, a_2, \ldots, a_n)$ and $(b_1, b_2, \ldots, b_n)$, if $(a_1, a_2, \ldots, a_n)$ is true and $(b_1, b_2, \ldots, b_n) \geq (a_1, a_2, \ldots, a_n)$, then $(b_1, b_2, \ldots, b_n)$ is also true. Since f is not a tautology, $(0, 0, \ldots, 0)$ is a false vertex. Consider the k vertices $S_1, S_2, \ldots, S_k$, which are the minimal† true vertices of the lattice. To each vertex S_i there corresponds a product term which consists of just those uncomplemented literals whose corresponding value in S_i is 1, e.g., if for a function $f(x_1, x_2, x_3, x_4)$ $S_i = (0, 1, 0, 1)$, then the corresponding product term is $x_2 x_4$. The expression formed of the disjunction of the k product terms, which correspond to all the minimal true vertices, is an expression for Φ. Since Φ is positive in all its variables, f is unate. ∎

Example For the unate function $f = x_1 x_2 + x_3 x_4$ there are two minimal true vertices, namely, $S_1 = (1, 1, 0, 0)$ and $S_2 = (0, 0, 1, 1)$. According to Theorem 7-1, every vertex (a_1, a_2, a_3, a_4) which is greater than S_1 or S_2 must be a true vertex. For example, $(1, 1, 1, 0)$ and $(0, 1, 1, 1)$ are true vertices, since $(1, 1, 1, 0) > (1, 1, 0, 0)$ and $(0, 1, 1, 1) > (0, 0, 1, 1)$. Indeed, these vertices correspond, respectively, to the products $x_1 x_2 x_3$ and $x_2 x_3 x_4$ which are covered by f. ∎

Linear separability

If we use the n-cube representation for threshold functions and regard the vertices as points in an n-dimensional space, we observe that the

---

† A true vertex S_i is said to be *minimal* if for no other true vertex $S_j < S_i$. A maximal vertex is defined analogously. (See Sec. 2-3.)

linear equation

$$w_1x_1 + w_2x_2 + \ldots + w_nx_n = T \qquad\qquad (7\text{-}10)$$

corresponds to an $(n-1)$-dimensional hyperplane which cuts through the n-cube. Now, since $f = 0$ when

$$w_1x_1 + w_2x_2 + \ldots + w_nx_n < T$$

and $f = 1$ when

$$w_1x_1 + w_2x_2 + \ldots + w_nx_n \geq T$$

we observe that the hyperplane separates the true vertices from the false ones. A switching function whose true vertices can be separated by a linear equation from its false ones is called a *linearly separable function,* and the functional property which makes such a separation possible is known as *linear separability.* Since, by definition, every function whose true vertices are separable from its false ones by Eq. (7-10) is a threshold function, we may conclude that all threshold functions are linearly separable, and vice versa. Indeed, the terms "threshold function" and "linearly separable function" are used interchangeably to describe the same functional property.

Let $f(x_1, x_2, \ldots, x_n)$ be a threshold function which depends upon and is positive in variable x_i and to which there corresponds the weight-threshold vector $V = \{w_1, w_2, \ldots, w_n; T\}$. Since f is positive in x_i, there exists a set of values $a_1, a_2, \ldots, a_{i-1}, a_{i+1}, \ldots, a_n$ for the input variables $x_1, x_2, \ldots, x_{i-1}, x_{i+1}, \ldots, x_n$, such that

$$f(a_1, \ldots, a_{i-1}, 1, a_{i+1}, \ldots, a_n) = 1$$

and

$$f(a_1, \ldots, a_{i-1}, 0, a_{i+1}, \ldots, a_n) = 0$$

Hence

$$w_1a_1 + \ldots + w_{i-1}a_{i-1} + w_i + w_{i+1}a_{i+1} + \ldots + w_na_n > T$$
$$w_1a_1 + \ldots + w_{i-1}a_{i-1} + w_{i+1}a_{i+1} + \ldots + w_na_n < T$$

and consequently, $w_i > 0$. Since the above argument may be applied to every x_i in $\{x_1, x_2, \ldots, x_n\}$, it follows that *the weights associated with a threshold function positive in all its variables are all positive.* A threshold function which is positive (negative) in all its variables is called a *positive (negative) threshold function.* Note that if f has a positive expression independent of x_i, then $w_i = 0$; but we shall not consider such functions.

Theorem 7-2 *Every threshold function is unate.*

Proof: Let $f(x_1, x_2, \ldots, x_n)$ be a threshold function whose true vertices can be separated from the false ones by the hyperplane

$$w_1 x_1 + w_2 x_2 + \ldots + w_n x_n = T$$

Suppose that f depends upon x_i and $w_i > 0$; then for every combination $(a_1, a_2, \ldots, a_{i-1}, a_{i+1}, \ldots, a_n)$ of the variables $x_1, x_2, \ldots, x_{i-1}, x_{i+1}, \ldots, x_n$, if vertex $(a_1, a_2, \ldots, a_{i-1}, 0, a_{i+1}, \ldots, a_n)$ is true, then $(a_1, a_2, \ldots, a_{i-1}, 1, a_{i+1}, \ldots, a_n)$ must also be true, because

$$w_1 a_1 + w_2 a_2 + \cdots + w_i + \cdots + w_n a_n > w_1 a_1$$
$$+ w_2 a_2 + \cdots + w_{i-1} a_{i-1} + w_{i+1} a_{i+1} + \cdots + w_n a_n$$

But since f is not independent of x_i, vertex $(a_1, a_2, \ldots, a_{i-1}, 0, a_{i+1}, \ldots, a_n)$ must be false, proving that f is positive in x_i. Now consider a variable x_i whose weight is negative, i.e., $w_i < 0$; then if vertex $(a_1, a_2, \ldots, a_{i-1}, 1, a_{i+1}, \ldots, a_n)$ is true, so is $(a_1, a_2, \ldots, a_{i-1}, 0, a_{i+1}, \ldots, a_n)$, because

$$w_1 a_1 + w_2 a_2 + \cdots + w_i + \cdots + w_n a_n < w_1 a_1 + w_2 a_2$$
$$+ \cdots + w_{i-1} a_{i-1} + w_{i+1} a_{i+1} + \cdots + w_n a_n$$

And since f is not independent of x_i, vertex $(a_1, a_2, \ldots, a_{i-1}, 1, a_{i+1}, \ldots, a_n)$ must be false, proving that f is negative in x_i. Consequently, f is either positive or negative in each of its variables, and thus it is unate. ∎

The converse of Theorem 7-2 is not true, because there exist many unate functions which are not linearly separable, e.g., $x_1 x_2 + x_3 x_4$.

Identification and realization of threshold functions

Our present objective is to present a procedure which will determine whether or not a given switching function is a threshold function and, if it is, will provide the values of the weights and threshold. The approach to be taken utilizes the linear separability property of threshold functions. In fact, it is a test to determine whether or not there exists a hyperplane which separates the true vertices of the function from the false ones. This is accomplished in several steps.

First, test the given function for unateness. This test is executed by examining a minimal expression of the function. And since a unate function has a unique minimal form (see Prob. 7-10), then if this expression is not unate, the function is not linearly separable. If it is unate, convert it into another function positive in all its variables.   For example, if $f = x_1x_2x_3'x_4 + x_2x_3'x_4'$, then its reduced expression is $f = x_1x_2x_3' + x_2x_3'x_4'$, and since it is unate, it is converted to $\Phi = x_1x_2x_3 + x_2x_3x_4$.

Next, find all minimal true and maximal false vertices of Φ.   In the above example there are two minimal true vertices, namely, $(1,1,1,0)$ and $(0,1,1,1)$.   The maximal false vertices are found by determining all false vertices with just one variable whose value is 0, then all false vertices with two variables whose value is 0, and so on, leaving out all vertices smaller than the ones already selected.   Clearly, the list of minimal true vertices contains all the necessary information for the determination of the maximal false vertices.   In our running example, the maximal false vertices are $(1,1,0,1)$, $(1,0,1,1)$, and $(0,1,1,0)$.

To determine whether or not Φ is linearly separable, and if it is to find an appropriate set of weights and threshold, it is necessary to determine the coefficients of the separating hyperplane.   This is accomplished by deriving and solving a system of pq inequalities, corresponding to the p minimal true and q maximal false vertices.   For each pair of vertices $A = \{a_1, a_2, \ldots, a_n\}$ and $B = \{b_1, b_2, \ldots, b_n\}$, where A and B are, respectively, minimal true and maximal false vertices, write the inequality

$$a_1w_1 + a_2w_2 + \ldots + a_nw_n > b_1w_1 + b_2w_2 + \ldots + b_nw_n$$

$$(7\text{-}11)$$

In our example, since $p = 2$ and $q = 3$, we find six inequalities, as follows:

$$w_1 + w_2 + w_3 > w_1 + w_2 + w_4$$
$$w_1 + w_2 + w_3 > w_1 + w_3 + w_4$$
$$w_1 + w_2 + w_3 > w_2 + w_3 \qquad\qquad (7\text{-}12)$$
$$w_2 + w_3 + w_4 > w_1 + w_2 + w_4$$
$$w_2 + w_3 + w_4 > w_1 + w_3 + w_4$$
$$w_2 + w_3 + w_4 > w_2 + w_3$$

Since Φ is a positive function, then, if it is linearly separable, the separating hyperplane [Eq. (7-10)] will have positive coefficients.   The hyperplane separating the minimal true vertices from the maximal false vertices separates all true vertices from all false ones, and thus yields the weight-threshold vector for Φ.   Solving the system of inequalities given in Eq. (7-12), we observe that the following are the necessary constraints which must be satisfied:

$$w_3 > w_4 \qquad\qquad w_3 > w_1$$
$$w_2 > w_4 \quad \text{and} \quad w_2 > w_1$$
$$w_1 > 0 \qquad\qquad w_4 > 0$$

Letting $w_1 = w_4 = 1$ and $w_2 = w_3 = 2$, we find, by substituting these values to any inequality in (7-12), that T must be smaller than 5 but larger than 4. Selecting $T = 9/2$ yields the weight-threshold vector for Φ, $V = \{1,2,2,1; 9/2\}$.

Finally, it is necessary to convert this weight-threshold vector to one which corresponds to the original function f. The conversion process is based on the properties established in (7-5), where for every input x_i which is complemented in the original function, w_i must be changed to $-w_i$ and T to $T - w_i$. In the above example inputs x_3 and x_4 appear in f in complemented form; thus, in the new weight-threshold vector, the weights are 1, 2, -2, and -1, and the threshold is $9/2 - 2 - 1 = 3/2$, to yield $V = \{1,2,-2,-1; 3/2\}$.

Example Determine whether the function

$$f(x_1,x_2,x_3,x_4) = \Sigma(0,1,3,4,5,6,7,12,13)$$

is a threshold function, and if it is, find a weight-threshold vector. $f = x_1'x_2 + x_1'x_4 + x_2x_3' + x_1'x_3'$ is unate, and therefore is converted into a positive function $\Phi = x_1x_2 + x_1x_4 + x_2x_3 + x_1x_3$. The minimal true vertices are

(1,1,0,0)　　　(1,0,0,1)　　　(0,1,1,0)　　　(1,0,1,0)

The maximal false vertices are

(0,1,0,1)　　　(0,0,1,1)　　　(1,0,0,0)

Consequently, we obtain a system of 12 inequalities:

$$\left.\begin{array}{l} w_1 + w_2 \\ w_1 + w_4 \\ w_2 + w_3 \\ w_1 + w_3 \end{array}\right\} > \left\{\begin{array}{l} w_2 + w_4 \\ w_3 + w_4 \\ w_1 \end{array}\right.$$

These inequalities impose several constraints on the weights associated with Φ, namely,

$w_1 > w_4$　　　$w_3 > w_4$　　　$w_2 > 0$

$w_1 > w_2$　　　$w_2 > w_4$　　　$w_3 > 0$

$w_1 > w_3$　　　　　　　　　　$w_4 > 0$

If we let $w_4 = 1$ and $w_2 = w_3 = 2$, it is necessary to assign $w_1 = 3$, because w_1 must be smaller than $w_2 + w_3$.

Now we have, for example, a true vertex (0,1,1,0), whose weighted sum is 4, and a false vertex (1,0,0,0), whose weighted sum is 3; consequently, $T = 7/2$ and the weight-threshold vector for Φ is

$V = \{3,2,2,1; \frac{7}{2}\}$. To find the corresponding vector for the original function f, note that x_1 and x_3 must be complemented. Thus f is a threshold function whose weight-threshold vector is

$$V = \{-3,2,-2,1; -\frac{3}{2}\} \quad \blacksquare$$

In more complex problems, and when the number of inequalities is large, it becomes necessary to resort to machine computations. By utilizing other properties of threshold functions it is possible to simplify somewhat the identification procedure, but all known methods still involve a solution of some complex system of equations. A listing of all threshold functions of up to seven variables can be found in various references (see, for example, Ref. 6). Such a listing, which usually contains the weights and threshold corresponding to each linearly separable function, is very helpful in the design of threshold networks.

The map as a tool in synthesizing threshold networks

So far we have been concerned mainly with the problem of identifying and realizing threshold functions. The next natural problem is that of syn-. thesizing networks constructed of threshold elements to realize any arbitrary switching function. One approach to such synthesis is to develop a procedure for the decomposition of nonthreshold functions into two or more factors, each of which will be a threshold function. In view of the difficulty of the problem and the lack of any effective procedures known to date, we shall limit our presentation to an introduction to the problem and two examples.

For functions of three or four variables, the identification problem may be solved by detecting certain patterns in the corresponding maps. A pattern of 1 cells is said to be an *admissible pattern* if it can be realized by a single threshold element. The admissible patterns for functions of three variables are shown in Fig. 7-7. Each admissible pattern may be

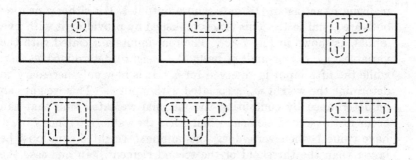

Fig. 7-7 Admissible patterns of three variables.

in any position on the map, provided that its basic topological structure is preserved. Clearly, any admissible pattern for functions of three variables is also an admissible pattern for functions of four or more variables, and so on. Note that, since the complement of a threshold function is also a threshold function, the patterns formed by 0 cells are admissible.

Analogously to the synthesis of AND-OR networks, a threshold-logic realization of an arbitrary switching function can now be accomplished by selecting a minimal number of admissible patterns such that each 1 cell of the map is covered by at least one admissible pattern.

Example Given the switching function

$$f(x_1,x_2,x_3,x_4) = \Sigma(2,3,6,7,10,12,14,15)$$

find a minimal threshold-logic realization. (By *minimal realization* we mean one which requires the smallest number of threshold elements.)

The map of f is shown in Fig. 7-8a, where the admissible patterns are marked by dotted lines. A quick test (see Prob. 7-10) reveals that f is not unate, and consequently not linearly separable. Hence we shall attempt to synthesize it as a cascade of two threshold elements, so that the first element realizes the admissible pattern g, and the second element realizes the admissible pattern h. By applying the techniques of the preceding section to the function $g(x_1,x_2,x_3,x_4) = \Sigma(2,3,6,7,15)$, the weight-threshold vector for the first element is found to be $V_g = \{-2,1,3,1; \frac{5}{2}\}$. Similarly, the weight-threshold vector for the element which realizes the admissible pattern h is found to be $V_h = \{2,1,1,-1; \frac{5}{2}\}$. These elements are shown in Fig. 7-8b.

If we select the threshold element which realizes g as the first element, then the second element must be such that it will realize h and at the same time allow g to propagate through it uninterrupted. In other words, the second element must, in addition to realizing h, act as an OR gate whose output is 1 if either g or h or both are equal to 1. This is accomplished by providing it with five inputs, as shown in Fig. 7-8c. The four inputs associated with the variables x_1, x_2, x_3, and x_4 have the weights determined earlier, while the fifth input is reserved for g. It is now only necessary to determine the weight w_g, associated with input g. This weight can be determined by computing the minimal weighted sum that can occur in the second element when g has the value 1. Since f must have value 1 whenever g does, this minimal weighted sum must be larger than the threshold of the second element. In our case the minimal weighted sum is w_g, and it occurs when $x_1 = x_2 = 0$ and

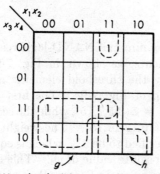

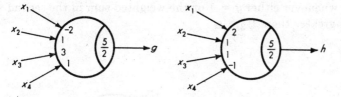

(a) Map for f exhibiting two admissible patterns.

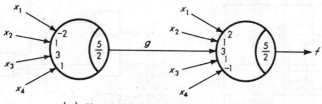

(b) Threshold elements realizing the admissible patterns.

(c) Threshold-logic realization of f.

Fig. 7-8 Synthesis of the function
$f(x_1,x_2,x_3,x_4) = \Sigma(2,3,6,7,10,12,14,15)$.

$x_3 = x_4 = 1$. Clearly, w_g must be larger than $\frac{5}{2}$, and therefore the value $w_g = 3$ has been selected. ∎

To simplify the computation of w_g, it can be set equal to (or larger than) the sum of the threshold and the absolute values of all negative weights of the second element. This, however, will not always yield a minimal value for w_g.

Example Consider the switching function

$f(x_1,x_2,x_3,x_4) = \Sigma(3,5,7,10,12,14,15)$

whose map is shown in Fig. 7-9a. Its minimal two-level AND-OR realization, shown in Fig. 7-9b, requires 20 diodes (or six transistors for the corresponding minimal NAND-logic realization) versus only two threshold elements, as shown in Fig. 7-9d. The admissible patterns realized by the threshold elements are indicated by the patches on the map of Fig. 7-9c. The first element realizes the threshold function $g = \Sigma(3,5,7,15)$, while the second element realizes the function $g + \Sigma(10,12,14,15)$. The weight w_g, associated with input g, has been specified to be $3\frac{1}{2}$, which is equal to the sum of the threshold and the absolute value of w_4. This ensures that f will be equal to 1 whenever g equals 1, regardless of the weighted sum of the variables within the second element. Hence the output f equals 1 whenever either $g = 1$ or the weighted sum in the second element is greater than $2\frac{1}{2}$. ∎

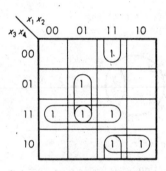

(a) Map showing a minimal set of prime implicants which cover f.

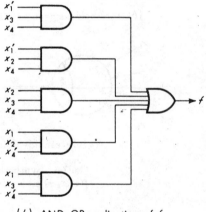

(b) AND-OR realization of f.

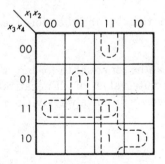

(c) Map showing the admissible pattern realized by each threshold element.

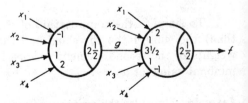

(d) A threshold-logic realization of f.

Fig. 7-9   Two realizations of $f(x_1,x_2,x_3,x_4) = \Sigma(3,5,7,10,12,14,15)$.

The synthesis procedure outlined in the preceding examples is particularly useful when the number of admissible patterns is small. Whenever the choice of admissible patterns is not obvious, it is necessary to construct a chart of patterns versus true vertices, analogous to the prime implicant chart, so that a minimal subset of admissible patterns can be determined. For functions of five or more variables it is possible to derive the set of all admissible patterns by a tabulation procedure [1], and then to construct the chart for selecting a minimal subset of admissible patterns.

By now the reader should have appreciated the complexity of the synthesis problem, which, like several other problems in threshold logic, is yet unsolved in its generality. Circuits may assume many different forms, and the cascade realization studied above is only one of them. A more comprehensive treatment of threshold logic is beyond the scope of this book, but is available in other sources, in particular, Refs. 1 and 3.

NOTES AND REFERENCES

Literally hundreds of papers and several books have been written on the subject of threshold logic. Most papers are concerned with the problems of identifying and realizing threshold functions. McNaughton [4] studied the properties of unate functions and established the unateness of a function as a necessary condition for its single-threshold-element realizability. Other properties of threshold functions, as well as synthesis procedures, have been studied by Elgot [2], Muroga et al. [5], Winder [6], Dertouzos [1], and Lewis and Coates [3].

1. Dertouzos, M.: "Threshold Logic: A Synthesis Approach," The MIT Press, Cambridge, Mass., 1965.
2. Elgot, C. C.: Truth Functions Realizable by Single Threshold Organs, *Proc. Ann. Symp. Switching Circuit Theory and Logical Design*, 1960; also in *AIEE Publ.* S-134, pp. 225–245, September, 1961.
3. Lewis, P. M., and C. L. Coates: "Threshold Logic," John Wiley & Sons, Inc., New York, 1967.
4. McNaughton, R.: Unate Truth Functions, *IRE Trans. Electron. Computers*, vol. EC-10, pp. 1–6, March, 1961.
5. Muroga, S., I. Toda, and S. Takasu, Theory of Majority Decision Elements, *J. Franklin Inst.*, vol. 271, pp. 376–418, May, 1961.
6. Winder, R. O.: Threshold Logic, doctoral dissertation for the Mathematics Department, Princeton University, Princeton, N.J., May, 1962.

PROBLEMS

7-1. Find the function $f(x_1, x_2, x_3, x_4)$ realized by each of the threshold networks shown in Fig. P7-1. Show the map of each function.

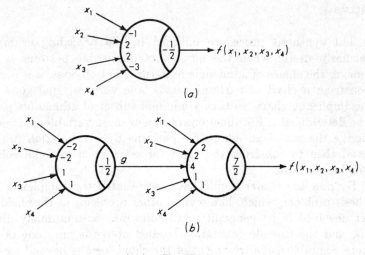

(a)

(b)

Fig. P7-1

7-2. By examining the linear inequalities, determine which of the following functions is a threshold function, and for each one that is, find the corresponding weight-threshold vector.

(a) $f_1(x_1,x_2,x_3) = \Sigma(1,2,3,7)$

(b) $f_2(x_1,x_2,x_3) = \Sigma(0,2,4,5,6)$

(c) $f_3(x_1,x_2,x_3) = \Sigma(0,3,5,6)$

7-3. For each of the functions of Prob. 7-2 which is realizable by a single threshold element, find a realization for $f'(x_1',x_2,x_3)$.

7-4. (a) Determine the function $f(x_1,x_2,x_3,x_4)$ realized by the network shown in Fig. P7-4.

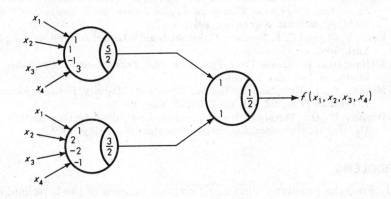

(b) Show that $f(x_1,x_2,x_3,x_4)$ can be realized by a single threshold element. Find such an element.

7-5. Consider the type of threshold functions for which all the weights are equal, that is, $w_1 = w_2 = \cdots = w_n$. In particular, those $f(x_1,x_2, \ldots ,x_n)$ for which

$$f(x_1,x_2, \ldots ,x_n) = 1 \qquad \text{if and only if} \qquad \sum_{i=1}^{n} x_i \geq \frac{T}{w}$$

$$f(x_1,x_2, \ldots ,x_n) = 0 \qquad \text{if and only if} \qquad \sum_{i=1}^{n} x_i < \frac{T}{w}$$

(a) Determine the value of f when (1) $T/w = 0$, (2) $T/w > n$, (3) $0 < T/w \leq n$.

(b) Show that for some positive integer k, f can be expressed as a symmetric function, i.e.,

$$f(x_1,x_2, \ldots ,x_n) = S_{k,k+1}, \ldots ,_n(x_1,x_2, \ldots ,x_n)$$

and determine k in terms of T and w.

A function of this type, which can be specified as a symmetric threshold function, is called a *voting function*. If, in addition, n is odd and $k = (n + 1)/2$, then the function $f(x_1,x_2, \ldots ,x_n)$ is said to be a *majority function*.

7-6. (a) Prove that if $f(x_1,x_2, \ldots ,x_n)$ is a threshold function with weight-threshold vector $V_1 = \{w_1,w_2, \ldots ,w_n; T\}$, then its dual, $f_d(x_1,x_2, \ldots ,x_n)$, is also a threshold function. Determine its weight-threshold vector.

(b) Prove that if f is a threshold function, then so is

$$g = x_i'f + x_if_d$$

where x_i may or may not be a member of the set $\{x_1,x_2, \ldots ,x_n\}$. Find the weight-threshold vector of g.

7-7. (a) Prove that if $f(x_1,x_2, \ldots ,x_n)$ is a threshold function with weight-threshold vector $\{w_1,w_2, \ldots ,w_n; T\}$, then $G = x_p + f$ and $H = x_pf$ are also threshold functions, where x_p may or may not be a member of the set $\{x_1,x_2, \ldots ,x_n\}$. Find w_p and the weight-threshold vectors for G and H.

Hint: Define two numbers M and N such that

$$M = \sum_{\substack{\text{all positive} \\ \text{weights}}} w_i \qquad N = \sum_{\substack{\text{all negative} \\ \text{weights}}} w_i$$

and if convenient, use them in the expression for w_p.

(b) Given that $f(x_1,x_2,x_3) = x_1x_2 + x_3'$ is a threshold function, utilize the foregoing result to show that

$$f_1(x_1,x_2,x_3,x_4) = x_2 + x_3' + x_4$$

and

$$f_2(x_1,x_2,x_3,x_4) = x_1x_2x_4 + x_2x_3'x_4$$

are threshold functions. Show in each case the weight-threshold vector.

7-8. The functions $f_1(x_1,x_2,x_3)$ and $f_2(x_1,x_2,x_3)$ are each realizable by a single threshold element. The weight-threshold vectors of these elements are, respectively,

$$V_1 = \{-1,-1,1;0\} \qquad V_2 = \{1,2,-1;2\}$$

Is the function

$$f(x_1,x_2,x_3,x_4) = x_4f_1(x_1,x_2,x_3) + x_4'f_2(x_1,x_2,x_3)$$

realizable by a single threshold element? If yes, give its weight-threshold vector. If not, indicate clearly why it is not a threshold function.

7-9. Prove that if an expression corresponding to a function that is positive (negative) in x_i contains both x_i and x_i', then every occurrence of the literal x_i' (x_i) is redundant.

7-10. (a) Prove that a necessary and sufficient condition for a function to be unate is that all its prime implicants intersect in a common implicant. [For example, the common implicant for

$$f(x_1,x_2,x_3,x_4) = \Sigma(0,1,3,4,5,6,7,12,13)$$

is the minterm 5.]

(b) Prove that the minimal sum-of-products form of a unate function is unique and consists of all prime implicants.

Hint: Use Prob. 7-9 and the fact that the conjunction of all product prime implicants of a unate function cannot be zero.

7-11. Use the result of Prob. 7-10 to determine which of the following functions is unate. Show its minimal form.

(a) $f_1(x_1,x_2,x_3,x_4) = \Sigma(1,2,3,8,9,10,11,12,14)$
(b) $f_2(x_1,x_2,x_3,x_4) = \Sigma(0,8,9,10,11,12,13,14)$
(c) $f_3(x_1,x_2,x_3,x_4) = \Sigma(2,3,6,10,11,12,14,15)$

7-12. For each of the following functions find a two-element cascade realization of the type illustrated in Fig. 7-8c.

(a) $f_1(x_1,x_2,x_3,x_4) = \Sigma(2,3,6,7,8,9,13,15)$
(b) $f_2(x_1,x_2,x_3,x_4) = \Sigma(0,3,4,5,6,7,8,11,12,15)$

7-13. (*a*) Show that the symmetric function $S_{1,2}(x_1,x_2,x_3)$ is not linearly separable.

(*b*) Find a two-element threshold-logic realization of $S_{1,2}(x_1,x_2,x_3)$. *Hint:* Note that

$$S_{1,2}(x_1,x_2,x_3) = S_{\text{all } a_i \geq 1}(x_1,x_2,x_3) \cdot S_{\text{all } a_i \leq 2}(x_1,x_2,x_3)$$

7-14. Show a threshold-logic realization of a full adder requiring only two threshold elements. (Note that both the sum and carry-out must be generated.)

8
Reliable Design and Fault Diagnosis

The problems of determining whether or not a digital circuit operates correctly, and of ensuring its correct operation even when some of its parts fail, are of both practical concern and theoretical interest. Present-day digital systems may be disabled by almost any internal failure, and the trend toward miniaturization makes the problems of maintenance and fault detection even more urgent. Digital systems may suffer two classes of faults: temporary faults, which occur due to noise and the nonideal transient behavior of switching components, and permanent faults, which result from component failures. The transient behavior of switching circuits is studied in Sec. 8-1, while the remaining sections are devoted to the diagnosis of switching circuits and to methods of improving their reliability by using various redundancy techniques.

8-1 HAZARDS

In the preceding chapters certain idealized assumptions regarding the operation of switching components have been made. Circuits have been assumed to respond instantaneously to input signals, and signal propagation time has been assumed to be zero. In practice, however, the delays associated with switching components cause noninstantaneous changes of states, which in turn may result in hazards. In this section we shall examine this transient phenomenon and present methods for the detection of hazards and the design of hazard-free switching circuits.

Static hazards

Consider the function $T(x,y,z) = \Sigma(2,3,5,7)$, whose map is shown in Fig. 8-1a. Two minimal implementations of T by means of gate and contact logics are shown in Fig. 8-1b and c, respectively. Suppose that the value of inputs y and z is 1 and that the value of input x is being changed from 0 to 1. Clearly, the value of T must remain 1 regardless of the value of x. As the value of x changes, the transmission path through the network of Fig. 8-1b changes from gate 1 to gate 2, or from the upper to the lower branch of the contact network of Fig. 8-1c. In

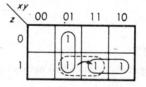

(a) Map for $T = x'y + xz$.

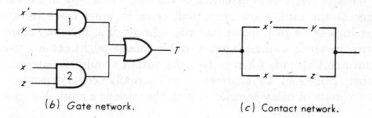

(b) Gate network.   (c) Contact network.

Fig. 8-1 Networks containing static hazards.

the ideal situation this change is instantaneous, and the value of T remains constantly 1. In practice, however, different delays are associated with gates 1 and 2, and the closing and opening of relay contacts do not always occur simultaneously. As a consequence, if the delay of gate 1, for example, is smaller than that of gate 2, and if x changes from 0 to 1 (while $y = z = 1$), then the transmission $x'y$ through gate 1 will become 0 shortly before the transmission xz through gate 2 becomes equal to 1. During this period the output T will be 0. Analogously, if contact x' opens before contact x closes, there will be a short time interval in which both x and x' are open and the value of T is incorrect. This phenomenon is known as *static hazard* and is indicated by the arrow in the map of Fig. 8-1a.

The static hazard shown may be removed by including the prime implicant yz in the expression for T, as indicated by the dotted subcube in the map of Fig. 8-1a, that is, $T = x'y + xz + yz$. The resulting circuits are shown in Fig. 8-2. Clearly, when $y = z = 1$, the output T will be 1 regardless of the delays associated with x' and x.

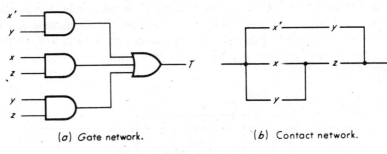

(a) Gate network.   (b) Contact network.

Fig. 8-2   Hazard-free networks.

We shall restrict our attention to the case where only single-variable changes at the inputs are permitted, since in other cases it becomes almost impossible to prevent hazards. In general, a *static hazard* is a situation in which a single input-variable change might cause a momentary incorrect output, when in fact the output should remain constant. Whether or not such an incorrect output actually occurs depends on the exact amounts of delay associated with the various circuit elements.

Design of hazard-free switching circuits

Two input combinations are said to be *adjacent* if they differ by the value of just a single input variable. For example, $x'yz$ and xyz are adjacent. A transition between a pair of adjacent input combinations which co spond to identical output conditions contains a static hazard if it makes possible the generation of a momentary spurious output. Such hazards may occur whenever there exists a pair of adjacent input combinations which produce the same output and there is no subcube (in the map) containing both combinations.

As a consequence, a switching circuit is hazard-free whenever all changes of adjacent input combinations which require constant output conditions occur within some subcube of the corresponding function; that is, every pair of adjacent 1 cells and every pair of adjacent 0 cells in the map of the corresponding function is covered by at least one subcube. An expression derived from such a collection of subcubes is called *hazard-free*. As an example, consider the function $T(x,y,z) = \Sigma(1,3,4,5)$, whose map is shown in Fig. 8-3a.

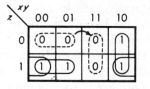

(a) Map for $T = \Sigma(1,3,4,5)$.

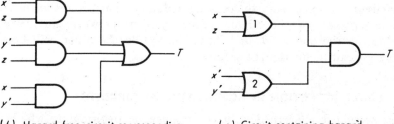

(b) Hazard-free circuit corresponding to $T = x'z + y'z + xy'$.

(c) Circuit containing hazard corresponding to $T = (x + z)(x' + y')$.

Fig. 8-3   Illustration of a hazard due to subcubes formed of 0 cells.

From the subcubes of the 1's, we conclude that the circuit which corresponds to $T = x'z + y'z + xy'$, as shown in Fig. 8-3b, is hazard-free. Indeed, a brief check verifies this conclusion. However, if we determine T as a product of sums by grouping the 0's, we obtain the circuit of Fig. 8-3c. Observing that $T = (x + z)(x' + y') = x'z + y'z + xy'$, we might jump to the conclusion that this circuit also is hazard-free. This is not the case, since the circuit contains a hazard, as indicated by the arrow on the map. If x changes from 0 to 1, while $y = 1$ and $z = 0$, and the delay of gate 1 is smaller than that of gate 2, both gates produce for a short duration a 1 output, and consequently the output T is equal to 1. This hazard may be eliminated by adding the subcube $y' + z$ to the expression of T so that $T = (x + z)(x' + y')(y' + z)$. It is easy to verify that the corresponding circuit, which is the dual to that of Fig. 8-3b, is completely hazard-free.

It follows that if a sum-of-products expression is hazard-free when formed of the 1 cells, the corresponding circuit must be constructed in the same unfactored form in order to remain hazard-free. And, analogously, if a hazard-free expression is derived from the 0 cells and is given in a product-of-sums form, it must be implemented in that form in order for the resulting circuit to be hazard-free. (The preceding must be regarded only as sufficient conditions, since there are certain hazard-free circuits which do not satisfy them.) In general, it can be shown that a two-level circuit which corresponds to a hazard-free expression formed of the 1 cells (0 cells) is also hazard-free in its 0 cells (1 cells). The proof is left to the reader as an exercise.

The necessity of eliminating hazards confronts the designer with two conflicting considerations. On the one hand, in order to obtain simpler circuits, it is advantageous to minimize the transmission functions. But minimal functions are the most vulnerable to hazards. As a consequence, in order to avoid hazards and increase the reliability of the circuit, it is necessary to add some redundant gates and thus increase the complexity of the circuit. This trade-off between simplicity of design, on the one hand, and its reliability, on the other, will become more evident in subsequent sections.

8-2 FAULT DETECTION IN COMBINATIONAL CIRCUITS

This section is concerned with the problem of determining whether a combinational circuit operates correctly or is impaired by some malfunction. We shall be primarily concerned with permanent faults due to component failures. It is assumed that other procedures will be employed to protect the circuit against the effects of transient faults.

The faults

One way of determining whether a combinational circuit operates properly is by applying to the circuit all possible input combinations and comparing the resultant outputs with either the corresponding truth table or a faultless version of the same circuit. Any deviation indicates the presence of some fault. Moreover, if a known relationship exists between the various possible faults and the deviations of output patterns, it is possible to diagnose the fault and to classify it at least within a subset of faults whose effects on the circuit outputs are identical.

Such exhaustive tests are generally very long, and consequently impractical. Moreover, for most circuits, they are unnecessary, and it is usually possible to detect faults within a circuit, or even to locate them, by considerably shorter tests. Such tests are referred to as either *fault-detection* or *fault-location tests*, depending on whether they just reveal the presence of a fault or in addition locate and diagnose it. The precise identification of the fault that has occurred is very complicated and often impossible, since two different faults may give rise to identical incorrect responses. Therefore the main effort is directed to devising tests which just locate the impaired module or subcircuit.

In order to arrive at fault-detection and diagnosis procedures which will be relatively easy to devise and short enough to be practical, it is necessary to make several simplifying assumptions. The testing procedures are developed for circuits composed of loop-free interconnections of AND, OR, NOT, NAND, and NOR gates; that is, feedback loops are not allowed in the circuits being tested. Initially we shall be concerned with procedures for the detection of *single* faults. This limitation does not, of course, exclude the detection of most double and other multiple faults, but it emphasizes that only single faults will be detected in all cases, while some multiple faults may not be detected. From a practical point of view this is not a severe limitation, since it still permits the detection of the *first* fault, and most circuits are reliable enough so that the probability of occurrence of multiple faults is rather small. Clearly, if a circuit contains logical redundancies, not all faults are detectable, since a redundant connection may be cut without altering the logical value of the function.

In the circuits most commonly used at present an open connection is logically equivalent to having that connection either "stuck-at-one" or "stuck-at-zero." In designing fault-detection tests we shall be concerned only with those faults which cause any wire to be (or appear logically to be) *stuck-at-zero* or *stuck-at-one* (abbreviated *s-a-*0 and *s-a-*1). Restricting our consideration to just this class of faults is technically justified, since most circuit failures fall in this class, and many other failures exhibit symptomatically identical effects.

The fault table

Let $x_1, x_2, \ldots, x_n$ be the inputs to a combinational circuit and let f be its fault-free output. Let f_α denote the output of the circuit in the presence of fault α. As an example consider the circuit shown in Fig. 8-4a and suppose that any one of its wires m, n, p, and q may be either *s-a-*0 or *s-a-*1. We shall denote by m_0 and m_1 the faults of wire m *s-a-*0 and *s-a-*1, respectively. Similar notation is used for the other wires. The truth table for this circuit is shown in Fig. 8-4b, where column f denotes the fault-free output while, for example, columns f_{m_0} and f_{m_1}

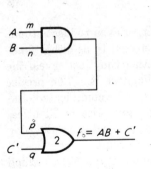

$f_0 = AB + C'$

(a) Circuit to be tested.

Inputs ABC	f	Outputs in presence of faults							
		f_{m_0}	f_{n_0}	f_{p_0}	f_{q_0}	f_{m_1}	f_{n_1}	f_{p_1}	f_{q_1}
000	1	1	1	1	0	1	1	1	1
001	0	0	0	0	0	0	0	1	1
010	1	1	1	1	0	1	1	1	1
011	0	0	0	0	0	1	0	1	1
100	1	1	1	1	0	1	1	1	1
101	0	0	0	0	0	0	1	1	1
110	1	1	1	1	1	1	1	1	1
111	1	0	0	0	1	1	1	1	1

(b) Truth table for the fault-free output and outputs in the presence of faults.

Inputs ABC	Possible faults				
	$\{m_0, n_0, p_0\}$	q_0	m_1	n_1	$\{p_1, q_1\}$
000		1			
001					1
010		1			
√ 011			①		1
100		1			
√ 101				①	1
110					
√ 111	①				

(c) Fault table.

Fig. 8-4 Derivation of minimal set of fault-detection tests.

correspond, respectively, to the circuit outputs in the presence of faults m_0 and m_1, and so on.

An input combination is referred to as a *test* for fault f_α if, in response to that input combination, the output of the correctly operating circuit is different from that of the circuit impaired by fault f_α. Hence, for example, the input combination 111 is the only test for detecting the fault f_{m_0} in the circuit of Fig. 8-4a, since it is the only input combination for which the values in columns f and f_{m_0} are different. On the other hand, fault f_{q_1} can be detected by the tests 001, 011, and 101, and so on, for other faults. More precisely, an input combination $a_1, a_2, \ldots, a_n$ is a test for detecting fault f_α if and only if

$$f(a_1, a_2, \ldots, a_n) \oplus f_\alpha(a_1, a_2, \ldots, a_n) = 1 \qquad (8\text{-}1)$$

where $f(a_1, a_2, \ldots, a_n)$ and $f_\alpha(a_1, a_2, \ldots, a_n)$ denote, respectively, the fault-free output and the incorrect output in response to the input $a_1, a_2, \ldots, a_n$. Thus, in order to determine all the tests that detect a fault f_α, it is necessary to take the modulo-2 sum of columns f and f_α in the truth table.

In the truth table shown in Fig. 8-4b, we observe that columns f_{m_0}, f_{n_0}, and f_{p_0} are identical, and so are columns f_{p_1} and f_{q_1}. In other words, the circuit output in the presence of fault f_{p_1} is identical with the output in the presence of f_{q_1}. Hence, there is no input combination which can distinguish fault f_{p_1} from f_{q_1}. Such faults are called equivalent faults. In general, two faults f_α and f_β are said to be *equivalent faults* if the function realized by the circuit with fault f_α is identical with the function realized by the same circuit with fault f_β. Faults that are not equivalent are said to be distinguishable faults. The truth table can usually be simplified by combining the columns that correspond to every set of equivalent faults. In the foregoing example, columns f_{p_1} and f_{q_1} may be combined, and similarly columns f_{m_0}, f_{n_0}, and f_{p_0} may be combined. In some situations it may occur that a column f_α is identical with the fault-free column f. As a result the modulo-2 sum of $f \oplus f_\alpha$ will be 0 for every input combination and, consequently, *fault f_α cannot be detected*. Undetectable faults usually occur in redundant circuits and they may be deleted from the truth table.

If we combine equivalent faults and take the modulo-2 sum of column f with all other columns which correspond to incorrect outputs, we obtain the fault table shown in Fig. 8-4c. This table is a valuable tool in determining the minimal set of tests for detecting all the faults in the circuit of Fig. 8-4a.

A *fault table* is a table in which there is a row for every possible test (i.e., input combination) and a column for every fault. A 1 is entered at the intersection of the ith row and the jth column if the fault corresponding to the jth column can be detected by the ith test. The problem of finding a minimal set of tests is now reduced to the problem of finding a minimal set of rows so that every column has a 1 entry in at least one row of the set. Such a set of rows will be said to *cover* the fault table. It is evident that the problem of finding a minimal set of rows which cover a fault table is identical with the prime-implicant covering problem studied in Chap. 4.

Covering the fault table

The fault table can now be further simplified by the removal of unnecessary rows and columns. A column i is said to *dominate* column j if i has a 1 in at least every row in which j has a 1. The dominating column

i may be removed, since any test which detects fault j will also detect fault i. For example, the column corresponding to p_1 and q_1 of Fig. 8-4c may be eliminated since it dominates column n_1. Analogously, a row j is *dominated* by row i if i has a 1 in at least every column in which j has a 1. The dominated row j may be eliminated, since it corresponds to a test that can always be replaced by test i. Thus, for example, row 001 can be removed since it is dominated by row 101 and, similarly, rows 010 and 100 can be removed because they are equivalent to and hence dominated by row 000. Clearly row 110 corresponds to a test which does not detect any fault and can therefore be removed from the table.

In order to find the smallest cover of the simplified fault table, the techniques of finding minimal switching expressions in Sec. 4-5 may be employed. The *essential tests* are determined by observing which faults can be detected by just a single test. Additional tests are added until a minimal cover is obtained. In our example there are three essential tests, 011, 101, and 111, which detect all faults except q_0. A fourth test 000 detects q_0 and thus completes the set of tests that detect all single faults in the circuit being tested.

It is convenient to distinguish between a *fault-detection test*, which refers to a single application of values to the input terminals, and a *fault-detection experiment*, which refers to a set of tests leading to a definite conclusion as to whether or not the circuit operates correctly for all input combinations. In our example the experiment consists of four tests as follows (though not necessarily in this order):

1. *Apply* 011: If the output is $T = 1$, circuit is faulty and the experiment may be stopped; if $T = 0$, apply second test.
2. *Apply* 101: If $T = 1$, circuit is faulty; otherwise, apply next test.
3. *Apply* 111: If $T = 0$, circuit is faulty; otherwise, apply next test.
4. *Apply* 000: If $T = 0$, circuit is faulty; if $T = 1$, circuit operates correctly.

The fault table provides a tool for the determination of a *minimal* set of fault-detection tests for combinational logic circuits. As a tool it is valid even if different sets of faults and different types of tests are assumed. But for larger circuits, because of the size of the fault table, the computation time and memory requirements become very large and the procedure becomes prohibitive. It can be made more efficient by considering only those tests which detect large numbers of faults, but the problem of finding such a set of tests is not simple. Different philosophies for more efficient design of fault-detection experiments are introduced in subsequent sections.

8-3 FAULT-LOCATION EXPERIMENTS

To locate, or diagnose, a fault it is not only necessary to detect it, but the fault must also be distinguished from all other nonequivalent faults. This can be accomplished by means of an expanded fault table which will subsequently be referred to as the fault-location table. We shall consider two types of experiments:

1. *Preset experiments* in which the entire set of tests is predetermined independently of the circuit's response.
2. *Adaptive experiments*, in which the test to be presently applied depends on the response of the circuit to the preceding tests.

Preset experiments

The *fault-location table* consists of all the rows and columns of the fault (detection) table and, in addition, it consists of a new column for each pair of faults of the fault table. Thus, if a fault table has k columns, the corresponding fault-location table will have $k + k(k - 1)/2 = k(k + 1)/2$ columns. The 1-entries in the new column $f_i f_j$ are obtained by taking the bit-by-bit modulo-2 sum of columns f_i and f_j. As in the fault-detection case, the problem of finding a minimal set of tests to locate all the nonequivalent faults in the circuit is transformed to the well-known prime-implicant covering problem, and the procedures studied in Chap. 4 are applicable in this case as well.

As an example, consider the fault table shown in Fig. 8-5a. It consists of six rows $T_1, T_2, \ldots, T_6$ corresponding to six possible tests, and six columns $f_1, f_2, \ldots, f_6$ corresponding to six possible faults. By taking all pairwise modulo-2 sums of these columns we obtain the entire fault-location table of Fig. 8-5a. The 1-entries of column $f_i f_j$ indicate the tests that distinguish between faults f_i and f_j, since either f_i or f_j (but not both) can be detected by each of these tests. For example, faults f_2 and f_4 can be distinghished by either T_3 or T_4, and so on.

To find a minimal set of fault-location tests that covers this table, we first identify T_3 and T_4 as the essential tests. The elimination of the essential rows and the (check-marked) columns covered by them yields the reduced table of Fig. 8-5b. Column $f_4 f_5$ can now be eliminated since it is equivalent to column $f_1 f_6$. Row T_5 can be eliminated because it is dominated by row T_6, and, subsequently, column $f_2 f_3$ can be eliminated since it becomes equivalent to column f_1. The final table can be covered by any two of the three tests $T_1, T_2,$ and T_6. If we choose T_2 and T_6 and add them to the essential tests, we obtain the complete set of preset fault-location tests $\{T_2, T_3, T_4, T_6\}$.

| | ✓ | ✓ | ✓ | ✓ | ✓ | ✓ | ✓ | ✓ | ✓ | ✓ | | ✓ | ✓ | ✓ | ✓ | ✓ | ✓ | | ✓ | ✓ |
	f_1	f_2	f_3	f_4	f_5	f_6	f_1f_2	f_1f_3	f_1f_4	f_1f_5	f_1f_6	f_2f_3	f_2f_4	f_2f_5	f_2f_6	f_3f_4	f_3f_5	f_3f_6	f_4f_5	f_4f_6	f_5f_6
T_1				1	1				1	1			1	1		1	1	1		1	1
T_2	1		1		1		1			1	1		1		1		1	1			1
✓ T_3			①	1				1	1			1	1		1	1			1	1	
✓ T_4	①	1					1	1				1	1	1	1	1	1				
T_5	1					1	1	1	1	1				1				1		1	1
T_6	1		1			1	1		1	1		1			1	1	1			1	1

Fault table

(a) Fault-location table.

Test	Faults				
	f_1	f_6	f_1f_6	f_2f_3	f_4f_5
T_1		1	1		1
T_2	1		1	1	1
T_5	1	1			
T_6	1	1		1	

(b) Reduced table.

Fault	Test			
	T_2	T_3	T_4	T_6
f	1	0	1	1
f_1	0	0	1	0
f_2	1	0	0	1
f_3	0	0	0	0
f_4	1	1	1	1
f_5	0	1	1	1
f_6	1	0	1	0

(c) Fault dictionary for preset experiment
(for the circuit output shown in Fig. 8-6a).

Fig. 8-5 Derivation of a minimal preset fault-location experiment.

In the case of preset fault-location experiments, it is convenient to have a *fault dictionary* which consists of a listing of the circuit outputs when any of the possible faults occur. The fault dictionary for the foregoing example for the outputs of the fault-free circuit shown in Fig. 8-6a is given in Fig. 8-5c, where the row corresponding to f shows the response of the correctly operating circuit. Given the dictionary and the circuit response to the set of tests, it is easy to determine whether a fault occurred and to locate that fault.

In most practical situations the circuit is constructed of modules, and it is only required to locate the faults within the limits of the modules. In such cases if a fault is located within a certain module, the entire module is replaced and hence it is not necessary to distinguish among faults which occur within the same module. For example, suppose that faults f_1 and f_6 of Fig. 8-5b occur within the same module and faults f_4 and f_5 occur within another module. Consequently, both columns f_1f_6 and f_4f_5 may be deleted and the reduced table thus consists of only two columns and can be covered by test T_6. In this case the entire fault-location experiment consists of the three tests $\{T_3, T_4, T_6\}$.

Adaptive experiments

In the preset testing procedure all the tests must always be applied regardless of the circuit output; moreover, the length of the experiment is independent of the order in which the various tests are applied. The location of the fault can be determined by means of the fault dictionary only after all the prespecified number of tests have been applied. We now consider *adaptive experiments*, which are also known as *sequential decision procedures*, and in which the selection of the next test to be applied is determined by the circuit response to the previous tests. A convenient way to describe adaptive experiments is by means of the adaptive tree.

The *adaptive* (or *sequential decision*) *tree* is a directed graph whose nodes correspond to the various tests and whose branches correspond to the different circuit responses to these tests. In particular, one of the branches emanating from some node T_j is associated with the correct circuit response to test T_j while the other branch is associated with an incorrect response to that test. These branches will be labeled P to indicate "pass" or correct response and F to indicate a failure. The initial branch that enters the first node is associated with the set of all possible faults $(f_0, f_1, \ldots, f_p)$, where for convenience we refer to f_0, the fault-free circuit, as a "fault." The branches emanating from the first node are each associated with a subset of faults that may affect the circuit, depending on the outcome of the first test. Clearly, these are disjoint subsets whose union includes the entire initial set of faults. The subset of faults associated with the branch entering a given node is partitioned into two disjoint subsets associated with the branches leaving that node. Each such subset contains those faults that can occur in the circuit, depending on whether the corresponding test passed or failed. The tree terminates when all its end branches are each associated with just a single fault. A sequence of branches, starting at the initial branch and terminating at an end branch, is referred to as a *path* in the tree. The *length* of the path is defined as the number of nodes in the path. Each path describes a sequence of tests which, when applied to the circuit, identifies and locates the fault associated with its end branch. Obviously each tree consists of $p + 1$ paths (not necessarily of equal length) corresponding to the fault-free circuit and to the p distinct faults.

The problem now is how to define the minimal adaptive tree and, having defined it, how to construct it. There are two common methods of defining minimal trees. The first one minimizes the total length of all $p + 1$ paths, that is, minimizes the sum of the lengths of all the paths. The second method minimizes the length of the longest path and thus yields a tree in which no path is longer than some value k. The minimal such k is then referred to as the length of the minimal tree.

Designing adaptive experiments

The next problem is how to determine the sequence of tests; or, to start with, what should be the first test. In general there is no algorithm for constructing the minimal tree, and an exhaustive trial and error is necessary. It is obvious, however, that such an exhaustive procedure is so complicated and time-consuming, even for relatively small circuits, that it is considered impractical. A different heuristic approach which usually yields nearly minimal trees and often yields minimal ones is to select in each step the row in the fault table which has the most nearly equal distribution of 0's and 1's. In other words, at each node we select a test that partitions the incoming subset of faults into the most nearly equal subsets of faults.

As an example consider the construction of an adaptive experiment for the fault table of Fig. 8-5a. If we add to this table a column corresponding to the fault-free output, we obtain the fault table of Fig. 8-6a. Following the heuristic approach we may choose either T_2 or T_6 as the first test, since each of these rows has three 1's and four 0's. The trees corresponding to these initial tests are shown in Fig. 8-6b and Fig. 8-6c, respectively. In the first case the initial set of faults $(f_0 f_1 f_2 f_3 f_4 f_5 f_6)$ is partitioned into two subsets: $(f_1 f_3 f_5)$ is the subset that corresponds to a test that failed, i.e., the response to T_2 indicates that one of the above three faults exists; $(f_0 f_2 f_4 f_6)$ is the subset of possible faults if the initial test passed. In the second step it is necessary to distinguish between these two subsets. To distinguish between f_1, f_3, and f_5 we need a test that partitions these faults into two subsets. Clearly, any one of the tests T_1, T_3, T_4, T_5, and T_6 can be selected. To distinguish between the faults f_0, f_2, f_4, and f_6 we must employ at least three tests, since there is no test that partitions the above subset into two equal-length subsets. Hence, the longest path in the tree whose initial node is T_2 is of length 4. This length is identical with the length of the preset experiment derived in the preceding section. However if we start the experiment with test T_6, we obtain the tree in Fig. 8-6c. This tree, which is the minimal one according to each of the previous definitions, has paths of maximal length 3 and leads, therefore, to experiments that are always shorter than the preset experiment discussed before.

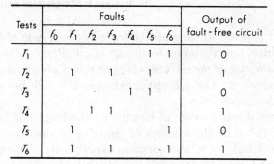

Tests	Faults							Output of fault-free circuit
	f_0	f_1	f_2	f_3	f_4	f_5	f_6	
T_1						1	1	0
T_2		1		1		1		1
T_3					1	1		0
T_4			1	1				1
T_5	1						1	0
T_6		1		1			1	1

(a) Fault table.

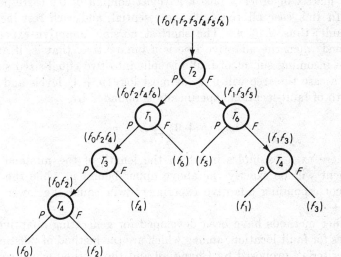

(b) Adaptive four-level tree with T_2 as initial test.

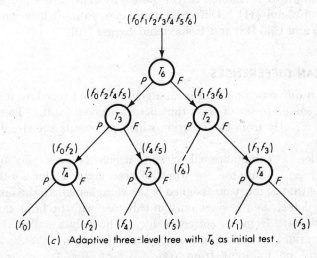

(c) Adaptive three-level tree with T_6 as initial test.

Fig. 8-6 Design of adaptive decision trees.

Clearly, the preset testing procedure is a special case of the adaptive testing procedure, and therefore *the length of an adaptive experiment need never exceed the length of the corresponding minimal preset experiment.* In most cases, however, the adaptive experiments will be considerably shorter than the preset ones.

We can establish a range of bounds on the length of fault-location experiments. Let p be the number of faults to be distinguished and let L designate the length of a fault-location experiment. The upper bound on the length of L may be provided by a fault table which consists of an identity matrix of order p plus a leftmost column of 0's corresponding to f_0. In this case all the tests are essential, and each test locates a single fault; thus, $L \leq p$. The shortest possible adaptive experiment is obtained when the adaptive tree is a binary tree, that is, if at each node the incoming subset of faults is split into two equal-sized subsets. In such a case the tree will have at most $\log_2 (p + 1)$ levels and hence the length of fault-location experiments is bounded by

$$\log_2 (p + 1) \leq L \leq p$$

There exist examples in which the length of the minimal preset experiment will be exactly the above upper bound p, while the length of the corresponding adaptive experiment will equal the lower bound $\log_2 (p + 1)$.

Other methods have been developed for generating adaptive decision trees for fault location, among which are the method of "distinguishability criteria" proposed by Chang [5] and the method which assigns a priori probabilities of failure to the nonequivalent faults proposed by Koren and Kohavi [11]. Different approaches to fault location can be found in Su and Cho [18] and Kohavi and Berger [10].

8-4 BOOLEAN DIFFERENCES

The Boolean difference method is an algebraic-type procedure for determining the complete set of tests that detect a given fault. These tests are derived directly from the function which represents the circuit being tested.

Consider a combinational circuit which realizes the function $f(x_1, x_2, \ldots, x_n)$. Suppose we want to test input x_i for s-a-0. The logical value that x_i must be assigned is the complement to the fault that we want to detect, i.e., 1, since only in this case will the fault cause the output to deviate from its correct value. The values assigned to the remaining variables (excluding x_i) are such that $f(x_1, \ldots, x_{i-1}, 1, x_{i+1}, \ldots, x_n)$ will be different from $f(x_1, \ldots, x_{i-1}, 0, x_{i+1}, \ldots, x_n)$ and, therefore, the value of x_i will determine the value of the output and the fault will be detectable.

Definition 8-1   The *Boolean difference* of a function $f(x_1,x_2, \ldots ,x_n)$ with respect to one of its variables x_i is defined

$$\frac{df(X)}{dx_i} = f(x_1, \ldots ,x_{i-1},0,x_{i+1}, \ldots ,x_n)$$

$$\oplus f(x_1, \ldots ,x_{i-1},1,x_{i+1}, \ldots ,x_n) \quad (8\text{-}2)$$

It will subsequently be convenient to denote $f(x_1, \ldots ,x_{i-1},0, \ldots ,x_n)$ by $f_i(0)$ and $f(x_1, \ldots ,x_{i-1},1, \ldots ,x_n)$ by $f_i(1)$, and we obtain

$$\frac{df(X)}{dx_i} = f_i(0) \oplus f_i(1) \qquad (8\text{-}2')$$

If $df(X)/dx_i \equiv 0$, then $f_i(0) \equiv f_i(1)$ and it implies that $f(X)$ is independent of x_i. If $df(X)/dx_i \equiv 1$, then any change in the value of x_i will affect the value of f, regardless of the values of the remaining variables. In general $df(X)/dx_i$ will be a function of some (or all) the variables. Our objective is to find those values of the variables for which $df(X)/dx_i = 1$, since these are the values that cause the output f to be incorrect when a fault exists on line x_i. Thus, in order to test x_i for a s-a-0 fault, it is necessary to assign the value 1 to x_i and to assign all other variables in such a way that $df(X)/dx_i = 1$. Consequently, the set of tests which detect the fault x_i s-a-0 is given by the equation

$$x_i \frac{df(X)}{dx_i} = 1 \qquad (8\text{-}3)$$

Analogously, the set of tests which detect the fault x_i s-a-1 is given by the equation

$$x_i' \frac{df(X)}{dx_i} = 1 \qquad (8\text{-}4)$$

As an example consider the circuit of Fig. 8-7. The Boolean difference with respect to x_3 is determined as follows:

$$f(X) = (x_1 + x_2)x_3' + x_3 x_4$$
$$\frac{df}{dx_3} = f_3(0) \oplus f_3(1) = (x_1 + x_2) \oplus x_4 = x_1'x_2'x_4 + x_1 x_4' + x_2 x_4'$$

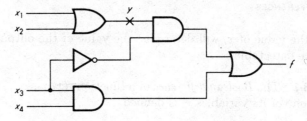

Fig. 8-7 A combinational circuit.

The tests for detecting a *s-a-0* fault at x_3 can now be determined from Eq. (8-3).

$$x_3 \frac{df}{dx_3} = x_1'x_2'x_3x_4 + x_1x_3x_4' + x_2x_3x_4' = 1$$

This expression is equal to 1 when any one of the three product terms equals 1. Thus, each of the following input combinations is a test for x_3 *s-a-0*.

$$(x_1,x_2,x_3,x_4) = \{(0,0,1,1),\ (1,\emptyset,1,0),\ (\emptyset,1,1,0)\}$$

Similarly, the tests for detecting a *s-a-1* fault at x_3 are determined from Eq. (8-4) as follows:

$$x' \frac{df}{dx_3} = x_1'x_2'x_3'x_4 + x_1x_3'x_4' + x_2x_3'x_4' = 1$$

Hence,

$$(x_1,x_2,x_3,x_4) = \{(0,0,0,1),\ (1,\emptyset,0,0),\ (\emptyset,1,0,0)\}$$

Properties of Boolean differences

For more complex circuits a significant amount of algebraic manipulations may be required for the determination of the Boolean differences. This problem can be simplified by using any of the following identities.

$$\frac{df(X)}{dx_i} = \frac{df'(X)}{dx_i} \tag{8-5}$$

$$\frac{df(X)}{dx_i} = \frac{df(x)}{dx_i'} \tag{8-6}$$

$$\frac{d}{dx_i}\left(\frac{df(X)}{dx_j}\right) = \frac{d}{dx_j}\left(\frac{df(X)}{dx_i}\right) \tag{8-7}$$

The following identities define the Boolean difference of the product and sum of two functions in terms of the Boolean differences of the individual functions.

230

$$\frac{d[f(X) \cdot g(X)]}{dx_i} = f(X) \cdot \frac{dg(X)}{dx_i} \oplus g(X) \cdot \frac{df(X)}{dx_i} \oplus \frac{df(X)}{dx_i} \cdot \frac{dg(X)}{dx_i} \quad (8\text{-}8)$$

$$\frac{d[f(X) + g(X)]}{dx_i} = f'(X) \frac{dg(X)}{dx_i} \oplus g'(X) \frac{df(X)}{dx_i}$$

$$\oplus \frac{df(X)}{dx_i} \cdot \frac{dg(X)}{dx_i} \quad (8\text{-}9)$$

$$\frac{d[f(X) \oplus g(X)]}{dx_i} = \frac{df(X)}{dx_i} \oplus \frac{dg(X)}{dx_i} \quad (8\text{-}10)$$

If $g(X)$ is independent of x_i we obtain

$$\frac{d[f(X) \cdot g(X)]}{dx_i} = g(X) \frac{df(X)}{dx_i} \quad (8\text{-}8')$$

$$\frac{d[f(X) + g(X)]}{dx_i} = g'(X) \frac{df(X)}{dx_i} \quad (8\text{-}9')$$

The proofs for these identities are quite straightforward and follow directly from the definition of the Boolean differences. They are therefore left to the reader.

Another useful tool in deriving Boolean differences is the *chain rule*, which in its simplest form can be stated as follows. Consider the circuit in Fig. 8-8. Let f be the output of the circuit. Let g be an internal wire

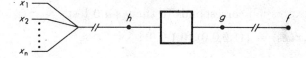

Fig. 8-8 Illustration of the chain rule.

and let h be either an internal wire or a primary input, such that every path from h to f passes through g. Then

$$\frac{df}{dh} = \frac{df}{dg} \cdot \frac{dg}{dh} \quad (8\text{-}11)$$

To prove the chain rule it is sufficient to show that df/dh assumes the value of the product $df/dg \cdot dg/dh$ for all the combinations of df/dg and dg/dh. Suppose, for example, that $df/dg = 0$. This implies that f is independent of g and, therefore, f must also be independent of h, since g is the only link between h and f. Thus, $df/dh = 0$. For the same reason, if $dg/dh = 0$, then $df/dh = 0$. Finally, let $df/dg = 1$ and $dg/dh = 1$. It is quite straightforward to show that, since the value of g depends on the value of h, while f depends on g, then f depends also on h. Thus, $df/dh = 1$. The details of the proof can be found in Ref. [21].

Further applications

The Boolean difference method can also be applied to derive tests for faults on internal circuit wires. Suppose, for example, that we want to test wire y in Fig. 8-7. The logical value of y can be expressed as a function of the external inputs and f can be expressed as a function of $x_1, x_2, \ldots, x_n$, and y. In this case

$$y = x_1 + x_2$$
$$f(X,y) = yx_3' + x_3x_4$$

Now, in the function $f(X,y)$, variable y may be treated as if it were an external input and the preceding method can be applied in this case as well. Thus,

$$\frac{df(X,y)}{dy} = x_3x_4 \oplus (x_3' + x_3x_4) = x_3'$$

The tests to detect y s-a-0 are determined from

$$y \frac{df(X,y)}{dy} = yx_3'$$
$$= (x_1 + x_2)x_3'$$
$$= x_1x_3' + x_2x_3'$$

This expression corresponds to the y s-a-0 tests

$$(x_1, x_2, x_3, x_4) = \{(1, \emptyset, 0, \emptyset), (\emptyset, 1, 0, \emptyset)\}$$

And for y s-a-1

$$y' \frac{df(X,y)}{dy} = y'x_3'$$
$$= x_1'x_2'x_3'$$
$$(x_1, x_2, x_3, x_4) = (0, 0, 0, \emptyset)$$

The chain rule can now be used to find tests for a fault on input x_1 of Fig. 8-7, in terms of the already known Boolean difference with respect to y. From Eq. 8-11 we obtain

$$\frac{df(X)}{dx_1} = \frac{df(X,y)}{dy} \cdot \frac{dy}{dx_1}$$
$$= x_3'[x_2 \oplus 1]$$
$$= x_2'x_3'$$

The s-a-0 tests are given by

$$x_1 \frac{df(X)}{dx_1} = x_1 x_2' x_3'$$

$$(x_1, x_2, x_3, x_4) = (1,0,0,\emptyset)$$

And the s-a-1 tests are derived as follows:

$$x_1' \frac{df(X)}{dx_1} = x_1' x_2' x_3'$$

$$(x_1, x_2, x_3, x_4) = (0,0,0,\emptyset)$$

Example Consider the circuit of Fig. 8-9.

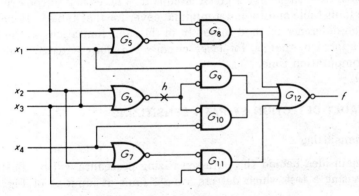

Fig. 8-9 A NOR-logic circuit.

To find a test for h s-a-0, we first express f as a function of x_1, x_2, x_3, x_4, and h, i.e.,

$$f(X,h) = x_1 x_2 x_3 x_4 + h(x_2 x_3 + x_1' x_2' x_3' x_4')$$

where

$$h(X) = x_2' x_3'$$

If we denote the first term in f by G (i.e., $G = x_1 x_2 x_3 x_4$) and the second term H and apply Eq. 8-9′, we obtain

$$\frac{df}{dh} = G' \frac{dH}{dh} = (x_1' + x_2' + x_3' + x_4')(x_2 x_3 + x_1' x_2' x_3' x_4')$$

$$= x_1' x_2 x_3 + x_2 x_3 x_4' + x_1' x_2' x_3' x_4'$$

To find tests for h s-a-0 we compute the values for which $h(df/dh) = 1$, that is,

$$h\frac{df}{dh} = x_2'x_3'(x_1'x_2x_3 + x_2x_3x_4' + x_1'x_2'x_3'x_4')$$

$$= x_1'x_2'x_3'x_4'$$

Thus, the test for h s-a-0 is

$$X = (0,0,0,0) \quad \blacksquare$$

The Boolean difference method enables us to determine all the tests which detect a given fault. This is in effect equivalent to determining in a systematic way the entries in the column (of the fault table) which corresponds to the given fault. In order to generate a minimal fault-detection experiment for a given circuit, it is necessary to construct the entire fault table and to find a minimal cover for that table. Hence, the Boolean difference method suffers from the same limitations as the fault-table approach, that is, for large circuits it requires excessive memory and computation time.

8-5 FAULT DETECTION BY PATH SENSITIZING

Path sensitizing

The main idea behind the path-sensitizing procedure will be illustrated by devising a test which detects a s-a-1 fault at input A of Fig. 8-10.

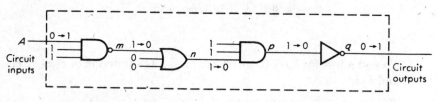

Fig. 8-10   A portion of a circuit describing a sensitized path.

Suppose that this path is the only one from A to the circuit output. In order to test a s-a-1 fault at input A, it is necessary to apply a 0 to A and 1's to all remaining inputs to the AND and NAND gates in the path, and 0's to all remaining inputs to the OR and NOR gates in the path. This ensures that all the gates will allow the propagation of the signal from A to the circuit output, and that only this signal will reach the circuit output. This assignment of values is shown in Fig. 8-10. The path is now said to be *sensitized*.

If input A is s-a-1, then m changes from 1 to 0, and this change propagates through connections n and p and causes q to change from 0 to 1. Clearly, in addition to detecting a s-a-1 fault at A, this test also detects s-a-0 faults at m, n, and p and a s-a-1 fault at q. A s-a-0 fault at A is detected in a similar manner. A 1 is applied to A, while other gate inputs remain as before. This second test would also detect the complementary set of faults to those detected by the previous test on this path. Thus the two tests together are sufficient to detect all s-a-0 and s-a-1 faults on this path.

The basic principles of the path-sensitization method, which is also known as the *one-dimensional path sensitization*, can thus be summarized as follows:

1. At the site of the fault assign a logical value complementary to the fault being tested, i.e., to test x_i for s-a-0 assign $x_i = 1$ and to test it for s-a-1 assign $x_i = 0$.
2. Select a path from the circuit inputs through the site of the fault to a circuit output. The path is said to be *sensitized* if the inputs to the gates along the path are assigned values so as to propagate to the path output any fault on the wires along the path. This process is called the *forward-drive phase* of the method.
3. Determine the primary inputs that will produce all the necessary signal values specified in the preceding steps. This is accomplished by tracing the signals backward from each of the gates along the path to the primary inputs. This process is called the *backward-trace phase* of the method.

Suppose we want to derive a test for a s-a-1 fault on wire h of Fig. 8-11. The forward drive starts by assigning a 0 to h and selecting a path to be sensitized. We choose to sensitize the path $G_7 G_9 G_{11} G_{13}$ to

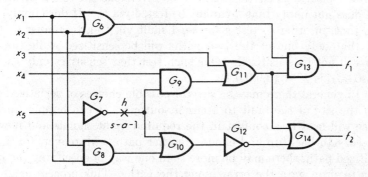

Fig. 8-11 Example for path sensitizing.

output f_1. Clearly, since G_9 and G_{13} are AND gates their other inputs must be 1's, while the second input to the OR gate G_{11} must be 0. This completes the forward drive and the path is now sensitized. Next, we must determine the primary inputs which will provide the required logical values to the gates along the sensitized path. This is accomplished by tracing back from each gate input to the corresponding primary inputs. In this example it is quite straightforward that we must set $x_5 = 1$, $x_4 = 1$, $x_3 = 0$, and $G_6 = 1$. To get $G_6 = 1$ we may set to 1 any one or both inputs to G_6. Suppose we choose $x_1 = 1$ and $x_2 = 0$, then we obtain the following test for h s-a-1

$$X = (1,0,0,1,1)$$

If, in response to these inputs, the circuit produces the output $f_1 = 0$, then the fault in question does not exist. If, on the other hand, $f_1 = 1$, the circuit has a fault. It does not necessarily mean that h is s-a-1, since such an erronous output may be caused by G_9 or G_{11} or G_{13} s-a-1 or by x_5 s-a-0. Thus, an erroneous output implies that some fault exists along the sensitized path.

Limitations of the method

Now suppose that we observe the circuit response to the above test at output f_2. An analysis shows that the input vector $X = (1,0,0,1,1)$ sensitizes the two paths $G_7G_9G_{11}G_{14}$ and $G_7G_{10}G_{12}G_{14}$ which emanate from h and terminate at f_2. It is easy, however, to verify that the fault h s-a-1 does not propagate to f_2 in spite of the fact that there are two sensitized paths connecting it to the circuit output. In fact, f_2 is equal to 1 via G_{10} and G_{12} if $h = 0$ and f_2 is equal to 1 via G_9 and G_{11} if $h = 1$. Such a phenomenon occurs whenever two or more paths which emanate from the site of a fault and reconverge at some forward point have unequal inversion parities, i.e., the number of inversions modulo-2 is unequal. This does not imply that h cannot be tested via f_2. It does imply, however, that, in order to test h for s-a-1 fault via f_2, a test must be found such that only one of the two paths will be sensitized while the other path will not be sensitized. One such test that sensitizes only the path $G_7G_{10}G_{12}G_{14}$ is $X = (0,0,0,0,1)$.

In general there may be several possible choices of sensitized paths from the site of the fault to a circuit output. It can happen that one choice will lead to a conflict in the required input signals and it will be necessary to back up and choose another path. Moreover, for a given sensitized path, there may be more than one way of specifying the inputs so as to propagate the error along the path. This process again may involve some trial and error. Furthermore, in many situations, a path may be sensitized by specifying values only to a subset of the primary inputs. In such cases, it may be possible to specify the other inputs so that several paths will be sensitized simultaneously by one test. Such efficient specifications will naturally lead to shorter fault-detection experiments.

A major advantage of the path-sensitization method, as illustrated by Fig. 8-10, is that in many cases a test for a primary input is also a test for all the wires along the sensitized path which connects that input to a circuit output. Consequently, if we can select a set of tests which sensitizes a set of paths containing all connections in the circuit, then it is sufficient to detect just those faults which appear on the circuit inputs. In fanout-free circuits, in which each gate output is connected to just one gate input, there is only one path from each circuit input to the output, and thus the set of paths originating at the inputs will indeed contain all connections. In circuits which contain fanout and in particular reconvergent fanout, the problem is considerably more complicated. In fact, the following example demonstrates that *the single-path-sensitization method does not always generate a test even if one is known to exist.*

Example Consider the fault h s-a-0 in the circuit of Fig. 8-9. We shall now show that it is impossible to find a test for this fault by sensitizing just a single path. Let us choose to sensitize the path $G_6 G_9 G_{12}$. This requires:

$G_6 = 1$, which implies $x_2 = 0$ and $x_3 = 0$.

$G_{10} = 0$ regardless of whether there is a fault or not, which implies $x_4 = 1$.

$G_{11} = 0$ implies $G_7 = 1$ (since $x_3 = 0$), which in turn implies $x_4 = 0$.

Evidently, to satisfy both $G_{10} = 0$ and $G_{11} = 0$, we must set conflicting requirements on x_4 and thus we have a contradiction. By the symmetry of the circuit it is obvious that an attempt to sensitize the path through G_{10} will also fail, and hence the method of one-dimensional path-sensitizing fails to generate the test $X = (0,0,0,0)$ which was shown to detect this fault. ∎

The one-dimensional path-sensitizing method failed in this case because it allows the sensitization of just a single path from the site of the fault. In fact, if we were allowed to sensitize both paths, through G_9 and G_{10}, simultaneously, the above test would be generated. This counterexample led to the development of the *two-dimensional path-*

sensitizing which is also known as the *d-algorithm*. The basic idea in the d-algorithm is to sensitize simultaneously all possible paths from the site of the fault to the circuit outputs. Details of the *d-algorithm* are beyond the scope of this book and can be found in Roth [16] and Refs. [3, 5, 6].

8-6 DETECTION OF MULTIPLE FAULTS

A circuit which consists of r wires may have as many as $2r$ distinct single faults, since each wire may be either s-a-0 or s-a-1. If we allow the occurrence of multiple faults, that is, more than one wire can have a fault at one time, the circuit may have as many as 3^r possible faults. To prove this, recall that each wire may be in one of three conditions: fault-free, s-a-0, or s-a-1, regardless of the condition of the other wires. It is evident that the fault table, the Boolean difference, or the path-sensitization methods are impractical for multiple faults, because the number of faults becomes very large. In fact, any method that considers every possible fault is highly inefficient for multiple faults. To overcome this limitation we present subsequently a method which considers the various *transformations* of a given circuit due to some faults, rather than the faults themselves. Many combinations of faults may cause the same transformation of the given circuit and therefore the number of transformations that must be considered is substantially smaller than 3^r. Clearly, any experiment that detects all multiple faults detects also all single faults. The converse, however, is not true, as is shown subsequently.

Experiments for two-level AND-OR networks

Consider the two-level AND-OR network shown in Fig. 8-12. Since it is assumed to be an irredundant network, the algebraic expression

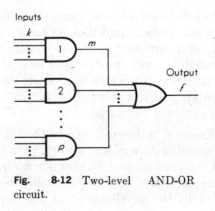

Fig. 8-12 Two-level AND-OR circuit.

describing it is an irredundant sum of prime implicants. Thus,

$$f = \sum_{i=1}^{n} P_i$$

where P_i denotes the ith prime implicant. In fact, each AND gate realizes one prime implicant. In analyzing the possible faults on the internal wires connecting the AND gates with the OR gate, it is evident that each such fault has an equivalent fault (or faults) on the inputs of the network (i.e., the inputs of the AND gates). For example, a s-a-0 fault on wire m is equivalent to a s-a-0 fault on one or more of the inputs of gate 1.

If a multiple fault includes both a primary input fault and a fault on the internal wire along the same path, the fault nearest the output overrides all other faults along the same path, and thus it determines the equivalent fault on the primary inputs and the response of the network. Consequently, an experiment designed to detect all multiple faults on the external inputs of the two-level AND-OR network detects all the faults within the network as well.

In constructing a fault-detection experiment our objective is actually to determine if the network under consideration realizes the required function f, or whether some fault caused it to realize a different function. This can be accomplished by testing the network to determine if it realizes only the required prime implicants and each of them. Consequently, it is first necessary to determine the effects of s-a-0 and s-a-1 faults on the function realized by the given network.

A s-a-0 fault at any of the inputs to the jth AND gate causes the output of this gate to be s-a-0, regardless of the values of the remaining variables. Such a fault in effect eliminates one prime implicant from the function realized by the network. Thus, to check whether a given prime implicant has completely "vanished," it is sufficient to test one minterm which is covered by that prime implicant and by no other prime implicant, and to verify that this minterm is indeed realized by the network. (Clearly, if the prime implicant is not redundant such a minterm always exists.) The requirement that the minterm chosen for testing must be one that is not covered by more than one prime implicant is essential, since a minterm covered by two (or more) prime implicants is realized by two (or more) AND gates, and a failure of one gate will not be detected if at least one of the remaining gates is operating correctly. Thus a complete set of tests for s-a-0 faults for a two-level AND-OR network consists of n tests corresponding to the n prime implicants in f. In other words, to test the jth AND gate for s-a-0 faults, it is necessary and sufficient to test one minterm a_j such that

$$a_j \, \varepsilon \, P_j \left(\sum_{i \neq j} P_i \right)'$$

The set of minterms that test each AND gate for $s\text{-}a\text{-}0$ faults is referred to as the set of $a\text{-}tests$.

A $s\text{-}a\text{-}1$ fault at an input to one of the AND gates causes the output of that gate to be independent of the variable associated with the $s\text{-}a\text{-}1$ input. Consequently, the gate will actually realize a product term that covers the original prime implicant but is independent of one of its variables. When using a map, this is equivalent to covering an additional subcube that is adjacent to the original one and in which the $s\text{-}a\text{-}1$ variable has a value complementary to its value in the original subcube. For example, if input z of gate 3 in Fig. 8-13a is $s\text{-}a\text{-}1$, the output of that gate will depend only on inputs w and x. In other words, the output of gate 3 can be represented by the expression $wx1 = wx(z + z')' = wxz + wxz'$, which means that gate 3 realizes an additional term wxz' that is adjacent to wxz. Since any of the inputs to gate 3 may be $s\text{-}a\text{-}1$, a test must be made to verify that none of the subcubes adjacent to wxz is realized by gate 3.

An input combination can be selected as a test for some $s\text{-}a\text{-}1$ fault only if the value of the function for that combination is 0. This is evident because a $s\text{-}a\text{-}1$ fault is detected by a 1 at the network output. But if some other AND gate is set to 1, the network output will be 1, regardless of the fault at the gate being tested. Therefore, to test whether the kth input of the jth AND gate is $s\text{-}a\text{-}1$, it is necessary and sufficient to test one minterm b_{jk} such that

$$b_{jk} \, \varepsilon \, P_{jk}^* \left(\sum_{i=1}^{n} P_i \right)'$$

where P_{jk}^* is the subcube adjacent to P_j and in which the value of the variable associated with the kth input is complementary to its value in P_j. Clearly, since P_j is a prime implicant, such a test can always be performed. The set of tests that check all possible subcubes adjacent to the original subcubes are referred to as $b\text{-}tests$.

A fault-detection experiment can now be constructed by selecting a set of a-tests and a set of b-tests. The number of a-tests is equal to the number of prime implicants and hence to the number of AND gates. The number of b-tests equals at most the number of literals in the function, but is usually considerably smaller because one b-test can serve for detecting $s\text{-}a\text{-}1$ faults at several gates simultaneously.

To detect a $s\text{-}a\text{-}0$ fault at the input to a certain AND gate, it is necessary to set to 1 the literal associated with this input and apply 1's to all remaining inputs of that gate. The yet unassigned variables must be assigned values in such a way that the outputs of all the other AND gates will be 0. Then, if the network output is 1, no *s-a-*0 fault exists. However, if the output is 0, the gate is faulty, because one (or more) of its inputs or its output is *s-a-*0. Clearly, such a set of values assigned to the switching variables will detect *s-a-*0 faults at *any* input of the given gate. Consequently it constitutes a *s-a-*0 test for the entire gate.

A *s-a-*1 fault at a gate input is detected in a similar manner. The input in question is assigned the value 0, while all other inputs to the AND gate are assigned 1's. The remaining variables are again assigned values in such a way that the output of each AND gate will be 0. Then, if the network output is 0, no *s-a-*1 fault exists at the input being tested. But if the output is 1, the network has a *s-a-*1 fault. The identification of the particular faulty input, however, is not always possible without additional tests, since any of the AND gate outputs may be *s-a-*1 and not necessarily the AND gate in question.

As an example consider the circuit shown in Fig. 8-13a which realizes the function

$$f(w,x,y,z) = w'y' + y'z + wxz + xyz'$$

The map in Fig. 8-13b illustrates the four prime implicants realized by the AND gates. A subcube in the map describing a prime implicant for which $f = 1$ is referred to as a *true* subcube. To test the four true subcubes for *s-a-*0 faults we select four minterms, one for each subcube, such that each minterm is contained in only one true subcube. The testing, for example, of the subcube (0,1,4,5)† can be accomplished by applying one of the input combinations represented by the decimal values 0 or 4, since each of these combinations is covered by only one true subcube. This is indicated in the map of Fig. 8-13b by the ✕ in cells 0 and 4 and the dotted line connecting them. Using a similar reasoning, it is evident that subcube (6,14) can be tested by applying to the circuit inputs either one of the combinations 6 or 14. On the other hand, subcube (1,5,9,13) contains only one minterm, 9, which is not contained in any other true subcube. Consequently, this input combination is an essential test and must be applied to the circuit in order to check gate 2. The complete set of *a-*tests for *s-a-*0 faults thus consists of four tests as follows:

$$\{a\} = \{0 \text{ or } 4, 6 \text{ or } 14, 9, 15\}$$

The *b-*tests (indicated in the map in Fig. 8-13c by the dark circles) must be selected in such a way that each subcube adjacent to a true sub-

---

† Subcube (0,1,4,5) denotes the subcube containing the four minterms whose decimal representation is given within the parentheses.

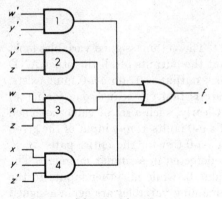

(a) Network.

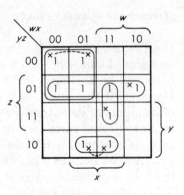

(b) Map for a-tests.

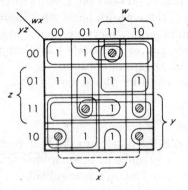

(c) Map for b-tests.

Fig. 8-13 Generating fault-detection tests.

cube is tested in at least one of its cells and the value of the function in the tested cells is 0. The adjacent subcubes are shown in Fig. 8-13c, where, for example, subcubes (5,7), (9,11), and (12,14) are adjacent to the true subcube (13,15), and so on. Since a single s-a-1 test can test simultaneously a number of gates, it is allowed (and generally desirable) to select cells common to a number of adjacent subcubes, so that the total number of tests will be minimal. In the running example

$$\{b\} = \{2 \text{ or } 10, 7, 11, 12\}$$

Thus, the minimal sets of fault-detection tests for the network of Fig. 8-13a are

$$\{0 \text{ or } 4, 2 \text{ or } 10, 6 \text{ or } 14, 7, 9, 11, 12, 15\}$$

Theorem 8-1 *The set T of a-tests and b-tests detects all multiple faults in the two-level AND-OR network.*

Proof: In order to prove the theorem it is sufficient to show that T detects all faults at the network inputs. If any single s-a-0 or s-a-1 fault occurs in one of these inputs, it will clearly be detected by the tests in T. If any input is s-a-1, its effect is to add a subcube to the network function. The only way that another fault can delete this subcube, and thus leave the s-a-1 fault undetected, is a s-a-0 fault on an input to the same AND gate, which has the s-a-1 fault. This s-a-0 fault cannot be masked by another s-a-1 fault at that gate and, therefore, it will be detected by the a-tests.

A s-a-0 fault at an input to an AND gate causes the corresponding prime implicant to vanish. This prime implicant is tested by a single a-test. If, however, this a-test (or minterm) is included in an adjacent subcube added to the function as a result of some s-a-1 fault, it will not detect the "vanished" prime implicant. The s-a-1 fault, however, will be detected by the b-tests. In all other situations the a-tests will detect all s-a-0 faults. Consequently, the a-tests and the b-tests together detect all multiple faults on the network inputs. ∎

Experiments for two-level OR-AND networks

Let N_1 and N_2 be two combinational networks, such that every fault-detection experiment for network N_1 is also a fault-detection experiment for network N_2. We say that N_1 *test covers* N_2 and denote it by $T(N_1) \supseteq T(N_2)$. If $T(N_1) \supseteq T(N_2)$ and $T(N_2) \supseteq T(N_1)$, we say that N_1 and N_2 are *test equivalent* and denote it by $T(N_1) = T(N_2)$. Fault-detection experiments for two-level OR-AND networks can be constructed by generating the experiments for the two-level AND-OR test-equivalent networks.

Theorem 8-2 *Every two-level OR-AND (AND-OR) network N_1 has a two-level AND-OR (OR-AND) test-equivalent network N_2 such that the inputs of N_2 are complements of the inputs of N_1.*

Proof: We can add an inverter to the network output, as shown in Fig. 8-14, without affecting the testing requirements of the network.

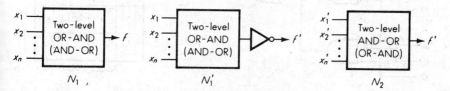

Fig. 8-14 Three test-equivalent networks.

Clearly, $T(N_1) = T(N_1')$. The inverter can now be propagated to the inputs while changing all OR gates into AND gates and vice versa. Finally, the inverters at the inputs can now be replaced by the complemented inputs and network N_2 results. This network is a two-level AND-OR network test-equivalent to N_1; that is, $T(N_1) = T(N_2)$. ∎

Example Consider the two-level OR-AND network of Fig. 8-15. The test-equivalent AND-OR network and its corresponding map are

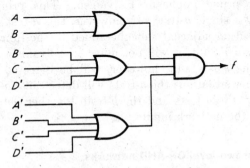

Fig. 8-15 OR-AND network.

shown in Fig. 8-16. Following the procedure outlined in the preceding section we find that

$$\{a\} = \{0 \text{ or } 2 \text{ or } 3,9,15\}$$

and

$$\{b\} = \{7,8,11,13,14\}$$

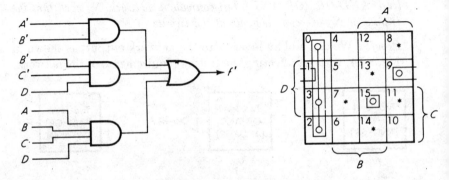

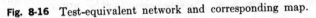

Fig. 8-16 Test-equivalent network and corresponding map.

Thus, the minimal sets of tests for the above network are

$$\{T\} = \{0 \text{ or } 2 \text{ or } 3,7,8,9,11,13,14,15\}$$

In this case the a-tests and b-tests correspond, respectively, to s-a-1 and s-a-0 tests, since they were generated for the complement of the function. ■

★Systematic generation of minimal fault-detection experiments for two-level networks

It is quite straightforward to use the map in order to find the a-tests and the b-tests for networks with five or fewer variables. In order to handle networks with larger numbers of variables, different techniques must be developed. In this section we present an algorithm for obtaining minimal fault-detection experiments. The algorithm is suitable for hand computation and has also been programmed.

Since the sets of a-tests and b-tests are disjoint, it is possible to determine each of these sets separately.

GENERATING THE a-TESTS

Step 1: Construct a *covering matrix* E whose column headings are the prime implicants realized by the AND gates and whose row headings are the minterms covered by the function.

Step 2: Delete all rows in E which contain two or more 1's.

Step 3: Choose, arbitrarily, for every P_j in E one minterm m_i, such that $e_{ij} = 1$, where

$$e_{ij} = \begin{cases} 1, & \text{if } m_i \, \varepsilon \, P_j \\ 0, & \text{if } m_i \notin P_j \end{cases}$$

$$E = \begin{array}{c} \\ m_1 \\ m_2 \\ \cdot \\ \cdot \\ \cdot \\ m_i \\ \cdot \\ \cdot \\ \cdot \\ m_k \end{array} \overset{\displaystyle P_1 \, P_2 \, \cdots \, P_j \, \cdots \, P_n}{\left[\begin{array}{ccccc} & & \cdot & & \\ & & \cdot & & \\ & & \cdot & & \\ \cdots & e_{ij} & & & \\ & & & & \\ & & & & \end{array} \right]}$$

GENERATING THE b-TESTS

As indicated before, the problem of generating a minimal set of b-tests is actually a problem of selecting a minimal set of tests such that each adjacent subcube is tested in at least one of its cells and the value of the function in each of these cells is 0. The procedure is summarized as follows.

Step 1: List all P_{jk}^* for all $j = 1, 2, \ldots, n$ and $k = 1, 2, \ldots, r_j$, when n is the number of prime implicants realized by the function and r_j is the number of literals in the jth prime implicant. This step actually lists all adjacent subcubes.

Step 2: For every $P_{is}^* \supseteq P_{jt}^*$, delete P_{is}^* from the list. (Since every test for P_{jt}^* is also a test for P_{is}^*, while the converse is not true.)

Step 3: Find all pairwise intersections of the terms that are now contained in the list. Whenever an intersection is nonempty and contains a minterm for which $f = 0$, checkmark the two intersected terms. This step actually lists the minterms (for which $f = 0$), which are contained in two or more adjacent subcubes.

Step 4: Repeat step 3 until no new terms are generated. The terms generated in step 3 and those not checkmarked from step 2 are called *prime intersections*. Steps 3 and 4 thus indicate those minterms that simultaneously test as many adjacent subcubes as possible.

Step 5: From the list of prime intersections construct a list of *prime tests* by selecting, arbitrarily, from each intersection an input combination for which the value of the function is 0.

Step 6: Construct the *prime-test chart*, whose column headings are the P_{jk}^* terms of the list found in step 2, and whose row headings are the prime tests of step 5. An $\times$ is inserted at the intersection of any one row and column P_{jk}^* if the corresponding prime test is covered by P_{jk}^*.

Step 7: Select a set of prime tests that check each of the P_{jk}^* terms, that is, find a cover for the prime test chart.

The proof that the foregoing algorithm is indeed valid is straightforward and follows the line of reasoning used in the map procedure.

As an example illustrating the foregoing procedure, consider the network of Fig. 8-17, which realizes the function

$$f = x_4 x_3 + x_4' x_3' x_2 + x_5 x_4 x_1 + x_5' x_4 x_2' x_1'$$

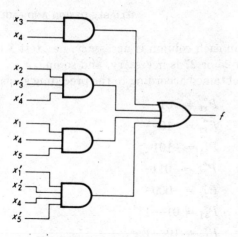

Fig. 8-17 Network to be tested.

The a-tests are as follows:

$$X_5 X_4 X_3 X_2 X_1 \quad \text{-11--} \quad \text{-001-} \quad \text{11--1} \quad \text{01-00}$$

		$X_5 X_4 X_3 X_2 X_1$	-11--	-001-	11--1	01-00
	(2)	0 0 0 1 0	0	1	0	0
	(3)	0 0 0 1 1	0	1	0	0
	(8)	0 1 0 0 0	0	0	0	1
	(12)	0 1 1 0 0	1	0	0	1
	(13)	0 1 1 0 1	1	0	0	0
	(14)	0 1 1 1 0	1	0	0	0
	(15)	0 1 1 1 1	1	0	0	0
$E =$	(18)	1 0 0 1 0	0	1	0	0
	(19)	1 0 0 1 1	0	1	0	0
	(25)	1 1 0 0 1	0	0	1	0
	(27)	1 1 0 1 1	0	0	1	0
	(28)	1 1 1 0 0	1	0	0	0
	(29)	1 1 1 0 1	1	0	1	0
	(30)	1 1 1 1 0	1	0	0	0
	(31)	1 1 1 1 1	1	0	1	0

Thus, the sets of a-tests are given by

$$\{a\} = \begin{cases} 13 \\ 14 & 2 \\ 15 & 3 \\ 28 & 18 & 25 \\ 30, & 19, & 27, & 8 \end{cases}$$

where only one test in each column is necessary, i.e., test 8 is essential, while only one out of 25 or 27 is necessary, and so on.

The b-tests are obtained according to the preceding steps as follows:

1. $P_1 = -11--$ $P_{11}^* = -01--$

                       $P_{12}^* = -10--$

   $P_2 = -001-$ $P_{21}^* = -101-$

                       $P_{22}^* = -011-$

                       $P_{23}^* = -000-$

   $P_3 = 11--1$ $P_{31}^* = 01--1$

                       $P_{32}^* = 10--1$

                       $P_{33}^* = 11--0$

   $P_4 = 01-00$ $P_{41}^* = 11-00$

                       $P_{42}^* = 00-00$

                       $P_{43}^* = 01-10$

                       $P_{44}^* = 01-01$

2. $P_{11}^* \supset P_{22}^*$, $P_{12}^* \supset P_{21}^*$, $P_{31}^* \supset P_{44}^*$, and $P_{33}^* \supset P_{41}^*$. Thus the new list is

$$-101- \checkmark$$
$$-011- \checkmark$$
$$-000- \checkmark$$
$$10--1 \checkmark$$
$$11-00$$
$$00-00 \checkmark$$
$$01-10 \checkmark$$
$$01-01$$

3. The pairwise intersections are found in a straightforward manner. The first term $-101-$, for example, has a nonempty intersection only with $01-10$. The intersection is 01010 and the two intersected terms are checkmarked. In the same way we find the remaining intersections, namely,

01010, 10111, 10001, 00000

4. The prime intersections therefore are

11-00, 01-01, 01010, 10111, 10001, 00000

5. To find a prime test from the intersection 11-00, we note that this intersection covers two combinations, 11000 and 11100.

But since the value of f is 1 for 11100, the prime test is 11000. In a similar manner we find the list of prime tests as follows:

11000, 01001, 01010, 10111, 10001, 00000

6. The prime-test chart is shown in Table 8-1. The checkmarks indicate that the corresponding tests are essential. In general, the method of covering a prime-test chart is similar to the covering of a fault table. However, the size of the prime-test chart is always very small in comparison with that of the corresponding fault table.

Table 8-1   Prime-test chart

		–101–	–011–	–000–	10--1	11–00	00–00	01–10	01–01
✓	11000					×			
✓	01001								×
✓	01010	×						×	
✓	10111		×		×				
	10001				×	×			
✓	00000				×			×	

In this specific example the essential tests cover the entire chart and the b-tests are

$\{b\} = \{24,9,10,23,0\}$

Consequently, the complete fault-detection experiment for the network of Fig. 8-17 consists of nine tests as follows:

$$T = \begin{Bmatrix} & & & & 13 & & & & \\ & & & & 14 & 2 & & & \\ & & & & 15 & 3 & & & \\ & & & & 28 & 18 & 25 & & \\ 24, & 9, & 10, & 23, & 0, & 30, & 19, & 27, & 8 \end{Bmatrix}$$

The method described in this section for the detection of multiple faults in two-level networks can be extended to multilevel networks as well. The interested reader may refer to Ref. 9. In multilevel networks, however, there is no guarantee that the experiments will be minimal. Indeed, so far, with the exception of the fault table, there is no algorithm for generating *minimal* fault-detection experiments for arbitrary networks.

8-7 FAILURE-TOLERANT DESIGN

With the exception of Sec. 8-1, we have so far been concerned only with the problem of establishing whether or not an existing network is operating correctly. The next natural question is whether it is possible to improve the reliability of a logic network and to design it so that, for specified classes of faults, it becomes self-checking or even self-correcting. As in the case of hazards, we shall show that any improvement in the reliability of logic networks involves the use of a certain amount of redundant hardware.

The problem

Physical devices used as switching components have nonzero probability of failure. As a result, in many applications where high reliability is of utmost importance, in addition to the selection of highly reliable components, special procedures must be employed in order to increase the mean failure-free time. In many cases digital systems cannot be repaired during too short intervals for economic, strategic, or physical (e.g., system is in space) reasons. On the other hand, since recent technology has contributed toward making component cost and size of secondary design importance, improved reliability can be achieved by such design techniques as the use of redundancies and of automatic self-checking.

Intuitively, it seems clear that if a logic network is to perform its logical function and at the same time correct errors, there must be some redundancy either in the inputs to the network or in its structure, or in both. In Chap. 1 we showed that a simple form of redundancy in the inputs to a network is the existence of parity and error-correcting digits which do not carry any information. Another way of arriving at circuits with error-detection and correction capabilities is by using multiplexing as a basic principle, whereby each gate is provided with multiple inputs. These inputs must be generated independently, so that a fault in one need not imply a fault in the others. Consequently, redundant, independent logic circuits must exist to generate these inputs.

As we shall subsequently see, there are several possible strategies to increase the reliability of a system. The selection of the strategy to be employed in each particular case depends on the designer's objectives, on the desired system capabilities, on the operating environment of the system, on the characteristics of the faults, and on the budget allotted for the system. In general these strategies can be subdivided into two basic approaches. The first approach is to design *self-checking* systems, which are continuously checked for faults. If a fault is detected, a standby unit is activated, replacing the faulty one. The second approach is to design systems with *fault-masking* capabilities, where the fault is masked by the presence of additional redundant hardware.

Many of the redundancy techniques covered in this section have been and are being employed in various practical computing systems. Among the better known, highly reliable systems are the Electronic Switching System (ESS) of Bell Laboratories, the Self-Testing and Repairing (STAR) computer of the Jet Propulsion Laboratories [2] and other computing systems used in space missions. A more extensive survey on fault-tolerant computing systems is available in Ref. 4.

Critical and subcritical errors

In the following discussion we shall study the properties of redundant switching circuits, each of whose inputs X_a, X_b, . . . , X_m consists of R versions of the signal, with each version designed to carry the same information, that is,

$$X_i = \{x_{i1}, x_{i2}, \ . \ . \ . \ , x_{iR}\}$$

where R is referred to as the circuit *redundancy*. Define a 0-*to*-1 error as one in which a correct 0 is permuted to an incorrect 1. Analogously define a 1-*to*-0 error as one in which a correct 1 is permuted to an incorrect 0. An error occurring on one of the redundant inputs x_{ij} to a specific gate is said to be *critical* if it causes an incorrect gate output. An error is said to be *subcritical* if its occurrence at one of the redundant inputs to a gate does not cause a fault in the gate output.

Example The various errors associated with some of the commonly used gates are summarized in Table 8-2. A 0-to-1 error (denoted $0 \rightarrow 1$) in an AND gate which has R identical inputs is subcritical, because the gate output remains 0 as long as one or more of the remaining $R - 1$ inputs is 0. However, such an error at the inputs to an OR gate is critical, because it changes the gate output from 0 to 1, regardless of the values of the remaining inputs. Similarly, a 1-to-0 error at any one input to an AND gate is critical since it is sufficient to change the gate output from 1 to 0. Clearly, this same fault is subcritical if it occurs at the inputs to an OR gate. Analogous arguments verify the remaining entries in the table. ∎

One of the most important properties displayed by the gates described in Table 8-2 (with the exception of the majority and modulo-2 gates) is that the output error, caused by a critical error in an AND gate, is a subcritical input error for an OR gate and that the output error, caused by a critical input error in an OR gate, is a subcritical input error

Table 8-2 Error classification in logical gates

Function	Logic symbol (redundancy = 3)	Sub-critical input error	Critical input error	Output error as a result of critical input error
AND	a_1 a_2 a_3 b_1 b_2 b_3	$0 \rightarrow 1$	$1 \rightarrow 0$	$1 \rightarrow 0$
OR	a_1 a_2 a_3 b_1 b_2 b_3	$1 \rightarrow 0$	$0 \rightarrow 1$	$0 \rightarrow 1$
NAND	a_1 a_2 a_3 b_1 b_2 b_3	$0 \rightarrow 1$	$1 \rightarrow 0$	$0 \rightarrow 1$
NOR	a_1 a_2 a_3 b_1 b_2 b_3	$1 \rightarrow 0$	$0 \rightarrow 1$	$1 \rightarrow 0$
Majority $\{a,b,c\}$	a_1 a_2 a_3 b_1 b_2 b_3 c_1 c_2 c_3 Maj	$0 \rightarrow 1$ $1 \rightarrow 0$	None	None
Modulo 2	a_1 a_2 a_3 b_1 b_2 b_3 $+$ z	None	$0 \rightarrow 1$ $1 \rightarrow 0$	$z \rightarrow z'$

for an AND gate. In a similar manner we find that the output error, caused by a critical error in a NAND (or NOR) gate, is a subcritical error in the next level of NAND (NOR) gates. These observations lead to the idea that error correction can be achieved by transforming critical input errors into output errors which are subcritical for the next level of gates and are corrected there.

Outline of possible strategies

The simplest approach to increase the reliability of a circuit is to test it often enough so that a fault is detected as soon as it has occurred. This can be accomplished either by using error-detecting codes or by attaching to the circuit a special subcircuit, called a *checker*, which automatically checks the circuit as it performs its computation.

After a fault has been diagnosed and located, it must be isolated to prevent it from affecting the entire computation. At this stage either a standby spare subsystem replaces the faulty one, then we say that the system is *self-correcting*, or the original system is reorganized to bypass the faulty module. The latter approach usually involves some degradation in the performance of the system and, hence, is referred to as *graceful degradation*, and the corresponding system is called a *fail soft* system. Fail soft systems do not require redundant hardware, but they are very difficult to design since they must possess two important properties. First, they must enable rapid fault detection and location; second, they must have the ability to reconfigurate themselves so that the faulty module will be isolated while the degradation in performance will be minimal.

In many practical situations one type of failure is more critical than another type. For example, if a traffic light control system fails, red lights are preferable to green ones in both directions; or if an elevator control system fails, the immediate stop of the elevator is preferable to its continued moving. The design of systems in which no single fault will produce the critical output is referred to as *fail safe* design.

Whenever a system must not malfunction, even in the presence of some faults, it becomes necessary to use *fault-tolerant systems*. A simple approach to fault-tolerant design is to duplicate the system and to compare the outputs of the two systems, as illustrated in Fig. 8-18. The two systems receive the same data, but only one of them is controlling the operation while the other serves as a standby and is being used for checking purposes only. The outputs of the two systems are fed into a matching circuit, which in its simplest form can be an EXCLUSIVE-OR gate. If a mismatch occurs, which indicates a fault, the gate produces a signal which, in turn, activates diagnostic programs to determine the

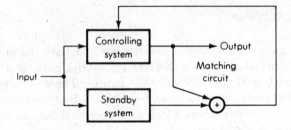

Fig. 8-18 Increasing the reliability by means of a standby system.

location of the fault. The fault-free unit becomes then the controlling one while the faulty unit is being repaired. This type of system design is used in the electronic telephone switching systems (ESS1) and in many other industrial applications.

Restoring organs

A restoring organ is a logical structure which receives redundant input information and generates more reliable output information. Its main task is to check the redundant inputs and to generate the desired number of independent outputs. A simple restoring organ, which uses straightforward multiplexing, is shown in Fig. 8-19a. The "decision element" may be a simple majority gate, a vote taker, or a threshold device. It receives R versions of the same input and is designed to compute R identical versions of the output. When the redundancy R is equal to 3, it is possible to use the majority circuit of Fig. 8-19b as a decision element. In this case three identical versions of input x, namely, x_1, x_2, and x_3, are fed into the majority circuit. A fault in any one of these input channels will not propagate to the output lines, and thus, except for faults within the decision element itself, this scheme corrects any

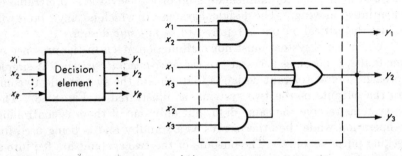

(a) General decision element.   (b) A majority gate as a decision element.

Fig. 8-19 A simple restoring organ.

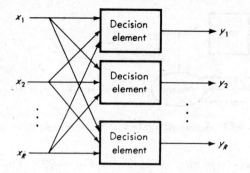

Fig. 8-20 A restoring organ used with unreliable decision elements.

single circuit failure. Note that no fault correction is possible by mere duplication of the number of inputs, although fault detection is possible; e.g., a modulo-2 gate can be used to detect the existence of different inputs.

The next obvious step is to improve the reliability of the decision elements themselves by using R identical copies, as shown in Fig. 8-20. The application of this scheme to the design of a redundant circuit for $f = a'b + ab'$ is shown in Fig. 8-21.

In practice it is important that the error-correction mechanism will not just correct errors but will also produce a warning signal indicating that an error has occurred. This can be done by means of a *disagreement*

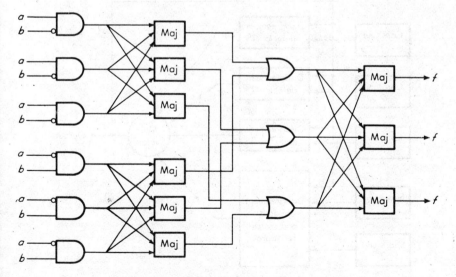

Fig. 8-21 Redundant circuit for $f = a'b + ab'$.

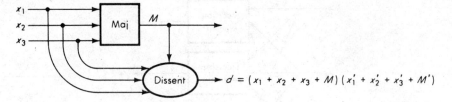

Fig. 8-22 A majority gate with disagreement detector.

detector (or *dissent circuit*), as shown in Fig. 8-22. The dissent circuit produces an output d which is equal to 1 for all input combinations except when x_1, x_2, x_3, and M assume identical values. Thus, $d = 1$ indicates the existence of an error, where

$$d = (x_1 + x_2 + x_3 + M)(x_1' + x_2' + x_3' + M')$$

A more reliable system organization is the *hybrid redundancy*. This system in its most general form consists of $N = 2n + 1$ identical units and a voter with threshold which is equal to $n + 1$. Thus, the voter produces an output according to the majority of its inputs. In addition the system consists of spare standby units such that, when one of the active units fails, a spare is automatically used to replace the faulty unit. The switching out of the faulty units and the switching in of the spare units are accomplished by means of special disagreement detectors and switching units. A hybrid redundancy with *triple modular redundancy* (TMR) core units and two standby units is shown in Fig.

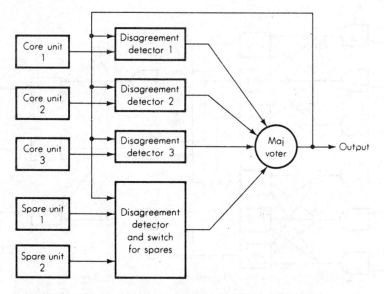

Fig. 8-23 Hybrid redundancy with triple modular redundancy core.

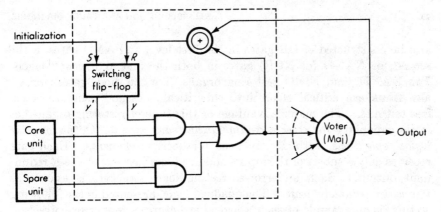

Fig. 8-24 A disagreement detector and switching unit for one core unit.

8-23. The disagreement detector associated with each core unit detects if the output of that core unit is different from the output of the voter.

A possible realization of the disagreement detector and switching unit (for just one core unit) is shown in Fig. 8-24. Initially the switching *flip-flop* is set and its output y is 1. In this case the core unit is connected to the voter while the spare, which is controlled by y', is disconnected from the voter. If the output of the voter is different from the output of the core unit, and hence the core unit is in the minority, the flip-flop is reset, the core unit is switched off, and the spare is switched on.

A different type of restoring organ constructed of diode gates is shown in Fig. 8-25. Any critical error at an input to the first level of gates causes two subcritical errors at the inputs to the second level of gates, in which one of them is corrected. Similar restoring organs can

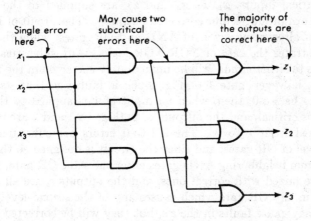

Fig. 8-25 Diode-gates restoring organ, shown for the case of redundancy $R = 3$.

also be constructed of OR gates in the first level and AND gates in the second, or NAND (or NOR) gates in both the first and second levels. The NAND (and NOR) restoring organs, like the diode-gates organs, also transform critical errors into subcritical ones and generate error-free outputs.   The major advantage of this type of restoring organs lies in its capability for *error correction in the same circuits that perform the logical operations*, without any need for decision elements.   Each gate receives only a subset of the inputs and produces just one of the R redundant outputs.   Such an error-correcting logic structure is known as *interwoven redundant logic*.   The quadded logic, presented in the following section, is an example of such a logical structure, where error correction is accomplished simultaneously with logical operations.

★8-8 QUADDED LOGIC

Quadded logic is a redundant logical structure which is protected against any type of single faults and many multiple ones.   It is provided with four versions of each input, and every logical circuit appears in quadruplicate.   Fault correction is accomplished in the same circuit which performs the logical operations by mixing the faulty signals with good ones so that most errors are corrected within one to two levels of propagation.

Basic structure

The basic structure of a quadded network is illustrated in Fig. 8-26. Four identical inputs, x_1, x_2, x_3, and x_4, are supplied to the network, which in turn produces four corrected outputs.   The circuit of Fig. 8-26a consists of alternating levels of AND and OR gates, while that of Fig. 8-26b illustrates the case of NOR-NOR logic.   Any subcritical error at the inputs to either circuit will be immediately corrected in the first gates level.   If, however, gate 1 of Fig. 8-26a is faulty so that its input x_1 appears to be s-a-0, then, when an input of 1 is applied to the circuit, the error is critical, and the outputs of both gates 1 and 2 are incorrectly transformed from 1 to 0.   These 1-to-0 errors are subcritical for the second level of OR gates, and since the circuit is designed so that no two outputs from neighboring AND gates enter the same OR gate, the faulty signals are mixed with correct ones, and the outputs z_i are all corrected. A failure in any OR gate which causes any of the second-level inputs to be s-a-1 may cause faults in the z's, but they will be corrected in a third level of gates.   A similar analysis demonstrates the error-correction capability of the NOR-NOR quadded structure of Fig. 8-26b.

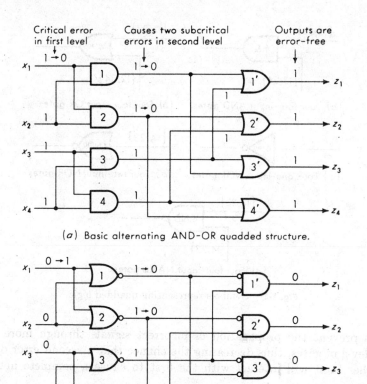

Critical error in first level $1 \to 0$

Causes two subcritical errors in second level

Outputs are error-free

(*a*) Basic alternating AND-OR quadded structure.

(*b*) Basic NOR-NOR quadded structure.

Fig. 8-26 Logic structures in quadded networks.

From the foregoing analysis it is evident that the error-correction capabilities of the basic quadded structure result from the specific interconnection patterns used in these networks, where the inputs x_1 and x_2 are connected to gates 1 and 2, while x_3 and x_4 are connected to gates 3 and 4. To prevent the propagation of any error through the second gates level, the outputs of AND gates 1 and 3 are connected to OR gates $1'$ and $3'$, while those of AND gates 2 and 4 are connected to OR gates $2'$ and $4'$. Such an interconnection pattern guarantees that each gate in the second level will receive at least one correct input, and will thus be able to produce the correct output.

As a result, we may conclude that in circuits which consist of alternating levels of AND and OR gates or successive levels of NAND (or NOR) gates, single-error correction is accomplished if the wiring interconnection patterns are chosen so that the same pattern is not enc untered twice consecutively as the signals flow. Such interconnec-

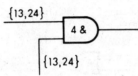
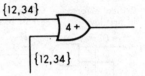

(a) Four four-input AND gates. (b) Four four-input OR gates.

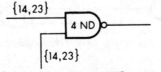

(c) Four one-input NOT gates. (d) Four two-input NOR gates.

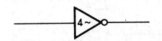

(e) Four four-input NAND gates.

Fig. 8-27 Symbols representing quadded logic.

tions prevent the propagation of incorrect signals through more than one level of gates, thus decreasing the chance that a second error due to another fault will interact with the first to cause a complete network failure.

The description of quadded logic may be facilitated by a compact notation, as shown in Fig. 8-27. Quadded connections are described by a single line, with which we associate a partition specifying the pairing of inputs to the logical gates. For example, the partition {13; 24} specifies that inputs 1 and 3 are paired in the cross connection, as are 2 and 4. The compact descriptions for the circuits of Fig. 8-26 are shown in Fig. 8-28. (Note that both forms of NOR gates, as well as those of NAND gates, may be employed.)

Example The circuit shown in Fig. 8-29b, in compact notation, is a quadded realization of the function $T = (AB + CD)(E + F)$. ∎

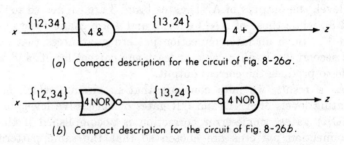

(a) Compact description for the circuit of Fig. 8-26a.

(b) Compact description for the circuit of Fig. 8-26b.

Fig. 8-28 Compact description of quadded circuits.

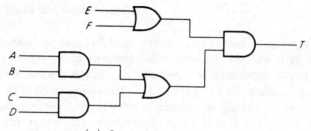

(a) Original irredundant circuit.

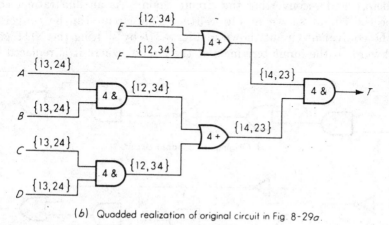

(b) Quadded realization of original circuit in Fig. 8-29a.

Fig. 8-29 A quadded realization of $T = (AB + CD)(E + F)$.

General quadded design procedure

In circuit design it often occurs that one AND gate feeds another AND gate or that one OR gate feeds another OR gate. If two different connection patterns are assigned to the two gates, a critical error at the input to the first gate will propagate and cause two errors at its output. But these errors are again critical because the second gate is logically identical with the first; consequently, the errors will propagate through the second gate as well and cause an error in all four outputs, which in turn will cause the entire circuit to fail. This situation is illustrated in Fig. 8-30, where, for example, the notation 1111 → 1110 means that the inputs to all four gates are 1's, but in gate 4 a 1-to-0 fault occurs.

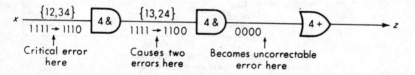

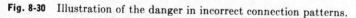

Fig. 8-30 Illustration of the danger in incorrect connection patterns.

As a result, we conclude that *whenever an AND gate feeds an AND gate (or an OR feeds an OR), the connection patterns at the inputs to the first and to the second gates must be identical.* (Is this rule valid for a NAND gate feeding another NAND gate or a NOR feeding a NOR?)

Quadding a circuit containing inverters is accomplished by first converting the given circuit to an equivalent one, whose inverters are either at the input terminals or at the output terminals, then quadding as before and reconverting the circuit again. As an illustration, consider the circuit shown in Fig. 8-31a. This circuit can be converted to the equivalent circuit shown in Fig. 8-31b by shifting the NOT gate backward to the input terminals of the circuit, where it is replaced by

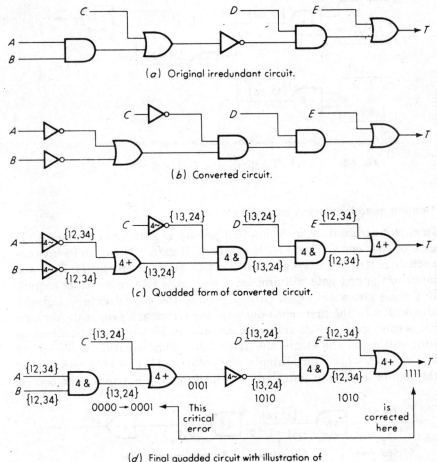

(a) Original irredundant circuit.

(b) Converted circuit.

(c) Quadded form of converted circuit.

(d) Final quadded circuit with illustration of correction of longest propagated error.

Fig. 8-31 Quadding of a circuit containing an inverter.

three NOT gates.   In the process, every AND gate encountered is transformed to an OR gate, and conversely, every OR gate is transformed to an AND gate, in accordance with De Morgan's theorem.   The converted circuit is then quadded using the above-developed procedure, with the result shown in Fig. 8-31c.   Finally, the circuit may be reconverted to its original form, as shown in Fig. 8-31d.   All errors are corrected by the quadded circuit within one level of propagation, with the exception of the error illustrated in Fig. 8-31d, where a critical error at the output of the first gate may propagate through three levels before it is corrected. (The actual propagation distance depends also on inputs C, D, and E.)

We observe in Fig. 8-31d that although the two gates adjacent to the NOT gate are of different types, their inputs have the same connection pattern.   This situation is clearly a consequence of our procedure and usually cannot be avoided when the circuit contains inverters.

In general, the connection patterns assigned to the various gate inputs are not unique, and their determination may involve some trial and error.   The quadding technique can be extended to logical circuits containing feedback and more complex digital devices, e.g., flip-flops and registers.   It may consequently be applied to all combinational as well as sequential circuits.

Quadding protects a circuit against single faults by masking the faults.   For multiple faults to cause a circuit failure, they must occur in gates which are close to each other.   And since most errors are corrected within one level of propagation, the probability of one error interacting with another is very small.   The price for this increase in reliability is a four- to fivefold increase in cost and a substantial increase in the complexity of the circuit, making the maintenance and repair problems extremely difficult.   These are some of the disadvantages of the quadding technique, and consequently, it is not very often used in practice.

NOTES AND REFERENCES

The subject of hazards in combinational circuits was first studied by Huffman in his paper [7], from which the material in Sec. 8-1 has been derived.   Numerous investigators have worked on the problems of fault detection and location and failure-tolerant design.   There are at least three books devoted to the subject (Refs. 3, 5, and 6) and numerous surveys, among which are Refs. 4 and 15.   The fault table has been extensively discussed in Kautz [8], of which parts of Sec. 8-3 are based. Fault location has also been studied in Koren and Kohavi [11], Kohavi and Berger [10], Su and Cho [18], and many others.   The Boolean difference method has been developed by Sellers et al. [17] and Yau and Tang

[21]. Path sensitization has been studied among many others by Armstrong [1] and Roth [16]. Most of the presentation in Sec. 8-6 on multiple faults is based on the work of Kohavi and Kohavi [9]. It was Von Neumann who initiated in his now famous paper [20] research in the subject of reliability through redundancy. Later Moore and Shannon [12], Pierce [13], and numerous other authors investigated various aspects and applications of redundancy techniques. An extensive collection of papers on the subject is available in a book edited by Wilcox and Mann [22]. Of particular interest in this volume is a paper by Tryon [19], titled Quadded Logic, on which the material in Sec. 8-8 is based. Other valuable sources of information on redundancy techniques and failure-tolerant design for digital systems are Pierce [14], Carter [4], and Ramamoorthy [15].

1. Armstrong, D. B.: On Finding a Nearly Minimal Set of Fault Detection Tests for Combinational Logic Nets, *IEEE Trans. Electron. Computers*, vol. EC-15, pp. 66–73, February, 1966.
2. Avizienis, A., et al.: The STAR (Self-Testing and Repairing) Computer: An Investigation of the Theory and Practice of Fault-Tolerant Design, *IEEE Trans. Computers*, vol. 20, no. 11, pp. 1312–1321, November, 1971.
3. Breuer, M. A., and A. D. Friedman: "Diagnosis and Reliable Design of Digital Systems," Computer Science Press, Inc., Woodland Hills, Calif., 1976.
4. Carter, W. C., and W. G. Bouricius: A Survey of Fault-Tolerant Computer Architecture and Its Evaluation, *Computer*, pp. 9–16, January, 1971.
5. Chang, H. Y., E. Manning, and G. Metze: "Fault Diagnosis of Digital Systems," Wiley Interscience, New York, 1970.
6. Friedman, A. D., and P. R. Menon: "Fault Detection in Digital Circuits," Prentice-Hall, Inc., Englewood Cliffs, N.J., 1971.
7. Huffman, D. A.: The Design and Use of Hazard-free Switching Networks, *J. Assoc. Computing Machinery*, vol. 4, no. 1, pp. 47–62, January, 1957.
8. Kautz, W. H.: Fault Testing and Diagnosis in Combinational Digital Circuits, *IEEE Trans. Computers*, vol. C-17, no. 4, pp. 352–366, April, 1968.
9. Kohavi, I., and Z. Kohavi: Detection of Multiple Faults in Combinational Logic Networks, *IEEE Trans. Computers*, vol. C-21, no. 6, pp. 556–568, June, 1972.
10. Kohavi, Z., and I. Berger: Fault Diagnosis in Combinational Tree Networks, *IEEE Trans. Computers*, vol. C-24, no. 12, pp. 1161–1167, December, 1975.
11. Koren, I., and Z. Kohavi: Sequential Fault Diagnosis in Combinational Networks, *IEEE Trans. Computers*, vol. C-26, no. 4, pp. 339–342, April, 1977.
12. Moore, E. F., and C. Shannon: Reliable Circuits Using Less Reliable Relays I-II, *J. Franklin Inst.*, vol. 262, no. 3, pp. 191–208; no. 4, pp. 281–297, 1956.
13. Pierce, W. H.: Adaptive Vote-takers Improve the Use of Redundancy, in R. H. Wilcox and W. C. Mann (eds.), "Redundancy Techniques for Computing Systems," pp. 229–250, Spartan Books, Washington, D.C., 1962.
14. Pierce, W. H.: "Failure-tolerant Computer Design," Academic Press Inc., New York, 1965.
15. Ramamoorthy, C. V., and R. C. Cheung: Design of Fault-Tolerant Computing Systems, in R. T. Yeh (ed.), "Applied Computation Theory," Prentice-Hall, Englewood Cliffs, N.J., 1976.

16. Roth, J. P.: Diagnosis of Automata Failures: A Calculus and a Method, *IBM Journal of Research and Development*, vol. 10, pp. 278–291, July, 1966.
17. Sellers, F. F., M. Y. Hsiao, C. L. Bearnson: Analyzing Errors with the Boolean Difference, *IEEE Trans. Computers*, vol. C-17, pp. 676–683, July, 1968.
18. Su, S. Y. H., and Y. C. Cho: A New Approach to the Fault Location of Combinational Circuits, *IEEE Trans. Computers*, vol. C-21, no. 1, pp. 21–30, January, 1972.
19. Tryon, J. G.: Quadded Logic, in R. H. Wilcox and W. C. Mann (eds.), "Redundancy Techniques for Computing Systems," pp. 205–228, Spartan Books, Washington, D.C., 1962.
20. Von Neumann, J.: "Probabilistic Logics and the Synthesis of Reliable Organisms from Unreliable Components," pp. 43–49, Automata Studies, Annals of Mathematics Studies, no. 34, Princeton University Press, Princeton, N.J., 1956.
21. Yau, S. S., and Y. S. Tang: An Efficient Algorithm for Generating Complete Test Sets for Combinational Logic Circuits, *IEEE Trans. Computers*, vol. C-10, no. 11, pp. 1245–1251, November, 1971.
22. Wilcox, R. H., and W. C. Mann (eds.): "Redundancy Techniques for Computing Systems," Spartan Books, Washington, D.C., 1962.

PROBLEMS

8-1. Analyze each of the circuits shown in Fig. P8-1 for static hazards. Redesign each circuit so that it becomes hazard-free.

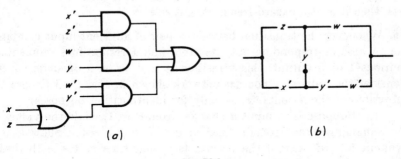

(a)   (b)

Fig. P8-1

8-2. Two different contact realizations, G_1 and G_2, of a function F are connected in parallel, as shown in Fig. P8-2. Discuss the hazards of the overall network in terms of the hazards in the individual networks. In particular, consider the cases:

(a) Both networks are hazard-free.
(b) One network is hazard-free.
(c) Neither network is hazard-free.

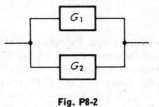

Fig. P8-2

8-3. Consider a network F which has both cut- and tie-set hazards and cannot be resynthesized. It is required to eliminate these hazards by adding terminal networks G_1, G_2, and G_3, as shown in Fig. P8-3. Derive an algorithm for determining G_1, G_2, and G_3, so that the overall network realizes F and has no static hazards.

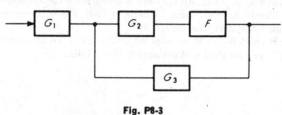

Fig. P8-3

8-4. Find all static hazards of the network shown in Fig. P5-5, assuming that the individual devices are hazard-free.

8-5. Prove that if a circuit is designed so that it is hazard-free in its tie sets, then it is also hazard-free in its cut sets.

8-6. Whenever the transition between a pair of adjacent input combinations whose corresponding outputs are 0 and 1 results in a momentary spurious 1 or 0 output, this transition is said to be a *dynamic hazard*. Consider the four-relay contact network shown in Fig. P8-6 (where the subscripts of the d contacts are only for identification purposes).

    (*a*) Suppose that input d changes from 0 to 1, while the values of the remaining inputs remain fixed at $a = 1$, $b = c = 0$. Show that a dynamic hazard exists if the d contacts change their states in the order given by their subscripts; i.e., d_1 closes first, d_2 opens second, etc.

    (*b*) Show all static hazards of this network.

    (*c*) Find a gate network which exhibits a dynamic hazard.

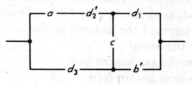

Fig. P8-6

8-7. (*a*) Find all the static hazards in the circuit shown in Fig. P8-7. (Assume the individual elements to be hazard-free.)

(*b*) Changing *only* the parameters of the threshold element, redesign the circuit so that all static hazards are eliminated.

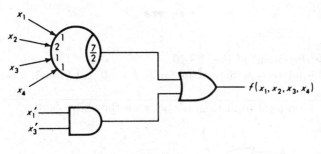

Fig. P8-7

8-8. For the network shown in Fig. P8-8:

(*a*) Show a map for $f(w,x,y,z)$.

(*b*) Find all static hazards of the network.

(*c*) Realize f with a single threshold element.

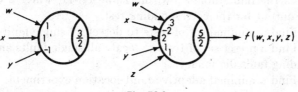

Fig. P8-8

8-9. In the gate network of Fig. P8-9, only wires m, n, p, and q may become either s-a-0 or s-a-1, while the remaining wires are considered "safe."

(*a*) Construct a fault table.

(*b*) Find a minimal cover of the table and use it to determine a minimal fault-detection experiment.

(*c*) Find a preset fault-location experiment and show its fault dictionary.

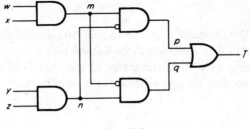

Fig. P8-9

8-10. For the circuit of Fig. P8-10:

(a) Find tests to detect the faults h s-a-0 and h s-a-1, k s-a-0 and k s-a-1.

(b) Find tests to distinguish between the above faults.

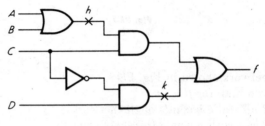

Fig. P8-10

8-11. Given the fault table shown in Table P8-11, where z denotes the fault-free output for the corresponding test.

(a) Find a minimal set of tests to detect all single faults.

(b) Find a preset set of tests to locate all single faults and show the corresponding fault dictionary.

(c) Find a minimal adaptive fault-location experiment.

Table P8-11

Tests \ Faults	f_1	f_2	f_3	f_4	f_5	z
T_1			1	1	1	0
T_2	1	1				1
T_3				1	1	1
T_4		1				0
T_5					1	1

8-12. For the circuit shown in Fig. P8-12:

(a) Find all the tests which detect each of the faults, B s-a-1 and h s-a-0.

(b) Find the tests which detect the multiple fault B s-a-1 and h s-a-0.

(c) Find all the tests that distinguish between the above two faults.

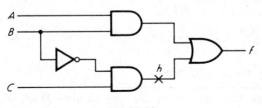

Fig. P8-12

8-13. For the circuit of Fig. P8-13:

(a) Find all the tests to detect input A' s-a-0 by using the sensitized-path approach and by using Boolean differences.

(b) Show all the single faults that can be detected by the test $(ABCD) = (1111)$.

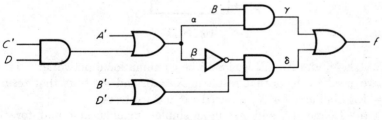

Fig. P8-13

8-14. Define *double Boolean difference* as follows:

$$\frac{df}{d(x_ix_j)} = f(x_1,x_2, \ldots ,x_i, \ldots ,x_j, \ldots ,x_n) \oplus$$
$$f(x_1, \ldots ,x_i', \ldots ,x_j', \ldots ,x_n)$$

From this equation we want to derive conditions under which a double fault at x_i and x_j will affect the output f.

(a) Show that

$$\frac{df}{d(x_ix_j)} = \frac{d^2f}{dx_idx_j} \oplus \frac{df}{dx_i} \oplus \frac{df}{dx_j}$$

when

$$\frac{d^2f}{dx_i dx_j} = \frac{d}{dx_i}\left(\frac{df}{dx_j}\right) = \frac{d}{dx_j}\left(\frac{df}{dx_i}\right)$$

(b) Show that, if g is not a function of x_i and x_j, then

(i) $\dfrac{d(fg)}{d(x_i x_j)} = g\,\dfrac{df}{d(x_i x_j)}$

(ii) $\dfrac{d(f + g)}{d(x_i x_j)} = g'\,\dfrac{df}{d(x_i x_j)}$

Hint: $AB \oplus AC = A(B \oplus C)$.

(c) Write the expression for the double Boolean difference for AND and OR function; that is, for $f_1 = x_1 x_2 \cdots x_n$ and $f_2 = x_1 + x_2 + \cdots + x_n$. Explain what combinations of multiple faults can be detected in the corresponding gates.

(d) Derive $df/[d(x_1 x_2)]$ for the Majority gate shown in Fig. P8-14 and explain the results.

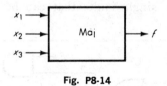

Fig. P8-14

8-15. Let N_x and N_y in Fig. P8-15 be combinational networks. To test N_x we need n_x^0 tests that result in $X = 0$, and n_x^1 tests that result in $X = 1$. Similarly for N_y we need n_y^0 and n_y^1 tests.

(a) Define n_f^0 and n_f^1 in a similar manner and find for them minimal values in terms of $n_x^0, n_x^1, n_y^0, n_y^1$.

(b) Repeat (a) when the OR gate in Fig. P8-15 is replaced by a NAND gate.

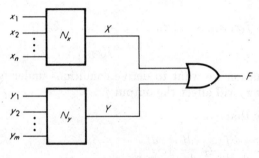

Fig. P8-15

8-16. The test $(ABCDEFGH) = (01111111)$ was applied to the circuit shown in Fig. P8-16 and the output f indicated an error.

(a) What are the single faults in this network that could cause the output to be erroneous?

(b) Which of the faults in (a) are equivalent?

(c) Show a minimal adaptive experiment that distinguishes between the nonequivalent faults.

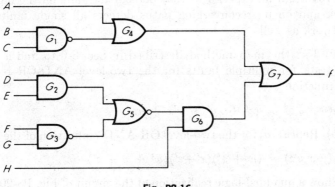

Fig. P8-16

8-17. The procedures presented in Sec. 8-6 can be generalized to fanout-free networks by: (1) Finding the equivalent sum of products; (2) selecting from this sum a *subset* of product terms which contains all the input variables; and (3) finding the a- and b-tests for the subset of these product terms.

(a) Prove that the above procedure detects all multiple faults in a fanout-free network.

(b) Apply the procedure to the network in Fig. P8-17 (six tests are sufficient).

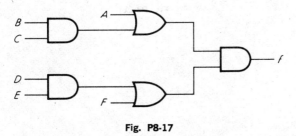

Fig. P8-17

8-18. The following will demonstrate that a fault-detection experiment that detects all single faults in a fanout-free network does not *necessarily* detect all multiple faults as well.

(a) Show that the following set of tests detects all single faults in the network of Fig. P8-17.

$$(ABCDEF) = \{111010,001001,011110,100100,101101,010111\}$$

(b) Prove that the multiple fault consisting of the four faults A and F s-a-0, B and E s-a-1, is not detected by the tests in (a).

8-19. Prove that an experiment that detects all faults on the inputs of a network and on its reconverging paths detects all single faults within the network as well.

8-20. (a) Use the map method described in Sec. 8-6 to find a minimal set of tests for multiple faults for the two-level AND-OR realization of the function

$$f_1(w,x,y,z) = wz' + xy' + w'x + wx'y$$

(b) Repeat (a) for the two-level OR-AND realization of the function

$$f_2(w,x,y,z) = (w + x')(x'+z')(w' + y + z')$$

8-21. Show a quadded-logic realization of the circuit of Fig. P8-20. Indicate the correction of the longest propagated error.

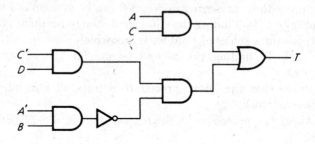

Fig. P8-21

Part Three
Finite-state Machines

9
Introduction to Synchronous Sequential Circuits and Iterative Networks

So far we have considered combinational switching circuits in which the outputs are functions of only the present circuit inputs. In most digital systems, however, additional circuits are necessary, capable of storing information and data, and also of performing some logical or mathematical operations upon these data. The outputs of these circuits at any given time are functions of the external inputs, as well as of the stored information at that time. Such circuits are called *sequential circuits*.†

A *finite-state machine* (or *finite automaton*) is an abstract model describing the synchronous sequential machine and its spatial counterpart, the iterative network. It is the basis for understanding and development of the various computation structures discussed in Part 3 of this book. The behavior, capabilities and limitations, and structure of finite-state machines are studied in Chaps. 12 through 16, while Chaps. 9 and

---

† Conventionally, the term *sequential machine* refers to the abstract model which represents the actual *sequential circuit*. In many cases, however, these terms are used interchangeably.

10 are devoted to the synthesis of these machines. Chapter 11 is concerned with asynchronous sequential circuits.

9-1 SEQUENTIAL CIRCUITS—INTRODUCTORY EXAMPLE

In our daily activities we all encounter the use of various sequential circuits. The elevator control which "remembers" to let us out before it picks up people going in the opposite direction; the traffic-light systems in our roads, trains, and subways; the lock on a safe which not only remembers the combination numbers but also their sequence; all these are examples of sequential circuits in action. Before deriving the basic model and general synthesis procedures, we shall investigate the properties of a simple sequential circuit.

The state table

Consider the *serial binary adder* whose block diagram is shown in Fig. 9-1. It is a synchronous circuit with two input terminals, designated X_1

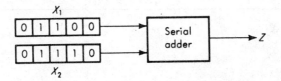

Fig. 9-1 Block diagram of a serial binary adder.

and X_2 and carrying the two binary numbers to be added, and one output terminal Z, which represents the sum. The inputs and the outputs consist of fixed-length sequences of 0's and 1's. The addition is to be performed serially; i.e., the least significant digits of the numbers X_1 and X_2 arrive at the corresponding input terminals at time t_1; a unit time later, the next significant digits arrive at the input terminals; and so on. The time interval between the arrival of two consecutive input digits is determined by the frequency of the circuit's clock. We shall assume that the delay within the combinational circuit is small with respect to the clock frequency, and as a consequence the sum digit arrives at the Z terminal immediately following the arrival of the corresponding input digits at the input terminals.

We shall denote by capital letters X and Z the input and output sequences, respectively, and by corresponding lowercase letters, i.e., x and

z, the input and output symbols at a specified point in time. We may often want to emphasize the precise time at which the input or output occurs. In such cases the notation $x(t_i)$ and $z(t_i)$ will be used.

Consider the following addition of two binary numbers:

$$
\begin{array}{cccccl}
t_5 & t_4 & t_3 & t_2 & t_1 & \\
0 & 1 & 1 & 0 & 0 & = X_1 \\
+\ 0 & 1 & 1 & 1 & 0 & = X_2 \\
\hline
1 & 1 & 0 & 1 & 0 & = Z
\end{array}
$$

An examination of the correlation between the inputs and the required output reveals the basic difference between a combinational circuit and the serial binary adder. While in a combinational circuit the output at time t_i is defined uniquely by the inputs at t_i, in the serial adder different outputs are required for identical input conditions. For example, at t_1 and t_5 the inputs are $x_1 x_2 = 00$, but the required outputs are $z = 0$ and $z = 1$, respectively. Similarly, at t_3 and t_4, the inputs are $x_1 x_2 = 11$, while the desired outputs are 0 and 1, respectively. It is therefore evident that *the output of the serial adder cannot be specified merely in terms of the external inputs*, and different design procedures must be employed.

Following the rules of elementary binary arithmetic, it is evident that the output at time t_i is a function of the inputs x_1 and x_2 at that time, and of the carry which has been generated at t_{i-1}. This carry (which may have either of the two values 0 or 1) in turn depends on the inputs at t_{i-1} and on the carry generated at t_{i-2}, and so on. Hence the adder must be able to preserve information regarding its inputs from the time it is set into operation up to time t_i. But since the starting time may be long past, it is impossible to preserve the whole history of the inputs. We therefore seek a different relation between the inputs $x_1(t_i)$ and $x_2(t_i)$ and the output $z(t_i)$.

In the case of the serial adder, we can distinguish two classes of past input histories, one resulting in production of a carry 0 and the other in producing a carry 1. These classes will be called the *internal states* (or simply *states*) of the adder. By "memorizing" the value of the carry, the adder actually shows some "trace" of its past inputs, at least to the extent of their influence on the response to the present inputs.

Let A designate the state of the adder at t_i if a carry 0 is generated at t_{i-1}, and let B designate the state of the adder at t_i if a carry 1 is generated at t_{i-1}. We refer to the state of the adder at the time when the present inputs are applied to it as its *present state*, and the state to which the adder goes, as a result of the new (not necessarily different) carry value, is referred to as the *next state*. The output $z(t_i)$ is a function of the inputs $x_1(t_i)$ and $x_2(t_i)$ and the state of the adder at time t_i. The next state of the adder depends only on the present inputs and on the present state. A convenient way of describing the behavior of the serial adder is by means of a *state table*, as shown in Table 9-1.

Table 9-1   State table for a binary serial adder

PS	$x_1x_2 = 00$	NS, z 01	11	10
A	A,0	A,1	B,0	A,1
B	A,1	B,0	B,1	B,0

PS = present state
NS = next state

Each row of the state table corresponds to a state of the adder, and each column corresponds to a combination of the external inputs x_1 and x_2. The entries of the table denote the state transitions and the outputs associated with these transitions. For example, if the adder is in state A, i.e., the present carry is 0, and it receives the input combination $x_1x_2 = 11$, it will go to state B, which corresponds to a carry 1, and produce an output $z = 0$. The remaining entries of the table can be verified in a straightforward manner, and since the table contains eight entries, corresponding to the eight combinations of states and inputs, it completely specifies the serial adder.

It is often convenient to use a directed graph as a counterpart to the state table. Such a graph, shown in Fig. 9-2, is known as the *state diagram* (or *state graph*). The vertices and directed arcs of the graph correspond to the states of the adder and to its state transitions, respectively. The labels of the directed arcs specify the inputs and the corresponding outputs; e.g., 10/0 represents the condition $x_1 = 1$, $x_2 = 0$, and $z = 0$. Clearly, both the state diagram and the state table provide the same information regarding the operation of the adder, and one can be obtained directly from the other. While in many cases these representations are equally suitable, in some applications one may be more convenient than the other.

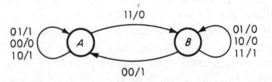

Fig. 9-2   State diagram for a serial adder.

The state assignment

In order to implement the serial adder, it is necessary to use some device capable of storing the information regarding the presence or absence of a carry. Such a device must have two distinct states, so that each of them can be assigned to represent a state of the adder. A number of such devices exist, among which is the *delay element*, which consists of a simple delay line or a D flip-flop which is described subsequently. The capability of the delay element to store information is a result of the fact that it takes a finite amount of time for the input signal Y to reach its output y. The length of the delay is usually equal to the interval between two successive clock pulses. For convenience, we assume that this delay is one time unit long.

The state of the delay element is specified by the value of its output y, which may assume either one of two values, namely, $y = 0$ and $y = 1$. Since the present input value Y of the delay is equal to its next output value, the input value is referred to as the *next state* of the delay, that is, $Y(t) = y(t + 1)$.

If we assign the states of the delay to those of the adder so that $y = 0$ is assigned to A and $y = 1$ to B, the value of y at t_i will correspond to the value of the carry generated at t_{i-1}. The process of assigning the states of a physical device to the states of the serial adder is known as the *state assignment* (or *secondary state assignment*). The output value y is referred to as the *state variable* (or *secondary variable*, to distinguish it from the external primary input variables).

The state assignment is completed by modifying the entries of the state table to correspond to the states of y, in accordance with the selected state assignment. The resulting table is given in Table 9-2, where the next-state and output entries have been separated into two sections. The entries of the next-state table define the necessary state transitions of the adder, and thus specify the next value of the output, $y(t + 1)$, of the delay. And since $Y(t) = y(t + 1)$, these entries specify also the required inputs to the delay at time t, so as to achieve the desired state transitions. Thus the next-state part of Table 9-2, which is called the *transition table*, serves also to specify the required *excitation* of the delay.

Table 9-2   Transition and output tables for a serial adder

y	Next state Y				Output z			
	x_1x_2 00	01	11	10	x_1x_2 00	01	11	10
0	0	0	1	0	0	1	0	1
1	0	1	1	1	1	0	1	0

The output part of Table 9-2, which is identical with that of Table 9-1, specifies the output z for every combination of x_1, x_2, and y. Consequently, using the map method, the following logical equations result:

$$Y = x_1x_2 + x_1y + x_2y$$
$$z = x_1'x_2'y + x_1'x_2y' + x_1x_2'y' + x_1x_2y$$

These equations are clearly identical with those obtained in Sec. 5-4 for the carry and sum functions of the full adder. The addition is accomplished by retransmitting the carry of the full adder through the delay Y into the full adder's input, as shown in Fig. 9-3. (Note that a delay whose input is Y is generally referred to as delay Y.) The additional input representing the clock pulse indicates that the serial adder is a synchronous circuit and all events occur only at discrete instants.

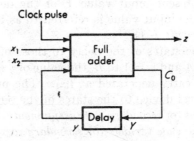

Fig. 9-3 Serial binary adder.

9-2 THE FINITE-STATE MODEL—BASIC DEFINITIONS

The behavior of a finite-state machine is described as a sequence of events that occur at discrete instants, designated $t = 1, 2, 3$, etc. Suppose that a machine M has been receiving input signals and has been responding by producing output signals. If now, at time t, we were to apply an input signal $x(t)$ to M, its response $z(t)$ would depend on $x(t)$, as well as on past inputs to M. And since a given machine M might have an infinite variety of possible histories, it would need an infinite capacity for storing them.

Since in practice it is impossible to implement machines which have infinite storage capabilities, *we shall concentrate on those machines whose past histories can affect their future behavior in only a finite number of ways.* For example, suppose that the serial binary adder of the previous section has been receiving input signals; its response to the signals at t is only a function of these signals and the value of the carry generated at $t - 1$. Thus, although the adder may have a large number of possible

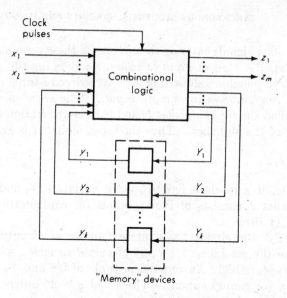

Clock
pulses

x_1

x_l

Combinational
logic

z_1

z_m

y_1 Y_1

y_2 Y_2

y_k Y_k

"Memory" devices

Fig. 9-4 Circuit representation of a synchronous
sequential machine.

input histories, they may be grouped into two classes, those resulting in
a 1 carry and those resulting in a 0 carry at t.

We shall study machines which can distinguish among a *finite* number of classes of input histories, and shall refer to these classes as the
internal states of the machine.   Every finite-state machine therefore contains a finite number of memory devices, which store the information
regarding the past input history.   Note that, although we restrict our
attention to machines which have finite storage capacity, no bound has
been set on the duration for which a particular input may affect the
future behavior of the machine.   A discussion of this subject is deferred
to Chap. 14.

Synchronous sequential machines

In general, a synchronous sequential machine is represented schematically
by the circuit of Fig. 9-4.†   The circuit has a finite number l of input

† It is appropriate to emphasize at this point that a synchronous circuit may take
a variety of forms. For example, it is possible to modify the basic model of Fig.
9-4 so that the inputs and outputs will be represented by levels, rather than pulses,
and the memory elements will be flip-flops whose state transitions are synchronized
by means of a clock. The combinational logic in this case receives level inputs and
produces level outputs. When properly interpreted, this form is equivalent to that
of Fig. 9-4, and all subsequent results are valid for either representation. This point
is further discussed in the next section.

terminals. The signals entering the circuit via these terminals constitute the set $\{x_1, x_2, \ldots, x_l\}$ of *input variables*, where x_j for all j may take on one of the two possible values, 0 or 1. An ordered l-tuple of 0's and 1's is an *input configuration* (or simply *input*). The set of $p = 2^l$ distinct inputs is called the *input alphabet I*, and each configuration is referred to as a *symbol* of the alphabet. Thus the input alphabet is given by

$$I = \{I_1, I_2, \ldots, I_p\}$$

For example, if a machine has two input variables, x_1 and x_2, then its input alphabet I consists of four symbols (or configurations), that is, $I = \{00, 01, 11, 10\}$.

Similarly, the circuit has a finite number m of output terminals which define the set $\{z_1, z_2, \ldots, z_m\}$ of *output variables*, where z_j for all j is a binary variable. An ordered m-tuple of 0's and 1's is an *output configuration* (or simply *output*). The set of $q = 2^m$ ordered m-tuples is called the *output alphabet* and is given by

$$O = \{O_1, O_2, \ldots, O_q\}$$

where each output configuration is a *symbol* of the output alphabet.

The signal value at the output of each memory element is referred to as the *state variable*, and the set $\{y_1, y_2, \ldots, y_k\}$ constitutes the set of state variables. The combination of values at the outputs of the k memory elements $y_1, y_2, \ldots, y_k$ defines the *present internal state* (or *state*) of the machine. The set S of $n = 2^k$ k-tuples constitutes the entire set of states of the machine, where

$$S = \{S_1, S_2, \ldots, S_n\}$$

The external inputs $x_1, x_2, \ldots, x_l$ and the values of the state variables $y_1, y_2, \ldots, y_k$ are supplied to the combinational circuit, which in turn produces the outputs $z_1, z_2, \ldots, z_m$ and the values $Y_1, Y_2, \ldots, Y_k$. The values of the Y's, which appear at the outputs of the combinational circuit at time t, are identical with the values of the state variables at $t + 1$, and therefore they define the *next state* of the machine, i.e., the state that the machine will assume next.

Synchronization is achieved by means of clock pulses. In practice, it may be accomplished by applying the clock pulses into the various AND gates which the inputs enter. This allows the gates to transmit signals only at instants which coincide with the arrival of the clock pulses. For a synchronous circuit to operate correctly, it is necessary to restrict the inherent delays within the combinational logic and to ensure that no input changes will occur while the clock pulse is present.

Specification of machine behavior

The relationship among the input, present state, output, and next state is described by either a *state table* or a *state diagram*. A state table has p columns, one for each input symbol, and n rows, one for each state. For each combination of input symbol and present state, the corresponding entry specifies the output that will be generated and the next state to which the machine will go. Although in practice every machine of the type shown in Fig. 9-4 has 2^l input symbols and 2^k states, some of them may be theoretically unnecessary. In other words, theoretically, a machine may have any number p of inputs and n of states. But in practice, when realizing such a machine, the actual circuit will have $l = \lceil \log_2 p \rceil$ input terminals and $k = \lceil \log_2 n \rceil$ memory elements, where $\lceil g \rceil$ is the smallest integer larger than or equal to g.

To each state of the machine there corresponds a vertex in the state diagram. From each vertex emanate p directed arcs, corresponding to the *state transitions* caused by the various input symbols. Each directed arc is labeled by the input symbol that causes the transition and by the output symbol that is to be generated. Since both the state table and the state diagram contain the same information, the choice between the two representations is a matter of convenience. Both have the advantage of being precise, unambiguous, and thus more suitable for describing the operation of a sequential machine than any verbal description.

The succession of states through which a sequential machine passes, and the output sequence which it produces in response to a known input sequence, are specified uniquely by the state diagram (or table) and the initial state, where by *initial state* we refer to the state of the machine prior to the application of the input sequence. The state of the machine after the application of the input sequence is called *final state*.

9-3 MEMORY ELEMENTS AND THEIR EXCITATION FUNCTIONS

In discussing the basic model for synchronous sequential machines we showed that a state table (or diagram) completely specifies the behavior of the machine. In order to design a circuit which operates according to the specifications of a given table, it is necessary to first select a number of memory elements, each of which is a device with two distinct states and is capable of storing a binary digit. The states of these elements are next assigned to the states of the machine, a process known as *state assignment*.

A *transition table* is derived from a state table by replacing each next-state entry with the corresponding state of the memory elements. A transition table thus specifies for every combination of inputs and state variables the next state of the memory elements, which is given by $Y_1, Y_2, \ldots, Y_k$. To generate these Y's, the memory elements must be supplied with the appropriate inputs. The switching functions which describe the effect of the circuit inputs $x_1, x_2, \ldots, x_l$ and the state variables $y_1, y_2, \ldots, y_k$ on the memory-element inputs are called _excitation functions_. These functions are derived from an _excitation table_, whose entries are the values of the memory-element inputs.

In Sec. 9-1 we have described the delay element as a memory device. Its storage capability is due to the fact that it takes a finite time for the signal to propagate through it. In practice, the most widely used memory element at present is the _flip-flop_.

Set-reset or SR flip-flop

The SR flip-flop, which is also known as the _bistable multivibrator_, has two inputs, S and R, and two outputs, y and y' (often denoted as the 1 and 0 outputs or Q and Q' outputs, respectively). A block diagram representing an SR flip-flop is shown in Fig. 9-5a. SR flip-flops are easily implemented with cross-coupled NOR or NAND gates, as shown in Fig. 9-5b and Fig. 9-5c, respectively. Such an implementation is available as an SSI integrated circuit and is known as the SR latch.

The SR flip-flop has two states, defined by $y = 1$ and $y = 0$. Output y' is the complement of y. The flip-flop possesses the property that it remains in one state indefinitely until it is directed by an input signal to do otherwise. The set (S) and reset (R) input signals may be either pulses or voltage levels, while the outputs are usually voltage levels. A signal at input S sets the flip-flop to the 1 state, i.e., sets $y = 1$; a signal at input R resets it to the 0 state. The excitation characteristics of the SR flip-flop are summarized in Table 9-3. If both R and S are excited simultaneously, the operation of the flip-flop becomes unpre-

Table 9-3 Excitation characteristics of SR flip-flops

	$y(t)$	$S(t)$	$R(t)$	$y(t+1)$
	0	0	0	0
$RS = 0$	0	0	1	0
$y(t+1) = R'y(t) + S$	0	1	1	?
	0	1	0	1
	1	1	0	1
	1	1	1	?
	1	0	1	0
	1	0	0	1

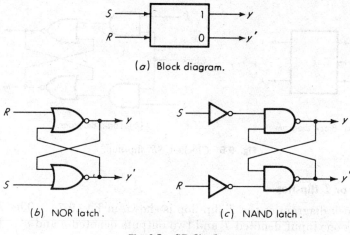

(a) Block diagram.

(b) NOR latch.

(c) NAND latch.

Fig. 9-5 *SR* flip-flop.

dictable. Consequently, the requirement $RS = 0$ must be imposed to ensure that the two invalid combinations in Table 9-3 will never occur. The excitation requirements of the SR flip-flop are summarized in Table 9-4, in which a dash (—) denotes a situation where the value of the input is a don't-care, since it does not affect the output value.

Table 9-4 Excitation requirements for *SR* flip-flops

Circuit change From:	To:	Required input S	R
0	0	0	—
0	1	1	0
1	0	0	1
1	1	—	0

In practice, a clocked, or synchronous, version of the SR flip-flop is generally used. In this version, shown in Fig. 9-6, all state changes can occur only in synchronization with the pulses from an electronic clock. To ensure proper operation, restrictions must be placed on the length of the clock pulses and on the frequency of the input changes so that the circuit will change state no more than once for each clock pulse. The synchronization of the S and R inputs with the clock is accomplished in Fig. 9-6b, by AND-gating them before they enter the latch inputs.

To simplify logic diagrams in subsequent sections we often ignore the clock, but it is important to note that *in all synchronous circuits the clock is implicit* whether shown or not.

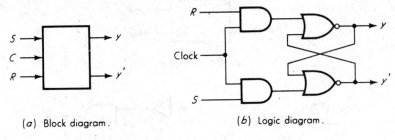

(a) Block diagram.

(b) Logic diagram.

Fig. 9-6 Clocked SR flip-flop.

Trigger or T flip-flop

The block diagram of the T flip-flop is shown in Fig. 9-7a. The T flip-flop has one input denoted T and two outputs denoted y and y'. It has

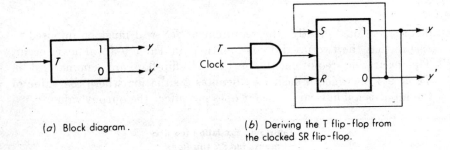

(a) Block diagram.

(b) Deriving the T flip-flop from the clocked SR flip-flop.

Fig. 9-7 Trigger (or T) flip-flop.

two distinct states, defined by the logical value of y; namely, the flip-flop is in the 1 state when $y = 1$ and it is in the 0 state when $y = 0$. Output y' is the complement of y. As in the case of the SR flip-flop, the T flip-flop remains in one state indefinitely until it is directed by an input signal to do otherwise. A value 1 applied to its input triggers the flip-flop and it changes state.

The terminal characteristics of the T flip-flop are summarized in Table 9-5. The next-state function $y(t + 1)$ can be expressed in terms

**Table 9-5 Excitation re-
quirements for T Flip-flops**

Circuit change From:	To:	Required Input T
0	0	0
0	1	1
1	1	0
1	0	1

of the present state and input values as follows:

$$y(t + 1) = Ty'(t) + T'y(t)$$
$$= T \oplus y(t)$$

A clocked T flip-flop can be realized by a cross-coupling of a clocked SR flip-flop, as shown in Fig. 9-7b.   (The clock in Fig. 9-6b is replaced by the AND combination of input T and a clock.)   If a nonclocked operation is desired, the clock and AND gate in Fig. 9-7b may be removed and T applied directly to the flip-flop.   In the clocked realization, if output y is equal to 1, then the reset input is 1.   The flip-flop will now change state (to $y = 0$) when $TC = 1$, that is, when both T and the clock are equal to 1.   Similarly, when $y = 0$ the set input equals 1 and the flip-flop will change state (to $y = 1$) when $TC = 1$.

Although the clock is not indicated in the block diagram, it will be understood to exist in all synchronous circuits.

The JK flip-flop

The JK flip-flop has the characteristics of both the set-reset and trigger flip-flops.   The inputs J and K, like the S and R, set and reset the flip-flop, respectively.   The combination $J = K = 1$ is permitted, and when it occurs the flip-flop acts like a trigger and switches to its complement state; that is, if $y = 1$, it switches to $y = 0$, and vice versa.   The block diagram and excitation requirements for the JK flip-flop are shown in Fig. 9-8a and Table 9-6, respectively.

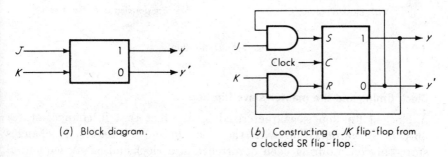

(a) Block diagram.

(b) Constructing a JK flip-flop from a clocked SR flip-flop.

Fig. 9-8 JK flip-flop.

One possible realization of a clocked JK flip-flop is by generalizing the clocked SR flip-flop, as shown in Fig. 9-8b.   Another realization, by means of a master-slave flip-flop, is discussed subsequently.

Table 9-6 Excitation requirements for JK flip-flops

Circuit change From:	To:	Required input J	K
0	0	0	—
0	1	1	—
1	0	—	1
1	1	—	0

The D flip-flop

The block diagram and a possible realization of the D flip-flop are shown in Fig. 9-9. The next state of this device is equal to its present excitation. Hence, it is characterized by the equation

$$y(t + 1) = D(t)$$

This flip-flop clearly behaves like the delay element discussed in the preceding sections and, consequently, its excitation requirements are specified by the transition table.

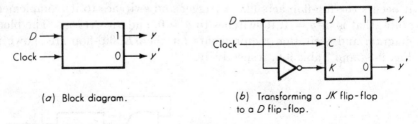

(a) Block diagram.

(b) Transforming a JK flip-flop to a D flip-flop.

Fig. 9-9 D flip-flop.

Clock timing and the master-slave flip-flop

A clocked flip-flop is characterized by the fact that it changes states only in synchronization with the clock pulse. Moreover, it changes state only once during each occurrence of a clock pulse. A sequential circuit operating under these restrictions is said to be a *synchronous sequential circuit*. The duration of the clock pulse is usually determined by the circuit delays and the signal propagation time through the flip-flops. In fact, *the clock pulse must be long enough to allow the flip-flop to change state, and at the same time must be short enough so that the flip-flop will not change state twice due to the same excitation.*

In general, referring to the sequential circuit model of Fig. 9-4, the outputs of a flip-flop (which serves as a memory element) are inserted into a combinational circuit, which, in turn, generates the excitation functions for that flip-flop. In such a case, illustrated in Fig. 9-10, the length of the clock pulse must be such that it will allow the flip-flop to generate the y's, but it will not be present when the values of the y's have propagated through the combinational circuit. Such a fine tuning of the length of the clock pulse is very difficult to accomplish. To overcome this difficulty a new type of flip-flop, called the *master-slave flip-flop*, can be used. This flip-flop eliminates the timing problems associated with the feedback loop by essentially isolating the inputs of the flip-flop from its outputs.

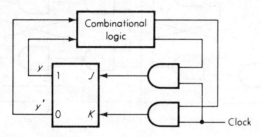

Fig. 9-10 The excitation of a JK flip-flop within a sequential circuit.

The master-slave flip-flop, shown in Fig. 9-11, is constructed of two set-reset flip-flops connected in series, with their clock inputs driven in complementary manner. The first flip-flop, called the *master*, can change state only when the clock pulse is 1, while the second flip-flop, called the *slave*, can change state only when the clock pulse is 0. A change in the excitation causes a change of state in the master flip-flop. During that period the slave flip-flop maintains its previous state and serves as a buffer between the master and the next stage. When the clock changes from 1 to 0, the state of the master flip-flop is frozen while the slave flip-flop is enabled and changes its state to that of the master flip-flop. The new state of the slave then determines the state of the entire master-slave flip-flop. Thus, when a master-slave flip-flop is substituted for the JK flip-flop in Fig. 9-10, the inputs into the combinational circuit do not change when the clock is 1. When the clock becomes 0, the y's change and consequently the output of the combinational circuit changes; but this cannot affect the state of the master flip-flop.

In practice, a master-slave flip-flop has three regular inputs, namely J, K (or S, R) and clock, and two additional inputs, called *direct set*

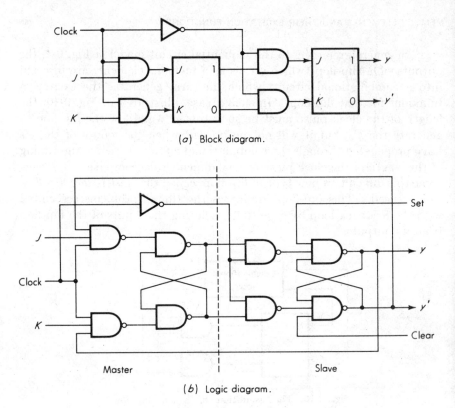

(a) Block diagram.

(b) Logic diagram.

Fig. 9-11 Master-slave flip-flop.

and *direct clear*. These latter inputs are added to the slave flip-flop and they override the regular input signals and the clock. They are used to either set the slave output to 1, by applying 0 to the set input and 1 to the clear input, or to clear the slave output to 0, by applying the complementary values to the set and clear inputs. It is not allowed to assign 0's to both the set and clear simultaneously. On the other hand, if we assign both of them 1's, the circuit returns to the normal clocked master-slave operation. Such external inputs are very useful, for example, in the design of counters, where it may be necessary to reset it to a prespecified count, or in the design of shift registers, which must be cleared before the start of certain computations.

To simplify the subsequent discussion, we shall synthesize sequential circuits using mainly the simplified basic flip-flops. The reader should keep in mind, however, that in each case a master-slave flip-flop can replace the simpler flip-flop with only minor modification in the design approach. Moreover, to simplify the resulting tables and circuits, the clock is generally not shown. However, as mentioned before, it is implicit in all synchronous circuits.

9-4 SYNTHESIS OF SYNCHRONOUS SEQUENTIAL CIRCUITS

We have seen in Sec. 9-1 a synthesis procedure for a serial binary adder using a delay as the memory element. In this section we shall develop the general method for designing sequential circuits, using various types of memory elements, and apply this method to the design of some of the commonly used circuits in current technology. The main steps in the method are summarized as follows:

1. From a word description of the problem, form a state table (or a state diagram) which specifies the circuit performance.
2. Check this table to determine whether it contains any redundant states. (The notion of a redundant state will be defined in Chap. 10, where we shall also present methods for detecting and eliminating such states. The state tables in this section will be developed so that they do not contain any redundant states.)
3. Select a state assignment and determine the type of memory elements to be used.
4. Derive transition and output tables.
5. Derive an excitation table and obtain the excitation and output · functions from their respective tables.
6. Draw a circuit diagram.

In step 5 we in effect convert the problem of sequential circuit synthesis into the more familiar problem of combinational circuit synthesis, since the construction of the excitation table is actually equivalent to the construction of a set of maps, from which the derivation of the excitation functions is straightforward.

The sequence detector

We wish to design a two-input, two-output sequence detector which produces an output 1 every time the sequence 0101 is detected, and an output 0 at all other times. For example, when the input sequence is 010101, the corresponding output sequence is 000101. In designing the sequence detector, we may find it more convenient to start the synthesis procedure by constructing the state diagram of the machine.

At time t_1 the machine is assumed to be in the initial state, designated (arbitrarily) as A. While in this state, the machine can receive either an input 0 or 1. For each of these inputs, an arc is drawn originating in state A and terminating in the appropriate next state, as shown in Fig. 9-12. The arc labeled 1/0 forms a self-loop around state A, since the machine does not initiate the detection process until it receives a 0

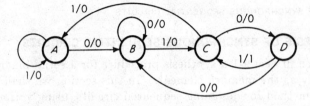

Fig. 9-12 State diagram for a sequence (0101) detector.

input. An input 0 indicates a possible start of the sequence to be detected, and therefore an arc labeled 0/0 leads from state A to B. When the machine is in state B, a 1 input takes it to state C, while a 0 input leaves it in the same state. If, when the machine is in state C, it receives a 1 input, its last two inputs are 11, and since this input sequence cannot be completed in any way as to yield 0101, the machine is directed to its initial state. The machine arrives at state D after having received an input sequence whose last three symbols are 010. An additional 1 input produces a 1 output and causes a transition from state D to C, which is the state corresponding to input sequences whose last symbols are 01. A 0 input, applied to the machine when in state D, causes a transition to B because the last 0 symbol may be a prefix of 0101.

The state table corresponding to the diagram of Fig. 9-12 is given in Table 9-7, where the input and output symbols are denoted by x and z, respectively.

Table 9-7   State table

PS	NS, z	
	$x = 0$	$x = 1$
A	$B,0$	$A,0$
B	$B,0$	$C,0$
C	$D,0$	$A,0$
D	$B,0$	$C,1$

Two state variables with $2^2 = 4$ states are needed for the representation of the four states of the sequence detector. If we select two delay elements, Y_1 and Y_2, as memory devices, and choose the state assignment shown in the left column of Table 9-8, we obtain the transition and output tables in the center and right columns of Table 9-8. The entries of the transition table specify, for each combination of present state and input, the values that the outputs of the delays should assume next. But since the *next* values of the delays are equal to their *present* excitation, the transition table entries in effect specify the required excitation of the delay elements. Consequently, whenever delay elements are used as memory devices, the transition and excitation tables are identical.

Table 9-8   Transition and output tables

y_1y_2	Y_1Y_2		z	
	$x = 0$	$x = 1$	$x = 0$	$x = 1$
$A \rightarrow 00$	01	00	0	0
$B \rightarrow 01$	01	11	0	0
$C \rightarrow 11$	10	00	0	0
$D \rightarrow 10$	01	11	0	1

The output table is, actually, a three-variable map in which the value of z is specified for every combination of x, y_1, and y_2, as shown in Fig. 9-13. The excitation table consists of two distinct three-variable

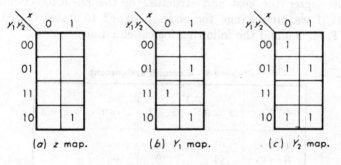

(a) z map.   (b) Y_1 map.   (c) Y_2 map.

Fig. 9-13   Excitation and output maps.

maps, corresponding to the excitation functions for Y_1 and Y_2. The entries of the map of $Y_1(Y_2)$ are given by the left-hand (right-hand) entries of the transition table. The logical equations, derived from the maps of Fig. 9-13, for the output and excitation functions are

$$z = xy_1y_2'$$
$$Y_1 = x'y_1y_2 + xy_1'y_2 + xy_1y_2'$$
$$Y_2 = y_1y_2' + x'y_1' + y_1'y_2$$

The implementation of these equations yields the sequence detector of Fig. 9-14.

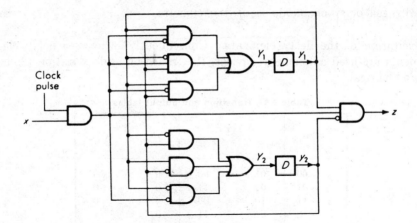

Fig. 9-14 Logic diagram of a sequence detector.

The reader will have observed that the state assignment employed in Table 9-8 is not the only possible one. In general, different state assignments yield different logical equations, which may affect to a considerable degree the cost and structure of the resulting circuit. For example, if we interchange the codes assigned to states C and D, we obtain Table 9-9 and the following logical equations.

Table 9-9 A second assignment

y_1y_2	Y_1Y_2		z	
	$x = 0$	$x = 1$	$x = 0$	$x = 1$
$A \rightarrow 00$	01	00	0	0
$B \rightarrow 01$	01	10	0	0
$C \rightarrow 10$	11	00	0	0
$D \rightarrow 11$	01	10	0	1

$$Y_1 = x'y_1y_2' + xy_2$$
$$Y_2 = x'$$
$$z = xy_1y_2$$

The implementation of the equations derived from the second assignment requires less than half the number of gates required for the circuit of Fig. 9-14. Also, the second excitation function for Y_2 is independent of the state variables y_1 and y_2 and depends only on the input. Unfortunately, there is no simple procedure which can be used to arrive at an assignment yielding a minimal circuit under some well-defined cost criterion. Some trial and error is consequently necessary until an acceptable assignment is achieved. The state-assignment problem, and in particular its effect on the machine structure, will be discussed extensively in Chap. 12.

A binary counter

A modulo-8 binary counter is to be designed with one input terminal which receives pulse signals and one output terminal. It should be capable of counting in the binary number system up to 7 and producing an output pulse for every eight input pulses. After a count of seven is reached, the next input pulse will reset the counter to its initial state, i.e., to a count of zero.

Let S_0, S_1, . . . , S_7 be the states of the counter after having received 0, 1, . . . , 7 input pulses, respectively. S_0, the state which designates the zero count, is the initial state. Transitions occur between successive states only when the counter receives an input pulse. The state diagram and table of the counter are shown in Fig. 9-15 and Table 9-10, respectively.

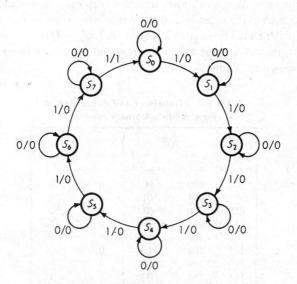

Fig. 9-15 State diagram for a modulo-8 binary counter.

From the correspondence between the states and the count, it is evident that no state in Table 9-10 is redundant. And since the counter has eight states, a state assignment requires three state variables (having

**Table 9-10   State table for a
modulo-8 binary counter**

	NS		Output	
PS	$x = 0$	$x = 1$	$x = 0$	$x = 1$
S_0	S_0	S_1	0	0
S_1	S_1	S_2	0	0
S_2	S_2	S_3	0	0
S_3	S_3	S_4	0	0
S_4	S_4	S_5	0	0
S_5	S_5	S_6	0	0
S_6	S_6	S_7	0	0
S_7	S_7	S_0	0	1

$2^3 = 8$ states).   The states of these variables, starting from the all-zero position, are 000, 001, . . . , 111.   The choice of assignment in this example should not be made arbitrarily since it determines the characteristics of the circuits and, in particular, it specifies the code and number system in which the counter actually counts.   Our objective is to design a counter which counts in the binary number system.   Accordingly, the code assigned to each state must be a binary representation of the actual count associated with that state, that is, $S_0 \rightarrow 000$, $S_1 \rightarrow 001$, . . . , $S_7 \rightarrow 111$. The transition and output tables corresponding to the foregoing assignment are shown in Table 9-11.

**Table 9-11   Transition and output tables
for a modulo-8 binary counter**

PS	NS		z	
$y_3 y_2 y_1$	$x = 0$	$x = 1$	$x = 0$	$x = 1$
000	000	001	0	0
001	001	010	0	0
010	010	011	0	0
011	011	100	0	0
100	100	101	0	0
101	101	110	0	0
110	110	111	0	0
111	111	000	0	1

Implementing the counter with T flip-flops

To complete the synthesis we should choose an appropriate set of memory elements and derive their excitation functions.   Let us select T flip-flops whose excitation requirements are specified by Table 9-5.

So far we have used a delay element whose output $y(t)$ equals its excitation at time $t - 1$, and consequently the transition table which specifies the required changes in the values of the y's yields the necessary present excitations as well. Table 9-11, however, does not yield the necessary excitations for the trigger flip-flops. Consider, for example, the entries 000 at the top of column $x = 0$ and the bottom of column $x = 1$. In the first case the flip-flops are to remain unchanged, since the transitions are from $S_0 = 000$ to $S_0 = 000$. In the second case, however, the transitions are from $S_7 = 111$ to $S_0 = 000$, and therefore all three flip-flops must change states. Hence, while in the first case no excitations are needed, in the second case all three flip-flops must be triggered, i.e., $T_1 = T_2 = T_3 = 1$. Similarly, the transition from $S_5 = 101$ to $S_6 = 110$, under 1 input, requires y_3 to remain unchanged, while y_1 and y_2 are to change states. Thus, from Table 9-5, it is evident that the required excitation is 011. In the same manner we specify the required excitations for each transition, and the excitation table shown in Table 9-12 results.

Table 9-12   Excitation table for T flip-flops

$y_3y_2y_1$	$T_3T_2T_1$ $x = 0$	$x = 1$
000	000	001
001	000	011
010	000	001
011	000	111
100	000	001
101	000	011
110	000	001
111	000	111

The excitation table consists of three distinct maps specifying T_1, T_2, and T_3 as functions of x, y_1, y_2, and y_3. The logical equations for the output and the excitation functions are derived from Tables 9-11 and 9-12, respectively, and are as follows. (Note that the code resulting from the binary state assignment is not cyclic, and thus the reader must be careful when "reading" the equations from the corresponding tables. Alternatively, it is possible to transform the tables into three maps and to determine the equations directly from these maps.)

$$T_1 = x$$
$$T_2 = xy_1$$
$$T_3 = xy_1y_2$$
$$z = xy_1y_2y_3$$

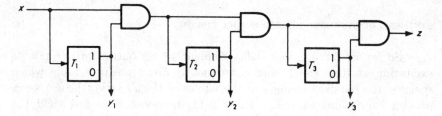

Fig. 9-16 Schematic diagram of a modulo-8 binary counter with T flip-flops.

The schematic diagram of a modulo-8 counter is shown in Fig. 9-16. The clock pulse has not been shown, but is implicit in this and subsequent figures. A pulse appears on terminal z whenever the total number of pulses received at the input line x is a multiple of 8. The actual count (modulo 8) of the number of incoming pulses is given by the values of the state variables y_1, y_2, and y_3, which have binary weights of 1, 2, and 4, respectively. For example, if $y_1 = 1$, $y_2 = 0$, and $y_3 = 1$, the number of incoming pulses has been 5 modulo 8.

Implementing the counter with SR flip-flops

The modulo-8 binary counter can also be implemented using SR flip-flops. The excitation table (Table 9-13) is derived from the transition table (Table 9-11) and from the excitation requirements of Table 9-4. As an example, consider the specification of the transition from $S_5 = 101$, under 1 input, to $S_6 = 110$. y_1 is to change from 1 to 0, and consequently, the flip-flop must be reset. From Table 9-4 it is evident that this is accomplished by setting $S_1 = 0$ and $R_1 = 1$, and thus the value 01 is entered in row 101, column S_1R_1, of Table 9-13. Similarly, y_2 must change from 0 to 1, and the value 10 is entered in column S_2R_2, row 101. y_3, however, is to remain unchanged; hence R_3 must not be 1, while S_3 may be either 0 or 1, which means that the appropriate entry in row 101, column S_3R_3, is -0. In a similar way the entire excitation table is specified.

Table 9-13   Excitation table for SR flip-flops

$y_3y_2y_1$	$x = 0$ S_3R_3	S_2R_2	S_1R_1	$x = 1$ S_3R_3	S_2R_2	S_1R_1
000	0 −	0 −	0 −	0 −	0 −	1 0
001	0 −	0 −	− 0	0 −	1 0	0 1
010	0 −	− 0	0 −	0 −	− 0	1 0
011	0 −	− 0	− 0	1 0	0 1	0 1
100	− 0	0 −	0 −	− 0	0 −	1 0
101	− 0	0 −	− 0	− 0	1 0	0 1
110	− 0	− 0	0 −	− 0	− 0	1 0
111	− 0	− 0	− 0	0 1	0 1	0 1

Table 9-13 consists of six distinct maps for S_1, R_1, S_2, R_2, S_3, and R_3 as functions of the variables x, y_1, y_2, and y_3. The logical equations for the excitation functions are

$$S_1 = xy_1' \qquad S_2 = xy_1y_2' \qquad S_3 = xy_1y_2y_3'$$
$$R_1 = xy_1 \qquad R_2 = xy_1y_2 \qquad R_3 = xy_1y_2y_3$$

The schematic diagram† corresponding to these equations is shown in Fig. 9-17.

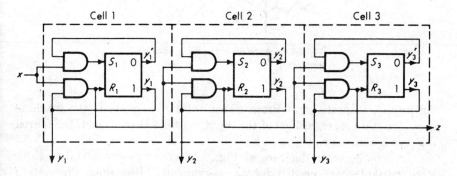

Fig. 9-17 Schematic diagram of a modulo-8 binary counter with SR flip-flops.

A parity-bit generator

A serial parity-bit generator is a two-terminal circuit which receives coded messages and is to add a parity bit to every m-bits message, so that the resulting outcome is an error-detecting coded message. The inputs in our example are assumed to arrive in strings of three symbols, i.e., $m = 3$, the strings spaced apart by single time units. The parity bits are to be inserted in the appropriate spaces, so that the resulting outcome is a continuous string of symbols without spaces. Even parity will be used; that is, a parity bit 1 is to be inserted if and only if the number of 1's in the preceding string of three symbols is odd.

The state diagram for the parity-bit generator is shown in Fig. 9-18. States B, D, and F correspond to even numbers of 1's, out of one, two, and three incoming inputs, respectively. Similarly, states C, E, and G correspond to odd numbers of 1's, out of one, two, and three incom-

---

† It is interesting to observe that the binary counter is an iterative network, in the sense that, from the terminal viewpoint, each cell, containing a flip-flop and its associated logic, is indistinguishable from the others. Consequently, in order to design a modulo-16 counter, all that is necessary is to add a fourth identical cell in cascade with the three cells shown in the figure.

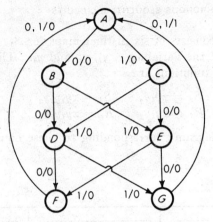

Fig. 9-18 State diagram for a parity-bit generator.

ing inputs, respectively. From either state F or state G the machine goes into state A, regardless of the input. (Note that, in fact, the fourth input is a blank, i.e., 0.)

Since the state diagram of Fig. 9-18 contains seven states, three state variables are needed for an assignment. But since three state variables have a total of eight states, one of the states will not be assigned, and its entries in the corresponding state table may be considered as don't-cares. We shall defer, however, the study of the properties of incompletely specified machines to Chap. 10. The state table and a possible state assignment are shown in Table 9-14. The reader can verify that the following logical equations result if JK flip-flops are used as memory elements.

Table 9-14 State table for a parity-bit generator

PS $y_1 y_2 y_3$	NS $x = 0$	$x = 1$	z $x = 0$	$x = 1$
$000 \rightarrow A$	B	C	0	0
$010 \rightarrow B$	D	E	0	0
$011 \rightarrow C$	E	D	0	0
$110 \rightarrow D$	F	G	0	0
$111 \rightarrow E$	G	F	0	0
$100 \rightarrow F$	A	A	0	0
$101 \rightarrow G$	A	A	1	1

$$J_1 = y_2 \qquad J_2 = y_1' \qquad J_3 = xy_1' + xy_2 \qquad z = y_2'y_3$$
$$K_1 = y_2' \qquad K_2 = y_1 \qquad K_3 = x'y_2' + x$$

Since the specification of the problem does not offer any clue as to which assignment to select, it may be chosen arbitrarily. The assignment shown in Table 9-14 has been selected so as to yield "reduced dependency" among the state variables; that is, J_1 and K_1 depend only on the second flip-flop, while J_2 and K_2 depend only on the first flip-flop. The method of selecting assignments which result in such circuit properties will be presented in Chap. 12.

A sequential circuit as a control element in a computation

In the preceding examples each sequential circuit received an input sequence and, in turn, produced an output sequence. This output sequence was the objective of the computation. Presently, however, many sequential circuits are used to control more complex computations. Indeed, the data for such computations do not even pass through the controlling circuit and are therefore not processed by it. The main role of a sequential circuit in the capacity of a control element is to streamline the computation by providing the appropriate control signals. Such circuits usually have a large number of inputs and outputs, and consequently more informal design techniques simplify considerably the design process. The following example illustrates a simple computation in which a sequential circuit is the control element.

The schematic diagram in Fig. 9-19 describes a digital system which computes the value of $(4a + b)$ modulo 16, where a and b are each a four-bit binary number. In this figure X is a register† containing four flip-flops while x is the number stored in X. The register can be loaded with either b or with $a + x$. The addition of a and x is performed by the four-bit parallel adder, denoted ADD. The input b to X is the channel through which the four-bit binary number b can be loaded into the register so that each bit enters the corresponding flip-flop. In general, if a number is loaded into the register, it replaces the number presently stored in it. The slash followed by the number 4 across a line in Fig. 9-19 indicates that each such line actually consists of four wires. K denotes a modulo-4 binary counter whose output L is equal to 1 whenever the count is 3 modulo 4.

The sequential circuit M has three inputs—an input u which initiates the computation, an input L that gives the count of K, and a clock. It has four outputs α, β, γ, z whose tasks are as follows: Outputs α and β are control lines for loading register X. Whenever α is 1 the contents of b are transferred into X. (This can actually be accomplished by AND-gating α with the wires corresponding to b.) Whenever β is 1

---

† A *k-bit register* is a cascade connection of k flip-flops so that each flip-flop can store one binary digit and the entire register thus stores a k-bit binary word.

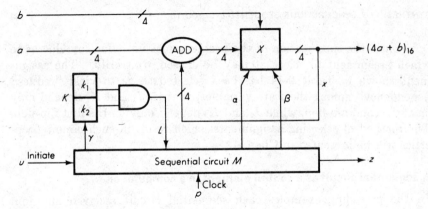

Fig. 9-19 A system to compute $(4a + b)$ modulo 16.

the values of x and a are added and transferred back into X. γ is the input of the counter. Hence, whenever $\gamma = 1$, the count of K increases by 1. The output z is to be 1 whenever the final result is available in X, that is, whenever $x = (4a + b)$ modulo 16. Output z can itself be a control input of another register that is to receive the final result of the computation. However, to simplify the design, this register is not shown.

Initially the count of K is zero, as are the values of u and z. When u becomes 1 the computation starts by setting $\alpha = 1$, which causes b to be loaded into X. Next, a is to be added to x. This is accomplished by setting β to 1 and, simultaneously, γ is set to 1 so that the count in K will keep track of the number of times that a has been added to x. After four such additions, z is to become 1 and the computation is complete. At this point, the count in K is again zero and, hence, it is ready for the start of the next computation.

A compact state diagram for M is shown in Fig. 9-20. In this state

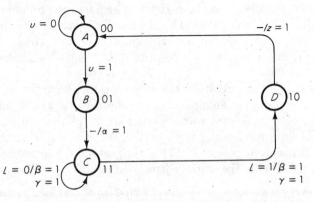

Fig. 9-20 State diagram for the circuit M.

diagram only part of the inputs and outputs are shown; in particular, only that part which changes during the transition and which is relevant for the transition in question. The clock p is usually omitted, although it is implicit. Initially M is in state A. When u becomes 1, M goes to state B without changing outputs. The next clock pulse causes M to go to state C and to produce output $\alpha = 1$, regardless of the other inputs. This is indicated by the symbol $-/\alpha = 1$ on the line going from B to C. Register X contains now the value of b. If u is a pulse, it may change to zero without affecting the computation; u was only needed to cause the transition from A to B and thus initiate the computation. Since $L = 0$, the machine remains in state C, and for each clock pulse it produces two outputs, namely, $\beta = 1$ and $\gamma = 1$. These outputs add a to x while advancing the count in K by one unit. After three such advances L becomes 1 and M goes to state D. During this transition a is added to x for the fourth time and K is set to zero. At this point $x = (4a + b)$ modulo 16 and consequently z becomes 1. The system is now back in state A ready to start a new computation.

Let the state variables y_1y_2 be assigned to the states of M as follows: $A \rightarrow 00$, $B \rightarrow 01$, $C \rightarrow 11$, $D \rightarrow 10$. This assignment is indicated in Fig. 9-20. The output functions can now be derived directly from the state diagram without any tables or maps. For example, α must become 1 whenever the state variables are $y_1y_2 = 01$ and the clock pulse p is 1. Thus,

$$\alpha = y_1'y_2p$$

The other outputs are obtained in a similar manner.

$$\beta = \gamma = y_1y_2p$$
$$z = y_1y_2'p$$

The next-state variables can be obtained with the aid of the transition table shown in Fig. 9-21a and the corresponding maps shown in Fig. 9-21b, assuming a realization of M by means of two D flip-flops. In this transition table some of the next-state entries are variables, and the treatment of such variables is analogous to the treatment of the map-entered variables discussed in Sec. 4-6. When the present state of M is $y_1y_2 = 00$, the next state depends on u; that is, the next state is 00 if $u = 0$ and is 01 if $u = 1$. Consequently, the next-state entry in row 00 is $0u$. On the other hand, if the present state is 01, the next state will be 11, regardless of the input sequence; hence, the next-state entry in row 01 is 11. In a similar manner we derive the entire transition table of Fig. 9-21a. The maps in Fig. 9-21b are obtained directly from the transition table. For example, the entry in row 11 of the transition

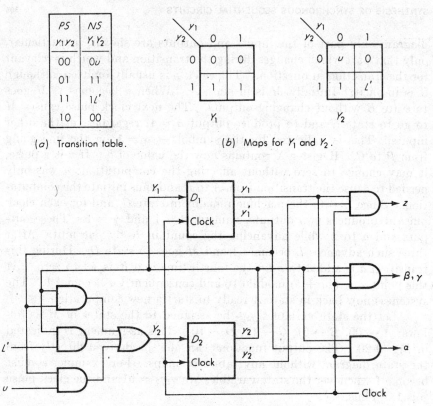

(a) Transition table. (b) Maps for Y_1 and Y_2.

(c) Logic diagram.

Fig. 9-21 Implementing the sequential circuit M with D flip-flops.

table is $Y_1Y_2 = 1L'$. Consequently, a 1 is entered in the Y_1 map in cell 11 while an L' is entered in the same cell in the Y_2 map. Following the procedure for covering maps with map-entered variables, we obtain the following next-state equations:

$$Y_1 = y_2$$
$$Y_2 = y_1'y_2 + uy_1' + L'y_2$$

It is useful to note that the next-state equations can also be derived directly from the state diagram. Y_1 is 1 in states C and D. Hence, it must change to 1 whenever the circuit is in either state B or C. Thus, from the state assignments of these states we obtain:

$$Y_1 = y_1'y_2 + y_1y_2 = y_2$$

This equation is clearly identical with the one obtained before. Similarly we can obtain the foregoing equation for Y_2 just by inspecting the state diagram. A logic diagram for M is shown in Fig. 9-21c.

9-5 AN EXAMPLE OF A COMPUTING MACHINE

So far we have considered sequential machines as independent units possessing finite and limited memory capabilities, whose task is to produce prespecified output sequences in response to the application of external input sequences. Such finite-state machines are known as *non-writing*, since they have no control on the external input and, in particular, cannot "write" or change their own inputs. We shall subsequently consider a simple example of a *writing machine*, that is, a finite-state machine which is capable of modifying its own input symbols.

The machine

Consider a system consisting of a finite-state machine M which is coupled through a *head* to an arbitrarily long storage register, called the *tape* (Fig. 9-22). The tape is divided into squares, so that each square stores

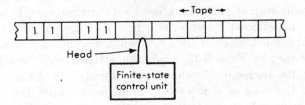

Fig. 9-22 An example of a writing machine.

at any moment a single symbol. (Blank squares will be said to store the symbol "blank," denoted 0.) The head is capable of performing three operations, *reading* the symbol contained in the square being scanned, *writing* a new (not necessarily distinct) symbol in the scanned square, and *shifting* the tape one square to either direction. When a new symbol is written on the tape, it replaces the symbol previously there. The finite-state machine acts as the control unit, specifying the operations to be executed by the head. In what is termed a *cycle of computation*, the machine starts in some state S_i, reads the symbol currently scanned by the head, writes there a new symbol, shifts right or left according to its state table, and then enters state S_j. For convenience, we shall assume that the tape is stationary, while the head is moving. Such a machine is usually called a *Turing machine*, after A. M. Turing.

The machine receives its inputs by reading the pattern of symbols written on the tape. Its output has the dual function of providing the head with the new symbols to be written on the tape and shifting the head to either direction. At the end of the computation, a new pattern of symbols is written on the tape. This pattern is the final objective of the entire computation.

The computation

As an example, let us design the finite-state machine which executes the following computation. The initial pattern of symbols on the tape consists of two finite blocks of 1's separated by a finite block of blanks. The machine is to shift the left-hand block of 1's to the right until it touches the right-hand block, and then halt. The machine is initially in state A, and its head is placed under the leftmost square containing a 1. Let the initial tape consist, for example, of the pattern $\cdots 011100011110 \cdots$, as shown in Fig. 9-23a, where the 0's designate blank squares. The desired final pattern is shown in Fig. 9-23e.

A simple way of performing the above computation is to erase, at each step, the leftmost 1 and write a new 1 in the first blank square to the right of the left block of 1's, as shown in Fig. 9-23b. This computation is described by Table 9-15, where the letters R and L designate right and left shifts, respectively, while 1 and 0 designate the symbols to be written on the tape in each cycle. Thus, for example, the entry $B,0R$ in row A, column 1, means that the machine is to write the symbol 0 in the currently scanned square, shift its head one square to the right, and go to state B.

Table 9-15   State table

PS	NS, write, shift 0	1
A	—	$B,0R$
B	$C,1R$	$B,1R$
C	$D,0L$	Halt
D	$A,0R$	$D,1L$
Halt	Halt	Halt

The computation starts when the machine erases the leftmost 1, currently under the head, shifts one square to the right, and enters state *B*. As long as it scans squares containing 1 symbols, it leaves them unchanged, shifts to the right, and stays in state *B*, in accordance 'with the specification *B*,1*R* in row *B*, column 1, of the state table. After the third right shift, the head scans a square containing a 0, and consequently, it must replace it by a 1, shift right, and go to state *C*. This situation is illustrated in Fig. 9-23*b*.

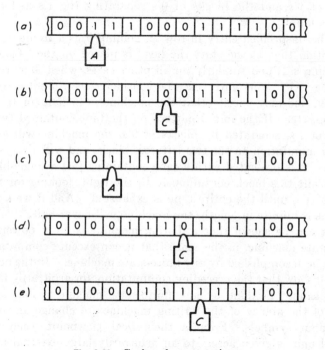

Fig. 9-23 Cycles of computations.

At this point the machine is in state *C*, scanning a 0. The entry in row *C*, column 0, indicates that the machine is to leave that symbol unchanged, shift left, and enter state *D*. The machine now moves to the left, leaving all 1's unchanged and remaining in state *D* until it reaches the first 0 symbol, where it changes direction, shifts right, and enters state *A*. (See Fig. 9-23*c*.)

The machine is now in a similar situation to that illustrated in Fig. 9-23*a*. Hence the foregoing sequence of operations will be repeated; that is, the 1 symbol under the head will be replaced by a 0, the machine will move right until it scans the first 0, which it replaces by a 1, shifts once again right, and enters state C.   It is now in the position illustrated in Fig. 9-23d.   The direction of shifts is now to the left until it scans the first 0 symbol, which once again causes a change in the shifting direction and sends the machine to state A, with its head scanning the leftmost 1 symbol.   After an additional cycle, the machine will be in the position shown in Fig. 9-23e, in state C, and scanning a 1.   This terminates the computation, and the machine halts.   Clearly, the computation described by Table 9-15 is independent of the precise size of the blocks of 1's and the blocks of 0's separating the 1's as long as each block is finite.

The unspecified entry in row A, column 0, is a result of our initial assumption that at the start the head is placed on the leftmost square containing a 1, and similarly, in all other cases, when M enters A, it is scanning a 1.   This entry may be considered as a don't-care, or alternatively, one may specify that the machine is to halt, or to cycle in a self-loop, etc.   If the initial pattern on the tape contained two or more blocks of 1's, separated by blocks of 0's, the machine will execute the above computation on the two leftmost blocks and will always halt.   If, however, it is presented with a tape containing just a single block of 1's, it will shift this block continuously to the right, looking for the second block of 1's, until the entire tape is exhausted.   And if we assume that the tape is infinite in length, the machine will never halt.

It can be shown that a Turing machine is more powerful than a finite-state machine, in the sense that it can execute computations that cannot be accomplished by any finite-state machine.   In the next chapter we shall show that the preceding computation, for arbitrarily large blocks of 1's, cannot be done by any finite-state machine.   This is clearly a result of the ability of the writing machines to change and write their own input symbols.   From a theoretical viewpoint, each finite-state control unit is given access to an arbitrarily large external memory, in which it executes the computations, stores partial results, modifies and replaces input information, and finally stores the output pattern and halts.   (We shall keep in mind that there exist, however, computations which never halt, as shown before, but will not refer to them further.)

From the nature of computations that can be performed by a Turing machine, we may suspect that it can serve as a theoretical model for digital computers.   Clearly, no physical computing machine operates as inefficiently as the preceding model, nor does it have arbitrarily large memory.   The model, however, can serve as a tool for studying the capabilities and limitations of physical computing machines, the nature of computations, and the type of functions which are not computable by any realizable machine.   The study of these important problems is, however, beyond the scope of this book.

Our main objectives in this section have been the introduction of a finite-state machine as the control unit of a larger computing system and the development of a simple model for future study of the power of computation of digital computers. There is no point in implementing Table 9-15, although it can be accomplished in the usual manner.

9-6 ITERATIVE NETWORKS

An *iterative network* is a digital structure composed of a cascade of identical circuits or *cells*. An iterative network may be sequential in nature, where each cell is a sequential circuit, e.g., the counter of Fig. 9-17 or a shift register which consists of a number of cascaded flip-flops, or it may be a combinational network where each cell is a combinational circuit, as, for example, are some symmetric circuits discussed in Chap. 6. The description and synthesis of combinational iterative networks are similar to those of synchronous sequential circuits. Moreover, it will be shown that every finite output sequence that can be produced *sequentially* by a sequential machine can also be produced *spatially* (or simultaneously) by a combinational iterative network.

Because an iterative network consists of identical cells, we shall restrict our attention to the design of any arbitrary cell, which will be referred to as a *typical cell.*

The analogy between iterative networks and sequential machines

The general structure of an iterative network has the form shown in Fig. 9-24. The external *cell inputs* applied to the ith cell are designated $x_{i1}, x_{i2}, \ldots, x_{il}$, where the ith (typical) cell is counted from the left.

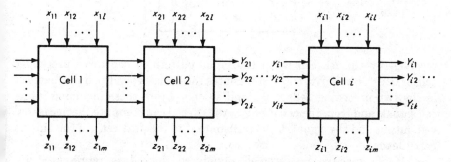

Fig. 9-24 General structure of an iterative network.

The *cell outputs* are designated $z_{i1}, z_{i2}, \ldots, z_{im}$. In addition, each cell receives information from the preceding cell via the intercell carry leads $y_{i1}, y_{i2}, \ldots, y_{ik}$, which are called *input carries*, and transmits information to the next cell via the intercell carry leads $Y_{i1}, Y_{i2}, \ldots, Y_{ik}$, called *output carries*. Often we are interested only in the output from the rightmost cell. In these cases the cell outputs are eliminated and the output is taken from the output carries of the last cell.

The operation of a cell can be described by means of a *cell table*, which specifies for each combination of cell inputs and input carries the values of the cell outputs and output carries. For example, let us construct the iterative network analogous to the sequence detector of Sec. 9-4. That is, we want to design an iterative network which consists of an arbitrarily large number of cells and whose typical cell contains a single cell input x_i and a single cell output z_i. The inputs are applied to all cells *simultaneously*, and the outputs are assumed to be generated *instantaneously*, so that the output z_i is 1 if and only if the input pattern of the four cells $i - 3$, $i - 2$, $i - 1$, and i is 0101, i.e., $x_{i-3} = x_{i-1} = 0$, and $x_{i-2} = x_i = 1$.

The technique of specifying the cell table for the ith cell is similar to that used in forming Table 9-7. The table must have four rows (or states), corresponding to the four possible distinct signals delivered by the intercell input carries. The resulting table, which is identical with Table 9-7, is repeated in Table 9-16. Row D designates the signals

**Table 9-16 Cell table for an
iterative pattern detector**

PS	NS, z_i	
	$x_i = 0$	$x_i = 1$
A	$B,0$	$A,0$
B	$B,0$	$C,0$
C	$D,0$	$A,0$
D	$B,0$	$C,1$

received by the ith cell when the input pattern in the three preceding cells is 010. Similarly, row C designates the signal when the input pattern in the two preceding cells is 01, and so on. From these incoming intercell signals and from the cell input x_i, the ith cell can compute the necessary cell output and the signals to be transmitted to the next cell via the output carry leads.

If we specify the intercell signals so that A is represented by $y_{i1}y_{i2} = 00$, B by 01, C by 11, and D by 10, the transition table shown in Table 9-8 results, and as a consequence the logical equations derived in Sec. 9-4 are obtained. In general, *if the same assignment is selected for the iterative network as for the sequential circuit, then the logic circuit of the ith cell and the combinational logic of the sequential circuit are identical.* While in the sequential case information is fed back through delays, in the iterative network the entire computation is executed instantaneously by using many identical cells. Clearly, the number of cells in an iterative network must equal the length of the input patterns applied to it. For example, if the input patterns are limited to length 6, and the specific input pattern applied to the above pattern detector has the form 010101, then the resulting output pattern will be 000101, as shown in Fig. 9-25. (The symbols along the intercell carry leads denote the transmitted signals.)

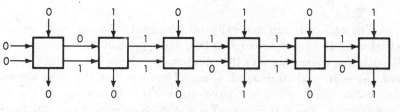

Fig. 9-25 Pattern detection.

The reader is encouraged to apply the foregoing procedure and to design a parallel parity-bit generator, as a counterpart to the sequential generator specified by Table 9-14.

Synthesis

The synthesis procedure for iterative networks is best illustrated by an example. We wish to design an n-cell network where each cell has one cell input x_i and one cell output z_i, such that $z_i = 1$ if and only if either one or two of the cell inputs $x_1, x_2, \ldots, x_i$ equal 1.

The cell table of the ith cell must have at least four rows to distinguish the following four distinct states. Row A designates the state where none of the cell inputs to preceding cells is equal to 1. Similarly, rows B, C, and D designate, respectively, the states where one, two, three or more of the cell inputs to preceding cells are equal to 1. The resulting cell table is shown in Table 9-17. The state assignment and output tables are shown in Table 9-18, and the typical cell is shown in Fig. 9-26c.

Table 9-17	Cell table	
PS	NS, z_i	
	$x_i = 0$	$x_i = 1$
A	A,0	B,1
B	B,1	C,1
C	C,1	D,0
D	D,0	D,0

Table 9-18   Output-carries and cell-output table

$y_{i1}y_{i2}$	$Y_{i1}Y_{i2}, z_i$	
	$x_i = 0$	$x_i = 1$
00	00,0	01,1
01	01,1	11,1
11	11,1	10,0
10	10,0	10,0

The logical equations corresponding to the output carries and the ith cell output are

$$Y_{i1} = y_{i1} + x_i y_{i2}$$
$$Y_{i2} = x_i' y_{i2} + x_i y_{i1}'$$
$$z_i = Y_{i2}$$

The end cells can generally be simplified. In our case, since the initial conditions are zero ($A \rightarrow 00$), both y_{11} and y_{12} are equal to 0. Substituting these values to the equations for the outputs yields $Y_{11} = 0$, and $Y_{12} = z_1 = x_1' \cdot 0 + x_1 \cdot 1 = x_1$. Thus the first cell is as shown in Fig. 9-26a. For cell 2 we have $y_{21} = Y_{11} = 0$, and $y_{22} = Y_{12} = x_1$. Consequently, $Y_{21} = 0 + x_2 x_1$, $Y_{22} = x_2' x_1 + x_2 = x_1 + x_2$, and the cell of Fig. 9-26b results. The simplification in the last cell (Fig. 9-26d) is possible because $Y_{n1} = 0$.

So far we have established the synthesis procedure of iterative net-

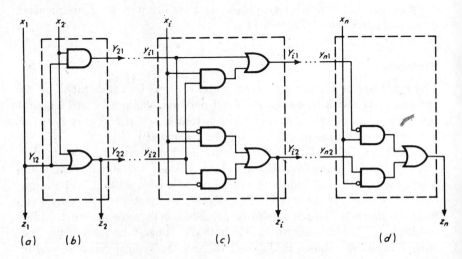

Fig. 9-26   Iterative network derived from Table 9-18.

works implemented with electronic gates. If, however, we wish to design a relay iterative network, care must be taken in selecting the state assignment. The logical equations generated from the assignment of Table 9-18 cannot be implemented with contacts, unless we insert in every cell two relays that will be energized by the input carries y_{i1} and y_{i2}, and whose contacts will be used to implement the above equations. But this would be a very costly and inefficient design. The simplest implementation of relay networks is achieved by assigning to each state of an n-state cell table a code consisting of n symbols, so that each code contains just a single 1. To prevent the formation of sneak paths from right to left appropriate diodes must be inserted in the y lines. These diodes are not shown in our figures, but it is implicit that signals propagate only from left to right. A possible assignment for Table 9-17 is shown in Table 9-19, from which we derive the following logical equations:

$$Y_{i1} = x_i'y_{i1} \qquad Y_{i3} = x_i'y_{i3} + x_iy_{i2}$$
$$Y_{i2} = x_i'y_{i2} + x_iy_{i1} \qquad z_i = Y_{i2} + Y_{i3}$$

Table 9-19 Transition and output table for relay implementation

$y_{i1}y_{i2}y_{i3}y_{i4}$	$Y_{i1}Y_{i2}Y_{i3}Y_{i4},\ z_i$ x_i'	x_i
$A \rightarrow 1000$	1000,0	0100,1
$B \rightarrow 0100$	0100,1	0010,1
$C \rightarrow 0010$	0010,1	0001,0
$D \rightarrow 0001$	0001,0	0001,0

An inspection of the above equations reveals that they are independent of y_{i4}. Therefore it is unnecessary to generate Y_{i4}, because it will never be used by the succeeding cells. The relay circuit of a typical cell is shown in Fig. 9-27. The dotted ground symbol designates the necessary insertion of initial conditions in the first cell, since state A is assigned 1000. The output z_i is therefore said to be 1, if it is grounded. If any two of the relays preceding X_i are energized, the ground appears at the ith cell on the input carry y_{13}. If X_i remains unenergized, the

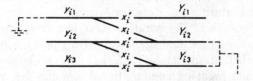

Fig. 9-27 Typical cell for a relay implementation of Table 9-19.

ground will propagate to Y_{i3} and to succeeding cells, until some relay X_j becomes energized and $x'_j = 0$; then the ground is blocked from propagating through the jth cell.

The circuit for the typical cell of Fig. 9-27 has been obtained by using the systematic procedure developed earlier for sequential machines and gate-type iterative networks. Actually, for relay-type networks, these steps are unnecessary, and the circuit can be obtained directly from the cell table. Row D in Table 9-17 designates the "open-circuit" state; that is, once any cell in the network has passed into state D, no output must be produced in any succeeding cells. In a relay circuit no special provisions need be made in order to take into account such a state, since "open-circuit" is equivalent to "no path" in this case. This situation has been clearly exhibited in our example, where Y_{i4} was shown to be unnecessary.

Now recall that the PS column designates the incoming input carries, while the NS entries designate the direction of propagation of these carries. Since the cell table consists of three "active" states, three input-carry leads are needed, and if we associate A, B, and C with the first, second, and third leads, respectively, then the circuit of Fig. 9-27 is obtainable by inspecting Table 9-17. The first input carry A is to be connected via an x'_i contact to the first output carry, and via an x_i contact to the second output carry, corresponding, respectively, to the state transitions specified in row A, columns x'_i and x_i. Similarly, the second input carry is connected via x_i to the third output carry, and so on. Thus the cell table of a relay-type iterative network serves as a complete wiring diagram.

In general, relay networks are asynchronous in nature. Cell inputs, as well as intercell carries, are constant levels of voltage (very often some high voltage and ground), and so are the cell outputs. Therefore, rather than associate the cell outputs with the state transitions, it is desirable to associate them with the states; that is, as long as the network is in a particular state, its cell output will be constant and equal to the output associated with that state. When the network changes state, the next cell output will be determined by the output associated with the corresponding next state of the network. Note that in this case the next output will be produced only after the network has actually reached the new state, and not during the state transition.

As a consequence of the iterative structure, iterative networks are easier to design, construct, and maintain. On the other hand, the time of operation is substantially longer than that of a two-level combinational realization. When realizing combinational circuits, for which speed of operation is not crucial and which can be composed of identical cells, the iterative networks prove to be very useful and economical. They are particularly effective for symmetric circuits and when conditions for an output can be specified in terms of the relative positions of blocks of 1's and 0's.

NOTES AND REFERENCES

The finite-state model described in this chapter was proposed by Mealy [8] in 1955, based on earlier models by Huffman [6] and Moore [10]. The applicability of the model to iterative combinational circuits was pointed out by McCluskey [7]. Today there are several texts devoted to finite-state machines, among which are Booth [1], Gill [2], Harrison [3], Hennie [4], and Miller [9]. A collection of original basic papers dealing with various aspects of finite automata is available in a book edited by Moore [11]. A comprehensive presentation of iterative networks is available in Hennie [5].

1. Booth, T. L.: "Sequential Machines and Automata Theory," John Wiley & Sons, Inc., New York, 1967.
2. Gill, A.: "Introduction to the Theory of Finite-state Machines," McGraw-Hill Book Company, New York, 1962.
3. Harrison, M. A.: "Introduction to Switching and Automata Theory," McGraw-Hill Book Company, New York, 1965.
4. Hennie, F. C.: "Finite-state Models for Logical Machines," John Wiley & Sons, Inc., New York, 1968.
5. Hennie, F. C.: "Iterative Arrays of Logical Circuits," The M.I.T. Press, Cambridge, Mass., 1961.
6. Huffman, D. A.: The Synthesis of Sequential Switching Circuits, *J. Franklin Inst.*, vol. 257, pp. 161–190, March, 1954; pp. 275–303, April, 1954. Reprinted in Moore [11].
7. McCluskey, E. J.: Iterative Combinational Switching Networks: General Design Considerations, *IRE Trans. Electron. Computers*, vol. EC-7, pp. 285–291, December, 1958.
8. Mealy, G. H.: A Method for Synthesizing Sequential Circuits, *Bell System Tech. J.*, vol. 34, pp. 1045–1079, September, 1955.
9. Miller, R. E.: "Switching Theory," vol. II, John Wiley & Sons, Inc., New York, 1965.
10. Moore, E. F.: "Gedanken-experiments on Sequential Machines," pp. 129–153, Automata Studies, Annals of Mathematical Studies, no. 34, Princeton University Press, Princeton, N.J., 1956.
11. Moore, E. F. (ed.): "Sequential Machines: Selected Papers," Addison Wesley Publishing Company, Inc., Reading, Mass., 1964.

PROBLEMS

9-1. Analyze the synchronous circuit of Fig. P9-1 (clock not shown but is implicit).

(a) Write down the excitation and output functions.

(b) Form the excitation and state tables.

(c) Give a word description of the circuit operation.

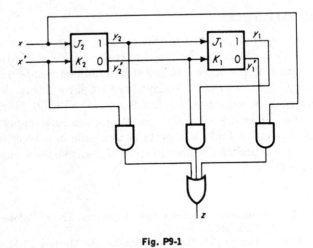

Fig. P9-1

9-2. A long sequence of pulses enters a two-input, two-output synchronous sequential circuit, which is required to produce an output pulse $z = 1$ whenever the sequence 1111 occurs. Overlapping sequences are accepted; for example, if the input is 01011111 $\cdots$, the required output is 00000011 $\cdots$

    (a) Draw a state diagram.

    (b) Select an assignment and show the excitation and output tables.

    (c) Write down the excitation functions for SR flip-flops, and draw the corresponding logic diagram.

9-3. Repeat Prob. 9-2 for the sequence 01101, and implement the circuit with T flip-flops as memory elements.

9-4. Construct the state diagram for a two-input, eight-state machine which is to produce an output $z = 1$ whenever the last string of five inputs contains exactly three 1's *and* the string starts with two 1's. After each string which starts with two 1's, analysis of the next string will not start until the end of this string of five, whether it produces a 1 output or not. For example, if the input sequence is 11011010, the output sequence is 00000000, while an input sequence 10011010 produces an output sequence 00000001.

9-5. For each of the following cases show the state table which describes a two-input, two-output machine having the following specification:

(a) An output $z = 1$ is to be produced coincident with every occurrence of an input 1 following a string of two or three consecutive input 0's. At all other times the output is to be 0.

(b) Regardless of the inputs, the first two outputs are 0's. Thereafter the output z is a replica of the input x, but delayed two unit times, that is, $z(t) = x(t - 2)$ for $t \geq 3$.

(c) $z(t)$ is 1 if and only if $x(t) = x(t - 2)$. At all other times z is to be 0.

(d) z is 1 whenever the last four inputs correspond to a BCD number which is a multiple of 3, i.e., 0, 3, 6, $\cdot$ $\cdot$ $\cdot$.

9-6. Design a two-input, two-output synchronous sequential circuit which produces an output $z = 1$ whenever any of the following input sequences occur: 1100, 1010, or 1001. The circuit resets to its initial state after a 1 output has been generated.

(a) Form the state diagram or table. (Seven states are sufficient.)

(b) Choose an assignment, and show the excitation functions for JK flip-flops.

9-7. Design a two-input, two-output synchronous sequential circuit which examines the input sequence in nonoverlapping strings of three inputs each and produces a 1 output coincident with the last input of the string if and only if the string consisted of either two or three 1's. For example, if the input sequence is 010101110, the required output sequence is 000001001. Use SR flip-flops in your realization.

9-8. Design a modulo-8 counter which counts in the way specified below. Use JK flip-flops in your realization.

Decimal	Gray code		
0	0	0	0
1	0	0	1
2	0	1	1
3	0	1	0
4	1	1	0
5	1	1	1
6	1	0	1
7	1	0	0

9-9. Construct the state diagram for a synchronous sequential machine which can be used to detect faults in 2-out-of-5 coded messages. That is, the machine examines the messages serially and produces an output of 1 whenever an illegal message of five binary digits is detected.

9-10. When a certain serial binary communication channel is operating correctly, all blocks of 0's are of even length and all blocks of 1's are of odd length. Show the state diagram or table of a machine which will produce an output pulse $z = 1$ whenever a discrepancy from the above pattern is detected.

Example: X: 0 0 1 0 0 0 1 1 1 0 1 1 0 0 · · ·
              Z: 0 0 0 0 0 0 1 0 0 0 1 0 1 0 · · ·

9-11. A new kind of flip-flop has been designed. It is equivalent to a *SR* flip-flop with gated inputs, as shown in Fig. P9-11.

A synchronous sequential circuit that generates an output $z = 1$ whenever the string 0101 is scanned in the input sequence is to be designed. Overlapping strings are accepted; for example, corresponding to the input sequence 0010101, the required output sequence is 0000101.

   (*a*) Construct the state diagram and table for the circuit, using the letters A, B, C, etc.

   (*b*) Make a state assignment (use a Gray code, starting with the all-0 assignment for the initial state).

   (*c*) Realize the sequential circuit using the new flip-flops as memory elements. Give the logical equations for the memory elements and the output.

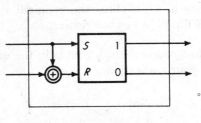

Fig. P9-11

9-12. The clocked memory device shown in Fig. P9-12 has one binary input Y and one binary output y. If $Y(t) = 0$, then $y(t + 1) = 0$; if $Y(t) = 1$, then $y(t + 1) = y'(t)$.

   (*a*) The state table given in Table P9-12 is to be realized using two such memory devices. Choose an appropriate state assignment and give the corresponding excitation and output equations.

   (*b*) Briefly discuss the possibility and practicality of using such memory devices to realize an arbitrary state table.

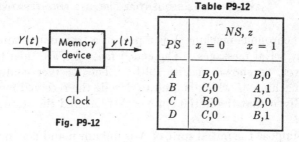

Table P9-12

PS	NS, z x = 0	x = 1
A	B,0	B,0
B	C,0	A,1
C	B,0	D,0
D	C,0	B,1

Fig. P9-12

9-13. Write the state table for a synchronous circuit, with one input x and one output z, which operates according to the following specifications. At time $t = 0$ the initial state is A, and $x(t) = 0$ for $t < 0$. The output function is either given by Eq. (a) or (b) as follows:

(a) $z(t) = x(t) + x(t - 1)$
(b) $z(t) = x(t) \cdot x(t - 1)$

where the change from Eq. (a) to Eq. (b) occurs at times τ such that

$$x(\tau) = x(\tau - 1) = x(\tau - 2) = 1$$

and the change from (b) to (a) occurs at times T such that

$$x(T) = x(T - 1) = x(T - 2) = 0$$

For example:

$t =$	0	1	2	3	4	5	6	7	8	9	10	11	12	$\cdots$
$x(t) =$	0	1	1	1	0	0	1	1	0	0	0	1	0	$\cdots$
$z(t) =$	0	1	1	1	0	0	0	1	0	0	0	1	1	$\cdots$

$$\underbrace{\qquad}_{a} \quad \underbrace{\qquad}_{b} \quad \underbrace{\qquad}_{a}$$

9-14. The synchronous circuit shown in Fig. P9-14, where D denotes a unit delay, produces a periodic binary output sequence. Assume that initially $x_1 = 1$, $x_2 = 1$, $x_3 = 0$, $x_4 = 0$ and that the initial output sequence is 1100101000. Thereafter this sequence repeats itself. Find a minimal expression for the combinational circuit $f(x_1, x_2, x_3, x_4)$. (The clock need not be included in the expression, although it is implicit.)

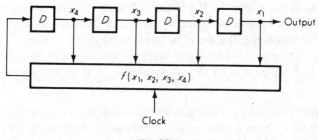

Fig. P9-14

9-15. A synchronous machine N is a part of a transmitter and is used to code binary serial messages. The coded messages are then transmitted to a receiver, as shown in Fig. P9-15. The receiver contains a synchronous machine M which is used to decode the received messages.

(a) Given that the initial state of N is A, find the state diagram of machine M.

(b) Suppose the initial state of N is unknown and machine M above received a 10-bit message; which of the ten bits can be uniquely decoded without an error? Explain.

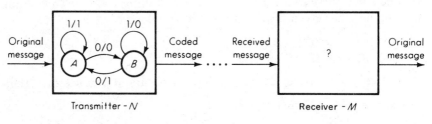

Fig. P9-15

9-16. A *palindrome* is a sequence which reads the same backward as forward, e.g., 11011 or 01010. Show the finite-state control of a Turing machine which is capable of detecting arbitrarily long palindromes. Assume you are given a tape initially marked only with the symbols #, 0, 1, where blanks (#) separate blocks of intermixed 0's and 1's. The machine will be started on a #, and should check whether the sequence to its right is a palindrome. If not, the machine should proceed to the next block. If the sequence is a palindrome, the machine should stop at the # to the right of the block.

Example:

$$\# \ 0 \ 1 \ 1 \ 1 \ \# \ 1 \ 0 \ 0 \ 1 \ 0 \ 0 \ 0 \ \# \ 1 \ 0 \ 1 \ \# \ 1 \ 1 \ 0 \ 0 \ 1 \ 1 \ 0 \ \#$$
$$\uparrow \qquad\qquad\qquad\qquad\qquad\qquad\qquad\qquad\qquad \uparrow$$
$$\text{start} \qquad\qquad\qquad\qquad\qquad\qquad\qquad\qquad \text{stop}$$

Hint: It is often useful in the course of computation to mark certain digits. This can be accomplished by replacing those digits with different symbols; for example, 0's may be replaced by 2's, while 1's may be replaced by 3's, etc. When these markers are no more necessary, they are erased and replaced with the old symbols. Use as many new symbols as necessary.

9-17. Assume you have a Turing machine which is started at the leftmost 1 in a block of n 1's on a tape, which otherwise contains only #'s (blanks). Using as many symbols as you would like:

(a) Show a finite-state control which will duplicate the block of 1's immediately to the right of the original block, leaving the original block and the rest of the tape intact when the machine stops (viz., the block is simply doubled in size—contains $2n$ 1's). The machine should stop at the leftmost 1.

(b) Show a finite-state control which will produce a number of replicas equal to the original number of 1's (stops with a block of n^2 1's).

(c) Show a finite-state control which will increase the number of 1's to 2^n and then stop.

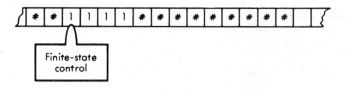

Fig. P9-17

9-18. An iterative network to be used for detecting faults in ringtail coded messages is to be designed. The network consists of five cells, each receiving a digit of the coded message, and is to produce an output of 1 when and only when an illegal message is detected. (The ringtail code is defined in Prob. 5-2.)

(a) Construct a cell table.

(b) Select an assignment and derive the logical equations for the output carries and the cell output.

(c) Construct a typical cell using AND, OR, NOT logic and show the simplified end cells.

9-19. The cell output of a typical cell of an iterative network is equal to 1 if and only if the input pattern of the preceding cells consists of groups of 0's and 1's, such that each group contains an odd number of members.

(a) Construct a cell table.

(b) Realize the typical cell using AND, OR, NOT logic.

(c) Realize the typical cell using relay contacts.

9-20. The typical cell of an iterative network has one binary input x_i and one binary output z_i. The output $z_i = 1$ if and only if $x_i \neq x_{i-2}$. For the first two cells (i.e., $i = 1, 2$) assume that $x_{-1} = x_0 = 0$.

(a) Write a cell table in standard form.

(b) Make a Gray-code state assignment and write the output and carry functions.

10

Capabilities, Minimization, and Transformation of Sequential Machines

This chapter extends some of the concepts introduced in Chap. 9 and presents important techniques for the synthesis of sequential machines and for other problems considered in later chapters. The first two sections are concerned with the general finite-state model, its definition, capabilities, and limitations. The last two sections are concerned with the minimization of completely, as well as incompletely, specified machines.

10-1 THE FINITE-STATE MODEL—FUTHER DEFINITIONS

Our attention will be primarily focused on *deterministic machines*, which possess the property that the next state $S(t + 1)$ is determined uniquely by the present state $S(t)$ and the present input $x(t)$. Thus

$$S(t + 1) = \delta\{S(t),x(t)\} \qquad (10\text{-}1)$$

where δ is called the *state transition function*. The value of the output $z(t)$ is, in the most general case, a function of the present state $S(t)$ and the inputs $x(t)$, i.e.,

$$z(t) = \lambda\{S(t),x(t)\} \tag{10-2}$$

where λ is called the *output function*. A machine possessing properties (10-1) and (10-2) is generally known as a *Mealy machine*. Another machine, known as the *Moore machine*, results when the output is a function of only the present state and is independent of the external input. In this case

$$z(t) = \lambda\{S(t)\} \tag{10-3}$$

Thus we arrive at the following formal definition of a sequential machine.

Definition 10-1 A *synchronous sequential machine* M is a quintuple

$$M = (I,O,S,\delta,\lambda)$$

where I, O, and S are finite, nonempty sets of inputs, outputs, and states, respectively;

  $\delta:I \times S \rightarrow S$ is the state transition function;
  λ is the output function such that
  $\lambda:I \times S \rightarrow O$ for Mealy machines;
  $\lambda:S \rightarrow O$ for Moore machines.

The cartesian product $I \times S$ is the set containing all pairs of elements (I_i,S_j). The state transition function δ associates with each pair (I_i,S_j) an element S_k from S, called the *next state*. In a Mealy machine the output function λ associates with each pair (I_i,S_j) an element O_k from O, while in a Moore machine a correspondence exists between the states and the outputs.

Input-output transformations

Consider machine M whose state diagram is given in Fig. 10-1. It is a four-state machine with one input variable and one output variable for which

$$S = \{A,B,C,D\} \qquad I = \{0,1\} \qquad O = \{0,1\}$$

Suppose that the initial state of M is A and the input sequence is 110; the machine will proceed through states B and C and return to state A, while producing the output sequence 001. Thus, for an initial state A, machine M *transforms* the input sequence 110 into 001. Similarly, for the same initial state, the input sequence 01100 is transformed into 00010. Since every computation involves some transformation of input-to-output sequences, a finite-state machine is capable of performing

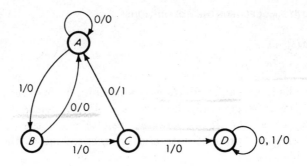

Fig. 10-1 State diagram of machine M.

a variety of computations and of solving a number of problems that can be expressed as transformation of sequences.

An important function of a sequential machine is to determine whether a given input sequence is a member of some prespecified set of sequences. The machine accomplishes this function by accepting those sequences which are members of the set, and rejecting the ones which are not. A machine, when started in its initial state, *accepts* an input sequence by producing an output 1 as it receives the last symbol of that sequence. Thus machine M accepts the sequences 110 and 0110 and rejects the sequence 01100, since its corresponding last output symbol is 0. The sequence detector of Fig. 9-8 can also be described as a machine which accepts those input sequences that are members of the set {all sequences whose last four symbols are 0101}.

The general problem of characterizing the machine's behavior by observing its input-output transformations is quite complex. Clearly, it is impractical to feed a machine with all possible input sequences in order to decide which ones it accepts. The problem increases in complexity if we wish to determine whether two arbitrary machines are related, in the sense that one machine accepts all the sequences accepted by the other. In this chapter we shall present finite experiments to determine the characteristics, capabilities, and limitations of a machine and the relations between machines. These subjects are further developed in Chaps. 13, 14, and 16.

Returning to the state diagram of M, we note that the application of an input 1 to M, when initially in state A, causes a transition to state B. We thus say that B is the 1-successor of A. In general, if an input sequence X takes a machine from state S_i to state S_j, then S_j is said to be the X-*successor* of S_i. For example, state D is the 111-successor of A. If M is known to be initially in either B or C, the 10-successor will be either state A or D. We say that (AD) is the 10-successor of (BC) to mean that A is the 10-successor of B and D of C.

It is evident that no input sequence exists which can take M out of state D, and thus D is said to be a terminal state. Generally, a state is called a *terminal state* if either of the following is true: (1) The corresponding vertex in the state diagram is a *sink* vertex; i.e., no outgoing arcs which emanate from it terminate in other vertices. (2) The corresponding vertex is a *source*; i.e., no arcs which emanate from other vertices terminate in it.

A source state is clearly not accessible from any other state, and similarly, no state is accessible from a sink state. These are extreme examples of situations which limit the state transitions in a sequential machine. In other cases certain subsets of states may not be reachable from other subsets of states, even if the machine does not contain any terminal state. If for every pair of states S_i, S_j of a machine M there exists an input sequence which takes M from S_i to S_j, then M is said to be *strongly connected*. Clearly, any nontrivial machine which has terminal states is not strongly connected.

10-2 CAPABILITIES AND LIMITATIONS OF FINITE-STATE MACHINES

At this point, after having established several behavioral properties and synthesis procedures for finite-state machines, we turn our attention to some basic questions regarding the capabilities of these machines. What can a machine do? Are there any limitations on the type of input-output transformations that can be performed by a machine? What restrictions are imposed on the capabilities of the machine by the finiteness of the number of its states? Although a precise answer to these questions will be deferred to Chap. 16, we will point out the existence of problems not solvable by any finite-state machine and determine a characteristic of transformations that are realizable by such machines.

Let the input to an n-state machine be an arbitrarily long sequence of 1's. In response, the machine will progress, starting from some initial state, through a succession of states, in accordance with its specified state transitions. Now, if we let the sequence be long enough so that it is longer than n, the machine must eventually arrive at a state it has previously been in. And consequently, from this point on, and because the input remains the same, the machine must continue in a periodically repeating fashion. Clearly, for an n-state machine, the period cannot exceed n, and could be smaller. Moreover, the transient time until the output reaches its periodic pattern cannot exceed the number of states n. The preceding result can easily be generalized to any arbitrary input consisting of a string of repeated symbols. In every such case the output will become periodic after a transient time no longer than n.

This conclusion leads to many interesting results which exhibit the limitations of finite-state machines. For example, suppose we want to design a machine which receives a long sequence of 1's and is to produce an output 1 when and only when the number of inputs that it has received so far is equal to $k(k + 1)/2$, for $k = 1, 2, 3, \ldots$. That is, the desired input-output transformation has the form

$$
\begin{array}{l}
\text{Input } = 1 \ \ 1 \ \ 1 \ \ 1 \ \ 1 \ \ 1 \ \ 1 \ \ 1 \ \ 1 \ \ 1 \ \ 1 \ \ 1 \ \ 1 \ \ 1 \ \ 1 \cdots \\
\text{Output } = 1 \ \ 0 \ \ 1 \ \ 0 \ \ 0 \ \ 1 \ \ 0 \ \ 0 \ \ 0 \ \ 1 \ \ 0 \ \ 0 \ \ 0 \ \ 0 \ \ 1 \cdots
\end{array}
$$

Clearly, since the output does not become eventually periodic, no finite-state machine can produce such an infinite sequence.

In Sec. 9-1 we designed a serial adder which is capable of adding serially two binary numbers of arbitrary length. As another example, demonstrating the limitations on the capabilities of finite-state machines, we shall show that the serial-multiplication problem is not solvable by a *fixed* finite-state machine; i.e., *no finite-state machine with a fixed number of states can multiply two arbitrarily large binary numbers.*

To prove the foregoing assertion, suppose that there exists an n-state machine capable of serially multiplying any two binary numbers. Let us select as the two numbers to be multiplied $2^p \times 2^p = 2^{2p}$, where $p > n$. The inputs are fed serially into the machine, least significant digits first. 2^p is represented by a 1 followed by p 0's, and 2^{2p} is to be represented by a 1 followed by $2p$ 0's. The inputs are fed into the machine during the first $p + 1$ time units, i.e., between t_1 and t_{p+1}, as shown below. During this period the machine produces 0's. At t_{p+1} the input stops, while the machine must go on producing p additional 0's followed by a 1.

t_{2p+1}	t_{2p}	$\cdots$	t_{p+1}	t_p	$\cdots$	t_2	t_1	= time
			1	0	$\cdots$	0	0	= first number
			1	0	$\cdots$	0	0	= second number
1	0	$\cdots$ 0	0	$\cdots$		0	0	= product

At this time period between t_{p+1} and t_{2p} the machine receives no input, but since $p > n$, it must have been during that time twice at one of the states. Following the same line of argument pursued earlier, we are led to the conclusion that its output must be periodic and the period is smaller than p. And therefore the machine will never produce the required 1 output.

Note that, for any two finite numbers, we can find a machine which is capable of multiplying them. However, the preceding result demonstrates that, for every finite-state machine capable of performing serial multiplication, we can find such numbers which it could not multiply. The reason for this limitation stems from the limited "memory" available to the machine. While in performing addition it had only to store information regarding a single-digit carry, in the multiplication problem it must be able to store arbitrarily large partial products.

In a similar manner we can show that no finite-state machine with a fixed number of states can perform, for arbitrarily large size blocks, the computation executed by the Turing machine of Sec. 9-5.

A more general and precise study of the capabilities and limitations of finite-state machines must be deferred to Chap. 16, where they will be defined in terms of regular expressions.

10-3 STATE EQUIVALENCE AND MACHINE MINIMIZATION

In constructing the state diagram (or table) of a finite-state machine, it often happens that the diagram contains redundant states, i.e., states whose functions can be accomplished by other states. The number of memory elements required for a realization of the machine is directly related to the number of states. (Recall that, for an n-state machine, $k = \lceil \log_2 n \rceil$ state variables are needed for an assignment.) Consequently, the minimization of the number of states does in many cases reduce the complexity and cost of the realization. Moreover, the diagnosis of sequential machines, which is studied in Chap. 13, is considerably simpler when the machine does not contain redundant states. It is therefore desirable to develop techniques for transforming a given machine into another machine which has no redundant states, so that both have the same terminal behavior.

k-equivalence

Two states, S_i and S_j, of machine M are *distinguishable* if and only if there exists at least one finite input sequence which, when applied to M, causes different output sequences, depending on whether S_i or S_j is the initial state. The sequence which distinguishes these states is called a *distinguishing sequence of the pair* (S_i, S_j). If there is uncertainty as to whether the state of M is S_i or S_j, the application of the corresponding distinguishing sequence yields an output sequence which is sufficient to determine uniquely the unknown state. If there exists for pair (S_i, S_j) a distinguishing sequence of length k, the states in (S_i, S_j) are said to be *k-distinguishable*.

As an example consider the pair (A, B) of machine M_1, whose state table is shown in Table 10-1. The pair (A, B) is 1-distinguishable, since a 1 input applied to M_1 when initially in A yields an output 1, versus an output 0 when it is initially in B. On the other hand, the pair (A, E) is 3-distinguishable, since there is no input sequence of length 2 which distinguishes A from E. The only sequence of length 3 which is a distinguishing sequence for the pair (A,E) is $X = 111$, and the output sequences corresponding to initial states A and E are 100 and 101, respectively. Note that 1101 is also a sequence which distinguishes A from E, although it is not the shortest such sequence. An all-zero sequence, on the other hand, will produce identical output sequences independently of whether the initial state is A or E.

The concept of k-distinguishability leads directly to the definition of k-equivalence and equivalence. States that are not k-distinguishable are said to be k-*equivalent*. For example, states A and E of M_1 are 2-equivalent. States which are k-equivalent are also r-equivalent, for all $r < k$. States that are k-equivalent for all k are said to be *equivalent*. Thus we arrive at the following definition.

Definition 10-2 States S_i and S_j of machine M are said to be *equivalent* if and only if, *for every possible input sequence*, the same output sequence will be produced regardless of whether S_i or S_j is the initial state.

Thus S_i and S_j are equivalent (indicated by $S_i = S_j$) if there is no input sequence which distinguishes them. It will be subsequently shown (see Theorem 10-2) that states that are k-equivalent for all $k \leq n - 1$ are equivalent. Clearly, if $S_i = S_j$ and $S_j = S_k$, then $S_i = S_k$. It therefore follows (see Sec. 2-2) that state equivalence is an equivalence relation, and in consequence of this characteristic, the set of states of the machine can be partitioned into disjoint subsets, known as the *equivalence classes*, so that two states are in the same equivalence class if and only if they are equivalent, and are in different classes if and only if they are distinguishable. Definition 10-2 can be generalized to the case where S_i is a possible initial state in machine M_1, while S_j is an initial state in machine M_2, where both M_1 and M_2 have the same input alphabet.

The procedure of determining the sets of equivalent states in a machine, i.e., the equivalence classes, ensues from the following property. *If S_i and S_j are equivalent states, their corresponding X-successors, for all X, are also equivalent*, since otherwise it would be trivial to construct a distinguishing sequence for (S_i,S_j) by first applying an input sequence that transfers the machine to the distinguishable successors of S_i and S_j.

The minimization procedure

The object of this section is to describe a procedure for determining the sets of equivalent states of a specified machine M. The result sought is a partition on the states of M such that two states are in the same block if and only if they are equivalent.

The first step is to partition the states of M into subsets such that all states in the same subset are 1-equivalent. This is accomplished by placing states having identical outputs under all possible inputs in the

Table 10-1   Machine M_1

PS	NS, z	
	$x = 0$	$x = 1$
A	E,0	D,1
B	F,0	D,0
C	E,0	B,1
D	F,0	B,0
E	C,0	F,1
F	B,0	C,0

$P_0 = (ABCDEF)$
$P_1 = (ACE)(BDF)$
$P_2 = (ACE)(BD)(F)$
$P_3 = (AC)(E)(BD)(F)$
$P_4 = (AC)(E)(BD)(F)$

same subset. Clearly, two states which are in different subsets are 1-distinguishable. As an example, consider machine M_1 given in Table 10-1. The first partition P_0 corresponds to 0-distinguishability, and it defines our initial "ignorance" regarding the response of the various states, prior to the application of any input. P_1 is obtained simply by inspecting the table and placing those states having the same outputs, under all inputs, in the same block. Thus A, C, and E are in the same block, since their outputs under 0 and 1 inputs are 0 and 1, respectively. A similar argument places B, D, and F in the other block. Clearly, P_1 establishes the sets of states which are 1-equivalent.

The next step is to obtain the partition P_2 whose blocks consist of the sets of states which are 2-equivalent, that is, equivalent under any input sequence of length 2. This is accomplished by observing that two states are 2-equivalent if and only if they are 1-equivalent and their I_i-successors, for all possible I_i, are also 1-equivalent. Consequently, two states are placed in the same block of P_2 if and only if they are in the same block of P_1, and for each possible I_i their I_i-successors are also contained in a block of P_1. This step is carried out by splitting blocks of P_1 whenever their successors are not contained in a common block of P_1. The 0- and 1-successors of (ACE) are (CE) and (BDF), respectively, and since both are contained in common blocks of P_1, the states in (ACE) are 2-equivalent, and therefore (ACE) constitutes a block in P_2. The 1-successor of (BDF) is (DBC), but since (DB) and (C) are not contained in a single block of P_1, the block (BDF) must be split into (BD) and (F), so that the successors of the blocks in the refined† partition are 1-equivalent. In a similar manner P_3 is obtained by splitting the block (ACE) of P_2 into (AC) and (E), since the 1-successors of A, C, and E are D, B, and F, which are not 2-equivalent.

In general, the P_{k+1} partition is obtained from P_k by placing in the same block of P_{k+1} those states which are in the same block of P_k and whose I_i-successors for every possible I_i are also in a common block of P_k.

† A partition P is said to be a *refinement* of a partition Q if P is smaller than Q.

This process places in the same block the states that are $(k + 1)$-equivalent, and in different blocks states that are $(k + 1)$-distinguishable. Note that no state can belong to more than one block, since this would make it distinguishable with respect to itself.

If for some k, $P_{k+1} = P_k$, the process terminates and P_k defines the sets of equivalent states of the machine; that is, all states contained in the same block of P_k are equivalent, while states belonging to different blocks are distinguishable. P_k is thus called the *equivalence partition*, and the foregoing procedure is referred to as the *Moore reduction procedure*. For machine M_1, P_3 is the equivalence partition, and therefore states A and C are equivalent, and so are B and D. Before proceeding with the minimization, we shall prove two theorems to establish its validity and determine its length.

Theorem 10-1 *The equivalence partition is unique.*

Proof: Suppose there exist two equivalence partitions, P_a and P_b, and that $P_a \neq P_b$. Then there exist two states, S_i and S_j, which are in the same block of one partition and are not in the same block of the other. Since S_i and S_j are in different blocks of (say) P_b, there exists at least one input sequence which distinguishes S_i from S_j, and therefore they cannot be in the same block of P_a. ∎

Theorem 10-2 *If two states, S_i and S_j, of machine M are distinguishable, then they are distinguishable by a sequence of length $n - 1$ or less, where n is the number of states in M.*

Proof: P_1 contains at least two blocks; otherwise M is reducible to a combinational circuit which has only a single state. At each step, the partition P_{k+1} is smaller than or equal to P_k. (Recall that a partition $P_i \leq P_j$ if every block of P_i is contained in a block of P_j, e.g., P_2 of M_1 is smaller than P_1.) If P_{k+1} is smaller than P_k, then it contains at least one more block than P_k. But since the number of blocks is limited to n, at most $n - 1$ partitions can be generated in the reduction procedure, and thus, if S_i and S_j are distinguishable, they are distinguishable by a sequence of length $n - 1$ or less. ∎

It can be shown (see Prob. 10-15) that the above is indeed the least upper bound.

Machine equivalence

Before proceeding with the determination of the minimal machine equivalent to M_1, we shall define precisely what we mean by equivalent and minimal machines.

Definition 10-3 Two machines, M_1 and M_2, are said to be *equivalent* if and only if, for every state in M_1, there is a corresponding equivalent state in M_2, and vice versa.

The equivalence partition has been shown to be unique. Thus the number of blocks in the equivalence partition of a machine M defines the *minimum* number of states that any machine equivalent to M must have. The machine which contains no equivalent states and is equivalent to M is called the *minimal*, or *reduced*, form of M.

If we denote the blocks of the equivalence partition P_3 of M_1 by α, β, γ, and δ, corresponding, respectively, to (AC), (E), (BD), and (F), we obtain machine M_1^* (Table 10-2). In constructing M_1^* we specify the 1-successor of α to be γ, since the 1-successor of (AC) is (BD), and so on. In this manner M_1^* is specified to duplicate the state transitions and response of M_1, and therefore is equivalent to it. And since it has been generated by the equivalence partition of M_1, it is its minimal form.

Table 10-2   Machine M_1^*

PS	NS, z	
	$x = 0$	$x = 1$
α	$\beta,0$	$\gamma,1$
β	$\alpha,0$	$\delta,1$
γ	$\delta,0$	$\gamma,0$
δ	$\gamma,0$	$\alpha,0$

Example   We shall further illustrate the reduction procedure by applying it to machine M_2 (Table 10-3) and finding its minimal form. The blocks of the equivalence partition P_4 are denoted by α, β, . . . , ϵ, and the reduced machine M_2^* (Table 10-4) results. ∎

Table 10-3   Machine M_2

PS	NS, z	
	$x = 0$	$x = 1$
A	$E,0$	$C,0$
B	$C,0$	$A,0$
C	$B,0$	$G,0$
D	$G,0$	$A,0$
E	$F,1$	$B,0$
F	$E,0$	$D,0$
G	$D,0$	$G,0$

$P_0 = (ABCDEFG)$
$P_1 = (ABCDFG)(E)$
$P_2 = (AF)(BCDG)(E)$
$P_3 = (AF)(BD)(CG)(E)$
$P_4 = (A)(F)(BD)(CG)(E)$
$P_5 = (A)(F)(BD)(CG)(E)$

Table 10-4   Machine M_2^*

PS	NS, z	
	$x = 0$	$x = 1$
$(A) \rightarrow \alpha$	$\epsilon, 0$	$\delta, 0$
$(F) \rightarrow \beta$	$\epsilon, 0$	$\gamma, 0$
$(BD) \rightarrow \gamma$	$\delta, 0$	$\alpha, 0$
$(CG) \rightarrow \delta$	$\gamma, 0$	$\delta, 0$
$(E) \rightarrow \epsilon$	$\beta, 1$	$\gamma, 0$

The selection of labels α, β, . . . , assigned to the blocks of P_4, is obviously arbitrary. A different assignment of labels would certainly have described a machine with the same behavioral properties. In general, if one machine can be obtained from the other by relabeling its states, they are said to be *isomorphic* to each other. The foregoing results lead to the following basic conclusion:

▶   To every machine M there corresponds a minimal machine M^* which is equivalent to M and is unique up to isomorphism.

The detection of isomorphism is not always easy and is best accomplished by using a canonical representation for the machine. Such a representation is obtained by selecting a state (preferably the starting state if specified) and labeling it A. The next labels are selected in such a way that when successive rows of the table, starting in A and going down through B, C, etc., are read from left to right, the first occurrence of each new label will be in alphabetical order. Whenever a machine is given in this canonical representation, it is said to be in *standard form*. Clearly, when the starting state of a reduced machine is specified, its standard form is unique.

The transformation of a machine into its standard form will be illustrated by means of M_2^*. Denoting α by A implies that its 0-successor ϵ must be denoted B, because it is the first occurrence of a new label. Similarly, its 1-successor δ must be denoted C. Row B (i.e., ϵ) must be relabeled next; its first entry is β, and since it is a new label, it is denoted D. Similarly, γ is denoted E, and the standard form of Table 10-5 results.

The detection of isomorphism when the starting states are not specified is in general not as simple. When the number of states, however, is not too large, isomorphism can be detected by inspecting the state diagrams of the machines. The necessary and sufficient condition for two machines to be isomorphic to each other is that their state diagrams be identical, except for the labeling of their vertices.

Table 10-5   Standard form
for M_2^*

PS	NS, z	
	$x = 0$	$x = 1$
$\alpha \rightarrow A$	B,0	C,0
$\epsilon \rightarrow B$	D,1	E,0
$\delta \rightarrow C$	E,0	C,0
$\beta \rightarrow D$	B,0	E,0
$\gamma \rightarrow E$	C,0	A,0

10-4 SIMPLIFICATION OF INCOMPLETELY SPECIFIED MACHINES

In practice, it often occurs that various combinations of states and inputs are not possible. For example, the machine of Table 9-15, when in state A, will never receive a 0 input, and consequently the corresponding transition and its associated output may be left unspecified. In other situations the state transitions are completely defined, but for some combinations of states and inputs the output values may not be critical, and thus are left unspecified. Such machines are said to be *incompletely specified;* the determination of their properties and methods for simplifying them are the subject of this section.

Whenever a state transition is unspecified, the future behavior of the machine may become unpredictable. In order to avoid such a situation we shall assume that the input sequences applied to the machine, when in any of its possible starting states, are such that no unspecified next state is encountered, except possibly at the final step. Such an input sequence is said to be *applicable* to the starting state S_i of M. Note that all outputs encountered need not be specified for a sequence to be applicable to S_i. The next states, however, must be specified, except possibly for the last symbol of the sequence.

Actually, the specified behavior of a machine with partially specified transitions can be described by another machine whose state transitions are completely specified. This transformation is accomplished by replacing all the dashes in the next-state entries by T and adding a terminal state T whose outputs are unspecified. As an illustration, consider machine M_3 shown in Table 10-6. The specified behavior of M_3 can be described by Table 10-7, in which all state transitions are specified, and only the outputs are partially defined.

Table 10-6   Machine M_3 with unspecified transitions

PS	NS, z $x=0$	$x=1$
A	B,1	—
B	—,0	C,0
C	A,1	B,0

Table 10-7   An equivalent description where all transitions are specified

PS	NS, z $x=0$	$x=1$
A	B,1	T,—
B	T,0	C,0
C	A,1	B,0
T	T,—	T,—

Compatible states

In Sec. 10-3 we defined state and machine equivalence. We shall find it useful to generalize these concepts as follows.

Definition 10-4 State S_i of M_1 is said to *cover*, or *contain*, state S_j of M_2 if and only if every input sequence applicable to S_j is also applicable to S_i, and its application to both M_1 and M_2 when they are initially in S_i and S_j, respectively, results in identical output sequences whenever the outputs of M_2 are specified.

The covering concept can be extended to machines as follows: *Machine M_1 is said to cover machine M_2 if and only if, for every state S_j in M_2, there is a corresponding state S_i in M_1 such that S_i covers S_j.* Clearly, the machine specified by Table 10-6 is covered by that of Table 10-7. If state S_i of machine M covers another state S_j of the same machine, then only S_i must be retained, while S_j may be deleted.

Definition 10-5 Two states, S_i and S_j, of machine M are *compatible* if and only if, for every input sequence applicable to both S_i and S_j, the same output sequence will be produced *whenever both outputs are specified* and regardless of whether S_i or S_j is the initial state.

Hence S_i and S_j are compatible if and only if their outputs are not conflicting (i.e., identical when specified) and their I_i-successors, for every I_i for which both are specified, are either the same or also compatible. In general, three or more states, S_i, S_j, S_k, . . . , are compatible if and only if, for every applicable input sequence, no two conflicting output sequences will be produced, without regard as to which of the above states is the initial state. Thus a set of states $(S_i,S_j,S_k, . . .)$ is called a *compatible* if all its members are compatible.

A compatible C_i is said to be *larger* than, or to *cover*, another compatible C_j if and only if every state contained in C_j is also contained in C_i. A compatible is *maximal* if it is not covered by any other compatible. (Note that a single state that is not compatible with any other state is a maximal compatible.) Thus, if we find the set of all the maximal compatibles, that in effect is equivalent to finding all compatibles, since every subset of a compatible is also a compatible.

Generalizing slightly, we find that in the case of incompletely specified machines, the analog to the equivalence relation studied earlier is the compatibility relation. The similarities and differences between these two relations will be pointed out subsequently.

The nonuniqueness of the reduced and minimal machines

Before developing the simplification procedure for incompletely specified machines, we shall illustrate some of the difficulties encountered in applying the minimization procedure of Sec. 10-3 to machine M_4 shown in Table 10-8.

Table 10-8   Machine M_4

PS	NS, z	
	$x = 0$	$x = 1$
A	C,1	E,—
B	C,—	E,1
C	B,0	A,1
D	D,0	E,1
E	D,1	A,0

The dashes in row A, column 1, and row B, column 0, mean that the outputs associated with these transitions will be ignored, and thus may be specified according to our convenience. If we replace both dashes by 1's, we find that states A and B become equivalent since their outputs and corresponding successors are identical. Consequently, we may combine these states by redirecting to A all the transitions presently leading to B. The resulting simplified machine, shown in Table 10-9, is in reduced form, and thus cannot be further simplified. If, however, we choose to specify the dashes as 0's, then it is easy to verify that states A and E are equivalent, and in addition states B, C, and D become equivalent. Thus we may relabel the blocks (AE) and (BCD) by α and β, respectively, and the minimal machine of Table 10-10 results.

Table 10-9 A simplified
reduced machine, M_4^*

PS	NS, z	
	$x = 0$	$x = 1$
A	$C,1$	$E,1$
C	$A,0$	$A,1$
D	$D,0$	$E,1$
E	$D,1$	$A,0$

Table 10-10 A minimal machine,
$M_4^{\#}$

PS	NS, z	
	$x = 0$	$x = 1$
$(AE) \rightarrow \alpha$	$\beta,1$	$\alpha,0$
$(BCD) \rightarrow \beta$	$\beta,0$	$\alpha,1$

From the foregoing example the following observations can be made. States A and B of M_4 are compatible, and if C and D are also compatible, so are A and E. But states B and E are 1-distinguishable, and therefore are incompatible. Consequently, since it is not transitive, the compatibility relation is not an equivalence relation. It thus follows that *a set of states is a compatible if and only if every pair of states in that set is compatible.* For example, states B, C, and D of M_4 form the compatible (BCD), since (BC), (BD), and (CD) are compatibles.

Both machines M_4^* and $M_4^{\#}$ cover M_4, and their numbers of states are each smaller than the number of states of M_4. Both are in reduced form; i.e., they contain no redundant states. This situation in which two different reduced machines cover a third one is evidently in contrast to Theorem 10-1. This poses serious difficulty in applying the previously derived minimization procedure, since we can no longer be content with finding a reduced machine covering the original one, and our aim must be to find a reduced machine which not only covers the original machine but also has a minimal number of states.

A further and very crucial difference between completely and incompletely specified machines is demonstrated by means of machine M_5 (Table 10-11). Because of the output entries, the only candidates for state equivalence are states A and B or B and C. And because of the next-state entries, A is equivalent to B only if B is equivalent to C. But for A and B to be equivalent, the dash must be replaced by a 0, while for B and C to be equivalent, the dash must be replaced by a 1. Evidently, there is no way of specifying the unspecified entry so as to achieve any state equivalence. However, a hasty conclusion that M_5 is in reduced form would be false, as is shown subsequently.

The augmented machine of Table 10-12 is obtained by a process known as *state splitting*. This process involves the replacement of a state S_i by two or more states, S_i', S_i'', . . . , such that each of the new states covers S_i. To ensure that the augmented machine covers the original one, it is necessary to modify the next-state entries, so that each

Table 10-11 Machine M_5

PS	NS, z	
	$x = 0$	$x = 1$
A	A,0	C,0
B	B,0	B,−
C	B,0	A,1

Table 10-12 Augmented machine

PS	NS, z	
	$x = 0$	$x = 1$
A	A,0	C,0
B'	B',0	B'',−
B''	B⁺,0	B',−
C	B⁺,0	A,1

transition to S_i is replaced by a transition to either S_i' or S_i'', etc. In our case, state B has been split into B' and B'', and the next-state entries modified as shown in Table 10-12, where the symbol B^+ means that the transition may be either B' or B''. Clearly, the augmented machine covers M_5 and is reducible to it by letting $B' = B'' = B$.

In general, since B' and B'' both cover B, we may specify the next-state entries B arbitrarily as B' or B''. If, however, we select the specification shown in Table 10-12, a simplification of M_5 becomes possible. States A and B' are compatible if their 1-successors C and B'' are. Similarly, states B'' and C are compatible if their 1-successors B' and A are. Thus, if we designate the compatibles (AB') and $(B''C)$ by α and β, respectively, we obtain the minimal machines of Table 10-13. The result is Table 10-13a or 10-13b, depending on whether B^+ is specified as B' or B''.

Table 10-13 Two minimal machines corresponding to M_5

PS	NS, z	
	$x = 0$	$x = 1$
$(AB') \to \alpha$	α,0	β,0
$(B''C) \to \beta$	α,0	α,1

(a) Setting $B^+ = B'$.

PS	NS, z	
	$x = 0$	$x = 1$
$(AB') \to \alpha$	α,0	β,0
$(B''C) \to \beta$	β,0	α,1

(b) Setting $B^+ = B''$.

The foregoing example demonstrates the nonuniqueness of the minimal machine in the case of incompletely specified machines. The minimal machines of Table 10-13 were obtained by allowing state B to be split so that it can be made equivalent to both A and C (by specifying the unspecified output differently). This points out the main difference between completely and incompletely specified machines. *While the equivalence partition consists of disjoint blocks, the subsets of compatibles may be overlapping.*

The merger graph

In reducing machine M_4 we actually specified the don't-care entries, and thus transformed the incompletely specified machine into a completely specified one. Such a specification may not be the optimal one, and thus will drastically reduce our freedom in simplifying the machine. It is therefore desirable first to generate the entire set of compatibles, and then to select an appropriate subset, which will form the basis for a state reduction leading to a minimal machine.

Since a set of states is compatible if and only if every pair of states in that set is compatible, it is sufficient to consider only pairs of states and to use them to generate the entire set. We shall refer to a compatible pair of states as a *compatible pair*. Let the I_k-successors of S_i and S_j be S_p and S_q, respectively; then $(S_p S_q)$ is said to be implied by $(S_i S_j)$. For example, the compatible (CF) of machine M_6 (Table 10-14) is implied by

Table 10-14   Machine M_6

PS	NS, z			
	I_1	I_2	I_3	I_4
A	—	C,1	E,1	B,1
B	E,0	—	—	—
C	F,0	F,1	—	—
D	—	—	B,1	—
E	—	F,0	A,0	D,1
F	C,0	—	B,0	C,1

(AC), and so on. Thus, if $(S_i S_j)$ is a compatible pair, then $(S_p S_q)$ is referred to as its *implied pair*. In general, a set of states P is *implied* by a set of states Q if, for some input I_k, P is the set of all I_k-successors of the states in Q. The merger graph presented subsequently serves as the major tool in the determination of the set of all compatibles.

The *merger graph* of an n-state machine M is an undirected graph defined as follows:

1. It consists of n vertices, each of which corresponds to a state of M.
2. For each pair of states $(S_i S_j)$ in M whose next-state and output entries are not conflicting, an undirected arc is drawn between vertices S_i and S_j.
3. If for a pair of states $(S_i S_j)$ the corresponding outputs under all inputs are not conflicting, but the successors are not the same, an interrupted arc is drawn between S_i and S_j, and the implied pairs are entered in the space.

Consider machine M_6 (Table 10-14) and its merger graph, shown in Fig. 10-2. Since the next-state and output entries of states A and B are not conflicting, an arc is drawn between vertices A and B. States A and C, on the other hand, have nonconflicting outputs, but the successors under input I_2 are C and F. Therefore (AC) is a compatible only if (CF) is, and consequently an interrupted arc is drawn between vertices A and C, and (CF) is entered in the space. Similarly, (AD) is a compatible if and only if (BE) is, and thus (BE) is entered in the space of the interrupted arc drawn between A and D. On the other hand, no arc is drawn between A and E, since these states are incompatible, their outputs under I_2 and I_3 being conflicting. In a similar manner, every possible pair of states is checked, and the entire merger graph completed.

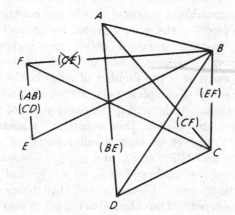

Fig. 10-2   Merger graph for machine M_6.

The merger graph displays all possible pairs of states and their implied pairs, and since a pair of states is compatible only if its implied pair is, it is now necessary to check and determine whether the implied pairs are indeed compatibles. A pair (S_pS_q) is incompatible if no arc is drawn between vertices S_p and S_q. In such a case, if (S_pS_q) is written in the space of an interrupted arc, the entry (S_pS_q) is crossed off, and the corresponding arc is ignored. For example, the condition for (BF) to be compatible is that (CE) be compatible, but since there is no arc drawn between C and E, (CE) is incompatible and the arc between B and F is ignored. Thus states B and F are incompatible. Next, it is necessary to check whether the incompatibility of (BF) does not invalidate any other implied pair, that is, if (BF) is not written in the space of another interrupted arc, and so on. The interrupted arcs which remain in the graph, after all the implied pairs have been verified to be compatible, are regarded as solid ones.

For machine M_6 the merger graph reveals the existence of nine compatible pairs:

$$(AB),(AC),(AD),(BC),(BD),(BE),(CD),(CF),(EF)$$

Moreover, since (AB), (AC), and (BC) are compatibles, then (ABC) is also a compatible, and so on. In this manner the entire set of compatibles of M_6 can be generated from its compatible pairs.

In order to find a minimal set of compatibles, which covers the original machine and can be used as a basis for the construction of a minimal machine, it is often useful to find the set of maximal compatibles. Recall that a compatible is maximal if it is not contained in any other compatible. In terms of the merger graph, we are looking for complete polygons which are not contained within any higher-order complete polygons. [A *complete polygon* is one in which all possible $(n - 3)n/2$ diagonals exist, where n is the number of sides in the polygon.] Since the states covered by a complete polygon are all pairwise compatible, they constitute a compatible; and if the polygon is not contained in any higher-order complete polygon, they constitute a maximal compatible.

In Fig. 10-2 the set of highest-order polygons are the tetragon $(ABCD)$ and the arcs (CF), (BE), and (EF). Generally, after a complete polygon of order n has been found, all polygons of order $n - 1$ contained in it can be ignored. Consequently, the triangles (ABC), (ACD), etc., are not considered. Thus the following set of maximal compatibles for machine M_6 results:

$$\{(ABCD),(BE),(CF),(EF)\}$$

The closed sets of compatibles

Consider the set of compatibles $\{(ABCD),(EF)\}$ of machine M_6. Since this is the minimal number of compatibles covering all the states of M_6, it defines a *lower bound* on the number of states in the minimal machine which covers M_6. But if we select the maximal compatible $(ABCD)$ to be a state in the reduced machine, its I_2- and I_3-successors, (CF) and (BE), respectively, must also be selected. However, since none of these compatible pairs is contained in the above set, the lower bound cannot be achieved, and the set of maximal compatibles $\{(ABCD),(EF)\}$ cannot be used to define the states of a minimal machine that covers M_6.

Definition 10-6   A set of compatibles (for machine M) is said to be _closed_ if, for every compatible contained in the set, all its implied compatibles are also contained in the set.   A closed set of compatibles which contains all the states of M is called a _closed covering_.

Example   For M_6 the set $\{(AD),(BE),(CD)\}$ is closed.   The set $\{(AB), (CD),(EF)\}$ is a closed covering.   ■

The closed covering serves, for incompletely specified machines, the same function that the equivalence partition serves for completely specified machines.   It specifies the states which are compatible and which may be covered by a single state of a reduced machine.   However, as demonstrated by the preceding examples, the closed covering is not unique, and our task is to select the one which has the minimum number of compatibles, and thus defines a minimal-state machine which covers the original one.

The set containing all the maximal compatibles is, clearly, a closed covering, since it covers all the states of the machine, and every implied compatible is contained in the set.   Consequently, the set of maximal compatibles places an _upper bound_ on the number of states in the machine which covers the original one.   For machine M_6, this bound is four.   It must be noted at this point that the upper bound is meaningless when the number of maximal compatibles is larger than the number of states in the original machine.

In the preceding discussion we showed that the bounds on the number of states in the minimal machine can be derived from the set of all the maximal compatibles.   For machine M_6 these bounds were found to be two and four, but since the lower bound cannot be achieved, it becomes necessary to determine whether a closed covering containing three compatibles can be found.   These compatibles need not necessarily be maximal; in fact, the maximal compatible $(ABCD)$ cannot be included in that set, since it implies the entire set of maximal compatibles.

An inspection of the merger graph of Fig. 10-2 reveals that states A and B can be covered by the compatible pair (AB), and similarly, states C and D can be covered by (CD); no pairs are implied by these compatibles, which thus form a closed set.   In order to obtain the desired covering, all we need is a single compatible which covers states E and F.   Fortunately, the pair (EF) is compatible, and it implies the pairs (AB) and (CD) which are contained in the above set.   Consequently, the set $\{(AB),(CD),(EF)\}$ is a closed covering containing three compatibles, and thus yields a minimal three-state machine which covers M_6.   This machine is shown in Table 10-15.   In a similar manner we can show that

Table 10-15   A minimal machine covering M_6

PS	NS, z			
	I_1	I_2	I_3	I_4
$(AB) \rightarrow \alpha$	$\gamma,0$	$\beta,1$	$\gamma,1$	$\alpha,1$
$(CD) \rightarrow \beta$	$\gamma,0$	$\gamma,1$	$\alpha,1$	—
$(EF) \rightarrow \gamma$	$\beta,0$	$\gamma,0$	$\alpha,0$	$\beta,1$

the set $\{(AD),(BE),(CF)\}$ is also a closed covering which corresponds to another minimal machine containing M_6.

The preceding closed coverings have been obtained by inspecting the merger graph and employing a "trial-and-error" procedure. In the following section we shall discuss in detail a more systematic procedure for determining the minimal closed coverings; but it should be pointed out from the outset that no straightforward procedure is known as yet, and a certain amount of search is unavoidable.

The compatibility graph

Consider machine M_7 and its merger graph, shown in Table 10-16 and Fig. 10-3, respectively. The merger graph is constructed in the usual manner; since states A and B are incompatible, the arc between C and E is crossed off, and as a result (AE) and (BD) are also found to be incompatible. The set of maximal compatibles derived from the merger graph contains four members and is given by

$$\{(ACD),(BC),(BE),(DE)\}$$

Table 10-16   Machine M_7

PS	NS, z			
	I_1	I_2	I_3	I_4
A	—	—	$E,1$	—
B	$C,0$	$A,1$	$B,0$	—
C	$C,0$	$D,1$	—	$A,0$
D	—	$E,1$	$B,-$	—
E	$B,0$	—	$C,-$	$B,0$

The *compatibility graph* is a directed graph whose vertices correspond to all compatible pairs, and an arc leads from vertex (S_iS_j) to vertex (S_pS_q) if and only if (S_iS_j) implies (S_pS_q). It is a tool which aids in the search for a minimal closed covering.

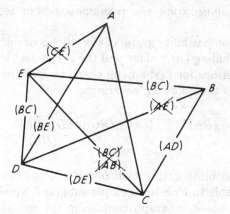

Fig. 10-3 Merger graph for machine M_7.

The compatible pairs and their implied pairs are usually obtained from the merger graph, and since a set of states is a compatible if and only if every pair of states in that set is compatible, then for a given machine, the set of compatible pairs defines uniquely the entire set of compatibles.† In the compatibility graph of machine M_7 (Fig. 10-4) an arc leads from vertex (AD) to vertex (BE) because the compatibility of (BE) is implied by that of (AD). No arcs emanate from (AC) since no other compatible is implied by it.

A subgraph of a compatibility graph is said to be closed if, for every vertex in the subgraph, all outgoing arcs and their terminating vertices also belong to the subgraph. If, in addition, every state of the machine is covered by at least one vertex of the subgraph, then the subgraph forms a closed covering for that machine.

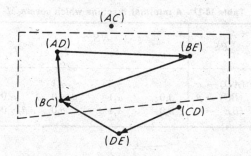

Fig. 10-4 Compatibility graph for machine M_7.

† In order to take into account those states which are incompatible with all other states, the definition of the set of compatible pairs must be generalized to include the pairs corresponding to self-compatibility, i.e., (AA), (BB), etc.

Example The compatibility graph of Fig. 10-4 contains seven closed subgraphs [including (AC) alone and the graph itself], six of which form closed coverings for M_7; among them we find the subgraphs corresponding to the following coverings:

$$\{(BC),(AD),(BE)\} \qquad \{(AC),(BC),(AD),(BE)\}$$
$$\{(DE),(BC),(AD),(BE)\} \quad \blacksquare$$

The compatibility graph itself forms a closed covering. However, it is often desirable to look for a closed subgraph which yields a simpler machine. If a closed subgraph containing the compatible pairs (S_iS_j), (S_jS_k), and (S_iS_k) has been found, the compatible $(S_iS_jS_k)$ can be formed, and so on. Although the number of states in the minimal machine is not necessarily proportional to the number of vertices in the closed graph, the inclusion of many redundant vertices in it does tend to increase the size of the machine. Unfortunately, there is no simple, precise procedure leading to the selection of the minimal closed covering, and trial-and-error technique cannot be avoided. The compatibility graph thus serves to display the various possible reduced machines which correspond to the different closed coverings.

In the compatibility graph of machine M_7, state B is covered by vertices (BE) and (BC); and since at least one of them must be included in any closed covering, the entire triangle $\{(BC),(AD),(BE)\}$ must also be included. This triangle, being a closed graph which covers every state of M_7, implies that the corresponding set of compatibles yields the desired minimal machine. Its state table is shown in Table 10-17, where the entry β/γ means that the next state may be either β or γ.

Table 10-17   A minimal machine which covers M_7

PS	NS, z			
	I_1	I_2	I_3	I_4
$(AD) \to \alpha$	—	$\gamma,1$	$\gamma,1$	—
$(BC) \to \beta$	$\beta,0$	$\alpha,1$	$\beta/\gamma,0$	$\alpha,0$
$(BE) \to \gamma$	$\beta,0$	$\alpha,1$	$\beta,0$	$\beta/\gamma,0$

The merger table

When dealing with machines having a large number of states, it may be more convenient to record the compatible pairs and their implications in a merger table of the form illustrated in Fig. 10-5, instead of using the

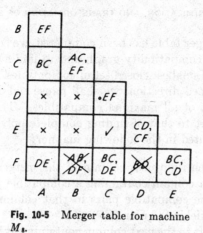

Fig. 10-5 Merger table for machine M_8.

merger graph. Each cell of the table corresponds to the compatible pair defined by the intersection of the row and column headings. The incompatibility of two states is recorded by placing an $\times$ in the corresponding cell, while their compatibility is recorded by a check mark ($\checkmark$). The entries in cell S_i,S_j are the pairs implied by (S_iS_j).

As an example, let us construct the merger table for machine M_8. The table is shown in Fig. 10-5. An $\times$ is inserted in cell (AD), since states A and D have conflicting outputs; a check mark is inserted in cell (CE), because state E contains state C. In a similar way the entire table is completed, and the implied compatibles are entered in the appropriate cells. Now it becomes necessary to check whether these entries indeed correspond to compatible pairs. Starting from the rightmost cell, we find no contradiction until we arrive at the entry (BD) in cell (DF). Since there is an $\times$ in cell (BD), the pair (DF) is incompatible and is therefore "crossed off." As a consequence of the incompatibility of (DF), the pair (BF) is also incompatible, and the corresponding cell is crossed off.

Table 10-18 Machine M_8

PS	NS, z	
	I_1	I_2
A	E,0	B,0
B	F,0	A,0
C	E,–	C,0
D	F,1	D,0
E	C,1	C,0
F	D,–	B,0

Once the merger table has been completed, we continue to construct the corresponding compatibility graph and to find a closed subgraph, in order to obtain the smallest closed set of compatibles. Before continuing in the above-outlined direction, we shall pause and describe a procedure for finding the set of all maximal compatibles. This procedure is the tabular counterpart to that of finding complete polygons in the merger graph. It is executed in the following manner:

1. Start in the rightmost column of the merger table and proceed left until a column containing a compatible pair is encountered. List all the compatible pairs in that column. In our example this step yields the pair (EF).
2. Proceed left to the next column containing at least one compatible pair. If the state to which this column corresponds is compatible with all members of some previously determined compatible, add this state to that compatible to form a larger compatible. If the state is not compatible with all members of a previously determined compatible, but is compatible with some members of such a compatible, form a new compatible which includes those members and the state in question. Next list all compatible pairs which are not included in any previously derived compatible.
3. Repeat step 2 until all columns have been considered. The final set of compatibles constitutes the set of maximal compatibles.

Applying this procedure to the merger table of machine M_8 yields the following sequence of compatibility classes:

Column E: (EF)
Column D: (EF), (DE)
Column C: (CEF), (CDE)
Column B: (CEF), (CDE), (BC)
Column A: (CEF), (CDE), (ABC), (ACF)

From column C it is evident that state C is compatible with states D, E, and F, and consequently the compatibles generated previously are enlarged to include state C. Column B, on the other hand, consists of a single compatible pair, which is added to the previously generated list. From column A, rows B and C, we obtain the compatible (ABC), while rows C and F, together with previously available compatibility relations, yield the compatible (ACF). The final list is the set of maximal compatibles of machine M_8.

The set of maximal compatibles clearly indicates that machine M_8 can be covered by a four-state machine, and cannot be covered by any two-state machine. To determine whether a three-state machine which

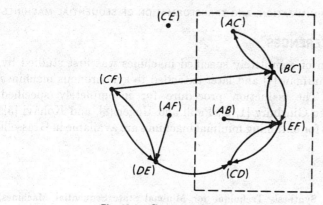

Fig. 10-6 Compatibility graph for machine M_8.

covers M_8 exists, we construct the compatibility graph, as shown in Fig. 10-6. It must be emphasized at this point that in many simple cases a shortcut can be taken, and the compatibility graph can be constructed directly from the state table, without the need to find first the merger graph or table.

An initial inspection of the compatibility graph does not reveal any subgraph which covers every state of M_8 and consists of just three vertices. In fact, any such graph must contain the subgraph whose vertices are (AC), (BC), (EF), and (CD). And since this graph is closed, it may seem that there exists no three-state machine which covers M_8. However, it has been pointed out earlier that it may be desirable to find a larger closed subgraph if the added vertices can be used to merge compatible pairs to yield larger compatibles. In the above example, if we add vertex (AB) to the preceding subgraph, we obtain a set which consists of five compatible pairs $\{(AB),(AC),(BC),(EF),(CD)\}$ and is reducible to the following closed covering:

$$\{(ABC),(CD),(EF)\}$$

Thus the minimum-state machine which covers M_8 consists of three states, and is given in Table 10-19.

Table 10-19 A minimal machine which covers M_8

PS	NS, z	
	I_1	I_2
$(ABC) \rightarrow \alpha$	$\gamma,0$	$\alpha,0$
$(CD) \rightarrow \beta$	$\gamma,1$	$\beta,0$
$(EF) \rightarrow \gamma$	$\beta,1$	$\alpha,0$

NOTES AND REFERENCES

The minimization of completely specified machines was first studied by Moore [7] and Huffman [4] and later extended to synchronous machines by Mealy [6]. The reduction procedure for incompletely specified machines is due to Ginsburg [1, 2], Paull and Unger [8], and Kohavi [5]. Other techniques for obtaining minimal machines are available in Grasselli and Luccio [3].

1. Ginsburg, S.: A Synthesis Technique for Minimal State Sequential Machines, *IRE Trans. Electron. Computers*, vol. EC-8, no. 1, pp. 13–24, March, 1959.
2. Ginsburg, S.: On the Reduction of Superfluous States in a Sequential Machine, *J. Assoc. Computing Machinery*, vol. 6, pp. 259–282, April, 1959.
3. Grasselli, A., and F. Luccio: A Method for Combined Row-Column Reduction of Flow Tables, *IEEE Conf. Record 1966 Seventh Symposium Switching and Automata Theory*, Oct. 26–28, 1966, pp. 136–147.
4. Huffman, D. A.: The Synthesis of Sequential Switching Circuits, *J. Franklin Inst.*, vol. 257, no. 3, pp. 161–190, 1954; no. 4, pp. 275–303, 1954.
5. Kohavi, Z.: Minimization of Incompletely Specified Sequential Switching Circuits, Research Report of the Polytechnic Institute of Brooklyn, PIBMRI, May, 1962, New York.
6. Mealy, G. H.: A Method for Synthesizing Sequential Circuits, *Bell System Tech. J.*, vol. 34, pp. 1045–1079, September, 1955.
7. Moore, E. F.: "Gedanken-experiments on Sequential Machines," pp. 129–153, Automata Studies, Princeton University Press, Princeton, N.J., 1956.
8. Paull, M. C., and S. H. Unger: Minimizing the Number of States in Incompletely Specified Sequential Switching Functions, *IRE Trans. Electron. Computers*, vol. EC-8, pp. 356–366, September, 1959.

PROBLEMS

10-1. (a) Prove that $n(n-1)/2$ is an upper bound on the length of the shortest input sequence which will take a strongly connected n-state machine through each of its states at least once, regardless of the initial state. Is this the least upper bound?

(b) Find a two-input, 12-state machine for which the length of such an input sequence is as large as possible. (A machine for which the length is 26 can be obtained after a number of trials.)

10-2. An n-state machine is supplied with a periodic input sequence whose period is p.

(a) Prove that the output sequence must eventually become periodic, and find a bound for the period.

(b) Show the response of machine M_1^* (Table 10-2) to the input sequence 010010010 · · · . In particular, find the period of the output sequence and the amount of time required for the periodic behavior to start.

⟂ **10-3.** Prove that there exists no finite-state machine that accepts precisely *all* those sequences that read the same forward as backward, i.e., sequences that are their own reverses. (Such sequences are called *palindromes*.)

Hint: Suppose that there exists an n-state machine that accepts all palindromes; then it accepts the sequence $00 \cdots 00100 \cdots 00$.
$$\underbrace{}_{n+1} \qquad \underbrace{}_{n+1}$$
But this implies that it also accepts a sequence that is not a palindrome.

10-4. Determine which of the machines with the following specifications is realizable with a finite number of states. If any machine is not realizable, explain why.

(*a*) A machine is to produce an output of 1 whenever the number of 1's in the input sequence, starting at $t = 1$, exceeds the number of 0's. For example, if the input is 01100111, the required output is 00100011.

(*b*) A machine with a single input line and 10 output lines numbered 0 through 9 is to be designed so that, following the nth input pulse, only one output pulse will be produced in the line whose corresponding number is equal to the nth digit of π (i.e., $3.14 \cdots$).

√ **10-5.** (*a*) Find the equivalence partition for the machine shown in Table P10-5.

(*b*) Show a *standard form* of the corresponding reduced machine.

(*c*) Find a minimum-length sequence that distinguishes state A from state B.

Table P10-5

PS	NS, z $x = 0$	$x = 1$
A	$B,1$	$H,1$
B	$F,1$	$D,1$
C	$D,0$	$E,1$
D	$C,0$	$F,1$
E	$D,1$	$C,1$
F	$C,1$	$C,1$
G	$C,1$	$D,1$
H	$C,0$	$A,1$

10-6. For each of the machines in Table P10-6, find the equivalence partition and a corresponding reduced machine in standard form.

Table P10-6

PS	NS, z x = 0	x = 1
A	B,0	E,0
B	E,0	D,0
C	D,1	A,0
D	C,1	E,0
E	B,0	D,0

(a)

PS	NS, z x = 0	x = 1
A	F,0	B,1
B	G,0	A,1
C	B,0	C,1
D	C,0	B,1
E	D,0	A,1
F	E,1	F,1
G	E,1	G,1

(b)

PS	NS, z x = 0	x = 1
A	D,0	H,1
B	F,1	C,1
C	D,0	F,1
D	C,0	E,1
E	C,1	D,1
F	D,1	D,1
G	D,1	C,1
H	B,1	A,1

(c)

10-7. Two columns of the state table of an eight-state, p-inputs finite-state machine are shown in Table P10-7. Prove that this machine has either no equivalent states or else no distinguishable states.

Table P10-7

PS	NS, z I_i	I_j
A	A,1	H,0
B	C,1	A,0
C	D,1	B,0
D	E,1	C,0
E	F,1	D,0
F	G,1	E,0
G	H,1	F,0
H	B,1	G,0

10-8. A *transfer sequence* $T(S_i,S_j)$ is defined as the shortest input sequence that takes a machine from state S_i to state S_j.

(a) Find a general procedure to determine the transfer sequence for a given machine and two specified states.

(b) Find a transfer sequence $T(A,G)$ for the machine shown in Table P10-8.

Hint: It is helpful to first determine which states can be reached from S_i by sequences of length 1, then by sequences of length 2, and so on.

Table P10-8

PS	NS, z $x = 0$	$x = 1$
A	A,0	B,0
B	C,0	D,1
C	E,0	D,0
D	F,0	E,1
E	G,0	A,0
F	G,0	B,1
G	C,0	F,0

10-9. (a) Develop a procedure to determine the shortest input sequence that distinguishes a state S_i from another state S_j of a given machine.

(b) Apply your procedure to determine the shortest input sequence that distinguishes state A from state G in the machine of Table P10-8.

Hint: Start from the first partition, P_k, in which S_i and S_j appear in separate blocks.

10-10. The *direct sum* $M_1 + M_2$ of two machines, M_1 and M_2, is obtained by combining the tables of the individual machines, as shown in Table P10-10, so that each state of the direct sum is denoted by a distinct symbol.

(a) Use the direct sum to determine whether state A of machine M_1 is equivalent to state H of machine M_2.

(b) Prove that machine M_1 is contained in machine M_2.

(c) Under what starting conditions are machines M_1 and M_2 equivalent?

Hint: Find the equivalence partition of the direct sum.

Table P10-10

PS	NS, z $x = 0$	$x = 1$
A	B,0	C,1
B	D,1	C,0
C	A,1	C,0
D	B,1	C,0

M_1

PS	NS, z $x = 0$	$x = 1$
E	H,1	E,0
F	F,1	E,0
G	E,0	G,1
H	F,0	E,1

M_2

PS	NS, z $x = 0$	$x = 1$.
A	B,0	C,1
B	D,1	C,0
C	A,1	C,0
D	B,1	C,0
E	H,1	E,0
F	F,1	E,0
G	E,0	G,1
H	F,0	E,1

$M_1 + M_2$

10-11. (a) Let M_1 and M_2 be strongly connected and completely specified machines, and suppose that a state S_i of M_1 is equivalent to a state S_j of M_2. Prove that M_1 is equivalent to M_2.

(b) Let M_1 be a strongly connected machine, and let M_2 be completely specified. Prove that if S_i of M_1 is equivalent to S_j of M_2, then M_1 is covered by M_2.

10-12. Determine the conditions under which two equivalent machines are isomorphic.

10-13. An unknown two-input, three-state machine produces the output sequence Z in response to the input sequence X:

$$X: \quad 0 \; 0 \; 0 \; 0 \; 1 \; 0 \; 1 \; 0 \; 0 \; 0 \; 1 \; 0$$
$$Z: \quad 1 \; 0 \; 1 \; 0 \; 0 \; 1 \; 1 \; 0 \; 0 \; 0 \; 0 \; 1$$

Assuming that A is the initial state, determine the reduced standard form description of the machine.

10-14. In this problem we shall establish a procedure for transforming a Mealy machine into a corresponding Moore machine, so that both accept exactly the same sets of sequences. To obtain the Moore machine, it is first necessary to split every state of the Mealy machine if different output values are associated with the transitions into that state. For example, state B of Table P10-14a can be reached from either state A or state C. But since different outputs are associated with these transitions, state B must be replaced by two equivalent states, B_0 with an output 0 and B_1 with an output 1, as shown in Table P10-14b. Every transition to B with a 0 output is directed to B_0, and every transition to B with a 1 output to B_1. Applying the same procedure to state D yields the state table of Table P10-14b, which can be transformed to the Moore machine of Table P10-14c.

We now observe that the Moore machine of Table P10-14c accepts those sequences accepted by the Mealy machine of Table P10-14a, but in addition it produces an output 1 when started in state A, without having been presented with any input sequence. Thus this Moore machine in fact accepts a zero-length sequence, called the *null sequence*. To prevent this situation, we add a new starting state A', whose state transitions are identical with those of A but whose output is 0, as shown in Table P10-14d.

(a) Prove that, to every q-output, n-state Mealy machine, there corresponds a q-output Moore machine which accepts exactly the same sequences and has no more than $qn + 1$ states.

(b) If the definition of acceptance by a Moore machine is modified so that acceptance of the null sequence is disregarded, show a procedure for transforming a Moore machine to a corresponding Mealy machine so that both accept the same sequences.

(c) Prove that if the Mealy machine is strongly connected and completely specified, the corresponding Moore machine will also be strongly connected and completely specified.

Table P10-14

PS	NS, z	
	x = 0	x = 1
A	C,0	B,0
B	A,1	D,0
C	B,1	A,1
D	D,1	C,0

(a)

PS	NS, z	
	x = 0	x = 1
A	C,0	B_0,0
B_0	A,1	D_0,0
B_1	A,1	D_0,0
C	B_1,1	A,1
D_0	D_1,1	C,0
D_1	D_1,1	C,0

(b)

PS	NS		z
	x = 0	x = 1	
A	C	B_0	1
B_0	A	D_0	0
B_1	A	D_0	1
C	B_1	A	0
D_0	D_1	C	0
D_1	D_1	C	1

(c)

PS	NS		z
	x = 0	x = 1	
A'	C	B_0	0
A	C	B_0	1
B_0	A	D_0	0
B_1	A	D_0	1
C	B_1	A	0
D_0	D_1	C	0
D_1	D_1	C	1

(d)

10-15. By referring to the machine shown in Fig. P10-15, prove that the bound established in Theorem 10-2 is the least upper bound; that is, show that for every n the pair of states $(S_1 S_2)$ cannot be distinguished by an experiment shorter than $n - 1$.

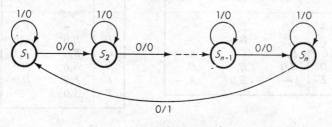

Fig. P10-15

10-16. A given machine is known to be either M_1 in state S_i or M_2 in state S_j, where S_i is not equivalent to S_j. Suppose you are given the state tables of M_1 and M_2 and assume that M_1 has n_1 states and M_2 has n_2 states. Prove that the given machine and its initial state can always be identified by means of an input sequence whose length L is bounded by $L \leq n_1 + n_2 - 1$.

10-17. Give a procedure that can be used to determine whether two incompletely specified machines, M_1 and M_2, are related, so that either M_1 contains M_2 or vice versa.

10-18. (a) Find all the state containments present in the machine shown in Table P10-18.

(b) Find two minimum-state machines that contain the given machine, and prove that these machines are indeed minimal.

Table P10-18

PS	NS, z $x = 0$	$x = 1$
A	B,0	C,1
B	D,0	C,1
C	A,0	E,0
D	—	F,1
E	G,1	F,0
F	B,0	—
G	D,0	E,0

10-19. For each of the incompletely specified machines shown in Table P10-19, find a minimum-state reduced machine containing the original one.

Table P10-19

PS	NS, z I_1	I_2	I_3
A	C,0	E,1	—
B	C,0	E,—	—
C	B,—	C,0	A,—
D	B,0	C,—	E,—
E	—	E,0	A,—

(a)

PS	NS, z I_1	I_2
A	—	F,0
B	B,0	C,0
C	E,0	A,1
D	B,0	D,0
E	F,1	D,0
F	A,0	—

(b)

10-20. Prove that the machine shown in Table P10-20 is minimal.

Table P10-20

PS	NS, z I_1	I_2	I_3	I_4	I_5	I_6	I_7
A	F,0	A,–	D,–	C,–	—	—	—
B	–,1	—	—	—	C,–	D,–	E,–
C	C,–	E,–	—	—	F,0	B,–	—
D	—	—	F,–	E,–	–,1	—	A,–
E	A,–	—	A,1	—	B,–	—	C,–
F	—	D,–	–,0	B,–	—	E,–	—

10-21. Find the reduced state table for the machine of Table P10-21. Design the circuit using a single SR flip-flop.

Table P10-21

PS	NS, $z_1 z_2$ 00	01	11	10
A	A,00	E,01	—	A,01
B	—	C,10	B,00	D,11
C	A,00	C,10	—	—
D	A,00	—	—	D,11
E	—	E,01	F,00	—
F	—	G,10	F,00	G,11
G	A,00	—	—	G,11

10-22. Design a serial to parallel, Excess-3 to BCD code converter. The circuit has a single input line, receiving messages in Excess-3 code, and four output lines, z_1, z_2, z_4, z_8, which are to reproduce the input messages in BCD code. The inputs arrive serially, with the least significant digit first. The outputs are specified only at the occurrence of every fourth input. For example, if the input sequence is 1001 (which is 6 in Excess-3 code), the required output is $z_1 = 0$, $z_2 = 1$, $z_4 = 1$, $z_8 = 0$.

11

Asynchronous Sequential Circuits

In many practical situations the synchronizing clock pulses are not available and asynchronous circuits must be designed. Moreover, within large synchronous systems it is often desirable to allow certain subsystems to operate asynchronously, thereby increasing the overall speed of operation. In this chapter we present some of the basic properties of asynchronous sequential circuits and methods for their synthesis.

11-1 FUNDAMENTAL-MODE CIRCUITS

Although there are many forms that an asynchronous sequential circuit might take, the one shown in Fig. 11-1 is the most straightforward and convenient for our purposes. Externally, the circuit is characterized by the fact that its inputs can change at any time, and that its inputs and outputs are represented by *levels* rather than pulses. Internally, it is characterized by the use of delay elements as memory devices.†

† In practice, when the inherent delay of the combinational logic is large enough, the external delay elements may not be necessary. But for clarity of presentation, we shall assume them present.

356

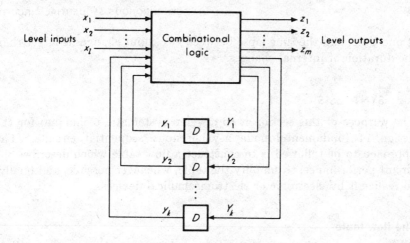

Fig. 11-1 The basic model for fundamental-mode circuits.

The combination of level signals that appear at the inputs and the outputs of the delays defines what is called the *total state* of the circuit. The combination of the input level signals $x_1, x_2, \ldots, x_l$ is referred to as the *input state;* the combination of the signals at the outputs of the delays, i.e., $y_1, y_2, \ldots, y_k$, is referred to as the *secondary state*, or *internal state*, of the circuit. The level outputs generated by the combinational logic define the outputs of the entire circuit, as well as the secondary state that the circuit will assume next. The variables y_1, $y_2, \ldots, y_k$ are referred to as *secondary*, or *internal*, *variables*, and the variables $Y_1, Y_2, \ldots, Y_k$ are called *excitation variables*.

For a given input state, the circuit is said to be in a *stable state* if and only if $y_i = Y_i$ for $i = 1, 2, \ldots, k$. In response to a change in the input state, the combinational logic produces a new set of values for the excitation variables, and as a result the circuit enters what is called an *unstable state*. When the secondary variables assume their new values, i.e., the y's become equal to the corresponding Y's, the circuit enters its "next" stable state. Thus *a transition from one stable state to another occurs only in response to a change in the input state.* We shall assume that, after a change in one input has occurred, no other change in any input occurs until the circuit enters a stable state. Such a mode of operation is often referred to as a *fundamental mode*. A different mode of operation, called a *pulse mode*, is discussed in Sec. 11-4.

In practice, because of stray delays and the nonideal characteristics of electronic devices, it is impossible to ensure that a change in two or more inputs will indeed occur simultaneously. Therefore, to ensure deterministic operation, we prohibit simultaneous changes of two or more inputs. This restriction in effect means that only one input can change at one time, and the time lapse between two input changes is larger than the duration of internal changes.

11-2 SYNTHESIS

The purpose of this section is to develop systematic techniques for the design of fundamental-mode asynchronous sequential circuits. The approach to be followed is to construct a flow table which describes the circuit performance, to simplify the table, whenever possible, and finally, to realize it by electronic or electromechanical devices.

The flow table

As in the case of synchronous circuits, the least systematic step in the synthesis procedure is that of transforming a verbal statement of the desired circuit performance into a precise description which specifies the circuit operation for every applicable input sequence. A convenient method of describing the performance of an asynchronous circuit is by means of a *flow table*. As an example, consider a sequential circuit with two inputs, x_1 and x_2, and one output, z. The initial input state is $x_1 = x_2 = 0$. The circuit output is to be 1 if and only if the input state is $x_1 = x_2 = 1$ and the preceding input state is $x_1 = 0$, $x_2 = 1$. Some possible input sequences and the corresponding output sequence are illustrated in Fig. 11-2.

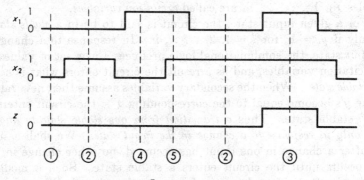

Fig. 11-2 Input-output sequences.

We now show how to construct the flow table for the given circuit. The column headings of Table 11-1 are the input combinations. The table entries are the states, state transitions, and outputs. Initially, the inputs are $x_1 = x_2 = 0$, and the circuit is in a stable state, designated

①, where the circle indicates that the state in question is stable. This is recorded in the table by entering a ① in the first row of column $x_1x_2 = 00$. To the right of the circled ① the output entry 0 is entered, since the output should be 0 when the circuit is in state ①. If now x_2 becomes 1 while x_1 remains 0, as illustrated in Fig. 11-2, the circuit enters a different state, designated ②, while its output is still 0. This is recorded in Table 11-1 by entering a ② in the second row, column $x_1x_2 = 01$, and a 0 in the corresponding output location. In the first row of the 01 column we enter the number 2 to indicate that, as a result of the change in the value of the input variables, a transition to state ② will occur. Thus, while the uncircled entry 2 designates an *unstable* transient condition, the circled entry ② designates the *stable* state assumed by the circuit as a result of the above input change. If input x_1 changes from 0 to 1 while the circuit is in state ②, the circuit should enter another stable state, designated ③, which is associated with an output $z = 1$. This is indicated by entering an uncircled 3 in the second row, column 11. In the same column and immediately below the uncircled 3, a circled ③ is entered to identify the stable state to which the circuit goes as a result of the last change of inputs. An output 1 is associated with the stable state ③.

A change in the value of the circuit inputs causes a *horizontal* move in the flow table to the column whose heading corresponds to the new input value. A change in the internal state of the circuit is reflected by a *vertical* move, as shown by the arrows in Table 11-1. (Note that, since a change in the inputs can occur only when the circuit is in a stable state, a horizontal move can emanate only from a circled entry.) For the time being we shall specify only the outputs of the stable states, leaving the outputs of the unstable states for later consideration.

So far we have specified the state transitions leading from the initial state to a state that generates a 1 output. Clearly, we must also specify what is to happen if an input sequence other than the one considered occurs. Suppose, for example, that initially x_1 changes before x_2. As a

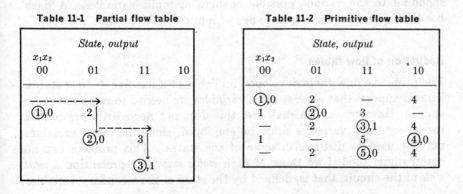

Table 11-1 Partial flow table

x_1x_2			
State, output			
00	01	11	10
①,0	2		
②,0	3		
	③,1		

Table 11-2 Primitive flow table

x_1x_2			
State, output			
00	01	11	10
①,0	2	—	4
1	②,0	3	—
—	2	③,1	4
1	—	5	④,0
—	2	⑤,0	4

result, the circuit will go through the unstable state 4 to the stable state ④, for which the output is 0. Since the two inputs are not allowed to change simultaneously, a dash is entered in the first row, column 11, and in the second row, column 10, of Table 11-2, and so on. In general, to specify the operation of a circuit, we use a partly developed table similar to Table 11-1 and specify the transitions for each allowable input change, starting from every stable state. If a new stable state is to be added, a *new* row is created in the column which corresponds to the values of the input variables. Any move from a stable state can be caused only by a change of input variables.

The table thus constructed is called a *primitive flow table*. Its main characteristic is that *only one stable state appears in each row, and the outputs are specified only for stable states*.

We now complete the flow table. Starting from the entry ② in column 01, if the inputs change to 00, it is necessary to send the circuit into a state which corresponds to input conditions $x_1 = x_2 = 0$ and output $z = 0$. Such a state is ①, and therefore an uncircled 1 is entered in column 00 of the row containing ②. The circuit can leave state ③ by either a change of inputs from $x_1x_2 = 11$ to $x_1x_2 = 01$ or to $x_1x_2 = 10$. In the first case the value of input x_1 has changed from 1 to 0, while x_2 remains equal to 1. If x_1 changes again (to 1), we want the circuit to go to state ③ and to produce a 1 output. This transition can be accomplished if we enter an uncircled 2 in column 01 in the third row. If, however, x_2 changes from 1 to 0 while x_1 remains 1, the circuit should go to state ④, which satisfies these conditions. Starting from state ④, we observe that if the value of x_2 changes from 0 to 1, the two circuit inputs are 1's. However, since the last input to change has been x_2 and not x_1, the circuit output should be 0. Consequently, a new state, designated ⑤, for which the output is 0, must be added in column 11.

At this point we have determined all the stable states shown in Table 11-2. The table is completed by entering the unstable states corresponding to the various possible changes of input variables. A dash has been entered wherever a change of input variables is not allowed.

Reduction of flow tables

The primitive flow table developed in Table 11-2 has five *distinct* states. Thus it appears that at least three variables are needed to represent these states. However, as we shall see, this does not necessarily mean that three secondary variables must be employed, since the input variables may be used to distinguish some of the states. This problem can be better understood if we think of each *stable state* as representing a *total state* of the circuit, that is, defined by the state of the secondary variables as well as by the state of the primary input variables. Accordingly, an asynchronous circuit can go from one stable state to another stable state without necessarily changing any of its internal variables. Such a situation simply means that these two states are distinguished by the states of the input variables. (Note that, in the case of synchronous circuits, the input variables cannot be used to specify the total state of the circuit since, although a synchronous circuit is stable when the clock pulses are absent, the inputs are not available to it.)

In general, when setting up a primitive flow table, it is not necessary to be concerned about adding states that may turn out to be redundant. All that is necessary is that a sufficient number of states be included, so that the circuit performance is completely specified for every allowable input sequence. The reduction of a primitive flow table thus has two functions, namely, eliminating redundant stable states and merging those stable states which are distinguishable by the input states. Since there is only one stable state in each row of the primitive flow table, we may think of it as the "present state" and rewrite Table 11-2 in the form shown in Table 11-3, where the circles serve only for the identification of stable states. The flow table in the form of Table 11-3 is now indistinguishable from a state table of an incompletely specified synchronous circuit, with possibly the exception that every row of the flow table contains one "next-state" entry which is identical with the "present state."

Table 11-3   Primitive flow table

"Present state"	x_1x_2 State, output			
	00	01	11	10
①	①,0	2	—	4
②	1	②,0	3	—
③	—	2	③,1	4
④	1	—	5	④,0
⑤	—	·2	⑤,0	4

The analogy between the minimization problem of synchronous circuits and the reduction of primitive flow tables of asynchronous circuits is now apparent. We may therefore utilize the techniques of Sec. 10-4 to reduce the number of rows in primitive flow tables. The merger graph for the flow table of Table 11-3 is shown in Fig. 11-3, where the maximal compatibles are

$$\{(123),(145)\}$$

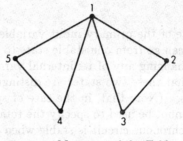

Fig. 11-3 Merger graph for Table 11-3.

Whenever a circled entry and an uncircled entry are to be combined, the resulting entry is circled, since the corresponding state must be stable. Thus, for example, the row which corresponds to the maximal compatible (123) is

$$①,0 \qquad ②,0 \qquad ③,1 \qquad 4,-$$

Two minimum-row flow tables corresponding to Table 11-2 are shown in Table 11-4. Table 11-4a corresponds to the closed covering $\{(123),(45)\}$, while Table 11-4b corresponds to the closed covering $\{(145),(23)\}$. The outputs associated with the unstable states have been specified to correspond to their respective stable states, e.g., the output associated with the unstable state 2 is 0, since the output of the stable state ② is 0, and so on.

Table 11-4 Reduced flow tables

x_1x_2	State, output					x_1x_2	State, output			
	00	01	11	10			00	01	11	10
	①,0	②,0	③,1	4 ,0			①,0	2 ,0	⑤,0	④,0
	1 ,0	2 ,0	⑤,0	④,0			1 ,0	②,0	③,1	4 ,0

(a) Closed covering $\{(123)(45)\}$.   (b) Closed covering $\{(145)(23)\}$.

Specifying the outputs

Our next step is to consider the assignment of output values to the unstable states in the reduced flow table. This assignment depends on the required output changes, as well as on a number of design objectives which are discussed subsequently. Suppose the circuit is to go from one stable state to another stable state associated with the same output, as is the case, for example, in Table 11-4a in the transition from state ① to

362

state ④. In such a case there must be no momentary false output. Consequently, the unstable state 4 must be assigned a 0 output. Similarly, the output associated with the unstable state 2 is specified as 0.

When a circuit changes from one stable state with a given output to another stable state with a different output, the transition may be associated with either of these outputs. The choice of output can be made according to whether it is desired that the output change will occur as soon as possible or as late as possible. When the relative timing of the output change is of no importance, the choice of output is made in such a way as to minimize the output logic. Consider, for example, the flow table in Table 11-5a. To determine the output associated with the unstable state 2, note that state ② can be reached from either state ① or from state ③. Since both are associated with a 0 output, while the output of state ② is 1, then, if a fast output change is desired, the output associated with 2 must be a 1. If, however, a slow output change is desired, the output of 2 should be set to 0. On the other hand, the output of unstable 1 must be set to 0, since the outputs of both states ① and ④ are 0's.

The output associated with the unstable state 4 must be a 0, as is the output associated with 3, since in each case the transition is between stable states associated with 0 outputs. Note that this output assignment means that the output associated with the transition from ② to ③ cannot be made to change as late as possible. An examination of the outputs associated with the unstable states in the last two rows shows that they are all optional. The output assignment shown in Table 11-5b has been made in such a way as to obtain fast output changes.

Table 11-5 Specification of outputs

State, output x_1x_2					State, output x_1x_2			
00	01	11	10		00	01	11	10
①,0	2	③,0	4		①,0	2 ,1	③,0	4 ,0
1	②,1	3	④,0		1 ,0	②,1	3 ,0	④,0
⑤,1	6	⑦,1	8		⑤,1	6 ,0	⑦,1	8 ,0
5	⑥,0	7	⑧,0		5 ,1	⑥,0	7 ,1	⑧,0

(a) Reduced flow table.   (b) Reduced flow table with outputs specified.

Excitation and output tables

To realize a reduced flow table, it is necessary to assign to its rows distinct combinations of values of secondary variables and to derive the corresponding excitation and output functions. For a state to be stable, the value of the Y's must be the same as that of the y's. Therefore the excitation required for any stable state is determined from the value of the secondary variables assigned to the row in which the stable state is contained. An uncircled entry represents an unstable state, which must eventually assume the value of the secondary state assigned to the circled entry having the same number. There are several difficulties associated with the state-assignment problem and with the transitions assigned to the unstable states. These problems are discussed in detail in the following section.

Table 11-6   Excitation and output table

y	x_1x_2	Y, z		
	00	01	11	10
0	0,0	0,0	0,1	1,0
1	0,0	0,0	1,0	1,0

To realize the reduced flow table of Table 11-4a, we assign a 0 to the first row and a 1 to the second row, as shown in Table 11-6. Every circled entry in the first row is now replaced by a 0, and in the second row by a 1. The uncircled entry 2 is assigned a 0, since the circuit must go into stable state ②. This assignment thus requires the variable y to change its state from 1 to 0 upon receiving the input levels 01. Similarly, the uncircled entries 1 and 4 are assigned 0 and 1, corresponding, respectively, to the assignments of the circled entries ① and ④. The excitation and output functions derived from Table 11-6 are

$$Y = x_1x_2' + x_1y$$
$$z = x_1x_2y'$$

Two corresponding realizations are shown in Fig. 11-4. The first realization uses conventional AND, OR, NOT logic. The second realization uses a relay Y as a memory element, while input signals are controlled by contacts of the input relays X_1 and X_2. The reader can (and should) analyze in detail the relay realization to make sure he fully understands how the notions of secondary variables, and stable and unstable states, are implemented in this realization.

A synthesis example

The synthesis procedure for fundamental-mode asynchronous circuits developed in the foregoing section consists of several steps, which can

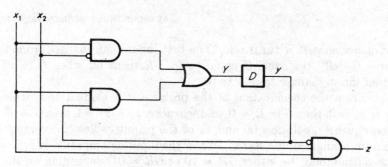

(a) A realization using conventional logic.

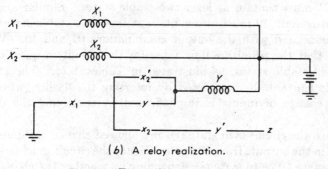

(b) A relay realization.

Fig. 11-4 Two realizations of Table 11-6.

be summarized as follows:

1. A primitive flow table is constructed from the verbal description of the circuit operation. In most cases we specify only those outputs that are associated with stable states.

2. A minimum-row reduced flow table is obtained by merging the rows in the primitive flow table. Either the merger graph or the merger table may be used to perform the reduction.

3. Secondary variables are assigned to the rows of the reduced flow table, from which excitation and output tables are constructed. The outputs associated with the unstable states are specified according to the various design requirements.

4. The excitation and output functions are derived, and the corresponding circuit is constructed.

We shall now illustrate the above procedure by designing an asynchronous sequential circuit with two inputs, x_1 and x_2, and two outputs, G and R, which is to behave in the following manner. Initially, both inputs and both outputs are equal to 0. Whenever $G = 0$ and either x_1 or x_2 becomes 1, G turns "on" (i.e., becomes 1). When the second

365

input becomes 1, R turns on. The first input that changes from 1 to 0 turns G "off" (i.e., sets G equal to 0). R turns off when G is off and either input changes from 1 to 0.

From the specification of the problem it is evident that whenever $x_1 = x_2 = 0$, then $G = R = 0$, and whenever $x_1 = x_2 = 1$, then $G = R = 1$. Consequently, columns 00 and 11 of the primitive flow table must each contain a single stable state. When the input combination is $x_1x_2 = 01$, the output may be either $GR = 10$ or $GR = 01$, depending on the preceding input combination. Since a different stable state must be included in each column of the flow table for every possible output condition, column 01 must contain at least two stable states. Similar arguments show that column 10 must also contain at least two stable states, which will be associated with the output combinations 01 and 10. We thus conclude that the primitive flow table for the circuit in question must contain six stable states, as illustrated in Table 11-7a. The primitive flow table can now be completed by inserting the dashes, whenever a multiple change of inputs is implied, and by specifying the unstable states.

When the circuit is in state ①, any allowed change of inputs causes a change in the outputs from 00 to 10. Hence the circuit must be directed to either state ② or to state ⑤, depending on whether the change in the inputs is from 00 to 01 or to 10, respectively. This is accomplished by entering a 2 in column 01 and a 5 in column 10 in the first row of Table 11-7b. It is a simple matter to complete the unstable entries in columns 00 and 11, since each of these columns contains just a single stable state. Therefore 1's and 4's are entered in the appropriate locations in Table 11-7b. The only as yet unspecified entries are those in the row containing ④ in columns 01 and 10. If we start from state ④ and change the inputs to 01 or to 10, G must be turned off. Hence we direct the transitions to states ③ and ⑥, which correspond to the output condition $GR = 01$.

Table 11-7   Primitive flow table

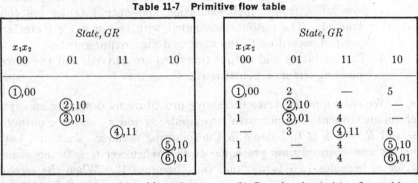

x_1x_2	State, GR		
00	01	11	10
①,00			
	②,10		
	③,01		
		④,11	
			⑤,10
			⑥,01

x_1x_2	State, GR		
00	01	11	10
①,00	2	—	5
1	②,10	4	—
1	③,01	4	—
—	3	④,11	6
1	—	4	⑤,10
1	—	4	⑥,01

(a) Table containing only stable states.   (b) Completed primitive flow table.

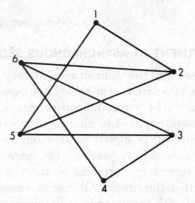

Fig. 11-5 Merger graph for the flow table of Table 11-7*b*.

The merger graph for the primitive flow table is shown in Fig. 11-5. It contains two triangles leading to the closed covering $\{(125),(346)\}$. The reduced flow table which consists of two rows is given in Table 11-8. The optional outputs associated with the outputs of the unstable states have been specified in such a way that R will be fast in turning on and slow in turning off.

Table 11-8   Reduced flow table

	State, GR		
x_1x_2			
00	01	11	10
①,00	②,10	4 ,11	⑤,10
1 ,01	③,01	④,11	⑥,01

The assignment of $y = 0$ to the first row and $y = 1$ to the second row of the reduced flow table leads to the excitation and output tables of Table 11-9.   The excitation and output functions are

$$Y = (x_1 + x_2)y + x_1x_2$$
$$G = (x_1 + x_2)y' + x_1x_2$$
$$R = y + x_1x_2$$

Table 11-9   Excitation and output table

	Y, GR			
y	x_1x_2			
	00	01	11	10
0	0,00	0,10	1,11	0,10
1	0,01	1,01	1,11	1,01

11-3 STATE ASSIGNMENT IN ASYNCHRONOUS SEQUENTIAL CIRCUITS

In Sec. 11-1 we discussed the difficulties that may arise as a result of the different delays associated with the various gates if multiple input changes are allowed. The same difficulties may arise if two or more secondary variables are required to change their values simultaneously. For practical reasons, it is clearly impossible to guarantee that all secondary elements indeed have precisely the same delays. As a result, the assignment of secondary variables to the rows of a reduced flow table must be such that the circuit will operate correctly even if different delays are associated with the secondary elements.

Races and cycles

A reduced excitation table is shown in Table 11-10. When both inputs are equal to 0 and $y_1y_2 = 00$, the required transition to state $y_1y_2 = 11$ involves a change in the values of two secondary variables. If these two changes occur simultaneously, the transition specified in the table will actually take place.   However, if either y_1 or y_2 changes first, instead of going directly to the secondary state 11, the circuit will go to either state 01 or to state 10.   Fortunately, since in either case the required transition is to state 11, as indicated by the entries 11 in rows 01 and 10, column 00, the circuit will finally reach its destination. Such a situation, where a change of more than one secondary variable is required, is called a *race*. If the final state which the circuit has reached does not depend on the order in which the variables change, as is the case discussed above, then the race is said to be a *noncritical race*.

Table 11-10 Illustration of races and cycles

Now suppose the circuit is in state $y_1y_2 = 11$ and the inputs are $x_1x_2 = 01$. The required transition is to state $y_1y_2 = 00$. If y_1 changes faster than y_2, the circuit will go to state 01, from which it will reach state 00, as indicated by the entry 00 in row 01, column 01. On the other hand, if y_2 changes faster than y_1, the circuit will go to state $y_1y_2 =$ (10) and remain there, since the total state $x_1x_2 = 01$, $y_1y_2 = 10$ is a stable state.   Thus the circuit operation will be incorrect.   Such a situation, where the final stable state reached by the circuit depends on the order in which the internal variables change, is referred to as a *critical race*, and must always be avoided.

Races can sometimes be avoided by directing the circuit through intermediate unstable states, before it reaches its final destination.   When the circuit of Table 11-10 is in secondary state $y_1y_2 = 01$ and input state $x_1x_2 = 11$, the required transition is to state (10).   But since such a transition, from 01 to 10, involves two simultaneous changes of the y's, the unstable state 11 is entered in row 01, column 11, thereby directing the circuit to row 11, from which it is directed to go to (10).   Such a situation, where a circuit goes through a *unique* sequence of unstable states, is called a *cycle*.   When a state assignment is made so that it introduces cycles, care must be taken to ensure that each cycle terminates on a stable state.   If a cycle does not contain a stable state, the circuit will go from one unstable state to another, until the inputs are changed.   Obviously, such a situation must always be avoided when designing asynchronous circuits.

To eliminate the critical race in column 01, it is necessary to select another secondary assignment so that all critical transitions involve single variable changes.   This can be accomplished by the assignment shown in Table 11-11.   It is of course necessary to check that no new critical races have been introduced by this assignment.   Having verified this, we can proceed to realize the flow table.

An assignment which contains no critical races or undesired cycles is referred to as a *valid* assignment.   As we shall subsequently see, in many situations a valid assignment cannot be obtained merely by interchanging the assignments of several states in an invalid assignment, and more sophisticated methods must be used.

Table 11-11   A valid assignment
for the flow table of Table 11-10

y_1y_2	x_1x_2	Y_1Y_2		
	00	01	11	10
00	10	(00)	10	01
01	10	00	11	(01)
10	(10)	00	11	(10)
11	10	(11)	(11)	10

Methods of secondary assignment

We now propose to consider methods for obtaining secondary-state assignments so that each transition is accomplished either by a change of secondary state in which only one secondary variable changes or by a change of secondary state in which a multiple change of secondary variables does not result in a critical race. One way of arriving at the desired result is to test each transition and to ensure that the assignment of rows containing an uncircled entry i will be adjacent to the assignment of the row containing (i). Subsequently, we shall refer to states which differ in only one variable as *adjacent* states.

The flow table of Table 11-12 contains three rows, denoted a, b, and c. Inspection of column 00 in the table reveals that the assignment of row a must be adjacent to that of row b, so that the transition from the unstable state 1 to the stable state (1) will involve just a single variable change. In a similar way we arrive at the following required adjacencies for race-free operation:

Column 00:   Row b must be adjacent to row a
Column 01:†   Rows a and b must be adjacent to row c
Column 11:   Row c must be adjacent to row b
Column 10:   Row c must be adjacent to row a

These required adjacencies can be demonstrated by the diagram shown in Fig. 11-6, where each row is represented by a vertex, and for each pair of adjacent rows an arc is drawn between the corresponding vertices. The arc labels (in parentheses) indicate the columns of the flow table in which the transitions are required. Such a diagram is known as a *transition diagram*. The problem now is to assign secondary states to the

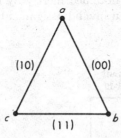

Fig. 11-6 Transition diagram for the flow table in Table 11-12.

Table 11-12   A flow table

x_1x_2	State			
	00	01	11	10
a	(1)	3	(4)	(6)
b	1	3	(5)	(7)
c	(2)	(3)	5	6

† If noncritical races are permitted, as is usually the case, then this requirement may be eliminated, since column 01 contains only one stable state.

vertices of the transition diagram, so that each pair of adjacent vertices is assigned a pair of adjacent secondary states.

If row a of Table 11-12 is assigned a combination of values of state variables with an even number of 1's, say 00, row b must contain an odd number of 1's, say 01. Now, for row c to be adjacent to both rows a and b, it must contain an odd number of 1's *and* an even number of 1's, which obviously cannot be achieved. To overcome this difficulty it is necessary to augment the flow table either by assigning two secondary states to row c or by introducing cycles which lead the circuit to the desired stable states. These possibilities are illustrated in Table 11-13a and b. In the first case each transition to state $\textcircled{c}$ is directed to the adjacent one, as illustrated in column 01. In the second case one of the entries in row 10 is used as an intermediate unstable state to direct the circuit to the desired stable state.

Table 11-13 Augmented flow tables

y_1y_2	x_1x_2 00	Y_1Y_2 01	11	10
$a \rightarrow$ 00	$\textcircled{00}$	10	$\textcircled{00}$	$\textcircled{00}$
$b \rightarrow$ 01	00	11	$\textcircled{01}$	$\textcircled{01}$
$c \rightarrow$ 11	$\textcircled{11}$	$\textcircled{11}$	01	10
$c \rightarrow$ 10	$\textcircled{10}$	$\textcircled{10}$	11	00

(a) Two assignments to row c.

y_1y_2	x_1x_2 00	Y_1Y_2 01	11	10
$a \rightarrow$ 00	$\textcircled{00}$	01	$\textcircled{00}$	$\textcircled{00}$
$b \rightarrow$ 01	00	11	$\textcircled{01}$	$\textcircled{01}$
$c \rightarrow$ 11	$\textcircled{11}$	$\textcircled{11}$	01	10
10	—	—	—	00

(b) Utilizing an unspecified entry as an unstable state.

The use of a fourth row does not increase the number of secondary variables. In other situations, however, the augmentation of a flow table may involve such an increase. To examine this problem in terms of a specific situation, consider the flow table in Table 11-14 and its transition diagram as shown in Fig. 11-7. We observe that row a must be

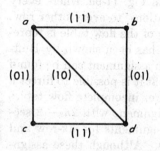

Fig. 11-7 Transition diagram for Table 11-14.

Table 11-14 A flow table which requires three secondary variables

	State x_1x_2 00	01	11	10
a	$\textcircled{1}$	$\textcircled{2}$	4	$\textcircled{6}$
b	1	3	$\textcircled{4}$	$\textcircled{7}$
c	1	2	$\textcircled{5}$	$\textcircled{8}$
d	1	$\textcircled{3}$	5	6

adjacent to three other rows, as must be row d. Clearly, there is no way of assigning four secondary states so that the above adjacencies will be satisfied. Hence a third secondary variable must be added.

The eight combinations of three secondary variables are represented by the cells of the map of Fig. 11-8. To find a valid assignment, we start by placing a circled ⓐ in cell $y_1y_2y_3 = 000$ to indicate that row a will be assigned the secondary state 000. Similarly, we place ⓑ, ⓒ, and ⓓ in the three cells adjacent to cell ⓐ. This, however, means that each of the transitions from rows b to d and from d to c requires two changes of secondary variables. These multiple changes can be accomplished by directing the circuit to its final destination through unstable states, as shown in Fig. 11-8. The flow table resulting from this assignment is shown in Table 11-15.

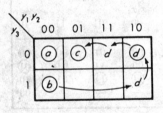

Fig. 11-8 Transition diagram.

Table 11-15   Race-free flow table

$y_1y_2y_3$	x_1x_2 00	01	11	10
$a \rightarrow$ 000	①	②	4	⑥
$b \rightarrow$ 001	1	3	④	⑦
011				
$c \rightarrow$ 010	1	2	⑤	⑧
110			5	
111				
101		3		
$d \rightarrow$ 100	1	③	5	6

State (spanning header above the x_1x_2 columns)

A race-free assignment can be obtained for any four-row flow table by assigning two combinations of secondary variables to each row of the table. Such a race-free assignment is shown in Fig. 11-9a, where every row is adjacent, in one of its assigned combinations, to every other row. This assignment in effect means that every row of the flow table is represented by two *equivalent* secondary states. It has been shown by Huffman [2] that for any flow table with 2^n rows, an assignment can be found with at most $2n - 1$ secondary variables, so that it is possible to direct a transition from each row to any other row. For incomplete flow tables which have only $(3/4)2^n$ rows, a race-free assignment with $2n - 2$ secondary variables can be found. Race-free assignments for six-row and eight-row flow tables are shown in Figs. 11-9. Although these assignments will satisfy the requirements for adjacencies of any flow table, in most cases they will not use the minimum numbers of secondary variables

It is reasonable, therefore, to first attempt to find a valid assignment by using the minimum number of variables before resorting to one of the general assignments of Fig. 11-9.

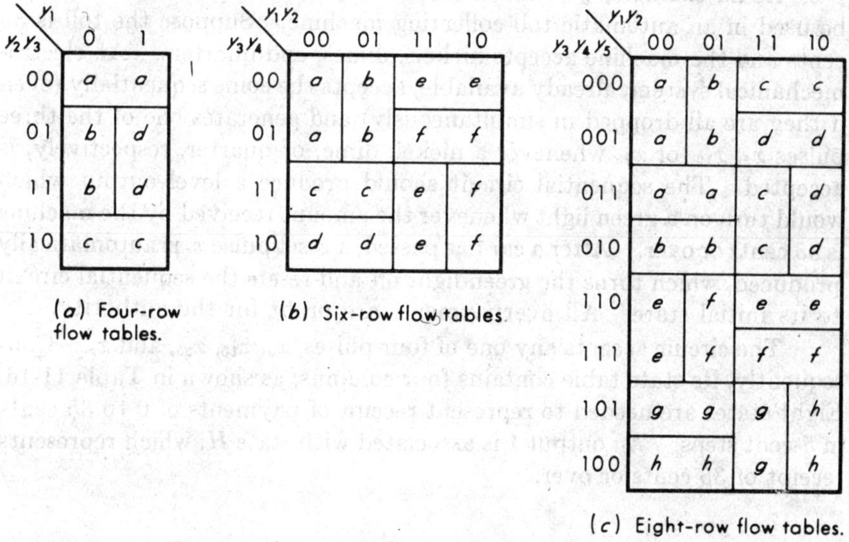

(a) Four-row flow tables.

(b) Six-row flow tables.

(c) Eight-row flow tables.

Fig. 11-9 Race-free assignments for flow tables in which every row is adjacent to all other rows.

11-4 PULSE-MODE CIRCUITS

In many practical situations it is desirable to design asynchronous sequential circuits with pulse inputs. As in the case of level inputs, we assume that input pulses may arrive at any time and no two pulses will arrive at the input lines simultaneously. For the operation of the circuit to be deterministic, two restrictions must be placed on the duration of the input pulses. First, the pulses must be long enough to cause a change in the state of the memory elements. Second, the pulses must be short enough so that they are no longer present after the memory elements have changed their states. The last restriction ensures that each input pulse will cause only one change of state.

When an input pulse occurs, it triggers the circuit and causes a transition from one stable state to another. To keep the circuit stable between two pulses, flip-flops whose outputs are level must be used as memory elements. But since the circuit is stable when there are no inputs, the model defined for fundamental-mode circuits is no longer valid. A modified version of the synchronous model will be shown to be

a convenient one to use in this case.   Clearly, since the absence of a pulse
conveys no information, the number of columns in the next-state table
is equal to the number of input terminals.   A circuit operating in the
above manner is said to operate in a *pulse mode*.

As an example, we shall design an asynchronous circuit which can
be used in an automatic toll-collecting machine.   Suppose the toll is 35
cents and the machine accepts nickels, dimes, and quarters.   An electromechanical system, already available, accepts the coins sequentially (even
if they are all dropped in simultaneously) and generates one of the three
pulses x_5, x_{10}, or x_{25} whenever a nickel, dime, or quarter, respectively, is
accepted.   The sequential circuit should produce a level output which
would turn on a green light whenever the amount received by the machine
is 35 cents or over.   After a car has passed, a reset pulse x_r is automatically
produced, which turns the green light off and resets the sequential circuit
to its initial state.   All overpayments are profit for the authority.

The circuit accepts any one of four pulses, x_5, x_{10}, x_{25}, and x_r.   Consequently, its state table contains four columns, as shown in Table 11-16.
Eight states are needed to represent receipt of payments of 0 to 35 cents
in 5-cent steps.   An output 1 is associated with state H, which represents
receipt of 35 cents or over.

Table 11-16   State table of a toll-collecting machine

Tolls	PS	NS				z
		x_5	x_{10}	x_{25}	x_r	
0¢	A	B	C	F	A	0
5¢	B	C	D	G	A	0
10¢	C	D	E	H	A	0
15¢	D	E	F	H	A	0
20¢	E	F	G	H	A	0
25¢	F	G	H	H	A	0
30¢	G	H	H	H	A	0
35¢ or more	H	H	H	H	A	1

The state table is clearly in reduced form, and consequently three
flip-flops are needed for a realization.   The state assignment and excitation tables are shown in Table 11-17.   Note that no critical race can occur
in a circuit which operates in pulse mode because the circuit is stable when
the input pulses are *not* present.   Since only one input pulse can occur

at a time, the excitation equations are found by considering each column separately.

Table 11-17   State assignment and excitation tables

$y_1y_2y_3$	x_5			x_{10}			x_{25}			x_r		
	S_1R_1	S_2R_2	S_3R_3	S_1R_1	S_2R_2	S_3R_3	S_1R_1	S_2R_2	S_3R_3	S_1R_1	S_2R_2	S_3R_3
$A \rightarrow 000$	0 −	0 −	10	0 −	10	10	10	10	10	0 −	0 −	0 −
$B \rightarrow 001$	0 −	10	−0	0 −	10	01	10	0 −	−0	0 −	0 −	01
$C \rightarrow 011$	0 −	−0	01	10	−0	01	10	01	01	0 −	01	01
$D \rightarrow 010$	10	−0	0 −	10	−0	10	10	01	0 −	0 −	01	0 −
$E \rightarrow 110$	−0	−0	10	−0	01	10	−0	01	0 −	01	01	0 −
$F \rightarrow 111$	−0	01	−0	−0	01	01	−0	01	01	01	01	01
$G \rightarrow 101$	−0	0 −	01	−0	0 −	01	−0	0 −	01	01	0 −	01
$H \rightarrow 100$	−0	0 −·	0 −	−0	0 −	0 −	−0	0 −	0 −	01	0 −	0 −

$$S_1 = x_5 y_2 y_3' + x_{10} y_2 + x_{25}$$

$$R_1 = x_r$$

$$S_2 = x_5 y_1' y_3 + x_{10} y_1' + x_{25} y_1' y_2' y_3'$$

$$R_2 = x_5 y_1 y_3 + x_{10} y_1 + x_{25} y_2 + x_r$$

$$S_3 = x_5(y_1 y_2 + y_1' y_2') + x_{10} y_3'(y_1' + y_2) + x_{25} y_1' y_2'$$

$$R_3 = x_5(y_1' y_2 + y_1 y_2') + x_{10} y_3 + x_{25}(y_2 + y_1) + x_r$$

$$z = y_1 y_2' y_3'$$

It is evident from the equations just derived that each product term contains at least one input variable, and that no input variable appears in a complemented form, since, in pulse-mode operation, a complement of an input variable corresponds to the absence of that input. It should also be noted that if pulse outputs are desired, the design techniques are similar to the above, except that a Mealy-type state table is formed.

NOTES AND REFERENCES

The first systematic treatment of asynchronous sequential circuits is due to Huffman [2], whose model for fundamental-mode circuits has been used in this chapter. Huffman [1] also studied the secondary-assignment problem for asynchronous circuits and proposed several race-free universal assignments. Some aspects of pulse-mode circuits were studied by McCluskey [3]. Unger [5] pointed out the existence of inherent hazards within fundamental-mode circuits and showed how to eliminate such hazards by inserting delays. Good presentations of asynchronous circuits are available in Miller [4] and Unger [6].

1. Huffman, D. A.: A Study of the Memory Requirements of Sequential Switching Circuits, *M.I.T., Res. Lab. Electron. Tech. Rept.* 293, April, 1955.
2. Huffman, D. A.: The Synthesis of Sequential Switching Circuits, *J. Franklin Inst.*, vol. 257, pp. 275–303, March–April, 1954.
3. McCluskey, E. J.: Fundamental and Pulse Mode Sequential Circuits, IFIP Congress, 1962, North Holland Publishing Company, Amsterdam, 1963.
4. Miller, R. E.: "Switching Theory," vol. 2, John Wiley & Sons, Inc., New York, 1965.
5. Unger, S. H.: Hazards and Delays in Asynchronous Sequential Switching Circuits, *IRE Trans. Circuit Theory*, vol. CT-6, no. 12, 1959.
6. Unger, S. H.: "Asynchronous Sequential Switching Circuits," John Wiley & Sons, Inc., New York, 1969.

PROBLEMS

11-1. From the excitation and output tables in Table P11-1 of a fundamental-mode asynchronous sequential circuit, determine what input sequences result in a 1 output. (Only single input changes are permitted.)

Table P11-1

	Y_1Y_2, z			
y_1y_2	x_1x_2 00	01	11	10
00	⓪⓪,0	10 ,0	01 ,0	⓪⓪,0
01	00 ,0	11 ,0	⓪①,1	11 ,0
11	00 ,0	①①,0	10 ,0	①①,0
10	00 ,0	①⓪,0	①⓪,0	11 ,0

11-2. Each of the following specifications describes a fundamental-mode sequential circuit with two inputs, x_1 and x_2, and one output, z. Show a primitive and a reduced flow table for each circuit.

(a) $z = 1$ if both x_1 and x_2 are equal to 1, but only if x_1 becomes 1 before x_2.

(b) When $x_2 = 1$, the value of the output z is equal to the value of x_1; when $x_2 = 0$, the output remains fixed at its last value prior to x_2 becoming 0.

(c) The output z is equal to 0 whenever $x_1 = 0$. The first change in input x_2, occurring while $x_1 = 1$, causes z to become 1. Thereafter z remains 1 until x_1 returns to 0.

11-3. Give a minimum-row, reduced-flow-table description of a two-input (x_1, x_2), one-output (z) sequential circuit which operates in the following manner: $z = 1$ if and only if $x_1 = x_2 = 1$ and the next-to-last input variable change was a change of x_1. Assume that the circuit is initially in the input state $x_1 = x_2 = 0$. Is the reduced flow table unique?

11-4. The output z of a fundamental-mode, two-input sequential circuit is to change from 0 to 1 only when x_2 changes from 0 to 1 while $x_1 = 1$. The output is to change from 1 to 0 only when x_1 changes from 1 to 0 while $x_2 = 1$.

(a) Find a minimum-row reduced flow table. The output should be fast and flicker-free.

(b) Show a valid assignment and write a set of (static) hazard-free excitation and output equations.

11-5. A sequential circuit with two inputs, x_1 and x_2, and two outputs, z_1 and z_2, is to be designed so that z_i (for $i = 1, 2$) takes on the value 1 if and only if x_i was the input that changed last.

(a) Find a minimum-row reduced flow table and a valid assignment.

(b) Assuming that all inputs are available in an uncomplemented as well as a complemented form, show a realization using NAND gates. (Fourteen gates are sufficient.)

11-6. Design an asynchronous sequential circuit with two inputs, x_1 and x_2, and two outputs, G and R, which is to operate in the following manner. Initially, both inputs and both outputs are equal to 0. The first input to become equal to 1, either x_1 or x_2, turns G "on" (i.e., sets G to 1). With the first input equal to 1, if the second input becomes equal to 1, then R turns on. Thereafter, as long as either input remains equal to 1, the input which first caused G to turn on controls the operation of G; i.e., it causes G to turn off when it becomes 0, and it turns it on again when it becomes 1. The second input controls the operation of R in the same manner.

(a) Show a minimum-row reduced flow table and find a valid assignment.

(b) Find the excitation and output equations.

11-7. At a junction of a single-track railroad and a road, traffic lights are to be installed. The lights are to be controlled by switches which are pressed or released by the trains. When a train approaches the junction from either direction and is within 1500 feet from it, the lights should change from green to red and remain red until the train is 1500 feet past the junction.

(a) Write a primitive flow table and reduce it. You may assume that the length of a train is smaller than 3000 feet.

(b) Show a relay realization of the light-control network.

(c) Repeat the design if it is known that the trains may be longer than 3000 feet.

11-8. Figure P11-8 illustrates an office for two students. Instead of light switches, the room has two photocells, one at each door. If either one or both students are in the office, the light is to be on. The students can enter or exit only as shown, with entrances and exits never occurring simultaneously. The photocells indicate a 1 when their beam is interrupted by a student entering or exiting and a 0 at all other times.

(a) Find a primitive and a minimum-row reduced flow table which describe the light-control operation.

(b) Show a valid assignment and find the excitation and output equations.

(c) Repeat (a) if it is allowed to enter and exit the room simultaneously.

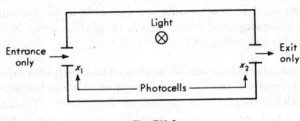

Fig. P11-8

11-9. A factory produces steel bars of length $L + \delta$ and $L - \delta$. It is required to sort these bars by placing them on a conveyor belt passing under two photocells, as shown in Fig. P11-9. The spacing between

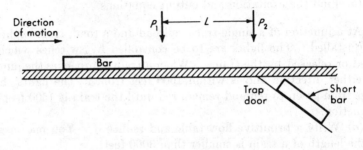

Fig. P11-9

bars on the belt is greater than δ. To the right of P_2 is a trap door through which short bars can drop. The door should not be open when the beam of P_2 is interrupted and should be open immediately after a short bar $(L - \delta)$ has completely passed P_2. Let the logical output x_i of P_i be 1 when the beam of P_i is interrupted. Let the trap-door control z be 1 when the door is open.

(a) Find a minimum-row reduced flow table with eight stable states that describes the trap-door control operation.

(b) Show a valid assignment and find the logical equations for the memory elements and the trap-door control.

11-10. A completely automatic and independent traffic-light system for the intersection of roads x and y consists of two radar sensors, some processing circuitry, and the lights. The sensors and circuitry generate two level outputs, z and w. The output z is 1 if and only if $m(x) - m(y) \geq 6$, where $m(x)$ indicates the number of cars waiting to cross road y. The output w is 1 if and only if $m(y) - m(x) \geq 6$. We wish to design a sequential circuit with inputs (z,w,z',w') and outputs (G_x,R_x,G_y,R_y), where G and R refer to green and red lights, respectively, and a subscript indicates the street from which the light is visible. The objective is to minimize intersection load by unloading whichever street is overloaded, i.e., has at least six cars more than the other. The lights of the street being unloaded should remain green until the other street becomes overloaded.

(a) Show a primitive flow table.

(b) Give a reduced flow table.

(c) Show a relay realization. The outputs are to be fast and flicker-free.

11-11. All the variables in the circuit of Fig. P11-11 are represented by voltage levels. The input variables x_1 and x_2 never change simultaneously.

(a) Describe in words the terminal behavior of the circuit.

(b) Derive the flow table for the circuit.

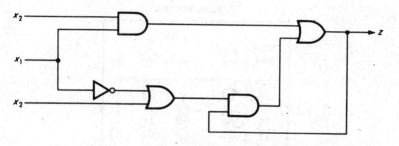

Fig. P11-11

(c) Show how one of the gates can be eliminated without changing the flow table. What physical problems might this cause, and how can they be prevented?

Hint: To derive the flow table, open the feedback loop.

11-12. The reduced flow table of Table P11-12a is to be assigned three secondary variables as shown in Table P11-12b. Note that several combinations of $y_1 y_2 y_3$ values have been assigned to the first two rows of the reduced table. Consequently, for example, the circuit will be stable when $x_1 x_2 = 00$ in any one of the $y_1 y_2 y_3$ combinations 000, 001, 011, and each of these stable configurations must be equivalent to ①. Complete the excitation table so that each transition requires as short a time as possible. Is the excitation table unique?

Table P11-12

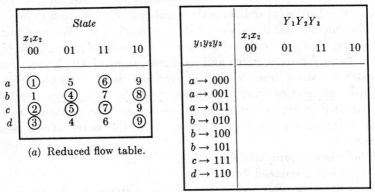

$x_1 x_2$	State			
	00	01	11	10
a	①	5	⑥	9
b	1	④	7	⑧
c	②	⑤	⑦	9
d	③	4	6	⑨

(a) Reduced flow table.

$y_1 y_2 y_3$	$x_1 x_2$	$Y_1 Y_2 Y_3$		
	00	01	11	10
$a \to 000$				
$a \to 001$				
$a \to 011$				
$b \to 010$				
$b \to 100$				
$b \to 101$				
$c \to 111$				
$d \to 110$				

(b) Excitation table.

11-13. (a) Find all the races in the flow table of Table P11-13 and indicate those that are critical and those that are not.

(b) Find another assignment which contains no critical races.

Table P11-13

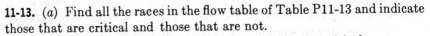

$y_1 y_2$	State			
	$x_1 x_2$ 00	01	11	10
00	ⓞⓞ	11	ⓞⓞ	11
01	11	ⓞ1	11	11
10	00	①ⓞ	11	11
11	①①	①①	00	①①

11-14. For each of the reduced flow tables in Table P11-14, find an assignment which contains no critical races and requires a minimum of secondary variables.

Table P11-14

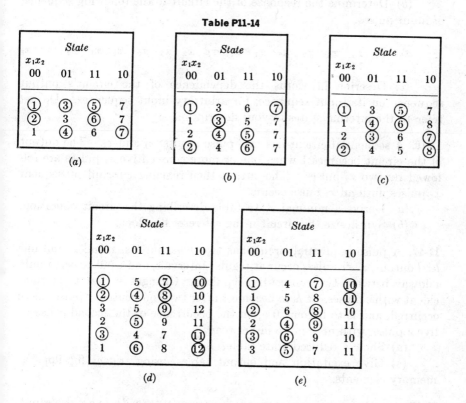

(a)

(b)

(c)

(d)

(e)

11-15. Table P11-15 describes a sequential circuit with two pulse inputs, x_1 and x_2, and one pulse output, z. The circuit is initially in state A, and no two input pulses occur simultaneously.

Table P11-15

PS	NS, z	
	x_1	x_2
A	$B,0$	$A,0$
B	$A,0$	$C,1$
C	$B,0$	$C,1$

(a) Show a realization of the circuit using trigger flip-flops and AND and OR gates. The circuit should start with both flip-flops in the 0 state.

(b) Determine the response of the circuit to the following sequence of input pulses:

$$x_2 \quad x_2 \quad x_1 \quad x_2 \quad x_2 \quad x_2 \quad x_1 \quad x_1 \quad x_1 \quad x_2 \quad x_2 \quad x_2 \quad x_1 \quad x_1 \quad x_2 \quad x_2 \quad x_1$$

(c) Describe in words the dependence of the circuit's output sequence on its input sequence, for arbitrary input sequences. Do *not* refer to the internal states in your description.

11-16. A sequential circuit has two pulse inputs, x_1 and x_2. The output of the circuit becomes 1 when one or more consecutive x_1 pulses are followed by two x_2 pulses. The output then remains 1 for all subsequent x_2 pulses until an x_1 pulse occurs.

(a) Derive a minimal state table describing the circuit operation.

(b) Synthesize the circuit using set-reset flip-flops.

11-17. A pulse sequential circuit has two *pulse* inputs, x and c, and one *level* output, z. c pulses occur at regular intervals, and x pulses occur only midway between two consecutive c pulses. Changes in z are to be coincident with c pulses. z is to become 1 after two consecutive x pulses have occurred, and is to become 0 upon the occurrence of the second consecutive c pulse, with no x pulse in between.

(a) Show a reduced state table.

(b) Give excitation and output tables, using trigger flip-flops as memory elements.

11-18. (a) Design an asynchronous binary counter with one pulse input, x, and two outputs, z_1 and z_2, capable of counting from zero to three. When the circuit is pulsed after the count has reached three, it should return to zero. The outputs should provide continuously the count modulo 4.

(b) Repeat the problem for *level* inputs and outputs.

11-19. The memory device shown in Fig. P11-19a has two binary (pulse) inputs, Y_1 and Y_2, and three binary (level) outputs, y_1, y_2, and y_3. When Y_1 is pulsed, y_1, y_2, and y_3 are complemented; when Y_2 is pulsed, y_2 and y_3 are complemented; when Y_1 and Y_2 are pulsed simultaneously (assume it can be done), only y_3 is complemented. Using only *one* such device, realize the state table of Fig. P11-19b. Use the part of the state assignment as specified, and show the excitation and output equations.

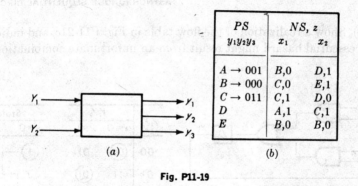

PS $y_1y_2y_3$	NS, z x_1	x_2
$A \rightarrow 001$	$B,0$	$D,1$
$B \rightarrow 000$	$C,0$	$E,1$
$C \rightarrow 011$	$C,1$	$D,0$
D	$A,1$	$C,1$
E	$B,0$	$B,0$

(a)   (b)

Fig. P11-19

11-20. A memory device has two binary (pulse) inputs, Y_1 and Y_2, and three binary (level) outputs, y_1, y_2, and y_3. When Y_1 is pulsed, both y_1 and y_2 are complemented; when Y_2 is pulsed, both y_2 and y_3 are complemented. It is not allowed to pulse Y_1 and Y_2 simultaneously. Use *one* such device to realize the pulse sequential circuit shown in Table P11-20.

Table P11-20

PS	NS x_1	x_2	z
A	D	A	0
B	C	D	0
C	A	B	0
D	B	B	1

11-21. The circuit of Fig. P11-21a realizes the flow table of Fig. P11-21b. An analysis of this circuit shows that if the delay associated with the NOT gate is very large, a change of input from $x = 0$ (while $y_1 = y_2 = 0$) to $x = 1$ may result in a transition to stable state ⑪ instead of to ⓪①. This phenomenon indeed occurs if, as a result of the above input change, y_2 changes faster than the propagation of the input through the NOT gate. Such a phenomenon is known as an *essential hazard*. Unger [6] proved that an essential hazard occurs in fundamental-mode circuits whenever three consecutive input changes take the circuit to a different stable state than the first change alone. Another example of a state table containing an essential hazard is given in Fig. P11-21c, where three consecutive changes take the circuit from state ① to state ④, while a single change takes it to state ②.

(a) Indicate a point (or points) in the circuit at which the insertion of a sufficiently large delay will prevent the hazardous behavior.

(b) Show a realization of the flow table in Fig. P11-21c, and indicate how an essential hazard might result from an unfortunate combination of delays.

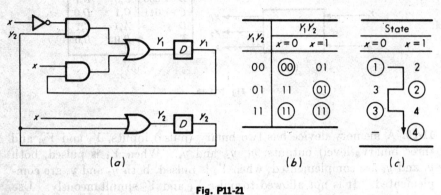

Fig. P11-21

11-22. For the flow table given in Table P11-22, determine *all* the essential output hazards and essential internal-variable hazards.

Table P11-22

$x_1 x_2$	State, output			
	00	01	11	10
	①,1	2,0	3,1	⑤,1
	4,0	②,0	3,1	8,1
	4,0	7,0	③,1	8,0
	④,0	6,1	9,0	⑧,0
	4,0	⑥,1	9,1	5,1
	1,0	⑦,0	⑨,1	5,1

12
Structure of Sequential Machines

One of the main problems in the synthesis of sequential machines is that of assigning combinations of state-variable values to the states of the machine. The selection of assignment determines the complexity and structure of the circuit which realizes the machine. Various restrictions and requirements may be imposed on the state assignment, depending on the design objectives and intended use of the circuit. It may be desirable, for example, to construct it using minimum amount of logic; or to build it from an interconnection of smaller circuits, and so on. By the *structure* of a sequential machine we mean the manner in which a machine can be realized from a set of smaller component machines, as well as the functional dependencies of its state and output variables. It is our aim in this chapter to study the state-assignment problem and how it affects the structure and complexity of sequential machines.

12-1 INTRODUCTORY EXAMPLE

The close relationship between the state-assignment problem and the structure of sequential machines will be demonstrated by means of machine M_1, shown in Table 12-1. Two possible state assignments for M_1 are shown in Table 12-2. The logical equations corresponding to assignment α, which are derived from the excitation and output tables, are

$$Y_1 = x'y_1 + xy_1' = f_1(x,y_1)$$
$$Y_2 = x'y_1 + xy_2 = f_2(x,y_1,y_2)$$
$$z = xy_2' = f_0(x,y_2)$$

Table 12-1   Machine M_1

PS	NS		z	
	$x = 0$	$x = 1$	$x = 0$	$x = 1$
A	A	D	0	1
B	A	C	0	0
C	C	B	0	0
D	C	A	0	1

From these equations it is evident that Y_1 is a function of y_1 and of the external input, and is independent of y_2. On the other hand, Y_2 depends

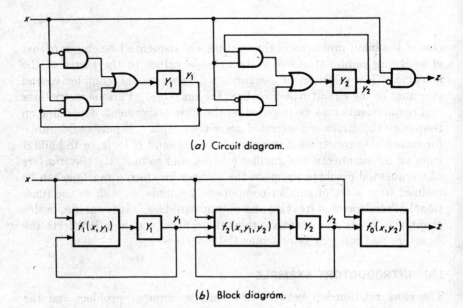

(a) Circuit diagram.

(b) Block diagram.

Fig. 12-1. First realization of machine M_1.

on the external input, as well as on y_1 and y_2. The output z is a function of x and y_2 only. The circuit diagram of M_1 is shown in Fig. 12-1a. The dependency of the next-state variables and the output is illustrated by the block diagram of Fig. 12-1b, where, for example, the "block" $f_1(x,y_1)$ corresponds to the combinational logic associated with the memory element Y_1, and so on.

Table 12-2   Excitation and output tables for machine M_1

$y_1 y_2$	$Y_1 Y_2$		z		$y_1 y_2$	$Y_1 Y_2$		z	
	$x = 0$	$x = 1$	$x = 0$	$x = 1$		$x = 0$	$x = 1$	$x = 0$	$x = 1$
$A \rightarrow 00$	00	10	0	1	$A \rightarrow 00$	00	11	0	1
$B \rightarrow 01$	00	11	0	0	$B \rightarrow 01$	00	10	0	0
$C \rightarrow 11$	11	01	0	0	$C \rightarrow 10$	10	01	0	0
$D \rightarrow 10$	11	00	0	1	$D \rightarrow 11$	10	00	0	1

(a) Assignment α.   (b) Assignment β.

The logical equations corresponding to assignment β, shown in Table 12-2b, are

$$Y_1 = x'y_1 + xy_1' = f_1(x,y_1)$$
$$Y_2 = xy_2' = f_2(x,y_2)$$
$$z = xy_1'y_2' + xy_1y_2 = f_0(x,y_1,y_2)$$

In this case Y_1 is independent of y_2, and Y_2 is independent of y_1. In other words, the next value of each state variable can be computed from its present value and the value of the present input, regardless of the value of the other state variable. The dependency of the output function, however, has increased as compared with its dependency in assignment α. The circuit and block diagrams corresponding to assignment β are shown in Fig. 12-2.

The preceding two realizations of machine M_1 clearly demonstrate that the choice of assignment affects the complexity of the circuit and determines the dependency of the next-state variables and the overall structure of the machine. Our objective in this chapter is to investigate the relationship between the state assignment and the reduction in the dependency of the state variables and the structure of sequential machines. These factors will be shown to affect the complexity and cost of the final circuits as well.

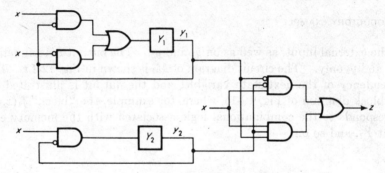

(a) Circuit diagram.

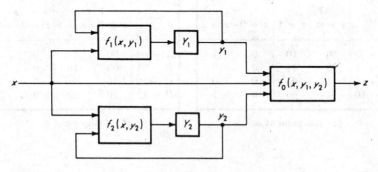

(b) Block diagram.

Fig. 12-2 Second realization of machine M_1.

12-2 STATE ASSIGNMENTS USING PARTITIONS

In this section we shall derive necessary and sufficient conditions for a sequential machine M to have assignments which result in reduced dependencies among the state variables. Such assignments generally yield simpler logic equations and circuits; they are also the fundamental means by which machine decompositions are obtained.

Closed partitions

Let machine M have a set of n states $S = \{S_1, S_2, \ldots, S_n\}$ and a set of p input symbols $I = \{I_1, I_2, \ldots, I_p\}$; then $k = [\log_2 n]$ state variables and $l = [\log_2 p]$ input variables are needed for a complete assignment, where $[g]$ is defined as the smallest integer equal to or greater than g. Each of the k next-state variables depends in general on the external inputs $x_1, x_2, \ldots, x_l$ and on the k state variables, i.e.,

$$Y_i = f_i(y_1, y_2, \ldots, y_k, x_1, x_2, \ldots, x_l) \qquad i = 1, 2, \ldots, k$$

Our objective is to obtain assignments in which the values of one or more subsets of the next-state variables can be determined independently of the values of the remaining variables, that is, assignments which yield logical equations for the variables $Y_1, Y_2, \ldots, Y_r$, where $1 \le r < k$, which are independent of the remaining $k - r$ variables. Thus

$$Y_i = f_i(y_1, y_2, \ldots, y_r, x_1, x_2, \ldots, x_l) \qquad i = 1, 2, \ldots, r$$

The subset $\{Y_1, Y_2, \ldots, Y_r\}$ of state variables whose values are independent of the values of $y_{r+1}, y_{r+2}, \ldots, y_k$ is said to be a *self-dependent* subset, and an assignment which yields such a subset is said to possess self-dependent subsets. Both assignments α and β of machine M_1 have this property.

The state-assignment problem may be viewed as either a coding problem or a partitioning problem. In viewing the state assignment as a coding problem, a distinct code is assigned to each row (state) of the stable table. From the partitioning point of view, which we shall adopt in this chapter, each state variable y_i induces a partition τ_i on the set of states of the machine, such that two states are in the same block of τ_i if and only if they are assigned the same value of y_i. For example, in assignment α for machine M_1, $y_1 = 0$ for states A and B, and $y_1 = 1$ for states C and D. Hence y_1 induces the partition $\tau_1 = \{\overline{A,B}; \overline{C,D}\}$ on the states of M_1. Similarly, y_2 induces the partition $\tau_2 = \{\overline{A,D}; \overline{B,C}\}$. Clearly, if the assignment is such that each state has a unique code, the product of the k partitions $\tau_1, \tau_2, \ldots, \tau_k$ corresponding to $y_1, y_2, \ldots, y_k$ is equal to zero, that is,

$$\tau_1 \cdot \tau_2 \cdot \tau_3 \cdot \ldots \cdot \tau_k = \pi(0)$$

We have shown how an assignment induces a set of partitions whose product is the zero partition. The inverse process, that of assigning the values of the state variables to distinguish the blocks of a set of partitions, is the one of significance in the synthesis procedure. Given a partition τ with $\#(\tau)$ blocks on the set of states of M, to distinguish between these blocks it is necessary to select $r = \lceil \log_2 \#(\tau) \rceil$ state variables and to assign a distinct combination of these variables to each block of τ; that is, all the states in each block are assigned the same values of $y_1, y_2, \ldots, y_r$. Each partition on the states of M provides some information regarding M's state. If M possesses two partitions, τ_1 and τ_2, such that $\tau_1 > \tau_2$, then τ_2 provides more information than τ_1. Clearly, the zero partition provides all the necessary information, since the knowledge of the block of $\pi(0)$, in which the machine is, is sufficient to determine uniquely the state of M. Thus, to obtain an assignment for M so that each state has a distinct code, it is necessary to assign the values of the state variables so that they distinguish the blocks of a set of partitions whose product is the zero partition.

Example   For machine M_1, the product of the partitions $\tau_1 = \{\overline{A,B}; \overline{C,D}\}$ and $\tau_2 = \{\overline{A,C}; \overline{B,D}\}$ is zero, i.e., $\tau_1 \cdot \tau_2 = \pi(0)$.   Hence, if we assign y_1 to distinguish block (A,B) from block (C,D), and assign y_2 to distinguish the blocks of τ_2, each state of M_1 will have a distinct code. One such assignment is assignment β, shown in Table 12-2b.   ■

Definition 12-1   A partition π on the set of states of a sequential machine M is said to be *closed* if, for every two states S_i and S_j which are in the same block of π and any input I_k in I, the states I_kS_i and I_kS_j are in a common block of π. I_kS_i denotes the I_k-successor of S_i.

Example   For machine M_1 in Table 12-1, the partitions $\pi_1 = \{\overline{A,B}; \overline{C,D}\}$ and $\pi_2 = \{\overline{A,C}; \overline{B,D}\}$ are closed.†   The 0- and 1-successors of (A,C) are (A,C) and (B,D), respectively, while the only successor of (B,D) is (A,C).   If we denote the blocks of π_2 (A,C) and (B,D) by P and Q, respectively, we may describe the successor relationships of these blocks by means of the graph of Fig. 12-3.   Clearly, the knowledge of the present block of M_1 and the input is sufficient to determine uniquely the next block. (We shall subsequently say that a machine is in a block to mean that it is in any one of the states contained in the block.)   ■

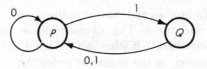

Fig. 12-3 Successor relationships of the blocks of the partition $\pi_2 = \{\overline{A,C};$ $\overline{B,D}\} = \{\overline{P}; \overline{Q}\}$.

Reduction of the functional dependency of the state variables

We shall now establish the relationship between the closed partitions and the reduction of the functional dependency of the state variables.

† In general, we shall reserve π to denote closed partitions, while τ, θ, etc., will denote arbitrary partitions.

Theorem 12-1 *Let M be a sequential machine with k state variables, y_1, y_2, . . . , y_k. If there exists a closed partition π on the states of M and if r state variables, where $r = [log_2 \#(\pi)]$, are assigned to the blocks of π, so that all the states contained in each block are assigned the same values of y_1, y_2, . . . , y_r, then the next-state variables, Y_1, Y_2, . . . , Y_r, are independent of the remaining $k - r$ variables. And conversely, if the first r next-state variables, Y_1, Y_2, . . . , Y_r $(1 \leq r < k)$, can be determined from the values of the inputs and the first r state variables, independently of the values of the remaining $k - r$ variables, then there exists a closed partition π on the states of M such that two states, S_i and S_j, are in the same block of π if and only if they are assigned the same values of the first r variables.*

Proof: Since each block of π is assigned the same values of the variables y_1, y_2, . . . , y_r, and since π is closed, the knowledge of the present block of π and the present inputs is sufficient to determine the next block of π. In other words, the knowledge of the present values of y_1, y_2, . . . , y_r and the present input values is sufficient to determine the values of Y_1, Y_2, . . . , Y_r, regardless of the values of the remaining variables. To prove the converse, form a partition π on the states of M such that all the states having the same assigned values of y_1, y_2, . . . , y_r are in the same block of π. To prove that π is closed, consider two states, S_i and S_j, which belong to the same block of π. Each of these states has the same assigned values of the first r variables, and since these variables are independent of the values of the remaining ones, an application of the same input sequence to both S_i and S_j causes the same change in the values of the first r variables for these two states. Therefore, for each value of I_k, the successors $I_k S_i$ and $I_k S_j$ have the same assignment of values of the first r variables, and consequently are contained in the same block of π. Thus π is closed. ∎

Example For machine M_1 the partitions $\pi_1 = \{\overline{A,B}; \overline{C,D}\}$ and $\pi_2 = \{\overline{A,C}; \overline{B,D}\}$ are closed. Since y_1 in assignment β has been assigned to distinguish the blocks of π_1, it is independent of y_2. Similarly, since y_2 has been assigned to distinguish the blocks of π_2, it is independent of y_1. ∎

Theorem 12-1 actually states a necessary and sufficient condition for the decomposition of sequential machines. The existence of a partition τ and a closed partition π on the set of states of a machine M, such that $\pi \cdot \tau = \pi(0)$, guarantees that M can be composed of two component machines connected in *series*. The first component in the connection consists of $[\log_2 \#(\pi)]$ memory elements (and their excitation circuitry), corresponding to the state variables assigned to distinguish the blocks of π. Since these variables are independent of the remaining variables, the first component is often referred to as the *independent* component. The second component in the serial connection, which is also referred to as the *dependent* component, contains $[\log_2 \#(\tau)]$ memory elements, corresponding to the state variables assigned to distinguish the blocks of τ. We shall refer to the independent component as the *predecessor* machine, and to the dependent component as the *successor* machine. It is often convenient to view the predecessor machine as the component which distinguishes between the blocks of π, and the successor machine as the component which distinguishes between the states within the blocks of π.

The existence of two closed partitions on the states of M such that their product is zero, i.e., $\pi_1 \cdot \pi_2 = \pi(0)$, implies that M can be composed of two components, operating in *parallel* independently of each other. One component consists of $[\log_2 \#(\pi_1)]$ memory elements, corresponding to the variables assigned to distinguish the blocks of π_1. The second component consists of $[\log_2 \#(\pi_2)]$ memory elements, corresponding to the variables assigned to distinguish the blocks of π_2.

The preceding arguments can thus be summarized as follows:

▶   An n-state machine M can be decomposed into two independent components operating in parallel if and only if there exist two nontrivial closed partitions π_1 and π_2 on the states of M such that $\pi_1 \cdot \pi_2 = \pi(0)$. This decomposition requires a minimal number (i.e., $[\log_2 n]$), of state variables if and only if

$$[\log_2 \#(\pi_1)] + [\log_2 \#(\pi_2)] = [\log_2 n]$$

Example   Consider machine M_2 given in Table 12-3. It can be shown that M_2 has seven closed partitions, which are listed in Fig. 12-4.

Table 12-3   Machine M_2

PS	NS $x = 0$	$x = 1$	z
A	H	B	0
B	F	A	0
C	G	D	0
D	E	C	1
E	A	C	0
F	C	D	0
G	B	A	0
H	D	B	0

$\pi_0 = \{\overline{A}; \overline{B}; \overline{C}; \overline{D}; \overline{E}; \overline{F}; \overline{G}; \overline{H}\} = \pi(0)$

$\pi_1 = \{A,B,C,D; E,F,G,H\}$

$\pi_2 = \{A,D,E,H; B,C,F,G\}$

$\pi_3 = \{A,D; B,C,F,G; E,H\}$

$\pi_4 = \{A,D,E,H; \overline{B,C}; \overline{F,G}\}$

$\pi_5 = \{A,D; \overline{B,C}; \overline{E,H}; \overline{F,G}\}$

$\pi_6 = \{A,B,C,D,E,F,G,H\} = \pi(I)$

Fig. 12-4   Closed partitions for machine M_2.

Since M_2 has eight states, three state variables are needed for an assignment. The existence of the closed partition π_5 suggests that machine M_2 can be realized as two component machines connected in series. The predecessor component has two state variables, y_1 and y_2, which are assigned to the blocks of π_5, and consequently are independent of y_3, while the successor component has a single variable, y_3, which distinguishes the states in the blocks of π_5.

The maximal reduction in the dependency of the state variables would be achieved if we could find three two-block closed partitions whose product is zero. In such a case each state variable would be independent of the remaining two variables, and the machine would be realized as a parallel connection of three component machines. It is evident, however, from the list of the nontrivial closed partitions of M_2, that only two two-block partitions can be found, namely, π_1 and π_2. In fact, since each of the nontrivial closed partitions is greater than π_5, no combination of closed partitions can be found whose product is zero. Therefore we must select a partition τ such that

$$\pi_1 \cdot \pi_2 \cdot \tau = \pi(0)$$

One possible partition τ is

$$\tau = \{\overline{A,B,G,H}\,;\,\overline{C,D,E,F}\}$$

Assigning y_1 to distinguish the blocks of π_1, y_2 to distinguish the blocks of π_2, and y_3 to distinguish the blocks of τ results in the assignment of Table 12-4. Clearly, y_1 and y_2, which are assigned to the blocks of closed partitions, will be self-dependent, while y_3, which is assigned to the blocks of τ, will be a function of the external input and all three state variables. The logical equations derived from Table 12-4 are

Table 12-4   Excitation and output table for machine M_2

$y_1y_2y_3$	$Y_1Y_2Y_3$ $x = 0$	$x = 1$	z
$A \to 000$	100	010	0
$B \to 010$	111	000	0
$C \to 011$	110	001	0
$D \to 001$	101	011	1
$E \to 101$	000	011	0
$F \to 111$	011	001	0
$G \to 110$	010	000	0
$H \to 100$	001	010	0

$$Y_1 = x'y_1'$$

$$Y_2 = x'y_2 + xy_2'$$

$$Y_3 = xy_3 + x'y_1'y_2y_3' + y_1'y_2'y_3 + y_1y_2y_3 + x'y_1y_2'y_3'$$

$$z = y_1'y_2'y_3$$

The corresponding schematic diagram is shown in Fig. 12-5. ∎

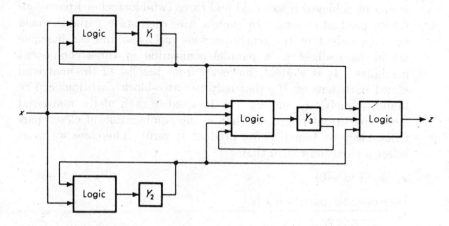

Fig. 12-5 Schematic diagram of machine M_2.

12-3 THE LATTICE OF CLOSED PARTITIONS

The closed partitions have been shown to play a significant role in the state-assignment problem and in determining the dependency of the state variables. We shall therefore present a method for generating these partitions and investigate their properties.

Theorem 12-2 *The product $\pi_1 \cdot \pi_2$ and sum $\pi_1 + \pi_2$ of two closed partitions on the set of states of M are also closed.*

Proof: Let π_1 and π_2 be two closed partitions on the states of M. We shall show that the partition $\pi_1 \cdot \pi_2$ is also closed, leaving the proof that $\pi_1 + \pi_2$ is closed as an exercise to the reader.

Let B be an arbitrary block of $\pi_1 \cdot \pi_2$. Since B is the intersection of some block B_1 of π_1 and B_2 of π_2, then B is contained in both B_1 and B_2. Since π_1 and π_2 are closed, the I_k-successor of B is also contained within some block I_kB_1 of π_1 and some block I_kB_2 of π_2, where I_kB_i is the I_k-successor of B_i. Therefore I_kB is contained within the intersection $I_kB_1 \cdot I_kB_2$. But the intersection

$I_k B_1 \cdot I_k B_2$ is contained in a block of $\pi_1 \cdot \pi_2$, and consequently, $I_k B$ is contained in a block of $\pi_1 \cdot \pi_2$. Therefore $\pi_1 \cdot \pi_2$ is closed. ∎

From this theorem it follows that, to each pair of closed partitions π_1 and π_2, there corresponds a *least upper bound*, $\pi_1 + \pi_2$, and a *greatest lower bound*, $\pi_1 \cdot \pi_2$. Consequently, the set of closed partitions on the states of a machine is closed under the $+$ and $\cdot$ binary operations and therefore forms a lattice (by Definition 2-2). This lattice is referred to as the π-*lattice*.

Let $\pi_{S_i S_j}$ be the *smallest* closed partition containing S_i and S_j in one block. We shall subsequently refer to the placing of S_i and S_j in one block as *identifying* them. To determine $\pi_{S_i S_j}$, we first identify S_i and S_j. This identification implies that we must also identify the successors $I_k S_i$ and $I_k S_j$, for every input I_k in I. The states $I_k S_i$ and $I_k S_j$ are said to be *implied* by S_i and S_j. Whenever a state S_i is identified with S_j and S_k, the transitive law must be applied so that (S_i, S_j, S_k) are placed in the same block of π. If we repeat the above procedure and find the smallest closed partition $\pi_{S_i S_j}$ for every pair of states $S_i S_j$, we obtain a set of partitions which are known as the *basic* partitions. The π-lattice can now be determined in two steps:

1. For every pair of states $S_i S_j$, determine $\pi_{S_i S_j}$.
2. Obtain all possible sums of the basic partitions.

Since every closed partition can be shown (see Prob. 12-5) to be the sum of one or more basic partitions, the above procedure indeed generates the set of all closed partitions.

Table 12-5 Machine M_3

PS	NS	
	$x = 0$	$x = 1$
A	E	B
B	E	A
C	D	A
D	C	F
E	F	C
F	E	C

As an illustration, we shall determine the π-lattice of machine M_3, shown in Table 12-5. The table in Fig. 12-6a shows all the possible initial identifications and their implications. Within the cell in row S_i, column S_j, we write the identifications implied by the initial identification of S_i and S_j. For example, if we start by identifying states A,B, we find that no other pair of states is implied. Consequently, the partition $\{\overline{A,B};\ \overline{C};\ \overline{D};\ \overline{E};\ \overline{F}\}$ is closed. We continue by identifying A,C, which in turn implies A,B and D,E. These implications may be described as

$$A,C \rightarrow A,B;\, D,E$$

It is already known that the identification of A,B does not imply any other pair; hence we check only the implications due to D,E. From the state table we find that D,E implies C,F. Since A,C and C,F are identified, the transitive law must be applied to yield A,C,F. This process is thus summarized as follows:

$$A,C \rightarrow A,B;\, D,E \rightarrow A,C,F;\, A,B;\, D,E \rightarrow A,B,C,F;\, D,E$$

In a similar manner the entire table is completed. Many shortcuts are possible. For example, while identifying B,D, the pair A,F is implied,

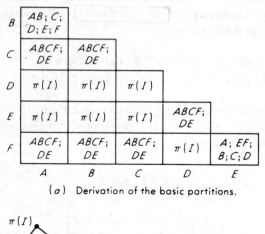

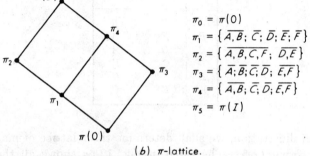

(a) Derivation of the basic partitions.

(b) π-lattice.

Fig. 12-6 Construction of the π-lattice of machine M_3.

but since the implications which result from the identification of A,F have already been determined, it becomes immediately evident that the identification of B,D implies the identity partition, i.e.,

$$B,D \rightarrow C,E; \; A,F \rightarrow A,B,C,F; \; D,E; \; C,E \rightarrow \pi(I)$$

The next step in the procedure is to determine the remaining (non-basic) closed partitions. This is done by computing the sums of pairs of basic partitions to obtain "second-level" partitions and then using only pairs of "second-level" partitions to obtain "third-level" partitions, and so on. For machine M_3 the basic partitions are

$$\pi_1 = \{\overline{A,B}; \overline{C}; \overline{D}; \overline{E}; \overline{F}\}$$
$$\pi_2 = \{\overline{A,B,C,F}; \overline{D,E}\}$$
$$\pi_3 = \{\overline{A}; \overline{B}; \overline{C}; \overline{D}; \overline{E,F}\}$$

The only sum that yields a nontrivial closed partition is

$$\pi_4 = \pi_1 + \pi_3 = \{\overline{A,B}; \overline{C}; \overline{D}; \overline{E,F}\}$$

The π-lattice for machine M_3 is shown in Fig. 12-6b.

12-4 REDUCTION OF THE OUTPUT DEPENDENCY

So far attention has been focused on the reduction of the dependency of the state variables. In assigning the states of these variables to the blocks of a closed partition, we have a considerable amount of freedom. It is our aim in the following discussion to show how this freedom can be used to obtain simpler output circuits with reduced dependencies. The problem is illustrated by considering two possible assignments for machine M_4, which is shown in Table 12-6.

Table 12-6   Machine M_4

PS	NS		z	
	$x = 0$	$x = 1$	$x = 0$	$x = 1$
A	B	D	1	0
B	A	C	0	1
C	D	A	0	1
D	C	B	1	0

Machine M_4 possesses the closed partition $\pi = \{\overline{A,B}; \overline{C,D}\}$. To obtain a state assignment we are looking for a partition τ such that

$\pi \cdot \tau = \pi(0)$. Assignments α and β shown in Table 12-7 correspond, respectively, to the partitions $\tau_a = \{\overline{A,C}; \overline{B,D}\}$ and $\tau_b = \{\overline{A,D}; \overline{B,C}\}$. The state variables and output function corresponding to assignment α are as follows:

$$Y_1 = x'y_1 + xy_1'$$
$$Y_2 = x'y_2' + y_1'y_2' + xy_1y_2$$
$$z = x'y_1'y_2' + x'y_1y_2 + xy_1'y_2 + xy_1y_2'$$

Table 12-7 Two possible assignments for machine M_4

$y_1\ y_2$	$y_1\ y_2$
$A \to 0\ 0$	$A \to 0\ 0$
$B \to 0\ 1$	$B \to 0\ 1$
$C \to 1\ 0$	$C \to 1\ 1$
$D \to 1\ 1$	$D \to 1\ 0$

(a) Assignment α.   (b) Assignment β.

The number of diodes required for a (two-level) realization of these functions is 32.

For assignment β we obtain

$$Y_1 = x'y_1 + xy_1'$$
$$Y_2 = x'y_2' + xy_1'y_2 + y_1y_2'$$
$$z = x'y_2' + xy_2$$

The realization of these functions requires only 22 diodes.

Evidently, the reduction in the circuit complexity is the outcome of decrease in the dependency of the output function. While in assignment α the output depends on x, y_1, and y_2, in assignment β it is independent of y_1. Although the reduction in the dependency of the output does not always ensure simpler output circuits, in most cases it does tend to decrease the complexity of the circuit. Our aim, therefore, is directed toward obtaining assignments which reduce the dependencies of the output logic.

Definition 12-2 A partition λ_o on the states of a machine M is said to be *output-consistent* if, for every block of λ_o and every input, all the states contained in the block have the same outputs.

Example $\lambda_o = \tau_b = \{\overline{A,D}; \overline{B,C}\}$ is an output-consistent partition of machine M_4. ∎

Let M have n states to which we assign k variables, where $k = [\log_2 n]$. Let $r = [\log_2 \#(\lambda_o)]$ variables be assigned to the blocks of M's output-consistent partition λ_o. Because λ_o is output-consistent, the outputs associated with the blocks of λ_o can be computed from these r variables, independently of the remaining $k - r$ variables which are assigned to the states in the blocks of λ_o. Consequently, we arrive at the following general result:

▶ The existence of an output-consistent partition λ_o on the states of a sequential machine M implies that there exists an assignment for M such that the outputs depend, at most, on the external inputs and on the variables assigned to the blocks of λ_o.

This result can be generalized as follows: Let $\Theta = \{\tau_1, \tau_2, \ldots, \tau_k\}$ be the set consisting of the partitions induced by the state variables $y_1, y_2, \ldots, y_k$. Let $\lambda_{o1}, \lambda_{o2}, \ldots, \lambda_{om}$ be the output-consistent partitions induced by the outputs $z_1, z_2, \ldots, z_m$. If, for some subset Q of Θ,

$$\lambda_{oi} \geq \prod_{j \in Q} \tau_j$$

then z_i is a function of the external input x and the variables assigned to the partitions contained in Q.

Example In machine M_4, $\lambda_o = \lambda_{o1} = \{\overline{A,D};\overline{B,C}\}$. Since y_2 in assignment β has been assigned to λ_o, the output z depends only on this variable and is independent of y_1. ■

In assignment β we obtained a reduction in the dependency of y_1 and (simultaneously) of the output z. This is possible since $\pi \cdot \lambda_o = \pi(0)$. In general, however, we cannot efficiently obtain a complete assignment based on any arbitrary closed partition π and any output-consistent partition λ_o. For example, if $\pi \cdot \lambda_o = \pi(0)$ but $[\log_2 \#(\pi)] + [\log_2 \#(\lambda_o)] > [\log_2 n]$, an assignment can be obtained in which the outputs depend on $[\log_2 \#(\lambda_o)]$ variables, and $[\log_2 \#(\pi)]$ variables are independent of the remaining ones. But such an assignment is not a minimal one, since it requires an excessive number of variables. For example, if $\pi = \{\overline{A,B};\overline{C,D};\overline{E,F};\overline{G,H}\}$ while $\lambda_o = \{\overline{A,C};\overline{B,E};\overline{D,G};\overline{F,H}\}$, then $\pi \cdot \lambda_o = \pi(0)$, but $\log_2 4 + \log_2 4 = 4$. If we use only π or only λ_o, we can obtain an assignment with only three variables. It should be noted that while λ_o simplifies the output circuit, the additional variables (the fourth one in the above case), which are not assigned to any closed partition, may add a significant amount of logic to the overall circuit. Consequently, we have two different requirements: to make an assignment based on an output-consistent partition λ_o and at the same time to reduce the dependencies of the state variables, i.e., to assign the variables to the blocks of a closed partition π. These two requirements often conflict. Various approaches have been tried in attempts to solve this problem (see, for example, Ref. 10). Presently, however, no simple solution is available, and some trial and error is needed.

12-5 INPUT INDEPENDENCE AND AUTONOMOUS CLOCKS

Some machines can be constructed of two components: an input-independent one and an input-dependent one. Our aim in this section is to determine necessary and sufficient conditions for the existence of state assignments which result in such a structure.

Definition 12-3 A partition λ_i on the states of a machine M is said to be *input-consistent* if, for every state S_i of M and all inputs $I_1, I_2, \ldots, I_p$, the next states, $I_1 S_i, I_2 S_i, \ldots, I_p S_i$, are in the same block of λ_i.

Example Consider machine M_5 shown in Table 12-8. State A implies the identification of states C and D. Similarly, the identification of E and F is implied by state C, while the identification of A and B is implied by state E. Thus the smallest input-consistent partition for M_5 is $\lambda_i = \{\overline{A,B}; \overline{C,D}; \overline{E,F}\}$. Clearly, any partition that contains λ_i is also input-consistent. Unless otherwise indicated, λ_i will subsequently designate the smallest input-consistent partition. ∎

Table 12-8   Machine M_5

PS	NS		z	
	$x = 0$	$x = 1$	$x = 0$	$x = 1$
A	D	C	0	1
B	C	D	0	0
C	E	F	0	1
D	F	F	0	0
E	B	A	0	1
F	A	B	0	0

Since the successor relationships among the blocks of λ_i are independent of the inputs, the $[\log_2 \#(\lambda_i)]$ variables assigned to distinguish the blocks of λ_i are input-independent. If, in addition to λ_i, machine M possesses a closed partition π such that $\pi \geq \lambda_i$, then, for a given state S_j

and every input $I_1, I_2, \ldots, I_p$ in I, the next states, $I_1S_j, I_2S_j, \ldots, I_pS_j$, must be in the same block of λ_i, and therefore in the same block of π as well. Consequently, for a given initial state, the block of π in which the state of M is contained after any finite input sequence depends only on the initial block and on the length of the sequence. This property may be summarized as follows:

▶ The existence of a closed partition π and a nontrivial input-consistent partition λ_i on the states of M, where $\pi \geq \lambda_i$, is a necessary and sufficient condition for the existence of an assignment for M such that the $[\log_2 \#(\pi)]$ variables assigned to the blocks of π are independent of the input and of the remaining state variables.

A component machine whose output at any time is independent of the input is called an *autonomous clock*. If M possesses an input-consistent partition λ_i and several closed partitions, each greater than or equal to λ_i, then the autonomous clock corresponding to the smallest such closed partition is referred to as the *maximal autonomous clock*.

Example For machine M_5 the input-consistent partition

$$\lambda_i = \{\overline{A,B}; \overline{C,D}; \overline{E,F}\}$$

is closed. The output-consistent partition is $\lambda_o = \{\overline{A,C,E}; \overline{B,D,F}\}$. Since $\pi = \lambda_i$ and $\pi \cdot \lambda_o = \pi(0)$, the assignment and logical equations in Table 12-9 result. The schematic diagram corresponding to this assignment is shown in Fig. 12-7. It clearly displays the existence of an autonomous clock, as well as the reduction in the dependency of z due to λ_o. The external clock pulses have not been drawn, but are implicit. In fact, they trigger the autonomous clock and cause it to change states. ■

Table 12-9 Assignment and equations for machine M_5

$y_1y_2y_3$		$Y_1 = y_2$
$A \rightarrow$	$0\ 0\ 0$	$Y_2 = y_1'y_2'$
$B \rightarrow$	$0\ 0\ 1$	$Y_3 = xy_3 + xy_2 + x'y_2'y_3' + y_2y_3$
$C \rightarrow$	$0\ 1\ 0$	$z = xy_3'$
$D \rightarrow$	$0\ 1\ 1$	
$E \rightarrow$	$1\ 0\ 0$	
$F \rightarrow$	$1\ 0\ 1$	(b) Logical equations.

(a) Assignment.

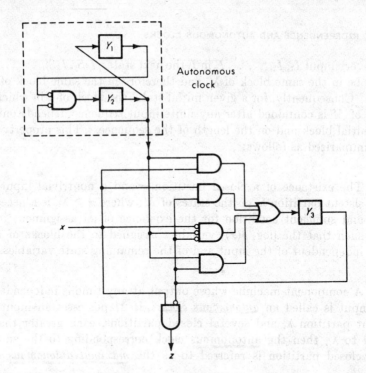

Fig. 12-7 Realization of machine M_5.

It is easy to show that if M is a strongly connected machine, then any component induced by a closed partition on the states of M is also strongly connected. Hence the autonomous clock of a strongly connected machine is also strongly connected, and furthermore it is a periodic machine. To find the period p of the autonomous clock, suppose that machine M possesses a closed partition π such that $\pi \geq \lambda_i$. The clock has $\#(\pi)$ states, and therefore, during $\#(\pi) + 1$ time units, it must pass at least twice through one of the states. Thus the period p is equal to or smaller than $\#(\pi)$.

Example The maximal autonomous clock of machine M_5 is determined from the partition $\pi = \lambda_i$.

$$\pi = \{\overline{A,B}; \overline{C,D}; \overline{E,F}\} = \{\overline{\alpha}; \overline{\beta}; \overline{\gamma}\}$$

In the state table of M_5 let us denote the blocks (A,B), (C,D), and (E,F) by α, β, and γ, respectively. The graph describing the block-successor relationships of π yields the state diagram of the maximal autonomous clock, as shown in Fig. 12-8. From the graph it is clear that the period of the clock is $p = 3$. ■

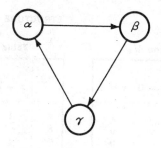

Fig. 12-8 The autonomous clock of machine M_6.

12-6 COVERS, AND GENERATION OF CLOSED PARTITIONS BY STATE SPLITTING

The correlation between the closed partitions and the existence of assignments with self-dependent and autonomous subsets has been established in the preceding sections. These assignments have been shown to yield simpler circuits and to affect the circuit's structure. Many machines, however, do not possess such partitions, and therefore cannot be implemented with independent components. Our objective in this section is to develop a method which will enable us to generalize the preceding structure theory and, by allowing the classification of the states into nondisjoint subsets, to augment a machine which does not possess any closed partition into an equivalent machine which possesses such partitions. Such an augmentation is achieved by splitting some states of the original machine. The basic tool in this procedure is the implication graph, which will be defined shortly.

Covers

To illustrate the basic ideas, consider machine M_6 shown in Table 12-10. It can be verified that no closed partition exists for this machine, and therefore it appears that it cannot be decomposed in any manner. Consider next machine M_6' (Table 12-11), which is reducible to machine M_6, since states C' and C'' are equivalent. Machine M_6' possesses the closed partition $\pi = \{\overline{A,C'}; \overline{B,C''}\}$. If we choose a partition $\tau = \{\overline{A,B}; \overline{C',C''}\}$ such that $\pi \cdot \tau = \pi(0)$, and if we assign y_1 and y_2 to the blocks of π and τ, respectively, the following equations result:

$$Y_1 = x$$
$$Y_2 = xy_2 + x'y_1y_2'$$
$$z = xy_1'y_2'$$

Clearly, machine M_6' is realizable as a serial connection of a predecessor component (Y_1) and a successor component (Y_2). Such decom-

Table 12-10   Machine M_6

PS	NS		z	
	$x = 0$	$x = 1$	$x = 0$	$x = 1$
A	A	B	0	1
B	C	B	0	0
C	A	C	0	0

Table 12-11   Machine M_6'

PS	NS		z	
	$x = 0$	$x = 1$	$x = 0$	$x = 1$
A	A	B	0	1
B	C'	B	0	0
C'	A	C''	0	0
C''	A	C''	0	0

position of machine M_6' is also a valid realization of the equivalent machine M_6, although the latter machine does not possess any closed partition. If we work backward from machine M_6' to M_6, we observe that the closed partition $\pi = \{\overline{A,C'}; \overline{B,C''}\}$ becomes equal to $\{\overline{A,C}; \overline{B,C}\}$ when the two equivalent states C' and C'' are merged. Although this collection of subsets covers all the states and is closed with respect to the states of M_6, it does not constitute a partition, since its blocks are not disjoint. In order to cover such situations, it becomes necessary to generalize the structure theory and to define sets consisting of overlapping subsets of states.

A collection φ of subsets, whose set union is S, such that no subset is included in another subset in the collection, is referred to as a *cover* on the set S. The subsets are called the *blocks* of φ. The cover φ on the set of states of a machine M is said to be *closed* if, for every two states S_i and S_j which are in the same block of φ and any input I_k in I, the states $I_k S_i$ and $I_k S_j$ are in a common block of φ. $\#(\varphi)$ and $\rho(\varphi)$ denote, respectively, the number of blocks in φ and the number of elements in the largest block of φ.

Example   The covers $\varphi = \{\overline{A,C}; \overline{B,C}\}$ and $\varphi_1 = \{\overline{A,B}; \overline{A,C}; \overline{B,C}\}$ on the set of states of M_6 are closed. ∎

If we denote the subsets (AC) and (BC) by P and Q, respectively, we obtain the successor relationships of Table 12-12. Since the predecessor machine in the serial connection of M_6 distinguishes the blocks of φ, the successor relationships of Table 12-12 define uniquely the state transitions of the predecessor component.

Table 12-12   State transitions of the predecessor component in the serial decomposition of machine M_6

	$x = 0$	$x = 1$
P	P	Q
Q	P	Q

In order to be able to decompose machines which do not possess any closed partition, it is necessary either to generalize the results of the previous sections to include covers or to develop a method whereby any such machine can be augmented to an equivalent machine which has one or more closed partitions, and therefore is decomposable. The approach taken in this section is the latter.

The implication graph

The main difference between machine M_6 and machine M_6' is that state C of M_6 has been split into states C' and C'' in M_6'. In general, state S_i is said to be *split* into states S_i' and S_i'' if (1) the outputs of S_i' and S_i'' are exactly the same as those of S_i; and (2) for every I_k in I, the states $I_k S_i'$ and $I_k S_i''$ are identical with $I_k S_i$, except where "primes" are necessary, as will be shown later.

An *implication graph* is a directed graph, with vertices representing subsets of the set of states of machine M. Each subset consists of states to be identified in the state table, or which are implied by previously identified subsets of states. The arc labeled I_k represents the transition from one subset of states $(S_i, S_j, \ldots)$ to the subset consisting of the I_k-successors $(I_k S_i, I_k S_j, \ldots)$.

Definition 12-4 A *closed* implication graph is a subgraph of an implication graph such that (1) for every vertex in the subgraph all outgoing arcs and their terminating vertices also belong to the subgraph; and (2) every state of M is represented by at least one vertex.

From the definition of the implication graph for a given machine M it is evident that the collection of subsets associated with the vertices of the closed graph constitutes a closed cover on the set of states of M. From now on we shall consider implication graphs whose vertices represent only pairs of states. It will be shown later that such graphs provide the necessary information regarding all closed covers.

An implication graph is constructed in the following manner. Identify any pair of states S_i and S_j and assign (S_i, S_j) to some initial vertex. For each input I_k draw an arc from vertex (S_i, S_j) to the vertex which represents the successors $(I_k S_i, I_k S_j)$. Repeat this process for all the vertices which are implied by the initial identification until no new vertex is generated.

If M is strongly connected, an initial identification of any pair of states will result in a closed graph. If, however, M is not strongly connected, the closed graph might have to be constructed of two or more disjoint subgraphs, that is, another pair of states not implied by (S_i, S_j) must be identified, its successors determined, and so on.

Example   To construct the implication graph for machine M_6, start by
identifying the pair of states (A,B).   This identification implies the
identification of (A,C), which in turn implies (B,C).   The graph
which is closed is shown in Fig. 12-9.   It is evident that the subgraph enclosed by the dotted lines is also closed, since it satisfies
Definition 12-4.   ■

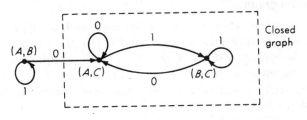

Fig. 12-9   Implication graph for machine M_6.

The general procedure of augmenting an arbitrary machine M into
an equivalent machine M', which possesses one or more closed partitions,
can now be summarized as follows:

1. Construct the implication graph of the given machine M.
2. From the implication graph choose a closed subgraph with minimal number of vertices.   This subgraph yields a closed cover φ
   on M.   If any state S_i is represented by more than one vertex,
   relabel S_i in the first vertex S_i', in the second vertex S_i'', and so
   on.
3. For each S_i which has been replaced by S_i', S_i'', . . . , split the
   corresponding state in M's state table.
4. Modify the entries of the new state table by inserting the necessary primes.   An entry S_p in row S_i, column I_k, is changed to
   S_p' if S_i is represented by some vertex (S_i,S_j) and the I_k-successor
   vertex is (S_p',S_q).

Example   In the implication graph of Fig. 12-9 only state C appears in
two vertices, and thus is split into C' and C'', as shown in Table
12-11.   The partition $\pi = \{\overline{A,C'}; \overline{B,C''}\}$, whose blocks correspond
to the subsets represented by the vertices of the implication graph,
is clearly closed.   ■

In general, the partition π, whose blocks correspond to the subsets
represented by the vertices of the closed implication graph, is closed with

respect to the set of states of the augmented machine M'. This partition has a finite number of blocks, since $(n - 1)n/2$ is the total number of distinct pairs of states. The closed implication graph actually describes graphically the successor relationship of the blocks of π, and consequently it represents the state diagram of the predecessor component in a possible serial realization of M'. The *implication table*, which is the tabular representation of the implication graph, is therefore the state table of the predecessor component. The implication table which corresponds to the closed graph of Fig. 12-9 was derived earlier and is shown in Table 12-12.

From the foregoing procedure it follows that *corresponding to every finite-state machine M, there exists at least one equivalent finite-state machine M' which possesses a closed partition and is therefore serially decomposable.* It should, however, be emphasized that such decompositions are not necessarily the most economical ways of realizing the machines. In fact, for an n-state machine, the closed cover may have up to $(n - 1)n/2$ blocks, which means that the predecessor component will have more states than the original machine. The primary case of practical interest is that in which none of the components in the decomposition is equal to or greater than the original machine. This condition is satisfied whenever the number of vertices in the closed implication graph is smaller than n.

In the foregoing discussion attention has been focused primarily on uniform closed covers containing two states per block. The remaining covers can be determined from this set of basic covers by obtaining all possible sums in a manner analogous to the method of generating the set of closed partitions. All the preceding techniques can be easily extended to blocks of any size and of uniform, as well as nonuniform, covers.

An application of state splitting to parallel decomposition

Machine M_7 and its π-lattice are given in Table 12-13 and Fig. 12-10, respectively. In addition to these closed partitions, it possesses an output-consistent partition λ_o and an input-consistent partition λ_i, namely,

$$\lambda_o = \{\overline{A,E,F}; \overline{B,D}; \overline{C,G}\}$$
$$\lambda_i = \{\overline{A,E,F}; \overline{B,C,D,G}\} = \pi_4$$

Our aim is to obtain a parallel decomposition of M_7. A brief inspection of the π-lattice reveals that no such decomposition is possible, since no two nontrivial closed partitions exist such that $\pi_i \cdot \pi_j = \pi(0)$ [the subset (C,D) is common for all nontrivial partitions]. Consequently, it becomes necessary to check whether there exist any closed covers which yield a parallel decomposition.

Table 12-13   Machine M_7

PS	NS		z	
	$x = 0$	$x = 1$	$x = 0$	$x = 1$
A	B	C	0	0
B	A	F	1	1
C	F	E	1	0
D	F	E	1	1
E	G	D	0	0
F	D	B	0	0
G	E	F	1	0

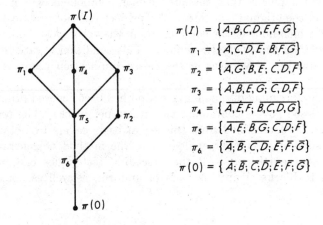

$$\pi(I) = \{\overline{A,B,C,D,E,F,G}\}$$
$$\pi_1 = \{\overline{A,C,D,E;\ B,F,G}\}$$
$$\pi_2 = \{\overline{A,G;\ B,E;\ C,D,F}\}$$
$$\pi_3 = \{\overline{A,B,E,G;\ C,D,F}\}$$
$$\pi_4 = \{\overline{A,E,F;\ B,C,D,G}\}$$
$$\pi_5 = \{\overline{A,E;\ B,G;\ C,D;F}\}$$
$$\pi_6 = \{\overline{A;\ B;\ C,D;\ E;F;G}\}$$
$$\pi(0) = \{\overline{A;\ B;\ C;D;\ E;F;G}\}$$

Fig. 12-10 π-lattice of machine M_7.

The implication graph, when started by the identification of (A,B), is given in Fig. 12-11. From the closed graph we obtain the closed cover

$$\varphi = \{\overline{A,G};\ \overline{B,E};\ \overline{C,F};\ \overline{D,F}\}$$

The corresponding augmented machine M_7' is given in Table 12-14.

In general, for every closed partition π on M, a corresponding closed partition π' on M' can be obtained by placing the states S_i', S_i'', etc., in π' for every split state S_i in π. The closed partitions on machine M_7'

which may be used to achieve a parallel decomposition are

$$\pi = \{\overline{A,G};\ \overline{B,E};\ \overline{C,F'};\ \overline{D,F''}\}$$
$$\pi_4' = \{\overline{A,E,F',F''};\ \overline{B,C,D,G}\}$$
$$\pi_3' = \{\overline{A,B,E,G};\ \overline{C,D,F',F''}\}$$

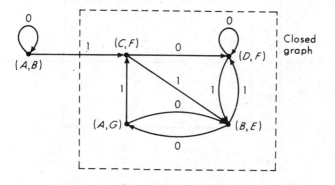

Fig. 12-11   Implication graph for machine M_7.

In addition, the augmented machine possesses the following output-consistent and input-consistent partitions

$$\lambda_o' = \{\overline{A,E,F',F''};\ \overline{B,D};\ \overline{C,G}\}$$
$$\lambda_i' = \pi_4'$$

From this set of partitions, the following observations can be made:

1. $\pi \cdot \pi_4' = \pi(0)$, which implies that a parallel decomposition is possible.
2. The component machine corresponding to π_4' consists of a single variable, y_1. It is an autonomous clock, since $\pi_4' = \lambda_i'$.
3. Since each block of π_3' contains exactly two blocks of π, we may assign y_2 to the blocks of π_3', and thus make it independent of the value of y_3.
4. The variable y_3 must be assigned to the blocks of a partition τ, such that $\pi_3' \cdot \tau = \pi$. The partition $\tau = \{\overline{A,C,F',G};\ \overline{B,D,E,F''}\}$ satisfies this condition.
5. The product $\tau \cdot \pi_4' = \{\overline{A,F'};\ \overline{B,D};\ \overline{C,G};\ \overline{E,F''}\}$ is smaller than λ_o'; consequently, the output z will be a function of only y_1 and y_3.

The assignment and logical equations resulting from the preceding observations are shown in Fig. 12-12a. The schematic diagram is shown in Fig. 12-12b.

Table 12-14   Machine M_7'

PS	NS		z	
	$x = 0$	$x = 1$	$x = 0$	$x = 1$
A	B	C	0	0
B	A	F''	1	1
C	F''	E	1	0
D	F''	E	1	1
E	G	D	0	0
F'	D	B	0	0
F''	D	B	0	0
G	E	F'	1	0

$$y_1\, y_2\, y_3$$

$A \to 0\ 0\ 0$

$B \to 1\ 0\ 1$

$C \to 1\ 1\ 0$ $Y_1 = y_1'$

$D \to 1\ 1\ 1$ $Y_2 = x'y_2 + xy_2'$

$E \to 0\ 0\ 1$ $Y_3 = y_2 + xy_3 + x'y_3'$

$F' \to 0\ 1\ 0$ $z = x'y_1 + y_1 y_3$

$F'' \to 0\ 1\ 1$

$G \to 1\ 0\ 0$

(a) Assignment and logical equations.

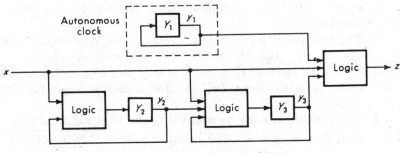

(b) Schematic diagram.

Fig. 12-12 Decomposition of machine M_7'.

12-7 INFORMATION FLOW IN SEQUENTIAL MACHINES

So far we have dealt mainly with serial and parallel decompositions. Of course, there are more complex structures, and our aim in this section is to define them and determine the conditions under which they exist. The main tool for accomplishing this task is the partition pair. It will be shown that the problem of finding state assignments leading to specified machine structures is equivalent to the problem of finding an appropriate set of partition pairs and determining their properties.

Introduction

Machine M_8, shown in Table 12-15, possesses two closed partitions: $\pi_1 = \{\overline{A,B,C}; \overline{D,E,F}\}$ and $\pi_2 = \{\overline{A,E}; \overline{B,F}; \overline{C,D}\}$, where $\pi_1 \cdot \pi_2 = \pi(0)$. Consequently, M_8 can be decomposed into two parallel components, as shown by assignment α in Table 12-16. The corresponding logical equations for the state variables are

$$Y_1 = x_1'y_1 + x_1y_1' = f_1(x_1,y_1)$$
$$Y_2 = x_2 + x_1y_2' + x_1y_3 + x_1'y_2y_3' = f_2(x_1,x_2,y_2,y_3)$$
$$Y_3 = x_1'x_2'y_2y_3' + x_2y_2' + x_1x_2'y_2y_3 = f_3(x_1,x_2,y_2,y_3)$$

Table 12-15   Machine M_8

PS	NS x_1x_2				z
	00	01	11	10	
A	A	C	D	F	0
B	C	B	F	E	0
C	A	B	F	D	0
D	E	F	B	C	0
E	E	D	C	B	0
F	D	F	B	A	1

Table 12-16   Two possible assignments for machine M_8

$y_1y_2y_3$	$y_1y_2y_3$
$A \to 0\,0\,0$	$A \to 0\,0\,0$
$B \to 0\,1\,0$	$B \to 0\,1\,1$
$C \to 0\,1\,1$	$C \to 0\,1\,0$
$D \to 1\,1\,1$	$D \to 1\,1\,0$
$E \to 1\,0\,0$	$E \to 1\,0\,0$
$F \to 1\,1\,0$	$F \to 1\,1\,1$
Assignment α.	Assignment β.

The two-level realization of the above equations requires 30 diodes, and the functional dependencies are such that two of the next-state variables (Y_2 and Y_3) depend, each, on two of the present-state variables (y_2 and y_3).

Next we examine assignment β, which yields the following equations:

$$Y_1 = x_1'y_1 + x_1y_1' = f_1(x_1,y_1)$$

$$Y_2 = x_2 + x_1'y_3 + x_1y_3' = f_2(x_1,x_2,y_3)$$

$$Y_3 = x_2y_2 + x_1x_2'y_2' = f_3(x_1,x_2,y_2)$$

The two-level realization of these equations requires only 20 diodes. This reduction in the number of diodes has been accomplished by reducing the functional dependencies of the variables, since each next-state variable now depends on just a single present-state variable. Evidently, this type of reduced dependencies (which actually contains "cross dependencies") could not have been predicted from just the closed partitions. Consequently, a more general tool is needed.

Partition pairs

In order to determine the cause for the cross dependencies obtained by assignment β, we first observe that y_1 induces π_1, while y_2 and y_3 induce the partitions $\tau(y_2) = \{\overline{A,E}; \overline{B,C,D,F}\}$ and $\tau(y_3) = \{\overline{A,C,D,E}; \overline{B,F}\}$, respectively, where $\pi_1 \cdot \tau(y_2) \cdot \tau(y_3) = \pi(0)$. Except for π_1, neither of these partitions is closed, although the product $\tau(y_2) \cdot \tau(y_3) = \pi_2$ is closed. However, the knowledge of the block of $\tau(y_2)$ and the inputs is sufficient to determine uniquely the successor block which is contained in some block of $\tau(y_3)$; that is, the successors of the blocks of $\tau(y_2)$ are contained in the blocks of $\tau(y_3)$. Similarly, it is evident that the blocks of $\tau(y_2)$ are the successors of the blocks of $\tau(y_3)$.

Definition 12-5 A *partition pair* (τ,τ') on the states of a sequential machine M is an ordered pair of partitions such that, if S_i and S_j are in the same block of τ, then for every input I_k in I, I_kS_i and I_kS_j are in the same block of τ'.

Thus τ' consists of all the successor blocks implied by τ. If $\tau = \tau'$, then τ is closed, since it contains its own successor blocks. Hence the set of closed partitions may be viewed as a special case of the (more general) set of partition pairs.

Example The following are partition pairs on the states of M_8:

$$(\pi_1, \pi_1') = (\{\overline{A,B,C}; \overline{D,E,F}\}, \{\overline{A,B,C}; \overline{D,E,F}\})$$

$$(\tau_1, \tau_1')' = (\{\overline{A,C,D,E}; \overline{B,F}\}, \{\overline{A,E}; \overline{B,C,D,F}\})$$

$$(\tau_2, \tau_2') = (\{\overline{A,E}; \overline{B,C,D,F}\}, \{\overline{A,C,D,E}; \overline{B,F}\})$$

In assignment β of Table 12-16, y_1, y_2, and y_3 have been assigned to π_1', τ_1', and τ_2', respectively. Note that in this example (τ_1', τ_1) and (τ_2', τ_2) are also partition pairs. ∎

In general, since τ consists of the blocks we want to identify, while τ' contains the implied successor blocks, it is evident that any partition τ_p' such that $\tau_p' \geq \tau'$ will also contain the successor blocks of τ. Similarly, the implied successors of any partition τ_q such that $\tau_q \leq \tau$ are smaller than those of τ, and therefore will be contained within the blocks of τ'. Thus the pairs (τ_q, τ') and (τ, τ_p') are also partition pairs on the states of M.

Example $(\tau_3, \tau_3') = (\{\overline{A,D}; \overline{B}; \overline{C,E}; \overline{F}\}, \{\overline{A,E}; \overline{B,D}; \overline{C,F}\})$ is a partition pair on M_8. The following are also partition pairs on M_8:

$$(\{\overline{A,D}; \overline{B}; \overline{C}; \overline{E}; \overline{F}\}, \{\overline{A,E}; \overline{B,D}; \overline{C,F}\})$$

$$(\{\overline{A,D}; \overline{B}; \overline{C,E}; \overline{F}\}, \{\overline{A,E}; \overline{B,D,C,F}\}) \quad ∎$$

A partial ordering on partition pairs is defined in the following way. If (τ_1, τ_1') and (τ_2, τ_2') are partition pairs, then $(\tau_1, \tau_1') \geq (\tau_2, \tau_2')$ if and only if $\tau_1 \geq \tau_2$ and $\tau_1' \geq \tau_2'$. We shall now prove that if (τ_1, τ_1') and (τ_2, τ_2') are partition pairs on the states of a machine M, then $(\tau_1 \cdot \tau_2, \tau_1' \cdot \tau_2')$ and $(\tau_1 + \tau_2, \tau_1' + \tau_2')$ are also partition pairs on the states of M and define, respectively, the glb and the lub of the given partition pairs. The assertion that $(\tau_1 \cdot \tau_2, \tau_1' \cdot \tau_2')$ is the glb of (τ_1, τ_1') and (τ_2, τ_2') can be proved by observing that if S_i and S_j are contained in some block of $\tau_1 \cdot \tau_2$, then they are contained in the same block in τ_1 and in τ_2. Therefore, for every input I_k, the successors $I_k S_i$ and $I_k S_j$ are also contained in the same block of τ_1' and τ_2', and hence of $\tau_1' \cdot \tau_2'$. The assertion that $(\tau_1 + \tau_2, \tau_1' + \tau_2')$ is the lub of (τ_1, τ_1') and (τ_2, τ_2') can be proved in a similar manner. Consequently, the set of all partition pairs forms a lattice under the above partial ordering.

Definition 12-6 Let τ' be a partition on the set of states of M. Define a partition $M(\tau')$ so that $M(\tau') = \Sigma \tau_i$, where the sum is over all τ_i such that (τ_i, τ') is a partition pair. Similarly, define the partition $m(\tau) = \Pi \tau_i'$, where the product is over all τ_i' such that (τ, τ_i') is a partition pair. A partition pair (τ,τ') is said to be an *Mm pair* if and only if $\tau = M(\tau')$ and $\tau' = m(\tau)$.

Since the lub of two partition pairs is a partition pair, it follows that $(M(\tau'),\tau')$ is a partition pair, where $M(\tau')$ is the lub of all τ_i such that (τ_i,τ') is a partition pair. In fact, $M(\tau')$ *is the largest partition the successors of whose blocks are contained in the blocks of* τ'. Similarly, since the glb of two partition pairs is a partition pair, it follows that $(\tau,m(\tau))$ is a partition pair, where $m(\tau)$ is the glb of all τ_i' such that (τ,τ_i') is a partition pair. $m(\tau)$ *is thus the smallest partition containing all the successors of the blocks of* τ. Hence $m(\tau)$ describes the largest amount of information that can be obtained from τ regarding the next state of machine M.

It can be shown (see Prob. 12-15) that the M and m partitions possess the following properties. If τ is a partition on machine M, then

$$
\left\{
\begin{aligned}
m[M(\tau)] &\le \tau \\
M[m(\tau)] &\ge \tau \\
M\{m[M(\tau)]\} &= M(\tau) \\
m\{M[m(\tau)]\} &= m(\tau)
\end{aligned}
\right.
$$

Consequently, for every partition τ on the states of M, $\{M(\tau),m[M(\tau)]\}$ and $\{M[m(\tau)],m(\tau)\}$ are Mm pairs on the states of M.

If (λ,λ') is an Mm pair, then λ is the largest partition from which we can determine λ', and at the same time λ' is the smallest partition which contains the successor blocks implied by λ. Thus, by enlarging λ' or by refining λ, we can obtain other partition pairs. Consequently, corresponding to every partition pair (τ,τ') there exists an Mm pair (λ,λ') such that $\lambda \ge \tau$ and $\lambda' \le \tau'$. Clearly, the set of all Mm pairs (which is in general substantially smaller than the set of all partition pairs) characterizes completely the set of all partition pairs on the states of M, since any partition pair can be generated from the corresponding Mm pair, as shown above.

Information-flow inequalities

In this section we shall derive the main theorem relating the algebraic properties of partitions to the dependencies of the state variables and to the structure of sequential machines. We shall also show that the existence of assignments with reduced dependencies of the state variables can be predicted from the set of Mm pairs associated with the machine.

Theorem 12-3 *Let the variables* y_1, y_2, $\ldots$, y_k *be assigned to the states of machine* M, *and let* $\tau(y_i)$ *be the partition induced by variable* y_i, *where $1 \leq i \leq k$. If the next-state variable Y_i can be computed from the external inputs and a subset P_i of the variables, then*

$$\Pi\tau(y_j) \leq M[\tau(y_i)]$$

where the product is taken over all $\tau(y_j)$, such that y_j is contained in the subset P_i. And conversely, a sufficient condition for the existence of an assignment, in which a next-state variable Y_i depends only on the external inputs and the value of a corresponding subset P_i of the state variables, is the existence of a partition pair $(\tau, \tau(y_i))$ on M so that, for each τ_i,

$$\Pi\tau(y_j) \leq M[\tau(y_i)]$$

where the product is taken over all $\tau(y_j)$, such that y_j is in P_i.

Proof: The blocks of the partition $\Pi\tau(y_j)$ consist of all the states which have the same value for the variables contained in P_i. Recalling that Y_i depends only on the variable y_j if y_j is in P_i, then, for any two states S_p and S_q which are in the same block of $\Pi\tau(y_j)$, and for all inputs I_k in I, the successor states $I_k S_q$ and $I_k S_p$ are in the same block of $\tau(y_i)$. Consequently,

$$(\Pi\tau(y_j), \tau(y_i))$$

is a partition pair. But since $M[\tau(y_i)]$ is the largest partition such that $(M[\tau(y_i)], \tau(y_i))$ is a partition pair, then

$$M[\tau(y_i)] \geq \Pi\tau(y_j)$$

Hence, if the next-state variable Y_i can be computed from a subset of the state variables, then we must have at least as much information about the present state as is contained in $M[\tau(y_i)]$.

To prove the converse, note that $(M[\tau(y_i)], \tau(y_i))$ is a partition pair and since $\Pi\tau(y_j) \leq M[\tau(y_i)]$, then

$$(\Pi\tau(y_j), \tau(y_i))$$

is also a partition pair. The knowledge of the value of the variables y_j in P_i is sufficient to determine the present block of $\Pi\tau(y_j)$, and therefore (by the definition of partition pairs) it is also sufficient to determine the successor block in $\tau(y_i)$. This, in turn, determines the value of the next state of y_i, that is, Y_i. Thus the theorem is proved. ∎

Returning to machine M_8, we note that $\pi_1' \cdot \tau_1' \cdot \tau_2' = \pi(0)$ and that $\pi_1 = \pi_1', \tau_1' = \tau_2$ and $\tau_2' = \tau_1$. Therefore a three-variable assignment exists, so that Y_1 (which is assigned to π'_1) is self-dependent, while Y_2 and Y_3 (which are assigned to τ'_1 and τ'_2) can be computed from y_3 and y_2, respectively. The above arguments lead to assignment β of Table 12-16.

The partition inequality in Theorem 12-3 is often referred to as *information-flow inequality*. It defines the minimal amount of information which we must have in order to compute the value of y_i for the next state. In other words, since $M[\tau(y_i)]$ is the largest partition (least amount of information regarding the machine's state) from which we can determine the block of $\tau(y_i)$ containing the next state of the machine, then, in order to compute the value of y_i for the next state, we must have at least as much information about the present state as is contained in $M[\tau(y_i)]$. Thus, knowing the information-flow inequalities is sufficient to specify the dependencies of the state variables and to determine the direction of "information flow" in the machine.

Computing the Mm pairs

Having established (in Theorem 12-3) the role of Mm pairs in the determination of assignments with reduced dependencies, we proceed to develop a systematic procedure to generate these pairs. Let a and b be two arbitrary states of machine M, and let τ_{ab} be the partition that includes a block (ab) and leaves all other states in separate blocks. Then $m(\tau_{ab})$ is the smallest partition containing the blocks implied by the identification of (ab). Clearly, $(\tau_{ab}, m(\tau_{ab}))$ is a partition pair.

Any partition τ can be expressed as a sum $\tau = \Sigma \tau_{ab}$, where the sum is taken over all τ_{ab} such that $\tau_{ab} \leq \tau$. And since the sum of partition pairs is also a partition pair, then $(\Sigma \tau_{ab}, \Sigma m(\tau_{ab}))$ is a partition pair. Therefore, if τ is the M-partition, then $(\tau, \Sigma m(\tau_{ab}))$ is an Mm pair.

The preceding result provides us with the basic tool for the computation of the Mm pairs. First we find the set $\{m(\tau_{ab})\}$ for all distinct a and b. This process requires $n(n-1)/2$ computations. Next we find all the possible sums of these partitions. From the preceding results it is evident that this process generates all the m-partitions. The M-partition $\tau = M(\tau')$ corresponding to every m-partition τ' is given by $\tau = \Sigma \tau_{ab}$, where the sum is taken over all τ_{ab} such that $m(\tau_{ab}) \leq \tau'$. This procedure actually generates the sum of all τ_{ab} which satisfy the requirement that (τ_{ab}, τ') be a partition pair. As an example, we shall compute the Mm pairs for machine M_9, given in Table 12-17.

First we compute the $m(\tau_{ab})$'s, starting from $m(\tau_{AB})$ and continuing through all possible pairs up to $m(\tau_{DE})$. $m(\tau_{AB})$ is found by determining the successors implied by the identification of A and B. From the state table we conclude that the identification of (AB) implies the identifications of (CE), (AC), and (BD). The application of the transitive rule

Table 12-17   Machine M_9

PS	x_1x_2				z
	00	01	11	10	
A	C	A	D	B	0
B	E	C	B	D	0
C	C	D	C	E	0
D	E	A	D	B	0
E	E	D	C	E	1

yields

$$m(\tau_{AB}) = \overline{\{A,C,E; B,D\}} = \tau_1'$$

Hence, if the uncertainty regarding the present state of M, which is specified by τ_{AB}, is (AB), then the uncertainty regarding the next state of M is given by $m(\tau_{AB}) = \tau_1'$. In a similar way we find the following set of distinct $m(\tau_{ab})$'s for machine M_9.

$$m(\tau_{AC}) = m(\tau_{DE}) = \overline{\{A,C,D; B,E\}} = \tau_2'$$

$$m(\tau_{AD}) = m(\tau_{CE}) = \overline{\{A; B; C,E; D\}} = \tau_3'$$

$$m(\tau_{AE}) = m(\tau_{CD}) = \pi(I)$$

$$m(\tau_{BC}) = m(\tau_{BE}) = \overline{\{A; B,C,D,E\}} = \tau_4'$$

$$m(\tau_{BD}) = \overline{\{A,C; B,D; E\}} = \tau_5'$$

The next step in the computation of the m-partitions is to form all possible sums of the $m(\tau_{ab})$'s. This is accomplished by performing all pairwise sums, then pairwise sums of the new partitions generated, and so on. In the above example no new nontrivial m-partitions are generated in this step.

Using the above set of m-partitions, we compute next the corresponding set of M-partitions. Recalling that $M(\tau_i') = \Sigma\tau_{ab}$, where the sum is taken over all τ_{ab} such that $m(\tau_{ab}) \leq \tau_i'$, we obtain

$$M(\tau_1') = \tau_{AB} + \tau_{AD} + \tau_{CE} + \tau_{BD} = \overline{\{A,B,D; C,E\}} = \tau_1$$

$$M(\tau_2') = \tau_{AC} + \tau_{DE} = \overline{\{A,C; B; D,E\}} = \tau_2$$

$$M(\tau_3') = \tau_{AD} + \tau_{CE} = \overline{\{A,D; B; C,E\}} = \tau_3$$

$$M(\tau_4') = \tau_{BC} + \tau_{BE} + \tau_{AD} + \tau_{CE} = \overline{\{A,D; B,C,E\}} = \tau_4$$

$$M(\tau_5') = \tau_{BD} = \overline{\{A; B,D; C; E\}} = \tau_5$$

Thus machine M_9 possesses a set of seven Mm pairs, of which two pairs are trivial, namely,

$$(\pi(I), \pi(I))$$

$$(\tau_1, \tau_1') = (\{\overline{A,B,D}; \overline{C,E}\}, \{\overline{A,C,E}; \overline{B,D}\})$$

$$(\tau_2, \tau_2') = (\{\overline{A,C}; \overline{B}; \overline{D,E}\}, \{\overline{A,C,D}; \overline{B,E}\})$$

$$(\tau_3, \tau_3') = (\{\overline{A,D}; \overline{B}; \overline{C,E}\}, \{\overline{A}; \overline{B}; \overline{C,E}; \overline{D}\})$$

$$(\tau_4, \tau_4') = (\{\overline{A,D}; \overline{B,C,E}\}, \{\overline{A}; \overline{B,C,D,E}\})$$

$$(\tau_5, \tau_5') = (\{\overline{A}; \overline{B,D}; \overline{C}; \overline{E}\}, \{\overline{A,C}; \overline{B,D}; \overline{E}\})$$

$$(\pi(0), \pi(0))$$

The Mm-lattice can now be drawn in a straightforward manner.

The above Mm pairs characterize the machine and contain all the information regarding its structure. In addition to numerous partition pairs that can be generated from these Mm pairs, two closed partitions, π_1 and π_2, exist, where

$$\pi_1 = \{\overline{A,D}; \overline{B}; \overline{C,E}\}$$

$$\pi_2 = \{\overline{A}; \overline{B}; \overline{C,E}; \overline{D}\}$$

The closed partitions are generated by enlarging the m-partition and refining the M-partition of the Mm pair (τ_3, τ_3').

State assignments based on partition pairs

We shall now apply the principles developed in this section, and our knowledge about the information flow in machine M_9, to obtain an assignment in which the dependencies of the variables will be reduced. For the example at hand, our aim is to obtain a three-variable assignment. Consequently, we are seeking three partitions, $\lambda_1, \lambda_2, \lambda_3$, of two blocks each, such that

$$\lambda_1 \cdot \lambda_2 \cdot \lambda_3 = \pi(0)$$

For each λ_i we shall determine the corresponding $\dot{M}(\lambda_i)$ and thus obtain three partition pairs, $(M(\lambda_1), \lambda_1)$, $(M(\lambda_2), \lambda_2)$, $(M(\lambda_3), \lambda_3)$, from which the structure of the machine can be determined.

To each partition λ_i we assign one state variable, y_i (in general, $[\log_2 \#(\lambda_i)]$ state variables). $M(\lambda_i)$ is then the partition containing the smallest amount of information from which we can compute the value of y_i assigned to the block of λ_i which contains the next state of the machine. From Theorem 12-3 it is evident that a reduction in the dependency of the variable assigned to a partition λ_i is achieved if $M(\lambda_i)$ is greater than or equal to the product of a small subset of the partitions $\lambda_1, \lambda_2, \lambda_3$. The variables assigned to the partitions in the subset provide y_i with at least that information specified by $M(\lambda_i)$.

In order to select the partitions $\lambda_1, \lambda_2, \lambda_3$, we look for two-block partitions in the set of m-partitions τ_i''s. In particular, if a variable y_i assigned to λ_i is to depend on just one other variable assigned to the blocks of λ_j, then $\lambda_j \leq M(\lambda_i)$ and $M(\lambda_i)$ can have at most two blocks. Thus, as our initial selection, let $\lambda_1 = \tau_1'$. Since $M(\tau_1')$ consists of two blocks, we may select it as the second partition, i.e., $\lambda_2 = M(\tau_1')$. Hence variable Y_1, which is defined by λ_1, will depend only on the information provided by y_2, which is defined by λ_2. As λ_1 and λ_2 have already been selected, the selection of λ_3 is simple, since it must make the product $\lambda_1 \cdot \lambda_2 \cdot \lambda_3 = \pi(0)$. We thus choose $\lambda_3 = \tau_2'$. The partitions $\lambda_1, \lambda_2, \lambda_3$ and their corresponding $M(\lambda_1), M(\lambda_2), M(\lambda_3)$ are given as follows:

$$(M(\lambda_1),\lambda_1) = (\{\overline{A,B,D}; \overline{C,E}\}, \{\overline{A,C,E}; \overline{B,D}\})$$

$$(M(\lambda_2),\lambda_2) = (\{\overline{A,D}; \overline{B}; \overline{C,E}\}, \{\overline{A,B,D}; \overline{C,E}\})$$

$$(M(\lambda_3),\lambda_3) = (\{\overline{A,C}; \overline{B}; \overline{D,E}\}, \{\overline{A,C,D}; \overline{B,E}\})$$

Note that λ_2 is not an m-partition, but since $\lambda_2 > \tau_3'$, then $M(\lambda_2) \geq M(\tau_3')$.

From the way we selected the above partition pairs, it is evident that Y_1 depends only on y_2, since λ_2 provides all the information which Y_1 requires as specified by $M(\lambda_1)$. In order to determine the dependencies of Y_2 and Y_3, we check to see if there exists a partition $\lambda_i \leq M(\lambda_2)$ or $\lambda_j \leq M(\lambda_3)$. Since there are no such partitions, the next step is to check if we can form a product of two partitions such that $\lambda_i \cdot \lambda_j \leq M(\lambda_2)$ or $\lambda_p \cdot \lambda_q \leq M(\lambda_3)$. Indeed, this can be accomplished, since

$$\lambda_2 \cdot \lambda_3 < M(\lambda_2)$$
$$\lambda_1 \cdot \lambda_3 < M(\lambda_3)$$

Consequently, Y_2 depends on the information supplied by y_2 and y_3, while Y_3 receives its inputs from y_1 and y_3. The functional dependencies of the next-state variable are summarized as follows:

$$Y_1 = f_1(x_1, x_2, y_2)$$
$$Y_2 = f_2(x_1, x_2, y_2, y_3)$$
$$Y_3 = f_3(x_1, x_2, y_1, y_3)$$

The schematic diagram of the circuit structure is shown in Fig. 12-13.

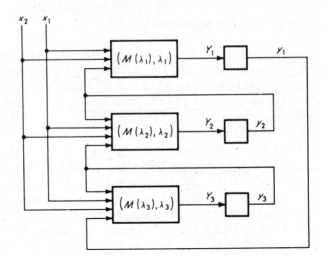

Fig. 12-13 Schematic diagram of the structure of machine M_9 when realized using λ_1, λ_2, and λ_3.

12-8 DECOMPOSITION

In the preceding sections we have studied the relation between the state-assignment problem and the structure of sequential machines and have determined necessary and sufficient conditions for a machine to be decomposable. Our objective in this section is to further investigate the properties of decomposable machines and of various component machines.

Serial decomposition

We shall first determine the conditions for a machine M to be decomposable into a serial (cascade) chain of components $\mathfrak{M}_1$, $\mathfrak{M}_2$, . . . , $\mathfrak{M}_m$ in which the outputs of any component may be used as inputs to other components. If an output of machine $\mathfrak{M}_i$ is an input of machine $\mathfrak{M}_j$, then $\mathfrak{M}_i$ is said to be a *predecessor* of $\mathfrak{M}_j$, and $\mathfrak{M}_j$ is said to be a *successor* of $\mathfrak{M}_i$. We shall assume that the component machines *operate concurrently;* that is, the next state of each component depends on its present state, on the present external inputs, and on the present state of its predecessors. We shall further assume that the component machines form a *loop-free interconnection;* i.e., if $\mathfrak{M}_i$ or any of its successors or successors of successors, etc., is a predecessor of $\mathfrak{M}_j$, then $\mathfrak{M}_j$ must not be a predecessor of $\mathfrak{M}_i$. A schematic diagram of such a serial decomposition is shown in Fig. 12-14a.

Theorem 12-4 *Let M be realizable as a serial loop-free connection of m components $\mathfrak{M}_1$, $\mathfrak{M}_2$, . . . , $\mathfrak{M}_m$; then there exists a set of m closed*

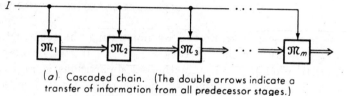

(a). Cascaded chain. (The double arrows indicate a
transfer of information from all predecessor stages.)

(b) Block diagram of the cascaded chain.

Fig. 12-14 Serial decomposition of a machine.

partitions $\{\pi_1, \pi_2, \ldots, \pi_m\}$ *such that* $\pi_1 \geq \pi_2 \geq \cdots \geq \pi_m$ *and*
$\pi_m = \pi(0)$. *Conversely, such a set of closed partitions is a sufficient
condition for the existence of a serial decomposition in which* $\mathfrak{M}_i$ *is a
predecessor of* $\mathfrak{M}_j$ *if and only if* $\pi_i \geq \pi_j$.

Proof: Suppose that machine M has been realized as a serial
connection of m components, as shown in Fig. 12-14a. For the
purpose of analysis, we may divide these components into two
groups, as shown in Fig. 12-14b. The first group, denoted M_a,
consists of k components, and the second group, denoted M_b, consists of $m - k$ components. If we let k equal 1, then by Theorem
12-1 there exists a closed partition π_1 on the states of M. Similarly,
if we group machines $(\mathfrak{M}_1, \mathfrak{M}_2)$ and $(\mathfrak{M}_3, \mathfrak{M}_4, \ldots, \mathfrak{M}_m)$, we obtain
another serial decomposition, of the type shown in Fig. 12-14b, to
which there corresponds another closed partition, π_2, on the states
of machine M.

To determine the relation between π_1 and π_2, note that, since
$\mathfrak{M}_1$ distinguishes the blocks of π_1, each block of π_1 in fact corresponds
to a state of $\mathfrak{M}_1$. Similarly, each block of π_2 corresponds to a state
of the composite machine $(\mathfrak{M}_1, \mathfrak{M}_2)$. But since $(\mathfrak{M}_1, \mathfrak{M}_2)$ can be
decomposed into $\mathfrak{M}_1$ in series with $\mathfrak{M}_2$, it follows that each state of
$\mathfrak{M}_1$ represents one or more states of the composite machine $(\mathfrak{M}_1, \mathfrak{M}_2)$.
Consequently, each block of π_1 contains one or more blocks of π_2,
i.e., $\pi_1 \geq \pi_2$. There exist m possible ways (one of which is
trivial) of grouping the component machines $(\mathfrak{M}_1, \ldots, \mathfrak{M}_k)$ and
$(\mathfrak{M}_{k+1}, \ldots, \mathfrak{M}_m)$. Hence there exist m closed partitions, $\pi_1 \geq
\pi_2 \geq \cdots \geq \pi_m$. Note that the equal sign in the above relation
can be omitted, since it corresponds to a degenerate case. In fact,
if $\pi_{k-1} = \pi_k$, then the component $\mathfrak{M}_k$ is redundant and may be
deleted.

421

The converse can be proved by illustrating the construction of the decomposed machine. Let $\pi_1 > \pi_2 > \cdots > \pi_m$ be a set of closed partitions on M. Select another set of partitions, $\tau_1, \tau_2, \ldots,$ τ_{m-1}, such that, for each value of i in the range $1 \leq i \leq m - 1$,

$$\pi_i \cdot \tau_i = \pi_{i+1}$$

and

$$\pi_1 \cdot \tau_1 \cdot \tau_2 \cdot \ldots \cdot \tau_{m-1} = \pi(0)$$

$\mathfrak{M}_1$ contains $[\log_2 \#(\pi_1)]$ state variables which are assigned to distinguish the blocks of π_1. Thus $\mathfrak{M}_1$ is independent of the remaining components. The second component, $\mathfrak{M}_2$, consists of the $[\log_2 \#(\tau_1)]$ variables assigned to the blocks of τ_1. Since τ_1 is not necessarily closed, $\mathfrak{M}_2$ depends on $\mathfrak{M}_1$. But since $\pi_1 \cdot \tau_1 = \pi_2$, $\mathfrak{M}_2$ is independent of the remaining components $\mathfrak{M}_3, \ldots, \mathfrak{M}_m$. In a similar manner the decomposed machine is constructed so that each component $\mathfrak{M}_k$ is independent of $\mathfrak{M}_{k+1}, \ldots, \mathfrak{M}_m$ and is a function of $\mathfrak{M}_1, \ldots, \mathfrak{M}_k$. ∎

Theorem 12-4 establishes the concept of *information flow* in a sequential machine which is realized as a serial connection of smaller components. In fact, we proved that, in the cascaded chain, information flows from component $\mathfrak{M}_i$ to component $\mathfrak{M}_j$ if and only if $\pi_i \geq \pi_j$.

Example   Consider machine M_{10} given in Table 12-18. It has three closed partitions (including the zero partition) and an output-con-

Table 12-18   Machine M_{10}

PS	NS		z
	$x = 0$	$x = 1$	
A	G	D	1
B	H	C	0
C	F	G	1
D	E	G	0
E	C	B	1
F	C	A	0
G	A	E	1
H	B	F	0

$$\pi_0 = \pi(0)$$
$$\pi_a = \{\overline{A,B,G,H}; \overline{C,D,E,F}\}$$
$$\pi_b = \{\overline{A,B}; \overline{C,D}; \overline{E,F}; \overline{G,H}\}$$
$$\lambda_o = \{\overline{A,C,E,G}; \overline{B,D,F,H}\}$$

sistent partition λ_o. Since $\pi_a > \pi_b > \pi_0$, machine M_{10} is decomposable into three components connected in series, so that each component is a two-state machine.

Machine $\mathfrak{M}_a$, which is derived from π_a, consists of $\#(\pi_a) = 2$ states, and therefore can be realized by a single state variable, y_a. The second component, $\mathfrak{M}_b$, is derived from a partition τ_1, such that $\pi_a \cdot \tau_1 = \pi_b$. One possible partition, τ_1, is

$$\tau_1 = \{\overline{A,B,C,D}; \overline{E,F,G,H}\}$$

Since $\#(\tau_1) = 2$, machine $\mathfrak{M}_b$ will consist of a single variable, y_b. The variables y_a and y_b are actually assigned to the blocks of the closed partition π_b, and therefore are independent of the remaining variable, which is assigned to the blocks of some partition τ_2, where $\tau_2 \cdot \pi_b = \pi(0)$. There are several partitions satisfying the last requirement. It is desirable, however, to select (whenever possible) a partition yielding simpler output circuits, i.e., $\tau_2 \leq \lambda_o$. A selection satisfying this condition is

$$\tau_2 = \lambda_o = \{\overline{A,C,E,G}; \overline{B,D,F,H}\}$$

An assignment based on the above partitions will yield the following functional relationships:

$$Y_a = f_a(x, y_a)$$
$$Y_b = f_b(x, y_a, y_b)$$
$$Y_c = f_c(x, y_a, y_b, y_c)$$
$$z = f_0(y_c)$$

The schematic diagram of this realization and the π-lattice of M_{10} are shown in Fig. 12-15. ∎

Machine M_{10} has thus been decomposed into three components connected in series. It is often necessary to determine the state table of each of these components, a task which is accomplished as follows. The state diagram of $\mathfrak{M}_a$ is obtained by constructing the implication graph of π_a. It consists of two vertices, P and Q, corresponding, respectively, to the blocks $(ABGH)$ and $(CDEF)$. The state table of $\mathfrak{M}_a$ which is identical with the implication table derived from π_a, is given in Table 12-19a. The output of $\mathfrak{M}_a$ is associated with its state and is identical with the value of y_a.

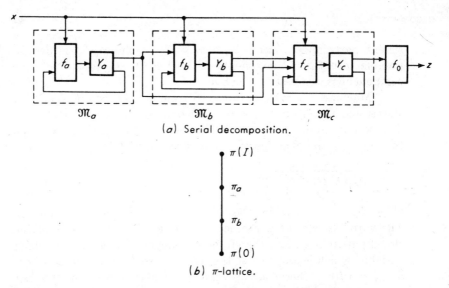

(a) Serial decomposition.

(b) π-lattice.

Fig. 12-15 Schematic diagram and π-lattice of machine M_{10}.

The inputs to $\mathfrak{M}_b$ are x and y_a, and its state-dependent output is y_b. It contains two states, α and β, corresponding, respectively, to the blocks $(ABCD)$ and $(EFGH)$ of τ_1. The state table of $\mathfrak{M}_b$ is shown in Table 12-19b. An input 00 to $\mathfrak{M}_b$ means that $\mathfrak{M}_a$ is in state P, i.e., $y_a = 0$, and the external input is $x = 0$. When $\mathfrak{M}_a$ is in state P and $\mathfrak{M}_b$ is in state α, then M_{10} is in either state A or B. From these states $\mathfrak{M}_b$ goes to state β, which corresponds to G and H. When $\mathfrak{M}_a$ is in state P and $\mathfrak{M}_b$ is in state β and an input $x = 0$ is applied, $\mathfrak{M}_b$ is to go to state α, which corresponds to states A and B in M_{10}. In a similar way the entire table is completed. The composite states of $\mathfrak{M}_a$ and $\mathfrak{M}_b$ correspond to the blocks of π_b. Since $\pi_a = \{P; Q\}$ and $\tau_1 = \{\alpha; \beta\}$, then

$$\pi_b = \pi_a \cdot \tau_1 = \{P\alpha; P\beta; Q\alpha; Q\beta\} = \{\overline{A,B}; \overline{G,H}; \overline{C,D}; \overline{E,F}\}$$

Finally, we note that $\mathfrak{M}_b$ can be reduced to a two-input machine, since the next-state entries in three columns of $\mathfrak{M}_b$ are identical. If we define i_1 and i_2 as

$$i_1 = x' + y_a$$
$$i_2 = xy_a'$$

we obtain the reduced form of $\mathfrak{M}_b$, as shown in Table 12-19c.

Machine $\mathfrak{M}_c$ consists of two states, γ and δ, corresponding to the blocks of $\tau_2 = \{\overline{A,C,E,G}; \overline{B,D,F,H}\} = \{\gamma; \delta\}$. It receives three inputs, x, y_a, and y_b, and produces one output, z. An input 000 to $\mathfrak{M}_c$ means that $\mathfrak{M}_a$ and $\mathfrak{M}_b$ are in states P and α, respectively, and $x = 0$. This in turn implies that M_{10} is in either state A or B, depending on whether $\mathfrak{M}_c$ is in state γ or δ, respectively. The 0-successors of A and B are G and H, which correspond to $P\beta\gamma$ and $P\beta\delta$, respectively. Therefore the entries in column 000 of $\mathfrak{M}_c$ are γ and δ. In a similar way the state table of $\mathfrak{M}_c$ is derived from Table 12-18 and the set of partitions π_a, τ_1, and τ_2. By making the appropriate input assignment the state table of machine $\mathfrak{M}_c$ may be reduced to the form shown in Table 12-19e.

Table 12-19 State tables of the component machines realizing M_{10}

PS	x		y_a
	0	1	
P	P	Q	0
Q	Q	P	1

(a) Machine $\mathfrak{M}_a$.

PS	$y_a x$				y_b
	00	01	10	11	
α	β	α	β	β	0
β	β	α	β	α	1

(b) Machine $\mathfrak{M}_b$.

PS	i_1	i_2	y_b
α	β	α	0
β	α	β	1

(c) Machine $\mathfrak{M}_b$—reduced form.

PS	$y_a y_b x$								z
	000	001	010	011	100	101	110	111	
γ	γ	δ	γ	γ	δ	γ	γ	δ	1
δ	δ	γ	δ	δ	γ	γ	γ	γ	0

(d) Machine $\mathfrak{M}_c$.

PS	I_1	I_2	I_3	z
γ	γ	δ	γ	1
δ	δ	γ	γ	0

(e) Machine $\mathfrak{M}_c$—reduced form.

Parallel decompositions

We have already shown that a necessary and sufficient condition for a sequential machine M to be decomposable into two independent components operating in parallel is the existence of two closed partitions (or covers), π_1 and π_2, such that $\pi_1 \cdot \pi_2 = \pi(0)$. This result can be easily generalized to a decomposition into m parallel components, which can be accomplished if and only if there exists a set of m closed partitions (or covers) on M, such that $\pi_1 \cdot \pi_2 \cdot \ldots \cdot \pi_m = \pi(0)$.

Machine M_{11} given in Table 12-20 has the π-lattice of Fig. 12-16a and the following nontrivial closed partitions:

$$\pi_a = \{\overline{A,B}; \overline{C,D}; \overline{E,G}; \overline{F,H}\}$$
$$\pi_b = \{\overline{A,H}; \overline{B,F}; \overline{C,G}; \overline{D,E}\}$$
$$\pi_c = \{\overline{A,B,F,H}; \overline{C,D,E,G}\}$$

Since $\pi_a \cdot \pi_b = \pi(0)$, a parallel decomposition of M_{11} is possible. However, since $[\log_2 \#(\pi_a)] + [\log_2 \#(\pi_b)] = 4$, such a decomposition requires four state variables. The state tables of the component machines M_a and M_b, which correspond, respectively, to π_a and π_b, are given in Table 12-21. The schematic diagram of the realization is shown in Fig. 12-16b.

Since the above realization requires four state variables, we next seek another decomposition which will require only three variables. Actually, our aim is to determine whether machines M_a and M_b can each be serially decomposed, in such a manner that both will have identical independent components. If such a component can be found, it may be

Table 12-20   Machine M_{11}

PS	NS		z
	$x = 0$	$x = 1$	
A	D	G.	0
B	C	E	0
C	H	F	0
D	F	F	0
E	B	B	0
F	G	D	0
G	A	B	0
H	E	C	1

Table 12-21   Parallel decomposition of machine M_{11}

PS	NS		z_1
	$x = 0$	$x = 1$	
$A,B \to a$	b	c	0
$C,D \to b$	d	d	0
$E,G \to c$	a	a	0
$F,H \to d$	c	b	1

PS	NS		z_2
	$x = 0$	$x = 1$	
$A,H \to \alpha$	δ	γ	1
$B,F \to \beta$	γ	δ	0
$C,G \to \gamma$	α	β	0
$D,E \to \delta$	β	β	0

(a) Machine M_a.   (b) Machine M_b.

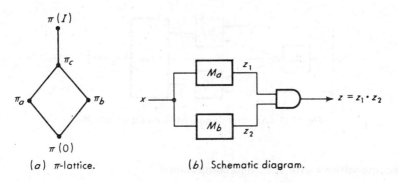

(a) π-lattice.　　　　　(b) Schematic diagram.

Fig. 12-16 Parallel decomposition of machine M_{11}.

"factored out" to serve as a common predecessor for both M_a and M_b. A necessary condition for the existence of such a common component is that both M_a and M_b can be serially decomposed; that is, both M_a and M_b have nontrivial closed partitions on their respective states. Clearly, the largest component machine that can be factored out is given by the smallest closed partition which is greater than π_a and π_b, i.e., the least upper bound $\pi_a + \pi_b$. For machine M_{11},

$$\pi_c = \pi_a + \pi_b = \{\overline{A,B,F,H}; \overline{C,D,E,G}\}$$

Since the least upper bound π_c is nontrivial, a two-state component can be factored out, and a decomposition of the form shown in Fig. 12-17 is possible for machine M_{11}. The common factor M_c in series with M_d realizes machine M_a, while M_c in series with M_e realizes machine M_b. The factor M_c, as well as the components M_d and M_e, are given in Table 12-22.

Table 12-22 The component machines corresponding to Fig. 12-17

PS	x 0	1	y_c
$A,B,F,H \rightarrow P$	Q	Q	0
$C,D,E,G \rightarrow Q$	P	P	1

(a) Machine M_c.

PS	$y_c x$ 00	01	10	11	z_d
$A,B,C,D \rightarrow r$	r	s	s	s	0
$E,F,G,H \rightarrow s$	s	r	r	r	1

(b) Machine M_d.

PS	$y_c x$ 00	01	10	11	z_e
$A,C,G,H \rightarrow u$	v	u	u	v	1
$B,D,E,F \rightarrow v$	u	v	v	v	0

(c) Machine M_e.

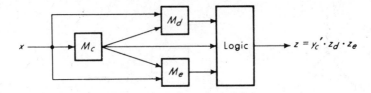

Fig. 12-17 Another decomposition of machine M_{11}.

Decompositions with specified components

So far we have studied several machine structures and determined the conditions for a machine to be decomposable into these structures. Our present objective is to determine if a machine can be decomposed in such a manner that one (or more) of its components is specified. One possible approach to the solution of this problem is to check all closed partitions and covers and determine if any of them yields the desired specified component. This approach, however, is long and impractical, and a new technique to handle this type of decompositions will be developed.

As an example, consider machines M_{12} and $\mathfrak{M}$, given in Tables 12-23 and 12-24, respectively. Our objective is to determine if machine M_{12} can be serially decomposed, so that $\mathfrak{M}$ is the predecessor component. In order to determine if such a decomposition is possible, it is necessary to establish what information regarding the states of M_{12} is contained in $\mathfrak{M}$. This can be accomplished by constructing a composite machine which contains both M_{12} and $\mathfrak{M}$ and is defined as follows.

<table>
<tr><td colspan="5" align="center">Table 12-23 Machine M_{12}</td></tr>
<tr><td rowspan="2">PS</td><td colspan="2">NS</td><td colspan="2">z</td></tr>
<tr><td>I_1</td><td>I_2</td><td>I_1</td><td>I_2</td></tr>
<tr><td>A</td><td>C</td><td>D</td><td>0</td><td>0</td></tr>
<tr><td>B</td><td>D</td><td>E</td><td>0</td><td>1</td></tr>
<tr><td>C</td><td>A</td><td>C</td><td>0</td><td>0</td></tr>
<tr><td>D</td><td>B</td><td>D</td><td>0</td><td>0</td></tr>
<tr><td>E</td><td>F</td><td>E</td><td>1</td><td>1</td></tr>
<tr><td>F</td><td>C</td><td>D</td><td>1</td><td>1</td></tr>
</table>

<table>
<tr><td colspan="3" align="center">Table 12-24 Machine $\mathfrak{M}$</td></tr>
<tr><td rowspan="2">PS</td><td colspan="2">NS</td></tr>
<tr><td>I_1</td><td>I_2</td></tr>
<tr><td>P</td><td>S</td><td>Q</td></tr>
<tr><td>Q</td><td>R</td><td>Q</td></tr>
<tr><td>R</td><td>S</td><td>Q</td></tr>
<tr><td>S</td><td>P</td><td>S</td></tr>
</table>

Let the *general composite machine*, corresponding to two machines, M_1 and M_2, having sets of states R and S, respectively, be that machine which contains the set of states $R \times S$. We shall use R_iS_j to denote the state of the general composite machine which corresponds to R_i in M_1 and (simultaneously) S_j in M_2. For two machines, M_1 and M_2, having simultaneous initial states, R_1 and S_1, the *composite machine* is the one which has an initial state R_1S_1 and consists of all subsequent states implied in chain fashion by R_1S_1 and its successors.

The composite machine corresponding to machines M_{12} and $\mathfrak{M}$ and to initial states A and P, respectively, is given in Table 12-25. Starting with AP, the application of input I_1 takes M_{12} to state C, and $\mathfrak{M}$ to state S. Therefore the I_1-successor of AP is CS. In a similar way we conclude that the I_2-successor of AP is DQ, and so on. Next we determine the successors of states CS and DQ, and this process continues until no new states are generated.

Table 12-25 Composite machine
for machines M_{12} and $\mathfrak{M}$ and
initial states A and P

PS	NS	
	I_1	I_2
AP	CS	DQ
CS	AP	CS
DQ	BR	DQ
BR	DS	EQ
DS	BP	DS
EQ	FR	EQ
BP	DS	EQ
FR	CS	DQ

In general, if M_1 has n_1 states and M_2 has n_2 states, the general composite machine has $n_1 \cdot n_2$ states. The composite machine may have as many as $n_1 \cdot n_2$ states, or as few as the smaller of n_1 or n_2 states. The I_k-successor of state R_iS_j of the composite machine is determined from the I_k-successors of R_i and S_j in their respective machines; that is, if I_kR_i is R_p and I_kS_j is S_q, then the I_k-successor of R_iS_j is R_pS_q.

For machine M_{12} to be serially decomposable so that $\mathfrak{M}$ is the predecessor component, it is necessary that M_{12} should have a closed cover whose corresponding implication graph is *equivalent* to the state diagram of $\mathfrak{M}$; that is, both graphs must be isomorphic, and the labels of arcs connecting corresponding vertices must be identical. This closed cover can be determined from the composite machine of Table 12-25 in a straightforward manner.

From the names of the states in the present-state column of the composite machine, it can be concluded that, when machine $\mathfrak{M}$ is in state P, the composite machine can be in either state AP or BP, and M_{12} can only be in A or B. Similarly, when $\mathfrak{M}$ is in state S, M_{12} can only be in state C or D, and so on. We can thus form a cover φ on the states of M_{12}, so that two states (say R_i and R_j) are in the same block of φ if and only if they are associated with the same state of $\mathfrak{M}$ (say S_k); that is, the composite machine of M_{12} and $\mathfrak{M}$ contains the states R_iS_k and R_jS_k. Thus, for machine M_{12}, we have

$$\varphi = \{\overline{A,B}; \overline{D,E}; \overline{B,F}; \overline{C,D}\}$$

The blocks (A,B) and (D,E) of φ correspond, respectively, to states P and Q in $\mathfrak{M}$, while (B,F) and (C,D) correspond to states R and S, respectively. Consequently, knowing the state of $\mathfrak{M}$ is always sufficient to determine the state of M_{12} to within at most two states.

In order to complete the synthesis, it is necessary to specify the successor component. A simple way to accomplish it is to first split states B and D of machine M_{12} so that $\pi = \{\overline{A,B'}; \overline{D',E}; \overline{B'',F}; \overline{C,D''}\}$ will be a closed partition on the states of the augmented machine. The predecessor component of the augmented machine is isomorphic to $\mathfrak{M}$, while the successor component, which consists of two states, distinguishes the blocks of a partition τ, such that

$$\tau \cdot \{\overline{A,B'}; \overline{D',E}; \overline{B'',F}; \overline{C,D''}\} = \pi(0)$$

A possible partition τ is

$$\tau = \{\overline{A,D',D'',F}; \overline{B',B'',E,C}\}$$

The state tables of the augmented machine and the successor component are obtained in the usual manner, as illustrated in the previous sections.

★12-9 SYNTHESIS OF MULTIPLE MACHINES

We shall now generalize the decomposition problem so that it includes simultaneous decomposition of two or more machines. More precisely, given two reduced machines, M_1 and M_2, having the same input alphabet I, and which are initially in states R_1 and S_1, respectively, we wish to find three machines, M_C, M_{1S}, and M_{2S}, where M_C is a common predecessor component whose output feeds into the successors M_{1S} and M_{2S} in such a way that M_C and M_{1S} form a serial decomposition of M_1, while M_C and M_{2S} form a serial decomposition of M_2. Figure 12-18 shows the desired structure, in which Z^1 and Z^2 are the outputs of M_{1S} and M_{2S}, respectively. When a maximum common predecessor component exists, the total state variables required for the realization is minimum, while the total output logic circuitry is not more complex than if the two machines were realized separately.

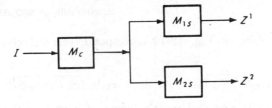

Fig. 12-18 Two machines having a common predecessor component, M_C.

The common predecessor machine

As an example, consider the two reduced Moore-type machines given in Table 12-26. The implication graphs of machines M_1 and M_2, for initial identifications of (R_1R_3) and (S_1S_3), respectively, are shown in Fig. 12-19. These closed graphs are equivalent, since they are isomorphic and the labels of arcs which connect corresponding vertices are identical. We have already established that the closed implication graph of a sequential machine M is actually equivalent to the state diagram of the predecessor component in a serial decomposition of M. Consequently, each of the graphs of Fig. 12-19 can serve as a state diagram of the predecessor component in the serial decomposition of the respective machine. And since the two graphs are equivalent, they correspond to two equivalent machines. Clearly, since the two predecessor components are equivalent, one of them may be removed, and the other one retained as the common predecessor component.

Table 12-26 Two machines to be decomposed simultaneously

R	NS		Z^1
	I_1	I_2	
R_1	R_1	R_2	$Z_1{}^1$
R_2	R_2	R_3	$Z_2{}^1$
R_3	R_3	R_4	$Z_3{}^1$
R_4	R_4	R_1	$Z_4{}^1$

(a) Machine M_1.

S	NS		Z^2
	I_1	I_2	
S_1	S_3	S_2	$Z_1{}^2$
S_2	S_4	S_3	$Z_2{}^2$
S_3	S_1	S_4	$Z_3{}^2$
S_4	S_2	S_1	$Z_4{}^2$

(b) Machine M_2.

(a) Machine M_1.

(b) Machine M_2.

Fig. 12-19 Implication graphs.

The graphs of Fig. 12-19 correspond, respectively, to the closed partitions

$$\pi_1 = \{\overline{R_1,R_3}; \overline{R_2,R_4}\} \qquad \text{and} \qquad \pi_2 = \{\overline{S_1,S_3}; \overline{S_2,S_4}\}$$

If we denote the first and second blocks of each partition by P and Q, respectively, we obtain the implication table of Table 12-27. This is the state table of the common predecessor component M_C. The successor components M_{1S} and M_{2S} can be obtained by using the methods developed in the foregoing section.

Table 12-27   Machine M_C

PS	NS	
	I_1	I_2
P	P	Q
Q	Q	P

From the preceding example it is evident that *a collection of two (or more) machines contains a common predecessor component M_C if and only if they possess equivalent implication graphs; the vertices and arcs of this common graph are in one-to-one correspondence with the states and state transitions, respectively, of M_C.* The procedure for finding the equivalent graphs is not, however, entirely systematic, since it depends on the selection of the initial state identifications. This limitation can be overcome by using the composite machine, as is shown subsequently.

The composite machine corresponding to M_1 and M_2 and to initial states R_1 and S_1 is given in Table 12-28. It consists of eight states.

Table 12-28   Composite machine for M_1 and M_2 and initial states R_1 and S_1

PS	NS		Z^1Z^2
	I_1	I_2	
R_1S_1	R_1S_3	R_2S_2	$Z_1{}^1Z_1{}^2$
R_1S_3	R_1S_1	R_2S_4	$Z_1{}^1Z_3{}^2$
R_2S_2	R_2S_4	R_3S_3	$Z_2{}^1Z_2{}^2$
R_2S_4	R_2S_2	R_3S_1	$Z_2{}^1Z_4{}^2$
R_3S_3	R_3S_1	R_4S_4	$Z_3{}^1Z_3{}^2$
R_3S_1	R_3S_3	R_4S_2	$Z_3{}^1Z_1{}^2$
R_4S_4	R_4S_2	R_1S_1	$Z_4{}^1Z_4{}^2$
R_4S_2	R_4S_4	R_1S_3	$Z_4{}^1Z_2{}^2$

While the composite machine includes all states of M_1 and M_2, it does not include all combinations of these states; e.g., R_1S_2 is not encountered when any of the eight states of the composite machine is selected as the initial state. Furthermore, if M_1 is initially in state R_1, then M_2 can be started only in either S_1 or S_3, since the only combinations of states included in the composite machine are R_1S_1 and R_1S_3. Thus the choice of an initial state in effect locks the two machines together, in the operational sense.'

Using the above procedure, we have transformed the two-machine problem into the well-known single-machine decomposition problem. The methods developed in the preceding sections are now applicable to the composite machine which contains the two machines M_1 and M_2.

Decomposing the composite machine

Let us now define two partitions, π_R and π_S, on the states of the composite machine so that two states are placed in the same block of π_R if and only if their names start with the same state R_i in M_1; two states are placed in the same block of π_S if and only if their names end with the same state S_j in M_2. Such partitions are often referred to as *state-consistent* partitions and are derived directly from the composite machine.

Example   The state-consistent partitions for the composite machine of Table 12-28 are

$$\pi_R = \{\overline{R_1S_1,R_1S_3};\ \overline{R_2S_2,R_2S_4};\ \overline{R_3S_3,R_3S_1};\ \overline{R_4S_4,R_4S_2}\}$$
$$\pi_S = \{\overline{R_1S_1,R_3S_1};\ \overline{R_2S_2,R_4S_2};\ \overline{R_1S_3,R_3S_3};\ \overline{R_2S_4,R_4S_4}\} \quad \blacksquare$$

Block (R_1S_1,R_1S_3) of π_R corresponds to state R_1 in M_1; block (R_1S_1,R_3S_1) of π_S corresponds to state S_1 in M_2; and so on. From the way the state-consistent partitions π_R and π_S are constructed, it is evident that they correspond to the zero partitions on the set of states of machines M_1 and M_2, respectively. Consequently, the implication graphs corresponding to π_R and π_S are equivalent to the state graphs of M_1 and M_2, respectively, and therefore these partitions are closed with respect to the states of the composite machine.

From the composite machine of Table 12-28 it is apparent that the required outputs Z^1 and Z^2 can be generated by a machine having three state variables and the appropriate output logic, rather than by two separate machines having a total of four state variables. This result is illustrated in Fig. 12-20a. We observe also that $\pi_R \cdot \pi_S = \pi(0)$, which, since both partitions are closed, is the condition for a parallel decomposition of the composite machine. In this case, of course, the result is simply

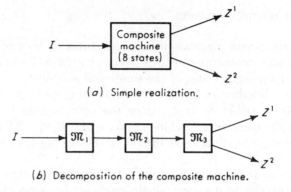

(*a*) Simple realization.

(*b*) Decomposition of the composite machine.

Fig. 12-20 Two possible realizations of the composite machine.

the original two machines M_1 and M_2, realized separately and having four state variables.

The composite machine is next examined for other possible decompositions, following the previously developed techniques. For example, the partitions

$$\pi_1 = \{\overline{R_1S_1,R_2S_2,R_3S_3,R_4S_4}; \ \overline{R_1S_3,R_2S_4,R_3S_1,R_4S_2}\}$$

and

$$\pi_2 = \{\overline{R_1S_1,R_3S_3}; \ \overline{R_2S_2,R_4S_4}; \ \overline{R_1S_3,R_3S_1}; \ \overline{R_2S_4,R_4S_2}\}$$

are easily shown to be closed, and since $\pi_1 > \pi_2$, a cascade realization of the type shown in Fig. 12-20*b* results, where each component, $\mathfrak{M}_1$, $\mathfrak{M}_2$, and $\mathfrak{M}_3$, is a two-state machine.

At this point we turn our attention to the question of determining if a common predecessor component exists for M_1 and M_2, and if several such components exist, how to find the largest one. From the results of the preceding section and from the properties of the composite machine and the state-consistent partitions π_R and π_S, it is evident that a common component exists if and only if we can find a closed partition π_C such that $\pi_C > \pi_R$ and $\pi_C > \pi_S$. Clearly, the smallest partition which satisfies these inequalities, and thus yields the largest common component M_C, is

$$\pi_C = \pi_R + \pi_S$$

For our example we obtain

$$\pi_C = \pi_R + \pi_S = \{\overline{R_1S_1,R_1S_3,R_3S_1,R_3S_3}; \ \overline{R_2S_2,R_2S_4,R_4S_2,R_4S_4}\}$$

Thus a common predecessor component consisting of one state variable exists. The resulting decomposition is shown in Fig. 12-18. It is easy to verify that this machine is identical with the one obtained using the implication graphs (Table 12-27). The successor machines M_{1S} and M_{2S}

(each consisting of one state variable) are determined by partitions τ_{1S} and τ_{2S}, respectively, such that

$$\pi_C \cdot \tau_{1S} = \pi_R \qquad \text{and} \qquad \pi_C \cdot \tau_{2S} = \pi_S$$

Possible partitions are

$$\tau_{1S} = \{\overline{R_1S_1, R_1S_3, R_2S_2, R_2S_4}; \ \overline{R_3S_1, R_3S_3, R_4S_2, R_4S_4}\}$$
$$\tau_{2S} = \{\overline{R_1S_1, R_3S_1, R_2S_2, R_4S_2}; \ \overline{R_1S_3, R_3S_3, R_2S_4, R_4S_4}\}$$

Clearly, Z^1 and Z^2 are each dependent upon only two state variables, and the entire machine requires a total of three state variables.

The lattice of all closed partitions on the set of states of the composite machine is shown in Fig. 12-21. However, it is interesting to point out that our two-machine cascade decomposition was obtained without searching for closed partitions; π_R and π_S were obtained directly by inspection of the composite machine, while π_C followed from the addition of the two partitions π_R and π_S. Thus the process involves a minimum of computation or manipulation.

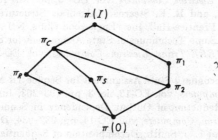

Fig. 12-21 π-lattice for the composite machine.

NOTES AND REFERENCES

The structure theory and the study of machine decomposition were originated by Hartmanis [5] in 1960, and further developed in a series of papers by Hartmanis and Stearns [6, 14], Karp [8], Yoeli [15, 16], and Kohavi [9, 10]. The concept of closed covers and the procedure of augmenting a machine by state splitting were introduced by Kohavi [9], and further developed to cover multiple machines in Kohavi and Smith [11, 13]. Other contributions to the general machine-structure theory include Krohn and Rhodes [12], Zeiger [17], and Gill [4]. A comprehensive treatment of structure and decomposition theory can be found in the book by Hartmanis and Stearns [7].

The state-assignment problem has been treated from different points of views by many authors. Of particular interest are the papers by Armstrong [1, 2] and Dolotta and McCluskey [3].

1. Armstrong, D. B.: A Programmed Algorithm for Assigning Internal Codes to Sequential Machines, *IRE Trans. Electron. Computers*, vol. EC-11, no. 4, pp. 466–472, August, 1962.
2. Armstrong, D. B.: On the Efficient Assignment of Internal Codes to Sequential Machines, *IRE Trans. Electron. Computers*, vol. EC-11, no. 5, pp. 611–622, October, 1962.
3. Dolotta, T. A., and E. J. McCluskey, Jr.: The Coding of Internal States of Sequential Circuits, *IEEE Trans. Electron. Computers*, vol. EC-13, no. 5, pp. 549–562, October, 1964.
4. Gill, A.: Cascaded Finite-state Machines, *IRE Trans. Electron. Computers*, vol. EC-10, no. 3, pp. 366–370, September, 1961.
5. Hartmanis, J.: Symbolic Analysis of a Decomposition of Information Processing Machines, *Information and Control*, vol. 3, no. 2, pp. 154–178, June, 1960.
6. Hartmanis, J.: On the State Assignment Problem for Sequential Machines I, *IRE Trans. Electron. Computers*, vol. EC-10, pp. 157–165, June, 1961.
7. Hartmanis, J., and R. E. Stearns: "Algebraic Structure Theory of Sequential Machines," Prentice-Hall, Inc., Englewood Cliffs, N.J., 1966.
8. Karp, R. M.: Some Techniques of State Assignment for Synchronous Sequential Machines, *IEEE Trans. Electron. Computers*, vol. EC-13, no. 5, pp. 507–518, October, 1964.
9. Kohavi, Z.: Secondary State Assignment for Sequential Machines, *IEEE Trans. Electron. Computers*, vol. EC-13, no. 3, pp. 193–203, June, 1964.
10. Kohavi, Z.: Reduction of Output Dependency in Sequential Machines, *IEEE Trans. Electron. Computers*, vol. EC-14, pp. 932–934, December, 1965.
11. Kohavi, Z., and E. J. Smith: Decomposition of Sequential Machines, *Proc. Sixth Ann. Symp. Switching Theory and Logical Design*, Ann Arbor, Mich., October, 1965.
12. Krohn, K. B., and J. L. Rhodes: Algebraic Theory of Machines, Proceedings Symposium on Mathematical Theory of Automata, Polytechnic Press, Brooklyn, N.Y., 1962.
13. Smith, E. J., and Z. Kohavi: Synthesis of Multiple Sequential Machines, *Proc. Seventh Ann. Symp. Switching and Automata Theory*, Berkeley, Calif., October, 1966.
14. Stearns, R. E., and J. Hartmanis: On the State Assignment Problem for Sequential Machines II, *IRE Trans. Electron. Computers*, vol. EC-10, no. 4, pp. 593–603, December, 1961.
15. Yoeli, M.: The Cascade Decomposition of Sequential Machines, *IRE Trans. Electron. Computers*, vol. EC-10, pp. 587–592, April, 1961.
16. Yoeli, M.: Cascade-Parallel Decompositions of Sequential Machines, *IEEE Trans. Electron. Computers*, vol. EC-12, no. 3, pp. 322–324, June, 1963.
17. Zeiger, H. P.: Loop-free Synthesis of Finite-state Machines, M.I.T. Ph.D. thesis, Dept. of Electrical Engineering, Cambridge, Mass., September, 1964.

PROBLEMS

12-1. Show that every n-state machine has N distinct state assignments, where

$$N = \frac{(2^k - 1)!}{(2^k - n)!k!} \qquad k = [\log_2 n]$$

Note that two assignments are said to be *distinct* if one cannot be obtained from the other by permuting or complementing the variables or by relabeling them.

Hint: Recall the fact that k binary variables can be permuted in $k!$ ways, and there are 2^k ways of complementing them.

12-2. (a) Given the machine shown in Table P12-2 and the two assignments α and β, derive in each case the logical equations for the state variables and the output function and compare the results.

(b) Express explicitly in each case the dependency of the output and the state variables.

Table P12-2

PS	NS $x=0$	$x=1$	z $x=0$	$x=1$
A	D	C	0	0
B	F	C	0	1
C	E	B	0	0
D	B	E	1	0
E	A	D	1	1
F	C	D	1	0

$y_1 y_2 y_3$	$y_1 y_2 y_3$
$A \to 0\,0\,0$	$A \to 1\,1\,0$
$B \to 0\,0\,1$	$B \to 1\,0\,1$
$C \to 0\,1\,0$	$C \to 1\,0\,0$
$D \to 0\,1\,1$	$D \to 0\,0\,0$
$E \to 1\,0\,0$	$E \to 0\,0\,1$
$F \to 1\,0\,1$	$F \to 0\,1\,0$
Assignment α.	Assignment β.

12-3. A six-state machine is said to have the five closed partitions shown below and *no* other closed partitions. Is this possible?

$$\pi_1 = \{\overline{A,C}; \overline{B}; \overline{D}; \overline{E,F}\} \qquad \pi_4 = \pi(0)$$
$$\pi_2 = \{\overline{A,D}; \overline{B,C}; \overline{E}; \overline{F}\} \qquad \pi_5 = \pi(I)$$
$$\pi_3 = \{\overline{A,B}; \overline{C,D}; \overline{E,F}\}$$

12-4. The machine shown in Table P12-4 has the following closed partitions:

$$\pi_1 = \{\overline{A,C,E}; \overline{B,D,F}\} \qquad \pi_2 = \{\overline{A,F}; \overline{B,E}; \overline{C,D}\}$$

(a) Find a state assignment which reduces the interdependencies of the state variables.

(b) Derive the logical equations and show the circuit diagram when unit delays are used as memory elements.

Table P12-4

PS	NS		z
	x = 0	x = 1	
A	D	C	1
B	A	D	0
C	B	E	0
D	E	B	0
E	F	C	0
F	C	D	0

12-5. (a) Show that every closed partition is the sum of some *basic* partitions. (Recall that a *basic* partition $\pi_{S_iS_j}$ is the smallest closed partition containing S_iS_j in one block.)

(b) Use the result of (a) to show that the procedure outlined in Sec. 12-3 for the construction of the π-lattice indeed gives all the closed partitions.

12-6. Let λ_o and λ_o' be two output-consistent partitions on the set of states of a machine M. Prove that $\lambda_o + \lambda_o'$ and $\lambda_o \cdot \lambda_o'$ are also output-consistent partitions.

12-7. (a) Let π be a closed partition on the set of states of a machine M. Prove that if π is also an output-consistent partition, i.e., $\pi \leq \lambda_o$, then M can be reduced to an equivalent machine which has only $\#(\pi)$ states. Conversely, if there are no closed partitions on M which are also output-consistent, then M is in reduced form.

(b) Demonstrate the above reduction procedure by first finding a closed partition which is also output-consistent for the machine shown in Table P12-7 and *then* reducing it.

Table P12-7

PS	NS		z
	x = 0·	x = 1	
A	E	C	0
B	B	A	1
C	B	D	0
D	E	C	1
E	E	F	1
F	B	C	0

12-8. The incompletely specified machine in Table P12-8 has a nontrivial closed partition which is also input-consistent. Does it have an autonomous clock? If yes, show its state diagram; if no, explain why.

Table P12-8

PS	NS		
	I_1	I_2	I_3
A	—	A	—
B	C	—	D
C	A	B	A
D	B	A	B

12-9. In each of the following sets of partitions, π_1 and π_2 designate closed partitions, while λ_o and λ_i designate output-consistent and input-consistent partitions, respectively.

(a) Construct for each case the corresponding π-lattice by obtaining all the necessary sums and products.

(b) Show schematic diagrams demonstrating in each case the possible machine decompositions that yield minimal interdependencies of the state variables, as well as the outputs.

(i) $\pi_1 = \{\overline{A,B,E,F}; \overline{C,D,G,H}\}$ $\lambda_o = \{\overline{A,B,G,H}; \overline{C,D,E,F}\}$
    $\pi_2 = \{\overline{A,F,C,H}; \overline{B,D,E,G}\}$ $\lambda_i = \{\overline{A,C}; \overline{B,D}; \overline{E,G}; \overline{F,H}\}$

(ii) $\pi_1 = \{\overline{A,B}; \overline{C,D}; \overline{E,F}; \overline{G,H}\}$ $\lambda_o = \lambda_i$
    $\pi_2 = \{\overline{A,E}; \overline{B,F}; \overline{C,G}; \overline{D,H}\}$ $\lambda_i = \{\overline{A,B,C,D}; \overline{E,F,G,H}\}$

(iii) $\pi_1 = \{\overline{A,C,E,G}; \overline{B,D,F,H}\}$ $\lambda_o = \{\overline{A,C}; \overline{B,D}; \overline{E,G}; \overline{F,H}\}$
    $\pi_2 = \{\overline{A,G}; \overline{B,F}; \overline{C,E}; \overline{D,H}\}$ $\lambda_i = 1$

12-10. (a) For the machine shown in Table P12-10, find the π-lattice and determine the input-consistent and output-consistent partitions.

(b) Show two assignments which result in autonomous clocks of different frequencies. In each case determine the period of the clock and

Table P12-10

PS	NS		z	
	$x=0$	$x=1$	$x=0$	$x=1$
A	D	C	0	0
B	C	D	0	1
C	E	F	0	0
D	F	F	0	1
E	G	H	0	0
F	H	G	0	1
G	B	A	0	0
H	A	B	0	1

draw a schematic diagram indicating the interdependencies within the decomposed machine.

12-11. (a) For the machine shown in Table P12-11 find λ_i and λ_o and construct the π-lattice.

    (b) Choose as a basis for your state assignment three partitions, τ_1, τ_2, and τ_3 (which may or may not be closed), such that the following functional dependencies will result:

$$Y_1 = f_1(y_1)$$
$$Y_2 = f_2(x, y_2, y_3)$$
$$Y_3 = f_3(x, y_2, y_3)$$
$$z = f_0(y_1, y_2)$$

Specify the desired relationship between the chosen τ's and λ_o and λ_i, and show a schematic diagram of the resulting structure.

    (c) Based on the chosen τ's, make a state assignment and derive the corresponding logical equations.

Table P12-11

PS	NS $x = 0$	$x = 1$	z
A	F	D	0
B	D	E	0
C	E	F	0
D	A	B	0
E	B	C	0
F	C	A	1

12-12. (a) Find a state assignment for the machine shown in Table P12-12 so that it will have the structure shown in Fig. P12-12.

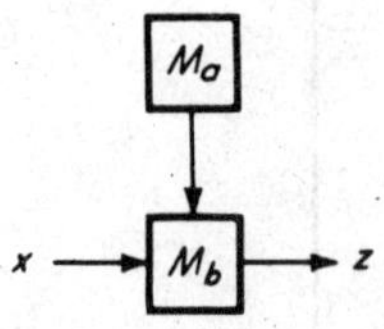

Table P12-12

PS	NS $x = 0$	$x = 1$	z $x = 0$	$x = 1$
A	D	B	0	0
B	A	C	1	0
C	B	E	1	0
D	F	A	0	1
E	F	C	0	0
F	E	D	0	1

Fig. P12-12

(b) Determine the logical equations for the output function and the state variables.

(c) Show the state diagram of the input-independent component.

12-13. (a) Find the π-lattice of machine M shown in Table P12-13, and specify all the possible ways of decomposing the machine.

(b) Identify states (A,B) and construct the implication graph. Augment the machine accordingly.

(c) Describe all the possible ways of decomposing the augmented machine M'. Specify in each case the dependencies of the state variables.

Table P12-13

PS	NS	
	$x = 0$	$x = 1$
A	B	C
B	C	D
C	D	C
D	E	B
E	D	A

12-14. The machine shown in Table P12-14 has the closed partition $\pi = \{\overline{A,C,D,F}; \overline{B,E,G}\}$.

(a) Can you find another closed partition so that a parallel decomposition is possible, without increasing the number of state variables?

(b) Construct an implication graph, starting with vertex (A,B), and show that there exists a machine M' equivalent to M which can be decomposed into the form shown in Fig. P12-14.

(c) Show the state tables of the component machines.

(d) Select an assignment that will lead to the structure of Fig. P12-14. Derive the corresponding logical equations.

Table P12-14

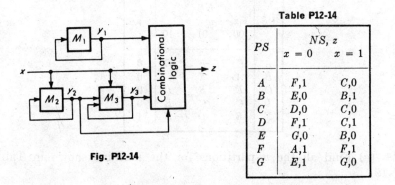

Fig. P12-14

PS	NS, z	
	$x = 0$	$x = 1$
A	F,1	C,0
B	E,0	B,1
C	D,0	C,0
D	F,1	C,1
E	G,0	B,0
F	A,1	F,1
G	E,1	G,0

12-15. (a) Prove that if τ is a partition on $\mathfrak{M}$, then

$$M\{m[M(\tau)]\} = M(\tau) \qquad \text{and} \qquad m\{M[m(\tau)]\} = m(\tau)$$

(b) Use the above to show that, for all τ of $\mathfrak{M}$,

$$\{M(\tau),m[M(\tau)]\} \qquad \text{and} \qquad \{M[m(\tau)],m(\tau)\}$$

are Mm pairs.

12-16. This problem is concerned with establishing a number of algebraic properties of Mm pairs and demonstrating that the set of all Mm pairs on a machine forms a lattice under the ordering defined in the text.

(a) Show that if $\lambda = M(\lambda')$ and $\tau = M(\tau')$, then $\lambda \cdot \tau = M(\lambda' \cdot \tau')$.

(b) Show that if $\lambda' = m(\lambda)$ and $\tau' = m(\tau)$, then $\lambda' + \tau' = m(\lambda + \tau)$.

(c) Prove that if (λ,λ') and (τ,τ') are Mm pairs, then their glb and lub are given by

$$\text{glb}\{(\lambda,\lambda'),(\tau,\tau')\} = [\lambda \cdot \tau, m(\lambda \cdot \tau)]$$

and

$$\text{lub}\{(\lambda,\lambda'),(\tau,\tau')\} = [M(\lambda' + \tau'),\lambda' + \tau']$$

12-17. Find the set of all Mm pairs for machine M_8 (Table 12-15) and draw its Mm-lattice.

12-18. (a) Determine the set of all Mm pairs for the machine shown in Table P12-18 and draw the corresponding Mm-lattice.

(b) Show a state assignment which results in the following functional dependencies:

$$Y_1 = f_1(x_1,x_2,y_1)$$
$$Y_2 = f_2(x_1,x_2,y_2,y_3)$$
$$Y_3 = f_3(x_1,x_2,y_1,y_2,y_3)$$

Table P12-18

PS	x_1x_2 00	NS 01	10	z
A	C	B	D	0
B	A	E	C	0
C	E	B	D	0
D	C	C	E	0
E	E	D	B	1

12-19. (a) Find all the m-partitions for the machine shown in Table P12-19.

(b) Select a number of m-partitions and find their corresponding M-partitions, so that they yield an assignment in which every variable depends on just one variable and the external input.

(c) Draw a schematic diagram of the resulting machine structure.

Table P12-19

PS	NS x_1x_2				z
	00	01	11	10	
A	A	A	D	A	1
B	C	C	D	A	0
C	D	A	A	A	0
D	B	A	D	B	0
E	E	C	A	B	0

12-20. Construct an arbitrary machine with five or six states and three or four inputs so that there exists at least one assignment which causes each state variable to be dependent only on the other variables and independent of itself, that is, Y_1 is independent of y_1, etc.

12-21. The machine shown in Table P12-21 can be serially decomposed into three components, without any increase in the number of state variables.

(a) Determine the period of the maximal autonomous clock.

(b) Select a set of partitions which induces an assignment such that the above serial decomposition is accomplished and the output logic is minimized.

(c) Show the state table of each component.

Table P12-21

PS	NS		z	
	$x = 0$	$x = 1$	$x = 0$	$x = 1$
A	D	C	0	0
B	C	D	0	1
C	E	F	0	0
D	F	F	0	1
E	G	H	0	0
F	H	G	0	1
G	B	A	0	0
H	A	B	0	1

12-22. The machine shown in Table P12-22 has the following partitions:

$$\pi_1 = \{\overline{A,B,C}; \overline{D,E,F}\} \qquad \lambda_o = \{\overline{A,D,E}; \overline{B,C,F}\}$$

$$\pi_2 = \{\overline{A,F}; \overline{B,E}; \overline{C,D}\} \qquad \lambda_i = \{\overline{A,C}; \overline{B}; \overline{D,F}; \overline{E}\}$$

(a) Draw a schematic diagram of the machine's structure induced by these partitions.

(b) Show complete state tables of the component machines.

Table P12-22

PS	NS		z	
	$x = 0$	$x = 1$	$x = 0$	$x = 1$
A	E	E	0	0
B	D	F	0	1
C	F	D	0	1
D	A	C	0	0
E	C	A	0	0
F	B	B	0	1

12-23. The machine of Table P12-23 is to be realized in the form shown in Fig. P12-23, where each of the blocks designated D represents a pure delay without internal feedback. Find a state table for the successor machine M_s, so that the number of state variables and the functional complexity of the output are minimized.

Table P12-23

PS	NS		z	
	$x = 0$	$x = 1$	$x = 0$	$x = 1$
A	E	A	0	0
B	D	B	0	1
C	D	B	0	0
D	F	C	1	1
E	E	C	1	0
F	F	B	1	1

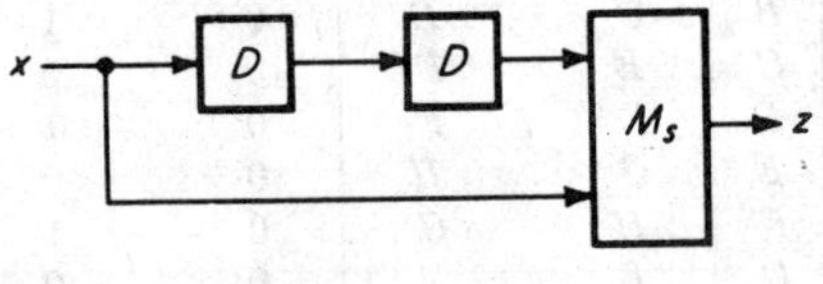

Fig. P12-23

12-24. Prove that if machines M_1 and M_2 are reduced, then, for specified initial states, the composite machine is also reduced.

12-25. Machine M_1 shown in Table P12-25 is to be realized in cascade form, with machine M_2 as the predecessor component. The starting states are A and P.

(a) Show the state table of an appropriate successor component.

(b) Choose a state assignment for M_1 which preserves the above structure and at the same time minimizes the complexity of the output function.

(c) Derive the logical equations for the state variables and the output function.

Table P12-25

PS	NS		z	
	$x = 0$	$x = 1$	$x = 0$	$x = 1$
A	B	E	0	1
B	D	C	1	1
C.	G	C	0	0
D	E	F	0	0
E	B	A	0	1
F	C	D	1	1
G	F	E	0	0

M_1

PS	NS	
	$x = 0$	$x = 1$
P	R	Q
Q	R	P
R	S	Q
S	Q	S

M_2

12-26. Machine M of Table P12-26 is to be realized in the form of Fig. P12-26. The state transitions of component M_a are specified as shown. The starting state of M is A, and that of M_a is G. Find the state table of M_b and specify the combinational logic which generates z.

Table P12-26

PS	NS, z	
	$x = 0$	$x = 1$
A	B,0	C,0
B	C,0	D,1
C	D,1	E,1
D	E,0	F,1
E	F,1	A,0
F	A,1	B,1

M

PS	NS	
	$x = 0$	$x = 1$
G	H	G
H	G	H

M_a

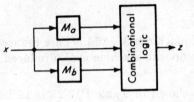

Fig. P12-26

12-27. Machines M_1 and M_2 of Table P12-27 can be jointly realized in the form shown in Fig. P12-27, with only three state variables.

(a) Construct the composite machine of M_1 and M_2 when the initial states are P and A for M_1 and M_2, respectively.

(b) Show the state tables for Mc and M_{2s}. Use state names $S_1, S_2, \ldots$ and $R_1, R_2, \ldots$, etc.

(c) Show the logical equations for the outputs.

Table P12-27

PS	NS $x = 0$	$x = 1$	Z^1
P	Q	R	0
Q	P	Q	0
R	Q	P	1

M_1

PS	NS $x = 0$	$x = 1$	Z^2
A	B	D	0
B	E	C	0
C	A	B	0
D	B	A	1
E	C	E	1

M_2

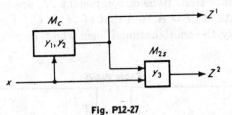

Fig. P12-27

12-28. Consider machines M_1 and M_2 shown in Table P12-28. Their starting states are R_1 and S_1, respectively.

(a) Find the π-lattice for each machine and determine whether or not a common predecessor machine exists.

(b) Show that if state S_2 is split into S_2' and S_2'', a common predecessor can be found.

(c) Realize the two machines in the form shown in Fig. 12-18. Show the state tables of the predecessor and the successor machines.

Table P12-28

PS	NS x = 0	x = 1	Z^1 x = 0	x = 1
R_1	R_2	R_4	1	0
R_2	R_1	R_3	0	1
R_3	R_1	R_4	0	1
R_4	R_2	R_3	1	0

M_1

PS	NS x = 0	x = 1	Z^2 x = 0	x = 1
S_1	S_1	S_3	0	0
S_2	S_1	S_2	0	1
S_3	S_2	S_3	1	1

M_2

12-29. A disjoint realization of M_1 and M_2, shown in Table P12-29, requires six state variables. Find another realization for these machines which requires just four state variables and has the form shown in Fig. P12-29. Assume that states S_1 and Q_1 are the initial states. Show the state table of each component and indicate the functional dependencies of the outputs.

Hint: You may find it necessary to split some states.

Table P12-29

PS	NS x = 0	x = 1	Z^1
S_1	S_6	S_3	0
S_2	S_5	S_2	0
S_3	S_4	S_3	0
S_4	S_6	S_2	0
S_5	S_7	S_2	0
S_6	S_1	S_6	0
S_7	S_5	S_7	1

M_1

PS	NS x = 0	x = 1	Z^2
Q_1	Q_3	Q_4	0
Q_2	Q_4	Q_5	0
Q_3	Q_1	Q_3	0
Q_4	Q_2	Q_4	0
Q_5	Q_6	Q_5	0
Q_6	Q_3	Q_4	1

M_2

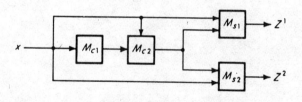

Fig. P12-29

12-30. Repeat Prob. 12-29 for machine M_1 as shown in Table P12-30 and machine M_2 as shown in Table P12-29.

Hint: It is quite straightforward to find a common factor machine which has two states. However, if you construct the composite machine for M_1 and M_2 and draw its implication graphs for initial identifications (S_1Q_1, S_2Q_1) and (S_1Q_1, S_1Q_2), you can show that a common factor machine which has four states can be found, while each of the successors has only two states.

Table P12-30

PS	NS $x = 0$	$x = 1$	Z^1
S_1	S_5	S_4	1
S_2	S_5	S_3	0
S_3	S_1	S_3	0
S_4	S_2	S_4	0
S_5	S_2	S_5	1

13
State-Identification and Fault-Detection Experiments

In this chapter we shall be concerned with experimental analysis of the behavior of finite-state machines. A machine is assumed to be reduced, strongly connected, and completely specified, and is available to the experimenter as a "black box," which means that he has access to its input and output terminals, but cannot inspect the internal devices and their interconnections. The experiments thus consist of a set of input sequences and their corresponding output sequences.

The state-identification experiments are designed to identify the unknown initial state of the machine and, whenever such an identification is unnecessary or impossible, to identify the final state of the machine. These experiments are known as the distinguishing and homing experiments, respectively. The machine-identification experiments are concerned with the problem of determining whether or not a given n-state machine is distinguishable from all other n-state machines. This problem is shown to be, under certain conditions, equivalent to the problem of determining whether or not a given machine is operating correctly.

13-1 EXPERIMENTS

The application of an input sequence to the input terminals of a machine is referred to as an *experiment* on the machine. An experiment designed to take the machine through all its transitions, in such a way that a definite conclusion can be reached as to whether or not the machine is operating correctly, is said to be a *fault-detection experiment* (or a *checking experiment*). At the beginning of an experiment the machine is said to be in an *initial* (or *starting*) *state*, and at the end of an experiment the machine is said to be in a *final state*. It is customary to distinguish between two types of experiments:

1. *Simple experiments*, which are performed on a single copy of the machine.
2. *Multiple experiments*, which are performed on two or more identical copies of the machine.

In practice, most machines are available in just a single copy, and therefore simple experiments are preferable to multiple ones.

According to performance, experiments are classified as:

1. *Adaptive experiments*, in which the input at any instant of time depends on the previous outputs.
2. *Preset experiments*, in which the entire input sequence is predetermined independently of the outcome of the experiment.

A measure of the efficiency and cost of an experiment is its *length*, which is the total number of input symbols applied to the machine during the execution of the experiment.

In Chap. 10 we studied the properties of experiments used to distinguish between two nonequivalent states, S_i and S_j. We showed that if S_i and S_j are distinguishable, then they are distinguishable by an experiment of length $n - 1$. We now consider the more general problems, that of identifying the initial or final state of a given machine, and that of distinguishing a given n-state machine from all other n-state machines which have the same input and output alphabets.

Introductory example

Consider machine M_1 (Table 13-1), which may initially be in any one of the states A, B, C, or D. The responses of M_1 to input sequences 01 and 111 are listed in Table 13-2. Knowing the output sequence that M_1 produces in response to the input sequence 01 is always sufficient to determine uniquely M_1's *final* state, since each of the output sequences that might result from the application of 01 is associated with just one final state. For example, the output sequence 00 indicates that the final state is B, while the output sequences 11 or 01 indicate that the final state is D or A, respectively. On the other hand, the knowledge of the response of M_1 to the input sequence 01 is not sufficient to determine M_1's *initial* state, since the production of output sequence 00 could mean that the initial state was A or that it was B. In fact, if M_1 was initially in either state A or B, it is impossible to determine the initial state by an experiment which starts with a 0, since the 0-successors of both A and B are C, and the output produced in both cases is 0. No sequence following the initial 0 input will yield any new information regarding the initial state.

Table 13-1   Machine M_1

PS	NS,z	
	$x = 0$	$x = 1$
A	$C,0$	$D,1$
B	$C,0$	$A,1$
C	$A,1$	$B,0$
D	$B,0$	$C,1$

Using the same line of argument, it is evident that the output sequence that M_1 produces in response to the input sequence 111 is always sufficient to determine uniquely M_1's final state, as well as its initial state. As shown in Table 13-2, each of the output sequences that might result from the application of 111 to M_1 is associated with just one initial state and one final state.

Before presenting the techniques to be used in the design of experiments, we shall introduce some of the terminology and define the successor tree, which will prove to be an effective tool in the design of minimal experiments.

Table 13-2   Responses of M_1 to input sequences 01 and 111

Initial state	Response to 01	Final state	Initial state	Response to 111	Final state
A	00	B	A	110	B
B	00	B	B	111	C
C	11	D	C	011	D
D	01	A	D	101	A
	(a)			*(b)*	

Uncertainties

Suppose that a machine M, which is given to the experimenter, can initially be in any one of its n states. In such a case we say that the initial uncertainty regarding the state of the machine is given by $(S_1 S_2 \cdots S_n)$. Thus the *initial uncertainty* is the minimal subset of S (including S itself) which is known to contain the initial state. For example, if machine M_1 can initially be in any one of its four states, then the initial uncertainty is $(ABCD)$.

Our aim is to perform experiments that reduce the initial uncertainty and whenever possible reveal the initial or final state. For example, suppose we apply an input 1 to machine M_1 and in response it produces an output 0. We may conclude that M_1 has initially been in state C, since only from that state is a response of 0 to a 1 input possible. The final state in this case is B. However, suppose the response of M_1 to an input 1 is 1; then all we can say regarding the final state of the machine is that it may be any of the states D, A, or C, depending on whether the initial state was A, B, or D, respectively. The set of states (ACD) thus represents the uncertainty regarding the final state of M_1 after the application of a 1 input. In general, the *uncertainty* regarding the state of M after the application of X is a specific subset of the X-successors of the states contained in the initial uncertainty. The elements of the uncertainty are not necessarily distinct.

Let U_0 be the initial uncertainty, and let the input I_i result in an uncertainty U_i; then U_i is said to be the I_i-*successor* of U_0. Suppose, for example, that the initial uncertainty regarding the state of M_1 is (ACD). If an input 1 is now applied to M_1, the successor uncertainty will be (B) or (CD), depending on whether the output is 0 or 1, respectively. We thus say that uncertainties $(B)(CD)$ are the 1-successors of (ACD). Subsequently, we shall refer to a collection of uncertainties as an *uncertainty vector*. The individual uncertainties contained in the vector are called the *components* of the vector. An uncertainty vector whose components contain a single state each is said to be a *trivial uncertainty vector*. An uncertainty vector whose components contain either single states or identical repeated states is said to be a *homogeneous uncertainty vector*. Thus, for example, the vectors $(AA)(B)(C)$ and $(A)(B)(A)(C)$ are homogeneous and trivial, respectively.

The successor tree

The *successor tree*, which is defined for a specified machine M and a given initial uncertainty, displays graphically the I_i-successor uncertainties for all I_i, and thus assists the experimenter in the selection of the most suitable input sequence. It is composed of branches arranged in successive *levels*, numbered $0, 1, \ldots, j, \ldots$. Each branch in the jth level splits into p branches, labeled $I_1, I_2, \ldots, I_p$, corresponding to the input symbols of the machine. The branches emanating from the jth level form the $(j + 1)$st level, and so on. Each node of the successor tree is associated with an uncertainty vector. The highest node (in level 0) is associated with the initial uncertainty U_0, and each of the p nodes in level 1 is associated with a successor of U_0. The jth level of the tree consists of p^j branches, each terminating at a node. A sequence of j branches, starting at the highest node and terminating at a node in the jth level, is referred to as a *path* in the tree; j is called the *length* of the path. Each path *describes* an input sequence which, when applied to the machine, results in the uncertainty vector associated with the terminal node in the jth level. Hence a tree with $j + 1$ levels contains p^j paths, describing the p^j input sequences of length j.

The successor tree for machine M_1 and an initial uncertainty $(ABCD)$ is shown in Fig. 13-1. It contains four levels numbered 0 through 3.

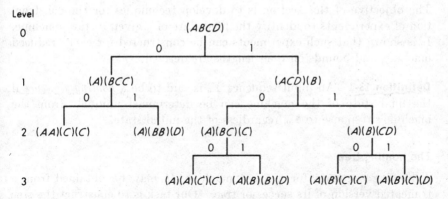

Fig. 13-1 Successor tree for machine M_1.

Each branch is labeled with the input symbol which it represents, and every node is associated with the corresponding uncertainty vector. The highest node is associated with the initial uncertainty, while the nodes in level 1 are associated with its 1- and 0-successors, and so on. For example, a 1 input applied to M_1 when the initial uncertainty is $(ABCD)$ results in the uncertainty vector $(ACD)(B)$, while a 0 input results in the uncertainty vector $(A)(BCC)$. The 1-successor of the vector $(ACD)(B)$ is determined by obtaining the 1-successors of (ACD) and (B) separately. For example, the 1-successor of (B) is (A), since the application of an input 1 to M_1 when in state B takes it to state A. The 1-successor of

(ACD), however, depends on the output; it is (CD) if the output is 1, and it is (B) if it is 0. Thus the corresponding uncertainty vector is $(A)(B)(CD)$. Similarly, the 0-successor of $(ACD)(B)$ is $(A)(BC)(C)$, since the 0-successor of (B) is (C), while that of (ACD) is $(A)(BC)$.

An uncertainty is said to be *smaller* than another uncertainty if it contains fewer elements; e.g., (BC) is smaller than (ACD). From the way the tree is constructed, it is evident that an uncertainty associated with a node in the jth level is either smaller than or contains the same number of elements as its predecessor in the $(j - 1)$st level. A homogeneous uncertainty vector will always have as its successors homogeneous uncertainty vectors. For example, in the tree of machine M_1, the successors of the uncertainty (BCC) are $(AA)(C)$ and $(A)(BB)$. The tree may be continued as far as is necessary, but for it to be of practical value, a truncated version must be defined by stipulating a number of termination rules.

13-2 HOMING EXPERIMENTS

The objective of this section is to develop techniques for the construction of experiments to identify the final state of a given n-state machine. It is shown that such experiments can be constructed for every reduced machine, and bounds on their lengths are derived.

Definition 13-1 An input sequence Y_0 is said to be a *homing sequence* if the final state of the machine can be determined uniquely from the machine's response to Y_0, regardless of the initial state.

The homing tree

A homing sequence for a given machine M may be obtained from a truncated version of its successor tree. Our task is to construct the tree and to determine the shortest path leading from the initial uncertainty to a trivial or a homogeneous uncertainty. The presence of such an uncertainty at the kth level of the tree guarantees that there exists an input sequence consisting of k symbols whose application to M is sufficient to specify uniquely M's final state.

A *homing tree* is a successor tree in which a jth-level node becomes terminal when any of the following occur:

1. The node is associated with an uncertainty vector whose non-homogeneous components are associated with some node in a preceding level;
2. Some node in the jth level is associated with a trivial or a homogeneous vector.

The homing tree of machine M_2 (Table 13-3) is shown in Fig. 13-2. The node associated with the vector $(AB)(DD)$ in level 2 is a terminal node, since its predecessor in level 1 is also associated with the vector $(AB)(DD)$.

Table 13-3   Machine M_2

PS	NS, z	
	$x = 0$	$x = 1$
A	$B,0$	$D,0$
B	$A,0$	$B,0$
C	$D,1$	$A,0$
D	$D,1$	$C,0$

Similarly, node $(ABCD)$ in level 1 is terminated, since it is identical with node $(ABCD)$ in level 0. The nodes in level 3 are terminal nodes, since $(A)(D)(DD)$ is a homogeneous uncertainty vector. The shortest homing sequence is 010, since it is the shortest sequence described by a path

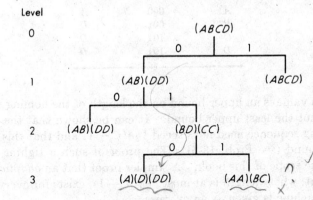

Fig. 13-2   Homing tree for machine M_2.

leading from the zeroth level to a homogeneous uncertainty. The response and final states corresponding to this sequence are given in Table 13-4.

We shall now establish the existence of the homing experiment and derive a bound on its length.

Theorem 13-1   *A preset homing sequence, whose length is at most $(n-1)^2$, exists for every reduced n-state machine M.*

Proof: Let the initial uncertainty be $(S_1 S_2 \cdots S_n)$. Since M is reduced, for every pair of states S_i, S_j there exists an experiment of length $n - 1$ or shorter which distinguishes S_i from S_j. Let us denote this experiment λ_i. Starting at the initial uncertainty, the application of the sequence λ_1, which distinguishes between some pair of states in M, yields the λ_1-successor uncertainty vector, which contains at least two components. Next, select any two states in one component and apply the appropriate sequence λ_2, which distinguishes between them. The $\lambda_1\lambda_2$-successor uncertainty vector contains at least three components. In a similar manner we obtain the $\lambda_1\lambda_2 \cdots \lambda_{n-1}$-successor vector which consists of n components, each of which contains only one state. Therefore the sequence $\lambda_1\lambda_2 \cdots \lambda_{n-1}$ is a homing sequence whose length is at most $(n - 1)^2$. ∎

Table 13-4 · Response of M_2 to the homing sequence 010

Initial state	Response to 010	Final state
A	000	A
B	001	D
C	101	D
D	101	D

This value is an upper bound on the length of the homing sequence, but it is not the least upper bound. It can be shown that the length of the homing sequence need not exceed $\frac{1}{2}n(n - 1)$ and that this is indeed a tight bound (see Prob. 13-5). The proof of such a tighter bound is beyond the scope of this book. A simpler proof that an *adaptive* homing experiment, whose length is at most $\frac{1}{2}n(n - 1)$, exists for every reduced n-state machine is given as an exercise.

Synchronizing experiments

A *synchronizing sequence* of a machine M is a sequence which takes M to a specified final state, regardless of the output or the initial state. Some machines possess such sequences; others do not.

For a given machine we can construct a successor tree, by ignoring the outputs and by associating with every node in the jth level the uncertainty regarding the final state which results from the application of the first j input symbols. For example, if the initial uncertainty of machine

M_2 is $(ABCD)$, then the 0-successor uncertainty is (ABD), and so on. Note that, since we are interested only in the final state regardless of the output, it is not necessary to write down repeated entries; e.g., $(ABDD)$ may be simply written as (ABD), etc. A jth-level node in the tree becomes terminal whenever any of the following occur:

1. The node is associated with an uncertainty that is also associated with some node in a preceding level;
2. Some node in the jth level is associated with an uncertainty containing just a single element.

A tree so constructed will be called a *synchronizing tree*. The synchronizing tree for machine M_2 is shown in Fig. 13-3.

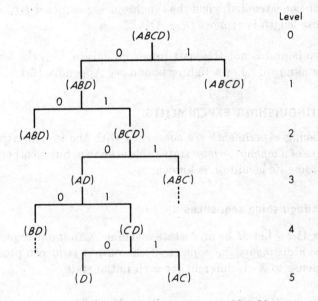

Fig. 13-3 Synchronizing tree for machine M_2.

A synchronizing sequence is described by a path in the tree leading from the initial uncertainty to a singleton uncertainty, i.e., an uncertainty containing just a single state. For machine M_2 the path 01010 describes a synchronizing sequence which, when applied to M_2, synchronizes the machine to state D, regardless of the output or the initial state. Note that if the initial uncertainty of machine M_2 is (BCD), the sequence 010 synchronizes M_2 to state D, since the 010-successors of B, C, and D are D, as shown in Table 13-4.

Theorem 13-2 *If a synchronizing sequence for an n-state machine M exists, then its length is at most $(n-1)^2 n/2$.*

Proof: Let the initial uncertainty be $(S_1 S_2 \cdots S_n)$. Select any two states S_i, S_j and apply to them a sequence ξ_1 which takes them into some state S_k. This task can always be accomplished, since M is known to possess a synchronizing sequence. The length of the sequence ξ_1 is at most $(n-1)n/2$, since the longest path for the synchronization of $(S_i S_j)$ is through all possible pairs of states, i.e., $(S_1 S_2), (S_1 S_3), \ldots, (S_{n-1} S_n)$. Consequently, S_k is the ξ_1-successor of $(S_i S_j)$. Next select a state S_p from the resultant uncertainty, and determine the sequence ξ_2, which takes $(S_k S_p)$ into some state S_q. The length of ξ_2 is also at most $(n-1)n/2$. In the same way it is possible to find the sequences $\xi_3, \xi_4, \ldots, \xi_{n-1}$, which, when concatenated, yield the synchronizing sequence $\xi_1 \xi_2 \cdots \xi_{n-1}$, whose length is at most $(n-1)^2 n/2$. ∎

The above bound is not the least upper bound; in fact, the least upper bound is unknown. For a tighter bound see Appendix 13-1.

13-3 DISTINGUISHING EXPERIMENTS

Distinguishing experiments are concerned with the identification of the initial state of a machine whose state table is known, but no other information regarding its condition is known.

Preset distinguishing sequences

Definition 13-2 Let M be an n-state machine. An input sequence X_0 is said to be a *distinguishing sequence* if the output sequence produced by M in response to X_0 is different for each initial state.

Knowing the output sequence that M produces in response to X_0 is sufficient to identify uniquely M's initial state. But the knowledge of the initial state and the input sequence is always sufficient to determine uniquely the final state as well. Consequently, *every distinguishing sequence is also a homing sequence*. The converse, however, is not true, since many homing sequences do not provide all the information regarding the initial state, e.g., the sequence 010 for machine M_2.

The distinguishing tree

A *distinguishing tree* is a successor tree in which a node in the jth level becomes terminal when any of the following occur:

1. The node is associated with an uncertainty vector whose non-homogeneous components are associated with some node in a preceding level;
2. The node is associated with an uncertainty vector containing a homogeneous nontrivial component;
3. Some node in the jth level is associated with a trivial uncertainty vector.

A path in the tree describes a distinguishing sequence of M if and only if it starts in the initial uncertainty (which is assumed to consist of the entire set of states S) and terminates in a node associated with a trivial uncertainty. A bound on the length of distinguishing sequences is shown in Appendix 13-2.

The distinguishing tree of machine M_1 is obtained from the corresponding successor tree (Fig. 13-1). The node associated with the homogeneous uncertainty vector $(A)(BCC)$ is terminated, since no further experiment can split the component (CC); i.e., there is no way of knowing, once the machine has passed to state C, whether the initial state was A or B. Machine M_1 has four distinguishing sequences of length 3: 111, 110, 101, and 100. The response of M_1 to the sequence 111 is summarized in Table 13-2b. This sequence clearly causes four distinct responses, depending on the initial state.

While every machine has at least one homing sequence, not every machine has a distinguishing sequence. For example, the distinguishing tree of machine M_2 must be terminated in level 1 (see Fig. 13-2), since the vector $(ABCD)$ is identical with the initial uncertainty, and the vector $(AB)(DD)$ has a nontrivial homogeneous component. An inspection of the state table of machine M_2 (Table 13-3) would have revealed the same result, since no experiment which starts with a 0 will distinguish between states C and D or between A and B, while no experiment which starts with a 1 will reduce the initial uncertainty.

The shortest distinguishing prefix

In many cases the initial state of a machine can be determined from only a prefix of the distinguishing sequence X_0. The length of the required prefix is a function of the initial state. Consider, for example, machine M_1, whose response to the distinguishing sequence 111 is given in Table 13-2b. It is evident that if the response of the machine to the first input symbol is 0, the initial state must have been C, and the distinguishing experiment may be terminated at this stage. On the other hand, if the response is 1, the initial state could have been either A, B, or D. The experiment must continue, and M_1 is supplied with the second 1 input. If M_1's response is now 0, the initial state must have been D, and the distinguishing experiment may be terminated. If, however, the response is 1, the uncertainty regarding the initial state is (AB), and a third 1 input must be applied to the machine. Thus, for machine M_1 and the distinguishing sequence 111, the shortest distinguishing prefix for state C is 1; for state D it is 11; for states A and B it is 111.

The shortest distinguishing prefixes can be determined by means of a modified distinguishing tree (see Ref. 5). They are particularly useful in the problems of fault detection and machine identification, where they lead to relatively short experiments.

Adaptive distinguishing experiments

So far we have considered preset experiments in which the choice of each input symbol is predetermined and is not influenced by the response of the machine to the preceding input symbols. We now consider adaptive experiments in which the choice of each input is determined by the machine's response to the previous inputs. As we shall see, the advantage of some adaptive experiments is that they are relatively short; in addition, there are machines for which only adaptive experiments can be constructed. On the other hand, the main disadvantage of using adaptive experiments is the relative difficulty in designing them and the need to inspect the output, after the application of each input, an act which tends to slow down the experiment.

As an example, consider machine M_3 (Table 13-5), for which the shortest preset distinguishing sequence is of length 3. Suppose that the

Table 13-5   Machine M_3

PS	NS, z $x = 0$	$x = 1$
A	C,0	A,1
B	D,0	C,1
C	B,1	D,1
D	C,1	A,0

initial uncertainty is $(ABCD)$ and an input symbol 0 is applied. As a result, the uncertainty is (CD) or (BC), depending on whether the response has been 0 or 1, respectively. This process can be described by means of an *adaptive tree*, as shown in Fig. 13-4a. In this tree, each horizontal line represents the application of a specific input symbol, as shown by the corresponding label. The downward lines represent the output symbols that the machine can produce with the given uncertainty.

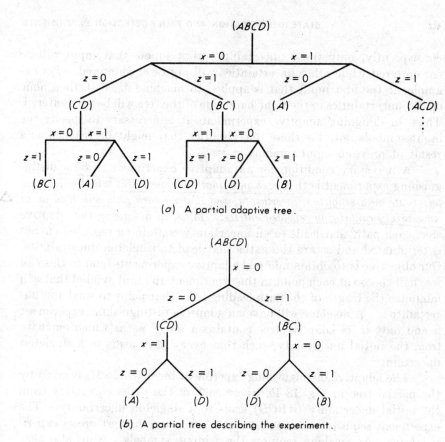

(a) A partial adaptive tree.

(b) A partial tree describing the experiment.

Fig. 13-4 Constructing an adaptive distinguishing experiment for machine M_3.

The next input symbol that must be applied to the machine after the application of the first 0 depends on whether the machine produced an output of 0 or 1, that is, whether the uncertainty is (CD) or (BC), respectively. In effect, each of these uncertainties can be viewed as an initial uncertainty for a new experiment. If the uncertainty is (CD), then in order to distinguish state C from state D, a 1 input is appropriate; but if it is (BC), a 0 input will distinguish between states B and C. In general, in designing adaptive experiments, each nontrivial component of every successor uncertainty vector represents the observer's knowledge of the present state of the machine, and consequently can be viewed as an initial uncertainty for a new independent experiment.

The adaptive tree usually lists all the possible successor uncertainties, and for each one it specifies the input symbols that can be applied next and the possible outcomes. However, in the course of an experiment, for a given uncertainty only one input will be applied and, consequently, only those uncertainties that follow that input will be encountered while other uncertainties will not be encountered. For example, if the first input that is applied to machine M_3 is 0, then none of the uncertainties in the right-hand side of the tree will be encountered. Thus, in designing adaptive experiments it is necessary to specify the input symbols only for those uncertainties that might be reached as a result of previous input symbols.

A necessary condition for an adaptive experiment to be a distinguishing experiment is that *each path that the experiment might follow will terminate on a singleton uncertainty, and that no such path will lead to an* $\triangle$ *uncertainty containing repeated entries*. Thus, in designing the adaptive tree, each path that leads to an uncertainty containing repeated entries is terminated and so are the paths that lead to singleton uncertainties. Our objective is to obtain minimal adaptive experiments, and to this end we shall choose at each point in the experiment an input symbol that will minimize the length of the path leading from that point to singleton uncertainties. A machine will have an adaptive distinguishing experiment if and only if its adaptive tree contains a set of paths which emanate from the initial uncertainty, such that every path leads to a singleton uncertainty.

The adaptive distinguishing experiment for machine $\dot{M}_3$ is given by the partial tree in Fig. 13-4b, where each of the paths emanating from the initial uncertainty $(ABCD)$ leads to a singleton uncertainty. The experiment requires two input symbols, while the shortest preset experiment for this machine requires three input symbols. Note also that since each of the paths in the experiment is minimal, according to the preceding definition, the adaptive experiment is minimal. The complete experiment is summarized as follows:

1. Apply an input 0 and inspect the corresponding output. If the output is 0, go to step 2; if it is 1, go to step 3.
2. Apply an input 1. The initial state can now be determined uniquely by observing the response. If it is 0, the initial state was B; if it is 1, the initial state was A.
3. Apply an input 0. If the response to this input is 0, the initial state was C; if it is 1, the initial state was D.

Some machines have both preset and adaptive distinguishing experiments, as demonstrated by machine M_3. Clearly in such a case, *the length of the minimal adaptive experiment need never exceed the length of the minimal preset experiment*. On the other hand, there are machines that have no distinguishing sequence, preset or adaptive, as demonstrated by M_2. Other machines may have no preset distinguishing sequences, but have adaptive ones (see, for example Prob. 13-13).

13-4 MACHINE IDENTIFICATION

So far we have been concerned with the problems of identifying the initial and final states of a known machine. We shall now address ourselves to a more general problem—that of identifying an unknown machine. The machine identification problem is essentially that of experimentally determining the state table of an unknown machine. In its most general form, when no information is available on the unknown machine, this problem cannot be solved for several reasons. First, the experimenter must have complete information regarding the input alphabet of the machine, since otherwise he or she can never be sure that the next input symbol will not reveal new information regarding the machine. Similarly, the machine cannot be identified unless there is an upper bound on the number of its states, since for any given machine and experiment of length L, it is possible to construct another machine that responds to the experiments of length L exactly like the given machine, but will respond differently to experiments of length greater than L. Finally, if a given machine M_i is in initial state S_i, it is indistinguishable experimentally from machine M_j whose initial state S_j is equivalent to S_i, although machines M_i and M_j may, in fact, be distinguishable. This situation clearly will not occur if both M_i and M_j are strongly connected.

To make the problem of machine identification solvable, we impose several restrictions on the machines. We assume that the input alphabet is known, as is an upper bound on the number of states of the machine. Moreover, the machine is assumed to be reduced and strongly connected.

An unknown machine with at most n states can now be identified in the following manner. Construct the direct-sum table (see Prob. 10-10) for all the tables that have n or fewer states and find a homing sequence for it. Clearly, such a homing sequence can always be found, and its application to the machine in question will reveal which set of equivalent states from the direct-sum table contains the final state of the machine. And if the direct-sum table contains only those tables that correspond to reduced and strongly connected machines, the homing sequence will uniquely identify the final state of the machine and, in turn, the machine itself. This demonstrates that under specified conditions the machine identification problem can be solved. However, as a procedure for actually designing experiments, the direct-sum approach is impractical, since the number of distinct tables is staggering even for relatively small n's. It will subsequently be shown that the problem of devising fault-detection experiments for sequential machines is directly related to the machine identification problem. More efficient procedures will be presented for the design of such experiments directly from the state table, without the use of the direct sum.

As an example, suppose a machine is known to have two states and its response to the input sequence X is the output sequence Z, as shown below.

Time:	t_1	t_2	t_3	t_4	t_5	t_6	t_7	t_8
X:	1	1	1	0	1	0	1	
Z:	0	1	0	0	1	0	0	

The first step in the analysis of these sequences is the identification of the distinct states of the tested machine. Let us name the two states A and B and suppose that at the start of the experiment the machine was in state A. The application of a 1 input results in a 0 output and a transition which is yet to be determined. However, since the second input symbol is also a 1 but the response is 1, the machine must have been at t_2 in a state other than A. Hence the experimenter may conclude that at t_2 the machine was in state B.

Since state A is the only state which responds to a 1 input by producing a 0 output, it is evident that at t_3 the machine was in state A. At t_4 it was again in state B, since it has already been verified (at t_2) that a 1 input causes a transition from state A to state B. In a similar manner it is easy to show that at t_5 the machine was again in state B, which in turn implies (see t_3) that at t_6 it was in state A. Finally, at t_7 it must have been in state A, since this is the only state in which the machine produces a 0 output as a response to a 1 input. As a result of the above analysis, the experimenter is able to demonstrate that the machine indeed has two states, named A and B, and that its transitions and outputs are given by the state table of Table 13-6. Thus, the above experiment is an identification experiment for machine M_4.

Table 13-6   Machine M_4

PS	NS, z	
	$x = 0$	$x = 1$
A	A,0	B,0
B	B,0	A,1

13-5 FAULT-DETECTION EXPERIMENTS

The problem of designing fault-detection experiments (or *checking experiments*) is actually a restricted problem of machine identification. An experimenter is supplied with a machine and its state table. His task is to determine from terminal experiments whether the given table accurately describes the behavior of the machine; that is, to decide whether the actual machine is isomorphic to the one described by the state table. As discussed before, we shall restrict our attention to strongly connected, completely specified and reduced machines. We also assume that the faults are permanent due to some component failure. This assumption excludes transient errors due to noise or incorrect inputs. At first we consider machines which possess at least one distinguishing sequence. In subsequent sections we shall relax this restriction and discuss machines that have no distinguishing sequence. Note that these experiments are intended to detect the presence of one or more faults, but will not locate or diagnose them.

Designing fault-detection experiments

In the procedure we shall use, each fault-detection experiment consists of two parts:

1. The first part is an *adaptive* experiment whose aim is to transfer the machine into a prespecified state, which is the initial state for the second part of the experiment.
2. The second part is a *preset* experiment in which the machine is taken through all possible transitions. This part is subdivided into two parts. In the first part the machine is caused to display the response of each of its states to the distinguishing sequence, while in the second part the actual transitions are verified.

As an example consider machine M_5, whose state table is given in Table 13-7 and whose responses to the sequences 00 and 01 are summarized in Table 13-8. Suppose that the preset part of the experiment is designed so that state A is the initial state, to which it is therefore

Table 13-7   Machine M_5

PS	NS, z	
	$x = 0$	$x = 1$
A	B,0	C,1
B	C,0	D,0
C	D,1	C,1
D	A,1	B,0

Table 13-8   Responses of machine M_5

Initial state	Response to 00	Final state		Initial state	Response to 01	Final state
A	00	C		A	00	D
B	01	D		B	01	C
C	11	A		C	10	B
D	10	B		D	11	C

| (a) | | | | (b) | | |

necessary to transfer the machine. To this end we apply the homing sequence 00 and observe the response.

1. If the response is 00, the machine is in state C. Apply the transfer sequence† $T(C,A) = 00$ to transfer the machine to state A;
2. If it is 01, apply $T(D,A) = 0$;
3. If it is 10, apply $T(B,A) = 10$;
4. If it is 11, the machine is in state A.

In designing the preset part of the fault-detection experiment, the first task is to ascertain that the starting state is indeed A and that the machine being tested actually contains four distinct states. This can be accomplished by displaying the response of each state to the same distinguishing sequence. Machine M_5 has two distinguishing sequences, 00 and 01, whose applications to the machine result in the responses shown in Table 13-8. The design of experiments based on the distinguishing sequence 00 is somewhat shorter, but will be left to the reader as an exercise.

To display the response of the starting state, we apply the distinguishing sequence $X_0 = 01$. If the machine has operated correctly up to this point, its output is 00, and it is now in state D. To display the response of this state, the distinguishing sequence 01 is applied again, and as a result, the machine goes to state C. The application of a third distinguishing sequence leaves the machine in state B and displays the response of state C. Applying X_0 twice more leaves the machine in state B, as shown below:

Input:	0	1	0	1	0	1	0	1	0	1
State:	A		D		C		B		C		B
Output:	0	0	1	1	1	0	0	1	1	0

† Recall that a *transfer sequence* $T(S_i,S_j)$ is the shortest input sequence that takes a machine from state S_i to state S_j.

The first eight symbols, by displaying four different responses to the sequence 01, i.e., 00, 11, 10, and 01, verify that the machine in question indeed has four distinct states. The last two symbols guarantee that the machine terminates in state B, since it has already been established that a response of 10 to the distinguishing sequence indicates a transition from state C to state B. The above sequence thus verifies the existence of at least four states, and since we assume that M_5 has no more than four states, then each state has been visited at least once, and its response to the distinguishing sequence has been determined. From this point on, if at any time during the course of the experiment one of the above responses to the distinguishing sequence is produced, the state of the machine at that time is uniquely identifiable. (It must be emphasized that the names given to the states are of no importance; a different set of names would result in an isomorphic machine.)

If the machine has not produced the expected output up to this point, we may conclude that a fault exists and terminate the experiment without any further tests. If, however, the above expected output has been produced, no conclusion can be reached as to whether the machine has operated correctly and is indeed in state B or a fault exists and the actual final state is different from B. We therefore assume that the machine actually started in state A and terminated in B. If this assumption is incorrect, it will be revealed in the next part of the experiment.

To complete the experiment, it is now necessary to verify every state transition. The general procedure to be followed is to apply the input symbol which causes the desired transition and to identify it by applying the distinguishing sequence. Since the machine is in state B, we shall start by applying an input 0, followed by the distinguishing sequence 01. This input sequence takes the machine back to state B, and thus a 101 input is applied to check the transition from B to D under a 1 input and to verify that the machine actually has moved to state D. In each of these three-bit sequences, the first bit causes the transition, while the distinguishing sequence ascertains that the transition is indeed the assumed one. At this point we have obtained additional information about another transition. It has earlier been shown that the application of 01 to the machine while in state B causes it to go to state C. But since an input of 0 takes the machine from B to C, we may conclude that, when a 1 input is applied to the machine while in state C, it stays in state C. In other words, since the 01-successor of state B is C and the 0-successor of B is also C, the 1-successor of C must be C.

At this point the machine is in state C. If, in response to the input sequence 001, the machine produces an output sequence 111, we may conclude that the 0-successor of C is D, and the final state is again C. But since it has already been established that the 01-successor of C is B, it means that the 1-successor of D is B. The experiment at this stage is as follows:

Input:	0 1 0 1 0 1 0 1 0 1 0 0 1 1 0 1 0 0 1
State:	A D C D B C C D B C D B D C D C
Output:	0 0 1 1 1 0 0 1 1 0 0 1 0 0 1 1 1 1 1

Up to this point we have checked every possible transition, except those from D to A and from A to B and to C. Since the machine is presently in state C, we must apply a transfer sequence to get to either state D or A. Such sequences can always be found for a strongly connected machine, and require at most $n - 1$ symbols. Furthermore, the transfer sequences should be applied in such a way that they will take the machine through "checked" transitions only. Thus the only possible transfer sequence in this case is $T(C,D) = 0$, because, as has already been demonstrated, the machine goes from C to D under an input 0. The application of a 0 followed by 01 ascertains the transition from D to A and returns the machine back to state D. This sequence provides enough information to verify the transition from A to C under a 1 input. This verification is achieved by inspection of the preceding sequence and observing that C is the 01-successor of D, and A is the 0-successor of D. Thus C is the 1-successor of A.

The last transition that needs to be checked is from state A to state B. Since the machine is in state D, a transfer sequence $T(D,A) = 0$ is applied, followed by 001. The complete experiment is shown below:

Input:	0 1 0 1 0 1 0 1 0 1 0 0 1 1 0 1 0 0 1 0 0 0 1 0 0 0 1
State:	A B D A C D B C C D B C D B D A C D A C D A B D A B C C
Output:	0 0 1 1 1 0 0 1 1 0 0 1 0 0 1 1 1 1 1 1 0 0 1 0 0 1

The preset part of the fault-detection experiment thus consists of the above input sequence, whose length is 27 symbols. If the machine at hand responds as shown above, it must be isomorphic to M_5, since it has been shown to contain four states whose responses are identical with corresponding responses of M_5, and all state transitions, which have been verified in terms of behavior exhibited at the beginning of the experiment, are also isomorphic to those of M_5. Clearly, if the machine has not produced the above expected output, it cannot be operating correctly. The location of the fault, however, cannot be determined merely by the above response.

Testing machines which have distinguishing sequences

The procedure can be summarized as follows. A fault-detection experiment starts with a homing sequence, followed by the appropriate transfer sequence, so as to maneuver the machine to the initial state of the preset part of the experiment. The machine is next supplied with an input sequence which causes it to visit each state and to display its response to the distinguishing sequence. Finally, the machine is made to go through every state transition, and in each case the transition is verified by displaying its response to the distinguishing sequence. In practice, it is not necessary to display all the responses at the beginning of the experiment. Any response or transition that is verified at a later point in the experiment may be used to determine a state transition at some earlier point.

More precisely, the procedure for constructing fault-detection experiments for machines having distinguishing sequences is as follows: Let $S_1, S_2, \ldots, S_n$ be the states of machine M, and suppose that X_0 is a distinguishing sequence for this machine. Let Q_i be the state to which M goes when initially in S_i as a result of the input sequence X_0. Also let $T(S_i, S_j)$ denote an input sequence (not necessarily unique) that transfers the machine from state S_i to state S_j. Now suppose that machine M is initially in its starting state S_1. Then, the sequence

$$X_0 T(Q_1, S_2) X_0 T(Q_2, S_3) X_0 T(Q_3, S_4) \cdots X_0 T(Q_n, S_1) X_0$$

will serve to take the machine through each of its states and to display all the different responses to the distinguishing sequence. For example, starting in S_1, X_0 leaves the machine in Q_1. Then $T(Q_1, S_2)$ transfers the machine to S_2, where X_0 is applied again, leaving the machine in Q_2. The corresponding output sequence clearly displays the response of M to X_0, when initially in either state S_1 or state S_2. The machine is similarly led through all its n states, and at each point the sequence X_0 is applied followed by the transfer sequence $T(Q_i, S_{i+1})$.

At the end of this part of the experiment the machine receives the sequence $X_0 T(Q_n, S_1)$. If it operates correctly, it will be in state S_1. This is verified by applying to it again the distinguishing sequence X_0. Clearly, if its response to the last X_0 is identical with its response to the first X_0, the machine will indeed be at the end of this part in state Q_1. Thus, the next part of the experiment can start at this point by identifying the transitions out of state Q_1.

In the second part of the experiment we establish the various state transitions. To check, for example, the 0-transition out of state S_i, when the machine is in some state Q_j, the appropriate sequence is

$$T(Q_j, S_{i-1}) X_0 T(Q_{i-1}, S_i) 0 X_0$$

The sequence $T(Q_j, S_{i-1}) X_0$ guarantees that the machine indeed went to state Q_{i-1}, as it has done in the previous part of the experiment. $T(Q_{i-1}, S_i)$ transfers M to state S_i, and then $0X_0$ is applied to cause and identify the 0-transition out of S_i. In a similar manner the machine can be taken through every transition, in each case identifying the transition by means of the response already established in the first part of the experiment. In general, however, to reduce the length of the experiment, it is possible to apply the two parts of the experiment simultaneously instead of sequentially.

The method outlined above can be applied to any reduced and strongly connected machine that has at least one distinguishing sequence. The design of fault-detection experiments for machines which do not have any distinguishing sequence is studied in Sec. 13-8. As will be shown, the design of such experiments is extremely complicated, and the resulting experiments are very long. This situation leads to the conclusion that, when designing a sequential machine, care must be taken to design it in such a way that whenever possible it will possess some distinguishing sequences and, thus, will be simpler to maintain and test. The development of such design procedures is the subject of the next section.

★13-6 DESIGN OF DIAGNOSABLE MACHINES

A *diagnosable* sequential machine is one which possesses one or more distinguishing sequences and thus permits us to identify uniquely the states of the machine by inspecting its response to such a sequence. In this section we shall present a method to modify the design of sequential machines in such a way that they will possess special distinguishing sequences so that relatively short fault-detection experiments can be constructed for them.

The testing graph

Machine M_2 (Table 13-3) does not possess any distinguishing sequence. We shall now show how it may be augmented, by adding to it an additional output terminal, so that the augmented machine will possess several distinguishing sequences.

The state table of M_2 may be rewritten as shown in the upper half of Table 13-9. The column headings consist of all input-output combinations, where the pair I_k/O_l corresponds to a combination of input I_k and output O_l. The row headings in the upper half of the table are the states of the machine. The entry in column I_k/O_l, row S_i, is the I_k-successor of S_i, if this successor is associated with an output O_l and is a dash (—) otherwise. For example, the 0-successor of A is B, and the corresponding output is 0. Consequently, a B is entered in row A, column 0/0, and a dash in column 0/1. In a similar manner the next-state entries of M_2 are entered in the upper half of the table.

Table 13-9 Testing table for machine M_2

	0/0	0/1	1/0	1/1
A	B	—	D	—
B	A	—	B	—
C	—	D	A	—
D	—	D	C	—
AB	AB	—	BD	—
AC	—	—	AD	—
AD	—	—	CD	—
BC	—	—	AB	—
BD	—	—	BC	—
CD	—	$\widehat{DD}$	AC	—

The lower half of the table is derived directly from the upper half. The row headings are all unordered pairs of states, while the table entries are their corresponding successors. If the entries in rows S_i and S_j, column I_k/O_l, of the upper half are S_p and S_q, respectively, then the entry in row S_iS_j, column I_k/O_l, of the lower half is S_pS_q. For example, since the entries in rows A and B, column 1/0, are D and B, respectively, the corresponding entry in row AB, column 1/0, is BD, and so on. If for some pair of states S_i and S_j either one or both corresponding entries in some column I_k/O_l are dashes, the corresponding entry in row S_iS_j, column I_k/O_l, is a dash. For example, the entry in row AC, column 0/0, is a dash, since the entry in row C, column 0/0, is a dash. The table thus completed is referred to as a *testing table*.

We shall refer to a pair (S_iS_j) as an *uncertainty pair* and to its successor (S_pS_q) as the *implied pair*. Thus, for example, the pair (BD) is implied by (AB). An uncertainty pair that does not imply any other pair, that is, all the entries in the corresponding row are dashes, can be omitted from the table. Whenever an entry in the testing table consists of a repeated state (e.g., DD in row CD), that entry is circled. A circle around DD means that states C and D are *merged* under input 0 into state D, and are indistinguishable by an experiment which starts with a 0 input.

Let us define a directed graph G, which will be called a *testing graph*, in the following way:

1. Corresponding to each row in the lower half of the testing table there is a vertex in G.
2. If there exists an entry S_pS_q, where $p \neq q$, in row S_iS_j, column I_k/O_l, of the testing table, then G has a directed arc leading from

the vertex labeled S_iS_j to the vertex labeled S_pS_q. The arc is labeled I_k/O_l. No arc is needed if S_iS_j implies S_pS_p, e.g., DD in row CD.

The testing graph for machine M_2 is derived directly from the lower half of the testing table and is shown in Fig. 13-5.

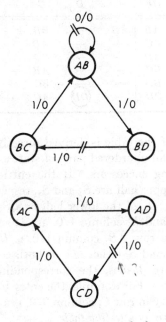

Fig. 13-5 Testing graph for machine M_2.

Definitely diagnosable machines

A machine M is defined as a *definitely diagnosable machine of order μ* if μ is the least integer, so that every sequence of length μ is a distinguishing sequence for M. In other words, a machine is definitely diagnosable if every node in level μ of the distinguishing tree is associated with a trivial uncertainty vector. The distinguishing tree can thus serve as a tool for recognizing definitely diagnosable machines. In this section, however, we shall derive a different test by means of the testing graph.

Theorem 13-3   *A machine M is definitely diagnosable if and only if its testing graph G is loop-free and no repeated states (i.e., circled entries) exist in the testing table.*

Proof: If the testing table contains a repeated entry in row S_iS_j, column I_k/O_i, then state S_i cannot be distinguished from S_j by an experiment which starts with I_k. Thus, if M is definitely diagnosable, its testing table does not contain repeated entries. Now suppose that G is not loop-free. Then, by repeatedly applying the symbols coinciding with the labels of the arcs in the loop, we find an arbitrarily long input sequence that cannot resolve the uncertainty regarding the initial state. Consequently, the machine is not definitely diagnosable. To prove sufficiency, assume that G is loop-free. If M is not definitely diagnosable, then there exists an arbitrarily long path in G corresponding to some input sequence X and some pair of states S_iS_j, so that S_i cannot be distinguished from S_j by X. But since the number of vertices in G cannot exceed $(n-1)n/2$ (corresponding to the number of distinct pairs of states), arbitrarily long paths in G are possible only if it contains a loop. Thus the theorem is proved. ∎

The above testing procedure is clearly equivalent to testing by means of the distinguishing tree. In fact, the graph being loop-free means that no node in the tree is associated with an uncertainty vector whose nonhomogeneous components are also associated with some node in a preceding level. Similarly, if the testing table is free of repeated entries, it means that no node in the tree is associated with an uncertainty vector containing a homogeneous nontrivial component. Hence every node in the μth level of the tree is associated with a trivial uncertainty vector.

Corollary *Let the testing table of machine M be free of repeated entries, and let G be a loop-free testing graph for M. If the length of the longest path in G is l, then $\mu = l + 1$.*

Proof: Since G is loop-free, M is definitely diagnosable. Assume that $\mu > l + 1$; then there exists at least one uncertainty pair (S_iS_j) which is transferred, by the application of an input sequence of length $l + 1$, to another pair (S_pS_q). Consequently, there must exist a path, between vertices S_iS_j and S_pS_q in G, whose length is $l + 1$. This contradicts our assumption, and thus μ cannot exceed $l + 1$. The proof that μ cannot be smaller than $l + 1$ is trivial. ∎

We thus arrive at the general result that *if a machine is definitely diagnosable of order μ, then $\mu \geq (n-1)n/2$.* In Prob. 13-28 we show that this bound is in fact the least upper bound for μ.

Designing definitely diagnosable machines

In order to obtain a machine M_2' which contains M_2 and possesses a distinguishing sequence, it is necessary to augment M_2 by adding to it an output terminal and assigning different output symbols to selected transitions. We shall in fact show that the addition of one output terminal is sufficient to make M_2' definitely diagnosable. The first step toward this end is to assign different outputs to each transition that may cause a repeated entry in the testing table. In the case of M_2, this is accomplished by assigning an output 10 to the transition from C to D, and an output 11 to the transition from D to D. Such an assignment of output values ensures that the testing table of M_2' will be free of repeated entries.

The testing graph of M_2 contains three loops: a self-loop around AB and two other loops, each containing three vertices. Clearly, these loops must be opened if M_2' is to be definitely diagnosable. In general, a loop is opened by the removal of any of its arcs. To remove an arc, it is necessary to assign different output symbols to the next-state entries represented by the vertex to which that arc leads. In other words, an arc leading from vertex S_iS_j to vertex S_pS_q is eliminated by assigning different output symbols to the transitions from S_i and S_j to S_p and S_q. For example, the self-loop around AB in Fig. 13-5 is opened by assigning the output symbols 01 and 00, respectively, to the next-state entries B and A in column $x = 0$. The loop $AB - BD - BC - AB$ can be opened by the removal of the arc from BD to BC. This is achieved by assigning the output symbols 00 and 01 to the next-state entries B and C in rows B and D, column $x = 1$. In a similar manner we open the loop $AC - AD - CD - AC$ by assigning a 00 output to the next-state entry D in row A, column $x = 1$, thus removing the arc from AD to CD. The resulting state table is shown in Table 13-10.

Table 13-10   Machine M_2'

PS	NS, zz_1	
	$x = 0$	$x = 1$
A	B,01	D,00
B	A,00	B,00
C	D,10	A,01
D	D,11	C,01

Since the length of a fault-detection experiment is directly proportional to the length of the distinguishing sequence for the machine, we attempt to open all loops, while simultaneously minimizing the length of the various paths in the graph. In opening the loops in the graph of Fig. 13-5, all the output entries, with the exception of the entry in row C, column $x = 1$, have been assigned new values. The longest path in the loop-free graph is of length 2, and consequently the order of the modified machine is $\mu = 3$. This result can, however, be improved by specifying the output entry in row C, column $x = 1$, as 01. This specification actually eliminates the arcs from AC to AD and from BC to AB. As a result, the length of the longest path in the graph is now 1, and M_2' is definitely diagnosable of order 2. The distinguishing tree of machine M_2' is shown in Fig. 13-6.

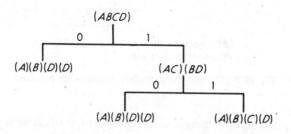

Fig. 13-6 Distinguishing tree for machine M_2'.

It is clear that, for any 2^k-state machine, the addition of k output terminals is sufficient to convert it into a definitely diagnosable machine. The problem of providing an algorithm for finding the minimal number of additional required output terminals is unsolved. But with some experience, a definitely diagnosable machine can be designed with a minimal, or nearly minimal, number of additional terminals. It is quite clear that, although the removal of a minimal number of arcs does not necessarily imply the addition of a minimal number of outputs, the elimination of too many arcs does tend to increase the number of necessary output terminals. Using presently available techniques, a certain amount of trial and error is unavoidable in attempting to add the minimal number of output terminals.

Since the procedure followed in the above example can be applied to any machine, we arrive at the following general result:

▶ To every reduced machine M there corresponds a definitely diagnosable machine M', which is obtained from M by the addition of one or more output terminals.

The block diagram of the definitely diagnosable machine M' which corresponds to machine M is shown in Fig. 13-7.

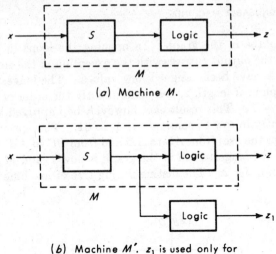

(a) Machine M.

(b) Machine M'. z_1 is used only for
diagnosing purposes.

Fig. 13-7 Design of a definitely diagnosable machine.

The question now arises as to the purpose of designing definitely diagnosable machines. Evidently, fault-detection experiments can be designed with just one distinguishing sequence. Moreover, even when a machine possesses two or more distinguishing sequences, there is no known procedure for utilizing them simultaneously in an experiment. The main motivation for designing definitely diagnosable machines and studying their properties is the expectation that such machines will prove easier to maintain, and that it will be possible to design for them fault-location experiments. Such experiments will be simpler to design for definitely diagnosable machines, since it is possible to cross-check the machine with every sequence of length μ, and not with just a single sequence.

★13-7 SECOND ALGORITHM FOR THE DESIGN OF FAULT-DETECTION EXPERIMENTS

The main feature of the algorithm presented in this section is that it involves the use of distinguishing sequences with repeated symbols, e.g., 000 or 111, and thus allows overlapping portions of the distinguishing sequences. This in turn will result in substantially shorter fault-detection experiments. For example, if 111 is a distinguishing sequence for a given machine, then the addition of just a single 1 following the initial three 1's is sufficient to identify the first transition, since the first three 1's identify the initial state, while the last three 1's identify its 1-successor. Before formulating the general algorithm, we shall construct a fault-detection experiment for machine M_2', using the distinguishing sequence 11.

A fault-detection experiment for machine M_2'

Suppose that machine M_2' is initially in state A. (Clearly, if M_2' is not in A, it is always possible to transfer it to A, since every sequence of length 2 is a homing sequence for M_2'.) In order to simplify the notation, we shall designate the binary outputs by decimal numbers; i.e., 00 will be designated by 0; 01 by 1; 10 by 2; and 11 by 3. The fault-detection experiment starts with the application of the distinguishing sequence $X_0 = 11$ to the machine, so as to display the response of the initial state. According to the state table, the 1-successor of A is D; to display its response to the distinguishing sequence, a single 1 input is needed following the initial two 1's. The input to the machine at this point consists of three consecutive 1's; the first two 1's identify the initial state, while the last two 1's identify its 1-successor.

If the machine is operating correctly, it will be at t_2 in state C. In order to display the response of state C to the distinguishing sequence, it is necessary to apply another 1 input. The machine will now be back in A, and this can be verified by the application of a fifth 1. At this point the experiment is as follows:

	t_0	t_1	t_2	t_3	t_4	t_5
Input:	1	1	1	1	1	
State:	A	D	C	A	D	C
Output:	0	1	1	0	1	

Since the machine has produced three different responses to the input sequence 11, it must have been at t_0, t_1, and t_2 in three different states. We denote these states A (at t_0), D (at t_1), and C (at t_2). Since the outputs produced by M_2' in response to X_0 at t_0 and t_3 are the same, and provided we can verify in the course of the experiment that the machine indeed has four distinct states, we may assume that at t_3 the machine was in state A. Moreover, since we know that the input sequence 11 takes the machine from A to C, at t_5 it will be in state C. In addition to displaying the responses of states A, D, and C to the distinguishing sequence, the above input sequence verifies the transitions from A to D, from D to C, and from C to A under 1 input.

It is evident that an application of another 1 at this point in the experiment will not yield any new transitions. Therefore a 0 must be applied, followed by X_0. This sequence will leave the machine in state A. Again, a continuation of the application of 1's is not useful, since the transition from A under input 1 has already been checked. Therefore we apply a 0 followed by 11. The 0 will take the machine to state B, which is identified by its response to 11. Then, to verify the transition from B under an input of 1, a 1 is applied, which leaves the machine in state B. An additional 0 followed by X_0 results in the following:

Input:	1	1	1	1	1	0	1	1	0	1	1	1	0	1	1
State:	A	D	C	A	D	C	D	C	A	B	B	B	B	A	D	C
Output:	0	1	1	0	1	2	1	1	1	0	0	0	0	0	1

At this point the machine is in state C. But since the two transitions from state C have already been checked, a transfer sequence must be applied, so that it takes the machine through only "checked" transitions. Since the only transition that has not yet been verified is from D to D under 0 input, the transfer sequence $T(C,D) = 0$ is applied, followed by 011. The complete experiment thus requires 19 symbols.

Input:	1	1	1	1	1	0	1	1	0	1	1	1	0	1	1	0	0	1	1
Output:	0	1	1	0	1	2	1	1	1	0	0	0	0	0	1	2	3	1	1

The general procedure

The procedure employed in the preceding example is valid for any machine that has a distinguishing sequence with repeated symbols. It can be summarized as follows:

1. Apply a homing sequence and if necessary a transfer sequence, so as to maneuver the machine into the specified initial state, denoted S_0.
2. Choose X_0 to be the shorter sequence between the sequences of all 0's or all 1's. (For the purpose of clarity of the procedure, assume that X_0 has been chosen as the all-1's sequence.)
3. Apply X_0 followed by a 1 to check the first transition from S_0 under an input of 1. (If the all-0's sequence has been chosen, apply an input 0 instead of 1, etc.)
4. If the 1-successor of S_0 is different from S_0, apply another 1. Similarly, if the 11-successor of S_0 is different from either S_0 or the 1-successor of S_0, apply another 1. In the same manner continue to add 1 inputs as long as new transitions are being checked.
5. When an additional 1 input does not yield any new transition, apply an input 0 followed by X_0.
6. As long as new transitions can be checked, apply inputs of 1's to the machine. When no new transitions can be checked, repeat steps 5 and 6.

7. When steps 5 and 6 do not yield any new transition, and the machine which is in state S_i is not yet completely checked, apply the sequence $T(S_i,S_k)$, which takes the machine only through checked transitions to a state S_k whose transition has not yet been verified.
8. Repeat the last three steps until all transitions have been checked.

Example The construction of a fault-detection experiment for machine M_2', using the shorter distinguishing sequence $X_0 = 0$, requires only 14 symbols and is illustrated as follows:

X:　　0　0　0　　　　　　　　X:　　1　0
　　　　A　B　A　B　　　　　　　　B　B　A
Z:　　1　0　1　　　　　　　　Z:　　0　0

(a) Steps 3, 4　　　　　　　　(b) Step 5

X:　　1　0　0　1　0　0　　　　X:　　1　1　0
　　　　A　D　D　D　C　D　D　　　　D　C　A　B
Z:　　0　3　3　1　2　3　　　　Z:　　1　1　1

(c) Step 6　　　　　　　　　　(d) Steps 7, 8

X:　　0　0　0　1　0　1　0　0　1　0　0　1　1　0
　　　　A　B　A　B　B　A　D　D　D　C　D　D　C　A　B
Z:　　1　0　1　0　0　0　3　3　1　2　3　1　1　1

(e) Complete checking experiment. ∎

★13-8 FAULT-DETECTION EXPERIMENTS FOR MACHINES WHICH HAVE NO DISTINGUISHING SEQUENCES

The procedures for designing fault-detection experiments for machines which have preset distinguishing sequences can be generalized without too much difficulty to machines which have only adaptive distinguishing sequences (see Prob. 13-28). The main difference is that in the latter case *different* distinguishing sequences may be used to identify the various states, while in the former case the *same* sequence X_0 was used for state identification. Moreover, adaptive distinguishing sequences may be used even for machines that do have preset sequences. The use of adaptive sequences will in most such cases yield shorter experiments. The adaptive distinguishing tree thus becomes an important tool in generating the distinguishing sequences. As we shall see, this tree is also instrumental in deriving fault-detection experiments for machines which have no distinguishing sequences at all. Note however that, although *adaptive* sequences are being used for state identification, the resulting fault-detection experiment is *preset*.

Characterizing and identifying sequences

The main difficulty in designing fault-detection experiments for machines which do not have any distinguishing sequence is due to the fact that the state of the machine at each point during the experiment cannot be determined merely by observing the machine's response at that point. Instead, it may be necessary to gather information from several points simultaneously, and to observe the response of the state in question to different input sequences. Only then will the state identification be possible. Our general approach in this case is to partition the states of the given machine in such a way that a simple (preset or adaptive) sequence exists which distinguishes the blocks of the partition. A different sequence (or sequences) is next found which distinguishes the states in each block. These sequences, which are referred to as *characterizing sequences*, serve to identify uniquely the states of the machine. We shall consider first the case of machines whose states are distinguishable by at most two characterizing sequences.

As an example, let us design a fault-detection experiment for machine M_2, whose state table is repeated in Table 13-11. As shown before, this machine does not have any distinguishing sequence. However, from the responses of M_2 shown in Table 13-12, it is evident that the input sequence 010 distinguishes the blocks of the partition $\pi_1 = \{A,B,CD\}$, while the sequence 10 distinguishes state C from D. Thus, the sequences 010 and 10 constitute a set of characterizing sequences for machine M_2. (Note that this set is not unique, since 0 and 10 also constitute a set of characterizing sequences.)

Table 13-11 Machine M_2

PS	NS, z $x = 0$	$x = 1$
A	B,0	D,0
B	A,0	B,0
C	D,1	A,0
D	D,1	C,0

Table 13-12 Response of M_2 to characterizing sequences

State	Response to 010	Response to 10
A	000	01
B	001	00
C	101	00
D	101	01

Clearly, the characterizing sequence 010, together with the corresponding response, is sufficient to distinguish each of the states A and B

from the remaining states. Specifically, the input sequences and their associated output sequences are:

$$A \quad \begin{matrix} 0 & 1 & 0 \\ 0 & 0 & 0 \end{matrix} \qquad B \quad \begin{matrix} 0 & 1 & 0 \\ 0 & 0 & 1 \end{matrix}$$

To determine the sequence that identifies state C, a different technique must be employed. First, we observe that, having identified uniquely states A and B, there may be at most two states that respond to a 0 input by producing a 1 output. (Note that both A and B respond to a 0 input by producing a 0 output.) Suppose now that the machine is supplied with the input sequence below and in turn produces the associated output sequence.

Input:	01	01	01	10
State:	S_i	S_j	S_k	S_p
Output:	10	10	10	00

Because the machine can have at most two states that respond to a 0 by producing a 1, state S_k must be identical to either S_i or to S_j (or to both). Consequently, S_p is identical to at least one of the states S_i, S_j, and S_k. Therefore, S_p is a state that responds to a 0 input by producing a 1 output, and to a 10 input by producing a 00 output. From Table 13-12 it is evident that these sequences identify uniquely state C. Similar reasoning shows that the sequences below identify state D, since they identify a state that responds to a 0 input by producing a 1 output and to a 10 input by producing a 01 output.

Input:	0	0	0	10
State:	S_i'	S_j'	S_k'	S_p'
Output:	1	1	1	01

The above sequences, which identify states C and D, may be written compactly as

$$C \begin{pmatrix} 0 & 1 \\ 1 & 0 \end{pmatrix}^3 \begin{matrix} 10 \\ 00 \end{matrix} \qquad D \begin{pmatrix} 0 \\ 1 \end{pmatrix}^3 \begin{matrix} 10 \\ 01 \end{matrix}$$

where the exponent indicates that the sequences within the parentheses are to be repeated three times. The set of input sequences used to identify the states of the machine are referred to as *identifying sequences*.

As we have seen in this example, the identifying sequences of some states may consist each of just a single characterizing sequence, e.g., states A and B, while those of other states, e.g., C and D, are more complex and contain two characterizing sequences. Before describing the procedure for designing these latter identifying sequences, we introduce some notation. Let $S_1, S_2, \ldots, S_n$ be the states of a machine for which X_1 and X_2 are characterizing sequences. Suppose the machine is in state S_i, and input X_1 is applied, then let Q_i denote the state of the machine at the end of this sequence. Again let $T(S_i, S_j)$ denote a transfer sequence which takes the machine from S_i to S_j.

Now suppose that we wish to find an identifying sequence for S_i by demonstrating its response to the two characterizing sequences X_1 and X_2. Suppose also that at most m states can respond in a given way to X_1. To ensure that the machine will *definitely* be in the same state (i.e., S_i) before the application of both X_1 and X_2, it is necessary to apply $m + 1$ times the sequence $X_1 T(Q_i, S_i)$. Therefore, during the sequence

$$[X_1 T(Q_i, S_i)]^{m+1} X_2$$

the state of the machine prior to the application of X_2 must be the same as the state prior to the application of some X_1. Thus, such a sequence exhibits the response of that state to both X_1 and X_2. This sequence therefore is an identifying sequence for that state. It is important to observe at this point that X_1 in the above sequence need not always be the complete characterizing sequence. Very often a prefix of the complete sequence is sufficient, as illustrated in the case of states C and D above, where the prefix 0 has been used instead of the complete sequence 010. Subsequently, we refer to identifying sequences consisting of just a single characterizing sequence as *identifying sequences of the first order*, and to sequences of the type $[X_1 T(Q_i, S_i)]^{m+1} X_2$ as *identifying sequences of second order*.

A testing procedure

Once the identifying sequences for all of the states of the machine have been determined, the checking experiment can be constructed. For the experiment to be a checking experiment, it must contain at least one identifying sequence for each state. By means of these sequences, we identify uniquely the n states of the machine in question. In addition, from the responses of the machine to the various identifying sequences, we can determine the responses of each of the machines' states to the characterizing sequences X_1 and X_2. The design of a checking experiment can now be described.

Let I_i be the identifying sequence for state S_i, and let P_i be the state which the machine enters at the end of I_i. One possible way of designing a checking experiment is to start with a sequence consisting of alternating identifying sequences and transfer sequences, i.e.,

$$I_1 T(P_1,S_2) I_2 T(P_2,S_3) I_3, \ldots , T(P_{n-1},S_n) I_n$$

This sequence takes the machine through all its n states and displays the response of each of the states to its identifying sequence.

The next problem is to determine the state of the machine at the end of I_n. In general, the determination of the state S_i of the machine at the end of some identifying sequence, say I_k, depends on the order of I_i. If it is of first order, then I_i is simply applied following I_k to identify S_i. If, however, I_i is of second order it is necessary to display the response of S_i to both X_1 and X_2. This can be achieved by means of the sequence

$$I_k X_1 T(Q_i,S_k) I_k X_2$$

If the circuit produces the same response in the two applications of I_k, then it must be in the same state, i.e., S_i, at the end of the two applications of I_k. Thus the foregoing sequence identifies uniquely S_i by displaying its response to X_1 and then to X_2.

Once the state of the machine can be established at a certain point during the experiment, the transitions leading out of that state can be determined. Suppose, for example, that we wish to examine the transition from S_i to S_j under an input of 0. If I_j is of first order, then the input sequence $0I_j$ checks this transition. If, however, I_j is of second order, the 0-successor, S_j, must be checked twice, once for each of the characterizing sequences. This check can be accomplished by applying the following sequence:

$$I_k T(P_k,S_i) 0 X_1 T(Q_j,S_k) I_k T(P_k,S_i) 0 X_2$$

The subsequence $I_k T(P_k,S_i)$ takes the machine to state S_i, while the subsequence $T(Q_j,S_k) I_k T(P_k,S_i)$ returns the machine to S_i for the second check. The transition under 1 input can be checked in the same way, and similarly for transitions from other states. The checking experiment can now be designed in a straightforward manner.

Following this procedure it is evident that each transition to a state for which the identifying sequence is of second order must be checked twice, while every transition to a state for which the identifying sequence is of first order need only be checked once. Consequently, in order to obtain minimal experiments, it is in most cases advantageous to select a set of identifying sequences in which a maximal number of states are distinguishable by identifying sequences of first order.

Example   The experiment shown below for machine M_2 is of length 35.

$$I_C \qquad\qquad I_B$$

$$I_D \qquad\qquad\qquad\qquad I_A$$

t:	1	2	3	4	5	6	7	8	9	10	11	12	13	14	15	16	17	18
X:	1	0	0	0	1	0	1	0	1	0	1	1	0	1	0	1	0
Z:	0	1	1	1	0	1	0	1	0	1	0	0	0	0	0	0	1

$$I_A \qquad I_A \qquad I_B$$

t:	18	19	20	21	22	23	24	25	26	27	28	29	30	31	32	33	34	35
X:	1	1	0	1	0	0	1	0	0	0	1	0	1	1	1	1	0	0
Z:	0	0	0	0	0	0	0	0	0	0	1	0	0	0	0	0	1	1

To prove that the experiment is indeed a checking experiment for M_2, it is sufficient to analyze the experiment and to show that it corresponds to a unique state table. By observing I_A, I_B, I_C, and I_D we identify four distinct states. Thus we have [where $S(i)$ is the state at time i]:

$$S(13) = S(20) = S(23) = A$$
$$S(15) = S(27) = B$$
$$S(12) = C$$
$$S(5) = D$$

From the above we find

1. Since $S(12) = C$ and $S(13) = A$, A is the 1-successor of C and the corresponding output is 0.
2. Since $S(20) = S(23) = A$, A is the 010-successor of A; consequently, $S(16) = S(26) = A$. From this we find that A is the 0-successor of B with an output of 0 and B is the 0-successor of A, also with an output of 0.
3. Since $S(14) = B$ we conclude that B is the 1-successor of B.
4. At $t = 15$ we see that A is the 01011-successor of B and since $S(27) = B$, we get $S(32) = A$. Also, since $S(16) = S(32) = A$, we conclude that $S(17) = S(33)$ is a state that responds to a 0 by producing a 1, and to a 10 by producing 01. Consequently, $S(17) = S(33) = D$ which implies that D is the 1-successor of A.
5. Now, since $S(12) = C$, C is the 1-successor of $S(11)$. But the 1-successors of states A, B, and C are D, B, and A, respectively. Thus, $S(11)$ must be D. Similarly, since A

is the 1-successor of $S(19)$, we find that $S(19) = C$ and
$S(18) = D$, which in turn implies that D is the 0-successor
of D.

6. Finally, since $S(5) = S(33) = D$, then $S(6) = S(34) = C$
and $S(7) = S(35)$. But this last state responds to a 0
by producing a 1 and to 10 by producing a 01. Consequently, it must be state D, and D is the 1-successor of C.

We have thus shown that the above experiment is a checking experiment for M_2. ∎

Partitions associated with input sequences

A partition π on the set of states of a machine M is said to be *associated*
with an input sequence X if it is the smallest partition whose blocks can
be distinguished by their responses to X; that is, two states belong to
the same block in π if and only if their responses to X are identical. For
example, in the case of M_2, $\pi_1 = \{A,B,CD\}$ is associated with the input
sequence 010, and $\pi_2 = \{AD,BC\}$ is associated with 10.

Following the discussion in the foregoing section, it is evident that
*a necessary and sufficient condition for a set of sequences to be characterizing
sequences is that the product of the partitions associated with these sequences
will be zero.* Indeed, in the case of machine M_1, $\pi_1 \cdot \pi_2 = \pi(0)$. Whenever a partition associated with an input sequence is the zero partition,
that sequence is known as a preset distinguishing sequence. Generalizing the definition of an "input sequence" to cover the case of an adaptive
sequence (which actually consists of a set of sequences), we conclude that
the existence of a zero partition associated with some (preset or adaptive)
input sequence X is a necessary and sufficient condition for X to be a
distinguishing sequence.

Although the length of the checking experiment is not necessarily
directly proportional to the length of the characterizing sequences or the
order of the identifying sequences, the use of longer and higher-order
sequences does tend to substantially increase the length of the experiment.
In particular, since we must check twice each transition leading to a state
whose identifying sequence is of second order, it is desirable to find sets
of identifying sequences containing as many sequences of first order as
possible. To simplify the identifying sequences of second order, it is
necessary to reduce the number of repetitions of sequences of the type
$XT(Q_i,S_i)$. In terms of partitions, the number of states distinguishable
by a first-order identifying sequence is equal to the number of single-
state blocks in the partition associated with the sequence in question.
For each block containing m states, at least two characterizing sequences

must be used in forming an identifying sequence, and the number of repetitions of the sequence $XT(Q_i,S_i)$ is at least $m + 1$.

The problem of determining an appropriate set of characterizing sequences is thus transformed to the equivalent problem of selecting a set of partitions whose product is zero and which correspond to simple and low-order identifying sequences. As the first step in the selection of this set of partitions we generate, by means of the *adaptive* distinguishing tree, the entire set of partitions associated with possible characterizing sequences. From this set we next select a subset which yields the necessary characterizing sequences.

As an example, consider machine M_6 whose state table is shown in Table 13-13. The partitions below are derived in a straightforward

Table 13-13   Machine M_6

PS	NS, z $x = 0$	$x = 1$
A	B, 1	C, 0
B	D, 0	B, 0
C	A, 0	D, 1
D	E, 1	D, 1
E	A, 0	B, 0

manner from the adaptive tree of Fig. 13-8.† (Note that many of these partitions cannot be generated by means of a preset tree.)

$\pi_1 = \{AD,BCE\}$ associated with the input symbol 0.
$\pi_2 = \{A,D,BCE\}$ associated with the (adaptive) set of input sequences $\{0,001\}$.
$\pi_3 = \{AD,B,CE\}$ associated with the input sequence 01.
$\pi_4 = \{A,B,CE,D\}$ associated with the (adaptive) set of input sequences $\{01,001\}$.
$\pi_5 = \{ABE,CD\}$ associated with the input symbol 1.
$\pi_6 = \{A,BE,CD\}$ associated with the input sequence 11.

From this set of partitions we must now choose a subset whose product is zero. The selection of such a subset, however, is not necessarily unique and there is no way of determining (except by actual con-

† In this adaptive tree, under each of the successor uncertainties, we kept records of the initial state that corresponds to each final state.

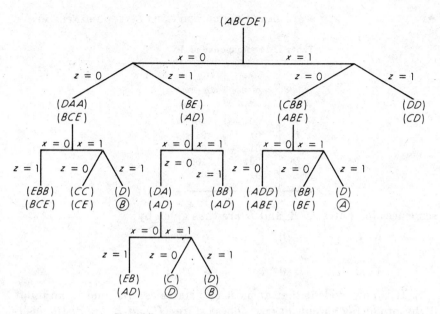

Fig. 13-8 Adaptive tree for machine M_6.

struction) which subset yields a minimal experiment. In general, a "good" selection of partitions is based on the following two criteria. First, *select a partition π that contains the largest number of single-state blocks* and thus yields the largest number of states whose identifying sequences are of first order. Second, *among the partitions satisfying the foregoing criterion, select one in which the number of repetitions of sequences of the type $XT(Q_i,S_i)$ is minimal.* Finally, select one or more partitions whose product with π is zero. If more than one selection of partitions that meet these criteria exists, select those partitions that are associated with shorter characterizing sequences. In most cases, such a selection will indeed result in nearly minimal checking experiments.

In our example, π_4 is clearly the only partition that leads to a set of identifying sequences such that three states, A, B, and D, are distinguishable by a first-order identifying sequence. Moreover, since the largest block in π_4 consists of just two states, C and E, the number of repetitions of the sequence $XT(Q_i,S_i)$ is minimal, i.e., 3. Of the two partitions, π_5 and π_6, whose product with π_4 is zero, π_5 is selected because it is associated with a shorter characterizing sequence, that is, 1. The selection of π_4 and π_5, where $\pi_4 \cdot \pi_5 = \pi(0)$, in effect determines the characterizing sequences for the states of M_6. This in turn determines the set of identifying sequences for M_6.

The response of machine M_6 to the (adaptive) input sequences associated with π_4 is summarized in Table 13-14. The identifying

Table 13-14 Response of M_6

State	Input sequence	Output sequence
A	001	101
B	01	01
C	01	00
D	001	100
E	01	00

sequences for states A, B, and D are thus given by:

$$A \quad \begin{matrix} 0 & 0 & 1 \\ 1 & 0 & 1 \end{matrix} \qquad B \quad \begin{matrix} 0 & 1 \\ 0 & 1 \end{matrix} \qquad D \quad \begin{matrix} 0 & 0 & 1 \\ 1 & 0 & 0 \end{matrix}$$

It is now evident that at most two states can respond to an input 01 by producing an output 00. These states, C and E, are distinguishable by the second characterizing sequence $X_2 = 1$ associated with π_5. We thus obtain the identifying sequences for states C and E as follows.

$$C \quad \begin{matrix} X_1 & X_2 \\ \left(\begin{matrix} 0 & 1 \\ 0 & 0 \end{matrix}\right)^3 & \begin{matrix} 1 \\ 1 \end{matrix} \end{matrix} \qquad E \quad \begin{matrix} X_1 & T(C,E) & X_2 \\ \left(\begin{matrix} 0 & 1 & 1 & 0 \\ 0 & 0 & 1 & 1 \end{matrix}\right)^3 & \begin{matrix} 1 \\ 0 \end{matrix} \end{matrix}$$

Having constructed the identifying sequences, the design of a checking experiment for machine M_6 is now straightforward. One such experiment is as follows.

	I_A															
	I_B		I_D				I_C								I_D	
X:	0	0	1	0	0	1	0	1	0	1	0	1	1	0	0	1
Z:	1	0	1	1	0	0	0	0	0	0	0	0	1	1	0	0
t:	1	2	3	4	5	6	7	8	9	10	11	12	13	14	15	16

	I_E													
	I_D				I_D								I_B	
X:	1	0	0	1	1	0	0	1	1	0	1	0	1
Z:	1	1	0	0	1	1	0	0	1	1	0	0	1
t:	17	18	19	20	21	22	23	24	25	26	27	28	29	30

$$I_A \qquad\qquad I_B \qquad\qquad I_D$$

```
X:  0  0  0  0  1  0  1  1  0  1  0  1  0  0  0  1
Z:  1  0  1  0  1  1  0  0  0  1  1  0  0  1  0  0
t:    31 32 33 34 35 36 37 38 39 40 41 42 43 44 45
```

The reader is encouraged to analyze this experiment and to verify that it indeed identifies uniquely machine M_6.

Machines characterized by three or more sequences

In the preceding example, the characterizing sequence X_1 was used to distinguish between the blocks of π_4, while X_2 was used to distinguish the states within the blocks. It may often occur that, while X_1 distinguishes the blocks of the partition, different sequences will be needed to distinguish the states in different blocks. For example, consider machine M_7 (Table 13-15) and the set of partitions below generated from its adaptive distinguishing tree. Clearly, there are no two partitions in this set whose product is zero. We must therefore search for a set of three or more partitions associated with an appropriate set of characterizing sequences.

Table 13-15 Machine M_7 and corresponding partitions

PS	NS, z x = 0	x = 1	
A	A, 0	B, 0	$\pi_1 = \{ABCDE,F\}$
B	A, 0	C, 0	$\pi_2 = \{ABDE,CF\}$
C	A, 0	D, 1	$\pi_3 = \{ABD,CF,E\}$
D	A, 0	E, 0	$\pi_4 = \{AD,BE,CF\}$
E	A, 0	F, 0	$\pi_5 = \{A,BE,CF,D\}$
F	A, 1	D, 1	

π_5 is chosen as the first partition because it contains two single-state blocks, and none of its blocks contains more than two states. States B and E can now be distinguished by the sequence associated with π_3, while states C and F are distinguishable by the sequence associated with π_1. Obviously, $\pi_1 \cdot \pi_3 \cdot \pi_5 = \pi(0)$. It is easy to verify from the distinguishing tree that π_5 is associated with the set of (adaptive) input sequences 1, 11, 110, 11_3 is associated with the sequence 10, and 11_1 is associated with the sequence 0. The identifying sequences derived from these characterizing sequences are summarized as follows:

$$A \quad \begin{matrix} 1 & 1 & 0 \\ 0 & 0 & 0 \end{matrix} \qquad\qquad D \quad \begin{matrix} 1 & 1 & 0 \\ 0 & 0 & 1 \end{matrix}$$

$$B \begin{pmatrix} 1 & 1 & 0 & 1 \\ 0 & 1 & 0 & 0 \end{pmatrix}^3 \quad \begin{matrix} 10 \\ 00 \end{matrix} \qquad E \begin{pmatrix} 1 & 1 & 1 \\ 0 & 1 & 0 \end{pmatrix}^3 \quad \begin{matrix} 10 \\ 01 \end{matrix}$$

$$C \begin{pmatrix} 1 & 0 & 1 & 1 \\ 1 & 0 & 0 & 0 \end{pmatrix}^3 \quad \begin{matrix} 0 \\ 0 \end{matrix} \qquad F \begin{pmatrix} 1 & 1 & 1 \\ 1 & 0 & 0 \end{pmatrix}^3 \quad \begin{matrix} 0 \\ 1 \end{matrix}$$

Higher-order identifying sequences

It is not always possible to distinguish all the states of an arbitrary machine by just two characterizing sequences. In such cases, higher-order identifying sequences are needed in order to distinguish some of the states of the machine. In general, *the states of every reduced n-state machine can always be distinguished by at most n − 1 characterizing sequences, where the length of each such sequence need never exceed n − 1 digits.* This follows immediately from the fact that any two given states in the reduced machine are distinguishable by an input sequence of length at most $n - 1$.

The design of experiments for machines whose states have identifying sequences of order k, where $k > 2$, is generally more complicated. First, the design of the kth order identifying sequences is more involved. Second, each transition to such a state must be checked k times to determine its response to each of the characterizing sequences. The order of identifying sequences is clearly dependent on the choice of partitions. Because at most $k - 1$ characterizing sequences are needed to distinguish k states, each of the states in a block containing k states can be distinguished by an identifying sequence whose order is at most k. Consequently, in order to reduce the order of identifying sequences, the selection of the first partition π must be such that it will contain as many single-state blocks as possible, and in addition each of its remaining blocks will contain as few states as possible.

Whenever a block in the partition π contains more than two states, higher-order identifying sequences may be needed to distinguish the states in such a block. Suppose we wish to design an identifying sequence for a state S_j contained in a k-state block. Let $X_1, X_2, \ldots, X_k$ be the characterizing sequences for the states in this block. Let Y_i designate the sequence $X_i T(R_i, S_j)$, which takes the machine from S_j to R_i

and back to S_j. Then, for the reasons outlined in the preceding sections, the sequence $Y_1^{k+1}Y_2$ can be used to display the response of S_j to X_1 and X_2 and finally to return the machine to state S_j. Extending the techniques used in constructing second-order identifying sequences to third-order sequences, it can be shown that the sequence

$$I_j = (Y_1^{k+1}Y_2)^{k+1}Y_1^{k+1}Y_3$$

is an identifying sequence of third order. In this case, the state of the machine prior to the last application of Y_2 must be identical to its state prior to one of the other applications of Y_2. But since this is the same state as the state prior to the application of Y_3, the above sequence displays the response of S_j to X_1, X_2, and X_3, and thus it is an identifying sequence of third order. Substituting the sequences represented by the Y's, we obtain

$$I_j = \{[X_1T(R_1,S_j)]^{k+1}X_2T(R_2,S_j)\}^{k+1}[X_1T(R_1,S_j)]^{k+1}X_3T(R_3,S_j)$$

The third-order identifying sequence $(Y_1^{k+1}Y_2)^{k+1}Y_1^{k+1}Y_3$ can be obtained from the second-order sequence $Y_1^{k+1}Y_2$ by repeating the latter sequence $n + 2$ times and substituting Y_3 for Y_2 in the last repetition. This same procedure can be followed again to obtain the fourth-order identifying sequence, namely,

$$I_j = [(Y_1^{k+1}Y_2)^{k+1}Y_1^{k+1}Y_3]^{k+1}(Y_1^{k+1}Y_2)^{k+1}Y_1^{k+1}Y_4$$

In a similar manner we can obtain higher-order identifying sequences.

APPENDIX 13-1 BOUNDS ON THE LENGTH OF SYNCHRONIZING SEQUENCES

Since the least upper bound on the length of a synchronizing sequence is unknown, we shall establish a range of values and show that the value of the least upper bound must be in that range.

Theorem 13-4 *If an n-state machine has a synchronizing sequence, or sequences, then it has one such sequence whose length is at most*

$$\frac{n(n + 1)(n - 1)}{6}$$

Proof: A necessary condition for a machine to have a synchronizing sequence is that, under at least one input I_k, the I_k-successors of some two states, S_i, S_j, will be identical. The synchronization of a machine whose initial state is unknown into some state S_c can be accomplished by applying I_k to the machine so that, if it is in either S_i or S_j, it will go to the common successor, then applying a sequence which transfers another pair of states, S_p, S_q, into S_i, S_j and again applying I_k to the machine to take it into the common successor, and so on. This process actually reduces the initial uncertainty $(S_1S_2S_3 \cdots S_n)$ to the singleton uncertainty (S_c).

Suppose now that $k - 1$ states have already been taken out of the uncertainty which presently consists of $n - k + 1$ states. We wish to determine an upper bound on the length of the sequence needed to reduce the uncertainty by another state, that is, to reduce it to $n - k$ states. Suppose also that S_u and S_v are the states that will now be taken by this sequence into a common successor. The present uncertainty U thus consists of S_u, S_v and the remaining $n - k - 1$ states. The length of the required sequence depends on the number of pairs of states through which S_uS_v pass before reaching the common successor. This number will be maximized if S_uS_v do not pass through any other pair of states contained in the remaining $n - k - 1$ states of the uncertainty. (Because in such a case we could use that pair of states to reduce the uncertainty.) For the same reason S_uS_v should not pass through any pair of states contained in the successors of these $n - k - 1$ states.

The length of the sequence to be determined will, thus, be maximized if all the uncertainty successors of U will contain the same $n - k - 1$ states and only S_uS_v will pass through various pairs of states. The successors of S_uS_v may be any pair of states not contained in these $n - k - 1$ states. Since there are

$$n - (n - k - 1) = k + 1$$

such states, there are $k(k + 1)/2$ pairs of possible successors to S_uS_v. Consequently, at most $k(k + 1)/2$ inputs (which is equal to $1 + 2 + 3 + \cdots + k$) are needed to take out the kth state from the uncertainty.

To reduce the initial uncertainty $(S_1S_2 \cdots S_n)$ to a singleton uncertainty, a sequence of length

$$1 + (1 + 2) + (1 + 2 + 3) + \cdots +$$
$$(1 + 2 + 3 + \cdots + n - 1) = \sum_{k=2}^{n} \frac{k(k - 1)}{2}$$

is needed. Since $k(k - 1)/2 = 0$ for $k = 1$, we can take the sum from 1 to n, i.e.,

$$\sum_{k=1}^{n} \frac{k(k-1)}{2} = \frac{1}{2} \sum_{k=1}^{n} k^2 - \frac{1}{2} \sum_{k=1}^{n} k$$

$$= \frac{1}{2} \left[\frac{n(n+1)(2n+1)}{6} - \frac{3n(n+1)}{6} \right]$$

$$= \frac{n(n+1)(n-1)}{6} \quad \blacksquare$$

Theorem 13-4 thus establishes an upper bound on the length of synchronizing sequences, which is lower by a constant factor from the bound shown in Sec. 13-2.

Theorem 13-5 *For every n, there exists an n-state machine which has a synchronizing sequence of length $(n-1)^2$.*

Proof: A machine that satisfies the theorem is given in Table 13-16. The proof that the shortest synchronizing sequence for this machine is of the form

$$0(1^{n-1}0)^{n-2}$$

is left to the reader as a (nontrivial) exercise. Note that the proof must consist of two parts: first, to prove that the above is indeed a synchronizing sequence, and second to show that it is the shortest synchronizing sequence.

Table 13-16 A machine having a synchronizing sequence of length $(n-1)^2$

PS	NS $x = 0$	$x = 1$
S_1	S_1	S_n
S_2	S_1	S_1
S_3	S_3	S_2
.	.	.
.	.	.
.	.	.
S_k	S_k	S_{k-1}
.	.	.
.	.	.
.	.	.
S_{n-1}	S_{n-1}	S_{n-2}
S_n	S_n	S_{n-1}

The length of the subsequence within the parentheses is n, since it consists of $n - 1$ 1's followed by a 0. There are $n - 2$ such subsequences, preceded by a single 0. Hence, the total length is

$$1 + (n - 2)n = n^2 - 2n + 1 = (n - 1)^2 \quad \blacksquare$$

Example A machine that illustrates Theorem 13-5 for $n = 5$ is shown in Fig. 13-9a. The corresponding path in the synchronizing tree which leads to the singleton uncertainty is given in Fig. 13-9b.

Combining the results in Theorems 13-4 and 13-5 we obtain the following corollary. $\blacksquare$

PS	NS	
	$x = 0$	$x = 1$
S_1	S_1	S_5
S_2	S_1	S_1
S_3	S_3	S_2
S_4	S_4	S_3
S_5	S_5	S_4

$(S_1 S_2 S_3 S_4 S_5)$
$\downarrow 0$
$(S_1 S_3 S_4 S_5)$
$\downarrow 1$
$(S_2 S_3 S_4 S_5)$
$\downarrow 1$
$(S_1 S_2 S_3 S_4)$
$\downarrow 1$
$(S_1 S_2 S_3 S_5)$
$\downarrow 1$
$(S_1 S_2 S_4 S_5)$
$\downarrow 0$
$(S_1 S_4 S_5)$
$\downarrow 1$
$(S_3 S_4 S_5)$
$\downarrow 1$
$(S_2 S_3 S_4)$
$\downarrow 1$
$(S_1 S_2 S_3)$
$\downarrow 1$
$(S_1 S_2 S_5)$
$\downarrow 0$
$(S_1 S_5)$
$\downarrow 1$
$(S_4 S_5)$
$\downarrow 1$
$(S_3 S_4)$
$\downarrow 1$
$(S_2 S_3)$
$\downarrow 1$
$(S_1 S_2)$
$\downarrow 0$
(S_1)

(a) Machine M_8.

(b) Shortest synchronizing sequence for machine M_8.

Fig. 13-9 Demonstrating Theorem 13-5 for $n = 5$.

Corollary 13-1 The least upper bound L on the length of synchronizing sequences is bounded by

$$(n - 1)^2 \leq L \leq \frac{n(n + 1)(n - 1)}{6} \quad \blacksquare$$

APPENDIX 13-2 A BOUND ON THE LENGTH OF DISTINGUISHING SEQUENCES

In the following we prove that the length of the distinguishing tree is bounded and consequently the construction of such a tree is a finite process.

Theorem 13-6 *If a preset distinguishing sequence for an n-state machine M exists, then its length is at most* $(n - 1)n^n$.

Proof: Let the uncertainty vector at some level in the distinguishing tree consist of m components whose sizes are $k_1, k_2, \ldots, k_m$. Clearly, the sum of the sizes of all the components must be equal to n; that is, $k_1 + k_2 + \cdots + k_m = n$. Let the numbers $k_1, k_2, \ldots, k_m$ be subsets in a partition μ, such that $\mu = \{k_1, k_2, \ldots, k_m\}$. Clearly, μ defines the *size distribution* of the components in the uncertainty vector. The number of different uncertainty vectors having the same size distribution μ is equal to $n^{k_1} n^{k_2} \cdots n^{k_m} = n^n$.

Consider now a path in the tree leading from the initial uncertainty vector to a trivial uncertainty vector. Let U_1 and U_2 be uncertainty vectors along this path, with corresponding partitions μ_1 and μ_2. Clearly, if U_2 is a successor of U_1, then the size distribution of U_2 is either equal to that of U_1 or is a refinement of that of U_1; i.e., $\mu_1 \geq \mu_2$. And since the initial uncertainty vector contains n states, there are at most $n - 1$ possible refinements of partitions along the path leading to the distinguishing sequence. Accordingly, the length of this path is $L \leq (n - 1)n^n$. $\blacksquare$

The above bound is not necessarily the least upper bound.

NOTES AND REFERENCES

The study of machine behavior from terminal experiments was first introduced by Moore [9], in 1956. He established the notions of homing, synchronizing, and distinguishing experiments and derived bounds on their lengths. Moore's ideas have been further developed by Gill [1], who simplified the search for the homing and distinguishing sequences; Ginsburg [2], Hibbard [4], and Kohavi and Winograd [8]. The material on fault-detection experiments is taken from Hennie [3], Kohavi and Lavallee [6], Kohavi and Kohavi [5], and Kohavi, Rivierre, and Kohavi [7].

1. Gill, A.: State-identification Experiments in Finite Automata, *Information and Control*, vol. 4, pp. 132–154, 1961.
2. Ginsburg, S.: On the Length of the Smallest Uniform Experiment Which Distinguishes the Terminal States of a Machine, *J. Assoc. Computing Machinery*, vol. 5, pp. 266–280, July, 1958.
3. Hennie, F. C.: Fault Detecting Experiments for Sequential Circuits, *Proc. Fifth Ann. Symp. Switching Circuit Theory and Logical Design*, pp. 95–110, Princeton, N.J., November, 1964.
4. Hibbard, T. N.: Least Upper Bounds on Minimal Terminal State Experiments for Two Classes of Sequential Machines, *J. Assoc. Computing Machinery*, vol. 8, pp. 601–612, October, 1961.
5. Kohavi, I., and Z. Kohavi: Variable-length Distinguishing Sequences and Their Application to the Design of Fault-detection Experiments, *IEEE Trans. Computers*, vol. C-17, pp. 792–795, August, 1968.
6. Kohavi, Z., and P. Lavallee: Design of Sequential Machines with Fault-detection Capabilities, *IEEE Trans. Electron. Computers*, vol. EC-16, pp. 473–484, August, 1967.
7. Kohavi, Z., J. A. Rivierre, and I. Kohavi: Checking Experiments for Sequential Machines, *Information Sciences*, vol. 7, no. 1, pp. 11–28, January, 1974.
8. Kohavi, Z., J. Winograd: Establishing Bounds Concerning Finite Automata, *Journal of Computer and System Sciences*, vol. 7, no. 3, pp. 288–299, June, 1973.
9. Moore, E. F.: "Gedanken-experiments on Sequential Machines," pp. 129–153, Automata Studies, Annals of Mathematics Studies, no. 34, Princeton University Press, Princeton, N.J., 1956.

PROBLEMS

13-1. For each of the machines shown in Table P13-1:

(a) Find the shortest homing sequences.

(b) Determine whether or not synchronizing sequences exist, and if any do exist, find the shortest ones.

Table P13-1

PS	NS, z	
	$x = 0$	$x = 1$
A	A,1	E,0
B	A,0	C,0
C	B,0	D,1
D	C,1	C,0
E	C,0	D,0

M_1

PS	NS, z	
	$x = 0$	$x = 1$
A	B,0	A,0
B	B,1	C,1
C	A,1	D,0
D	C,0	A,1

M_2

PS	NS, z	
	$x = 0$	$x = 1$
A	C,0	D,1
B	C,0	A,1
C	A,1	B,0
D	B,0	C,1

M_3

13-2. It is necessary to synchronize the machine of Table P13-2 to state A with a minimum number of input symbols. Devise such a procedure, which may be adaptive.

Table P13-2

PS	NS, z x = 0	x = 1
A	C,1	E,1
B	A,0	D,1
C	E,0	D,1
D	F,1	A,1
E	B,1	F,0
F	B,1	C,1

13-3. You are presented with a machine that is known to be described by one of the two state tables shown in Table P13-3. No information is available regarding the initial state of the machine. Devise a procedure for identifying the machine, and find all minimal *preset* experiments which can perform this task.

Hint: Construct a machine which is the *direct sum* of the two machines.

Table P13-3

PS	NS, z x = 0	x = 1
A	A,0	B,0
B	C,0	A,0
C	A,1	B,0

PS	NS, z x = 0	x = 1
D	E,0	F,1
E	F,0	D,0
F	E,0	F,0

13-4. Find the shortest homing sequence for the machine shown in Table P13-4. (Note that this machine is a special case, $n = 4$, of the machine of Fig. P13-5.)

Table P13-4

PS	NS, z I_1	I_2	I_3
S_1	$S_1,0$	$S_1,0$	$S_1,0$
S_2	$S_3,0$	$S_2,0$	$S_2,0$
S_3	$S_2,0$	$S_4,0$	$S_3,0$
S_4	$S_4,0$	$S_3,0$	$S_4,1$

13-5. It can be shown that every n-state machine has a *preset* homing sequence whose length does not exceed $(n-1)n/2$. By referring to Fig. P13-5, prove that this bound cannot be lowered; that is, there exists a class of machines the length of whose homing sequences is precisely $(n-1)n/2$.

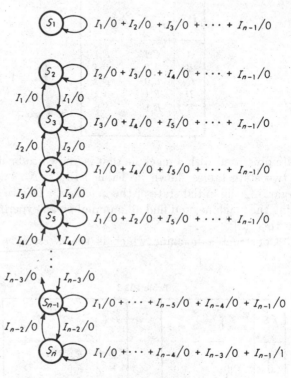

Fig. P13-5

13-6. (*a*) Find a single sequence of 0's and 1's which can serve as a homing sequence for all reduced and strongly connected three-state machines whose input symbols are 0 and 1.

(*b*) Can you generalize the result of part *a* to n-state machines? Show a bound on the length of such sequences.

13-7. Prove that, in a reduced n-state machine, every set of $n-k$ states $(n-2 \geq k \geq 0)$ contains at least one pair of states which is distinguishable by an experiment of length $k+1$.

13-8. Prove that every n-state machine has an *adaptive* homing sequence whose length is at most $(n-1)n/2$.

　　Hint: Use the result of Prob. 13-7.

13-9. Construct a minimal adaptive homing-experiment for the machine shown in Table P13-2.

Hint: Construct an *adaptive* homing tree analogous to the tree shown in Fig. 13-4.

13-10. It is necessary to determine the final state of the machine shown in Table P13-10 when the initial state is unknown and only output sequences from the machine are available to the experimenter; that is, no information regarding the input to the machine is available.

(a) Devise a procedure to determine whether a specific output sequence can be used to identify the final state of the machine.

(b) Find the reduced standard-form state table that accepts precisely those output sequences which can be used to identify the final state of the machine. Use state names A, B, etc.

Table P13-10

PS	NS, z $x = 0$	$x = 1$
A	B,0	C,0
B	A,0	D,1
C	D,1	B,0
D	A,1	D,1

13-11. For each of the machines shown in Table P13-11 determine whether or not preset distinguishing sequences exist, and if any do exist, find the shortest ones.

Table P13-11

PS	NS, z $x = 0$	$x = 1$
A	C,1	A,0
B	D,0	D,0
C	A,0	D,0
D	B,0	C,0

M_1

PS	NS, z $x = 0$	$x = 1$
A	D,0	C,1
B	A,0	B,1
C	E,0	B,1
D	B,0	D,1
E	C,1	E,1

M_2

PS	NS, z $x = 0$	$x = 1$
A	A,0	E,1
B	E,1	A,0
C	F,1	B,0
D	B,0	F,1
E	C,1	G,0
F	G,0	C,1
G	H,0	D,1
H	D,1	H,0

M_3

13-12. (a) Find a preset distinguishing experiment that determines the initial state of the machine shown in Table P13-12, given that it cannot be initially in state E.

(b) Can you identify the initial state when the initial uncertainty is $(ABCDE)$?

Table P13-12

PS	NS, z	
	$x = 0$	$x = 1$
A	B,1	A,1
B	E,0	A,1
C	A,0	E,1
D	C,1	D,1
E	E,0	D,1

13-13. (a) For each of the machines shown in Table P13-13 devise a preset or an adaptive experiment which identifies the initial state.

·(b) Find a five-state machine which has no preset distinguishing sequence but has an adaptive one.

Table P13-13

PS	NS, z		PS	NS, z	
	$x = 0$	$x = 1$		$x = 0$	$x = 1$
A	B,1	C,1	A	B,0	E,0
B	C,0	D,1	B	E,1	B;0
C	D,1	E,0	C	D,1	A,1
D	A,0	F,0	D	B,0	C,0
E	A,0	A,0	E	E,0	D,1
F	A,0	B,0			

M_1 M_2

13-14. Specify the entries marked * in the machine of Table P13-14 so that it will be strongly connected and the sequences 000 and 111 will be distinguishing sequences.

Table P13-14

PS	NS, z	
	$x = 0$	$x = 1$
A	*,0	*,0
B	C,0	D,0
C	A,0	B,0
D	D,1	A,1

13-15. Prove that the length L of the minimal distinguishing sequence for a machine with n states and q output symbols is bounded by

$$L \geq \frac{\log_2 n}{\log_2 q}$$

13-16. Let M be a reduced n-state machine with input alphabet $I = \{I_1, I_2, \ldots, I_p\}$.

(a) Prove that if, for every input I_i in M, there exists a pair of states whose successors are identical, while producing the same output in response to I_i, then M does not have any distinguishing sequence.

(b) Prove that if, for no input I_i in M, there exists such a pair of states, then M has a preset distinguishing sequence whose length is at most $n(n - 1)/2$.

13-17. Recall that experiments that require several copies of the same machine are called *multiple experiments*. Suppose that two copies of the machine shown in Table P13-17 are available and that each of them is in the same unknown initial state.

(a) Design an adaptive experiment to distinguish their initial state.

(b) Repeat (a) if the output associated with the 1-successor of state D in Table P13-17 is 0 instead of 1.

Hint: You may apply different input symbols to each copy.

Table P13-17

PS	NS, z $x = 0$	$x = 1$
A	$B,0$	$D,0$
B	$C,1$	$D,0$
C	$B,0$	$A,1$
D	$D,1$	$C,1$

13-18. (a) Show that every machine of the form in Fig. P14-18 has a synchronizing sequence. Find such a sequence and specify its length.

(b) Does every machine of this form have also a distinguishing sequence? Prove that it does or show a counter example.

(c) Can every finite-state machine be realized in this form?

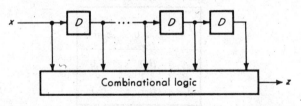

Fig. P13-18

13-19. The response of the machine shown in Table P13-19 to an unknown input sequence is given to the experimenter. Devise a procedure that the experimenter may use in order to identify the initial state. What are the minimum-length sequences that will make such an identification possible?

Table P13-19

PS	NS, z	
	$x = 0$	$x = 1$
A	A,0	B,0
B	C,0	D,0
C	D,1	C,1
D	B,1	A,1

13-20. The machine shown in Table P13-20 is initially provided with an input sequence 01 to which it responds by producing an output sequence 10. It is next provided with the sequence 1010101010010011010001. Assuming that no malfunction increases the number of states, show that this sequence is a fault-detection experiment for this machine, and find the correct output sequence.

Table P13-20

PS	NS, z	
	$x = 0$	$x = 1$
A	A,1	B,0
B	C,0	A,0
C	B,0	C,1

13-21. The initial state of the machine of Table P13-21 is unknown, as is the entry in row *B*, column 1, of the state table. Design an adaptive experiment that can be used to determine the unknown entry. (Six input symbols should be sufficient for such an experiment.)

Table P13-21

PS	NS, z	
	$x = 0$	$x = 1$
A	B,0	C,0
B	A,1	*
C	B,1	C,1

13-22. The initial state of the machine shown in Table P13-22 is A, but its entry in row D, column 1, is unknown. An input sequence 0110 has been applied to the machine, which produces an output sequence whose last two symbols are 00. Following this sequence, a sequence 101 has been applied to the machine, which in turn produces an output sequence whose last symbol is a 0. Determine the missing entry.

Table P13-22

PS	NS, z	
	$x = 0$	$x = 1$
A	$B,0$	$C,1$
B	$A,1$	$D,1$
C	$C,0$	$A,1$
D	$E,1$	*
E	$A,0$	$E,0$

13-23. The input sequence X shown below has been applied to a reduced five-state machine whose state table is to be determined. In response the machine produced the output sequence Z. Show the state table of the machine in standard form if it is known that its starting state is A.

X: 0 0 0 0 1 0 1 0 1 0 1 0 0 1 0 1 0 0 0 1 0 0 1 0

Z: 0 1 2 0 1 3 2 1 1 0 1 3 3 2 0 1 3 3 3 2 1 2 1 1

13-24. Construct a fault-detection experiment for the machine of Table P13-24 that is *entirely preset*, that is, with no initial adaptive part. (Such an experiment need not require more than 24 symbols.)

Table P13-24

PS	NS, z	
	$x = 0$	$x = 1$
A	$D,0$	$C,0$
B	$C,0$	$D,0$
C	$A,0$	$B,0$
D	$D,1$	$A,1$

13-25. The following experiment has been proposed as a fault-detection experiment for the machine shown in Table P13-25, when started in state A and under the assumption that the number of states will not increase as a result of a malfunction.   Either prove that it is a proper fault-detection experiment, i.e., it identifies uniquely the machine, or show by means of a counter example that it is not such an experiment.

Input:	0	0	1	0	0	1	0	1	0	1	1	0	0	0	1	0	0
Output:	2	2	2	0	1	0	2	2	0	0	2	1	2	1	1	2	2

Table P13-25

PS	NS, z	
	$x = 0$	$x = 1$
A	A,2	B,2
B	C,0	A,1
C	D,1	E,0
D	E,2	A,0
E	B,1	C,2

13-26. A four-state machine received the input sequence X, shown below, and in response produced the output sequence Z.

    (a) What are the distinguishing sequences for the machine?

    (b) Assuming the machine starts in state A, do the sequences below correspond to a unique machine?   If yes, show its state table; if not, show all possible state tables.

X:	0	0	0	0	0	1	0	1	0	1	0	0	0	0	0	1	0	1
Z:	0	0	1	1	0	0	1	1	1	0	0	1	1	0	0	1	1	0

13-27. By referring to the machine in Table P13-27, where $[g]$ is the largest integer not exceeding g, prove that the bound established in Sec. 13-6 for definite diagnosability is the least upper bound.   That is, prove that for every n there exists an n-state machine, as given by Table P13-27, which is definitely diagnosable of order $\mu = n(n - 1)/2$.

Table P13-27

PS	I_1	I_2	I_3
1	2,0	3,0	2,0
2	3,0	4,0	3,0
3	4,0	5,0	4,0
.	.	.	.
.	.	.	.
.	.	.	.
i	$i+1,0$	$i+2,0$	$i+1,0$
.	.	.	.
.	.	.	.
$\left[\dfrac{n}{2}\right]-1$	$\left[\dfrac{n}{2}\right],0$	$\left[\dfrac{n}{2}\right]+1,0$	$\left[\dfrac{n}{2}\right],0$
$\left[\dfrac{n}{2}\right]$	$\left[\dfrac{n}{2}\right]+1,0$	$\left[\dfrac{n}{2}\right]+2,1$	$\left[\dfrac{n}{2}\right]+1,1$
.	.	.	.
.	.	.	.
j	$j+1,0$	$j+2,1$	$j+1,1$
.	.	.	.
.	.	.	.
$n-2$	$n-1,0$	$n,1$	$n-1,1$
$n-1$	$n,0$	$1,1$	$n,0$
n	$1,1$	$1,0$	$n,1$

13-28. The following problem demonstrates that *preset* fault-detection experiments can be constructed for machines having only *adaptive* distinguishing sequences. Construct a *preset* fault-detection experiment for machine M_2 of Table P13-13. Assume that the machine has been homed into state B and that no malfunction will increase the number of its states. (Forty-four symbols are sufficient.)

13-29. (*a*) Show the testing table and graph for the machine given in Table P13-29.

(*b*) Add to the machine one output terminal so that the sequence 11 will be a distinguishing sequence.

(*c*) Design a fault-detection experiment for the augmented machine. (Twenty-four symbols are sufficient.)

Table P13-29

PS	NS, z	
	$x = 0$	$x = 1$
A	A,0	B,0
B	A,0	C,0
C	A,0	D,0
D	A,1	A,0

13-30. An unknown three-state machine with two input symbols 0 and 1 is provided with the input sequence X, and it responds by producing the output sequence Z, as shown below:

X: 1 1 0 0 1 0 1 0 1 1 1 1 1 0 0 0 1 1 0 0 1 0 1

Y: 1 0 0 0 0 0 0 0 0 1 0 1 0 0 0 0 0 1 1 1 0 0 0

Show that this experiment is sufficient to identify the machine uniquely (up to isomorphism).

14
Memory, Definiteness, and Information Losslessness of Finite Automata

An important characteristic of a finite-state machine is that it has a "memory"; i.e., the behavior of the machine is dependent upon its past history. While the behavior of some machines depends on remote history, the behavior of others depends only on more recent events. The amount of past input and output information needed in order to determine the machine's future behavior is called the *memory span* of the machine.

If the initial state of a deterministic, completely specified machine and the input sequence to it are known, the corresponding final state and output sequence can be determined uniquely. However, there are special situations in which either the initial state is unknown or some past input symbols are unknown. In such situations the behavior of the machines cannot always be predicted in advance. In this chapter we shall try to answer the following questions: For a given machine, what is the minimum amount of past input-output information required in order to render its future behavior completely predictable? Under what conditions can the input to the machine be reconstructed from its output? Finally, we shall investigate some aspects of the relationship between finite-state machines and coding theory.

14-1 MEMORY SPAN WITH RESPECT TO INPUT-OUTPUT SEQUENCES (FINITE-MEMORY MACHINES)

A finite-state machine M is defined as a *finite-memory machine* of *order* μ if μ is the least integer, so that the present state of M can be determined uniquely from the knowledge of the last μ inputs and the corresponding μ outputs. In other words, a machine is finite memory of order μ if and only if every input sequence of length μ is a homing sequence. Consequently, the homing tree can serve as a possible tool for detection and recognition of a finite memory for M. In this section, however, we shall derive a different test, which will be shown to be valid for all memory aspects of automata.

The testing table and testing graph†

Consider machine M_1, whose state table is shown in Table 14-1. We may rewrite that state table as shown in the upper half of Table 14-2. The column headings of Table 14-2 consist of all input-output combinations, and the entries of the upper half of the table are the next-state entries corresponding to these combinations. For example, the 1-successor of state C is B, and the corresponding output is $z = 1$. Consequently, a B is entered in row C, column 1/1, of the table, and a dash (—) is entered in row C, column 1/0. In a similar manner the entire upper half of Table 14-2 is completed.

The row headings in the lower half of the table are all unordered pairs of states, while the table entries are the corresponding successors. If the entries in rows S_i and S_j, column I_k/O_l, of the upper half are S_p and S_q, respectively, then the entry in row S_iS_j, column I_k/O_l, of the lower half is S_pS_q. For example, the entries in rows A and C, column 1/1, are C and B, respectively. Consequently, the entry in row AC, column 1/1, is BC. If for some pair of states S_i and S_j, either one or both corresponding entries in some column I_k/O_l are dashes, the entry in row S_iS_j, column I_k/O_l, is a dash. For example, the entry in row AB, column 1/0, is a dash, since the entry in row A, column 1/0, is a dash, and so on. The table so completed is called a *testing table for finite memory*, or simply, a *testing table*.

We shall refer to a pair of states (S_iS_j) as an *uncertainty pair*, and to its successor (S_pS_q) as the *implied pair*. Thus, for example, the pair (AC) is implied by (BD).

Let us now define a directed graph G, which will be called a *testing graph (for finite memory)*, in the following way:

---

† The testing table and graph are similar to those presented in Sec. 13-6, but are redefined here for completeness of the presentation.

Table 14-1 Machine M_1

PS	NS, z	
	$x = 0$	$x = 1$
A	B,0	C,1
B	D,0	C,0
C	D,0	B,1
D	C,0	A,0

Table 14-2 Testing table for machine M_1

PS	0/0	0/1	1/1	1/0
A	B	—	C	—
B	D	—	—	C
C	D	—	B	—
D	C	—	—	A
AB	BD	—	—	—
AC	BD	—	BC	—
AD	BC	—	—	—
BC	DD	—	—	—
BD	CD	—	—	AC
CD	CD	—	—	—

1. Corresponding to each row in the lower half of the testing table there is a vertex in G. The vertex label is the same as the row heading.
2. An arc is drawn leading from the vertex labeled S_iS_j to the vertex labeled S_pS_q, where $p \neq q$, if and only if there exists an entry S_pS_q in row S_iS_j, column I_k/O_l, of the testing table. The arc is labeled I_k/O_l. No arc is needed if S_iS_j implies S_pS_p, e.g., DD in row BC.

The testing graph G_1 for machine M_1 is derived directly from the lower half of the testing table and is shown in Fig. 14-1.

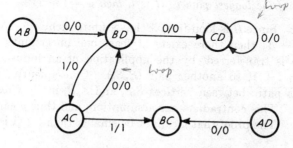

Fig. 14-1 Testing graph for machine M_1.

Conditions for finite memory

Let the initial uncertainty regarding the state of machine M be $(S_1S_2 \cdots S_n)$. M is finite memory of order μ if the application of any input sequence of length μ transfers the machine into an identifiable state, and if there exists an input sequence of length $\mu - 1$ which, together with the corresponding output sequence, does not provide enough information for a unique identification of the final state.

Theorem 14-1 *A sequential machine M has a finite memory if and only if its testing graph G is loop-free.*

Proof: Assume that G is not loop-free. Then, by repeatedly applying the symbols coinciding with the labels of the arcs in the loop, we find an arbitrarily long input sequence that cannot resolve the uncertainty regarding the final state, and thus the machine is not finite memory. To prove sufficiency, assume that G is loop-free. If M is not finite memory, there exists an arbitrarily long path in G, corresponding to some input sequence X and some pair of states $(S_i S_j)$, so that S_i and S_j cannot be distinguished by X. But since the number of vertices in G cannot exceed $(n-1)n/2$ (corresponding to the number of distinct pairs of states), arbitrarily long paths in G are possible only if it contains a loop. Thus the theorem is proved. ∎

Example From the testing graph of M_1 (Fig. 14-1) it is evident that, since G_1 contains two loops, M_1 is not finite memory. An arbitrarily long string of 0 inputs will never resolve the uncertainty (CD); and similarly, if the initial uncertainty is (AC), the input sequence $0101 \cdots 01$ will transfer the machine to (BD), (AC), (BD), $\cdots$, and so on. ∎

Corollary *Let G be a loop-free testing graph for machine M. If the length of the longest path in G is l, then $\mu = l + 1$.*

Proof: Since G is loop-free, M has a finite memory. Assume that $\mu > l + 1$; then there exists at least one uncertainty pair $(S_i S_j)$ which is transferred, by the application of an input sequence of length $l + 1$, to another pair $(S_p S_q)$. Consequently, there must exist a path, between vertices $S_i S_j$ and $S_p S_q$ in G, whose length is $l + 1$. This contradicts our assumption, and thus μ cannot exceed $l + 1$. The proof that μ cannot be smaller than $l + 1$ is trivial. ∎

From the preceding results it is evident that *if a machine is finite memory of order μ, then $\mu \le (n-1)n/2$.*

A machine for which $\mu = (n-1)n/2$

Machine M_2, shown in Table 14-3, illustrates the case where the bound of μ is achieved. The corresponding testing table and graph are given in Table 14-4 and Fig. 14-2, respectively.

Table 14-3	Machine M_2	
PS	NS, z	
	$x = 0$	$x = 1$
A	B,0	D,0
B	C,0	C,0
C	D,0	A,0
D	D,0	A,1

Table 14-4   Testing table for M_2

PS	0/0	0/1	1/1	1/0
A	B	—	—	D
B	C	—	—	C
C	D	—	—	A
D	D	—	A	—
AB	BC	—	—	CD
AC	BD	—	—	AD
AD	BD	—	—	—
BC	CD	—	—	AC
BD	CD	—	—	—
CD	DD	—	—	—

Clearly, the testing graph of M_2 is loop-free, and its maximal path, emanating from AB and terminating at CD, is of length 5.   Hence $\mu = 6$. In general, it can be shown (see Prob. 14-3) that there exists a class of machines for which $\mu = (n - 1)n/2$, and therefore the bound of μ is the least upper bound and cannot be improved.

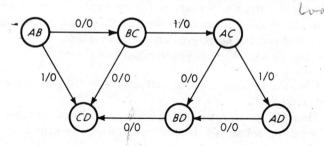

Loop ?

Fig. 14-2   Testing graph for machine M_2.

★An algorithm to determine whether a graph is loop-free

When the number of vertices in the testing graph G is large, it is desirable to have a more systematic algorithm to determine if it is loop-free, and if it is, the length of the longest path l.   We present here one such algorithm which does not require the actual drawing of the graph and can be easily executed by a computer.

Let G be a directed graph with p vertices.   Define the *connection matrix* of G to be a $p \times p$ matrix, whose (i,j)th entry is 1 if there is an arc emanating from vertex i and terminating at vertex j, and is 0 otherwise.   The labels associated with the rows and columns of the matrix are the same as the labels of the vertices of G.   The labels associated with corresponding rows and columns are identical; i.e., the ith row and the ith column have the same label.

The procedure for determining whether a graph is loop-free can be illustrated by means of machine M_2. The connection matrix of M_2 is derived directly from the testing table and is as follows:

$$
\begin{array}{c}
(AB) \\
(AC) \\
(AD) \\
(BC) \\
(BD) \\
(CD)
\end{array}
\begin{bmatrix}
0 & 0 & 0 & 1 & 0 & 1 \\
0 & 0 & 1 & 0 & 1 & 0 \\
0 & 0 & 0 & 0 & 1 & 0 \\
0 & 1 & 0 & 0 & 0 & 1 \\
0 & 0 & 0 & 0 & 0 & 1 \\
0 & 0 & 0 & 0 & 0 & 0
\end{bmatrix}
$$

Two arcs emanate from vertex AB: to BC and to CD. Therefore the entries in row AB, columns BC and CD, are 1, and so on.

If a directed graph G is loop-free, then it has one or more terminal vertices.† Furthermore, the subgraph, resulting from the removal of a terminal vertex and all arcs leading to it, is also loop-free. This can be proved by observing that if G has no terminal vertex, we can construct arbitrarily long paths in G. But since G is finite, this means that G has a loop. In the matrix representation, the removal of a vertex and all arcs leading to and from it is accomplished by the deletion from the matrix of the row and column corresponding to this vertex.

The testing algorithm is summarized as follows:

1. Given a testing table, construct the corresponding connection matrix.
2. Delete all those rows having 0's in all positions and remove corresponding columns. If there are none, go to step 4.
3. Repeat step 2.
4. If the matrix has not completely vanished, then G is not loop-free. If the matrix has vanished, G is loop-free. (By "vanished" we mean that the resulting matrix contains no rows or columns.)

Returning to the connection matrix of M_2, the first application of step 2 results in the removal of row (CD) and its corresponding column. The resulting matrix is

$$
\begin{array}{c}
(AB) \\
(AC) \\
(AD) \\
(BC) \\
(BD)
\end{array}
\begin{bmatrix}
0 & 0 & 0 & 1 & 0 \\
0 & 0 & 1 & 0 & 1 \\
0 & 0 & 0 & 0 & 1 \\
0 & 1 & 0 & 0 & 0 \\
0 & 0 & 0 & 0 & 0
\end{bmatrix}
$$

† A vertex from which no arcs emanate is called a *terminal vertex*.

Repeated applications of step 2 result in the removal of rows (BD), (AD), (AC), and so on.

$$
\begin{array}{c}
(AB) \\
(AC) \\
(AD) \\
(BC)
\end{array}
\begin{bmatrix}
0 & 0 & 0 & 1 \\
0 & 0 & 1 & 0 \\
0 & 0 & 0 & 0 \\
0 & 1 & 0 & 0
\end{bmatrix}
\quad
\begin{array}{c}
(AB) \\
(AC) \\
(BC)
\end{array}
\begin{bmatrix}
0 & 0 & 1 \\
0 & 0 & 0 \\
0 & 1 & 0
\end{bmatrix}
\quad
\begin{array}{c}
(AB) \\
(BC)
\end{array}
\begin{bmatrix}
0 & 1 \\
0 & 0
\end{bmatrix}
\quad
(AB) \quad [0]
$$

Clearly, on the next step the matrix vanishes.

We observe that at each application of step 2 we remove the terminal vertices and all arcs leading to them. Consider the terminal vertices at the end of the longest paths whose length is l. It takes $l + 1$ applications of step 2 to remove all the vertices in these paths and to eliminate the matrix. Consequently, *the number of times that step 2 is applied is equal to the order μ of the memory.* In the preceding example step 2 was applied six times; consequently M_2 is finite memory of order $\mu = 6$, as is already known. Note that, if at some time the matrix contains two (or more) rows consisting of 0's in all their positions, all these rows and their corresponding columns must be deleted simultaneously, and this step counts as a single application of step 2.

14-2 MEMORY SPAN WITH RESPECT TO INPUT SEQUENCES (DEFINITE MACHINES)

A sequential machine M is called a *definite machine of order μ* if μ is the least integer, so that the present state of M can be determined uniquely from the knowledge of the last μ inputs to M. A definite machine is thus said to have a finite input memory. On the other hand, for a nondefinite machine there always exists at least one input sequence of arbitrary length, which does not provide enough information to identify the state of the machine. A definite machine of order μ is often called a *μ-definite machine.* Clearly, if a machine is μ-definite, it is also finite memory of order equal to or smaller than μ.

The knowledge of any μ past input values is always sufficient to completely specify the present state of a μ-definite machine. Therefore any μ-definite machine can be realized as a cascade connection of μ delay elements, which store the last μ input values, and a combinational circuit which generates the specified output. This realization, which is often referred to as the *canonical realization of a definite machine,* is shown in Fig. 14-3.

Properties of definite machines

We shall now study some of the properties of definite machines, from which we shall derive tests for definiteness. The first obvious property

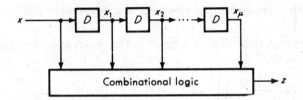

Fig. 14-3 Canonical realization of a μ-definite machine.

is that a machine is definite of order μ if and only if every sequence of length μ is a synchronizing sequence. This property can be detected by means of the synchronizing tree presented in Sec. 13-2. The tree is terminated whenever any of the following occur:

1. An uncertainty in the kth level is also associated with some node in a preceding level;
2. All nodes of the kth level are associated with singleton uncertainties, i.e., uncertainties which consist of only a single state each.

Clearly, if the tree terminates by virtue of rule 1, the corresponding machine is not definite. On the other hand, if the tree terminates by virtue of rule 2, the corresponding machine is definite, since it means that every input sequence (i.e., path in the tree) leads to a unique final state. Furthermore, the length of the path determines the order of definiteness; that is, if the tree is terminated in level k and rule 2 is satisfied, then the corresponding machine is k-definite. Note that if some node is associated with a singleton uncertainty, that node may become terminal, but the successors of other nodes must be determined. The order of the definiteness is determined by the length of the longest path.

Example Consider machine M_3, whose state table is given in Table 14-5. The output entries have been omitted, since only the inputs to the machine play a role in the determination of definiteness. The synchronizing tree for machine M_3 is shown in Fig. 14-4. Its length is $k = 3$, and consequently M_3 is definite of order 3. ■

Table 14-5   Machine M_3

PS	NS	
	$x = 0$	$x = 1$
A	A	B
B	C	B
C	A	D
D	C	B

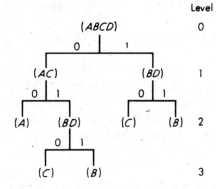

Level

Fig. 14-4 Synchronizing tree for machine M_3.

Let M be a μ-definite machine, and let $(S_i S_j)$ be a nontrivial uncertainty in the $(\mu - 1)$st level of the corresponding synchronizing tree. Since the μth level of the tree consists of only single states, the I_k-successors of both S_i and S_j must be identical for every possible I_k in I; that is, every definite machine contains at least two distinct states for which $I_k S_i = I_k S_j$ for all I_k in I. Define the <u>contracted table</u> $\bar{M}$ as the table obtained by deleting row S_j and replacing in the entire table all the appearances of S_j by S_i. It is easy to show that the application of any input sequence X to $\bar{M}$ or to M, when initially in any state S_k such that $S_k \neq S_j$, will pass both $\bar{M}$ and M to the same final state if the final state is different from S_j, and will pass $\bar{M}$ to S_i if the final state of M is S_j.

Let $\bar{M}$ be the contracted table which is obtained from M by replacing each set of states whose I_k-successors are identical with a single member from that set. Clearly, the synchronizing tree of $\bar{M}$ has only $\mu - 1$ levels, and its last level consists of only singleton uncertainties. But since such a tree corresponds to a machine which is $(\mu - 1)$-definite, we arrive at the following general result:

▶ If M is a μ-definite machine, the contracted machine $\bar{M}$ is $(\mu - 1)$-definite. Conversely, if $\bar{M}$ is k-definite, then M is $(k + 1)$-definite. If $\bar{M}$ is not definite, neither is M.

Tests for definiteness

The synchronizing tree can be used to test for definiteness. In this section we shall illustrate two additional testing procedures. The first procedure, which utilizes the previously derived properties of definite machines, involves repeated derivations of contracted tables. The second procedure is based on the familiar testing graph.

515

The first test for definiteness is as follows:

1. Determine the subsets of states whose I_k-successors are identical;
2. Select one representative state in each subset;
3. Obtain the contracted table $\bar{M}$ by replacing each subset with its representative and modifying the table entries accordingly;
4. Regard $\bar{M}$ as a new table and repeat the previous steps until no new contractions are possible.

M is definite if and only if the final contracted table obtained in step 4 consists of just a single state.

Example Test machine M_4 of Table 14-6 for definiteness. The non-trivial subsets of states whose corresponding successors are identical are (B,F) and (C,D). Select B and C as the representative states, and obtain the contracted table $\bar{M}_4$, which consists of four states, as shown in Table 14-7. States B and C in the contracted table can now be represented by state B, and the contracted table shown in Table 14-8a results. The fourth contraction yields a single-state machine. Thus M_4 is definite. ∎

Table 14-6   Machine M_4

PS	NS	
	$x = 0$	$x = 1$
A	A	B
B	E	B
C	E	F
D	E·	F
E	A	D
F	E	B

Table 14-7   The contracted table $\bar{M}_4$

PS	NS	
	$x = 0$	$x = 1$
A	A	B
B	E	B
C	E	B
E	A	C

Table 14-8   Repeated contractions of M_4

PS	$x = 0$	$x = 1$
A	A	B
B	E	B
E	A	B

(a)

PS	$x = 0$	$x = 1$
A	A	B
B	A	B

(b)

PS	$x = 0$	$x = 1$
A	A	A

(c)

We shall now show that the test for definiteness is always finite, and determine the bound on its length.

Theorem 14-2 *If machine M is μ-definite, then $\mu \le n - 1$. Moreover, the order of definiteness is equal to the number of contractions needed to obtain a one-state machine.*

Proof: Since M is μ-definite, then $\bar{M}$ is $(\mu - 1)$-definite. Each contracted table must contain at least one state less than its predecessor. Consequently, after at most $n - 1$ repeated contractions, we obtain a one-state machine which is 0-definite; i.e., no input is required in order to determine its present or final state. To determine the order of definiteness, it is necessary to count backward; that is, the last contracted table is 0-definite, its predecessor is 1-definite, and so on. ∎

For machine M_4, $\mu = 4$, since four contractions are necessary in order to obtain a one-state machine.

The second test for definiteness is based on a testing table and graph, which are defined as follows. The *testing table* (*for definiteness*), which is divided into two parts, has p columns, corresponding to $I_1, I_2, \ldots, I_p$. The rows in the upper part of the table correspond to the states of the machine, and the table entries are the state transitions. The row headings in the lower part of the table are all unordered pairs of states, while the table entries are the corresponding successors. The *testing graph* (*for definiteness*) is defined as in the previous section, and is derived directly from the lower part of the testing table. The arc labels, however, are now input symbols instead of input-output combinations.

Example The testing table for machine M_3 is shown in Table 14-9, and the corresponding testing graph, which is loop-free, is shown in Fig. 14-5. ∎

Theorem 14-3 *A machine M is μ-definite if and only if its corresponding testing graph G is loop-free. If the length of the longest path in G is l, then $\mu = l + 1$.*

Proof: The proof is similar to that of Theorem 14-1 and is left to the reader as an exercise. ∎

Machine M_3 is definite of order $\mu = 3$, since its testing graph is loop-free and the longest path in the graph is of length $l = 2$.

The relationship between the testing graph and the synchronizing tree is evident. A loop-free graph means that no uncertainty in the kth level of the tree is also associated with some node in a preceding level,

Table 14-9 Testing table for machine M_3

PS	$x = 0$	$x = 1$
A	A	B
B	C	B
C	A	D
D	C	B
AB	AC	BB
AC	AA	BD
AD	AC	BB
BC	AC	BD
BD	CC	BB
CD	AC	BD

and, conversely, a loop in the graph means that such a situation does occur.

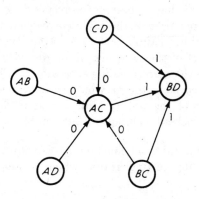

Fig. 14-5 Testing graph for machine M_3.

14-3 MEMORY SPAN WITH RESPECT TO OUTPUT SEQUENCES

A finite-state machine M is said to have an *output memory* of *order* μ if μ is the least integer, so that the knowledge of the last μ outputs suffices to determine the state of M at some time during the last μ transitions. In this section emphasis is placed on the specification of the state of M at *some time* during the experiment, instead of on the identification of the final state. The case of identifying the final state is more restricted and is left to the reader as an exercise.

Test for output memory

The major tools for testing whether or not a given machine has a finite output memory are a modified testing table and its corresponding testing graph. The *testing table (for output memory)*, which consists of two parts, has q columns corresponding to the output symbols of the machine, i.e., $O_1, O_2, \ldots, O_q$. The row names of the upper part of the table are the states of M. The entries in row S_i, column O_j, are the states that can be reached from S_i by single transitions associated with the output symbol O_j. We shall call these states the *(output) O_k-successors* of S_i. The entire upper half of the testing table is, actually, a listing of the output successors of the states of M, and is therefore called an *output successor table*. Thus, for machine M_5 of Table 14-10, the output 1-successors of B are A and C; state B has no output 0-successors. This is recorded in Table 14-11 by entering AC in row B, column 1, and a dash in row B, column 0. When reference to output successors is self-evident in the context, we shall omit the adjective "output."

Table 14-10   Machine M_5

PS	NS, z $x = 0$	$x = 1$
A	$B,0$	$D,1$
B	$C,1$	$A,1$
C	$B,0$	$C,0$
D	$C,0$	$C,1$

Table 14-11   Testing table for machine M_5

PS	$z = 0$	$z = 1$
A	B	D
B	—	(AC)
C	(BC)	—
D	C	C
AB	—	$(AD)(CD)$
AC	$(BB)(BC)$	—
AD	(BC)	(CD)
BC	—	—
BD	—	$(AC)(CC)$
CD	$(BC)(CC)$	—

For each unordered pair of states there is a row in the lower half of the testing table. The table entries are the corresponding output successors. The output O_k-successors of S_iS_j are all pairwise combinations of the output O_k-successors of S_i and S_j. For example, if the successors of S_i and S_j are S_pS_q and S_rS_t, respectively, then the corresponding successors of S_iS_j are S_pS_r, S_pS_t, S_qS_r, S_qS_t. If for some pair of states S_i and S_j either one or both O_k-successors are dashes, the O_k-successor of S_iS_j is also a dash. Thus, since the output 1-successor of C is a dash, the output 1-successor of AC is also a dash, as shown in the lower half of Table 14-11.

A *testing graph (for output memory)* G is a directed graph, such that:

1. Corresponding to each row in the lower half of the testing table there is a vertex in G. The vertex label is the same as the row heading.
2. An arc labeled O_k is drawn from vertex S_iS_j to vertex S_pS_q, where $p \neq q$, if and only if S_pS_q is an entry in row S_iS_j, column O_k.

The testing graph of machine M_5 is shown in Fig. 14-6. Note that two or more arcs having the same label may emanate from a single vertex, e.g., vertex AB.

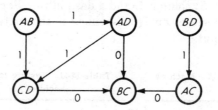

Fig. 14-6   Testing graph G_5 for machine M_5.

Theorem 14-4   *A finite-state machine M has a finite output memory if and only if its corresponding testing graph G is loop-free. Furthermore, if G is loop-free and the longest path in G is of length l, then M has an output memory of order $\mu = l + 1$.*

Proof: If G contains a loop, choose any two vertices in the loop, say S_iS_j and S_pS_q; then there exist two identical output sequences, produced by M while in transition from S_i via S_p to S_i and from S_j via S_q to S_j. Since these sequences may be repeated as many times as we wish, they will never distinguish the states associated with any vertex contained in the loop, and consequently M does not have a finite output memory. If G is loop-free but M does not have a finite output memory, then, for every possible positive integer μ, there exists a path, emanating from some vertex S_iS_j, which does not pass M into an identifiable state. This implies arbitrarily long paths in G. But since G is finite and loop-free, this cannot be achieved, and thus M has a finite output memory. The proof that $\mu = l + 1$ follows from the same line of argument used in the corollary in Sec. 14-1.   ■

For example, G_5 in Fig. 14-6 is loop-free, and its longest path is of length 3, i.e., the path from AB through AD and CD to BC. Thus M_5 has a finite output memory of order $\mu = 4$.

Note that the testing graph does not contain any vertex corresponding to pairs consisting of repeated entries, e.g., BB, etc. The existence of such a pair means, in effect, that there is no uncertainty regarding the state of the machine. Therefore the deletion of such pairs from the graph (or even from the testing table) does not affect the test for finite output memory.

Determining the state of the machine

If machine M has a finite output memory, it is possible to determine the state of M at some point during any experiment of length μ. We shall now show how to identify this state when the only available information is the output sequence.

Suppose, for example, that the output sequence produced by machine M_5, in response to some unknown input sequence, is 1110. Initially, the machine could have been in either state A, B, or D, since no 1 output can be generated by a transition from state C. Thus the initial uncertainty is (ABD). From the output successor table we find that the output 1-successor of A is D, of B is (AC), and of D is C. Consequently, the 1-successor uncertainty of (ABD) is (ACD). (In general, the output successor of a set of states Q is the set consisting of all output successors of the members of Q.) In a similar manner we find that the 1-successor of (ACD) is (CD), and so on. The next state is clearly C, as shown below:

Possible uncertainties	$\begin{matrix} A \\ B \\ D \end{matrix}$	$\begin{matrix} A \\ C \\ D \end{matrix}$	$\begin{matrix} C \\ D \end{matrix}$	$\begin{matrix} C \\ \\ \end{matrix}$	$\begin{matrix} B \\ C \end{matrix}$
Output sequence	1	1	1	0	

Note that although the state of M_5 has been identified at one point during the above experiment, the uncertainty increases to (BC) one time unit later.

The reason for suggesting the above definition of output memory, which is somewhat different from those of input-output memory or definiteness, is the fact that the output successor table might have multivalued entries. Therefore the identification of the state of the machine at some point during the experiment does not guarantee the identification of its successor.   All we can say is that, within μ transitions corresponding to any output sequence, there must be at least one time period during which the machine is unambiguously in a certain state, regardless of the initial state.

14-4 INFORMATION LOSSLESS MACHINES

One of the central problems in coding and information transmission is the determination of conditions under which it is possible to reconstruct the input sequence to the machine from the corresponding output sequence. It will be shown that whenever a machine is used as an encoding device (i.e., the machine is provided with an input sequence and its output is the coded message) and when its initial and final states are known, its information losslessness guarantees that the coded message can always be deciphered.   Thus we define a machine M to be (*information*) *lossless* if the knowledge of the initial state, the output sequence, and the final state is sufficient to determine uniquely the input sequence.

Conditions for lossiness

A machine that is not lossless is said to be *lossy*.   A simple example of a lossy machine is one in which, for some state S_i and two distinct input symbols I_p and I_q, the I_p- and I_q-successors and the corresponding outputs are identical.   Clearly, in such a case, the knowledge of the output, as well as the initial and final states, is not sufficient to determine whether I_p or I_q was applied to the machine.

Loss of information occurs whenever two states, S_i and S_j, which can be reached from a common state S_c by means of two distinct input sequences while producing identical output sequences, merge into a final state, S_f, and produce the same output.   Clearly, once the machine has reached state S_f, no future experiment will make possible the retrieval of the input sequence which transferred M from S_c to S_f.   This case, which is necessary and sufficient for a machine to be lossy, is illustrated in Fig. 14-7.

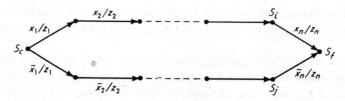

Fig. 14-7 Condition for information loss.

Example   Machine M_6 of Table 14-12 is lossy, as demonstrated in Fig. 14-8.   Two distinct input sequences (01 and 10) take the machine

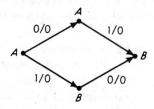

Fig. 14-8   Demonstration that machine M_6 is lossy.

from state A to state B, while producing identical output sequences (00).   After M_6 has reached state B, it is impossible to determine which input sequence actually occurred.   ■

Table 14-12   Machine M_6

PS	NS, z	
	$x = 0$	$x = 1$
A	$A,0$	$B,0$
B	$B,0$	$A,1$

From the foregoing discussion it is evident that in order to test a machine for losslessness, it is first necessary to determine if, for some state, two or more successors and their corresponding outputs are identical or if any merger of the type illustrated in Fig. 14-7 exists.   Before presenting a test for information losslessness, we shall define an "order" of losslessness.

Information losslessness of finite order

Suppose that a system of lossless machines is used for encoding and decoding purposes.   The "encoder" receives an input sequence and in turn produces an output sequence, which is transmitted to a "decoder."   Clearly, if the encoder is lossless, its input can be reconstructed from its output, as well as the information regarding its initial and final states.   The major drawback in such a decoding process lies in the fact that the information regarding the final state is transmitted by the encoder only after the entire message has been transmitted.   Consequently, the entire message must be stored before the deciphering process can begin.   And since the output sequence may be arbitrarily long, the lossless machine cannot serve as a practical tool for encoding and decoding purposes. In view of this limitation, it becomes desirable to look for machines for which it is not necessary to store the entire message, but where the deciphering process can start when only the initial state and a finite length of the output sequence are available.

A machine is said to be (*information*) *lossless of finite order* if the knowledge of the initial state and the first μ output symbols is sufficient to determine uniquely the first input symbol. The knowledge of the initial state and the first input symbol is sufficient to determine the next state, and thus the second input symbol can be computed from the $(\mu + 1)$st output symbol, and so on. The integer μ, which is a measure of the delay in the deciphering of the input symbols, is said to be the *order* of losslessness if μ is the least integer satisfying the above definition, that is, if for some initial state and a sequence of $\mu - 1$ output symbols, there exist at least two possible input sequences, differing in their initial input symbols.

The simplest example of lossless machines of finite order is that of first order, where the first input symbol can be determined from the knowledge of the initial state and the first output symbol. Hence there is no delay in deciphering the inputs for this class of machines. As an example, consider machine M_7, shown in Table 14-13. Since for every state of M_7 the output associated with the 0-successor is different from the output associated with the 1-successor, knowing the initial state and first output symbol is sufficient for the identification of the first input symbol. For example, if M_7 is initially in state A, and if in response to an as yet unknown input symbol an output of 1 is produced, we can unambiguously identify the input symbol as a 0.

Table 14-13   Machine M_7

PS	NS, z	
	$x = 0$	$x = 1$
A	C,1	D,0
B	D,0	A,1
C	D,1	B,0
D	C,0	B,1

Test for information losslessness

We now derive a test to determine whether or not a given machine is lossless, and to find its order of losslessness if it is finite. Before proceeding with the testing procedure, we introduce some terminology that facilitates discussion on information losslessness. Two states, S_i and S_j, are said to be (*output*) *compatible* if there exists some state S_p such that both S_i and S_j are its O_k-successors, or if there exists a compatible pair of states S_r, S_t such that S_i, S_j are their O_k-successors. In such a case we say that the compatible $(S_i S_j)$ is *implied* by $(S_r S_t)$.

The first step in the testing procedure is to check each row of the state table for an appearance of two identical next-state entries associated with the same output symbol. If no identical entries appear, the next step is to construct the output successor table. A *testing table* (*for information losslessness*) is now constructed in two parts. The upper part consists of the output successor table, while the lower part is constructed in the following manner. Every compatible pair appearing in the successor table is made a row heading in the lower part of the testing table. The successors of these pairs are found in the usual way, and consist of all implied compatible pairs. Any implied pair which has not yet been used as a row heading is now made a row heading, its successors found, and so on. The process terminates when all compatible pairs have been used as row headings.

Machine M_8, given in Table 14-14, may be used to illustrate the testing procedure. The output successor table is shown in the upper half of Table 14-15. (AC) is a compatible pair, since both A and C are

Table 14-14   Machine M_8

PS	NS, z	
	$x = 0$	$x = 1$
A	$A,1$	$C,1$
B	$E,0$	$B,1$
C	$D,0$	$A,0$
D	$C,0$	$B,0$
E	$B,1$	$A,0$

Table 14-15   Testing table for machine M_8

PS	$z = 0$	$z = 1$
A	—	(AC)
B	E	B
C	(AD)	—
D	(BC)	—
E	A	B
AC	—	—
AD	—	—
BC	$(AE)(DE)$	—
AE	—	$(AB)(BC)$
DE	$(AB)(AC)$	—
AB	—	$(AB)(BC)$

the output 1-successors of A. Similarly, the pairs (AD) and (BC) are compatible pairs. Consequently, these pairs are used as row headings for the lower part of the testing table. Pairs (AE) and (DE), which are implied by (BC), are now made row headings, and so on. Note that, contrary to the testing procedure for finite output memory, the testing table for information losslessness does not necessarily include all distinct pairs of states, but only the compatible ones.

At this point we are ready to derive necessary and sufficient conditions for a machine to be information lossless. Suppose that the testing table contains a compatible pair consisting of repeated entries, e.g., $(S_k S_k)$; then there exists either some compatible pair $(S_i S_j)$ which implies $(S_k S_k)$ or some state S_i which has identical output successors for two or more inputs. But since these cases have been shown to be necessary and sufficient for lossiness, the machine in question must be lossy. We thus arrive at the following general result:

▶   A machine is lossless if and only if its testing table does not contain any compatible pair consisting of repeated entries.

A *testing graph* (*for information losslessness*) G is a directed graph such that:

1. Corresponding to every compatible pair there is a vertex in G.
2. An arc labeled O_k is drawn from vertex $S_i S_j$ to vertex $S_p S_q$, where $p \neq q$, if and only if $(S_p S_q)$ is a compatible implied by $(S_i S_j)$.

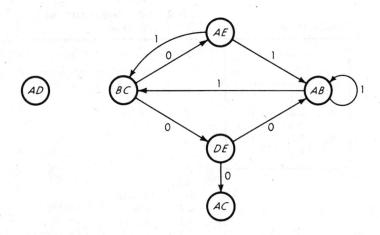

Fig. 14-9   Testing graph for machine M_8.

The testing graph G_8 of machine M_8 is derived in the usual way from the lower half of the testing table and is shown in Fig. 14-9. M_8 is clearly lossless, because there are no compatible pairs consisting of repeated

entries.   Before determining the order of losslessness, we prove the following theorem.

Theorem 14-5   *A machine M is lossless of order* $\mu = l + 2$ *if and only if
its testing graph is loop-free and the length of the longest path in the
graph is l.*

Proof: Assume that M is lossless.   Suppose that G is not loop-free,
and let S_iS_j be some vertex in the loop.   Clearly, every compatible
pair is accessible from some state of M by a pair of distinct input
sequences which yield identical output sequences.   Thus we can
find a pair of different input sequences which take M to S_iS_j, while
producing identical output sequences.   If we now observe the output symbols that the machine produces, while going through all the
compatible pairs in the loop, we find that the machine is back in
S_iS_j, without supplying any additional information to make possible
the identification of the first input symbol.   And since this loop may
be repeated as many times as we wish, we may construct a pair of
arbitrarily long input sequences that start in the same state of M
and differ in the first symbol but produce identical output sequences.
Thus M is not lossless of finite order.   The proof that the loop-free
condition is indeed. sufficient for finite order is trivial, and follows
the line of arguments used in the proof of Theorem 14-1.

   To determine the order of losslessness, consider the longest path
in G.   It takes one input symbol to get from a state of M into the
first compatible, and it takes l inputs to go through the longest path
in G.   Since the compatible that has been reached after $l + 1$ inputs
does not imply any other compatible, one more input will yield
different outputs, depending on which of the states of the compatible
the machine is in.   This in turn determines the initial input symbol.
Thus $\mu = l + 2$ output symbols (plus the knowledge of the initial
state) are sufficient to determine the first input symbol.   ∎

From Theorem 14-5, we conclude that, if M is lossless of order μ,
then $\mu \leq 1 + n(n - 1)/2$.   The proof that this is indeed the least upper
bound is given in Appendix 14-1.

   The case of $\mu = 1$ is detected by the absence of compatible pairs (see
machine M_7), while the case of $\mu = 2$ is detected by the absence of arcs
in the graph.

   Returning to machine M_8, we observe that, since G_8 is not loop-free,
M_8 is not lossless of finite order.   It is interesting to note that M_8 is
lossless, although state A can be reached by a 1 input from both states
C and E, and the output produced is 0.   This situation does not imply
lossiness, since the pair (CE) is not compatible; i.e., C and E cannot be

reached from any initial state by means of two distinct input sequences while producing identical output sequences.

Example   As another illustration, the above test is applied to machine M_9 of Table 14-16.   This machine is shown to be lossless of order 3, since its testing graph (Fig. 14-10) is loop-free and the longest path is of length 1.   ∎

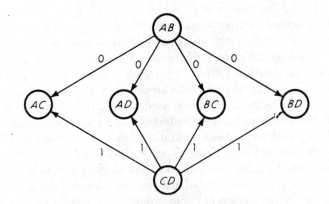

Fig. 14-10   Testing graph for machine M_9.

Table 14-16   Machine M_9

PS	NS, z	
	$x = 0$	$x = 1$
A	A,0	B,0
B	C,0	D,0
C	D,1	C,1
D	B,1	A,1

Table 14-17   Testing table for M_9

PS	$z = 0$	$z = 1$
A	(AB)	—
B	(CD)	—
C	—	(CD)
D	—	(AB)
AB	(AC)(AD) (BC)(BD)	—
CD	—	(AC)(AD) (BC)(BD)

Retrieval of the input sequence

The knowledge of the output sequence produced by a lossless machine, as well as its initial and final states, is sufficient to determine the inputs applied to the machine.   We shall now present a procedure to retrieve the input sequence by first reconstructing the state sequence.   The machine being lossless ensures that the input sequence is uniquely specified by the state sequence.

Let M be a lossless machine which is initially in a known state, and after producing a given output sequence of length r, it terminates in a known final state. Suppose we now wish to determine the state of the machine just after it has produced the jth output symbol. By applying the first j output symbols to the output successor table, starting from the known initial state, we find a set of states in which the machine could be. In an analogous way we can trace the predecessors of the final state by applying (in reverse order) the $r - j$ output symbols to the output predecessor table (which will be defined shortly). This last step yields a set of possible predecessors just prior to the production of the $(j + 1)$st output symbol. Clearly, since the machine is lossless, it could have been in just one state at the time in question, and thus the intersection of the set derived from the successor table and the set derived from the predecessor table will reveal this state.

As an example, consider machine M_8. Assume that this machine was initially in state A, has in response to a yet unknown input sequence produced the output sequence 110001100101, and has terminated in state B. From the output successor table (Table 14-15) we find that the 1-successors of A are A and C, and the 1-successors of AC are also A and C. Just after the third output symbol, the machine could have been in either state A or D, since AD is the 0-successor of AC. Similar reasoning is used to find the states in which the machine may be after the production of every output symbol. These steps can be summarized as follows:

$$
A \quad
\begin{matrix} A \\ C \end{matrix} \;
\begin{matrix} A \\ C \end{matrix} \;
\begin{matrix} A \\ D \end{matrix} \;
B \;
\begin{matrix} A \\ D \\ E \end{matrix} \;
\begin{matrix} A \\ B \\ C \end{matrix} \;
\begin{matrix} A \\ B \\ C \end{matrix} \;
\begin{matrix} A \\ D \\ E \end{matrix} \;
\begin{matrix} A \\ B \\ C \end{matrix} \;
\begin{matrix} A \\ B \\ C \end{matrix} \;
\begin{matrix} A \\ D \\ E \end{matrix} \;
B
$$

$$
1 \quad 1 \quad 0 \quad 0 \quad 0 \quad 1 \quad 1 \quad 0 \quad 0 \quad 1 \quad 0 \quad 1
$$

We have not yet utilized the information that can be obtained from the final state. This is best accomplished by an *(output) predecessor table*, which is constructed as follows. There is a column labeled O_k in the table for each output symbol O_k in O, and there is a row for each state of the machine. The entries in row S_i, column O_k, are those states for which S_i is an output O_k-successor. These states are often referred to as the *(output) O_k-predecessors* of state S_i. The output predecessors of each of the machine states can be found directly from the state table. For convenience, the row headings of the predecessor table are placed on the right-hand side of the table. This emphasizes the fact that the row headings are the successors of the corresponding table entries.

For example, state B of machine M_8 can be reached by a single transition from states B and E while producing an output of 1, and from state D while producing an output of 0. Thus the entry in row B, column 1, of the output predecessor table (Table 14-18) is BE, while the entry in row B, column 0, is D. In a similar manner we obtain the entire predecessor table.

**Table 14-18   Output prede-
cessor table for machine M_8**

$z = 0$	$z = 1$	NS
CE	A	A
D	BE	B
D	A	C
C	—	D
B	—	E

If we now wish to determine the state of M_8 just prior to the production of the last output symbol, we look for the output 1-predecessors of state B, which is known to be the final state. As shown before; the 1-predecessors of B are B and E. But from the output successor table we have found that at the time in question the machine could be in either state A, D, or E. And since it can be in only one state at that time, that state must be given by the intersection of (B,E) and (A,D,E). Therefore the 1-predecessor of B is E. The entire procedure is summarized in Fig. 14-11. It is easy to verify by means of the state table that the input sequence, which corresponds to the state sequence of Fig. 14-11, is 010010101100.

Possible successors to initial state	A	$\begin{matrix}A\\C\end{matrix}$	$\begin{matrix}A\\C\end{matrix}$	$\begin{matrix}A\\D\end{matrix}$	$\begin{matrix}B\\C\end{matrix}$	$\begin{matrix}A\\D\\E\end{matrix}$	$\begin{matrix}A\\B\\C\end{matrix}$	$\begin{matrix}A\\B\\C\end{matrix}$	$\begin{matrix}A\\D\\E\end{matrix}$	$\begin{matrix}A\\B\\C\end{matrix}$	$\begin{matrix}A\\B\\C\end{matrix}$	$\begin{matrix}A\\D\\E\end{matrix}$	B
Output sequence	1	1	0	0	0	1	1	0	0	1	0	1	
Possible predecessors to final state	A	A	$\begin{matrix}C\\D\end{matrix}$	$\begin{matrix}B\\D\end{matrix}$	$\begin{matrix}C\\E\end{matrix}$	A	A	$\begin{matrix}C\\D\end{matrix}$	$\begin{matrix}B\\D\end{matrix}$	$\begin{matrix}B\\E\end{matrix}$	$\begin{matrix}B\\D\end{matrix}$	$\begin{matrix}B\\E\end{matrix}$	B
The state sequence	A	A	C	D	C	A	A	C	D	B	B	E	B
Input sequence	0	1	0	0	1	0	1	0	1	1	0	0	

Fig. 14-11   Retrieval of an input sequence.

Whenever a given output sequence has been generated by a lossless machine, the state transitions and input sequence can be determined uniquely. If, however, at some point the intersection of the sets containing the possible successors and predecessors consists of two or more states, then there exist at least two distinct input sequences which produce identical output sequences. Therefore the machine in question is not lossless. If at some point the intersection is empty, the corresponding output sequence could not have been produced by the given machine subject to the specified initial and final states. In fact, if the intersection is empty at one point, it must be empty at all points.

Inverse machines

An *inverse* M^i is a machine which, when excited by the output sequence of a machine M, produces (as its output) the input sequence to M, after at most a finite delay. Evidently, a deterministic inverse can be constructed only if M is lossless, and it can be constructed so that it produces M's input sequence after just a finite delay if and only if M is lossless of finite order.

Consider, for example, machine M_7 of Table 14-13, which is lossless of first order. For any possible initial state and output sequence, the knowledge of the initial state of M_7 and the first output symbol is sufficient to determine uniquely the first input symbol to the machine. Hence there is no delay in deciphering the inputs to this machine. The state transitions of the inverse machine $M_7{}^i$ are therefore given by the output successor table, as shown in Table 14-19. The outputs associated with these state transitions are found by means of the state table of machine M_7. If machine $M_7{}^i$ is placed in cascade with machine M_7, it will produce as its output an exact replica of the input sequence to M_7.

Table 14-19   Machine $M_7{}^i$

PS	NS, x	
	$z = 0$	$z = 1$
A	D,1	C,0
B	D,0	A,1
C	B,1	D,0
D	C,0	B,1

For every lossless machine of order μ, the knowledge of the state at time $t - \mu + 1$ and the last μ output symbols, i.e., $z(t - \mu + 1)$, $z(t - \mu + 2)$, . . . , $z(t)$, is sufficient to determine uniquely the input symbol $x(t - \mu + 1)$. Consequently, if we send the output sequence produced by a lossless machine M of order μ into a register which consists of $\mu - 1$ delay units, we can design a combinational circuit that has as inputs the contents of that register, as well as the state of M at time $t - \mu + 1$, and in turn produces the value of $x(t - \mu + 1)$.

The combinational circuit can be specified by a truth table in which the value of $x(t - \mu + 1)$ is specified for every possible combination of $S(t - \mu + 1)$ and $z(t - \mu + 1), z(t - \mu + 2), \ldots, z(t)$. The information regarding the state of M can be supplied to the combinational circuit by a copy of the original machine M, which is set to be at $t = \mu - 1$ in the same state that M was in at $t = 0$, and receives as its inputs a delayed (by $\mu - 1$ time units) version of the inputs to M. The schematic diagram of such a deciphering system is shown in Fig. 14-12.

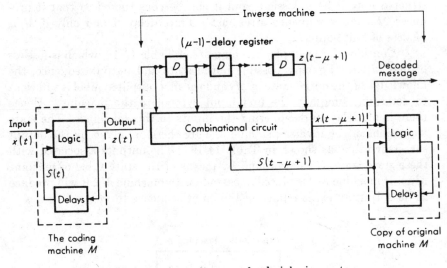

Fig. 14-12 Schematic diagram of a deciphering system.

The foregoing deciphering system does not yield an economical realization, since it requires a copy of the original machine as well as a $(\mu - 1)$-delay register. In fact, if we were to construct a composite state table for the inverse machine (i.e., a composite table for both the register and the copy of M), we would find that in many cases it can be considerably simplified. The question that now arises is whether we can find directly from M's description a minimal inverse, without going through the above construction procedure. Indeed, this can be accomplished, as is shown subsequently.

★The minimal inverse-machine

We shall demonstrate a construction procedure that yields a minimal inverse-machine by finding the inverse of machine M_{10}, shown in Table 14-20. This machine is lossless of third order, and therefore, if we know the initial state and the values of three successive outputs produced by transitions from this state, we can determine the first input to the machine. Let us now define a set of triples, denoted $(S(t),z(t + 1),z(t + 2))$. The first member of each triple is a possible initial state of M_{10}; the second member is one of the output symbols that can be produced by a single transition from this state; and the third member is another output symbol that can follow this initial state and the first output symbol. A triple is defined for each possible initial state and for all possible sequences of outputs of length 2. For machine M_{10} we obtain the following triples:

$$(A,0,0) \quad (B,0,1) \quad (C,0,0) \quad (D,1,0)$$
$$(A,1,1) \quad (B,1,0) \quad (C,0,1) \quad (D,1,1)$$

The triple $(A,0,1)$, for example, is not defined, because the output sequence 01 cannot be generated by M_{10} when started initially in state A.

Table 14-20   Machine M_{10}

PS	NS, z	
	$x = 0$	$x = 1$
A	C,0	D,1
B	D,0	C,1
C	A,0	B,0
D	C,1	D,1

The set of triples so generated contains all possible combinations of initial states and output sequences of length 2. To determine the input symbol that causes the transition from the initial state, while producing the output symbol specified by the second member of the triple, all that is necessary is one additional output symbol. Accordingly, if we construct a machine each of whose states corresponds to a triple and represents the "information" carried by that triple, and if we supply the machine with the outputs of the original machine, then it will have all the necessary information to compute the input symbols in question.

The inverse of machine M_{10}, denoted $M_{10}{}^i$, has eight states, corresponding to the eight triples derived earlier. We shall often refer to a state of the inverse-machine as an *inverse state*. For every state of $M_{10}{}^i$, the next inverse state is a triple whose members are determined in the following manner:

1. The first member is the state to which machine M_{10} goes when it is initially in the state that is the first member of the present inverse state, and when it is supplied with the first input symbol.
2. The second member is the third member of the corresponding present inverse state.
3. The third member is the present output of M_{10}.

The state table of machine $M_{10}{}^i$ is given in Table 14-21. Suppose, for example, that $M_{10}{}^i$ is in state $(A,0,0)$ and its present input is 0. To determine its 0-successor, we observe that machine M_{10}, when initially in state A, can produce three consecutive 0 outputs only if the first input symbol is 0; as a result, M_{10}'s first transition is to state C, and the 0-successor of $(A,0,0)$ contains C as its first member. The second member of the triple $(C,0,0)$ equals the third member of $(A,0,0)$, while its third member is the present output of M_{10}, which is, actually, the present input to $M_{10}{}^i$ and is given by $M_{10}{}^i$'s column heading. The output of $M_{10}{}^i$ is a delayed replica of the input to M_{10}; that is, the output of $M_{10}{}^i$ at t is equal to M_{10}'s input at $t - 2$.

Table 14-21   Machine $M_{10}{}^i$

PS	NS, x	
	z = 0	z = 1
$(A,0,0)$	$(C,0,0),0$	$(C,0,1),0$
$(A,1,1)$	$(D,1,0),1$	$(D,1,1),1$
$(B,0,1)$	$(D,1,0),0$	$(D,1,1),0$
$(B,1,0)$	$(C,0,0),1$	$(C,0,1),1$
$(C,0,0)$	$(A,0,0),0$	$(B,0,1),1$
$(C,0,1)$	$(B,1,0),1$	$(A,1,1),0$
$(D,1,0)$	$(C,0,0),0$	$(C,0,1),0$
$(D,1,1)$	$(D,1,0),1$	$(D,1,1),1$

The set of states generated by the set of triples is clearly sufficient for a realization of the inverse-machine. It does not, however, yield the smallest set of states. Machine $M_{10}{}^i$, for example, can be reduced, since $(A,0,0)$ is equivalent to $(D,1,0)$, and similarly $(A,1,1)$ is equivalent to $(D,1,1)$. If we denote $(A,0,0)$ by S_1, $(A,1,1)$ by S_2, and so on, we obtain the minimal inverse of Table 14-22.

The foregoing procedure is applicable to any lossless machine of finite order. In general, for a machine of order μ, we define a set of

**Table 14-22   Minimal
inverse $M_{10}{}^i$**

PS	NS, x	
	$z = 0$	$z = 1$
S_1	$S_5,0$	$S_6,0$
S_2	$S_1,1$	$S_2,1$
S_3	$S_1,0$	$S_2,0$
S_4	$S_5,1$	$S_6,1$
S_5	$S_1,0$	$S_3,1$
S_6	$S_4,1$	$S_2,0$

μ-tuples which constitutes the set of states of the inverse-machine.   The first member of each μ-tuple is a state of the original machine M; the remaining members are possible output sequence of length $\mu - 1$, which can be produced by successive transitions from that state.   The fact that this procedure yields more economical realizations than the "canonic" realization of the preceding section can be explained as follows.   In the canonic realization we have stored the output sequence in a shift register and used a copy of the original machine to provide the information regarding the state of the original machine.   In this realization we actually utilize the same memory devices to store information regarding both the states and the output sequences, thus achieving reduction in the number of states of the inverse-machine.

Suppose that machine M_{10} is initially in state A and, in response to some input sequence, it produces one of the output sequences 00 or 11. Then $M_{10}{}^i$ must be, two units of time later, in the state which corresponds to A and the appropriate output sequence, i.e., $(A,0,0)$ or $(A,1,1)$.   But since $S_4 = (B,1,0)$ is the only state from which $M_{10}{}^i$ can reach $(A,0,0)$ and $(A,1,1)$ when supplied with inputs 00 and 11, respectively, it follows that, if the initial state of M_{10} is A, the initial state of $M_{10}{}^i$ must be $(B,1,0)$. In a similar way the reader can verify that if machine M_{10} is initially in state B, $M_{10}{}^i$ can initially be in either S_1 or S_4, and when M_{10} is initially in either state C or D, $M_{10}{}^i$ can initially be in either one of S_2, S_3, S_5, or S_6.

As an example, demonstrating the deciphering capability of $M_{10}{}^i$, let M_{10} and $M_{10}{}^i$ be initially in states A and S_4, respectively, and let the input sequence 010001101 be applied to M_{10}.   The deciphering process is shown in Fig. 14-13.   The first two output symbols of $M_{10}{}^i$, as well as the last two input symbols to M_{10}, must be ignored.   In the remaining positions, both sequences, the input to M_{10} and output of $M_{10}{}^i$, are identical, although shifted in time.

State of M_{10}	A	C	B	D	C	A	D	D	C	B
Input to M_{10}	0	1	0	0	0	1	1	0	1	
Output of M_{10}	0	0	0	1	0	1	1	1	0	
State of $M_{10}{}^i$	S_4	S_5	S_1	S_5	S_3	S_1	S_6	S_2	S_2	S_1
Output of $M_{10}{}^i$	—	—	0	1	0	0	0	1	1	

Fig. 14-13 Deciphering process by means of $M_{10}{}^i$.

★14-5 SYNCHRONIZABLE AND UNIQUELY DECIPHERABLE CODES

The objective of this section is twofold: to introduce some of the basic issues in coding theory, and to demonstrate the applicability of the preceding testing techniques to the area of information transmission and codes. We do not intend to develop the entire subject of coding theory, but rather to illustrate some aspects of this subject which are relevant to the memory and information-losslessness aspects of automata. These concepts will therefore be introduced without formal definitions and proofs.

Introduction

Let the symbols $\{A,B,C, \ldots\}$ denote a finite *source alphabet*, and let $L = \{0,1,2, \ldots\}$ be a *code alphabet*. We shall be concerned with only binary codes, where $L = \{0,1\}$. A concatenation of a finite number of code symbols is referred to as a *code word*. A *code* consists of a finite number of distinct code words of finite length, each representing a source symbol. A coded message is constructed by concatenating code words, without spacing or any other punctuation. For example, let the code alphabet be $L = \{0,1\}$, and let the set of code words γ_1 be $\{00,01,11,10\}$. The code shown in Table 14-23 is a mapping from the source alphabet $\{A,B,C,D\}$ to γ_1. Thus the sequence $ABDC$ would be coded as 00011011.

Table 14-23 A binary code

Source symbols	Code words
A	00
B	01
C	11
D	10

By the use of the code in Table 14-23, we may obtain a sequence of binary digits for any sequence of source symbols. We may also work backward to obtain a sequence of source symbols for any sequence of binary digits arising from this code.   In fact, since each source symbol is represented by a distinct code word and all code words are of equal length, to every sequence of code words from this code there corresponds a unique sequence of source symbols.   Not in every case can we work backward and find a unique sequence of source symbols which corresponds to a given binary sequence.   For example, if $\gamma_2 = \{0,00,01\}$ is the code representing $\{A,B,C\}$, then the sequence 0001 may be decoded as either AAC or as BC.

A code is said to be *uniquely decipherable* if and only if every coded message can be decomposed into a sequence of code words in only one way.   Thus γ_1 is uniquely decipherable, while γ_2 is not.   Whenever the number of code symbols is not the same for all code words, the code is not necessarily uniquely decipherable, as illustrated by γ_2.   On the other hand, the code $\gamma_3 = \{1,01,001,0001\}$ is uniquely decipherable, since the symbol 1 actually serves as a separator between successive code words. Such a separator is referred to as a *comma*, and such a code is called a *comma code*.   A code in which all code words contain the same number of symbols is called a *block code*.   A code in which the number of symbols representing code words is not the same is called a *variable-length code*.

Whenever each code word can be deciphered without knowing the succeeding code words, the code is said to be an *instantaneous code*.   For example, γ_1 and γ_3 are instantaneous codes, while $\gamma_4 = \{1,10,100\}$ is not, since the sequence 10 cannot be deciphered until we verify that the next symbol is a 1.

Let $\xi = \xi_1\xi_2 \cdots \xi_n$ be a code word; then the sequence of code symbols $\xi_1\xi_2 \cdots \xi_m$, where $m \leq n$, is called a *prefix* of ξ.   It can be shown that a necessary and sufficient condition for a code to be instantaneous is that no code word is a prefix of some other code word.   Clearly, γ_4 is not instantaneous, because 1 is a prefix of both 10 and 100.

One of the major reasons for using variable-length codes is the reduction in the average length of the coded messages.   Certain symbols of the source alphabet are more frequently used than others.   For example, in English, the letter e is more often used than the letter q.   It is advantageous to assign shorter code words to those symbols which appear most often, and longer code words to other symbols.   If we let P_i and l_i denote, respectively, the probability of occurrence and the length of the code word representing the ith source symbol, we obtain the average length of the code, which is defined as the sum $\Sigma P_i l_i$, where the sum is taken over all code words.   For a given source alphabet and a given code alphabet, it is usually possible to construct many uniquely decipherable codes.   In many codes, however, if an error occurs at the beginning of the coded message, it may invalidate the entire message.   It is therefore desirable to have codes which are *synchronizable,* that is, for which the propagation of an error is bounded to only a fixed portion of the message.

A test for unique decipherability

A code is said to be *uniquely decipherable with a finite delay* μ if and only if μ is the least integer, so that the knowledge of the first μ symbols of the coded message suffices to determine its first code word. We now present a testing procedure to determine whether or not a code is uniquely decipherable, and if it is, the delay μ. This procedure is analogous to the tests for information losslessness and information losslessness of finite order.

Let us insert a separation symbol S at the beginning and end of each code word in γ. In addition, in every code word representing the source symbol N, we insert the symbol N_i between its ith symbol and its $(i + 1)$st symbol. For example, if the source symbols are $\{A,B,C\}$ and $\gamma = \{0,01,1010\}$, then the code words with the inserted symbols are

$$
\begin{aligned}
A &\to S \quad 0 \quad S \\
B &\to S \quad 0 \quad B_1 \quad 1 \quad S \\
C &\to S \quad 1 \quad C_1 \quad 0 \quad C_2 \quad 1 \quad C_3 \quad 0 \quad S
\end{aligned}
$$

Each code symbol ξ_k is now situated between two separation symbols. We say that the separation symbol to the right of the code symbol is the ξ_k-*successor,* denoted R_i, of the left separation symbol. For example, C_1 is the 1-successor of S, because $S1C_1$ occurs in the third code word. Two successors, R_i and R_j, are *compatible* if $S\xi_kR_i$ and $S\xi_kR_j$ occur, or if $R_p\xi_kR_i$ and $R_q\xi_kR_j$ occur, and R_p and R_q are compatible. In such a case (R_iR_j) is said to be the compatible *implied* by (R_pR_q).

A *testing table (for unique decipherability)* can now be constructed in the following manner:

1. The column headings of the table are the symbols of the code alphabet.
2. The first row heading is S. The other row headings are the compatible pairs.
3. The entries in row R_pR_q, column ξ_k, are the compatibles implied by (R_pR_q) under ξ_k.

The testing table for our example is given in Table 14-24. The entry in row S, column 0, is (SB_1), since $S0S$ and $S0B_1$ occur in the first and second words. The compatible implied by (SB_1) is (SC_1), since S is the 1-successor of B_1 in code word B, while C_1 is the 1-successor of S in code word C; i.e., $B_1 1 S$ and $S 1 C_1$ occur in the code words. If $(R_i R_j R_k)$ are compatible, we enter into the table all unordered pairs $(R_i R_j)$, $(R_i R_k)$, $(R_j R_k)$. The table is completed when all the compatible pairs have been used as row headings.

Table 14-24 Testing table for
$$\gamma = \{0,01,1010\}$$

	0	1
S	(SB_1)	—
SB_1	—	(SC_1)
SC_1	$(SC_2)(B_1C_2)$	—
SC_2	—	(C_1C_3)
B_1C_2	—	(SC_3)
C_1C_3	(SC_2)	—
SC_3	$(SB_1)(SS)$	—

If during the construction of the testing table a repeated pair (SS) occurs, the code is not uniquely decipherable. The occurrence of such a compatible pair means that there exists some compatible pair $(R_i R_j)$ such that S is the ξ-successor of both R_i and R_j. But since both R_i and R_j (like all compatible pairs) are reachable from S by a binary sequence that corresponds to two or more different sequences of source symbols, the code is not uniquely decipherable. Moreover, by tracing back the compatibles which implied the pair (SS), we can find one of the shortest ambiguous messages, which in our example is 01010, as shown in Fig. 14-14. The pair (SS) is written in the rightmost position, and its 0-pre-

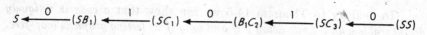

$$S \longleftarrow^{0} (SB_1) \longleftarrow^{1} (SC_1) \longleftarrow^{0} (B_1C_2) \longleftarrow^{1} (SC_3) \longleftarrow^{0} (SS)$$

Fig. 14-14 Determination of an ambiguous message.

decessor is written in the next left position, and so on. The sequence of arrow labels leading from S to (SS) is an ambiguous message. Indeed, 01010 may be interpreted as AC or as BBA.

It is easy to show that if the pair (SS) is not generated, the code is uniquely decipherable. Hence *a necessary and sufficient condition for a code to be uniquely decipherable is that the pair (SS) is not generated in the testing table.*

A *testing graph* (*for unique decipherability*) G can now be constructed as follows:

1. Corresponding to every row in the testing table there is a vertex in G.
2. A directed arc leads from a vertex to each of the vertices corresponding to the implied compatible pairs.

The testing table for the code $\gamma = \{1,10,001\}$ is shown in Table 14-25. The corresponding testing graph is shown in Fig. 14-15. Since the pair

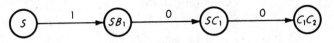

Fig. 14-15   Testing graph.

(SS) has not been generated in the testing table, the code is uniquely decipherable.

Table 14-25   Testing table for $\gamma = \{1,10,001\}$

		0	1
$A \to S1S$	S	—	(SB_1)
$B \to S1B_10S$	(SB_1)	(SC_1)	—
$C \to S0C_10C_21S$	(SC_1)	(C_1C_2)	—
	(C_1C_2)	—	—

In analogy to Theorem 14-5 we can show that *a code is uniquely decipherable with a finite delay μ if and only if its testing graph is loop-free*. The delay μ is equal to $l + 1$, where l is the length of the longest path in G. The longest path in the graph of Fig. 14-15 is 3, and thus $\mu = 4$.

Deciphering a coded message

We now describe a procedure to decipher a coded message. The decoding procedure is similar to the input-retrieval procedure for lossless machines and will be illustrated by means of an example. Consider the code $\gamma = \{11,011,001,01,00\}$, which is known to be uniquely decipherable, and suppose we want to decode the sequence 00111011000110100011. Scanning the message from the left, we insert a lower comma whenever a sequence which corresponds to a legitimate code word is detected. For example, the first comma from the left follows the initial 00, since 00 is a word in γ. Next, a comma follows the 1, since the sequence 001 is also a word in γ, and so on. Although the tenth and eleventh symbols are 0's, no lower comma is inserted between the eleventh and the twelfth symbols, because there is no comma between the ninth and the tenth symbol, and a new word cannot start unless a comma indicates the end of the preceding word. The procedure is illustrated in Fig. 14-16.

$$0\ '\ 0\ ,\ 1\ \overset{!}{.}\ 1\ ,\ 1\ ;\ 0\ '\ 1\ ,\ 1\ ;\ 0\ '\ 0\ ;\ 0\ '\ 1\ ,\ 1\ ;\ 0\ 1\ ;\ 0\ '\ 0\ ;\ 1\ ,\ 1$$

Fig. 14-16   Deciphering of a coded message.

Next we scan the coded message from the right and inset an upper comma whenever a sequence which corresponds to the inverse of a legitimate code word is scanned. The inverses of the code words in our example are {11,110,100,10,00}. If the code is uniquely decipherable, the message can be decoded by retaining only those commas that occur in the upper and lower spaces simultaneously. In our example we find the following message:

001; 11; 011; 00; 011; 01; 00; 11

Although the above procedure will in general require keeping track of a number of sequences and the locations of the various commas, it is in principle a simple procedure that can be carried out by a finite-state machine.

A test for synchronizability of codes

A code is said to be *synchronizable of order* μ if μ is the least integer, so that the knowledge of any μ consecutive code symbols is sufficient to determine a separation of code words within these symbols. Although there exist synchronizable codes which are not uniquely decipherable, we shall restrict our attention to synchronizable codes which are uniquely decipherable with a finite delay, since these are the only ones of practical interest.

The problem of testing a code for synchronizability is analogous to the problem of testing a machine for finite output memory. In fact, since in both cases the objective is to specify the sequence at some point, we can use the same testing procedure. Let us construct a *testing table* (*for synchronizability*) in the following manner. The row headings in the upper half of the table consist of all the separation symbols. The column headings are the code symbols. The entries in row R_i, column ξ_k, of the upper half of the table are the ξ_k-successors of R_i. The row headings in the lower half of the table are all pairs of separation symbols. The entries in row R_iR_j, column ξ_k, are the pairs implied by (R_iR_j) and symbol ξ_k. The *testing graph* (*for synchronizability*) has a vertex for each row in the lower half of the testing table. A directed arc labeled ξ_k leads from vertex R_iR_j to vertex R_pR_q, where $p \neq q$, if and only if (R_pR_q) is the ξ_k-successor of (R_iR_j). We can now state, without proof, a necessary and sufficient condition for a code to be synchronizable.

▶   A code is synchronizable if and only if it is uniquely decipherable and its testing graph is loop-free. It is synchronizable of order μ if and only if the longest path in the graph is of length $\mu - 1$.

Example   Consider the code $\gamma = \{1,10,001\}$, whose testing table is shown in Table 14-26 and whose testing graph is shown in Fig. 14-17. Since the code is uniquely decipherable and the graph is loop-free, γ is synchronizable of order 5. ∎

Table 14-26   Testing table for $\gamma = \{1,10,001\}$

	0	1
S	C_1	(SB_1)
B_1	S	—
C_1	C_2	—
C_2	—	S
SB_1	(SC_1)	—
SC_1	(C_1C_2)	—
SC_2	—	(SB_1)
B_1C_1	(SC_2)	—
B_1C_2	—	—
C_1C_2	—	—

The main advantage of using a synchronizable code is that the propagation of errors within messages composed of such a code is bounded. In other words, if an error occurs in transmitting a coded message, its effect on the decipherability of the message is limited to at most μ symbols, since the knowledge of any μ code symbols is sufficient to determine a

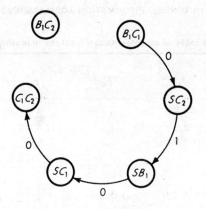

Fig. 14-17 Testing graph.

single separation within these symbols. And since synchronizable codes are also uniquely decipherable with a finite delay, the determination of a single separation of code words is sufficient for the decoding of the message from that point on.

★APPENDIX 14-1 THE LEAST UPPER BOUND FOR INFORMATION LOSSLESSNESS OF FINITE ORDER

In the following we shall prove that the bound for information losslessness established by Theorem 14-5 is the least upper bound. Specifically, we shall show that for every n there exists a four-input seven-output machine which is information lossless of maximal order, that is, for which $\mu = 1 + (n - 1)n/2$. Such a machine is shown in Table 14-27, where $[g]$ is the largest integer not exceeding g.

Theorem 14-6 *For every n, there exists an information lossless machine of order*

$$\mu = \frac{1 + n(n - 1)}{2}$$

Proof: We prove the theorem by demonstrating that the class of machines described in Table 14-27 is information lossless of order $1 + n(n - 1)/2$. The upper part of the testing table for this machine is given in Table 14-28. The testing graph is derived directly from the table and is shown for an even n in Fig. 14-18. The graph contains no vertex with repeated entries because all the entries in every column of the upper part of the testing table are distinct. The graph contains $n(n - 1)/2$ vertices arranged in

543

Table 14-27 State table of an information lossless machine of maximal order

PS	NS, z			
	I_1	I_2	I_3	I_4
1	2,0	3,2	2,3	2,5
2	3,0	4,2	3,3	3,5
3	4,0	5,2	4,3	4,5
$\cdot$	$\cdot$	$\cdot$	$\cdot$	$\cdot$
$\cdot$	$\cdot$	$\cdot$	$\cdot$	$\cdot$
i	$i+1,0$	$i+2,2$	$i+1,3$	$i+1,5$
$\cdot$	$\cdot$	$\cdot$	$\cdot$	$\cdot$
$\cdot$	$\cdot$	$\cdot$	$\cdot$	$\cdot$
$\left[\dfrac{n}{2}\right]-1$	$\left[\dfrac{n}{2}\right],0$	$\left[\dfrac{n}{2}\right]+1,2$	$\left[\dfrac{n}{2}\right],3$	$\left[\dfrac{n}{2}\right],5$
$\left[\dfrac{n}{2}\right]$	$\left[\dfrac{n}{2}\right]+1,0$	$\left[\dfrac{n}{2}\right]+2,1$	$\left[\dfrac{n}{2}\right]+1,3$	$\left[\dfrac{n}{2}\right]+1,5$
$\cdot$	$\cdot$	$\cdot$	$\cdot$	$\cdot$
j	$j+1,0$	$j+2,1$	$j+1,3$	$j+1,5$
$\cdot$	$\cdot$	$\cdot$	$\cdot$	$\cdot$
$n-2$	$n-1,0$	$n,1$	$n-1,3$	$n-1,5$
$n-1$	$n,0$	$1,1$	$1,6$	$n,5$
n	$1,4$	$1,2$	$n,3$	$2,4$

$n-1$ columns. The maximal path which connects all these vertices is shown in Fig. 14-18 by the solid line. The maximal path is constructed in the following manner: The first compatible pair $(1,2)$ is introduced in column 4 of the testing table. This pair in turn implies pairs $(2,3)$, $(3,4)$, . . . , $(n-2,n-1)$. Because of the arrangement of the entries in column 1 of Table 14-28 pair $(1,n)$ is implied by $(n-2,n-1)$. And because of the entries in column 2, pair $(1,3)$ is implied by $(1,n)$. And similarly for every column of vertices in the graph. The path goes from vertex $(1,k)$, for all $2 \le k \le n/2$, to vertex $(n-k,n-1)$, from which it then goes to vertex $(1,n-k+2)$ as implied by the entries in column 1 of the testing table.

The path continues from vertex $(1,h)$, for all $(n/2)+1 < h \le n$ to vertex $(n-h+1,n)$ and from which it goes to $(1,n-h+3)$ as implied by the entries in column 2 of the testing table. Finally,

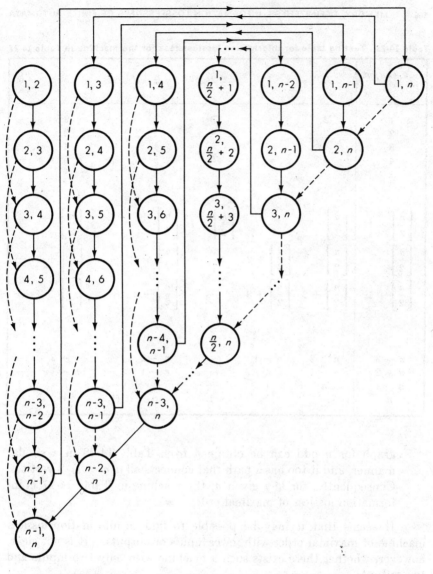

Fig. 14-18 Testing graph for an even n for the lossless machine of Table 14-27.

the path goes from vertex $(n/2,n)$ to $(n/2 + 1,n)$ and so on, to $(n - 1,n)$, as implied by the entries in column 3 of Table 14-28. Vertex $(n - 1,n)$ is a terminal vertex since the corresponding compatible pair implies no other compatible pair.

It is evident from the structure of the graph that it has no loops, although it contains a number of shorter paths. The testing

Table 14-28   Testing table for information losslessness for the machine in Table 14-27

Output PS	0	1	2	3	4	5	6
1	2	—	3	2	—	2	—
2	3	—	4	3	—	3	—
3	4	—	5	4	—	4	—
4	5	—	6	5	—	5	—
.	.	.	.	.	.	.	.
$\left[\frac{n}{2}\right]-1$	$\left[\frac{n}{2}\right]$	—	$\left[\frac{n}{2}\right]+1$	$\left[\frac{n}{2}\right]$	—	$\left[\frac{n}{2}\right]$	—
$\left[\frac{n}{2}\right]$	$\left[\frac{n}{2}\right]+1$	$\left[\frac{n}{2}\right]+2$	—	$\left[\frac{n}{2}\right]+1$	—	$\left[\frac{n}{2}\right]+1$	—
$\left[\frac{n}{2}\right]+1$	$\left[\frac{n}{2}\right]+2$	$\left[\frac{n}{2}\right]+3$	—	$\left[\frac{n}{2}\right]+2$	—	$\left[\frac{n}{2}\right]+2$	—
.	.	.	.	.	.	.	.
$n-3$	$n-2$	$n-1$	—	$n-2$	—	$n-2$	—
$n-2$	$n-1$	n	—	$n-1$	—	$n-1$	—
$n-1$	n	1	—	—	—	n	1
n	—	—	1	n	(1,2)	—	—

graph for n odd can be obtained from Table 14-28 in a similar manner, and it too has a path that connects all $n(n-1)/2$ vertices. Consequently, for any given n, the machine in Table 14-27 is information lossless of maximal order. ∎

It seems that it may be possible to find an information lossless machine of maximal order with fewer inputs or outputs. It is not clear, however, whether there exists such a machine with only two inputs and two outputs.

NOTES AND REFERENCES

The various memory aspects of automata have been investigated by numerous authors, among whom are Liu [6, 7, 8], McCluskey [10], Massey [9], Simon [12], and Perles, Rabin, and Shamir [11]. Lossless machines were first studied by Huffman [4], who devised tests for losslessness and losslessness of finite order. Even [1] devised a different testing procedure, the one adopted in this chapter. The least upper bound developed in the appendix is due to Kohavi and Winograd [5]. The tests for decipherability and synchronizability of codes are due to Even [2, 3].

1. Even, S.: On Information Lossless Automata of Finite Order, *IEEE Trans. Electron. Computers*, vol. EC-14, pp. 561–569, August, 1965.
2. Even, S.: Test for Synchronizability of Automata and Variable Length Codes, *IEEE Trans. Information Theory*, vol. IT-10, pp. 185–189, July, 1964.
3. Even, S.: Tests for Unique Decipherability, *IEEE Trans. Information Theory*, vol. IT-9, pp. 109–112, April, 1963.
4. Huffman, D. A.: Canonical Forms for Information Lossless Finite-state Machines, *IRE Trans. Circuit Theory*, vol. CT-6, Special Supplement, pp. 41–59, May, 1959.
5. Kohavi, Z., and J. Winograd: Establishing Bounds Concerning Finite Automata, *Journal of Computer and System Sciences*, vol. 7, no. 3, June, 1973, pp. 288–299.
6. Liu, C. L.: Some Memory Aspects of Finite Automata, *M.I.T. Res. Lab. Electron. Tech. Rept.* 411, May, 1963.
7. Liu, C. L.: Determination of the Final State of an Automaton Whose Initial State Is Unknown, *IEEE Trans. Electron. Computers*, vol. EC-12, December, 1963.
8. Liu, C. L.: kth-order Finite Automaton, *IEEE Trans. Electron. Computers*, vol. EC-12, October, 1963.
9. Massey, J. L.: Note on Finite-memory Sequential Machines, *IEEE Trans. Electron. Computers*, vol. EC-15, pp. 658–659, 1966.
10. McCluskey, E. J.: Reduction of Feedback Loops in Sequential Circuits and Carry Leads in Iterative Networks, *Proc. Third Ann. Symp. Switching Theory and Logical Design*, Chicago, 1962, pp. 91–102.
11. Perles, M., M. O. Rabin, and E. Shamir: The Theory of Definite Automata, *IEEE Trans. Electron. Computers*, June, 1963, pp. 233–243.
12. Simon, S. M.: A Note on Memory Aspects of Sequence Transducers, *IRE Trans. Circuit Theory*, vol. CT-6, Special Supplement, pp. 26–29, May, 1959.

PROBLEMS

14-1. For each of the following machines determine whether or not it has a finite memory, and if it does, find its order.

PS	NS, z $x = 0$	$x = 1$
A	B,0	B,0
B	C,0	D,0
C	D,0	C,0
D	A,0	C,1

(a)

PS	NS, z $x = 0$	$x = 1$
A	D,0	C,1
B	A,0	E,0
C	C,1	E,0
D	C,1	C,1
E	B,0	B,1

(b)

PS	NS, z $x = 0$	$x = 1$
A	B,0	E,0
B	C,0	D,0
C	D,0	C,0
D	E,0	A,0
E	E,0	A,1

(c)

14-2. The *canonical realization of finite-memory machines* is shown in Fig. P14-2. Verify that the machine of Table P14-2 has a finite memory, and show its canonical realization. In particular, design the combinational logic.

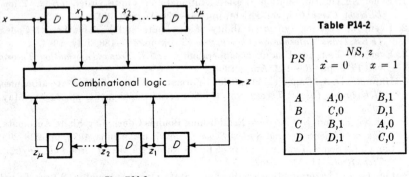

Fig. P14-2

Table P14-2

PS	NS, z	
	$x = 0$	$x = 1$
A	A,0	B,1
B	C,0	D,1
C	B,1	A,0
D	D,1	C,0

14-3. Prove that, for every n, the machine of Table P14-3 has a finite memory of order $\mu = (n - 1)n/2$. (Recall that $[g]$ is the least integer greater than or equal to g.)

Hint: Use the testing graph for finite memory.

Table P14-3

PS	NS		z	
	$x = 0$	$x = 1$	$x = 0$	$x = 1$
1	2	3	0	0
2	3	4	0	0
3	4	5	0	0
4	5	6	0	0
.	.	.	.	.
.	.	.	.	.
.	.	.	.	.
$[(n - 3)/2]$	$[(n - 1)/2]$	$[(n + 1)/2]$	0	0
$[(n - 1)/2]$	$[(n + 1)/2]$	$[(n + 3)/2]$	0	1
$[(n + 1)/2]$	$[(n + 3)/2]$	$[(n + 5)/2]$	0	1
.	.	.	.	.
.	.	.	.	.
.	.	.	.	.
$n - 3$	$n - 2$	$n - 1$	0	1
$n - 2$	$n - 1$	n	0	1
$n - 1$	n	1	0	1
n	n	1	0	0

14-4. Let M be a p-input, q-output, n-state, strongly connected machine. Prove that if M has a finite memory of order μ, then $(pq)^\mu \geq n$.

14-5. (a) Test the machine of Table P14-5 for definiteness.

(b) Show the canonical realization of this machine (see Fig. 14-3). In particular, specify the combinational logic.

Table P14-5

PS	NS, z	
	$x = 0$	$x = 1$
A	D,1	E,0
B	A,0	B,1
C	C,0	B,0
D	C,1	B,1
E	A,0	B,0

14-6. (a) Specify the unspecified entries in Table P14-6a so that the resulting machine will be definite. Is your answer unique? If not, show all the possible ways to specify the table.

(b) Is it possible to specify Table P14-6b so that it corresponds to a definite machine? Justify your answer.

Table P14-6

PS	NS	
	$x = 0$	$x = 1$
A	A	B
B	—	B
C	E	—
D	—	F
E	—	D
F	E	—

(a)

PS	NS	
	$x = 0$	$x = 1$
A	A	B
B	C	C
C	—	—
D	—	—

(b)

14-7. Determine which of the following machines has a finite output memory, and find its order.

Table P14-7

PS	NS, z $x = 0$	$x = 1$
A	A,0	B,1
B	C,1	D,0
C	D,0	C,1
D	B,1	A,0

(a)

PS	NS, z $x = 0$	$x = 1$
A	C,0	C,0
B	D,1	A,0
C	C,1	B,0
D	D,1	D,1

(b)

PS	NS, z $x = 0$	$x = 1$
A	B,0	C,0
B	D,0	E,1
C	F,1	D,0
D	F,1	F,1
E	B,0	B,0
F	A,1	A,1

(c)

14-8. Given the state table of machine M shown in Table P14-8. Specify the missing output entries in such a way that the machine will be finite memory of maximal order.

Table P14-8

PS	NS, z $x = 0$	$x = 1$
A	B,0	C,1
B	D,0	D,–
C	C,–	A,0
D	C,0	A,1

14-9. Given machine M with n states $S_1, S_2, \ldots, S_n$.

(a) Devise a procedure to determine whether the machine has n preset sequences $X_1, X_2, \ldots, X_n$, such that X_i is the shortest sequence that takes M from any unknown initial state to state S_i.

(b) Apply your procedure to find the appropriate sequences for machine M in Table P14-9.

(c) Find an upper bound on the length of X_i.

(d) Does the existence of such a set of sequences imply that M must be a definite machine?

Table P14-9

PS	NS, z $x = 0$	$x = 1$
A	C,0	B,0
B	E,1	F,0
C	A,1	F,1
D	E,0	B,1
E	C,1	D,0
F	E,0	F,0

14-10. Consider the class of machines which have a finite output memory of order μ, so that the knowledge of the last μ outputs suffices to determine the *final* state of the machine.

(a) Devise a test to determine whether a given machine belongs to the above class.

(b) Find such a four- or five-state machine and apply your test to it.

14-11. For each of the following machines determine whether or not it is lossless. If it is lossy, find a shortest output sequence produced by two different input sequences with the same initial and final states. If it is lossless, determine its order.

Table P14-11

PS	NS, z $x = 0$	$x = 1$
A	B,1	C,0
B	A,0	D,1
C	B,0	A,0
D	C,1	A,1

(a)

PS	NS, z $x = 0$	$x = 1$
A	B,0	C,1
B	D,1	A,0
C	E,1	F,1
D	F,0	E,0
E	C,1	A,0
F	B,0	D,1

(b)

PS	NS, z $x = 0$	$x = 1$
A	B,0	C,0
B	D,0	E,1
C	E,0	A,1
D	E,0	D,0
E	C,1	B,1

(c)

PS	NS, z $x = 0$	$x = 1$
A	B,0	A,1
B	C,0	D,1
C	E,1	A,0
D	E,0	C,0
E	C,1	E,0

(d)

14-12. You are presented with only the lower half of a testing table (for losslessness) of an unknown machine. Specify the upper half of the table and find a corresponding four-state machine. Is your answer unique?

Table P14-12

	$z = 0$	$z = 1$
A		
B		
C		
D		
AB	—	(BC)(CC)
AC	—	(AB)(AC)
AD	—	—
BC	(BD)	(AC)
BD	(AD)(CD)	—
CD	(AB)(BC)	—

14-13. (a) The machine described in Table P14-13 has two binary outputs, z_1 and z_2. Some of the output entries are incompletely specified.

Specify all the output entries so that the machine will be lossless of first order.

(b) Prove that any binary-input, binary-output machine can be transformed into a lossless machine of first order by adding to it a single binary output terminal.

Table P14-13

PS	NS, $z_1 z_2$	
	$x = 0$	$x = 1$
A	$B, -1$	$C, 1\ 1$
B	$D, 0 -$	$D, 0 -$
C	$D, 0 -$	$E, -$
D	$B, 0 -$	$D, -0$
E	$C, 0 -$	$D, -0$

14-14. The machine described in Table P14-14 has two binary outputs z_1 and z_2, some of whose entries are incompletely specified. Specify all output entries so that the machine will be lossless of the least order. Is such a specification unique?

Table P14-14

PS	NS, $z_1 z_2$	
	$x = 0$	$x = 1$
A	$B, 10$	$C, 10$
B	$C, 00$	$C, 1 -$
C	$A, 1 -$	$D, 00$
D	$D, 1 -$	$A, 00$

14-15. Prove that the machine of Table P14-15 is lossless of maximal order, i.e., $\mu = 11$.

Table P14-15

PS	NS, Z	
	$x = 0$	$x = 1$
S_1	$S_2, 1$	$S_1, 1$
S_2	$S_3, 1$	$S_5, 3$
S_3	$S_4, 1$	$S_4, 3$
S_4	$S_5, 1$	$S_3, 2$
S_5	$S_1, 2$	$S_1, 3$

14-16. For the machine shown in Table P14-16:

(a) Find in a systematic way the output sequence Z_2 when the output sequence Z_1 is $Z_1 = 001001$, and it is known that the initial and final state is B.

(b) Given the initial and final states as well as the output sequence Z_1, is it always possible to determine the output sequence Z_2?

Table P14-16

PS	NS, z_1z_2	
	$x = 0$	$x = 1$
A	A,11	B,10
B	D,00	A,00
C	E,00	C,10
D	B,01	C,01
E	C,11	A,01

14-17. For the machine shown in Table P14-17:

(a) Is the machine finite output memory? If yes, find the order λ.

(b) Is the machine information lossless of finite order? If yes, find the order μ.

(c) The machine produced the output sequence $Z = 0101000$. What is the corresponding input sequence? Is it unique?

(d) What is the minimal length of output sequence Z that enables us to determine at least one input symbol?

Table P14-17

PS	NS, z	
	$x = 0$	$x = 1$
A	B,0	C,0
B	D,0	E,1
C	A,1	E,0
D	E,0	D,0
E	A,1	E,1

14-18. Given the cascade connection of machines M_1 and M_2 as shown in Fig. P14-18.

(a) For M_1 and M_2 shown in Table P14-18, given that the output sequence $z = 110011$ and the final state of M_2 is B, determine the initial state of M_1.

(b) For the machines in Table P14-18 prove that, for every given output sequence z of length L, the knowledge of the final state of M_2 is sufficient to determine the state of M_1 at some time during the experiment. Find the value of L.

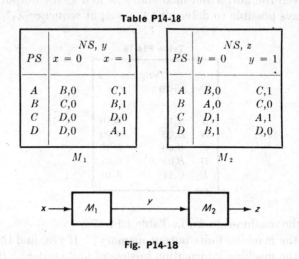

Table P14-18

PS	NS, y x = 0	x = 1
A	B,0	C,1
B	C,0	B,1
C	D,0	D,0
D	D,0	A,1

M_1

PS	NS, z y = 0	y = 1
A	B,0	C,1
B	A,0	C,0
C	D,1	A,1
D	B,1	D,0

M_2

Fig. P14-18

14-19. Machines M_1 and M_2 shown in Table P14-19 are connected in cascade as shown in Fig. P14-18. The initial state of M_1 is A. Find in a systematic way all the shortest input sequences which, when applied to M_1, will make it possible to identify the initial state of M_2 by means of its response z.

Table P14-19

PS	NS, y x = 0	x = 1
A	B,0	C,1
B	C,1	A,0
C	A,0	B,0

M_1

PS	NS, z y = 0	y = 1
D	E,1	D,0
E	F,1	G,0
F	D,1	E,0
G	F,0	D,0

M_2

14-20. (a) In response to an unknown input sequence, the machine of Table P14-20 produces the following output sequence:

1 0 0 1 1

Find the input sequence if it is known that the *final* state is B.

(b) Prove that the knowledge of the final state of this machine and the last output symbol is sufficient for the determination of the next-to-final state.

(c) Devise a test to determine whether a given machine is lossless, so that the knowledge of the *final* state and the last μ output symbols is sufficient to identify the next-to-final state.

Hint: Use the output-predecessor table.

Table P14-20

PS	NS, z	
	$x = 0$	$x = 1$
A	B,0	C,1
B	A,0	C,0
C	D,1	A,1
D	B,1	D,0

14-21. (a) In response to an unknown input sequence, the machine of Table P14-21 produces the output sequence

1 1 1 0 0 0 0 0 1 0

Find the input sequence to the machine if it is known that its initial state is A and its final state is F.

(b) Can the machine produce the output sequence 11011000 when both its initial and final states are A?

Table P14-21

PS	NS, z	
	$x = 0$	$x = 1$
A	B,1	C,0
B	D,1	B,1
C	E,1	B,0
D	A,0	E,0
E	F,0	D,1
F	D,0	A,1

14-22. Find a reduced, four-state machine that is lossless of first order and is isomorphic to its own inverse.

14-23. Design an inverse of the machine shown in Table P14-23. Give a reduced, standard-form state table, assuming that the initial state of the lossless machine is A. For each of the other possible initial states of this machine, specify appropriate initial states of the inverse.

Table P14-23

PS	NS, z	
	$x = 0$	$x = 1$
A	$B,1$	$C,1$
B	$D,0$	$E,0$
C	$A,1$	$F,1$
D	$C,0$	$B,0$
E	$F,1$	$A,1$
F	$E,0$	$D,0$

14-24. (a) Prove that the inverse of a lossless machine of finite order is a lossless machine of finite order.

(b) Demonstrate, by finding the inverse of machine $M_{10}{}^i$ (Table 14-22), that the inverse of the inverse of a lossless machine of finite order is isomorphic to the original machine; i.e., show that the inverse of $M_{10}{}^i$ is isomorphic to M_{10}.

14-25. The output of a finite-state machine is the modulo-2 sum of the present input and the second and third past inputs, i.e.,

$$z(t) = x(t) \oplus x(t - 2) \oplus x(t - 3)$$

(a) Prove that such a machine is lossless of finite order.
(b) Realize the machine and its inverse.

14-26. Show that the code $\gamma = \{1,110,010,100\}$ is uniquely decipherable. Is it also uniquely decipherable with a finite delay? If so, find the delay; if not, show a message that cannot be deciphered in a finite time.

14-27. Given the uniquely decipherable code $\gamma = \{0,001,101,011\}$. Decipher the following message:

$$0 \quad 0 \quad 1 \quad 0 \quad 1 \quad 0 \quad 0 \quad 1 \quad 1 \quad 0 \quad 1 \quad 0 \quad 0 \quad 1 \quad 1 \quad 0 \quad 0 \quad 0 \quad 1$$

15
Linear Sequential Machines

Linear sequential machines constitute a subclass of linear systems in which the input, output, and state transitions occur in discrete steps. Consequently, the tools and techniques available for the analysis and synthesis of linear systems can be applied to linear machines as well. The numerous applications of linear machines give further incentive to the investigation of their properties and to development of efficient synthesis procedures.

In the first sections we present an intuitive, though well-justified, approach which requires only a limited knowledge of modern algebra. In subsequent sections (i.e., Secs. 15-4 through 15-6) the matrix formulation is presented, and methods for minimizing and detecting linear machines are developed.

15-1 INTRODUCTION

A *linear sequential machine* (called also *linear machine*) is a network which has a finite number of input and output terminals and is composed of interconnections of three types of basic components, to be introduced shortly. The input signals applied to the machine are elements of a finite field† $GF(p) = \{0,1, \ldots, p-1\}$, and the operations performed by the basic components on their inputs are carried out according to the rules of $GF(p)$. A block-diagram representation of a linear machine with l input terminals and m output terminals is shown in Fig. 15-1.

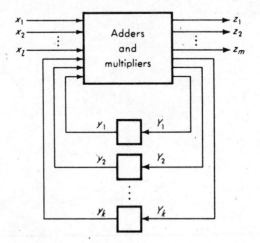

Fig. 15-1 Block diagram of a linear machine.

For a machine to be linear, its response to a linear combination of inputs must preserve the scale factor and the principle of superposition. Thus each of the basic components which are used to realize a linear machine must be linear. This requirement clearly precludes the use of an AND gate whose output is the product of its inputs; e.g., if the inputs are x_1 and x_2 and the signal values are elements of $GF(2)$, the output is $z = x_1 x_2$ modulo 2. Using similar arguments we observe that the OR gate is not linear since, for example, the output‡ of a two-input gate is $z = x_1 + x_2 + x_1 x_2$ modulo 2. The following three types of basic components are clearly linear:

    1. *Unit delays.* A unit delay is a two-terminal element whose output $y(t)$ is related to its input $Y(t)$ by $y(t) = Y(t-1)$.

† Some of the relevant basic properties of finite fields are summarized in Appendix 15-1. The understanding of these properties is essential in the study of linear machines.

‡ In this chapter the symbol $+$ represents the addition operation in accordance with the rules of $GF(p)$ (i.e., modulo p).

2. *Modulo-p adders.* An adder has l input terminals and one output terminal. The output is the modulo-p sum of the inputs; i.e., if the inputs are $x_1, x_2, \ldots, x_l$, the output is $x_1 + x_2 + \cdots + x_l$ (modulo p).

3. *Modulo-p scalar multipliers.* A multiplier c [where c is an element of $GF(p)$] has one input and one output terminal. If the input is x, the output is cx (modulo p).

Modulo-p addition and scalar multiplication are assumed to be executed instantaneously. For most purposes we shall restrict p to prime numbers. The symbols representing the above components are shown in Fig. 15-2.

Any network which is constructed by interconnecting components of the types shown in Fig. 15-2 is referred to as a linear circuit, provided

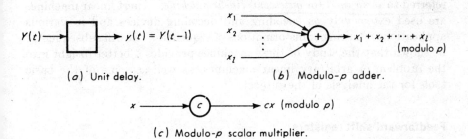

(a) Unit delay.   (b) Modulo-p adder.

(c) Modulo-p scalar multiplier.

Fig. 15-2 Basic components for linear circuits.

that every closed loop contains at least one delay element. The unit delay is equal to the discrete interval of time between two successive clock pulses. The state variables of a linear machine are the outputs $y_1, y_2, \ldots, y_k$ of the delay elements. The state of a machine at time t is specified by the value of the y's at t, i.e., $y_1(t), y_2(t), \ldots, y_k(t)$. The number of delay elements (or state variables) in a linear machine is referred to as the *dimension* of the machine. A linear machine whose components are modulo p and whose input signals are elements of $GF(p)$ is said to be a linear machine *over* $GF(p)$.

Example Figure 15-3 illustrates a four-terminal, four-dimensional linear machine over $GF(3)$. ∎

A linear machine over $GF(2)$ is called a *binary* machine. Binary machines are practical and simple to construct, and are widely used in various applications. Consequently, although we shall develop the

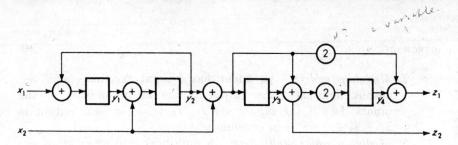

Fig. 15-3 A four-terminal, four-dimensional linear machine over $GF(3)$.

theory of linear machines over $GF(p)$, most examples will be selected from linear machines over the field $GF(2)$.

15-2 INERT LINEAR MACHINES

A linear machine whose delay elements are initially in the zero state is referred to as an *inert* (or *quiescent*) *linear machine*.   Inert linear machines are used extensively as encoding and decoding devices and in various applications requiring transformations of sequences.   It will subsequently be shown that the study of these machines provides a better insight into the problem of arbitrary linear machines, as well as some of the basic tools for the analysis of the subject.

Feedforward shift registers

The simplest type of inert linear machines is a two-terminal shift register which contains only feedforward paths and whose output is a modulo-p sum of selected input digits.   The schematic representation of a feedforward shift register over $GF(p)$ is shown in Fig. 15-4.

The output z can be described by a polynomial in D over the field $GF(p)$, i.e.,

$$z = a_0x + a_1Dx + \cdots + a_kD^kx \tag{15-1}$$

where the symbol D^i is an i-unit *delay operator*, which delays by i time units the variable on which it operates.   For example, the equation

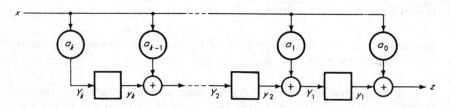

Fig. 15-4 A feedforward shift register.

$z = D^2x$ means that, for all $t \geq 2$, $z(t) = x(t - 2)$. $D^0 = 1$ is referred to as the *identity operator*.   Equation (15-1) is a valid description of the shift register of Fig. 15-4 only if the initial conditions of the delays are zero, i.e., $y_1(0) = y_2(0) = \cdots = y_k(0) = 0$, since otherwise the output cannot be expressed for all times as only a function of the input.   Equation (15-1) can be rewritten as

$$z = (a_0 + a_1D + \cdots + a_kD^k)x$$

or as

$$\frac{z}{x} = a_0 + a_1D + \cdots + a_kD^k = T(D) \tag{15-2}$$

where the polynomial $T(D)$, which expresses the ratio of z/x, is defined as the *transfer function* of the inert linear machine.

Example   Consider the inert linear machine over $GF(2)$ of Fig. 15-5, where the output is a modulo-2 sum of the present input and the first and third past inputs, i.e., $z(t) = x(t) + x(t - 1) + x(t - 3)$.   The corresponding polynomial in the delay operator is

$$z = x + Dx + D^3x$$

and the transfer function is

$$T_1 = \frac{z}{x} = 1 + D + D^3$$

Note that, for $GF(2)$, the scalar multiplier a_i is either 1 or 0, depending on whether there is or is not a connection to the ith modulo-2 adder.   ∎

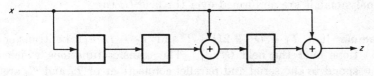

Fig. 15-5   Realization of $z = x + Dx + D^3x$.

To show that the circuit represented by Eq. (15-1) and Fig. 15-4 is indeed linear, let z and z^* be the responses to two distinct input sequences x and x^*, respectively, and let v and v^* be scalars taken from $GF(p)$. Then

$$z = a_0x + a_1Dx + \cdots + a_kD^kx$$

and

$$z^* = a_0x^* + a_1Dx^* + \cdots + a_kD^kx^*$$

The response Z to a linear combination of the inputs is given by

$$Z = a_0(vx + v^*x^*) + a_1D(vx + v^*x^*) + \cdots + a_kD^k(vx + v^*x^*)$$

or

$$Z = v[a_0x + a_1Dx + \cdots + a_kD^kx]$$
$$+ v^*[a_0x^* + a_1Dx^* + \cdots + a_kD^kx^*]$$

Hence

$$Z = vz + v^*z^* \tag{15-3}$$

The response of the machine to a linear combination of the inputs preserves the scale factor and the principle of superposition, and consequently the machine is linear. As a result, we may apply the linear theory of polynomials to the delay polynomials as well.

Consider now a serial connection of two linear machines of the type shown in Fig. 15-4; that is, the output of the predecessor machine is the input to the successor machine. Let x_1, z_1, and T_1 denote the input, output, and transfer function of the predecessor machine, and let x_2, z_2, and T_2 denote the input, output, and transfer function of the successor machine. The transfer function T_3 of the serial connection is given by

$$T_3 = \frac{z_2}{x_1}$$

But since x_2 and z_1 are identical, we have

$$T_3 = \frac{z_1}{x_1} \cdot \frac{z_2}{x_2} = T_1 \cdot T_2$$

Similarly, the transfer function of a parallel connection of the above machines is given by $T_4 = T_1 + T_2$. The multiplication and addition of polynomials are performed over the field $GF(p)$.

Example Let $T_1 = D^2 + 2D + 1$ and $T_2 = D + 1$ be transfer functions over the field $GF(3)$. The transfer functions which correspond to the serial and parallel connections of T_1 and T_2 are given by

$$T_3 = (D^2 + 2D + 1)(D + 1) = D^3 + 1$$
$$T_4 = (D^2 + 2D + 1) + (D + 1) = D^2 + 2 \quad \blacksquare$$

Impulse response and null sequences

It is useful to define the *impulse response* h of an inert linear machine as its response to the input sequence $100 \cdots 0$. For example, the impulse response of the (inert) feedforward shift register of Fig. 15-4 is

$a_0 a_1 a_2 \cdots a_k 0 \cdots 0$. After at most $k + 1$ time units, the output of the k-dimensional feedforward shift register will be a sequence of 0's. In analogy to linear system theory we can determine the response of an inert linear machine to an arbitrary input sequence from its impulse response. This is accomplished by performing a discrete "convolution" in $GF(p)$.

Example The impulse response of $T_1 = 1 + D + D^3$ is $h = 110100$ $\cdots$ 0. The response of T_1 to the input sequence 1011 is determined by adding (modulo 2) the sequences $h + D^2 h + D^3 h$ as follows:

Impulse:	1	0	0	0	0	$\cdots$	0				
Impulse response h:	1	1	0	1	0	$\cdots$	0				
Input sequence:	1	0	1	1							
h:	1	1	0	1	0	0	0	0	$\cdots$	0	
$D^2 h$:	0	0	1	1	0	1	0	0	$\cdots$	0	
$D^3 h$:	0	0	0	1	1	0	1	0	$\cdots$	0	
Output sequence:	1	1	1	1	1	1	1	0	$\cdots$	0	

The reader can similarly verify that the response of T_1 to the input sequence 11101 is 10000001. ∎

If the initial state at $t = 0$ of an inert linear machine is $00 \cdots 0$, i.e., $y_1(0) = y_2(0) = \cdots = y_k(0) = 0$, and the input to the machine is a sequence of 0's, the output is also a sequence of 0's. However, it is possible to generate an output sequence consisting of 0's by providing the machine with a nonzero input sequence. Such a sequence is called a *null sequence* of the linear machine T and is denoted X_0, so that TX_0 is a sequence of 0's. If X_0 and X_0^* are null sequences for a machine T, that is, $TX_0 = 00 \cdots 0$ and $TX_0^* = 00 \cdots 0$, then $v_1 TX_0 + v_2 TX_0^* = T(v_1 X_0 + v_2 X_0^*) = 00 \cdots 0$, where v_1 and v_2 are scalars from $GF(p)$. Thus *any linear combination of null sequences is also a null sequence for the machine.*

Example A null sequence of $T_1 = 1 + D + D^3$ is determined as follows:

$$0 = X_0 + DX_0 + D^3 X_0$$
$$X_0 = DX_0 + D^3 X_0$$

Thus the present digit of X_0 is found by adding (modulo 2) the first and third past input digits of X_0. The null sequence is determined by selecting an arbitrary (nonzero) sequence of length 3 (in general, of length equal to the dimension k) and specifying subsequent digits.

For T_1 the selection of 001 as the initial sequence yields the following null sequence:

$$X_0 = (0 \quad 0 \quad 1) \quad 1 \quad 1 \quad 0 \quad 1 \quad 0 \quad 0 \quad 1$$

After seven digits, the null sequence, which consists of the last seven digits, repeats itself. ■

Example · The null sequence for the polynomial $T = 1 + 2D^2 + D^3$ over $GF(3)$ is found from

$$0 = X_0 + 2D^2X_0 + D^3X_0$$

Adding $2X_0$ to both sides and recalling that $2X_0 + X_0 = 0$ in modulo 3 yields

$$2X_0 = 2D^2X_0 + D^3X_0$$

Multiplying both sides by 2 yields

$$X_0 = D^2X_0 + 2D^3X_0$$

Starting with 111, we obtain the null sequence

$$X_0 = (1 \quad 1 \quad 1) \quad 0 \quad 0 \quad 2 \quad 0 \quad 2 \quad 1 \quad 2 \quad 2 \quad 1 \quad 0 \quad 2 \quad 2 \quad 2$$
$$0 \quad 0 \quad 1 \quad 0 \quad 1 \quad 2 \quad 1 \quad 1 \quad 2 \quad 0 \quad 1 \quad 1 \quad 1 \quad ■$$

The preceding null sequences are known as *maximal* sequences, since each of them contains $(p^k - 1)$ digits, and includes all possible k-tuples, except $00 \cdots 0$. Additional properties of null sequences and their relationships to the delay polynomials are discussed in Ref. 7.

Inverse-machines

Feedforward shift registers are often used for encoding purposes. It is useful to determine whether an inverse-machine that can be used as a decoder exists, and if it does, how to construct it. We shall say that a polynomial $T(D)$, where $z = Tx$, has an inverse, which will be denoted by $1/T(D)$, if there exists a network which realizes $x = (1/T)z$. We shall consider only those inverses that decode without any delay. The inverse of the feedforward shift register of Fig. 15-4 is obtained by reversing the directions of z and x in the schematic diagram of Fig. 15-4 and inversing the scalar multipliers, as shown in Fig. 15-6.

If we provide the inverse-machine of Fig. 15-6 with the impulse response of the original machine of Fig. 15-4, i.e., $a_0a_1 \cdots a_{k-1}a_k00 \cdots 0$, its response will be the original message $x = 100 \cdots 0$. Since the inverse-machine is linear and initially inert, it will decode any message

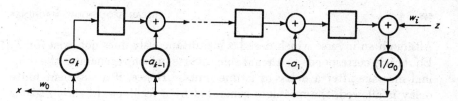

Fig. 15-6 Inverse-machine for the shift register of Fig. 15-4.

produced by the original machine. [Note that the negative scalars are actually positive integers since $(-a)$ modulo $p = (p - a)$ modulo p.]

From Fig. 15-6 it is evident that the inverse is realizable only if $a_0 \neq 0$. In general, *an inert linear machine described by a delay polynomial T has a linear inverse described by T^{-1}, which decodes without a delay, if and only if T contains a nonzero constant term which is prime to the modulo p.* The general proof of this result is left to the reader as an exercise. The following demonstrates it for the case of $GF(2)$.

An inert linear machine over the field of integers modulo 2 has an inverse, which decodes the output of the original machine without a delay, if and only if $a_0 = 1$ in T. To prove this assertion, consider the polynomial $T = a_1D + a_2D^2 + \cdots + a_kD^k$, for which $a_0 = 0$. Let the input to and the output from the inverse-machine be denoted w_i and w_o, respectively; then the transfer function is given by

$$\frac{w_o}{w_i} = \frac{1}{a_1D + a_2D^2 + \cdots + a_kD^k}$$

or

$$a_1Dw_o = w_i + a_2D^2w_o + \cdots + a_kD^kw_o$$

The above equation means that a *past* output of the inverse-machine (i.e., Dw_o) is a function of past outputs, as well as of the *present* input to the inverse-machine. Such a condition is clearly not physically realizable. (If $a_1 = 0$, the above argument holds for the term containing the lowest order $a_i \neq 0$.)

If T does not contain a nonzero constant term, no instantaneous inverse can be found. However, an "inverse" which decodes the original input after a finite delay can be found. Let a_i be the scalar associated with the lowest power of D for which $a_i \neq 0$, i.e.,

$$T = D^i + a_{i+1}D^{i+1} + \cdots + a_kD^k$$

(modulo 2). The "inverse" is given by

$$\frac{w_o}{w_i} = \frac{1}{D^i + a_{i+1}D^{i+1} + \cdots + a_kD^k} \tag{15-4}$$

or

$$\frac{D^iw_o}{w_i} = \frac{1}{1 + a_{i+1}D + \cdots + a_kD^{k-i}} \tag{15-5}$$

Although an inverse which decodes instantaneously does not exist for T, Eq. (15-5) corresponds to a realizable inverse, which regenerates the original message after a delay of i time units. Hence, if a sufficient finite delay is allowed, the messages generated by a feedforward shift register can always be decoded. This actually means that the shift register of Fig. 15-4 is lossless of order μ, where $\mu < k$.

Example The inverse of the inert linear machine of Fig. 15-5 is given by $T_1^{-1} = 1/(1 + D + D^3)$, and is shown in Fig. 15-7. (Note that, for binary inert linear machines, $-a_i = a_i$.) ∎

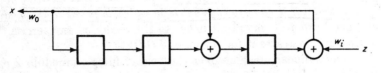

Fig. 15-7   An inverse to the machine of Fig. 15-5.

Linear machines with nonzero initial conditions

The inverse of an inert linear machine might not be inert. Consequently, its response to a sequence of zero inputs is not necessarily a sequence of zero outputs, but may be the null sequence X_0, whose starting digits are determined by the initial state of the inverse. This can be shown by observing that the transfer function of the inverse is $x/z = T^{-1}$, or $z = Tx = 0$, because the input z to the inverse is assumed to be the all-0's sequence. Clearly, the solution of the equation $Tx = 0$ is the null sequence X_0.

Let the inputs to the linear machine T_1 and its inverse T_1^{-1} (Figs. 15-5 and 15-7, respectively) be 0's. If they are inert, their respective outputs will also be 0's. If, however, they are not inert, their respective outputs will not be 0's but will depend on their initial states. Since T_1 contains only feedforward paths, its response to a sequence of 0's might initially be nonzero, depending on the initial state. However, after at most three time units, the response will be a sequence of 0's. In general, for every k-dimensional feedforward shift register, the response to a sequence of 0's will also be a sequence of 0's, after a transient period of at most k time units in which the output might be nonzero. In the case of a noninert shift register which contains feedback paths, e.g., T_1^{-1}, the response to a sequence of 0's is not necessarily a sequence of 0's. The behavior of a noninert linear machine whose input is a sequence of 0's is often referred to as *autonomous* behavior, and it can be described by the state diagram of the corresponding machine whose input terminals are ignored. The state diagrams describing the autonomous behavior of T_1 and T_1^{-1} are given in Fig. 15-8.

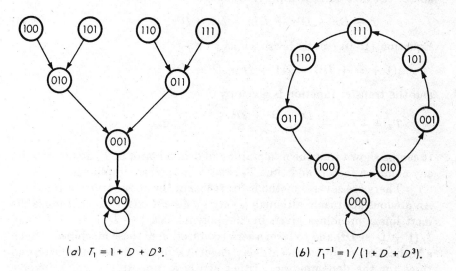

(a) $T_1 = 1 + D + D^3$.

(b) $T_1^{-1} = 1/(1 + D + D^3)$.

Fig. 15-8 State diagrams for autonomous behavior of linear machines.

An *autonomous linear machine* is a linear machine which contains no inputs (except a clock). A transition is caused by the clock pulse, and since the machine is deterministic, only one transition is permitted from each state. While the state diagram of T_1 contains only a single loop, corresponding to the case where the initial condition is 000, the diagram of T_1^{-1} contains two loops, which are called the *cycle sets*. The non-trivial cycle contains seven states and is maximal. (In general, the maximum number of distinct states in a k-dimensional modulo-p machine is p^k, and therefore a maximal cycle contains $p^k - 1$ states.) For a more comprehensive study of the properties of autonomous linear machines, the reader is referred to Gill [9].

15-3 INERT LINEAR MACHINES AND RATIONAL TRANSFER FUNCTIONS

In the preceding section the output of an inert linear machine was assumed to be a function of the present and some of the past input digits. In this section we develop the more general case where the present output depends on the present and selected past inputs and also on a finite number of past outputs. In this latter case the transfer function is a rational polynomial in the delay operator, i.e., $T = P(D)/Q(D)$.

Realization of rational polynomials

As an example, consider the inert linear machine whose output z is the modulo-2 sum of the present, first, second, and fourth previous inputs and of the first and third previous outputs, i.e.,

$$z = x + Dx + D^2x + D^4x + Dz + D^3z \tag{15-6}$$

Equation (15-6) can be rewritten as

$$z(1 + D + D^3) = x(1 + D + D^2 + D^4)$$

and the transfer function is given by

$$T_2 = \frac{z}{x} = \frac{1 + D + D^2 + D^4}{1 + D + D^3}$$

It can be shown that the numerator and denominator of T_2 do not contain any common factor, and thus T_2 cannot be further simplified.

There are several methods for realizing the above transfer function. An obvious approach, although a very inefficient one, is to synthesize the inert linear machines given by the polynomials $1 + D + D^2 + D^4$ and $1/(1 + D + D^3)$ and to form a serial connection of these machines. Such a realization requires seven delay elements, four for the numerator and three for the denominator. Other synthesis procedures which involve factoring of the numerator, partial fraction expansion, and ladder-type expansions, although useful, do not necessarily yield a minimal realization. (A *minimal realization* is one which yields a machine of smallest dimension.) Clearly, the minimal possible dimension is determined by the degree of the polynomial and is equal to the highest degree in either the numerator or the denominator of the transfer function. The chain realization described below yields in an efficient manner a minimal realization.

For T_2 the number of delay elements required in the minimal realization is four—the degree of the numerator. To demonstrate this assertion let us rewrite Eq. (15-6) in increasing powers of D as follows:

$$x + z = D(x + z) + D^2x + D^3z + D^4x$$

or

$$x + z = D\{(x + z) + D\{x + D(z + Dx)\}\} \tag{15-7}$$

The realization of Eq. (15-7), which is known as a *chain realization*, and that of its inverse, which corresponds to

$$T_2^{-1} = x/z = (1 + D + D^3)/(1 + D + D^2 + D^4)$$

are shown in Fig. 15-9. The output z is generated by adding x to $x + z$, i.e., $(x + z) + x = z$ (modulo 2). This realization uses only EXCLU-

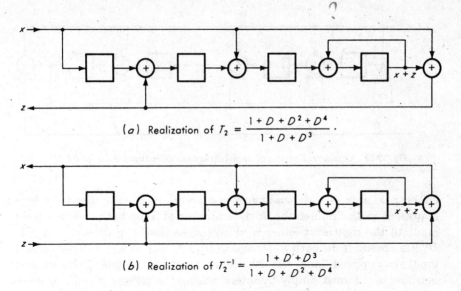

(a) Realization of $T_2 = \dfrac{1 + D + D^2 + D^4}{1 + D + D^3}$.

(b) Realization of $T_2^{-1} = \dfrac{1 + D + D^3}{1 + D + D^2 + D^4}$.

Fig. 15-9 Chain realization of an inert linear machine and its inverse.

SIVE-OR adders, i.e., two-input modulo-2 adders, which are relatively inexpensive and readily available. In general, one of the characteristics of the chain realization is that it employs modulo-2 adders with only two inputs.

To present the chain realization of an arbitrary transfer function over $GF(2)$, note that the transfer function $T = P(D)/Q(D)$ of any realizable inert linear machine over $GF(p)$ has the form

$$T = \frac{z}{x} = \frac{a_0 + a_1 D + \cdots + a_k D^k}{1 + b_1 D + \cdots + b_k D^k} = \frac{P(D)}{Q(D)} \qquad (15\text{-}8)$$

where the a_i's and b_i's are elements of $GF(p)$. The denominator $Q(D)$ must contain the term 1 if T is to be realizable, as shown in the preceding section. Clearly, a realizable instantaneous inverse T^{-1} exists if and only if the numerator contains a nonzero constant term a_0 which is prime to the modulo p. Machine T_2 has such an instantaneous inverse, as illustrated in Fig. 15-9b, since the numerator of T_2 contains a nonzero constant term, i.e., $a_0 = 1$.

For any invertible transfer function over $GF(2)$ of the form of Eq. (15-8) we can write an expression for $x + z$ as a sum of *past* inputs and outputs, e.g., Eq. (15-7). This expression can be realized by an alternating chain of delay elements and modulo-2 adders, as shown in Fig. 15-10. In general, the chain realization of a k-dimensional inert linear machine requires k delay elements and at most k two-input modulo-2 adders. One of the inputs to the ith adder from the right (except the first adder) is the output of the ith delay element. The second input, if required, is

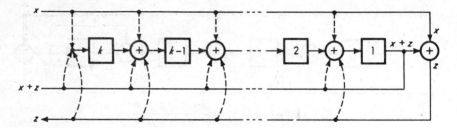

Fig. 15-10 Chain realization of an arbitrary transfer function over $GF(2)$.

either x, z, or $x + z$, depending, respectively, on whether the term D^{i-1} is present in the numerator or denominator of T or both. The second input to the rightmost adder is always x, so that $x + (x + z) = z$. If D^{i-1} is absent from both $P(D)$ and $Q(D)$, i.e., $a_{i-1} = b_{i-1} = 0$, no second input is required, and the ith adder may be deleted. The inverse machine is obtained simply by interchanging the roles of x and z as illustrated in Fig. 15-9b.

The realization of a two-terminal k-dimensional inert linear machine, over the field $GF(p)$, whose transfer function is given by Eq. (15-8), is shown in Fig. 15-11. Note that, for $p \geq 3$, it is generally not sufficient to employ only two-terminal adders, unless the number of adders is increased. The realization of Fig. 15-11 is obtained in a direct manner from the realizations in Figs. 15-4 and 15-6. The verification that it indeed realizes Eq. (15-8) is left to the reader as an exercise.

Example The realization of

$$T_3 = \frac{1 + 2D + D^2 + 2D^4}{1 + 2D + D^2 + D^3}$$

over $GF(3)$ is shown in Fig. 15-12. ∎

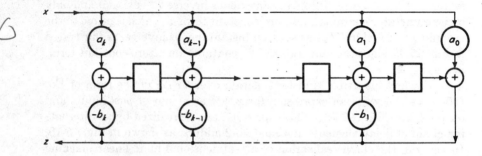

Fig. 15-11 Realization of $T = \dfrac{a_0 + a_1D + \cdots + a_kD^k}{1 + b_1D + \cdots + b_kD^k}$ (modulo p).

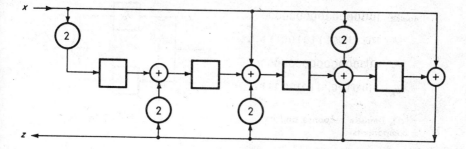

Fig. 15-12 Realization of $T_3 = \dfrac{1 + 2D + D^2 + 2D^4}{1 + 2D + D^2 + D^3}$ (modulo 3).

Impulse response and transfer function

The impulse response h of an inert linear machine has been defined as its response to the input sequence $100 \cdots 0$. For any given impulse response a transfer function can always be specified, and if the impulse response is realizable, a corresponding machine can be synthesized. We shall now show how to synthesize an inert linear machine from its impulse response. In particular, we shall prove that if the impulse response is realizable, then it consists of two components: a transient component denoted h_t and a periodic component denoted h_p.

In Sec. 10-2 it was shown that the response of an arbitrary sequential machine to a periodic excitation is periodic. In particular, the response to a sequence of 0's is periodic, with the period shorter than or equal to n, where n is the number of states. For a k-dimensional inert linear machine, the period of the response to a sequence of 0's is at most $p^k - 1 = n - 1$, since this is the maximal nontrivial cycle set (excluding the zero state). Consequently, a necessary condition for an impulse response h to be realizable is that it will ultimately become periodic. And since the length of the transient response is at most $k + 1$, the transfer function of a realizable two-terminal k-dimensional inert linear machine can be specified uniquely by observing the first $k + p^k$ symbols of the impulse response.

As an example, consider the impulse response $h = 1010100, 1110100,$ $1110100, \ldots$ of an inert linear machine over $GF(2)$. The impulse response can be separated into a transient and a periodic component, so that $h = h_t + h_p$, as shown in Fig. 15-13a. The synthesis of the corresponding inert linear machine can be accomplished by specifying separately the transfer functions T_t and T_p, corresponding, respectively, to h_t and h_p, so that the overall transfer function $T = T_t + T_p$ (see Fig. 15-13b). T_t is found from h_t to be $T_t = D$. The periodic component h_p can be described by $1 + D + D^2 + D^4$, and since the period is 7, the

Impulse: 10000000000000000...

h: 10101001110100111...

h_t: 01000000000000000...

h_p: 1110100,1110100,111...

(a) Impulse response and its components.

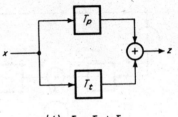

(b) $T = T_p + T_t$.

Fig. 15-13 Synthesis of an inert linear machine from its impulse response.

entire periodic transfer function is specified by

$$T_p = (1 + D + D^2 + D^4)(1 + D^7 + D^{14} + \cdots)$$

or

$$T_p = \frac{1 + D + D^2 + D^4}{1 + D^7}$$

Hence

$$T = T_p + T_t = \frac{1 + D + D^2 + D^4}{1 + D^7} + D$$

$$= \frac{1 + D^2 + D^4 + D^8}{1 + D^7}$$

This function can be simplified as (see Appendix 15-2)

$$T = \frac{(1 + D + D^2 + D^4)^2}{(1 + D + D^2 + D^4)(1 + D + D^3)} = \frac{1 + D + D^2 + D^4}{1 + D + D^3}$$

A minimal realization of this transfer function is shown in Fig. 15-9a.

Multiterminal machines

In the preceding sections we developed the properties of two-terminal inert linear machines, characterized by rational polynomials in the delay operator D. A multiterminal inert linear machine with l input terminals and m output terminals can be characterized by a set of lm transfer functions, where

$$T_{ij}(D) = \frac{z_j}{x_i} \qquad \text{for all } i = 1, 2, \ldots, l \text{ and } j = 1, 2, \ldots, m$$

T_{ij} is evaluated when $x_i = 0$ for all $i \neq j$; i.e., the transfer function T_{ij} specifies the dependency of output z_j on input x_i when all other inputs are held at zero. The synthesis problem of a multiterminal inert linear machine can thus be transformed to the well-known problem of synthesiz-

572

ing a set of two-terminal inert linear machines. A realization of an arbitrary multiterminal inert linear machine from an appropriate set of two-terminal machines is shown in Fig. 15-14. It must be emphasized that this is not always a minimal realization; rather it demonstrates that a realization exists. More efficient methods which yield minimal realizations are developed in subsequent sections.

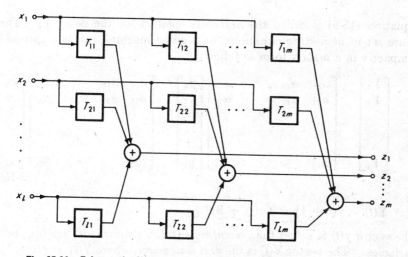

Fig. 15-14 Schematic diagram of a multiterminal inert linear machine.

15-4 THE GENERAL MODEL

The specification of the outputs of an inert linear machine by means of a set of polynomials, so that $z_j = \sum_{i=1}^{l} T_{ij} x_i$, is actually a "black box" type of specification; that is, each output is specified only in terms of the external inputs and the characterizing polynomials. Such a specification is possible since the machine is assumed to be initially inert, i.e., $x(t) = 0$ for all $t < 0$, and therefore $y_i(t) = 0$ for all $t < 0$ and $i = 1, 2, \ldots, k$. The specification of an arbitrary (not necessarily inert) linear machine is accomplished by specifying the output and the next-state functions in terms of the inputs, as well as the present states of the machine.

The matrix formulation

Consider a k-dimensional linear machine over $GF(p)$, with l inputs and m outputs, as shown in Fig. 15-1. Since the combinational logic consists of only adders and scalar multipliers, the next state of the delay Y_i can be expressed as a function of the external inputs to the machine and its present state as follows:

$$Y_i = (\alpha_{i1}y_1 + \alpha_{i2}y_2 + \ldots + \alpha_{ik}y_k) + (\beta_{i1}x_1 + \beta_{i2}x_2 + \ldots + \beta_{il}x_l)$$

or

$$Y_i = \sum_{j=1}^{k} \alpha_{ij}y_j + \sum_{j=1}^{l} \beta_{ij}x_j \tag{15-9}$$

Equation (15-9) is called the *next-state equation* for the delay Y_i. The entire set of next-state equations for a given machine can be expressed compactly in a matrix form as follows:

$$\begin{bmatrix} Y_1 \\ Y_2 \\ \cdot \\ \cdot \\ \cdot \\ Y_k \end{bmatrix} = \begin{bmatrix} \alpha_{11} & \alpha_{12} & \cdots & \alpha_{1k} \\ \alpha_{21} & \alpha_{22} & \cdots & \alpha_{2k} \\ \cdot & \cdot & \cdots & \cdot \\ \alpha_{k1} & & \cdots & \alpha_{kk} \end{bmatrix} \begin{bmatrix} y_1 \\ y_2 \\ \cdot \\ \cdot \\ y_k \end{bmatrix} + \begin{bmatrix} \beta_{11} & \beta_{12} & \cdots & \beta_{1l} \\ \beta_{21} & \beta_{22} & \cdots & \beta_{2l} \\ \cdot & \cdot & \cdots & \cdot \\ \beta_{k1} & & \cdots & \beta_{kl} \end{bmatrix} \begin{bmatrix} x_1 \\ x_2 \\ \cdot \\ \cdot \\ x_l \end{bmatrix}$$

$$\tag{15-10}$$

or

$$\mathbf{Y}(t) = \mathbf{y}(t+1) = \mathbf{A}\mathbf{y}(t) + \mathbf{B}\mathbf{x}(t)$$

The vector $\mathbf{y}(t)$ is called the *present-state vector;* its elements are the state variables. The vector $\mathbf{Y}(t)$ is the *next-state vector*, where $\mathbf{Y}(t) = \mathbf{y}(t+1)$. The vector $\mathbf{x}(t)$ is the *input vector;* its elements are the *input variables*, where $x_i(t)$ is the input applied to the ith terminal at time t. The dimensions of the state and input vectors are k and l, respectively, i.e.,

$$\mathbf{y}(t) = \begin{bmatrix} y_1 \\ y_2 \\ \cdot \\ \cdot \\ \cdot \\ y_k \end{bmatrix} \qquad \mathbf{Y}(t) = \begin{bmatrix} Y_1 \\ Y_2 \\ \cdot \\ \cdot \\ Y_k \end{bmatrix} \qquad \mathbf{x}(t) = \begin{bmatrix} x_1 \\ x_2 \\ \cdot \\ \cdot \\ x_l \end{bmatrix}$$

When t is understood, $y_i(t)$ and $x_i(t)$ are written as y_i and x_i, respectively.

In a similar manner each output function can be specified in terms of the present state and the inputs to the machine. The ith output is expressed as

$$z_i = (\gamma_{i1}y_1 + \gamma_{i2}y_2 + \cdots + \gamma_{ik}y_k) + (\delta_{i1}x_1 + \delta_{i2}x_2 + \cdots + \delta_{il}x_l)$$

or

$$z_i = \sum_{j=1}^{k} \gamma_{ij}y_j + \sum_{j=1}^{l} \delta_{ij}x_j \tag{15-11}$$

Equation (15-11) is called the *output equation*. The entire set of output equations for a given machine can also be expressed in a matrix form as follows:

$$
\begin{bmatrix} z_1 \\ z_2 \\ \cdot \\ \cdot \\ \cdot \\ z_m \end{bmatrix} = \begin{bmatrix} \gamma_{11} & \gamma_{12} & \cdots & \gamma_{1k} \\ \gamma_{21} & \gamma_{22} & \cdots & \gamma_{2k} \\ \cdot & & & \\ \cdot & & & \cdot \\ \gamma_{m1} & & \cdots & \gamma_{mk} \end{bmatrix} \begin{bmatrix} y_1 \\ y_2 \\ \cdot \\ \cdot \\ \cdot \\ y_k \end{bmatrix} + \begin{bmatrix} \delta_{11} & \delta_{12} & \cdots & \delta_{1l} \\ \delta_{21} & \delta_{22} & \cdots & \delta_{2l} \\ \cdot & & & \\ \cdot & & & \cdot \\ \delta_{m1} & & \cdots & \delta_{ml} \end{bmatrix} \begin{bmatrix} x_1 \\ x_2 \\ \cdot \\ \cdot \\ \cdot \\ x_l \end{bmatrix}
$$

$$(15\text{-}12)$$

or

$$ \mathbf{z}(t) = \mathbf{C}\mathbf{y}(t) + \mathbf{D}\mathbf{x}(t) $$

where $\mathbf{z}(t)$ is the *output vector;* its ith element $z_i(t)$ is the output generated at terminal i at time t.

The matrices $\mathbf{A}$, $\mathbf{B}$, $\mathbf{C}$, and $\mathbf{D}$, defined by Eqs. (15-10) and (15-12), are the *characterizing matrices* of the linear machine. $\mathbf{A}$ is referred to as the *characteristic matrix;* it specifies the autonomous behavior of the machine. The matrix formulation characterizes completely any linear machine, and thus leads to a precise definition of a linear machine in terms of the characterizing matrices.

Definition 15-1 A machine is said to be *linear* over a finite field $GF(p)$ if its states can be identified with the elements of a vector space, and its next-state and output functions can be specified by a pair of matrix equations over $GF(p)$.

$$ \mathbf{Y}(t) = \mathbf{A}\mathbf{y}(t) + \mathbf{B}\mathbf{x}(t) \tag{15-13a} $$
$$ \mathbf{z}(t) = \mathbf{C}\mathbf{y}(t) + \mathbf{D}\mathbf{x}(t) \tag{15-13b} $$

The *dimension* of the machine is the dimension of its state vector.

Equations (15-13) represent a Moore or a Mealy machine, according to whether $\mathbf{D}$ is or is not identically zero. We subsequently refer to a machine whose characterizing matrices are $\mathbf{A}$, $\mathbf{B}$, $\mathbf{C}$, and $\mathbf{D}$ as machine $\{\mathbf{A},\mathbf{B},\mathbf{C},\mathbf{D}\}$.

The entries of the characterizing matrices are determined from the next-state and output equations, given by Eqs. (15-9) and (15-11), respectively, in the following way. α_{ij} denotes the product of the scalar multipliers contained in the path leading from y_j to Y_i. If there are two or more paths from y_j to Y_i, α_{ij} denotes the sum of all such products; if no path exists between y_j and Y_i, $\alpha_{ij} = 0$. β_{ij} denotes the corresponding values for the paths leading from input x_j to Y_i. Similarly, γ_{ij} denotes the sum of products of the scalar multipliers contained in the paths leading from y_j to the output terminal z_i; if no path exists between y_j and z_i, $\gamma_{ij} = 0$. δ_{ij} denotes the corresponding values for the paths originating at input x_j and terminating at output z_i.

Example   The characterizing matrices for the four-terminal linear machine of Fig. 15-3 are

$$A = \begin{bmatrix} 0 & 1 & 0 & 0 \\ 1 & 0 & 0 & 0 \\ 0 & 1 & 0 & 0 \\ 0 & 2 & 2 & 0 \end{bmatrix} \qquad B = \begin{bmatrix} 1 & 0 \\ 0 & 1 \\ 0 & 1 \\ 0 & 2 \end{bmatrix}$$

$$C = \begin{bmatrix} 0 & 2 & 0 & 1 \\ 0 & 1 & 1 & 0 \end{bmatrix} \qquad D = \begin{bmatrix} 0 & 2 \\ 0 & 1 \end{bmatrix} \quad \blacksquare$$

The response of linear machines

The relationship between the input sequence to machine $\{A,B,C,D\}$ and its corresponding output sequence is obtained by iterating Eqs. (15-13a) and (15-13b), i.e.,

$$y(1) = Ay(0) + Bx(0)$$

$$z(0) = Cy(0) + Dx(0)$$

$$z(1) = CAy(0) + CBx(0) + Dx(1)$$

$$z(2) = CA^2y(0) + CABx(0) + CBx(1) + Dx(2)$$

$$z(3) = CA^3y(0) + CA^2Bx(0) + CABx(1) + CBx(2) + Dx(3)$$

$$. . . . .$$

$$z(t) = CA^t y(0) + \sum_{j=0}^{t-1} CA^{t-1-j}Bx(j) + Dx(t)$$

or

$$z(t) = CA^t y(0) + \sum_{j=0}^{t} H(t - j)x(j) \qquad (15\text{-}14)$$

where

$$H(t - j) = \begin{cases} D & \text{when } t - j = 0 \\ CA^{t-1-j}B & \text{when } t - 1 - j \geq 0 \end{cases} \qquad (15\text{-}15)$$

From Eq. (15-14) we see that the response of a linear machine consists of two components.   The first component, known as the *autonomous response*, is obtained by setting $x(t) = 0$ for all $t \geq 0$, i.e.,

$$z_a(t) = CA^t y(0) \qquad (15\text{-}16)$$

The second component, known as the *forced response*, is obtained by setting $\mathbf{y}(0) = \mathbf{0}$, i.e.,

$$\mathbf{z}_f(t) = \sum_{j=0}^{t} \mathbf{H}(t - j)\mathbf{x}(j) \tag{15-17}$$

The total response is thus given by

$$\mathbf{z}(t) = \mathbf{z}_a(t) + \mathbf{z}_f(t) \tag{15-18}$$

Equation (15-17) actually describes in matrix form the response of inert machines, which have been studied extensively in earlier sections by means of the polynomial representation.   The total response [Eq. (15-18)] of a linear machine, for a given input sequence and an arbitrary initial state, can be found by separately determining the forced and autonomous responses and adding them up.

The autonomous response is generally determined from the analysis of the internal circuit.† The state behavior of the internal circuit is completely characterized by the characteristic matrix $\mathbf{A}$, since Eq. (15-13a) becomes

$$\mathbf{Y}(t) = \mathbf{y}(t + 1) = \mathbf{A}\mathbf{y}(t)$$

Since the internal circuit is autonomous, the λ-successor S_j of state S_i [where $S_i = \mathbf{y}_i(t)$] is given by

$$\mathbf{y}_j(t) = \mathbf{A}^\lambda \mathbf{y}_i(t)$$

where λ denotes the number of state transitions.   (Note that, while y_j denotes the state of the jth delay, $\mathbf{y}_i$ denotes state S_i of the machine.)

The sequence of predecessors of a given state is established by constructing the inverse internal circuit; such an inverse exists only if each state has a unique predecessor.   For an internal circuit given by $\mathbf{A}$, the inverse is given by $\mathbf{A}^{-1}$, since

$$\mathbf{y}(t) = \mathbf{A}^{-1}\mathbf{Y}(t)$$

Thus the inverse circuit exists if and only if A is nonsingular, i.e., the determinant $|\mathbf{A}|$ is different from zero.

The autonomous linear machines are best analyzed either by means of their state diagrams (as illustrated earlier in Fig. 15-8) or by means of the characteristic polynomials derived from $\mathbf{A}$.   For further discussion of autonomous linear machines see Ref. 9.

---

† The *internal circuit* is that part of the circuit which can be specified by $\mathbf{A}$ alone; that is, it contains only the delay elements and their interconnections, while the input and output lines have been deleted.

15-5 REDUCTION OF LINEAR MACHINES

We now determine conditions, in terms of the characterizing matrices, for linear machines to be finite memory and definitely diagnosable. The length of the shortest distinguishing sequence for arbitrary initial uncertainty is determined. A procedure is presented to determine whether or not a given linear machine is minimal, and if it is not, how to minimize it. The techniques developed in earlier chapters for arbitrary sequential machines are valid for linear machines as well. Our present objective, however, is to develop an *analytical* procedure, rather than an enumerative one, which is valid only for linear machines and which utilizes the matrix formulation.

The diagnostic matrix

Let $\mathfrak{M}$ be a k-dimensional linear machine over $GF(p)$. To describe an experiment of length k, the set of equations represented by Eqs. (15-14) and (15-15) can be expressed compactly as

$$Z^{(k)} = K_k y(0) + V_k X^{(k)} \tag{15-19}$$

where

$$
Z^{(k)} = \begin{bmatrix} z(0) \\ z(1) \\ \cdot \\ \cdot \\ \cdot \\ z(k-1) \end{bmatrix}
\qquad
K_k = \begin{bmatrix} C \\ CA \\ \cdot \\ \cdot \\ \cdot \\ CA^{k-1} \end{bmatrix}
\qquad
X^{(k)} = \begin{bmatrix} x(0) \\ x(1) \\ \cdot \\ \cdot \\ \cdot \\ x(k-1) \end{bmatrix}
$$

and

$$
V_k = \begin{bmatrix}
D & 0 & 0 & \cdots & & 0 \\
CB & D & 0 & \cdots & \cdots & \\
CAB & CB & \cdots & \cdots & \cdots & \\
\cdots & \cdots & \cdots & \cdots & \cdots & \\
\cdots & \cdots & \cdots & \cdots & \cdots & 0 \\
CA^{k-2}B & \cdots & & CB & D
\end{bmatrix}.
$$

The vector $y(0)$ denotes the initial state at $t = 0$. For initial states S_a and S_b the corresponding state vectors are denoted $y_a(0)$ and $y_b(0)$, respectively. The matrix K_k, which consists of submatrices corresponding to the different outputs, is called the *diagnostic* (or *distinguishing*) *matrix*. From Eq. (15-19) it is evident that if S_a is equivalent to S_b, then

$$K_k y_a(0) = K_k y_b(0) \tag{15-20}$$

since the second term $\mathbf{V}_k\mathbf{X}^{(k)}$ is independent of the initial state and depends only on the input sequence. Moreover, since the inputs enter Eq. (15-19) additively, all input sequences are equally effective in state-distinguishing experiments. Consequently, to simplify the computation, $\mathbf{X}^{(k)}$ may be selected as the all-zero sequence $\mathbf{X}^{(k)} = \mathbf{0}$, reducing Eq. (15-19) to

$$\mathbf{Z}^{(k)} = \mathbf{K}_k\mathbf{y}(0) \tag{15-21}$$

The proof that Eq. (15-20) is a necessary and sufficient condition for S_a and S_b to be equivalent follows from Theorem 15-1, and is left to the reader as an exercise.

Before proceeding with the investigation of the properties of minimal linear machines, it is necessary to show that the first r linearly independent rows of the diagnostic matrix $\mathbf{K}_k$ occur in a consecutive sequence in $\mathbf{C}$, $\mathbf{CA}, \ldots , \mathbf{CA}^i$, where $i < r$. To prove this assertion, assume that all the rows of $\mathbf{CA}^i$ are linear combinations of the rows of $\mathbf{K}_i$, i.e., the rows of $\mathbf{C}, \mathbf{CA}, \ldots , \mathbf{CA}^{i-1}$. Then rows of $\mathbf{CA}^{i+1}$ are the same linear combinations of rows of $\mathbf{K}_i\mathbf{A}$, i.e., $\mathbf{CA}, \mathbf{CA}^2, \ldots , \mathbf{CA}^i$. But since the rows of $\mathbf{CA}^i$ are linear combinations of rows of $\mathbf{C}, \mathbf{CA}, \ldots , \mathbf{CA}^{i-1}$, the rows of $\mathbf{CA}^{i+1}$ are also linear combinations of rows of $\mathbf{C}, \mathbf{CA}, \ldots , \mathbf{CA}^{i-1}$. Consequently, the process of finding the linearly independent rows of $\mathbf{K}_k$ terminates as soon as some submatrix $\mathbf{CA}^i$ is generated whose rows are linearly dependent on rows of the preceding submatrices.

Theorem 15-1 *A k-dimensional linear machine* {$\mathbf{A},\mathbf{B},\mathbf{C},\mathbf{D}$} *is definitely diagnosable of order k if and only if the diagnostic matrix* $\mathbf{K}_k$ *has k linearly independent rows.*

Proof: The state vector $\mathbf{y}$ is k-dimensional, and consequently $\mathbf{K}_k$ has exactly k columns. Thus the rank of $\mathbf{K}_k$ cannot exceed k. If $\mathbf{K}_k$ contains k linearly independent rows, then, under the sequence of all-zero inputs, the outputs corresponding to these rows in Eq. (15-21) impose k linearly independent constraints on $\mathbf{y}(0)$. Since $\mathbf{y}(0)$ is k-dimensional, it is specified uniquely by these constraints, and thus the all-zero sequence of length k is a distinguishing sequence. But since all input sequences of a given length have been shown to be equally effective in the distinguishing experiments, every input sequence of length k or more is a distinguishing sequence, and the machine is definitely diagnosable.

To prove that it is definitely diagnosable of order k, it is sufficient to note that the rows of $\mathbf{CA}^k, \mathbf{CA}^{k+1}, \ldots$ are linearly dependent on rows of $\mathbf{K}_k$, and thus the length of the distinguishing sequences need not exceed the rank of $\mathbf{K}_k$. If $\mathbf{K}_k$ contains fewer than k linearly independent rows, there must exist some nonzero $\mathbf{y}(0) \neq \mathbf{0}$ which is annihilated by $\mathbf{K}_k$, and hence results in the same input-output behavior as in the case $\mathbf{y}(0) = \mathbf{0}$. This means that the machine in question is not reduced. ∎

From Theorem 15-1 it follows that a linear machine is in reduced form if and only if the rank of K_k is k. Moreover, *every reduced k-dimensional linear machine is definitely diagnosable of order k, and is finite memory of order less than or equal to k.* These properties are known also as the *observability* and *predictability* properties of linear machines.

Example Consider the linear machine $\mathfrak{M}_1$ over $GF(2)$ given by the following matrices:

$$\mathbf{A} = \begin{bmatrix} 0 & 1 & 1 \\ 1 & 0 & 0 \\ 1 & 0 & 0 \end{bmatrix} \qquad \mathbf{B} = \begin{bmatrix} 1 \\ 1 \\ 0 \end{bmatrix} \qquad \mathbf{C} = \begin{bmatrix} 1 & 1 & 0 \\ 1 & 1 & 1 \end{bmatrix} \qquad \mathbf{D}_/ = \begin{bmatrix} 0 \\ 1 \end{bmatrix}$$

The diagnostic matrix $\mathbf{K}_3$ is determined, and Eq. (15-21) becomes

$$\mathbf{K}_3 = \begin{bmatrix} \mathbf{C} \\ \mathbf{CA} \\ \mathbf{CA}^2 \end{bmatrix} \quad \text{and} \quad \begin{bmatrix} z_1(0) \\ z_2(0) \\ z_1(1) \\ z_2(1) \\ z_1(2) \\ z_2(2) \end{bmatrix} = \begin{bmatrix} 1 & 1 & 0 \\ 1 & 1 & 1 \\ \hline 1 & 1 & 1 \\ 0 & 1 & 1 \\ \hline 0 & 1 & 1 \\ 0 & 0 & 0 \end{bmatrix} \cdot \begin{bmatrix} y_1(0) \\ y_2(0) \\ y_3(0) \end{bmatrix}$$

The rank of $\mathbf{K}_3$ is 3, and hence the dimension of $\mathfrak{M}_1$ cannot be reduced. For a given initial state, the values of $y_1(0)$, $y_2(0)$, and $y_3(0)$ are specified, and the matrix $\mathbf{Z}^{(t)}$ yields the response of $\mathfrak{M}_1$ to the distinguishing sequence 000. For example, if the initial state is (111), then in response to 000, the sequences $z_1 = 010$ and $z_2 = 100$ are produced. It is suggested that the reader draw the circuit diagram and compare the actual circuit responses with the responses obtained in an analytical manner. ∎

The minimization procedure

Let $\mathfrak{M}$ be a k-dimensional linear machine $\{\mathbf{A},\mathbf{B},\mathbf{C},\mathbf{D}\}$ over $GF(p)$, and let r be the rank of the diagnostic matrix, where $r < k$. Define an $r \times k$ matrix $\mathbf{T}$ consisting of the first r linearly independent rows of $\mathbf{K}_k$, and a $k \times r$ matrix $\mathbf{R}$ denoting the right inverse of $\mathbf{T}$, so that $\mathbf{TR} = \mathbf{I}_r$, where $\mathbf{I}_r$ is the $r \times r$ identity matrix. Define an r-dimensional machine $\mathfrak{M}^*$ with characterizing matrices $\{\mathbf{A}^*,\mathbf{B}^*,\mathbf{C}^*,\mathbf{D}^*\}$, such that

$$\begin{aligned} \mathbf{A}^* &= \mathbf{TAR} & \mathbf{C}^* &= \mathbf{CR} \\ \mathbf{B}^* &= \mathbf{TB} & \mathbf{D}^* &= \mathbf{D} \end{aligned} \tag{15-22}$$

At this point we shall state and prove a major theorem, which establishes the validity of the following minimization procedure.

Theorem 15-2   *State* y *of* $\mathfrak{M}$ *is equivalent to state* $y^* = Ty$ *of* $\mathfrak{M}^*$. *Machine* $\mathfrak{M}^*$ *is a reduced machine equivalent to* $\mathfrak{M}$.

Proof:† In order to prove the first part, it is necessary and sufficient to show that, for every state of $\mathfrak{M}$, y^* and Ty have equivalent successors and yield identical outputs, i.e., to show that

$$T(Ay + Bx) = A^*y^* + B^*x$$

and

$$Cy + Dx = C^*y^* + D^*x$$

Define $\bar{y} = y - RTy$; then, since $TR = I_r$, we obtain

$$T\bar{y} = Ty - TRTy = Ty - Ty = 0$$

Since $T\bar{y} = 0$, then $K_k\bar{y} = 0$. Therefore [by Eq. (15-20)] state $\bar{y}$ is equivalent to state 0. And since $A0 = 0$,

$$A\bar{y} = 0 \qquad \text{and} \qquad TA\bar{y} = 0$$

Also, since the rows of C are spanned by those of T, $C\bar{y} = 0$. The next-state and output equations are

$$T(Ay + Bx) = T[A(\bar{y} + RTy) + Bx] = TA\bar{y} + TARTy + TBx$$
$$= 0 + (TAR)(Ty) + (TB)x = A^*y^* + B^*x$$
$$Cy + Dx = C(\bar{y} + RTy) + Dx = C\bar{y} + CRTy + Dx$$
$$= 0 + (CR)(Ty) + Dx = C^*y^* + D^*x$$

Hence $y^* = Ty$ under the transformation of Eq. (15-22). Similarly, since $Ry^* = RTy = y$, state y^* of $\mathfrak{M}^*$ is equivalent to state $y = Ry^*$ of $\mathfrak{M}$.

   We shall now show that $\mathfrak{M}^*$ is a reduced machine, and thus is the minimal machine equivalent to $\mathfrak{M}$. Since K_k has a rank less than k, it partitions the states of $\mathfrak{M}$ into subsets (usually called cosets) as follows. Let G_0 denote the subset containing all the states which are equivalent to the zero state $y = 0$. From Eq. (15-20) we conclude that G_0 denotes the null space of K_k. Let us

---

† This proof requires some knowledge of matrix algebra and may be skipped at first reading.

now generate a set of subsets from G_0 so that two states, $\mathbf{y}_a$ and $\mathbf{y}_b$, are in the same subset if and only if $\mathbf{y}_a - \mathbf{y}_b$ is in G_0. Hence $\mathbf{K}_k(\mathbf{y}_a - \mathbf{y}_b) = \mathbf{0}$ and $\mathbf{K}_k\mathbf{y}_a = \mathbf{K}_k\mathbf{y}_b$, which means that $\mathbf{y}_a$ is equivalent to $\mathbf{y}_b$, and the subsets so generated are the equivalence classes of $\mathfrak{M}$. Moreover, since states in different subsets are distinguishable by the all-zero sequence (or any other input sequence), the subsets generated by $\mathbf{K}_k$ correspond to the states of the reduced form of the original machine. (These subsets are actually identical with the blocks of the final partition in the reduction procedure outlined in Chap. 10.)

Since G_0 generates $p^r - 1$ distinct subsets, the reduced form of $\mathfrak{M}$ over $GF(p)$ has p^r states, where r is the rank of $\mathbf{K}_k$. Since $\mathfrak{M}$ and $\mathfrak{M}^*$ are equivalent and $\mathfrak{M}^*$ has exactly p^r states, it is the minimal machine which is equivalent to $\mathfrak{M}$. ∎

Example   Consider the linear machine $\mathfrak{M}_2$ over $GF(2)$, defined by the matrices

$$\mathbf{A} = \begin{bmatrix} 0 & 1 & 0 \\ 1 & 0 & 0 \\ 0 & 1 & 1 \end{bmatrix} \qquad \mathbf{B} = \begin{bmatrix} 1 \\ 1 \\ 1 \end{bmatrix} \qquad \mathbf{C} = [1 \quad 0 \quad 0] \qquad \mathbf{D} = [1]$$

$$\mathbf{K}_3 = \begin{bmatrix} \mathbf{C} \\ \mathbf{CA} \\ \mathbf{CA}^2 \end{bmatrix} = \begin{bmatrix} 1 & 0 & 0 \\ 0 & 1 & 0 \\ 1 & 0 & 0 \end{bmatrix}$$

The rank of $\mathbf{K}_3$ is 2, and thus $\mathfrak{M}_2$ is reducible. The first two rows of $\mathbf{K}_3$ are linearly independent; therefore

$$\mathbf{T} = \begin{bmatrix} 1 & 0 & 0 \\ 0 & 1 & 0 \end{bmatrix}$$

The right inverse $\mathbf{R}$ of $\mathbf{T}$ is constructed by selecting a set of r linearly independent columns from $\mathbf{T}$. Since the rank of $\mathbf{T}$ is r and column rank equals row rank, such a set always exists. Form an $r \times r$ matrix $\mathbf{Q}$ from these columns and find its inverse, $\mathbf{Q}^{-1}$. The right inverse $\mathbf{R}$, which is a $k \times r$ matrix, is formed by placing in it the rows of $\mathbf{Q}^{-1}$ in positions corresponding to the columns selected from $\mathbf{T}$, and where all other rows are set to zero. In our case

$$\mathbf{Q} = \begin{bmatrix} 1 & 0 \\ 0 & 1 \end{bmatrix} \qquad \mathbf{Q}^{-1} = \begin{bmatrix} 1 & 0 \\ 0 & 1 \end{bmatrix} \qquad \mathbf{R} = \begin{bmatrix} 1 & 0 \\ 0 & 1 \\ 0 & 0 \end{bmatrix}$$

Following the definitions of the characterizing matrices of $\mathfrak{M}_2^*$, we obtain

$$\mathbf{y^*} = \mathbf{Ty} = \begin{bmatrix} 1 & 0 & 0 \\ 0 & 1 & 0 \end{bmatrix} \cdot \mathbf{y}$$

$$\mathbf{A^*} = \mathbf{TAR} = \begin{bmatrix} 1 & 0 & 0 \\ 0 & 1 & 0 \end{bmatrix} \cdot \begin{bmatrix} 0 & 1 & 0 \\ 1 & 0 & 0 \\ 0 & 1 & 1 \end{bmatrix} \cdot \begin{bmatrix} 1 & 0 \\ 0 & 1 \\ 0 & 0 \end{bmatrix} = \begin{bmatrix} 0 & 1 \\ 1 & 0 \end{bmatrix}$$

$$\mathbf{B^*} = \mathbf{TB} = \begin{bmatrix} 1 & 0 & 0 \\ 0 & 1 & 0 \end{bmatrix} \cdot \begin{bmatrix} 1 \\ 1 \\ 1 \end{bmatrix} = \begin{bmatrix} 1 \\ 1 \end{bmatrix}$$

$$\mathbf{C^*} = \mathbf{CR} = \begin{bmatrix} 1 & 0 & 0 \end{bmatrix} \cdot \begin{bmatrix} 1 & 0 \\ 0 & 1 \\ 0 & 0 \end{bmatrix} = \begin{bmatrix} 1 & 0 \end{bmatrix}$$

$$\mathbf{D^*} = \mathbf{D} = [1]$$

The circuit diagram of the reduced machine $\mathfrak{M}_2^*$, given by $\{\mathbf{A^*, B^*, C^*, D^*}\}$, is shown in Fig. 15-15. ■

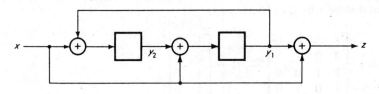

Fig. 15-15 Realization of the reduced machine $\mathfrak{M}_2^*$.

The minimal machine $\mathfrak{M}_2^*$ has been determined without explicitly constructing the equivalence classes of $\mathfrak{M}_2$. We shall now find them to demonstrate the procedure outlined in the proof of Theorem 15-2. From Eq. (15-21) we have

$$\begin{bmatrix} z_1(0) \\ z_1(1) \end{bmatrix} = \mathbf{Ty}(0) = \begin{bmatrix} 1 & 0 & 0 \\ 0 & 1 & 0 \end{bmatrix} \cdot \begin{bmatrix} y_1(0) \\ y_2(0) \\ y_3(0) \end{bmatrix} \tag{15-23}$$

G_0 contains all the states, designated by their corresponding vectors, for which $\mathbf{0} = \mathbf{Ty}(0)$, i.e.,

$$G_0 = \left\{ \begin{bmatrix} 0 \\ 0 \\ 0 \end{bmatrix}, \begin{bmatrix} 0 \\ 0 \\ 1 \end{bmatrix} \right\}$$

The remaining subsets, which yield the equivalence classes of $\mathfrak{M}_2$, are determined by adding to G_0 any element not contained in G_0, so that two states, $\mathbf{y}_a$ and $\mathbf{y}_b$, are in the same subset if and only if $\mathbf{y}_a - \mathbf{y}_b$ is in G_0. Let the first such element be the vector

$$\begin{bmatrix} 0 \\ 1 \\ 0 \end{bmatrix} \quad \text{which yields} \quad G_1 = \left\{ \begin{bmatrix} 0 \\ 1 \\ 0 \end{bmatrix}, \begin{bmatrix} 0 \\ 1 \\ 1 \end{bmatrix} \right\}$$

Similarly, we obtain the remaining equivalence classes,

$$G_2 = \left\{ \begin{bmatrix} 1 \\ 0 \\ 0 \end{bmatrix}, \begin{bmatrix} 1 \\ 0 \\ 1 \end{bmatrix} \right\} \quad G_3 = \left\{ \begin{bmatrix} 1 \\ 1 \\ 0 \end{bmatrix}, \begin{bmatrix} 1 \\ 1 \\ 1 \end{bmatrix} \right\}$$

Note that since $\mathbf{y}^* = \mathbf{T}\mathbf{y}$, the output vector of Eq. (15-23) actually specifies the state of $\mathfrak{M}_2^*$ which corresponds to the equivalence class given by G_i.

Example   Consider the linear machine $\mathfrak{M}_3$ given by $\{\mathbf{A},\mathbf{B},\mathbf{C},\mathbf{D}\}$ over $GF(2)$ and shown in Fig. 15-16.

$$\mathbf{A} = \begin{bmatrix} 1 & 0 & 0 & 0 \\ 0 & 0 & 1 & 1 \\ 1 & 1 & 0 & 0 \\ 1 & 0 & 1 & 0 \end{bmatrix} \quad \mathbf{B} = \begin{bmatrix} 1 & 0 \\ 0 & 0 \\ 1 & 1 \\ 1 & 1 \end{bmatrix}$$

$$\mathbf{C} = \begin{bmatrix} 0 & 1 & 0 & 1 \\ 1 & 1 & 1 & 0 \end{bmatrix} \quad \mathbf{D} = \begin{bmatrix} 1 & 0 \\ 0 & 0 \end{bmatrix}$$

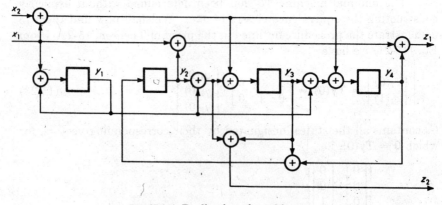

Fig. 15-16   Realization of machine $\mathfrak{M}_3$.

$$K_3 = \begin{bmatrix} C \\ CA \\ CA^2 \end{bmatrix} = \begin{bmatrix} 0 & 1 & 0 & 1 \\ 1 & 1 & 1 & 0 \\ \hline 1 & 0 & 0 & 1 \\ 0 & 1 & 1 & 1 \\ \hline 0 & 0 & 1 & 0 \\ 0 & 1 & 0 & 1 \end{bmatrix}$$

$$T = \begin{bmatrix} \overbrace{0 \quad 1 \quad 0}^{Q} & 1 \\ 1 & 1 & 1 & 0 \\ 1 & 0 & 0 & 1 \end{bmatrix} \qquad Q = \begin{bmatrix} 0 & 1 & 0 \\ 1 & 1 & 1 \\ 1 & 0 & 0 \end{bmatrix}$$

$$Q^{-1} = \begin{bmatrix} 0 & 0 & 1 \\ 1 & 0 & 0 \\ 1 & 1 & 1 \end{bmatrix} \qquad R = \left. \begin{bmatrix} 0 & 0 & 1 \\ 1 & 0 & 0 \\ 1 & 1 & 1 \\ 0 & 0 & 0 \end{bmatrix} \right\} Q^{-1}$$

Q^{-1} occupies the first three rows of R, since the linearly independent columns in T have been selected from positions 1, 2, and 3.

$$A^* = TAR = \begin{bmatrix} 0 & 1 & 0 & 1 \\ 1 & 1 & 1 & 0 \\ 1 & 0 & 0 & 1 \end{bmatrix} \cdot \begin{bmatrix} 1 & 0 & 0 & 0 \\ 0 & 0 & 1 & 1 \\ 1 & 1 & 0 & 0 \\ 1 & 0 & 1 & 0 \end{bmatrix} \cdot \begin{bmatrix} 0 & 0 & 1 \\ 1 & 0 & 0 \\ 1 & 1 & 1 \\ 0 & 0 & 0 \end{bmatrix} = \begin{bmatrix} 0 & 0 & 1 \\ 0 & 1 & 1 \\ 1 & 1 & 1 \end{bmatrix}$$

$$B^* = TB = \begin{bmatrix} 0 & 1 & 0 & 1 \\ 1 & 1 & 1 & 0 \\ 1 & 0 & 0 & 1 \end{bmatrix} \cdot \begin{bmatrix} 1 & 0 \\ 0 & 0 \\ 1 & 1 \\ 1 & 1 \end{bmatrix} = \begin{bmatrix} 1 & 1 \\ 0 & 1 \\ 0 & 1 \end{bmatrix}$$

$$C^* = CR = \begin{bmatrix} 0 & 1 & 0 & 1 \\ 1 & 1 & 1 & 0 \end{bmatrix} \cdot \begin{bmatrix} 0 & 0 & 1 \\ 1 & 0 & 0 \\ 1 & 1 & 1 \\ 0 & 0 & 0 \end{bmatrix} = \begin{bmatrix} 1 & 0 & 0 \\ 0 & 1 & 0 \end{bmatrix}$$

$$D^* = D = \begin{bmatrix} 1 & 0 \\ 0 & 0 \end{bmatrix}$$

The reduced circuit corresponding to $\{A^*, B^*, C^*, D^*\}$ is shown in Fig. 15-17. ∎

It is useful to note that the first three linearly independent rows of the diagnostic matrix K_3^* of the reduced machine $\mathfrak{M}_3^*$ are the rows of I_3

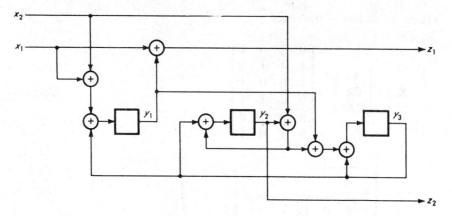

Fig. 15-17 Reduced machine $\mathfrak{M}_3^*$.

in natural order, that is,

$$\mathbf{K}_3^* = \begin{bmatrix} 1 & 0 & 0 \\ 0 & 1 & 0 \\ 0 & 0 & 1 \\ 0 & 1 & 1 \\ 1 & 1 & 1 \\ 1 & 0 & 0 \end{bmatrix} \begin{matrix} \checkmark \\ \checkmark \\ \checkmark \\ \\ \\ \end{matrix}$$

From Eq. (15-22) we can show that the matrix $(\mathbf{A}^*)^t$ of the reduced machine is related to the original $\mathbf{A}^t$ by

$$(\mathbf{A}^*)^t = \mathbf{TA}^t\mathbf{R}$$

and that the diagnostic matrix $\mathbf{K}^*$ is related to $\mathbf{K}$ by

$$\mathbf{K}^* = \mathbf{KR}$$

The formal proof of the above relationships is left to the reader as an exercise (see Prob. 15-23). Their immediate consequence is summarized as follows:

 The first r linearly independent rows of the matrix $\mathbf{K}_r^*$ of a reduced linear machine are the rows of the identity matrix $\mathbf{I}_r$.

Applying the above results to Eq. (15-21) suggests that, for an initial state $\mathbf{y}_a^* = [y_1^*, y_2^*, \ldots, y_r^*]^T$ (where $[\mathbf{y}]^T$ denotes the transpose of $\mathbf{y}$) and under the all-0's input sequence, the outputs corresponding to the unit vector rows of $\mathbf{K}_r^*$ are identical with the values $y_1^*, y_2^*, \ldots, y_r^*$. This result is of paramount importance in the identification problem of linear machines, which is discussed in the following section.

15-6 IDENTIFICATION OF LINEAR MACHINES

We shall now establish certain conditions under which a reduced sequential machine will be linearly realizable. If the machine is linearly realizable, we shall determine an appropriate state assignment and define the characterizing matrices of a linear machine of smallest dimension. We assume that the input and output symbols of the machine are taken from $GF(p)$ and that the zero element of the field is specified. If the machine is not linearly realizable, one of several tests in the procedure will fail.

The identification procedure

From the discussion in Sec. 15-5 we know that a linearly realizable machine must have exactly p^k states for some integer k. Moreover, *a machine is equivalent to a linear machine if and only if its reduced form is linear.*

Let the sequential machine M have p^k states, denoted S_a, S_b, . . . , S_{p^k}, and let the l-dimensional vector $\mathbf{x}$ and the m-dimensional vector $\mathbf{z}$ denote its input and output, respectively. We construct for M a *distinguishing table* which contains the *outputs generated by M in response to a sequence of 0's.* The table contains p^k columns corresponding to the states of M. It is formed block by block, where the ith block corresponds to the output vector $\mathbf{z}(t)$ at $t = i$. The table thus contains at most k blocks of m rows each, corresponding to the output vectors $\mathbf{z}(0)$, $\mathbf{z}(1)$, . . . , $\mathbf{z}(k - 1)$. The process of adding blocks to the table is terminated when, for some t, the set of rows contained in the block $\mathbf{z}(t)$ is linearly dependent on the rows in the preceding blocks.

As an example, we construct the distinguishing table for machine M_4 of Table 15-1. The entries in column A are 11, 01, corresponding to the outputs of M_4 when initially in state A and given the input sequence 00. The construction of Table 15-2 terminates after the second block, since the rows of $\mathbf{z}(1)$ are linear combinations of those of $\mathbf{z}(0)$. We shall subsequently denote the distinguishing table by U.

Table 15-1   Machine M_4

PS	NS, $z_1 z_2$	
	$x = 0$	$x = 1$
A	B,11	D,01
B	A,01	C,11
C	C,10	A,00
D	D,00	B,10

Table 15-2   Distinguishing table for machine M_4

	A	B	C	D
$\mathbf{z}(0)$	1	0	1	0
	1	1	0	0
$\mathbf{z}(1)$	0	1	1	0
	1	1	0	0

Since the input and output symbols of M_4 are limited to 0 and 1, the linear realization has to be over $GF(2)$. The first test is based on the fact that, for every linear machine, the all-0's sequence is a distinguishing sequence. If M is reduced, the columns of U must be distinct, since otherwise there would be two or more states in M which are indistinguishable under the all-0's sequence, and M is not linear. Clearly, Table 15-2 "passes" this test.

Let U^* be the table consisting of the first r linearly independent rows of U, and let S_i denote the ith column of U^*. Assuming that a linear realization of M is possible, let states $A, B, \ldots$ of M correspond to $\mathbf{y}_a, \mathbf{y}_b, \ldots$ of its linear realization $\mathfrak{M}$. This is accomplished by selecting the p^k columns of U^* as the state assignment for the p^k states of $\mathfrak{M}$. For machine $\mathfrak{M}_4$, which is to be the linear realization of M_4, we have

$$\mathbf{y}_a = \begin{bmatrix} 1 \\ 1 \end{bmatrix} \qquad \mathbf{y}_b = \begin{bmatrix} 0 \\ 1 \end{bmatrix} \qquad \mathbf{y}_c = \begin{bmatrix} 1 \\ 0 \end{bmatrix} \qquad \mathbf{y}_d = \begin{bmatrix} 0 \\ 0 \end{bmatrix}$$

In the above step it has been implicitly assumed that if a linear realization exists, its state assignment is given by U^*. This assertion follows directly from the result of the preceding section, in which it has been shown that, under the all-0's input sequence, the outputs corresponding to the r linearly independent rows of $\mathbf{K}_r^*$ are identical with the state assignment given by $(y_1^*, y_2^*, \ldots, y_r^*)$. And since the rows of U^* are the linearly independent outputs associated with the states of $\mathfrak{M}$, they are also equal to the state assignment of $\mathfrak{M}$.

In order to determine the set of characterizing matrices $\{\mathbf{A}, \mathbf{B}, \mathbf{C}, \mathbf{D}\}$ of $\mathfrak{M}$, we select r linearly independent columns from U^*, corresponding to r state vectors of $\mathfrak{M}$, and form an $r \times r$ matrix $\mathbf{v}$ such that

$$\mathbf{v} = [\mathbf{y}_a, \mathbf{y}_b, \ldots, \mathbf{y}_r]$$

From Eq. (15-13a) we find that the next-state function of $\mathfrak{M}$ under 0 inputs is

$$[\mathbf{Y}_a{}^0, \mathbf{Y}_b{}^0, \ldots, \mathbf{Y}_r{}^0] = \mathbf{Av}$$

where $\mathbf{Y}_i{}^0$ denotes the 0-successor of $\mathbf{y}_i$. Since $\mathbf{v}$ is nonsingular,

$$\mathbf{A} = [\mathbf{Y}_a{}^0, \mathbf{Y}_b{}^0, \ldots, \mathbf{Y}_r{}^0]\mathbf{v}^{-1} \qquad\qquad (15\text{-}24)$$

If all r unit vectors appear in U^*, $\mathbf{v}$ can be chosen as $\mathbf{I}_r$, which yields $\mathbf{v} = \mathbf{v}^{-1}$, and Eq. (15-24) is reduced to

$$\mathbf{A} = [\mathbf{Y}_a{}^0, \mathbf{Y}_b{}^0, \ldots, \mathbf{Y}_r{}^0] \qquad\qquad (15\text{-}25)$$

Whenever the number of states $p^k = p^r$, i.e., $k = r$, $\mathbf{v}$ can be specified as $\mathbf{I}_r$.

Similarly, from Eq. (15-13b) and for $\mathbf{x}(t) = \mathbf{0}$, we find

$$[z_a{}^0, z_b{}^0, \ldots, z_r{}^0] = \mathbf{Cv}$$

where $z_i{}^0$ denotes the output produced by $\mathfrak{M}$ when in state $\mathbf{y}_i$ and excited by input $\mathbf{x} = \mathbf{0}$. Thus

$$\mathbf{C} = [z_a{}^0, z_b{}^0, \ldots, z_r{}^0]\mathbf{v}^{-1} \qquad (15\text{-}26)$$

and when $\mathbf{v} = \mathbf{I}_r$,

$$\mathbf{C} = [z_a{}^0, z_b{}^0, \ldots, z_r{}^0] \qquad (15\text{-}27)$$

In order to determine $\mathbf{B}$ and $\mathbf{D}$, let us denote a unit input vector as $\mathbf{u}_i$, where the ith component of $\mathbf{u}_i$ is 1 and all other components are 0's. From Eq. (15-13a) we obtain

$$\mathbf{Bx} = \mathbf{Y} - \mathbf{Ay}$$

In order to determine $\mathbf{B}$, we select some state $\mathbf{y}_i$ (preferably the zero state if it exists in U^*) and specify $\mathbf{B}$ in terms of the constraints imposed on it by $\mathbf{y}_i$ and the unit input vectors. Clearly, such a process does not guarantee that the selection of another $\mathbf{y}_j$ will specify the same $\mathbf{B}$ matrix, unless the machine being identified is indeed linear. For the time being we shall specify a set of characterizing matrices, and will check them for all possible input and state combinations at the end of the test.

Let the input consist of the unit vectors

$$\mathbf{u} = [\mathbf{u}_1, \mathbf{u}_2, \ldots, \mathbf{u}_l]$$

The next-state vector, $\mathbf{Y}_i{}^{u_j}$, denotes the u_j-successor of y_i. Thus

$$\mathbf{Y}_i{}^u = [\mathbf{Y}_i{}^{u_1}, \mathbf{Y}_i{}^{u_2}, \ldots, \mathbf{Y}_i{}^{u_l}]$$

and

$$\mathbf{Bu} = \mathbf{Y}_i{}^u - \mathbf{Ay}_i$$

or

$$\mathbf{B} = [\mathbf{Y}_i{}^u - \mathbf{Ay}_i]\mathbf{u}^{-1} \qquad (15\text{-}28)$$

Since $\mathbf{u}$ generally consists of unit vectors, and when $\mathbf{y}$ is the zero state, Eq. (15-28) reduces to

$$\mathbf{B} = [\mathbf{Y}_i{}^{u_1}, \mathbf{Y}_i{}^{u_2}, \ldots, \mathbf{Y}_i{}^{u_l}] \qquad (15\text{-}29)$$

Similarly, from Eq. (15-13b) we obtain

$$\mathbf{D} = \{[z_i{}^{u_1}, z_i{}^{u_2}, \ldots z_i{}^{u_l}] - \mathbf{Ay}_i\}\mathbf{u}^{-1} \qquad (15\text{-}30)$$

where $z_i{}^{u_j}$ is the output vector associated with the transition from $\mathbf{y}_i$ under input $\mathbf{u}_j$. In analogy to Eq. (15-29) the reduced equation is

$$\mathbf{D} = [z_i{}^{u_1}, z_i{}^{u_2}, \ldots, z_i{}^{u_l}] \qquad (15\text{-}31)$$

Returning to machine M_4, we specify $\mathbf{v}$ to be

$$\mathbf{v} = [\mathbf{y}_c, \mathbf{y}_b] = \begin{bmatrix} 1 & 0 \\ 0 & 1 \end{bmatrix} = \mathbf{I}_2$$

From Eqs. (15-25) and (15-27) we obtain

$$\mathbf{A} = [\mathbf{Y}_c^0, \mathbf{Y}_b^0] = \begin{bmatrix} 1 & 1 \\ 0 & 1 \end{bmatrix} \qquad \mathbf{C} = [\mathbf{z}_c^0, \mathbf{z}_b^0] = \begin{bmatrix} 1 & 0 \\ 0 & 1 \end{bmatrix}$$

The only unit input vector is $\mathbf{u} = [1]$, and hence $\mathbf{Y}_i^1$ is the 1-successor of $\mathbf{y}_i$. Since the zero state is contained in U^*, let $\mathbf{y}_i = \mathbf{y}_d$, and by Eqs. (15-29) and (15-31) we obtain

$$\mathbf{B} = [\mathbf{Y}_d^1] = [\mathbf{y}_b] = \begin{bmatrix} 0 \\ 1 \end{bmatrix} \qquad \mathbf{D} = [\mathbf{z}_d^1] = \begin{bmatrix} 1 \\ 0 \end{bmatrix}$$

The state and output equations are

$$\mathbf{Y}(t) = \begin{bmatrix} 1 & 1 \\ 0 & 1 \end{bmatrix} \mathbf{y}(t) + \begin{bmatrix} 0 \\ 1 \end{bmatrix} \mathbf{x}(t)$$

$$\mathbf{z}(t) = \begin{bmatrix} 1 & 0 \\ 0 & 1 \end{bmatrix} \mathbf{y}(t) + \begin{bmatrix} 1 \\ 0 \end{bmatrix} \mathbf{x}(t)$$

The final test is to verify that the above equations indeed represent machine M_4 under *all* input and state combinations. This is accomplished by verifying each state transition and its corresponding output. For example, substituting $\mathbf{y}_a$ for A and $\mathbf{0}$ for $\mathbf{x}(t)$, the machine should go to state $\mathbf{y}_b$ and produce output 11, corresponding to the entry $B,11$ in column 0, row A, in Table 15-1. And indeed,

$$\begin{bmatrix} 1 & 1 \\ 0 & 1 \end{bmatrix} \cdot \begin{bmatrix} 1 \\ 1 \end{bmatrix} + \begin{bmatrix} 0 \\ 1 \end{bmatrix} \cdot [0] = \begin{bmatrix} 0 \\ 1 \end{bmatrix} \rightarrow \mathbf{y}_b$$

$$\begin{bmatrix} 1 & 0 \\ 0 & 1 \end{bmatrix} \cdot \begin{bmatrix} 1 \\ 1 \end{bmatrix} + \begin{bmatrix} 1 \\ 0 \end{bmatrix} \cdot [0] = \begin{bmatrix} 1 \\ 1 \end{bmatrix} \rightarrow \mathbf{z}_a^0$$

The characterizing matrices are thus verified, and the linear realization of Fig. 15-18 results.

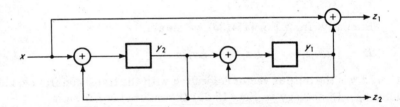

Fig. 15-18   Machine $\mathfrak{M}_4$.

Example Machine M_5 and its distinguishing table are given in Tables 15-3 and 15-4, respectively. The "checked" rows are linearly independent, and since U^* contains all possible eight 3-tuples, the identification procedure is continued.

Table 15-3 Machine M_5

PS	NS, z_1z_2	
	$x = 0$	$x = 1$
A	$A,00$	$E,10$
B	$A,10$	$E,00$
C	$B,11$	$F,01$
D	$B,01$	$F,11$
E	$C,01$	$G,11$
F	$C,11$	$G,01$
G	$D,10$	$H,00$
H	$D,00$	$H,10$

Table 15-4 Distinguishing table for machine M_5

	A	B	C	D	E	F	G	H	
$z(0)$	0	1	1	0	0	1	1	0	✓
	0	0	1	1	1	1	0	0	✓
$z(1)$	0	0	1	1	1	1	0	0	
	0	0	0	0	1	1	1	1	✓
$z(2)$	0	0	0	0	1	1	1	1	
	0	0	0	0	0	0	0	0	

Select

$$\mathbf{v} = [\mathbf{y}_b, \mathbf{y}_d, \mathbf{y}_h] = \begin{bmatrix} 1 & 0 & 0 \\ 0 & 1 & 0 \\ 0 & 0 & 1 \end{bmatrix} = \mathbf{I}_3$$

From Eqs. (15-25) and (15-27) we obtain

$$\mathbf{A} = [\mathbf{Y}_b^0, \mathbf{Y}_d^0, \mathbf{Y}_h^0] = \begin{bmatrix} 0 & 1 & 0 \\ 0 & 0 & 1 \\ 0 & 0 & 0 \end{bmatrix} \qquad \mathbf{C} = [\mathbf{z}_b^0, \mathbf{z}_d^0, \mathbf{z}_h^0] = \begin{bmatrix} 1 & 0 & 0 \\ 0 & 1 & 0 \end{bmatrix}$$

Setting $\mathbf{u} = [1]$ and $\mathbf{y}_i = \mathbf{y}_a = \mathbf{0}$, Eqs. (15-29) and (15-31) yield

$$\mathbf{B} = [\mathbf{Y}_a^1] = \begin{bmatrix} 0 \\ 1 \\ 1 \end{bmatrix} \qquad \mathbf{D} = [\mathbf{z}_a^1] = \begin{bmatrix} 1 \\ 0 \end{bmatrix}$$

Thus

$$\mathbf{Y}(t) = \begin{bmatrix} 0 & 1 & 0 \\ 0 & 0 & 1 \\ 0 & 0 & 0 \end{bmatrix} \mathbf{y}(t) + \begin{bmatrix} 0 \\ 1 \\ 1 \end{bmatrix} \mathbf{x}(t)$$

$$\mathbf{z}(t) = \begin{bmatrix} 1 & 0 & 0 \\ 0 & 1 & 0 \end{bmatrix} \mathbf{y}(t) + \begin{bmatrix} 1 \\ 0 \end{bmatrix} \mathbf{x}(t)$$

The matrices are verified to correspond to M_5, and their linear realization is given in Fig. 15-19. ∎

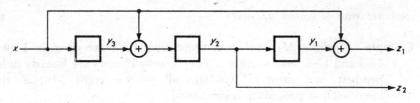

Fig. 15-19 Machine $\mathfrak{M}_5$.

Example As another example, consider the four-stage up-down Gray-code counter of Table 15-5, whose distinguishing table is given in Table 15-6.

Table 15-5 Machine M_6

PS	NS $x = 0$	$x = 1$	$z_1 z_2$
A	B	D	00
B	C	A	01
C	D	B	11
D	A	C	10

Table 15-6 Distinguishing table

	A	B	C	D	
$z(0)$	0	0	1	1	✓
	0	1	1	0	✓
$z(1)$	0	1	1	0	
	1	1	0	0	✓
$z(2)$	1	1	0	0	
	1	0	0	1	

The state assignment is given by

$$\mathbf{y}_a = \begin{bmatrix} 0 \\ 0 \\ 1 \end{bmatrix} \qquad \mathbf{y}_b = \begin{bmatrix} 0 \\ 1 \\ 1 \end{bmatrix} \qquad \mathbf{y}_c = \begin{bmatrix} 1 \\ 1 \\ 0 \end{bmatrix} \qquad \mathbf{y}_d = \begin{bmatrix} 1 \\ 0 \\ 0 \end{bmatrix}$$

Note that although M_6 has only four states, its minimal linear realization is of a third dimension; that is, if M_6 is linearly realizable, it is realizable as a submachine of an eight-state linear machine. Note also that $\mathbf{v}$ cannot be chosen as the identity matrix, and the zero state $\mathbf{y}_i = \mathbf{0}$ is not contained in the state assignment. Consequently, the simplified equations cannot be used, and matrix inversion cannot be avoided. Let

$$\mathbf{v} = [\mathbf{y}_d, \mathbf{y}_b, \mathbf{y}_a] = \begin{bmatrix} 1 & 0 & 0 \\ 0 & 1 & 0 \\ 0 & 1 & 1 \end{bmatrix} \quad \text{then} \quad \mathbf{v}^{-1} = \begin{bmatrix} 1 & 0 & 0 \\ 0 & 1 & 0 \\ 0 & 1 & 1 \end{bmatrix}$$

From Eqs. (15-24) and (15-26) we obtain

$$\mathbf{A} = \begin{bmatrix} 0 & 1 & 0 \\ 0 & 1 & 1 \\ 1 & 0 & 1 \end{bmatrix} \mathbf{v}^{-1} = \begin{bmatrix} 0 & 1 & 0 \\ 0 & 0 & 1 \\ 1 & 1 & 1 \end{bmatrix}$$

$$\mathbf{C} = \begin{bmatrix} 1 & 0 & 0 \\ 0 & 1 & 0 \end{bmatrix} \mathbf{v}^{-1} = \begin{bmatrix} 1 & 0 & 0 \\ 0 & 1 & 0 \end{bmatrix}$$

Let $\mathbf{y}_i^1 = \mathbf{y}_a$. Then, from Eq. (15-28) we obtain

$$\mathbf{B} = \begin{bmatrix} 1 \\ 0 \\ 0 \end{bmatrix} - \mathbf{A} \begin{bmatrix} 0 \\ 0 \\ 1 \end{bmatrix} = \begin{bmatrix} 1 \\ 1 \\ 1 \end{bmatrix} \qquad \mathbf{D} = \begin{bmatrix} 0 \\ 0 \end{bmatrix}$$

The minimum dimensional linear circuit realizing the counter is shown in Fig. 15-20. ∎

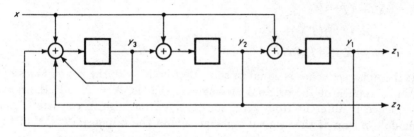

Fig. 15-20   Linear realization of the Gray-code counter.

15-7 APPLICATION OF LINEAR MACHINES TO ERROR CORRECTION

The availability of analysis and synthesis techniques for linear machines, as well as their economical realization by means of shift registers, have made them widely applicable in communication and digital computation. Linear machines are particularly useful in computations involving multiplication and division of polynomials and in error detection and correction. In this section we describe in detail how they can be used in a simple error-correcting coding scheme.   For a more complete survey of coding and digital computation applications, the reader is referred to Peterson [15] and Gill [9].

Consider the communication-system model shown in Fig. 15-21. The *message*, denoted X, consists of a sequence over $GF(p)$ of length n. The *encoder*, whose transfer function is T, transforms the message into another sequence over $GF(p)$ of length n.   This sequence is referred to as the *transmitted sequence* and is designated Z, where $Z = TX$.   The

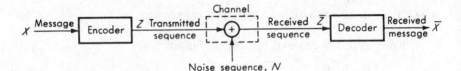

Fig. 15-21 A model for a communication system.

sequence Z is transmitted through a noisy *channel*, whose output $\bar{Z}$ is called the *received sequence*. In the channel a *noise sequence* over $GF(p)$, denoted N, is added to the transmitted sequence, so that the received sequence is equal to

$$\bar{Z} = Z + N$$
$$= TX + N$$

The *decoder*, whose transfer function is T^{-1}, processes the received sequence and produces a sequence $\bar{X}$ such that

$$\bar{X} = (T^{-1})\bar{Z}$$
$$= (T^{-1})(TX + N)$$
$$= X + (T^{-1})N$$

If the noise sequence is equal to zero, that is, $N = 0$, the *received message* $\bar{X}$ is a replica of the original message X, that is, $X = \bar{X}$. If the noise sequence is different from zero, the received message $\bar{X}$ consists of the modulo-p sum of the original message X and the response $(T^{-1})N$ of the decoder to the noise sequence.

As an illustration of the error-correction procedure, let us analyze in detail the communication system shown in Fig. 15-22, where the encoder's transfer function is given by $T = 1 + D^2 + D^3$, and the message as well as the noise are over $GF(2)$. We assume that the noise sequence contains only a single nonzero digit; i.e., the communication system is *single-error-correcting*. Suppose that a seven-bit message X is to be transmitted, where the first four digits are the *information digits*, and the remaining three digits are the *checking digits*. The checking digits in X are always 0's. Consequently, if $\bar{X}$ is received with three 0's in the last three positions, it means that no noise is present in the channel,

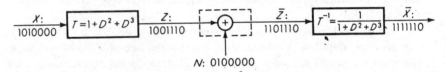

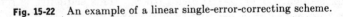

Fig. 15-22 An example of a linear single-error-correcting scheme.

and $\bar{X}$ is an identical replica of X. If, however, the received message $\bar{X}$ contains nonzero digits in the last three positions, this indicates that an error occurred during the transmission, and an error-correcting procedure must be employed to recover the original message.

When an error occurs, it is necessary to determine the sequence $(T^{-1})N$ and to subtract it from the received message $\bar{X}$. To determine $(T^{-1})N$, we observe that, since the last three digits of X were originally 0's, then the last three digits of $\bar{X}$ must consist only of digits of $(T^{-1})N$, without any contribution from X. In fact, if only a single error occurred at time t, then the sequence $(T^{-1})N$ is simply the response of the decoder T^{-1} to a unit impulse occurring at t. Therefore the checking digits of $\bar{X}$ consist of a subsequence of three digits of the impulse response of T^{-1}. (Clearly, if the error occurs in one of the checking digits, say in the second checking digit, then the first digit will be a zero, and the remaining two checking digits will be the first two digits of the impulse response of T^{-1}.)

The decoder is chosen so that its impulse response has a maximal period of seven digits. This ensures that, by observing the subsequence contained in the last three digits of $\bar{X}$, we can determine uniquely the entire sequence $(T^{-1})N$. Since a maximal impulse response contains all seven possible combinations of three successive nonzero digits, each noise impulse corresponds to only one pattern of checking digits, and thus its location can be uniquely determined.

As an example, suppose that the sequence 1010000 is to be transmitted by means of the communication system of Fig. 15-22. The transmitted sequence Z is found to be 1001110. If an error occurs in the second digit, the received sequence $\bar{Z}$ is 1101110. Since the impulse response of the decoder, whose transfer function is $T^{-1} = (1 + D^2 + D^3)^{-1}$, is 1011100, the received message $\bar{X}$ is equal to 1111110. The checking digits of $\bar{X}$ are identical with the fourth, fifth, and sixth digits of the impulse response. Consequently, we may conclude that the noise impulse has occurred in the second information digit. The sequence $(T^{-1})N$ is thus found to be 0101110, and it may now be added (same as subtracting, modulo 2) to $\bar{X}$ to obtain the original message X, i.e.,

$$
\begin{array}{llllllll}
\text{Decoder's impulse response:} & 1 & 0 & 1 & 1 & 1 & 0 & 0 \\
\bar{X}: & 1 & 1 & 1 & 1 & 1 & 1 & 0 \\
\underline{(T^{-1})N:} & \underline{0} & \underline{1} & \underline{0} & \underline{1} & \underline{1} & \underline{1} & \underline{0} \quad + \\
X: & 1 & 0 & 1 & 0 & 0 & 0 & 0
\end{array}
$$

In a similar manner the reader can verify that if the message 1110000 is transmitted by means of the system of Fig. 15-22, and the noise N is given by 0010000, then the received message is 1100111. The checking digits contain the third, fourth, and fifth digits of the decoder's impulse response.

Consequently, $(T^{-1})N$ is equal to 0010111, and the message X can be reconstructed.

To obtain single-error correction for messages over $GF(2)$ containing m information digits and k checking digits, we need a decoder whose impulse response is of length $m + k$, with each string of k successive digits different from every other subsequence of length k. Such an impulse response can be obtained from a decoder whose transfer function is of degree k and whose impulse response is maximal, i.e., of length $m + k = 2^k - 1$. If the last k digits of the received message $\bar{X}$ are not zeros, the sequence $(T^{-1})N$ must be subtracted from $\bar{X}$. This can be accomplished by shifting $\bar{X}$ over the decoder's impulse response until the last k digits of $\bar{X}$ match a corresponding subsequence of the impulse response. This is always possible, since the impulse response contains every nonzero subsequence of length k. The modulo-2 sum of $\bar{X}$ and the digits of the impulse response appearing directly below it yield the original message X.

APPENDIX 15-1 BASIC PROPERTIES OF FINITE FIELDS†

A set R is said to form a *ring* if two operations, addition and multiplication, are defined for every pair of elements in R, and if it satisfies the following postulates:

1. *Closure.* For every a and b in R, $a + b$ and ab are in R.
2. *Associativity.* For every a, b, and c in R, $(a + b) + c = a + (b + c)$ and $(ab)c = a(bc)$.
3. R contains a *unique zero element*, denoted 0, such that, for every a in R $a + 0 = 0 + a = a$.
4. To each a in R there corresponds a unique element $-a$ in R such that $a + (-a) = (-a) + a = 0$. $-a$ is called the *inverse* of a.
5. *Distributivity.* Multiplication distributes over addition; that is, $a(b + c) = ab + ac$, for all a, b, and c in R.
6. *Commutativity.* For all a and b in R, $a + b = b + a$.

If multiplication is also commutative, i.e., $ab = ba$, R is said to be a *commutative ring*.

Example The set of integers $\{0,1, \ldots, p - 1\}$ under the modulo-p addition and multiplication operations forms a commutative ring. (Note that modulo p means that $a = b$ whenever $a - b$ is a multiple

† This is only a short summary of several definitions and results in the area of fields. For a more complete coverage, the reader is referred to any book on algebra.

of p.) The definition of the modulo-4 operations is shown in Table A15-1. ∎

Table A15-1   Addition and multiplication modulo 4

+	0	1	2	3			0	1	2	3
0	0	1	2	3		0	0	0	0	0
1	1	2	3	0		1	0	1	2	3
2	2	3	0	1		2	0	2	0	2
3	3	0	1	2		3	0	3	2	1

The set F is said to be a *field* if it is a commutative ring and, in addition, satisfies the following two postulates:

1. There is a unique nonzero element 1 in F such that $a1 = a$ for every a in F.
2. To each nonzero a in F there corresponds a unique element a^{-1} (or $1/a$) in F such that $aa^{-1} = 1$.

The set of real numbers and that of complex numbers each form an infinite field. Fields containing a finite number of elements are usually called *finite fields*.

Example   The modulo-4 ring defined in Table A15-1 is not a field, since the element 2 does not have a multiplicative inverse; that is, the equation $2a = 1$ does not have a solution for a, as can be seen from the defining table.   On the other hand, the equation $2a = 2$ (modulo 4) has two solutions, $a = 1$ and $a = 3$. ∎

The above example illustrates the reason for restricting our discussion of linear machines to the modulo p of prime numbers, since multiplication by numbers which are not prime to the modulo may be irreversible, and consequently do not preserve information. It can be shown that if p is a prime integer, then the ring of integers, modulo p, forms a field.   This finite field is called a *Galois field* and is denoted $GF(p)$.

Example   The set of integers $\{0,1,2\}$ and the operations defined in Table A15-2 form the finite field $GF(3)$. ∎

Table A15-2   Modulo-3 operations

+	0	1	2		·	0	1	2
0	0	1	2		0	0	0	0
1	1	2	0		1	0	1	2
2	2	0	1		2	0	2	1

Any Galois field with prime characteristic p contains exactly p^k elements, for some integer k. This field is denoted $GF(p^k)$. It can also be shown that for any finite field there exists a prime integer p and a positive integer k, so that the given field is equivalent to $GF(p^k)$.

In this chapter the fields were defined over $GF(p)$, where p is a prime. The theory and results obtained can be generalized to include linear machines defined over any finite field. It can be shown [17] that there exists an equivalence between a linear machine defined over any finite field and a linear machine defined over $GF(p)$. Consequently, any linear machine defined over any finite field can be synthesized by the techniques developed for machines defined over $GF(p)$, where p is a prime integer.

APPENDIX 15-2   THE EUCLIDEAN ALGORITHM

The Euclidean algorithm provides a procedure for determining the greatest common divisor of two polynomials over a field F.

Let $P(D)/Q(D)$ be a rational polynomial of the form

$$\frac{P(D)}{Q(D)} = \frac{a_0 + a_1 D + \cdots + a_m D^m}{b_0 + b_1 D + \cdots + b_n D^n}$$

where the degree of $P(D)$ is smaller than that of $Q(D)$. [The degree of the polynomial $P(D)$ is the greatest i, such that $a_i \neq 0$.] The Euclidean algorithm is based on the result that every rational polynomial can be divided in a unique manner so that

$$Q(D) = q(D)P(D) + r(D)$$

When the remainder $r(D) = 0$, $P(D)$ is said to divide $Q(D)$. To find the greatest common divisor we use successive divisions as follows:

$$Q(D) = q_1(D)P(D) + r_1(D)$$
$$P(D) = q_2(D)r_1(D) + r_2(D)$$
$$r_1(D) = q_3(D)r_2(D) + r_3(D)$$

$$\cdots \cdots \cdots \cdots \cdots \cdots \cdots$$

$$r_{i-2}(D) = q_i(D)r_{i-1}(D)$$

Then $r_{i-1}(D)$ is the greatest common divisor of $P(D)$ and $Q(D)$.

Example   Determine the greatest common divisor for the polynomial

$$T(D) = \frac{P(D)}{Q(D)} = \frac{1 + D + D^4 + D^6}{D + D^3 + D^4 + D^6 + D^8 + D^9} \qquad [\text{over } GF(2)]$$

$$
\begin{array}{r}
D^3 + D^2 + D \\
\hline
D^6 + D^4 + D + 1 \,\big|\, D^9 + D^8 + D^6 + D^4 + D^3 + D \\
\end{array}
$$

$$
\begin{array}{l}
\quad D^9 + D^7 + D^4 + D^3 \\
\hline
\quad D^8 + D^7 + D^6 + D \\
\quad D^8 + D^6 + D^3 + D^2 \\
\hline
\quad D^7 + D^3 + D^2 + D \\
\quad D^7 + D^5 + D^2 + D \\
\hline
\quad D^5 + D^3 \qquad \leftarrow \text{determination of } r_1(D)
\end{array}
$$

$$
\begin{array}{r}
D \\
\hline
D^5 + D^3 \,\big|\, D^6 + D^4 + D + 1 \\
\end{array}
$$

$$
\begin{array}{l}
\quad D^6 + D^4 \\
\hline
\quad D + 1 \qquad \leftarrow \text{determination of } r_2(D)
\end{array}
$$

$$
\begin{array}{r}
D^4 + D^3 \\
\hline
D + 1 \,\big|\, D^5 + D^3 \\
\end{array}
$$

$$
\begin{array}{l}
\quad D^5 + D^4 \\
\hline
\quad D^4 + D^3 \\
\quad D^4 + D^3 \qquad \leftarrow r_3(D) = 0 \\
\hline
\end{array}
$$

Since $r_3(D) = 0$, $r_2(D) = D + 1$ is the greatest common divisor. To find the reduced polynomial, it is necessary to divide $P(D)$ and $Q(D)$ by $D + 1$. This division yields

$$T(D) = \frac{1 + D^4 + D^5}{D + D^2 + D^4 + D^5 + D^8} \qquad \blacksquare$$

NOTES AND REFERENCES

Linear machines were first investigated by Huffman in 1956 [13]. This original work, which was restricted to inert machines, was later expanded by several people, notably Cohn [3, 4], Elspas [7], Friedland [8], Hartmanis [10], and Stern and Friedland [17]. The problem of identifying linear machines was treated by numerous authors, among them Brzozowski and Davis [2, 6] and Hartmanis [11]. The most general minimization and identification procedure is due to Cohn and Even [5], whose approach has been followed in this chapter. Other aspects of linear machines have been studied by Booth [1], Pugsley [16], and Zierler [18]. The applications of linear machines to error-correcting codes are due to Huffman [12] and Peterson [15]. A good collection of papers on linear machines is available in Kautz [14]. The best general treatment of linear machines can be found in the book by Gill [9].

1. Booth, T. L.: An Analytic Representation of Signals in Sequential Networks, Proceedings Symposium on Mathematical Theory of Automata, vol. 12, pp. 301–340, Polytechnic Institute of Brooklyn, New York, 1963.
2. Brzozowski, J. A., and W. A. Davis: On the Linearity of Autonomous Sequential Machines, *Trans. IEEE*, vol. EC-13, pp. 673–679, 1964.
3. Cohn, M.: Controllability in Linear Sequential Networks, *Trans. IRE*, vol. CT-9, pp. 74–78, 1962.
4. Cohn, M.: Properties of Linear Machines, *J. Assoc. Computing Machinery*, vol. 11, pp. 296–301, 1964.
5. Cohn, M., and S. Even: Identification and Minimization of Linear Machines, *Trans. IEEE*, vol. EC-14, pp. 367–376, 1965.
6. Davis, W. A., and J. A. Brzozowski: On the Linearity of Sequential Machines, *Trans. IEEE*, vol. EC-15, pp. 21–29, 1966.
7. Elspas, B.: The Theory of Autonomous Linear Sequential Networks, *Trans. IRE*, vol. CT-6, pp. 45–60, 1959.
8. Friedland, B.: Linear Modular Sequential Circuits, *Trans. IRE*, vol. CT-6, pp. 61–68, 1959.
9. Gill, A.: "Linear Sequential Circuits," McGraw-Hill Book Company, New York, 1967.
10. Hartmanis, J.: Linear Multivalued Sequential Coding Networks, *Trans. IRE*, vol. CT-6, pp. 69–74, 1959.
11. Hartmanis, J.: Two Tests for the Linearity of Sequential Machines, *Trans. IEEE*, vol. EC-14, pp. 781–786, 1965.
12. Huffman, D. A.: A Linear Circuit Viewpoint of Error-correcting Codes, *Trans. IRE*, vol. IT-2, pp. 20–28, 1956.
13. Huffman, D. A.: The Synthesis of Linear Sequential Coding Networks, in C. Cherry (ed.), "Information Theory," pp. 77–95, Academic Press Inc., New York, 1956.
14. Kautz, W. H. (ed.): "Linear Sequential Switching Circuits: Selected Technical Papers," Holden-Day, Inc., Publisher, San Francisco, 1965.
15. Peterson, W. W.: "Error-correcting Codes," The M.I.T. Press, Cambridge, Mass., 1961.
16. Pugsley, J. H.: Sequential Functions and Linear Sequential Machines, *Trans. IEEE*, vol. EC-14, pp. 376–382, 1965.
17. Stern, T. E., and B. Friedland: The Linear Modular Sequential Circuit Generalized, *Trans. IRE*, vol. CT-8, pp. 79–80, 1961.
18. Zierler, N.: Linear Recurring Sequences, *J. Soc. Ind. Appl. Math.*, vol. 7, pp. 31–48, 1959.

PROBLEMS

15-1. A *combinational linear circuit* is a circuit constructed of only modulo-p adders and multipliers. The block diagram in Fig. P15-1 represents a combinational linear circuit over $GF(2)$. The circuit outputs can be expressed as

$$z_a = x_a$$

$$z_b = x_a + x_b$$

$$z_c = x_b + x_c$$

(a) Show the circuit diagram.

(b) Find the output sequences in response to the following input sequences:

x_a: 0 1 0 1 1 1 1 0 0 0 1 0 1 1
x_b: 1 1 0 1 0 0 0 0 1 0 1 1 0 1
x_c: 0 0 1 1 0 1 1 0 1 0 0 0 0 1

(c) Design the inverse of this circuit; i.e., express the inputs as functions of the outputs and show the inverse circuit.

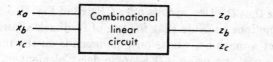

Fig. P15-1

15-2. (a) Determine the transfer function of the shift register shown in Fig. P15-2.

(b) Find its null sequence and show that it is maximal.

(c) Find the inverse machine.

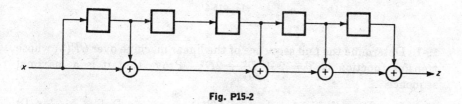

Fig. P15-2

15-3. For each of the following polynomials over $GF(2)$,

$$z_1 = x + D^3x + D^4x \qquad z_2 = x + D^2x + D^4x + D^5x$$

(a) Show the corresponding linear circuit and its inverse.

(b) Find the null sequence and determine whether or not it is maximal.

(c) Utilize the impulse response to determine the response of each circuit to the input sequence 000001101.

15-4. Show the state diagram of the linear machine whose transfer function is $T = 1 + D + D^3$.

15-5. Prove that the two circuits over $GF(3)$ of Fig. P15-5 are equivalent.

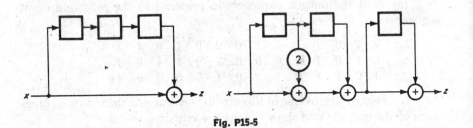

Fig. P15-5

15-6. Prove that the two circuits over $GF(16)$ of Fig. P15-6 have the same transfer functions. (Note that the use of feedback allows us in this case to construct a machine, whose output depends on the inputs three time units in the past, by using just a single delay element.)

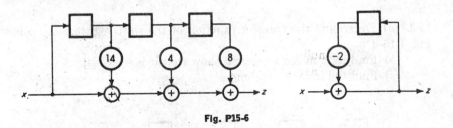

Fig. P15-6

15-7. Determine the null sequence of the linear machine over $GF(3)$ whose transfer function is $T = 2 + D^2 + 2D^3$. Prove that it is a maximal sequence.

15-8. Prove that the delay polynomial $T(D) = a_0 + a_1D + \cdots + a_kD^k$ has a linear inverse which decodes without a delay if and only if $T(D)$ has a nonzero constant term which is relatively prime to p.

Hint: Assume initially $a_0 = 1$. Expand $1/T(D)$ into the form

$$\frac{1}{T(D)} = \frac{1}{1 + \sum_{1}^{n} a_iD^i} = 1 - \sum_{1}^{n} a_iD^i + \left(\sum_{1}^{n} a_iD^i\right)^2 - \cdots$$

15-9. Figure P15-9 shows an inert linear machine over $GF(3)$. Prove that its transfer function is

$$T = \frac{z}{x} = \frac{2D + 2D^2 + D^3}{1 + D^2}$$

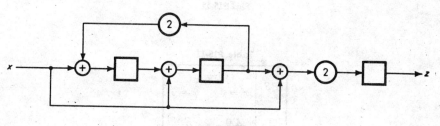

Fig. P15-9

15-10. (a) Prove that the transfer function of the inert linear machine of Fig. P15-10 is given by

$$T = \frac{z}{x} = \frac{T_1}{1 - T_1 T_2}$$

where T_1 and T_2 are the transfer functions of the individual submachines.

(b) Use the result of part a to find the transfer function of the machine in Fig. P15-9.

Hint: In part b determine first the direct paths through which the input signal can reach the output terminal.

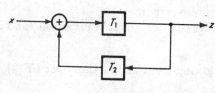

Fig. P15-10

15-11. (a) Determine the transfer function of the linear machine over $GF(2)$ shown in Fig. P15-11 and find its impulse response. Assume that it is initially inert.

(b) Prove that its state table is isomorphic to Table P15-11.

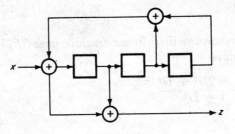

Fig. P15-11

Table P15-11

PS	NS, z $x = 0$	$x = 1$
A	A,0	E,1
B	E,1	A,0
C	F,1	B,0
D	B,0	F,1
E	C,1	G,0
F	G,0	C,1
G	H,0	D,1
H	D,1	H,0

15-12. For each of the following transfer functions,

$$T_1 = \frac{1 + D^2}{1 + D + D^3} \qquad \text{over } GF(2)$$

$$T_2 = \frac{D^2}{2D^2 + D + 1} \qquad \text{over } GF(3)$$

(a) Show the corresponding network.

(b) Find its impulse response.

(c) Determine whether or not it is invertible, and if it is, show the inverse.

15-13. Given the following transfer function over $GF(2)$,

$$T = \frac{D^{10} + D^9 + D^8 + D^7 + D}{D^7 + D^4 + D^2 + D + 1}$$

(a) Determine by means of the Euclidean algorithm the greatest common divisor of the numerator and the denominator and simplify the function.

(b) Show a minimal chain realization, using no more than eight delay elements.

15-14. Show minimal realizations of the transfer function below and its inverse.

$$T = \frac{1 + D + 2D^2 + D^3}{1 + D + D^3 + 2D^4} \qquad \text{over } GF(3)$$

15-15. Design a four-dimensional linear machine over $GF(2)$ whose impulse response is

$$h = 1\ 1\ 1\ 1\ 1\ 0\ 0\ 1\ 0\ 1\ 1\ 1\ 0\ 0\ (1\ 0\ 1\ 1\ 1\ 0\ 0) \cdots$$

(The sequence in parentheses repeats itself thereafter.)

15-16. Show the linear circuit over $GF(2)$ whose characterizing matrices are

$$\mathbf{A} = \begin{bmatrix} 1 & 1 & 0 \\ 1 & 1 & 1 \\ 1 & 0 & 0 \end{bmatrix} \quad \mathbf{B} = \begin{bmatrix} 1 & 1 \\ 0 & 0 \\ 0 & 1 \end{bmatrix} \quad \mathbf{C} = \begin{bmatrix} 1 & 0 & 0 \\ 1 & 0 & 0 \end{bmatrix} \quad \mathbf{D} = \begin{bmatrix} 0 & 0 \\ 0 & 1 \end{bmatrix}$$

15-17. (a) Find the characteristic matrix $\mathbf{A}$ which is realized by the internal circuit of Fig. P15-17.

(b) Determine the transpose of the matrix $\mathbf{A}$ found in part a, and show a circuit which realizes the transposed matrix.

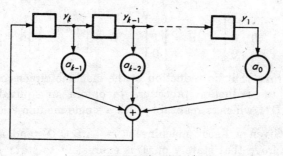

Fig. P15-17

15-18. (a) Prove that a linear machine $\{\mathbf{A},\mathbf{B},\mathbf{C},\mathbf{D}\}$ is μ-definite if and only if μ is the least integer, so that $\mathbf{A}^\mu = \mathbf{0}$.

(b) Prove that if a k-dimensional linear machine is μ-definite, then $\mu \le k$.

Hint: See Ref. 4.

15-19. (a) Design the linear circuit over $GF(2)$ whose characterizing matrices are

$$A = \begin{bmatrix} 1 & 0 & 0 & 0 & 1 \\ 0 & 0 & 1 & 1 & 1 \\ 1 & 1 & 0 & 0 & 0 \\ 1 & 0 & 1 & 0 & 0 \\ 0 & 0 & 1 & 0 & 1 \end{bmatrix} \quad B = \begin{bmatrix} 1 & 0 \\ 0 & 0 \\ 1 & 1 \\ 1 & 1 \\ 1 & 1 \end{bmatrix}$$

$$C = \begin{bmatrix} 0 & 1 & 0 & 1 & 1 \\ 1 & 1 & 1 & 0 & 1 \end{bmatrix} \quad D = \begin{bmatrix} 1 & 0 \\ 0 & 0 \end{bmatrix}$$

(b) Minimize the machine of part a, and show that it is independent of x_2.

15-20. (a) Minimize the linear machine over $GF(2)$ given by the following characterizing matrices:

$$A = \begin{bmatrix} 0 & 1 & 0 & 1 \\ 0 & 1 & 1 & 1 \\ 1 & 1 & 0 & 0 \\ 1 & 1 & 1 & 1 \end{bmatrix} \quad B = \begin{bmatrix} 0 \\ 0 \\ 0 \\ 1 \end{bmatrix} \quad C = [1 \quad 0 \quad 1 \quad 0] \quad D = [0]$$

(b) For each state of the reduced machine, show the equivalent states of the original machine.

15-21. (a) Design the linear circuit over $GF(2)$ whose characterizing matrices are

$$A = \begin{bmatrix} 0 & 1 & 1 \\ 1 & 0 & 0 \\ 1 & 0 & 0 \end{bmatrix} \quad B = \begin{bmatrix} 1 \\ 1 \\ 0 \end{bmatrix} \quad C = \begin{bmatrix} 1 & 1 & 0 \\ 1 & 1 & 1 \end{bmatrix} \quad D = \begin{bmatrix} 0 \\ 1 \end{bmatrix}$$

(b) Prove that no reduction in the machine dimension is possible, but apply the reduction procedure to obtain an equivalent machine $\{A^*, B^*, C^*, D^*\}$ which is realizable with a single modulo-2 adder.

15-22. (a) Given a linear machine $\mathfrak{M} = \{A, B, C, D\}$ and a nonsingular matrix G, prove that state y of $\mathfrak{M}$ is equivalent to state $\bar{y} = Gy$ of $\overline{\mathfrak{M}}$, where $\overline{\mathfrak{M}}$ is the linear machine characterized by

$$\bar{A} = GAG^{-1} \quad \bar{B} = GB \quad \bar{C} = CG^{-1} \quad \bar{D} = D$$

(b) Prove that machines $\mathfrak{M}$ and $\overline{\mathfrak{M}}$ are isomorphic.

15-23. (a) Prove that, for all $t \geq 0$,

$$(A^*)^t = TA^tR$$

where A^* is the characteristic matrix of the reduced machine, defined in Eq. (15-22).

Hint: Prove the assertion for $t = 0$ and use induction on t.

(b) Use the result of part a to prove that the diagnostic matrix $\mathbf{K}^*$ of the reduced machine is related to $\mathbf{K}$ by

$$\mathbf{K}^* = \mathbf{KR}$$

(c) Prove that if $\mathbf{T}^*$ is the $r \times r$ matrix consisting of the first r linearly independent rows of $\mathbf{K}_r^*$ of a reduced linear machine, then $\mathbf{T}^* = \mathbf{I}_r$, where $\mathbf{I}_r$ is the identity matrix.

15-24. A k-dimensional linear machine $\{\mathbf{A},\mathbf{B},\mathbf{C},\mathbf{D}\}$ is said to be μ-*controllable* if, for every pair of states S_i and S_j, there is an input sequence of *exactly* length μ which takes the machine from state S_i to state S_j.

(a) Prove that a k-dimensional machine $\mathfrak{M}$ is μ-controllable if and only if the rank of the $k \times \mu l$ matrix

$$\mathbf{G}_\mu = [\mathbf{A}^{\mu-1}\mathbf{B}, \mathbf{A}^{\mu-2}\mathbf{B}, \ldots, \mathbf{AB}, \mathbf{B}]$$

is k; i.e., there are k linearly independent columns in $\mathbf{G}_\mu$.

(b) Determine whether the following machine over $GF(2)$ is μ-controllable.

$$\mathbf{A} = \begin{bmatrix} 0 & 1 & 0 \\ 1 & 0 & 0 \\ 0 & 0 & 1 \end{bmatrix} \qquad \mathbf{B} = \begin{bmatrix} 0 \\ 1 \\ 1 \end{bmatrix}$$

Hint: Try first 3-controllable and show that $\mathbf{G}_3$ is singular.

15-25. For each of the machines in Table P15-25 determine whether it is linear, and if it is, show a linear realization.

Table P15-25

PS	NS, z	
	$x = 0$	$x = 1$
A	A,0	E,1
B	E,1	A,0
C	F,1	B,0
D	B,0	F,1
E	C,1	G,0
F	G,0	C,1
G	H,0	D,1
H	D,1	H,0

(a)

PS	NS				z_1z_2			
	00	01	11	10	00	01	11	10
A	E	F	A	B	10	11	00	01
B	G	H	C	D	11	10	01	00
C	B	A	F	E	01	00	11	10
D	D	C	H	G	00	01	10	11
E	B	A	F	E	11	10	01	00
F	D	C	H	G	10	11	00	01
G	E	F	A	B	00	01	10	11
H	G	H	C	D	01	00	11	10

(b)

15-26. Test the machine of Table P15-26 for linearity. In particular, determine if the state transitions are linear and if the outputs are linear.

Table P15-26

PS	NS, z	
	$x = 0$	$x = 1$
A	A,0	B,0
B	C,0	D,0
C	A,1	B,1
D	C,1	D,0

16
Finite-state Recognizers

This chapter is concerned with the characterization of finite-state machines and the sets of sequences that they accept. We investigate a number of generalized forms of finite-state machines and prove that these forms are equivalent, with respect to the sets of sequences that they accept, to the basic deterministic finite-state model. In Secs. 16-2 and 16-3 we study the properties of nondeterministic state diagrams, called transition graphs, which will prove a useful tool in the study of regular expressions. Procedures are developed whereby any transition graph can be converted into a deterministic state diagram.

Section 16-4 presents the language of regular expressions, which provides a precise characterization of the sets of sequences accepted by finite-state machines. In the next two sections we prove that any finite-state machine can be characterized by a regular expression, and every regular expression can be "realized" by a finite-state machine. Finally, Sec. 16-7 is concerned with a generalized form of finite-state machines, known as two-way machines.

16-1 DETERMINISTIC RECOGNIZERS

So far we have regarded a finite-state machine as a *transducer* that *transforms* input sequences into output sequences. In this chapter we shall view a machine as a *recognizer* which *classifies* input strings into two classes, the strings that it accepts and the strings that it rejects. The set consisting of all the strings that a given machine accepts is said to be *recognized* by that machine.

The finite-state model that we shall use is shown in Fig. 16-1, where a *finite-state control* is coupled through a *head* to a finite linear sequence of

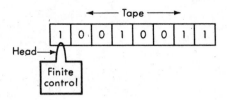

Fig. 16-1   A finite-state recognizer.

squares, each containing a single symbol of the alphabet. Such a sequence of squares is called an (*input*) *tape*. Initially, the finite-state control is in the starting state, and the head scans the leftmost symbol of the string that appears on the tape. The head then scans the tape from left to right. In what is termed a *cycle of computation* the machine starts in some state S_i, reads the symbol currently scanned by the head, shifts one square to the right, and then enters state S_j.

Clearly, the concept of a head reading from left to right the symbols contained in a linear tape is equivalent to a string of inputs which enter the machine at successive times. In fact, the finite-state control is a Moore finite-state machine.† The states whose assigned output is 1 are referred to as *accepting* (or *terminal*) *states*, while the states whose assigned output is 0 are called *rejecting* (or *nonterminal*) *states*. A string (or a tape) is *accepted* by a machine if and only if the state that the machine enters after having read the rightmost tape symbol is an accepting state. Otherwise the string is rejected. The set of strings recognized by a machine thus consists of all the input strings that take the machine from its starting state to an accepting state.

The machine of Fig. 16-1 can be described by a state diagram in which the starting state is marked by an incoming short arrow, and the

---

† By allowing the head to write on the tape, while restricting its motion to left-to-right, we can generalize the model to include Mealy machines.

accepting states are indicated by double circles. For example, the state diagram of Fig. 16-2a describes a machine that accepts a string if and only if the string begins and ends with a 1, and every 0 in the string is preceded and followed by at least a single 1. The machine consists of three states, of which A is the starting state and B is an accepting state. Note that,

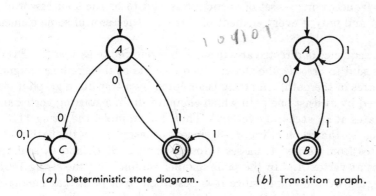

(a) Deterministic state diagram.   (b) Transition graph.

Fig. 16-2 Two ways of describing a set of strings.

in general, a starting state may also be an accepting state. In such a case the machine is said to accept the null string.

16-2 TRANSITION GRAPHS

Because a state diagram describes a *deterministic* machine, the next state transition must be determined *uniquely* by the present state and the presently scanned input symbol. No alternative behavior is allowed. Moreover, in a deterministic state diagram, a transition must be specified for each input symbol. Consequently, a state diagram consists of a vertex for every state and a directed arc labeled α emanating from each vertex for every input symbol α. However, if our prime objective is to study and classify sets of sequences, some of these restrictions may be removed, and different diagrams, called transition graphs, may prove more convenient.

Nondeterministic recognizers

A *transition graph* (or *transition system*) is a directed graph. It consists of a set of vertices labeled A, B, C, etc., and various directed arcs connecting them. At least one of the vertices is specified as a *starting vertex*, and at least one is specified as an *accepting* (or *terminal*) *vertex*. The arcs are labeled with symbols from the (*input*) *alphabet* of the graph. If the graph contains an arc labeled α leading from vertex V_i to vertex V_j, then V_j is said to be the α-*successor* of V_i. For a given input α, a vertex may have one or more α-successors or none. Thus, for example, in the transition graph of Fig. 16-2b, vertex A has two 1-successors, namely, A and B, but has no 0-successor. A set of vertices S is said to be the α-successor of a set R if and only if every element of S is an α-successor of some element of R.

A sequence of directed arcs in a graph is referred to as a *path*. Every path is said to *describe* the string which consists of the symbols assigned to the arcs in the path. A string is accepted by a transition graph if it is described by at least one path which emanates from a starting vertex and terminates at an accepting vertex. Thus, for example, the string 1110 is accepted by the graph of Fig. 16-3, since it is described by the path which emanates from vertex A, passes through vertices B, D, and C, and terminates at vertex A. In the same manner we find that the string 11011 is accepted by the graph, since it is described by a path that emanates from the starting vertex B, passes through D, C, B, D, and terminates at the accepting vertex C. On the other hand, the string 100, for example, is rejected, since there is no path in the graph which describes it.

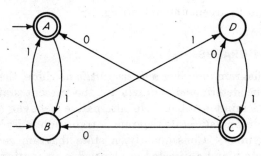

Fig. 16-3 A transition graph.

As in the case of state diagrams, the set of strings that are accepted by a transition graph is said to be _recognized_ by the graph. For example, the transition graph of Fig. 16-2b recognizes the same set of strings recognized by the state diagram of Fig. 16-2a. If two or more graphs recognize the same set of strings, they are said to be _equivalent graphs_. Thus the graphs in Fig. 16-4 are equivalent, since each graph accepts a string if and only if each 1 in the string is preceded by at least two 0's.

Clearly, a state diagram is a special case of a transition graph, and is therefore referred to as a *deterministic (transition) graph*. Other transition graphs are referred to as *nondeterministic (transition) graphs*. The two graphs in Fig. 16-2, for example, are equivalent, although one is deterministic and the other one is not. Because deterministic graphs describe the behavior of deterministic finite-state machines, we often regard nondeterministic graphs as describing the behavior of nondeterministic finite-state machines. It must, however, be emphasized that the

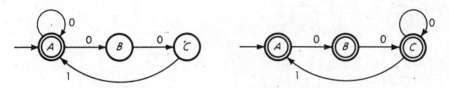

Fig. 16-4 Two equivalent transition graphs.

notion of nondeterministic recognizers is useful for classifying sets of strings, but should not be confused with realizable machines.

Graphs containing λ-transitions

Nondeterministic transition graphs can be further generalized by allowing transitions that are associated with a *null symbol λ*. Such transitions are referred to as λ-*transitions*, and they can occur when no input is applied. When determining the string described by a path which contains arcs labeled λ, the λ symbols are disregarded and deleted from the string.

The use of λ-transitions may sometimes simplify the transition graph by reducing the number of labeled arcs, as is the case in the graph of Fig. 16-5a. This graph recognizes the set of strings that start with an even number of 1's, followed by an even number of 0's, and end up with the substring 101. (Note that zero is considered an even number.) Thus, for example, the strings 101, 11101, 110000101, and 00101 are accepted by the graph, while 110011101 and 0011101 are rejected.

It is a simple matter to convert a transition graph containing λ-transitions into an equivalent graph which contains no such transitions. A λ-transition from vertex V_1 to vertex V_2 of a given graph can always be replaced by a set of arcs emanating from V_1 and duplicating the transitions which emanate from V_2. In addition, if V_1 is a starting vertex, V_2 must also be made a starting vertex. If V_2 is an accepting vertex, V_1 must also be made an accepting vertex. To remove the λ-transition from the graph of Fig. 16-5a, it is necessary to duplicate the transitions from

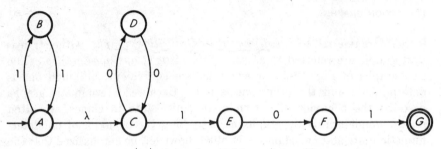

(a) A graph containing a λ-transition.

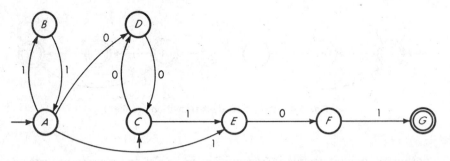

(b) An equivalent graph without λ-transitions.

Fig. 16-5 Elimination of λ-transition.

vertex C to vertices D and E by directing arcs, correspondingly labeled, from vertex A to vertices D and E. The equivalent graph which contains no λ-transition is shown in Fig. 16-5b.

16-3 CONVERTING NONDETERMINISTIC INTO DETERMINISTIC GRAPHS

A natural question which now arises is whether a nondeterministic graph can recognize sets of strings which cannot be recognized by a deterministic graph. At first one might suspect that the added flexibility of nondeterministic graphs increases their computational capabilities. However, as we shall now show, *there exists an effective procedure for converting a nondeterministic transition graph into an equivalent deterministic one.* This leads to the conclusion that nondeterministic graphs and deterministic graphs have identical computational capabilities.

Introductory example

Consider the nondeterministic transition graph of Fig. 16-6a. A tabular description of the graph, called a *transition table*, is shown in Fig. 16-6b, where the starting vertices are indicated by small arrows next to rows A

and B, and the accepting vertex is indicated by a circle around row heading C. The table entry in row V_i, column α, consists of the α-successors of vertex V_i.

Suppose now that we wish to determine whether a given string $w = a_1a_2a_3 \cdots a_k$ is accepted by the graph of Fig. 16-6a; that is, whether the graph contains a path that emanates from a starting vertex, terminates at an accepting vertex, and describes the string w. Since A and B are the starting vertices, any such path must include as its first arc one of the arcs emanating from either A or B. Specifically, if the first symbol in w is a_1, then the first arc in the path can reach any of the vertices in the

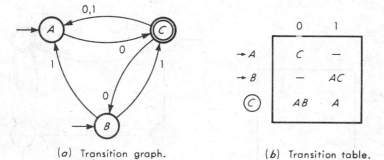

(a) Transition graph.   (b) Transition table.

Fig. 16-6 A nondeterministic graph to be converted to a deterministic one.

subset which consists of the a_1-successors of $\{A,B\}$. Using similar reasoning, we find that the ith arc in a path that describes w must lead to one of the vertices contained in the subset which consists of the $a_1a_2 \cdots a_i$-successors of $\{A,B\}$. If the final subset of vertices reached by the path contains an accepting vertex, the string w is accepted; otherwise it is rejected. For example, any path that describes the string 0010 must start with the arc leading from vertex A to vertex C. And since the 0-successors of C are A and B, one of these vertices must be encountered next in the path describing the given string. In the same manner, since $\{AC\}$ is the 1-successor of $\{AB\}$, we find that the third arc in the path leads to either one of the vertices A or C. The fourth symbol might lead to either one of the vertices A, B, or C, and since vertex C is an accepting vertex, the string is accepted. A similar argument shows, for example, that the string 1100 is rejected, since it might lead to either vertex A or vertex B, and neither of these vertices is an accepting one.

The foregoing example suggests a procedure for determining whether a specified string is accepted by a given graph. The procedure involves tracing the various paths that describe the given string, and determining the sets of vertices that can be reached from the starting vertices by applying the symbols of the string. The procedure can be facilitated and applied to arbitrary strings by the use of a *successor table*, which lists all the subsets of vertices that are reachable from the starting vertices. The successor table for the graph of Fig. 16-6 is shown in Fig. 16-7a. Its column headings are the symbols of the alphabet. The first row heading is the set of starting vertices, while the remaining row headings are the subsets of vertices reachable from the starting vertices. The entry in a given row—say Q—column α is determined from the transition table and consists of the α-successor of {Q}.

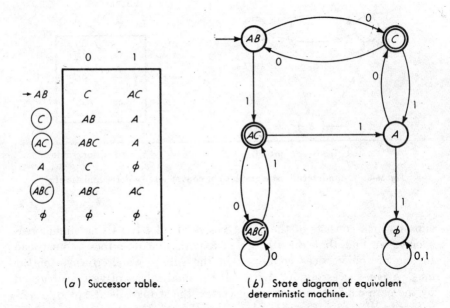

	0	1
→ AB	C	AC
C	AB	A
AC	ABC	A
A	C	φ
ABC	ABC	AC
φ	φ	φ

(*a*) Successor table.

(*b*) State diagram of equivalent deterministic machine.

Fig. 16-7 Deterministic form of the graph of Fig. 16-6.

The first row heading in Fig. 16-7a is *AB*, since *A* and *B* are the starting vertices. The entries in row *AB* are the 0- and 1-successors of {*AB*}, namely, {*C*} and {*AC*}, respectively. *C* and *AC* are now made row headings, and their successors found, and so on. Since vertex *A* has no 1-successor, the 1-successor of row *A* must correspond to the set that contains none of the vertices of the transition graph. Such a set is referred to as the *empty*, or *null*, set and is denoted φ. Finally, the row headings of rows *C*, *AC*, and *ABC* are circled to indicate that each of the sets {*C*},

$\{AC\}$, and $\{ABC\}$ contains the accepting vertex C of the original transition graph.

Proof of the conversion procedure

The graph in Fig. 16-7b is derived directly from the successor table. It is clearly a deterministic graph, since in its construction only one transition is allowed for each input symbol. To verify that this graph indeed accepts a string if and only if that string is accepted by the corresponding nondeterministic graph, note that the last vertex of the deterministic graph reached by the given string corresponds to the subset of vertices that can be reached by the same string in the nondeterministic graph. The string is accepted by the deterministic graph if and only if there is in the nondeterministic graph at least one path which results in the string being accepted, that is, if one of the vertices reachable by the string is an accepting one. The foregoing procedure, which is also known as the *subset construction,* can be applied to any nondeterministic graph. Thus we arrive at the following theorem.

Theorem 16-1 *Let S be a set of strings that can be recognized by a non-deterministic transition graph G_n. Then S can also be recognized by an equivalent deterministic graph G_d. Moreover, if G_n has p vertices, G_d will have at most 2^p vertices.*

Proof: The existence of a deterministic graph G_d that is equivalent to the given nondeterministic graph G_n is guaranteed by the subset construction developed above. If we denote the p vertices of G_n by $V_1, V_2, \ldots, V_p$, then, by the subset construction, the equivalent deterministic graph may have at most 2^p vertices labeled ϕ; V_1, $V_2, \ldots, V_p$; V_1V_2, $V_1V_3, \ldots, V_2V_3, \ldots, V_{p-1}V_p$; $V_1V_2V_3$, $\ldots, V_{p-2}V_{p-1}V_p$; $\cdots$; $V_1V_2 \cdots V_p$. ∎

Theorem 16-1 permits us to describe deterministic finite-state machines by means of nondeterministic transition graphs. Such descriptions will prove very convenient in the following discussion of regular expressions.

16-4 REGULAR EXPRESSIONS

In this chapter we are mainly concerned with the characterization of sets of strings recognized by finite automata. It is therefore appropriate to develop a compact language for describing such sets of strings. The language developed in this section is known as *type-3 language* or as the language of *regular expressions.*

Describing sets of strings

We shall first consider informally some sets recognized by simple graphs, leaving the formal presentation to subsequent sections. Consider the transition graph in Fig. 16-8a, which recognizes the set {101} that contains just one string. We shall describe the set {101} by the *expression†* **101.**

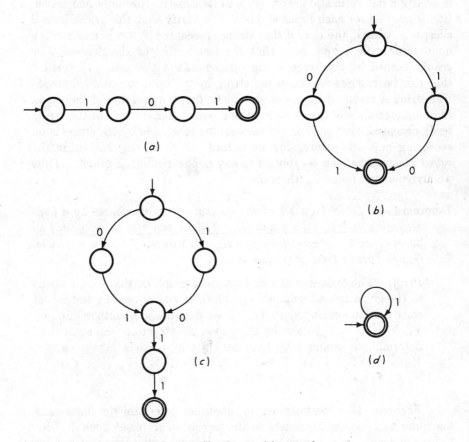

Fig. 16-8 Simple transition graphs.

Similarly, for arbitrary alphabet {a,b}, the set {abba} is described by the expression **abba**, and so on.

The graph of Fig. 16-8b recognizes the set of strings {01,10}, which consists of two strings, 01 and 10. To represent such a set, we employ the set union operation +, and express the set {01,10} as **01 + 10.** In

† In this chapter, boldface type is used to describe expressions.

the same manner the set $\{abb,a,b,bba\}$ can be described by the expression **abb + a + b + bba**. Clearly, since the set union operation is commutative and associative, the union operation of expressions is also commutative and associative.

Next consider the graph of Fig. 16-8c, which recognizes the set $\{0111,1011\}$. This set can be described by the expression **0111 + 1011**. However, we observe that this graph recognizes precisely those strings which are recognized by the graph in Fig. 16-8b *and* are followed immediately by the substring 11. In other words, the graph of Fig. 16-8c recognizes the set whose members are those strings formed by concatenating strings of $\{01,10\}$ and $\{11\}$. In general, the *concatenation* of two sets, $\{P\}$ and $\{Q\}$, is the set consisting of strings formed by taking any string of $\{P\}$ and attaching to it any string of $\{Q\}$. The above set can thus be described by the *concatenation* of the two corresponding expressions **01 + 10** and **11**, i.e., **(01 + 10)11**. Clearly, the concatenation operation is associative, that is, if **P**, **Q**, and **R** are expressions, then **(PQ)R = P(QR)**, but is not commutative, that is, **PQ ≠ QP**. To simplify notation we omit the parentheses and write the product **(PQ)R** as **PQR**.

The graph in Fig. 16-8d recognizes the set of strings whose members consist of an arbitrary number (possibly zero) of 1's, i.e., $\{\lambda,1,11,111,1111, \ldots \}$. This set can be described by the infinite expression $\lambda + 1 + 11 + 111 + 1111 + \cdots$, or compactly by **1***, where

$$1^* = \lambda + 1 + 11 + 111 + 1111 + \cdots$$

The symbol * is referred to as the *star* (or *closure*) *operation*. In general, **R*** describes the set consisting of the null string λ and those strings that can be formed by concatenating a finite number of strings from $\{R\}$. For example, the expression **01(01)*** describes the set consisting of those strings that can be formed by concatenating one or more 01 substrings, that is,

$$01(01)^* = 01 + 0101 + 010101 + 01010101 + \cdots$$

For convenience, **RR** may be abbreviated as $\mathbf{R^2}$, **RRR** as $\mathbf{R^3}$, etc. Thus

$$R^* = \lambda + R + R^2 + R^3 + \cdots$$

We are now able to describe some sets of strings on a given alphabet by means of the operations $+$, $\cdot$, *. For example, the set of strings on $\{0,1\}$ beginning with a 0 and followed only by 1's can be described by **01***, while the set of strings containing exactly two 1's can be described by **0*10*10***. An important expression is $\underline{(0 + 1)^*}$, which describes the set containing all the strings that can be formed on the binary alphabet;

that is,

$$(0 + 1)^* = \lambda + 0 + 1 + 00 + 01 + 11 + 10 + 000 + \cdots$$

Thus, for example, the set of strings that begin with the substring 11 is described by the expression $11(0 + 1)^*$.

Example The transition graph of Fig. 16-9a accepts those strings that can be formed by concatenating a finite number of 01 and 10 substrings followed by a 11. Accordingly, it can be described by the expression $(01 + 10)^* 11$. In a similar manner the reader can verify that the set of strings recognized by the graph of Fig. 16-9b can be described by $(10^*)^*$. ∎

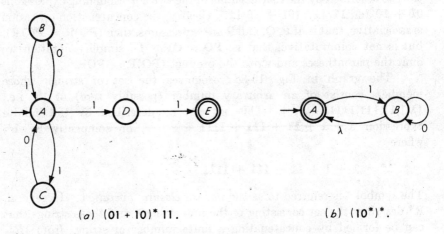

(a) $(01 + 10)^* 11$.   (b) $(10^*)^*$.

Fig. 16-9 Transition graphs and sets of strings they recognize.

We have thus shown that some sets of strings may be described by expressions formed of symbols from the alphabets of these sets and the operations union, concatenation, and star. We now formalize these ideas.

Definition and basic properties

Let $A = \{\alpha_1, \alpha_2, \ldots, \alpha_p\}$ be a finite *alphabet*; then the class of *regular expressions over the alphabet A* is defined recursively as follows:

1. Any of the *symbols* $\alpha_1, \alpha_2, \ldots, \alpha_p$, alone, is a regular expression, as are the *null string* λ and the *empty set* ϕ.

2. If P and Q are regular expressions, then so is their *concatenation* PQ and their *union* P + Q. If P is a regular expression, then so is its *closure* P*.

3. No other expressions are regular unless they can be generated in a *finite* number of applications of the above rules.

By convention, the precedence of the operations in decreasing order is *, ·, +.

At this point it is appropriate to consider the significance of the expressions λ and ϕ. The expression λ describes the set which consists of just the null string. It can be recognized, for example, by the graph of Fig. 16-10*a*. The expression ϕ, on the other hand, describes the set

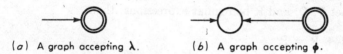

(*a*) A graph accepting λ. (*b*) A graph accepting ϕ.

Fig. 16-10 Recognizers for λ and ϕ.

that has no strings at all. In other words, ϕ describes the set recognized by a graph which accepts no strings, such as the graph shown in Fig. 16-10*b*. The reader may verify that each of the following identities, which involve the expressions ϕ and λ, exhibits different ways of describing the *same* sets of strings.

$$\phi + R = R \tag{16-1}$$

$$\phi R = R\phi = \phi \tag{16-2}$$

$$R\lambda = \lambda R = R \tag{16-3}$$

$$\lambda^* = \lambda \tag{16-4}$$

$$\phi^* = \lambda \tag{16-5}$$

A set of strings that can be described by a regular expression is called a *regular set*. Not every set of strings is regular. For example, the set over the alphabet $\{0,1\}$, which consists of k 0's (for all k), followed by a 1, followed in turn by k 0's, is not regular, as will be proved later. This set can be described by the expression $010 + 00100 + 0001000 + \cdots + 0^k10^k + \cdots$. But such a description involves an infinite number of applications of the union operation. Consequently, it is not a regular expression. There are, however, certain infinite sums which are regular. For example, the set which consists of alternating 0's and 1's, starting and ending with a 1, i.e., $\{1,101,10101,1010101, \ldots\}$, can be described by the expression $1 + 101 + 10101 + \cdots$, or $1(01)^*$, which is clearly regular.

Manipulating regular expressions

A regular set may be described by more than one regular expression. For example, the above set of alternating 0's and 1's can be described by the expression $1(01)^*$, as well as by $(10)^*1$. Two expressions which describe the same set of strings are said to be *equivalent*. Unfortunately, no straightforward methods are available to determine whether two given expressions are equivalent. In certain cases, however, a regular expression can be converted into another equivalent expression by the use of simple identities. Some of these identities (whose proofs are left to the reader as an exercise) are listed as follows:

Let P, Q, and R be regular expressions; then

$$R + R = R \qquad\qquad (16\text{-}6)$$

$$PQ + PR = P(Q + R) \qquad PQ + RQ = (P + R)Q \qquad (16\text{-}7)$$

$$R^*R^* = R^* \qquad\qquad (16\text{-}8)$$

$$RR^* = R^*R \qquad\qquad (16\text{-}9)$$

$$(R^*)^* = R^* \qquad\qquad (16\text{-}10)$$

$$\lambda + RR^* = R^* \qquad\qquad (16\text{-}11)$$

$$(PQ)^*P = P(QP)^* \qquad\qquad (16\text{-}12)$$

To prove the last identity, note that each of the expressions $(PQ)^*P$ and $P(QP)^*$ can be written in the form $P + PQP + PQPQP + \cdots$.

The set described by the expression $(P + Q)^*$ consists of all the strings that can be formed by concatenating P's and Q's, including the null string λ. It is easy to verify that the expression $(P^* + Q^*)^*$ describes the same set of strings, as does the expression $(P^*Q^*)^*$. Thus we find

$$(P + Q)^* = (P^*Q^*)^* = (P^* + Q^*)^* \qquad\qquad (16\text{-}13)$$

but note that $(P + Q)^* \neq P^* + Q^*$.

The following identity will be proved in Sec. 16-5.

$$(P + Q)^* = P^*(QP^*)^* = (P^*Q)^*P^* \qquad\qquad (16\text{-}14)$$

This identity leads in turn to

$$\lambda + (P + Q)^*Q = (P^*Q)^* \qquad\qquad (16\text{-}15)$$

Indeed, by Eqs. (16-11) and (16-14),

$$(P^*Q)^* = \lambda + (P^*Q)^*P^*Q$$
$$= \lambda + (P + Q)^*Q$$

The preceding identities can sometimes be used to simplify regular expressions or to demonstrate their equivalence, as illustrated in the following examples.

Example Prove that the set of strings in which every 0 is immediately followed by at least two 1's can be described by both R_1 and R_2, where

$$R_1 = \lambda + 1^*(011)^*(1^*(011)^*)^*$$
$$R_2 = (1 + 011)^*$$

Proof:
$$R_1 = \lambda + 1^*(011)^*(1^*(011)^*)^* \qquad [\text{by } (16\text{-}11)]$$
$$= (1^*(011)^*)^* \qquad\qquad [\text{by } (16\text{-}13)]$$
$$= (1 + 011)^* = R_2$$

The reader can verify that R_2 indeed decribes the set in question. ∎

Example Prove the identity

$$(1 + 00^*1) + (1 + 00^*1)(0 + 10^*1)^*(0 + 10^*1) = 0^*1(0 + 10^*1)^*$$

Proof:
$$(1 + 00^*1) + (1 + 00^*1)(0 + 10^*1)^*(0 + 10^*1)$$
$$= (1 + 00^*1)[\lambda + (0 + 10^*1)^*(0 + 10^*1)]$$
$$= [(\lambda + 00^*)1][\lambda + (0 + 10^*1)^*(0 + 10^*1)] \qquad [\text{by } (16\text{-}11)]$$
$$= 0^*1(0 + 10^*1)^* \quad ∎$$

In many situations, however, algebraic manipulations of regular expressions are extremely involved, and thus are not a suitable tool for determining the equivalence of two regular expressions. As we shall see in the next section, perhaps the best approach is to convert the expressions in question into their equivalent state diagrams and to test the diagrams for equivalence by the techniques of Chap. 10. Other procedures for establishing equivalence of regular expressions can be found in Ref. 3.

16-5 TRANSITION GRAPHS RECOGNIZING REGULAR SETS

We have already seen in several examples that transition graphs are capable of recognizing regular sets. We wish to show now that to every regular set, there corresponds a transition graph (and hence a deterministic finite-state machine) which recognizes that set of strings.

Constructing the transition graphs

We now prove the following theorem.

Theorem 16-2 *Every regular expression* $\mathbf{R}$ *can be recognized by a transition graph.*

Proof: We shall prove the theorem by constructing the required transition graph. The construction procedure is inductive on the total number of characters in $\mathbf{R}$, where by a *character* we refer to an appearance of any of the expressions $\alpha_1, \alpha_2, \ldots, \alpha_p, \lambda, \phi$ or the star operation $*$ in $\mathbf{R}$. For example, the number of characters in $\mathbf{R} = \lambda + (1*0)*1*$ is seven.

BASIS: Let the number of characters in $\mathbf{R}$ be one. Then $\mathbf{R}$ must be either ϕ, λ, or a symbol, say α_i, from the alphabet. The graphs in Fig. 16-11 recognize these regular sets.†

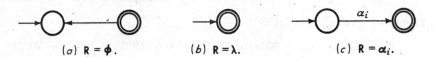

(a) $\mathbf{R} = \phi$.   (b) $\mathbf{R} = \lambda$.   (c) $\mathbf{R} = \alpha_i$.

Fig. 16-11 Transition graphs recognizing elementary regular sets.

INDUCTION STEP: Assume the theorem is true for expressions with n characters or less. We now show that it must also be true for any expression $\mathbf{R}$ having $n + 1$ characters. $\mathbf{R}$ must be in one of the three following forms:

1. $\mathbf{R} = \mathbf{P} + \mathbf{Q}$
2. $\mathbf{R} = \mathbf{PQ}$
3. $\mathbf{R} = \mathbf{P}*$

where $\mathbf{P}$ and $\mathbf{Q}$ are expressions, each having n or fewer characters. According to the induction hypothesis, the sets $\mathbf{P}$ and $\mathbf{Q}$ can be

† Although there is a distinction between regular expressions and the sets that they describe, it is customary to speak of the regular set $\mathbf{R}$ as meaning the set that can be described by $\mathbf{R}$.

recognized by transition graphs, which we shall denote G and H, respectively, as shown in Fig. 16-12a. (Note that each of the graphs in Fig. 16-12 contains just one starting and one accepting vertex.)

The set described by **P + Q** can be recognized by a transition graph composed of G and H, as shown in Fig. 16-12b. The set

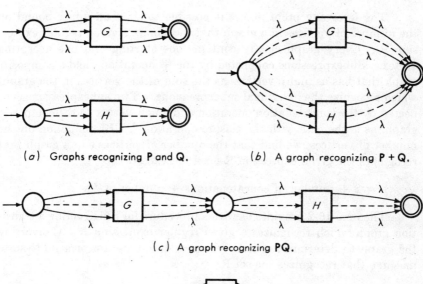

(a) Graphs recognizing **P** and **Q**. (b) A graph recognizing **P + Q**.

(c) A graph recognizing **PQ**.

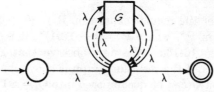

(d) A graph recognizing **P***.

Fig. 16-12 Construction of composite graphs.

described by **PQ** can be recognized by a transition graph constructed in the following manner. Coalesce the accepting vertex of G with the starting vertex of H and regard the combined vertex as one that is neither starting nor accepting. The resulting graph is shown in Fig. 16-12c. The starting vertices of this graph are the starting vertices of G, while the accepting vertices are those of H. Clearly, this graph will accept a string if and only if that string belongs to **R = PQ**. Finally, to recognize the set **P***, construct the graph of

Fig. 16-12*d*. The graphs in Fig. 16-12, which are composed of G and H, are referred to as *composite graphs*.

Since every regular set can be described by an expression obtained by a finite number of applications of the operations +, ·, * on the alphabet $\{\alpha_1, \alpha_2, \ldots, \alpha_p\}$, ϕ, and λ, the theorem is proved. ∎

The foregoing proof makes it possible to state an upper bound on the number of vertices in a graph that recognizes a given regular expression R. Every graph clearly contains one starting and one accepting vertex. Subexpressions connected by the + operation yield a composite graph that has as many vertices as the sum of the vertices in the graphs which recognize the individual subexpressions. Two subexpressions connected by the concatenation operation add a new vertex to the composite graph, as is the case with the closure operation *. By induction on the number of vertices, we find that the number of vertices v in a graph that recognizes the given expression R need not exceed

$$v = 2 + \text{number of concatenations} + \text{number of *'s}$$

Theorem 16-2 provides us with a procedure for constructing a transition graph which recognizes a given regular expression R. Converting the graph to deterministic form yields a state diagram of a finite-state machine that recognizes the set R.

Example   Consider the regular expression $R = (0 + 1(01)^*)^*$. Since it is of the form P^*, where $P = 0 + 1(01)^*$, it is recognized by the graph of Fig. 16-13*a*. We now observe that $P = 0 + Q$, where $Q = 1(01)^*$, and the resulting graph is shown in Fig. 16-13*b*. The subexpression Q can be decomposed into $Q = ST$, where $S = 1$ and $T = (01)^*$. This yields the graph of Fig. 16-13*c*. The process is continued in a similar manner until each subexpression consists of only a single symbol. The final transition graph that recognizes R is shown in Fig. 16-13*d*. Note that the number of vertices in the graph is six, in agreement with the value of v derived above. ∎

We can now prove the identity in Eq. (16-14) by demonstrating that both expressions $(P + Q)^*$ and $P^*(QP^*)^*$ can be recognized by equivalent transition graphs. The graph in Fig. 16-14*a* recognizes the set described by $P^*(QP^*)^*$. Removal of the λ-transitions results in the graph of Fig. 16-14*b*, which can be converted to the deterministic graph of Fig. 16-14*c*. Clearly, this graph recognizes the set $(P + Q)^*$, and thus the two expres-

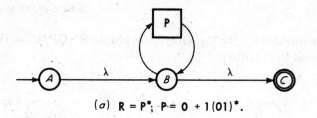

(a) R = P*; P = 0 + 1(01)*.

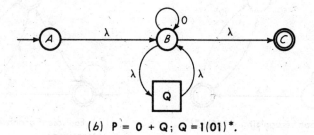

(b) P = 0 + Q; Q = 1(01)*.

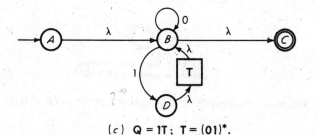

(c) Q = 1T; T = (01)*.

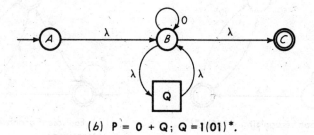

(d) Final step.

Fig. 16-13 Construction of a transition graph recognizing
R = (0 + 1(01)*)*.

sions are equivalent. By Eq. (16-12) we obtain $\mathbf{P^*(QP^*)^* = (P^*Q)^*P^*}$, which proves the identity.

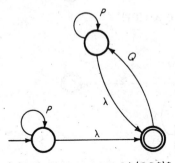

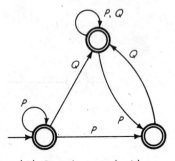

(a) Graph recognizing $\mathbf{P^*(QP^*)^*}$.   (b) Equivalent graph with no λ-transitions.

(c) Equivalent deterministic graph recognizing $(\mathbf{P + Q})^*$.

Fig. 16-14 Illustration of proof that $\mathbf{P^*(QP^*)^* = (P + Q)^*}$.

Informal techniques

In practice, in many cases it is possible to construct transition graphs from their corresponding regular expressions in a straightforward manner, without resorting to the above induction procedure.

Example Construct a graph that recognizes the regular set

$$\mathbf{P = (01 + (11 + 0)1^*0)^*11}$$

As an introduction we shall construct a graph that recognizes the subexpression $\mathbf{Q = (11 + 0)1^*0}$. Every string in Q starts with either the substring 11 or 0, followed by an arbitrary number of 1's, and ends with a 0. The graph of Fig. 16-15 clearly recognizes just this set of strings. The subexpressions **11** and **0** are represented by parallel paths between vertices A and C, while 1^* corresponds to a self-loop around vertex C. To ensure that a string is accepted only if it ends with a 0, an arc labeled 0 leads from vertex C to the accepting vertex D.

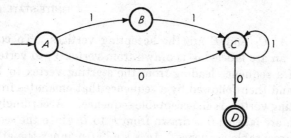

Fig. 16-15 A graph recognizing $Q = (11 + 0)1*0$.

Now consider the expressions **P**. The graph that recognizes **P** is constructed so that paths are provided for strings from the sets **01** and **(11 + 0)1*0**, followed by a string from the set **11**. One possible such graph is shown in Fig. 16-16. ■

In a number of cases it is convenient to use λ-transitions to preserve the order in which substrings appear. As an example, consider the expression **R = (11)*(00)*101**. In this expression substrings from **(00)*** must *follow* substrings from **(11)***. One way of ensuring that this order is preserved is by using a λ-transition, as shown in Fig. 16-5a. This graph accepts only those strings which start with a string from **(11)***, followed by a string from **(00)***, and end with the string 101.

Example Construct a transition graph that recognizes the set

$R = (1(00)*1 + 01*0)*$

We begin by setting up paths for the subexpressions **1(00)*1** and **01*0**, as shown in Fig. 16-17a. Vertex A is the starting vertex,

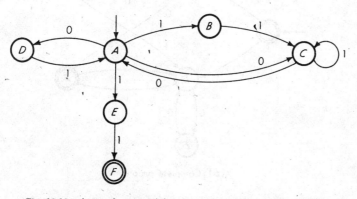

Fig. 16-16 A graph recognizing $P = (01 + (11 + 0)1*0)*11$.

while A, C, and F are the accepting vertices. To complete the graph, an arc labeled α_i is drawn from vertex V_j to vertex V_k if and only if a sequence leading from the starting vertex to V_j, followed by α_i and then followed by a sequence that emanates from V_k to an accepting vertex, is an acceptable sequence. Accordingly, for example, an arc labeled 0 is drawn from F to B, since the sequence 1100 is an acceptable sequence. In a similar manner the graph is completed, as shown in Fig. 16-17b. ■

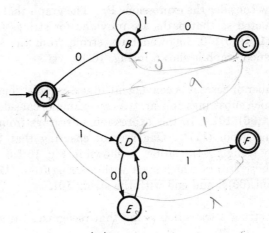

(a) Partial graph.

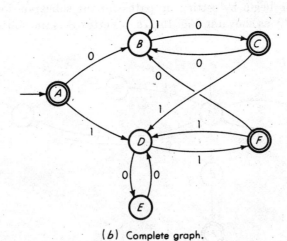

(b) Complete graph.

Fig. 16-17 Transition graph recognizing $\mathbf{R} = (1(00)^{*}1 + 01^{*}0)^{*}$.

In conclusion, we have established that every regular set can be recognized by a finite-state machine. Moreover, there is a routine procedure for determining the machine that recognizes a given regular set. This procedure involves the use of nondeterministic transition graphs, which can later be converted into the equivalent deterministic graphs. Other methods, however, are available [6] which provide directly the state-diagram description of the machine, without the need to resort to nondeterministic graphs.

16-6 REGULAR SETS CORRESPONDING TO TRANSITION GRAPHS

We now consider the problem of deriving regular expressions that describe specified transition graphs. Specifically, we shall show that the set of strings that can be recognized by a transition graph (and hence a finite-state machine) is a regular set.

Proof of uniqueness

Before proceeding with our main topic, we shall establish the following theorem:

Theorem 16-3 *Let* Q, P, *and* R *be regular expressions on a finite alphabet. Then, if* P *does not contain* λ, *the equation*

$$R = Q + RP \tag{16-16}$$

has a unique solution given by

$$R = QP^* \tag{16-17}$$

Proof: $R = QP^*$ is clearly a solution to the equation $R = Q + RP$, since [by substitution and Eq. (16-11)]

$$R = Q + RP = Q + QP^*P = Q(\lambda + P^*P) = QP^*$$

To prove uniqueness, expand

$$
\begin{aligned}
R &= Q + RP \\
&= Q + (Q + RP)P = Q + QP + RP^2 \\
&= Q + QP + (Q + RP)P^2 = Q + QP + QP^2 + RP^3 \\
& \cdots \cdots \cdots \cdots \cdots \cdots \cdots \cdots \cdots \cdots \cdots \\
&= Q(\lambda + P + P^2 + \cdots + P^{i-1} + P^i) + RP^{i+1} \tag{16-18}
\end{aligned}
$$

where i is any arbitrary integer.   Choose some string w in $\mathbf{R}$, suppose the length of w is k, and then substitute $i = k$ in Eq. (16-18).

$$\mathbf{R} = \mathbf{Q}(\lambda + \mathbf{P} + \mathbf{P}^2 + \cdots + \mathbf{P}^k) + \mathbf{R}\mathbf{P}^{k+1}$$

Since $\mathbf{P}$ does not contain λ, the length of the shortest string in the set $\mathbf{R}\mathbf{P}^{k+1}$ is at least $k + 1$.   Consequently, w is not contained in $\mathbf{R}\mathbf{P}^{k+1}$, but is contained in $\mathbf{Q}(\lambda + \mathbf{P} + \mathbf{P}^2 + \cdots + \mathbf{P}^k)$.   But since $\mathbf{Q}(\lambda + \mathbf{P} + \mathbf{P}^2 + \cdots + \mathbf{P}^k)$ is contained in $\mathbf{Q}\mathbf{P}^*$, then w is contained in $\mathbf{Q}\mathbf{P}^*$.

To prove the converse, suppose that w is a string in $\mathbf{Q}\mathbf{P}^*$. Then there exists some integer k such that w is in $\mathbf{Q}\mathbf{P}^k$. This in turn implies that w is contained in $\mathbf{Q}(\lambda + \mathbf{P} + \mathbf{P}^2 + \cdots + \mathbf{P}^k)$, and hence in $\mathbf{R} = \mathbf{Q} + \mathbf{R}\mathbf{P}$.   ■

In an analogous manner we can show that, if $\mathbf{P}$ does not contain λ, then $\mathbf{R} = \mathbf{P}^*\mathbf{Q}$ is the unique solution to the equation $\mathbf{R} = \mathbf{Q} + \mathbf{P}\mathbf{R}$. Note that if $\mathbf{P}$ contains λ, the solution of Eq. (16-16) is not unique.   If $\mathbf{P} = \phi$, then $\mathbf{R} = \mathbf{Q}$.

Systems of equations

Consider the transition graph of Fig. 16-18 whose starting vertex is A and accepting vertex C.   The set of strings recognized by this graph consists of all the strings that can be described by paths emanating from

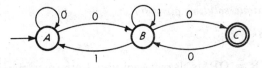

Fig. 16-18   A transition graph to be analyzed.

vertex A and terminating at C.   But since vertex C can be reached only through vertex B, each of these strings must end with a 0 and have as prefix a string leading from A to B.   Let us denote the set of strings leading from A to B by $\mathbf{B}$ and the set of strings that take the graph from A to C by $\mathbf{C}$.   The set $\mathbf{C}$ can then be expressed as $\mathbf{C} = \mathbf{B}0$.

Next consider the set $\mathbf{A}$, which consists of exactly those strings that take the graph from vertex A to itself.   Vertex A can be reached from B with a 1, from A with a 0, and with the null string λ.   Thus $\mathbf{A}$ can be expressed as $\mathbf{A} = \lambda + \mathbf{A}0 + \mathbf{B}1$.   Finally, vertex B can be reached from

A with a 0, from B with a 1, and from C with a 0.   As a result, we obtain the equation $\mathbf{B} = \mathbf{A0} + \mathbf{B1} + \mathbf{C0}$.

The foregoing analysis yields a system of three simultaneous equations which characterize the sets of strings that take the graph from its starting vertex to each of its vertices.   In Theorem 16-4 we shall prove that each of these sets of strings is regular.

$$\mathbf{A} = \lambda + \mathbf{A0} + \mathbf{B1} \tag{16-19}$$

$$\mathbf{B} = \mathbf{A0} + \mathbf{B1} + \mathbf{C0} \tag{16-20}$$

$$\mathbf{C} = \mathbf{B0} \tag{16-21}$$

These equations can now be solved for the variables $\mathbf{A}$, $\mathbf{B}$, and $\mathbf{C}$.   Substituting Eq. (16-21) for $\mathbf{C}$ in Eq. (16-20) yields

$$\mathbf{B} = \mathbf{A0} + \mathbf{B1} + \mathbf{B00} = \mathbf{A0} + \mathbf{B}(1 + 00) \tag{16-22}$$

Equation (16-22) is now of the form of Eq. (16-16):

$$\mathbf{R} = \mathbf{Q} + \mathbf{RP}$$

and its solution is given by Eq. (16-17), i.e.,

$$\mathbf{R} = \mathbf{QP}^*$$

Applying Eq. (16-17) to Eq. (16-22), we obtain

$$\mathbf{B} = \mathbf{A0}(1 + 00)^* \tag{16-23}$$

$\mathbf{B}$ can now be substituted into Eq. (16-19) to give

$$\mathbf{A} = \lambda + \mathbf{A0} + \mathbf{A0}(1 + 00)^{*}1 = \lambda + \mathbf{A}(0 + 0(1 + 00)^{*}1) \tag{16-24}$$

Equation (16-24) is again of the general form of Eq. (16-16) and thus has the solution

$$\mathbf{A} = \lambda(0 + 0(1 + 00)^{*}1)^* = (0 + 0(1 + 00)^{*}1)^* \tag{16-25}$$

Since the set recognized by the graph is given by $\mathbf{C}$, we want to find a solution for this variable.   Substituting Eq. (16-25) for $\mathbf{A}$ in Eq. (16-23), we obtain a solution for $\mathbf{B}$ which, in turn, may be substituted into Eq. (16-21) to yield the solution for $\mathbf{C}$, i.e.,

$$\mathbf{B} = (0 + 0(1 + 00)^{*}1)^{*}0(1 + 00)^* \tag{16-26}$$

$$\mathbf{C} = (0 + 0(1 + 00)^{*}1)^{*}0(1 + 00)^{*}0 \tag{16-27}$$

The above procedure can now be applied to find a system of simultaneous equations for any transition graph which contains no λ-transitions and has a single starting vertex.   (Recall that every transition graph can be converted to an equivalent graph with no λ-transitions and just one starting vertex.)   Suppose V_1 is the starting vertex in a graph containing n vertices, $V_1, V_2, \ldots, V_n$. Let V_i denote the set of strings that take the graph from V_1 to V_i, and let α_{ij} denote the set of strings that take the graph from vertex V_i to vertex V_j without going through any other vertex. $\alpha_{ij} = \phi$ if no direct transition exists from V_i to V_j. Then we arrive at the following equations:

$$V_1 = V_1\alpha_{11} + V_2\alpha_{21} + \cdots + V_n\alpha_{n1} + \lambda$$
$$V_2 = V_1\alpha_{12} + V_2\alpha_{22} + \cdots + V_n\alpha_{n2}$$
$$\cdot \cdot \cdot \cdot \cdot \cdot \cdot \cdot \cdot \cdot \cdot \cdot \cdot \cdot \cdot \cdot \cdot \cdot \cdot \cdot \cdot \cdot \cdot \cdot \cdot \cdot \cdot \quad\quad (16\text{-}28)$$
$$V_n = V_1\alpha_{1n} + V_2\alpha_{2n} + \cdots + V_n\alpha_{nn}$$

This system of equations can now be solved for $V_1, V_2, \ldots, V_n$ by repeated substitutions and successive applications of Eq. (16-17) in the following manner. Whenever an equation is of the form $V_i = V_j\alpha_{ji} + V_k\alpha_{ki}$ or $V_i = V_j\alpha_{ji} + V_k\alpha_{ki} + \lambda$, where $i \neq j \neq k$, then V_i can be substituted into all other equations to yield a system with fewer equations and unknowns. Whenever an equation has the form $V_i = V_i\alpha_{ii} + V_j\alpha_{ji}$ (plus λ if appropriate), then Eq. (16-17) can be applied to yield $V_i = V_j\alpha_{ji}(\alpha_{ii})^*$, which can now be substituted for V_i in the other equations. Note that, since the graph is assumed to contain no λ-transitions, the condition in Theorem 16-3, that α_{ii} should not contain λ, can always be met. This procedure will finally lead to a single equation in one variable. This variable can in turn be determined by another application of Eq. (16-17).

The set of strings recognized by a given graph can be described by the union of the V's which correspond to accepting vertices. For example, if vertices B and C in the graph of Fig. 16-18 were accepting vertices, then the set of strings recognized by the graph could be described by $B + C = (0 + 0(1 + 00)^*1)^*0(1 + 00)^*(\lambda + 0)$.

Clearly, any system of equations of the form of Eq. (16-28) can be uniquely solved by the procedure just outlined, provided that we prove that each of the V_i's and α_{ij}'s is a regular expression. This proof is given in the following theorem.

Theorem 16-4 *The set of strings that take a finite-state machine M from an arbitrary state S_i to another state S_j is a regular set.*

Proof: Let Q be any subset of the states of M containing both S_i and S_j, and let $R_{ij}{}^Q$ denote the set of strings that take the machine from state S_i to state S_j without passing through any state that is outside Q. Since Q may consist of all the states in M, the theorem will be proved if we show that $R_{ij}{}^Q$ is regular. The proof will be by induction on the number of states in Q.

BASIS: Suppose that Q consists of just a single state, which we shall call S_i. Then, the set of strings that take S_i into itself, without passing through any other state, consists of only a finite number of single input symbols. Since by definition each such input symbol is regular, the above set of strings is regular. The corresponding regular expression will be denoted $\mathbf{T}_{ii}$.

INDUCTION STEP: Assume that $R_{ij}{}^Q$ is regular for all subsets of states containing m or fewer states. Thus, $R_{ij}{}^Q$ can be described by the regular expression $\mathbf{R}_{ij}{}^Q$. We shall now prove that the set of strings $R_{ij}{}^P$ is also regular, where P is a set containing $m + 1$ states, including states S_i and S_j. Suppose now that we remove state S_i from P. The resulting subset consists of only m states and will be referred to as Q, for which the theorem is assumed to hold.

Consider a string from $R_{ij}{}^P$. In general it will cause the machine to go through state transitions as follows:

$$S_i, S_t, \ldots, S_u, S_i, \ldots, S_i, \ldots, S_j$$

where the dots correspond to transitions within the set Q and, therefore, do not contain occurrences of S_i. The substrings that take the machine from S_i and back into S_i may consist of either single input symbols from the regular set $\mathbf{T}_{ii}$ or of sequences of symbols that take the machine from S_i through some states, say $S_t, \ldots, S_u$, and back into S_i. Such an input sequence actually consists of a single symbol, denoted T_{it}, that takes M from S_i to S_t, followed by a sequence from $\mathbf{R}_{tu}{}^Q$ and ending with a symbol T_{ui} that returns M to S_i. Each of the symbols T_{it} and T_{ui} is clearly regular and, consequently, the set of strings that take M from S_i into S_i can be described by the regular expression

$$\mathbf{T}_{ii} + \sum_{tu} \mathbf{T}_{it} \mathbf{R}_{tu}{}^Q \mathbf{T}_{ui}$$

where the sum is taken over all possible pairs of states in Q. And since the machine can be taken an arbitrary number of times from S_i through states in Q and back into S_i, the set of the corresponding strings can be described by the regular expression

$$\left(\mathbf{T}_{ii} + \sum_{tu} \mathbf{T}_{it} \mathbf{R}_{tu}{}^Q \mathbf{T}_{ui} \right)^*$$

This set of strings is followed by the set of substrings that take the machine from S_i into S_j. This latter set of substrings consists of all the single symbols T_{ij} that take the machine from S_i to S_j and all other strings that take the machine from S_i to S_j via some states

$S_t, \ldots, S_u$. Clearly, this set can be described by the regular expression

$$T_{ij} + \sum_{tu} T_{it}R_{tu}{}^Q T_{uj}$$

Consequently, the set of strings $R_{ij}{}^P$ is regular and can be described by the expression

$$R_{ij}{}^P = (T_{ii} + \sum_{tu} T_{it}R_{tu}{}^Q T_{ui})^* (T_{ij} + \sum_{tu} T_{it}R_{tu}{}^Q T_{uj}) \quad \blacksquare$$

Combining Theorems 16-2 and 16-4, we obtain the following general result, which is known as Kleene's theorem.

▶ A finite-state machine recognizes a set of strings if and only if it is a regular set.

Applications

The correspondence between regular sets and finite-state machines enables us to determine whether certain sets are regular. For example, let R denote a regular set on the alphabet A that can be recognized by (the Moore) machine M_1. Define the complement of R, denoted R', as the set containing all the strings on A that are not contained in R. R' describes a regular set, since it can be recognized by a machine M_2, which is obtained from M_1 by complementing the output values associated with the states of M_1.

As another example, let us define the intersection of two sets, P and Q, denoted $P \,\&\, Q$, as the set consisting of all the strings that are contained in both P and Q. We can show that the set $P \,\&\, Q$ is regular by observing that each of the sets P' and Q' are regular and, consequently, $P' + Q'$ and $(P' + Q')'$ are regular. And since $P \,\&\, Q = (P' + Q')'$, the set $P \,\&\, Q$ is regular. Regular expressions containing the complementation and intersection operations, as well as the union, concatenation, and closure, are called *extended regular expressions*.

The added operations increase our versatility in describing regular sets. For example, consider the set of strings on the alphabet $\{0,1\}$ such that no string in the set contains three consecutive 0's. This set can be described by the expression $[(0 + 1)^*000(0 + 1)^*]'$, whereas a more complicated expression, like $(1 + 01 + 001)^*(\lambda + 0 + 00)$, would be required if the complementation operation were not used. On the other hand, since expressions containing complementation and intersection operations are difficult to manipulate or to transform to the corresponding graphs, their usefulness is limited.

The following example will illustrate some additional techniques that can be used to determine whether certain sets are regular.

Example Let M be a finite-state machine whose input and output alphabets are $\{0,1\}$. Assume that the machine has a designated starting state. Let $z_1 z_2 \cdots z_n$ denote the output sequence produced by M in response to the input sequence $x_1 x_2 \cdots x_n$. Define a set S_M which consists of all the strings w such that $w = z_1 x_1 z_2 x_2 \cdots z_n x_n$, for any $x_1 x_2 \cdots x_n$ in $(0 + 1)^*$. Prove that S_M is regular.

Given the state diagram of M, replace each directed arc with two directed arcs and a new state, as shown in Fig. 16-19. Retain the original starting state and designate all the original states as accepting states. The resulting nondeterministic transition graph recognizes the set S_M. Therefore S_M must be regular.

Fig. 16-19   Illustration of the procedure for designing a recognizer for S_M.

This procedure will now be applied to find a deterministic machine that recognizes the set S_N, where N is the machine described in Fig. 16-20. Replacing every arc of machine N with two directed arcs, and following the procedure just outlined, we arrive at the transition graph in Fig. 16-21a. Converting this graph into deterministic form yields the state diagram of Fig. 16-21b. ∎

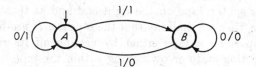

Fig. 16-20   Machine N.

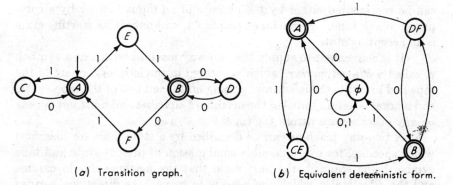

(a) Transition graph.   (b) Equivalent deterministic form.

Fig. 16-21   Constructing a finite-state machine that recognizes S_N.

★16-7 TWO-WAY RECOGNIZERS

In Sec. 16-1 we introduced the concept of a recognizer as a finite-state control coupled through a head to a linear input tape. We assumed that the recognizer could move its head in only one direction, to the right. In an attempt to further generalize the model, we consider recognizers which are not confined to a strict forward motion, but can move two ways on their input tapes, that is, to the right and to the left. A natural question that now arises is whether the option given to the machine to move left and reexamine the input tape increases its computational capabilities. In other words, what characterizes the sets of tapes that are recognized by this class of machines? As we shall see, machines that can move both ways, but *cannot* change tape symbols, are no more (nor less) powerful than machines that can move in only one direction.

Description of the model

A *two-way recognizer*, or a *two-way machine*, consists of a finite-state control coupled through a head to a tape. Initially, the finite-state control is in its designated starting state, with its head scanning the leftmost square of the tape. The machine then proceeds to read the symbols of the tape, one at a time. In each cycle of computation the machine examines the symbol currently scanned by the head, shifts the head one square to the right or to the left, and then enters a new (not necessarily distinct) state.

If, when operating in this manner on a given tape, the machine eventually *gets off* the tape on the right end and at that time enters an accepting state, then we shall say that the tape is *accepted* by the machine. A machine can *reject* a tape either by getting off its right end while entering a rejecting state or by looping within the tape. As in the case of one-way machines, the set of tapes that are accepted by a given two-way machine is said to be *recognized* by that machine. The null string λ can be represented either by the absence of an input tape or by a completely blank tape. A machine accepts λ if and only if its starting state is an accepting state.

It is convenient to supply the two-way machine with a new symbol, ¢, called a *left-end marker*, which is entered in the leftmost square of the tape and prevents the head from getting off the left end of the tape. The end marker is not a symbol of the machine's alphabet and must not appear on any other square within the tape.

A two-way machine can be described by a state table (or diagram) which specifies, for every possible combination of present state and tape symbol being scanned, the next state that the machine should assume and the direction in which the head is to move. As directional entries we use the letters L, to denote a shift to the left, and R, to denote a shift to the right.

Example   Table 16-1 describes a two-way machine having four states and two tape symbols, 0 and 1, plus the ¢ marker. The starting state is A, and the accepting state is C. A blank tape entry indicates that the corresponding state-symbol combination cannot occur. Figure 16-22a illustrates the computation that the machine will perform when supplied with a tape that starts with the symbols ¢0. The computation begins with the machine in state A and with its head scanning the left-end marker. According to the state table, the machine will move one square to the right while remaining in state A. The machine will then be scanning a 0, and consequently will enter state B and move one square to the left. From now on the machine will oscillate between these two squares, and thus all strings beginning with a 0 will be rejected.

Table 16-1   A two-way machine recognizing the set 100*

	¢	0	1
→ A	A,R	B,L	B,R
B	A,R	C,R	D,R
©		C,R	D,R
D		D,R	D,R

Next suppose that the machine is presented with a tape that starts with ¢11. We have the computation illustrated in Fig. 16-22b. When the third symbol is reached, the machine will be in state D. Thereafter it will remain in state D, regardless of the tape content, until it gets off the tape. Since D is a rejecting state, all sets of tapes starting with 11 are rejected. Finally, let the tape

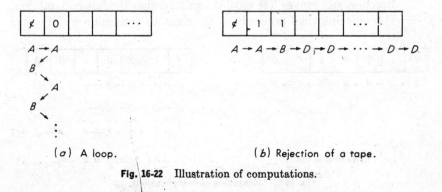

(a) A loop.   (b) Rejection of a tape.

Fig. 16-22 Illustration of computations.

consist of the string ¢10. Again the machine starts by moving to
the right, and it goes through a succession of states until it gets off
the tape in state C. Since C is an accepting state, the tape in
question is accepted. By similar reasoning we can verify that the
machine recognizes the set **100***. ∎

In the next section we shall prove that two-way machines are as
powerful as one-way machines with respect to the classes of tapes that
they can recognize. For some computations, however, it is convenient
to use two-way recognizers, since they may require fewer states than the
equivalent one-way recognizers. On the other hand, for the ability of a
two-way machine to back up and reread its tape, we pay by an increased
computation time.

Example Consider the two-way machine shown in Table 16-2, which
accepts a tape if and only if it contains at least three 1's and at least

Table 16-2 A two-way machine

	¢	0	1
→ A	A,R	A,R	B,R
B		B,R	C,R
C		C,R	D,L
D	E,R	D,L	D,L
E		F,R	E,R
F		G,R	F,R
Ⓖ		G,R	G,R

two 0's. Some typical computations are shown in Fig. 16-23. The
operation of the machine can be summarized as follows. Initially,
the machine is in state A and the head is scanning the left-end
marker. It then proceeds to the right to determine whether the
tape contains at least three 1's. If the tape contains two or fewer
1's, it is rejected; if it contains three 1's, the head reverses its
direction and moves left until it again reaches the left-end marker.
The machine then proceeds to the right to determine whether the

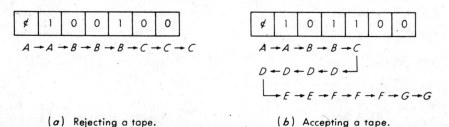

(a) Rejecting a tape.   (b) Accepting a tape.

Fig. 16-23 Examples of computations.

tape contains two or more 0's.   If it does, the machine enters state
G and will eventually accept the tape; otherwise the tape will be
rejected.   ■

The minimal one-way machine that is equivalent to the two-way
machine in Table 16-2 has 12 states.   This larger number of states is
necessary because of the way a one-way machine operates.   Any one-way
machine that recognizes the above set of tapes must examine the tapes
for the proper number of 0's and 1's *simultaneously*.   This can be done,
for example, by the use of two separate counters, one for the 1's and the
other for the 0's.   The state of the machine in such a case is the composite state of the two counters.   Consequently, the number of states
required to perform the above computation is proportional to the *product*
of the numbers of states required to test the tapes for the number of 0's
and the number of 1's separately.   On the other hand, the two-way
machine in this example tests the tapes first for the proper number of 1's,
and then it tests them for the proper number of 0's.   Thus the number of
states is proportional to the *sum* of the numbers of states required to
test the tapes for the two requirements separately.

Conversion to one-way recognizers

We now turn to proving that two-way machines can recognize sets of
tapes (or strings) if and only if they are regular sets.   Specifically, we
shall show that, for every given two-way machine, there is an equivalent
one-way machine that recognizes the same set of tapes.   Since the details
of the construction procedure do not add significantly to its understanding, we shall confine our discussion to sketching the main ideas of
the proof.
   Since a one-way machine makes as many moves as there are symbols
on the tape, while a two-way machine generally makes many more moves
by backing up, the one-way machine cannot keep track of all the moves
of the two-way machine or simulate them.   It is therefore necessary to
isolate the significant information, gained by a two-way machine by
moving to the left, from the particular sequence of moves.   Consider an
initial segment at the left of the input tape, and suppose that the head is
scanning the rightmost square of this segment.   The only way that this
segment can influence the future behavior of the two-way machine is via
the state which the machine is in when (and if) it leaves this segment.
Thus, when a two-way machine backs up and reexamines a segment of
the tape, the state S_i in which the machine reenters the segment and the
corresponding S_i' which the machine would be in if it left the segment are
the only two factors of significance in predicting the future behavior of the
machine.

A two-way machine having n states can be in any one of these states when it scans the rightmost square of the initial segment. Two cases must be considered. First, the machine may never leave the segment, but oscillate within it. Second, the machine will ultimately leave the segment on the right in one of its n states. Thus a reentry into a segment may have $n + 1$ outcomes, that is, leaving the segment in one of the n states or not leaving it. Consequently, the effect of the segment on the computation can be determined by specifying, for each state S_i in which the machine might reenter the segment, which of the $n + 1$ outcomes would indeed result. Such a specification is accomplished by means of a *crossing function* (or *crossing table*), denoted $C(S)$.

The following is extracted from Shepherdson's proof [11]. It summarizes the informal arguments in support of his proof. (Note that M denotes the given two-way machine and t denotes an initial tape segment.)

"If we think of the different states which M could be in when it re-entered t as the different questions M could ask about t, and the corresponding states M would be in when it subsequently left t again, as the answers, then we can state the result more crudely and succinctly thus: A machine can spare itself the necessity of coming back to refer to a piece of tape t again, if, before it leaves t, it thinks of all the possible questions it might later come back and ask about t, answers these questions now and carries the table of question-answer combinations forward along the tape with it, altering the answers where necessary as it goes along."

As an example, consider the two-way machine M given in Table 16-3 and the initial tape segment $\cent001$. Figure 16-24 illustrates, for each possible initial state, the computation performed by the machine if its head is initially scanning the rightmost symbol of the given segment. If the initial state is A, the machine immediately leaves the segment in

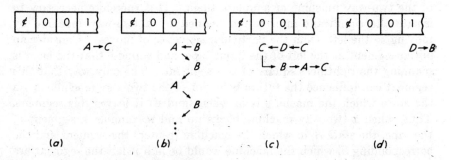

Fig. 16-24 Computations on the segment $\cent001$.

state C. If, however, the initial state is B, the machine will oscillate between states B and A and will never leave the segment. From Fig. 16-24 we can derive the crossing function associated with the segment ¢001, as shown in the first two columns of Table 16-4. The first column, S_i, of this table lists the states of the machine, while the second column, $C(S_i)$, lists the states in which the machine crosses the given segment to the right. A 0 entry indicates that the tape will be rejected.

Table 16-3 Two-way machine M

	¢	0	1
→ A	A,R	B,R	C,R
B		A,R	A,L
Ⓒ		B,R	D,L
D		C,L	B,R

Table 16-4   Crossing functions for machine M

S_i	$C(S_i)$ for ¢001	$C(S_i)$ for ¢0011
A	C	C
B	0	0
C	C	0
D	B	B

An important property of crossing functions is that the crossing function of a $(k + 1)$-symbol segment can be obtained from the crossing function of a k-symbol segment. The rightmost column of Table 16-4 contains the crossing function associated with the segment ¢0011. This crossing function can be determined from the crossing function of the segment ¢001. Suppose, for example, that the machine is in state A scanning the rightmost symbol of ¢0011. According to the state table in Table 16-3, the machine will move to the right and enter state C, as illustrated in Fig. 16-25a. Accordingly, the entry in row A in the rightmost column is C. If, however, the machine is in state B while scanning the rightmost symbol of the given segment, it will move left and enter state A. But according to the crossing function associated with the seg-

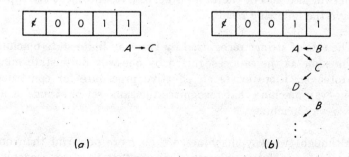

(a)   (b)

Fig. 16-25   Illustration of computations on the segment ¢0011.

ment ¢001, the machine will leave this segment in state C, as shown in Fig. 16-25b. It will then be scanning again the rightmost symbol of ¢0011, and according to the state table, it will move left again and enter state D. According to the crossing function for ¢001, the machine will ultimately leave this segment on the right and enter state B. Evidently, such a sequence of moves indicates that the computation will never halt, and consequently a 0 is entered in row B of Table 16-4. The same line of reasoning leads to the specification of the entries in rows C and D.

The procedure followed in this example leads to the conclusion that, *given the crossing functions associated with the initial segments containing k symbols, we can readily determine the crossing functions associated with all initial segments containing $k + 1$ symbols.* In fact, since the number of distinct crossing functions associated with a specific two-way machine cannot exceed $(n + 1)^n$, where n is the number of states, it is possible to construct a one-way machine that will read the tape from left to right and compute with each move the crossing function associated with the corresponding initial segment. Such a machine will have as many states as there are crossing functions. Its input alphabet is the same as that of the corresponding two-way machine. The next-state entries of the one-way machine are determined as follows. For a given state, which corresponds to a crossing function of the two-way machine, the next-state entry under input α corresponds to the new crossing function, obtained from the given one and the symbol α, in the manner illustrated in the above example in Fig. 16-25.

Once we have a one-way machine that scans the tape from left to right and computes the crossing functions associated with successive initial segments, and since the starting state of the two-way machine is specified, it is a simple matter to determine, after each move of the one-way machine, the corresponding next state of the two-way machine. Consequently, we can determine the state of the two-way machine when it gets off the tape. If this state is an accepting state, the one-way machine will also accept the tape; otherwise it will reject the tape. We thus have the following result:

▶ The sets of strings recognized by two-way finite-state machines are the same as the sets recognized by one-way finite-state machines. Moreover, there exists an effective procedure for constructing a one-way machine that recognizes the same set of strings as a given two-way machine.

Although two-way machines are no more powerful than one-way machines with respect to the sets of strings that they can recognize, it is often more convenient to describe certain computations in terms of two-way machines. The equivalence of the two models, however, makes it generally possible to use either one.

NOTES AND REFERENCES

Nondeterministic graphs were first used by Myhill [8] and further developed by numerous investigators, in particular those working on languages. The initial concept of regular expressions and the equivalence between regular expressions and finite-state machines were presented by Kleene [5]. Simpler techniques for converting regular expressions into transition graphs, and vice versa, have been subsequently developed by Copi, Elgot, and Wright [4], McNaughton and Yamada [6], and Ott and Feinstein [9]. The procedure presented in this chapter of constructing transition graphs from regular expressions is due to Ott and Feinstein [9], while the procedure used to derive regular expressions which describe transition graphs is due to Arden [1]. A survey of regular expressions is available in Brzozowski [2].

Two-way machines were first investigated by Rabin and Scott [10], who provided the first proof that two-way machines are equivalent to one-way machines. Shepherdson [11] subsequently provided a simpler proof, the one outlined in Sec. 16-7.

1. Arden, D. N.: Delay Logic and Finite State Machines, *Proc. Second Ann. Symp. Switching Theory and Logical Design*, October, 1961, pp. 133–151.
2. Brzozowski, J. A.: A Survey of Regular Expressions and Their Applications, *IRE Trans. Electron. Computers*, vol. EC-11, pp. 324–335, June, 1962.
3. Brzozowski, J. A.: Derivatives of Regular Expressions, *J. Assoc. Computing Machinery*, vol. 11, pp. 481–494, 1964.
4. Copi, I. M., C. C. Elgot, and J. B. Wright: Realization of Events by Logical Nets, *J. Assoc. Computing Machinery*, vol. 5, pp. 181–196, April, 1958; reprinted in Moore [7].
5. Kleene, S. C.: Representation of Events in Nerve Nets and Finite Automata, *Automata Studies*, Princeton University Press, Princeton, N.J., 1956, pp. 3–41.
6. McNaughton, R., and H. Yamada: Regular Expressions and State Graphs for Automata, *IRE Trans. Electron. Computers*, vol. EC-9, pp. 39–47, March, 1960; reprinted in Moore [7].
7. Moore, E. F. (ed.): *Sequential Machines: Selected Papers*, Addison-Wesley Publishing Company, Inc., Reading, Mass., 1964.
8. Myhill, J.: Finite Automata and the Representation of Events, *WADC Tech. Rept.* 57-624, pp. 112–137, 1957.
9. Ott, G. H., and N. H. Feinstein: Design of Sequential Machines from Their Regular Expressions, *J. Assoc. Computing Machinery*, vol. 8, pp. 585–600, October, 1961.
10. Rabin, M. O., and D. Scott: Finite Automata and Their Decision Problems, *IBM J. Res. Develop.*, vol. 3, no. 2, pp. 114–125, April, 1959; reprinted in Moore [7].

11. Shepherdson, J. C.: The Reduction of Two-way Automata to One-way Automata, *IBM J. Res. Develop.*, vol. 3, no. 2, pp. 198–200, April, 1959; reprinted in Moore [7].

PROBLEMS

16-1. For each of the sets described as follows, find a transition graph that recognizes the set.

(a) The set of strings on the alphabet {0,1} that start with 01 and end with 10.

(b) The set of strings on the alphabet {0,1} that start and end with a 1, and every 0 is immediately preceded by at least two 1's.

(c) The set of strings on the alphabet {0,1,2} in which every 2 is immediately followed by exactly two 0's, and every 1 is immediately followed by either a 0 or else by a 20.

16-2. Consider the class of transition graphs containing no λ-transitions.

(a) Show a procedure for converting a specified transition graph with several starting vertices into a graph with just one starting vertex. Apply your procedure to the graph in Fig. P16-2.

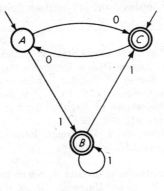

Fig. P16-2

Hint: Add a new vertex and designate it as the starting vertex.

(b) Show a procedure for converting a given transition graph with several accepting vertices into a graph with just one accepting vertex. Apply your procedure to the graph in Fig. P16-2.

(c) Is it always possible to convert an arbitrary transition graph into a graph with just one starting vertex and just one accepting vertex? Determine the conditions under which such a conversion is possible.

16-3. For each of the nondeterministic graphs in Fig. P16-3, find an equivalent deterministic graph (in standard form) that recognizes the same set of strings.

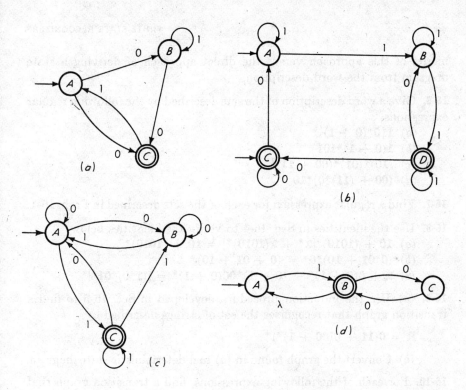

Fig. P16-3

16-4. Show that the two graphs in Fig. P16-4 are equivalent by converting them to deterministic forms.

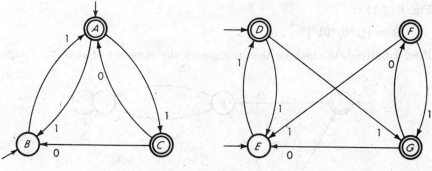

Fig. P16-4

16-5. Design a finite-state machine that accepts only those input sequences which end with either 101 or with 0110. Construct, first, a nondeterministic graph that recognizes the above set of sequences, and then convert this graph into an equivalent deterministic graph. Discuss the merits of this approach versus the direct approach of deriving a state diagram from the word description.

16-6. Give a word description of the sets described by the following regular expressions.

    (a) **110*(0 + 1)**
    (b) **1(0 + 1)*101**
    (c) **(10)*(01)*(00 + 11)***
    (d) **(00 + (11)*0)*10**

16-7. Find a regular expression for each of the sets described in Prob. 16-1.

16-8. Use the identities in Sec. 16-4 to verify the identities below:

    (a) $10 + (1010)^*[\lambda^* + \lambda(1010)^*] = 10 + (1010)^*$
    (b) $(0^*01 + 10)^*0^* = (0 + 01 + 10)^*$
    (c) $\lambda + 0(0 + 1)^* + (0 + 1)^*00(0 + 1)^* = [(1^*0)^*01^*]^*$

16-9. (a) Use the induction procedure developed in Sec. 16-5 to find a transition graph that recognizes the set of strings described by

$$R = 0(11 + 0\overline{(}00 + 1)^*)^*$$

    (b) Convert the graph found in (a) to a deterministic state diagram.

16-10. For each of the following expressions, find a transition graph that recognizes the corresponding set of strings.

    (a) $(0 + 1)(11 + 0^*)^*(0 + 1)$
    (b) $(1010^* + 1(101)^*0)^*1$
    (c) $(0 + 11)^*(1 + (00)^*)^*11$

16-11. The regular expression that corresponds to the transition graph in Fig. P16-11 is

$$R = [(1^*0)^*01^*]^*$$

Find a finite-state machine that recognizes the same set of strings.

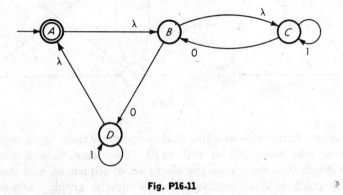

Fig. P16-11

16-12. The nondeterministic graph in Fig. P16-12 has A and B as starting vertices and C as an accepting vertex.

(a) Find a regular expression that describes the set of strings accepted by this graph.

(b) Derive a reduced deterministic machine equivalent to this graph.

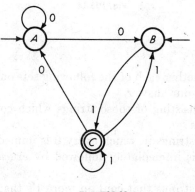

Fig. P16-12

16-13. For each of the machines in Table P16-13, find a regular expression which describes the set of input strings recognized by the machine. In each case the starting state is A.

Table P16-13

PS	NS $x = 0$	$x = 1$	z
A	A	B	0
B	B	A	1

(a)

PS	NS $x = 0$	$x = 1$	z
A	B	A	1
B	B	C	0
C	A	B	1

(b)

PS	NS, z $x = 0$	$x = 1$
A	B,0	A,1
B	A,1	C,1
C	C,0	B,0

(c)

16-14. Find a regular expression on the alphabet $\{0,1,2\}$ for the set of strings recognized by the graph of Fig. P16-14.

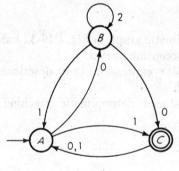

Fig. P16-14

16-15. Determine whether each of the following sets on the alphabet $\{0,1\}$ is regular. Justify your answer.

(a) The set consisting of those strings which contain, for all k's, k ones and $k + 1$ zeros.

(b) The set of strings in which every 0 is immediately preceded by *at least* k ones and is immediately followed by *exactly* k ones, where k is a specified integer.

(c) The set of strings that contain more 1's than 0's.

(d) The set of strings consisting of a block of k^2 zeros immediately followed by a single 1, where $k = 0, 1, 2, \cdots$.

16-16. (a) Let M be a deterministic Mealy-type finite-state machine with a starting state A. Prove that if T is the set of strings that can be produced as output strings by M, then T is a regular set. Show a procedure to design a finite-state machine that will recognize T.

'*Hint:* Use the output successor table of. M.

(b) Apply your procedure to find a finite-state machine that will recognize the set of output strings that can be produced by the machine in Table P16-16.

Table P16-16

PS	NS, z	
	$x = 0$	$x = 1$
A	$B,1$	$A,1$
B	$A,0$	$C,0$
C	$D,1$	$B,0$
D	$C,0$	$A,1$

16-17. The reverse R^r of a set R is the set that consists of the reverses of the strings in R. Thus, for example, if 0101 is in R, then 1010 is in R^r.

(a) Prove that if R is regular, then so is R^r.

Hint: Develop a systematic procedure to convert a given regular expression into its reverse.

(b) Apply your procedure to find the reverse of the expression

$$R = (00)*(0 + 10*)* + 10*(01*10*)*$$

16-18. Either prove each of the following statements or show a counter example.

(a) Every *finite* subset of a nonregular set is regular.

(b) The expressions $P = (1*0 + 001)*01$ and $Q = (1*001 + 00101)*$ are equivalent.

(c) Let R denote a regular set. Then the set consisting of all the strings in R which are identical with their own reverses is also a regular set.

(d) Every subset of a regular set is also regular.

16-19. Consider the nondeterministic machine M^d, which is obtained from a strongly connected deterministic machine M by interchanging the sets of starting and accepting states and by reversing the arrows on the state diagram.

(a) If machine M recognizes the set R, what is the set recognized by M^d?

(b) Prove that the deterministic machine obtained by applying the "subset construction" to M^d has no equivalent states.

16-20. Let P be a regular set consisting of strings of even length. Define a set Q which consists of exactly those strings that can be formed by taking the first half of each member of P. (For example, if 10110100 is contained in P, then 1011 will be contained in Q.) Prove that Q is a regular set.

Hint: Design a machine that recognizes Q.

16-21. Let P be a regular set, and let Q be the set formed of all the strings from P with "even-numbered" symbols deleted; that is, if $a_1a_2a_3a_4a_5 \cdots$ is a string in P, then $a_1a_3a_5 \cdots$ is a string in Q. Prove that Q is a regular set.

16-22. Let P be an arbitrary regular set. Consider those strings w in P such that both w and ww are in P. Define Q to be the set consisting of all the above w's. Thus, for example, if 101 and 101101 are in P, then 101 is in Q. Prove that Q is a regular set.

16-23. Let R be a regular set on the alphabet $\{0,1\}$. The *derivative of R with respect to x*, denoted R_x, is defined as the set consisting of all the substrings y such that xy is in R. For example, if $R = 01^* + 100^*$, then $R_0 = 1^*$ and $R_{10} = 0^*$.

(a) Prove that for all x, R_x is a regular set.

(b) Show that there is only a finite number of distinct derivatives for any regular set, although there is an infinite number of choices for x. Find an upper bound on this number if it is known that R can be recognized by a transition graph with k vertices.

16-24. The *right quotient* of the sets X and Y, denoted X/Y, is defined as the set Z which consists of all the strings z such that $x = zy$ is a string in X, and y is a string in Y. Prove that if X is a regular set, then $Z = X/Y$ is also a regular set. Y may or may not be a regular set.

16-25. Determine which of the following tapes is accepted by the two-way machine shown in Table P16-25.

    (a) ¢010101

    (b) ¢010110

    (c) ¢10101

Table P16-25

	¢	0	1
→ A	A,R	B,R	C,R
B		D,L	C,L
C		C,R	D,R
Ⓓ		B,R	C,L

16-26. A two-way machine with n states is started at the left end of a tape containing p squares. What is the maximum number of moves that the machine can make before accepting the tape?

16-27. Construct a two-way machine whose tape may contain symbols from the alphabet $\{0,1,2\}$ plus the left-end marker, and which accepts a string if and only if it starts and ends with a 2, and if every 2, except the first one, is immediately preceded by a substring from the set $0(01)^*$.

16-28. A given two-way machine recognizes the set of tapes A, rejects the set B, and does not accept (by never halting) the set C. Can a two-way machine be designed so that it:

    (a) Recognizes B, rejects A, does not accept C?

    (b) Recognizes A, rejects B and C?

    (c) Recognizes A, but does not accept B and C?

    (d) Recognizes A and C, rejects B?

    (e) Recognizes C, rejects B, does not accept A?

Hint: Determine first which of the sets A, B, and C is regular.

Index

PZZ